# CENTURY
# OF
# WAR

ALSO BY GABRIEL KOLKO

Confronting the Third World:
United States Foreign Policy, 1945–1980

Anatomy of a War:
Vietnam, the United States, and the Modern Historical Experience

Main Currents in Modern American History

The Limits of Power:
The World and United States Foreign Policy, 1945–1954 (with Joyce Kolko)

The Roots of American Foreign Policy:
An Analysis of Power and Purpose

The Politics of War:
The World and United States Foreign Policy, 1943–1945

Railroads and Regulation, 1877–1916
(Transportation History Prize, Organization of American Historians)

The Triumph of Conservatism:
A Reinterpretation of American History, 1900–1916

Wealth and Power in America:
An Analysis of Social Class and Income Distribution

# CENTURY OF WAR

## Politics, Conflicts, and Society Since 1914

## Gabriel Kolko

THE NEW PRESS   •   *New York*

Published in the United States by The New Press, New York. Distributed by W. W. Norton & Company, Inc., 500 Fifth Avenue, New York, NY 10110

**Library of Congress Cataloging-in-Publication Data**

Kolko, Gabriel.
    Century of War: politics, conflicts, and society since 1914 /
Gabriel Kolko.
        p. cm.
    Includes bibliographical references and index.
    ISBN 1-56584-191-3
    1. War and society—History—20th century.   2. War and
civilization—History—20th century.   I. Title
HM36.5.K65   1994
303.48'5—dc20                                           94-22344

Book design by Paul Chevannes

Production by Kim Waymer

Established in 1990 as a major alternative to the large, commercial publishing houses, The New Press is the first full-scale nonprofit American book publisher outside of the university presses. The Press is operated editorially in the public interest, rather than for private gain; it is committed to publishing in innovative ways works of educational, cultural, and community value that, despite their intellectual merits, might not normally be "commercially" viable. The New Press's editorial offices are located at the City University of New York.

Printed in the United States of America

HC 94 95 96 97      9 8 7 6 5 4 3 2 1

PB 95 96 97 98      9 8 7 6 5 4 3 2 1

To Iris and Stan Ovshinsky

Who have combined idealism and humanism with genius in science
Cherished friends and a great inspiration since the beginning

# CONTENTS

# PREFACE

The astonishingly complex epoch that we are living through mocks description. The growing political and intellectual uncertainty that dominates this rare period in human history is the culmination of a century of political and social developments and crises that have frequently evolved in convoluted ways. Not only have innumerable decisive events been difficult to perceive, but they often have occurred simultaneously and with increasing rapidity throughout vast parts of the globe, defying our abilities to make coherent linkages between disparate experiences in many places. The unprecedented and wholly unexpected ideological and organizational collapse of the Marxist-Leninist states alone challenges our capacity to comprehend our own century; but the reemergence of virulent nationalisms and ethnic turmoil make it imperative that we begin to diagnose our times far more profoundly lest the dragons of atavism and irrationality once again wreak havoc on more and more of mankind. For we are also confronting imminent dangers that include the very real possibilities of war in growing portions of a world in which there is now an abundance of incredibly destructive weapons.

It is simple enough to criticize the paucity of analytic writing and research that has been done to explain effectively the nature of the modern historical experience, but contributing to a deeper understanding of our times is quite another matter. This demands not merely a searching assessment of the logic and premises of the existing state of the art but also an alternative synthesis of reality as well as credible explanations grounded upon it, and this is an immeasurably more daunting challenge. So much that is valuable has been printed that observations about the fact it has not been even more insightful, or integrated in ways to illuminate even more crucial issues, can very justifiably be dismissed as carping. I, for one, do not want to minimize the importance of the many books from which I have learned so much and which have been indispensable for this effort—as, indeed, they will be for anyone's. But at the end of this century we simply do not know nearly enough—nor have we thought sufficiently—about the social and human processes and events that have gone into the making of our century, and that in many decisive ways have made the future of humanity more precarious than it has been at any time in the past fifty years. Old "laws" and grand theories, whether Marxist, capitalist, or the ostensibly neutral reflections of social theorists, have in vital regards proven worse than useless, often substituting the desires or obfuscating rationalizations of vested interests where real clarity is required. At this critical point in history they all offer far less than what is essential both to describe and cope with humanity's grave predicaments.

In a word, there is a vast, growing disjunction between conventional wisdom and the historical experience of this century. What we do know about these and comparable matters—and it is very important and valuable on its own terms—is invariably confined to developments in specific countries, and the traditionally circumscribed way that most writers and scholars work tends to discourage linking trends in one nation to those elsewhere. In a vital sense, our best knowledge is compartmentalized by nations or narrowly defined issues. And this is both a good and bad thing: poor theory, of which there is a surfeit, is worse than none at all; still, we nonetheless also desperately require unifying notions and syntheses, but those that are far less timeless and pretentious than past writers of all political stripes have offered, and which remain flexible, contingent, and open to constant modifications even while we strive to understand the relationships between events in more than one place. It is infinitely easier to say that knowledge should triumph over dogmatism and error than to make it do so, but traditional beliefs and old shibboleths, whether mainstream capitalist or socialist in its various mutations, have left us disarmed to understand the past century or to face the next, and the sheer magnitude and difficulty of the tasks of social reasoning before us in no way diminish the urgency of our transcending modern civilization's cherished but dangerous illusions.

In both Europe and Asia, wars have been the single most important catalyst of the great political and ideological transformations that have characterized this century, and they remain humanity's principal nemesis both today and in the future. If we can comprehend the characteristics of war more acutely, we can more clearly articulate the nature of the past century, and war's monumental consequences for social institutions and people. Indeed, to grasp precisely the interaction between war and modern social change explains, to a crucial degree, the roots of Leninism's initial successes and its subsequent failures, and how communism's astonishing demise was later possible—and this relationship is one of the principal focuses of my volume. Confronting these and comparable issues helps to illuminate how mankind at the end of the twentieth century has arrived at the precarious point at which it now stands.

This book is an effort to diagnose afresh the nature of war in the twentieth century and to see how its political and human implications have defined our historical experience. The topics I deal with are very important, yet remain only a portion of a significantly larger picture. For one thing, while I treat both world wars, the Korean and Vietnam wars, and two important civil wars, I have nonetheless not considered hundreds of other conflicts that are also of great significance. It is only a beginning, cast at a very broad level of generalization, far more concerned with the impact of modern wars on societies and the men and women in them, with people's responses to their miseries and trauma, rather than with the wars' causes, even though at various points causes and effects inextricably merge. The processes rather than the origins of wars interest me much more because they largely define the political results of armed conflict, and these consequences have a far greater role in explaining the emergence and strength of very diverse socialist and fascist movements than the essentially peacetime factors that nearly all theorists have largely concentrated upon. Much of this book, especially Part Two, probes the impact of war on ordinary human beings. Invariably, however, the ways wars have been fought, the character of military technology, and what leaders and elites anticipated when they embarked upon them are integral to the manner in which modern wars have unfolded in reality, and defining some fairly general linkages between rulers and the results of their decisions for the masses is unavoidable.

In Part One, I treat rulers' and generals' expectations, and this necessarily leads to my concern for the perceptions, power, and capacities of those who command nations and armies: their beliefs, myopia, social roles, and abilities are all very significant. Such a focus on history as the heads of states or generals have shaped it is more traditional and the mainstay of most books on war. By itself, it distorts reality, but it unquestionably provides an indispensable framework and, analyzed properly, it also explains how and why leaders and social systems are shaken or even toppled. In Part Two, I consider the countless ways that wars between 1914 and 1949 profoundly altered the lives of ordinary people, from peasants in China to workers in Paris, and how their responses to such challenges evolved, both in their immediate lives and in their relationships to their societies. These reactions and changing thoughts and goals produced all of the significant movements of the Left in this century, and not only Communist revolutions that succeeded, about which much has been written and which we comprehend thoroughly, but also those that failed, a subject that tells us a great deal that is crucial about the nature of international affairs and which has previously been inadequately considered and understood.

Part Three deals with the period after 1945, when wars, while no longer global in the same way as the two great wars, and nominally "limited" to countries or regions, in fact over time have affected vast areas and were frequently limited principally in the sense that there was no direct military conflict between the great powers—which is to say the United States and the Soviet Union. "Limited war," in practice, has also involved unprecedented firepower and violence. Such increasingly complex realities demand that I weave progress in military technology, the nature of the Left, and causes of war together with those structural and other changes in the Third World that have been, or threaten to become, major sources of future conflicts.

*Century of War* therefore employs a variety of approaches, and focuses on many levels, from war's impact on the daily lives of unknown people to the strategic calculations of famous men—or all that is a part of the grand tapestry that is modern history. Important developments in Asia as well as Europe concern me also, and this book is therefore longer than I would have liked but far shorter than had I sought also to deal with yet other significant questions.

In essence, what follows is a panorama of our labyrinthine century, but many of the key players in it are relatively unfamiliar, and the recognizable figures are presented in a way that reveals them in other than conventional perspectives. While I have synthesized the work of innumerable writers on various topics that I describe quite generally, I also plunge into details essential to substantiate more analytic points and to convey an adequate sense of reality. Where I become quite specific, I have also sought to evoke comparative social developments so as to draw the reader back to some larger, more globally significant generalization. The conflict in Greece after 1946 therefore fits logically with that in the Philippines at about the same time, and the lessons of Korea are spelled out in Vietnam. We live in one increasingly integrated world, and only by juxtaposing major events can one illuminate crucial dimensions of this century's inordinately complex experiences. *Century of War* is therefore a comparative history of wars and the people and societies engulfed in their fire and suffering.

Although I use many secondary accounts, those familiar with my two long books on the Second World War and the Vietnam War will appreciate the time I have also spent mining diverse primary sources. My study of the Vietnam experience, *Anatomy of a War,* is a detailed application of many of the analytic methods for assessing war and society that I utilize in the pages that follow. Three other books I have written on post-1945 foreign and military affairs also employ primary sources. But notwithstanding having done the research and spent the time that is a prerequisite for offering the reader what is an exceedingly ambitious undertaking, I must also point to this effort's unavoidable limits.

War deals with monumental, unimaginable tragedies, and words often profane the human experience regardless of a writer's intentions. Historians, however sensitive, rarely can devote the space essential for plumbing the intensity of calamities or the dilemmas and choices that people confronted in the face of mortal dangers, and I am no exception. Suffice it to say, few can describe precisely what they often feel, and after three decades in which wars have been my principal concern, and having directly witnessed one of them on its edges, I am acutely conscious of this deficiency. Words mock our emotions; it is a dilemma precious few ever transcend. It offends our sense of real human experiences to seek to reduce suffering to aggregate measurable proportions, but to attempt to fathom the meaning and significance of those experiences is also to understand, as fully as human capacities allow, the decisive factors in war and history, the forces that decide the outcome of the much more easily described and studied battles or of decision making. At the same time, I wish to forewarn the reader that all efforts to quantify war, whether numbers killed, costs, or whatever, are at best approximate, and sometimes only speculative. A nation at war seeks to win it, or at least to avert defeat, and none has ever considered devoting the staff necessary to gather data sufficiently precise to completely satisfy later researchers. I have attempted to do the best with what is available, and often give ranges of quite disparate estimates. All wars are terrible, and, if not chaotic from their inception, they all become so.

As with all of my earlier books, without the indispensable financial, moral, and physical support of many institutions and people, I unquestionably could not have written this volume, and it is with both gratitude and deep appreciation that I acknowledge them—adding, too, the usual caveat that no person or organization mentioned here should be assumed to approve or share in any way the views contained in this volume. York University continues to play a crucial role—as it has since 1970—allowing me freedom for research and writing. It has in countless ways permitted me to organize my life in the manner I most desire, and I once again am pleased to reiterate my deep gratitude for its liberal assistance and encouragement. The Social Sciences and Humanities Research Council of Canada during 1989–91 once again generously provided research expenses and free time, for which I am greatly indebted. I particularly appreciate five valuable weeks of total freedom the Rockefeller Foundation gave me to work during early 1992 in their superb Bellagio Study Center at a crucial point in the development of this book. The library and especially Dick van Galen Last of the Netherlands Institute for War Documentation in Amsterdam were exceedingly helpful in keeping me abreast of World War Two scholarship and in facilitating my research.

I cannot do adequate justice to the countless precious ways that Nicole and Louis Evrard have since 1962 shown their friendship and made my life and work far more agreeable and interesting. They have also kept me in touch with important French writing and ideas. Professor Michael Kater has patiently, generously guided my readings in German history; he illuminated many complex matters, and I am very much indebted to him for his insight and friendship. Professor Renato Constantino has long directed my efforts to understand all aspects of Philippine history and life, for which I remain deeply grateful. Professor Robert Cuff came to the rescue in diverse ways on problems of war organization, and Professor Lars Bærentzen kindly clarified some crucial issues dealing with Greece. Professor Jürgen Kocka showed great courtesy, as did his colleagues at the University of Bielefeld, in responding to my queries regarding research in Germany and then in patiently listening to an early, quite primitive formulation of some of the issues that this book deals with.

As with everything I have ever done, my wife, Joyce, once again gave both indispensable support and criticism, simultaneously providing both encouragement and posing some very acute questions that compelled me to think much harder—even if less than she would have desired. I have gained immeasurably from both roles, and my appreciation to her far transcends these mere words.

Needless to say, I alone assume sole responsibility for everything contained in this book and any errors of fact or interpretation.

# INTRODUCTION

The twentieth century began with profound self-confidence. Whatever their objectives, virtually everyone who envisioned the future shared a common optimism and belief that they would attain their often very different goals and that both the weight of their own wisdom and social and historical forces justified their optimism. Whether they aspired to preserve the status quo or to replace it, the people and parties that conjured images of the coming decades were blithely oblivious to what would actually occur, and the enormity of the gap between their expectations and subsequent history's reality demands deep reflection.

The sanguine consensus on modern civilization's future among rulers and ruled, oppressors and oppressed, reflected an intellectual legacy rooted in the Enlightenment belief in the inexorably progressive stages of mankind's social and economic development, one that Marxist theories reinforced, but there was also a stolidly traditional and far less intellectually elegant basis for great hopes. Those who had power and authority were loath to question either their right to rule or the wisdom of their judgments, and they faced the future confidently. That their decisions might be gravely flawed, much less prove fatally dangerous not only to their societies but to themselves as well, was scarcely deemed possible before 1914—not even to the overwhelming majority of socialists.

Whether ruling classes, with all of their component constituencies, could behave rationally, at least in the sense of preserving the social orders on which their legitimacy was based, became a decisive issue in Europe as soon as the stage for World War One was set. How military technology would affect the people and societies of nations at war, or how long modern wars might endure, were questions of grave significance. The premises that led to the readiness on the part of all of Europe's leaders to embark on that war, the rival generals' calculations on how best to fight it, their common visions of its length and social costs—and whether or not it would be gravely traumatic—leads directly to the fundamental problem of the very function of intelligence and insight in guiding human destinies in our century. Did those who made history ever anticipate the meaning and consequences of their decisions? And how and why were such crucial individuals and social strata, sharing largely similar strategic conclusions, selected to lead armies and organize nations for warfare? Whether those civilians and generals alike who endorsed wars could also manage them effectively became a crucial factor in the eventual length of time it took to attain victory, for time has increasingly grave social and political effects whose military implications, as we shall see, were decisive.

Creating a war organization capable of meeting the needs of the nation's military branches, at least to the greatest extent possible, meant that the distribution of power among domestic social forces became a vital issue in the prosecution of the war. Would military officers be able to cope with the escalating demands of increasingly sophisticated weapons technology and logistics, or would the businessmen called upon to assist them sacrifice their own personal and industry objectives on behalf of a greater common interest? And whether workers and peasants would forgo their own opportunity to take advantage of shortages of labor or food remained an issue also. Would the new responsibilities and powers that war's exigencies pushed into the hands of the once less-favored sectors of society leave the traditional structure of prewar power intact once the conflict ended?

Such questions, along with many others like them, were intimately linked to the impact of the two world wars on European and Asian societies and the people in them. These issues involved not whole nations, treated as monolithic abstract entities, but especially how the wars affected those social groups and classes least able to cope with the conflicts' exactions. When we focus on the repercussions of war on social systems, such topics as inflation, with its consequences especially for the middle and working classes and their access to food, or the ways invading armies traumatized peoples with forced migrations, deprivation, and incalculable tolls on their ways of life and often their very existence, move to the fore. Obviously, over many decades the weight of such problems varies from place to place, but as wars have become far more destructive, they erode, if not shatter, prewar societies more profoundly than ever. As awkward as the seemingly dry subjects of economics and living standards may appear on paper, in daily experience they were translated into ever-present issues of existence and often hunger, and it was such realities, perhaps more than any other single factor, including the results of battles, that were to turn individuals into agents of real or potential political and social change, produce mass movements and parties everywhere, and define the political outcome of wars.

At the same time, just as wars have affected civilians in ways leaders and strategists scarcely considered, their impact upon the men mobilized to fight them emerged as a crucial factor after 1916; it became exceedingly important in much of central Europe after 1917, and decisive in Russia. The nature of armies and the men in them, their aspirations and abilities, as well as their weaknesses in the face of monumental, protracted terror, assumed a significance that neither optimistic conventional wisdom nor socialist theory ever considered. The stages by which rural and working-class men, if not youths, might be transformed into socially and politically dangerous actors, or at least unwilling defenders of the constituted order, is but one crucial aspect of the total meaning of conflicts for societies—one that was especially prominent in much of Europe during the latter part of the First World War, but which subsequently in France, China, or Vietnam after 1939 remains basic to analyzing how and why wars end the way they do.

The human conditions that wars create, whether for soldiers or civilians, constitute the larger backdrop for the diplomacy, battles, and events that grow out of the struggles between nations and on which most historians have traditionally fixed their attention. The very trauma of wars profoundly affects the entire complex institutional and social fabric of states that engage in them—victors often as much as those that are defeated—and focusing on this indispensable framework as the century progresses becomes vitally important in trying to comprehend both the immediate repercussions of wars and their indelible aftermaths and implications for social change, international relations, and the endless mutations between them that shaped world events throughout this century—during peace as well as war. For wars increasingly have become struggles between competing social systems, involving the viability of the political, cultural, and economic institutions of various adversaries, and their outcome has with time reflected these domains at least as much as the balance of military power on which traditionalists are still wont to concentrate. What has been unpredictable is the point at which a nation will reach an impasse, when its society's integrative abilities or capacities to muddle along will cease to function and it is defeated not as a result of direct military events, as we think of them in terms of battles or the weight of competing military forces, but because of the inability or unwillingness of a people to carry on as its leaders or rulers dictate or require.

Wars have vastly telescoped social time and dynamics in the twentieth century as they transmute human and social realities. They have frequently wiped out vast sections of privileged classes economically, or even seen them destroyed, and it has affected workers and peasants in numerous nations and compelled them to think and act in ways unimaginable during peacetime. Such alterations of consciousness occur for many reasons, ranging from economic hardships and forced labor, to an abhorrence—to cite but two instances—of the behavior of fellow Frenchmen or Filipinos during wartime; we shall examine many cases where such processes occurred, and we must comprehend how and why wars in this century have imposed the necessity of choice and action upon countless numbers of people who would otherwise have remained socially passive very much longer, if not forever. For we must understand how the destruction of conventional wisdom and icons takes place, and how the transformation of attitudes and the creation of new desires as well as needs accompanies it. The stages by which wartime mobilization and common suffering produced many mutations after 1914 that were indispensable to the emergence of diverse fascist as well as communist movements in the war's wake is intimately linked to such experiences. After 1945, structural changes in the Third World, as a result of either wars or the emergence of export-based economies that displaced large numbers of peasants, or both, resulted in the social breakdown of any number of once relatively stable countries; the reasons why the indigenous radical forces emerging in such environments eventually were engulfed in the ceaseless vortex of violence and war that has plagued much of the Third World since 1945 brings us to our own epoch.

War in this century became an essential precondition for the emergence of a numerically powerful Left, moving it from the margins to the very center of European politics during 1917–18 and of all world affairs after 1941— where it became the permanent object of the United States' obsessive concerns until just a few years ago, when Communist and socialist parties, in virtually all of the forms they took, became gravely, perhaps even fatally, defensive and isolated. More powerful socialist parties and the appearance of communism and the creation of the Soviet Union were inextricably linked to the very social and political dynamics that the war produced in Europe after 1916, especially, but by no means exclusively, among soldiers. The Left's most important impact during World War One was the direct consequence of the profound alienation and protests of ordinary soldiers throughout Europe, which revealed the extent to which the world's leaders had misunderstood the social implications of the fatal strategies on which they embarked. This first serious conflict between the forces of order and those of change had, notwithstanding the fears of contemporaries, fairly limited repercussions, confined to the emergence of the USSR, because the war's domestic effects, while far greater than those of any other modern war, were nonetheless much less significant than those after 1939, when a very large part of Asia was also traumatized profoundly.

World War One was the first event to pose the fundamental question of how the modern Left would emerge in reality, and what roles its leaders and parties would play, as opposed to radicalism surfacing in the form of quite inchoate, self-generating movements that frustrated those who aspired to steer them in directions they deemed best. Bolshevism and even social democracy assumed the party would play an indispensable leadership role, performing the decisive catalytic role in the calculations of the former and a necessary function in the case of the latter. But whether the Left in the twentieth century would grow under the aegis of either, or in its own inconsistent, even disorderly, fashion, depended greatly on how wars affected the masses as well as the spatial (including the nature of all forms of communication) and organizational environment in each nation. In a word, we remain with the classic question of what causes people to act: Leaders? Events? Objective conditions? Changed consciousness? Parties? And to what extent have leaders followed the masses in order to channel and exploit their political potential? The causal significance to be attached to orthodox Marxist prognoses, from increasing immiserization of the proletariat to more arcane theorems in *Capital*, can largely be resolved when explaining how, why, and when workers changed and began to emerge as potentially key social actors in Europe—and then failed to attain socialism. Such a comprehensive historical reappraisal of the origins and roles of leftist movements and parties in our era has long been overdue, and it is a major focus of this volume.

More specifically, although the Second World War affected every aspect of European civilian life far more profoundly and extensively than the war of 1914–18, an absolutely crucial political as well as historical question remains why there was far less change in southern and western Europe after 1944, when armed Resistance forces might have filled the immense vacuum that the discredited traditional conservative classes created because so many of them were collaborators and fascists. Why, in such a context, there was no serious political crisis in any European country where the masses were radicalized, save Greece, reveals a great deal about the nature and objectives of the Soviet Union and the Communist parties, as well as the origins of the long peace in Europe that has begun to erode dramatically since their demise.

Stated yet another way, the question is whether communism after 1917, but especially since 1945, was the cause of the world's crises in international relations, including many wars, or essentially the reflection of a sustained period of intense disorder that the traditional world's wars created. The character of the USSR, the complexity and motives of those millions who joined diverse Communist movements, the manner in which armed, nominally Communist-led insurgencies emerged after 1945 in Greece, the Philippines, Vietnam, and elsewhere, all demand very critical reassessments now that the Soviet Union and most Communist parties have virtually ceased to exist (and those states that still claim to be Leninist are in practice economically anything but socialist in the traditional meaning of that term). For the world nonetheless is now experiencing violence and instability in more places than at virtually any time since the end of World War Two. The issue we must also consider, among many others, is whether the very existence of the Soviet Union itself, and its hegemony over Communist parties, indeed spared the remainder of Europe the basic political and social challenges they might have confronted, challenges comparable to the far greater dangers Europe's rulers faced after the much less destructive war of 1914–18.

And if this was indeed the case, now that politics and social change in the world no longer have the USSR and Communist parties to fetter it, what does our future hold?

# PART ONE

# Making and Managing Wars: The View from the Top

# CHAPTER 1

# Preparing the World for War

To comprehend the nature of this century as mankind approaches its culmination necessitates both complex and simple analyses of the forces and influences that have molded it: complex lest we fail to appreciate the richly textured field of factors that affect nations and people in the contemporary world; and simple, lest our necessary but inherently demanding concern with often reciprocal, interrelated, but variable ideas and institutions causes us to slight war's most essential realities. For the ultimate outcome of the modern historical experience for countless tens of millions of people, whatever the precise reasons for it at any given point, or whether or not we can describe it exactly, has been that their lives have been traumatized and often destroyed, and that mankind's achievements by the conclusion of the twentieth century, with strife and hunger in dozens of nations and the mounting risks of far more destructive conflicts both within and between states than was possible even thirty years ago, have been far less impressive than its tragic failures in ameliorating the human condition. Although we must think more acutely and honestly than ever to fathom how the world has arrived at its present impasse, there is no conflict whatsoever between iconoclastic candor and the anger and impatience that is essential if humanity is to escape the destructive legacies and illusions of past conflicts and to survive the next century.

We have lived nearly an entire century with the ghosts of nationalism—its aspirations, its delusions, its awesome dangers—a nationalism that during the nineteenth century culminated in the unification of Germany and Italy and then proceeded for over half a century to inspire much of eastern Europe and the colonial world with a passion for self-determination that was eventually to destroy empires. After a century of strife it has helped enormously to inspire, nationalism's grip on the minds of much of the globe, from cynical leaders of states to common folk whose notion of politics is essentially to be left alone, remains as potent as ever in much of the world. The logic of self-determination has divided regions and continents into smaller and smaller units whose inability to survive independently or to live with their neighbors has produced great tension and conflict. This comes at a point in human development when the nature and quantity of weaponry makes war so dangerous and destructive that surviving another century without terrible nuclear or chemical-biological catastrophes remains the greatest single challenge confronting people everywhere.

Whatever redeeming role nationalism may have played proved ephemeral as the concept inevitably assumed all of the most negative aspects of its ideological heritage. The mass attitudes it spawned throughout the European continent encompassed racist dogmas of varying degrees of virulence, commitments to the triumph of one linguistic or ethnic group over another as part of an ostensibly logical, natural order of things, and often a nostalgic attraction to violence in its own right as an ennobling aspect of human endeavor. By 1900 the ideological preconditions for war existed not just in Europe but throughout much of the globe, and these have persisted in diverse ways up to the present.

Fathoming this ideological world is both simple—for in fact its roots were based on a few primitive, remarkably similar premises to be found everywhere—as well as complex insofar as the ideas and impulses it embodied possessed countless intellectual and cultural expressions, particularly among the ruling social groups who historically have been nationalism's strongest advocates everywhere. But to linger on these many intriguing, very diverse, and nuanced attributes at the expense of a clear understanding of nationalism's remarkably common institutional foundations in the twentieth century not only prevents our comprehending both its principal consequences and historical role but also the remarkably similar crises that each of the various chauvinisms it spawned confronted during and after the wars they have all been so crucial in causing.

## The Nationalist and Militarist Consensus

In its most extreme jingoist form, nationalism before 1914 produced influential Frenchmen who were convinced of their superiority over Germans, and were consequently committed to a greater French power in Europe, or

Germans close enough to decision makers to matter who honed biologically justified doctrines of racial superiority to rationalize preventive-war theories. But notwithstanding such common and well-known crude examples of the nationalist mission, whose ultimate expression was militarism, it is more crucial for one to understand that similar notions also emerged out of the European and American ruling classes' consensual and frequently more subtle and less obviously virulent visions of the role of martial conduct and human values, as well as of the nature of the international system and the politics of nations. For while the purely xenophobic and the more cultivated intellectual threads in the nationalist tradition ultimately merged and produced a unified world view, ideology, and culture, they also ironically created universal but inherently irreconcilable class aspirations and objectives that were inevitably to lead to wars and the ruination of traditional social orders.

European militarism's intellectual and social legacies initially descended principally from the real or pretended aristocracies' values and class needs, but various bourgeois constituencies often aided and encouraged them, reinforcing the doctrine's influence and increasing its role. It would be an error, however, to attribute militarism's origins to Europe and ignore the United States' important contributions to it and its own synthesis and use of the notion later, or how Japanese imperialism concocted its own distinctive rationalizations to parallel those emerging in the rest of the world. Indeed, we can best appreciate militarism as a very general concept and basis for social and military policy, one often simply a truculent mood devoid of sharp, clearly defined components. In practice, it has embodied everything ranging from highly intellectualized doctrines of power and Darwinian biological theory, or a national ruling class's much cruder rationalization for acquiring colonies, to mindless xenophobic bellicosity on the part of ordinary people.

The very universality of such ideas and values on the legitimacy of conflict among nations, which eminently respectable civilian political leaders in all of the world's major nations shared and have sustained in many guises to our own day, meant that although they contributed in a general way to producing wars in this century they were not necessarily their primary causal or the most determining factors—much less defined when wars began. To understand the complex reasons why and when wars occur and even, to a critical degree, why the ideas that militarism and nationalism encompassed gained a serious hearing among decision makers also demands an understanding of the dynamics of specific societies and their power structures and internal economic and social contexts. Ideas had an autonomous status, which were important among the principal contestants in the wars of this century, but their practical social consequences were inextricable from a much larger field of factors and influences. By the turn of this century the ideas of Clausewitz, Darwin, and Mahan had directly or indirectly influenced a great many of the men guiding the destinies of much of the industrialized world, so that their behavior often reflected their common impulses and myopia. Clausewitz infused a new moral and pseudoscientific vision into thinking about war, providing the otherwise anti-intellectual warrior castes of Europe with a rationale for their power in an aggressively empiricist industrializing era that the vast majority of officers deplored as crassly commercial and devoid of sufficient spirituality. The social thinkers that Darwin's work spawned rounded off Clausewitz's influences with their primitively conservative notions of struggle, survival-of-the-fittest, and death for the weak. War now also had a putative scientific sanctification and presumably could now be conducted in a rational fashion, and Clausewitz's stress on the importance of the military leader of genius further made it appear as an inevitable part of the natural order of things.

With Captain Alfred T. Mahan's influential 1890 treatise on sea power, a justification for naval expansion or the acquisition of bases and colonies coincided with the very significant nascent imperialist constituencies emerging in Europe and the United States after 1890 to create yet another seemingly coherent rationalization for expansive economic and strategic impulses that were already growing, whatever the ostensible reasons, in Germany, the United States, and elsewhere. Ironically, the nationalist impulses that culminated in imperialism and conflict all flourished under the aegis of an essentially competitive but transnational doctrine. And they all shared, as well, a fatal, complete blindness to the domestic social costs, the effects of war on the cohesion and internal tranquility of their own nations—a myopia that was to prove the traditional orders' single most catastrophic miscalculation in this century.

Many senior officers in the industrialized nations of the world also shared a profound common distaste for the egoist morality of commerce and capitalism. Ironically, a remarkable antimodernist consensus later united them not only in their belief in the restorative spiritual values of warfare per se but also in their strategic approach to each others' armies on the battlefield, as well as in their responses to the First World War on their respective social systems once it began to cause Europe's nations to begin to tremble and, for some, capsize. Innumerable British, French, and German generals, as well as civilians such as Theodore Roosevelt and his circle in the U.S. and the aristocratic "diehards" in England, employed a cult of action and physical fitness prevalent among all the ruling classes of the industrialized nations to romanticize combat and its sacrifices as personally ennobling—if not a sacred experience. Echoes of this creed survive to this day.

The warrior cult that gained transnational respectability by the turn of the century was essentially romantic and feudal, suffused with a chivalric code of personal norms of discipline and courage, and founded on Clausewitz's belief in the primacy of morale in warfare. It provided military leaders in various nations with the self-confidence they needed to rationalize the astonishingly obsolete norms of warfare they were then justifying to themselves as well as to their civilian peers. And it was a crucial source of the myopia that was to turn war in this century into the fundamental origin of crisis and change. The ideological accretions that emerged to abet warfare's rise to overwhelming legitimacy before and after 1914 integrated the cult of personal action with a narrowly defined anti-economic behavior—a denial of egoism on behalf of an alleged transcendent national destiny—to strengthen measurably both professional warriors' and their civilian equivalents' power within the ruling classes of much of the industrialized world. Such moods found immediate expressions in forms as diverse as Robert Baden-Powell's scouting movement, with its militarily organized anti-urban idealization of primitive survival and manliness, and Italian Fascism's emotional advocacy of action and the readiness for fighting sacrifices.[1]

These visions of warfare emphasizing personal qualities—qualities that most officers felt the urban masses generally lacked—resulted in all of the major enemies in the First World War adhering to a common strategy that assumed there would be a quick and decisive war of mobility and offensives, one largely employing elite cavalry possessing unflinching morale and ready to fight the enemy at close quarters using the cold steel of swords and bayonets. "Both sides," the head of France's army in 1914, Marshal Joseph Joffre, later wrote when contemplating this vision of an essentially medieval jousting match, "were in agreement that only a vigorous offensive could bring success." And since the Germans also possessed what Joffre called "an unflinching will," what was so surprising about the first grand theater war of this century was not that it quickly became stalemated but that it was so obvious in advance that this would occur and that the generals and leaders of all sides were so totally unprepared for it.[2] Their common conviction that wars would be fought in a way congenial to their side's strategy, priorities, equipment, and budget, in a strategically convenient manner, has persisted in various guises to this day. Yet without such illusions the very idea of war as a plausible means of advancing a nation's interests would have lost most of its adherents.

The major powers' acquisitive territorial and economic goals existed in tandem with influential ideological, cultural, and strategic premises to reinforce one another, in Germany's case long antedating Hitler's desire to obtain *Lebensraum* for his nation in eastern Europe's vast space. The values

and objectives Hitler evoked were but continuations of an anti-Slav sentiment that had a respectable grip on the most important German leaders
from the late nineteenth century onward. The French military, sharing the
German officers' antidemocratic visions, also imagined a France that would
expand not only overseas but in Europe, and comparable strains of
thought—both expansionist and hostile to the role of the masses in politics—existed in Britain as well.

   Residues of this common body of shared ideas, values, and impulses
reappeared constantly after the First World War as the world's ruling elites
revealed their endemic inability to reflect upon and change as a consequence of the war's immense carnage and profound social and political dislocations. The war's romantic illusions infected Italian politics immediately, as well as Japanese officers who concocted a lethal synthesis of
reverence for action and self-abnegation, total respect for the imperial system of authority, hostility to commerce and democracy, and belief in
expansion. While the principal causes of Japanese imperialism after 1931
were geopolitical and especially economic, the military's ideological inheri-
tance was also persuasive. Ultimately, war has been the outcome of ideological, materialist, and strategic influences, and its consistent inability to
fulfill its promises as painlessly as desired has reflected the fatal blindness
that has invariably accompanied it whatever the precise combination of
forces producing conflicts. And that ideas and doctrinal fixations can be
transcendentally influential in negating the lessons of repeated failure was
seen later in the United States' dogged counterinsurgency efforts after
1947.[3]

### Individual Consensus and Social Myopia
Any account of war in our times must confront the fact that the rulers of
nations have persistently exhibited a myopia that has compounded the
impact of war on the populations of innumerable countries throughout this
century. Given the striking repetitive eccentricities and perverse obstinacy
of countless important men in this century, we cannot avoid either contemplating their causal role or probing how such types manage to lead
states during their most critical hours. But ultimately one is also forced to
ask whether critical personalities are principally a cause or a reflection of
the endemic, recurrent failures that social systems produce.

   Biography is surely relevant, but as fascinating as it is, it hardly exhausts
the complexity of the relationship between men and the cultures, milieus,
and politics that bring them to the fore. Anyone reading the many portraits
of Field Marshal Earl Douglas Haig and his command of the British
Expeditionary Force in France after late 1915 will marvel at his ability to
see the war as an abstract, routinized, and structured exercise warranting
his remaining far behind the front, rarely visiting it, having precious little

contact with most of his senior officers, and working regular hours without any exceptions for the emergencies that arose continuously. Certain that he was guided by divine wisdom, he would not allow facts to alter his preconceptions. Yet Haig's obtuseness is much more interesting both as a mirror of the values of the British elite that chose him, and as a fairly typical example of a mentality that many of his peers in the German, Russian, or French armies also shared in a world where men such as himself inexorably created protracted misery—and also ran armies.

Haig's ascendancy was due to his wealth, high social status, and resulting friendships, above all with the king, and to his ability to articulate the cavalryman's personal, heroic Victorian qualities that his fellow officers believed would prove crucial in wartime. Whatever his utterly impersonal work style, these qualities alone made it possible for him to remain in command in spite of his essential mediocrity and the fact that vast numbers of British lives were being destroyed in constant, futile efforts that implemented his larger vision of a war in which courage and persistence in doing what was assumed to be correct strategically would decide its outcome. Haig reflected superbly all the qualities of an entire generation of aristocratic British leaders both in and out of the military. Field Marshal Earl Horatio Kitchener, who was secretary of state for war until June 1916, was far more acerbic than even Haig, ruthless in advancing his career, and no better able to cope administratively with the real problems of fighting a modern war in a political context. And while Haig sincerely regarded himself as God's chosen instrument, so too did General Paul von Hindenburg in Germany—who became far more important than Haig and was later the president who helped Hitler to take power in 1933. And General Helmuth J. L. von Moltke, scion of the most famous German military family and chief of the general staff in August 1914, was even more out of touch with reality in believing that the United States might be persuaded to join the war against England in return for being given Canada.

Personal foibles and weaknesses are much smaller obstacles to attaining leadership roles and waging war than a lack of essential social contacts and a thorough socialization in the elite structures of a society—including intimate acquaintance with the men who influence command selections. And this very comprehensive process of socializing aspiring decision makers intensifies a nation's inability to transcend its own analytic limits in order to be better able to either avoid or win a war. A typical case during the Vietnam War can be found in the inability of the highest decision makers in Washington to counteract erroneous or irrelevant information coming from those subordinates who knew that the presentation of facts that undermined the rationale for the aggressive but hopeless policies the Johnson administration implemented until 1968 would make them look like defeatist bearers of bad tidings—and damage their careers. Policies, biases, and interests decisively influence the uses made of information in all societies and also what is legitimized as genuine or relevant facts, so that the function of knowledge is not to help the system make truly objective decisions but to reinforce those, however untenable they may be, it has adopted for other reasons. Colorful or eccentric men in high places are ultimately less the cause of a nation's incapacity to adapt or succeed than a reflection of a far deeper endemic myopia that its leadership selection system, interests, and official dogmas impose as a binding consensus upon all those who aspire to lead it. Leaders sharing collective illusions and conforming to predetermined canons of behavior and thought inevitably entrap societies they control in those difficulties that are inherent in their sanctioned values and doctrines.[4]

### Grand Strategies as Rationalizations for Domestic Imperatives

Although it is the consensus around a society's dominant ideology and goals rather than specific personalities that creates the tightly circumscribed parameters of thought and action among those who aspire to rule or actually do so, the problem still remains as to how a nation articulates and then implements its concrete social and political objectives in the first place. Above all, how does it so often make erroneous estimates, frequently for purposes of sheer convenience, that then cause it to get into far deeper troubles than it ever imagined possible?

The principal examples in this century suggest that rulers or heads of state and the military during periods of international crises quite consistently define their nations' overall external priorities and role in accordance with their general vision of war and violence in the spectrum of human priorities and values. But the manner in which they apply those values concretely has usually, although not always, interacted with and reflected the interests and objectives of the dominant ruling institutions and class at a given point in time, and also whether its component elites are disunited in ways that reduce their overall influence when crucial decisions for war or peace are taken. These motives may be—indeed, often are—largely domestic and internal in nature, and further distort a broad ruling class's understanding of the risks and character of armed conflicts or cause it to project illusory scenarios that reconcile it to adventures that otherwise would appear sheer folly. While obvious self-interest will have its own, less intellectually elegant justifications, both the more general and immediate causes of the behavior of those who lead nations toward war usually exist in tandem in various combinations, notwithstanding the contradictions or tensions that frequently exist between them. This often complex interaction between domestic needs, constraints, and priorities and the choice of strategies and military planning of the dominant classes is a recurrent, universal theme in the evolution of wars in this century, often illuminating not just why and how a nation fights a war but also the often inordinately convoluted reasons it chooses for doing so.

One of the most glaring examples of the ways by which a military's biases and interests profoundly influenced its definition of reality and subsequent military strategy emerged in France before World War One. An officer corps, whose leaders were overwhelmingly antidemocratic, deepened its commitment to the doctrine of a short war, based on a professional elite army employing high mobility and the offensive, mainly to protect itself from antagonistic civilian encroachments in the wake of the profoundly contentious Dreyfus affair. And it advocated this policy notwithstanding the military leadership's knowledge since 1904 of the basic German military plan when war broke out, which along with the changing nature of modern warfare in fact justified relying wholly on a defensive strategy using nonelite conscripts. The army's leaders were far more concerned with hostile politicians' efforts to democratize the military by enlarging the reserves and preparing for a defensive war, especially after the army's critics in 1905 passed a two-year military-service law. The generals' principal objective was to prevent civilian control over the army, and the increase in Germany's military spending and manpower after 1912 as well as anti-German chauvinist appeals allowed them to gain passage in August 1913 of their much-coveted restoration of military service to three years. The officers' fears of the perils of democracy received much more sympathy from the mainly chauvinist bourgeoisie when the ostensibly antimilitarist Socialists increased their strength in the April 1914 National Assembly elections by thirty-four seats. When war broke out, it was this prewar domestic challenge to elite hegemony—as much as any other factor—that defined France's initial choice of strategies.[5]

In Germany, notwithstanding that the democratic, antimilitarist forces were still relatively underdeveloped, domestic factors also proved crucial to the conduct of its foreign policy and in defining the total-war military doctrines of the offensive on which its generals planned the conflict. Both in Germany and France, and for many of the same reasons, political leaders and their officers produced visions of the war that were mirror images of each other, fantastically expecting the enemy to engage in combat in precisely those ways for which they were most prepared and which would thus enhance their own political power. In the course of the monumental bloodletting that was to follow, a perverse oneness of assumptions and reflexes that evolved from the shared impulses and illusions of many past decades was to unify the men who sent millions of youths to die.

Prussia's ultimate political veto over the political process after 1871 gave the military in Germany a much more dominant position than it held elsewhere in Europe. Given this reality, and the cultural-ideological premises that mixed fear and respect to obtain habitual obedience from the masses, Germany's rulers initially thought less than their French equivalents about protecting their authority. The alliance of industry and the military after the 1890s to support greatly expanded naval armaments capable of reducing domestic economic problems and the risks of growing workers' radicalism may not have been absolutely essential to social stability, but the manner by which a merger of conservatism's internal and external policies coincided with its generalized commitment to the growth of German power in Europe and elsewhere made war inevitable eventually. By enlarging the navy and obviating the need for a bigger army that would produce a less elitist and presumably less controllable officer corps and politically reliable soldiery, Prussia's leaders threatened to challenge Britain's naval supremacy while avoiding France's painful confrontations with efforts to democratize the army.

The emergence of the Social Democratic party (SPD) in 1912 as the largest single party in the Reichstag also profoundly defined the German rulers' policies on war and peace. Although Germany's political structure was far more autocratic than France's, the SPD's sustained growth in the face of antisocialist laws after 1879 presented a serious challenge to the alliance of Prussia, the monarchy, and big business that dominated the state. Just as the rulers applied sufficient repression to let the Social Democrats understand the limits of the political order within which they functioned, and considered far more draconian steps, so too did they calculate how their foreign policy and arms spending could cope with internal political opposition. The question of whether its foreign policy was based wholly or only partly on domestic considerations is less important to resolve than the indisputable fact that Germany's expansion was always to some vital extent a function of its internal political crises. The increasing instability of its politics after 1909, and the failure of a Center-Right coalition to stem the SPD's growth, was to lead to the conservative attempt to produce a national consensus around an aggressive, militarist foreign policy as a means of integrating the working class into a nationalist design and, in effect, to suspend the political dialogue on domestic issues so threatening to the hegemony of the status quo. The problem was that the SPD's latent social-patriotic enthusiasm could be mobilized only for a short war against czarist Russia, one portrayed as a defense against encirclement, but this coincided neatly with the rising preventive-war school's belief that the Russian menace had best be confronted earlier rather than later.

Such a war, given Russia's alliances, automatically also meant war with France, which the army and various industrialists also supported. Around such a broad consensus, linked to a successful but brief offensive, Germany could unite in ways impossible in peacetime. No one thought a long war to be conceivable, and Germany's rulers believed that a quick triumph, while politics was suspended in the Reichstag until December 1914, would greatly enhance the military's reputation and solidify the conservative order, thereby reversing the red tide and resolving domestic and foreign challenges at one and the same time.[6]

Given such social imperatives and goals and the parameters they imposed on Europe's major nations before 1914, the men who rose to lead those states never modified their goals in any significant manner. While some had profound ideological motives, others saw clearly how practical political alliances required policies culminating inexorably in expansion and, eventually, war. The latter group's more prosaic materialist concerns in no way eliminated the influence of ideas and conceptions leading to war, but only increased the causal role of internal politics and economic considerations and interests.

This proved true later, even in the case of Nazi Germany. Notwithstanding Hitler's mad rhetoric and romanticism, he was also fully aware of the turbulent events during and after World War One and he consciously refused to test his population's tolerance of war's hardships. To avert social crises such as those that had plagued Germany after 1917, he carefully sustained living standards at the expense of a far greater armaments program that very well might have produced military victory. Japan's leaders possessed pan-Asian doctrines and diverse racial doctrines, but they vindicated their expansionist policies after 1930 with essentially material justifications, and Hideki Tojo—as aggressive as any political leader after 1931—had no need whatsoever for elaborate ideologies but saw war exclusively in terms of material power.

These parallel responses of similar national ruling elites to domestic considerations continuously, repeatedly shaped relations between states, for better or worse, as varying combinations of internal and foreign objectives merged to define the future of war and peace for a century. But their superficially more objective responsiveness to impersonal factors involving economic and political gain was in itself also the outcome of an inherently biased perception, one that was mostly convenient rather than accurate, and quite dismissive of realism and facts; it placed the attainment of group and class interests as well as individual careers far above a candid effort to estimate accurately the possible political and economic outcome of modern military technology or war's implications for their nation's future well-being.

## The Causes of Consensus

Notwithstanding that they were quite distinct societies politically, the nations involved in the great bloodletting of 1914–18 initially shared a consensus on making war as well as unifying illusions regarding the obligations it would impose upon each of them. It is this broad area of agreement, which produced an amazingly parallel response to European realities, that requires much more emphasis. Even more important, however, is the question of whether the existence of a general accord on a nation's foreign policy among all classes of society was the necessary and sufficient reason for its embarking on expansion and conflict. Stated another way, had only the ruling classes favored them and not been able to count on support from workers and peasants at their inception, might the conflicts of this century have been averted? In the broadest sense, how decisive is the role of the ruling classes' hegemonic definition of the values and assumptions touching the issues of war and peace in actually producing conflict?

It would be foolish to ignore the specific intellectual and political qualities of Germany, for example, in the decades preceding 1914, or the reasons why its bourgeoisie sanctioned a military and foreign policy that produced a preventive or preemptive war mentality among the nation's rulers. The middle classes and civilian elites unquestionably overwhelmingly supported either the notion of expansionism or war itself and, at the very least, those arms and economic policies that guaranteed the military undisputed ascendancy and made war inevitable. But the Prussian landed elite and its allies were careful not to undermine the material interests of the modernizing industrial and commercial classes. Had Germany's rulers not created an economy based on militarism and a statist industrial policy, one that enabled the existing social order to maintain the unity of the middle and military-aristocratic classes on the basic issues of war and peace, the nation's common shared values and their presumed hegemony may have been weakened or even shattered. For the consensus that existed was not merely one of values, though it was most assuredly also that, but of interests as well, and all of these combined made Germany's path toward war all the more certain.

In a situation where officers with neofeudal ideas accept modernization, the principal strategic elites of a nation can accommodate to each other—and each others' ideas—with little loss to their own vital interests, and it is mainly for this reason that the broad consensus between the military and civilian elites in this century has emerged in so many nations.

As I noted earlier, martial and sacrificial chivalric values in England synthesized Victorian and middle-class beliefs; and in the United States, civilian politicians linked to the Theodore Roosevelt Progressives preached them to make the political ethos of militarism largely civilian in origin. This did not mean that the unanimity between civilians and officers for expansion and war was always quickly or smoothly attained, but the way interests and ideas coincided is crucial to understanding why wars were eventually begun. The Japanese war party and civilians differed on tactics until 1941 but not on the basic issue of a qualitative expansion of Japan's power in East Asia. When powerful civilians share the same misconceptions with officers, as in the case of the White House and the Pentagon in 1964, the case for embarking on dangerous courses requires no serious justifications; so that in 1964 the Pentagon could cite war games it had played without the participation of any Asia experts to argue that the struggle in Vietnam could be won quickly. The criterion of rationality for judging warlike policies is ultimately socially conditioned, in many major nations having affected generals and civilians alike and produced predictably common optimistic prognoses. And the career imperatives compelling individuals to work within limited boundaries automatically assure that only a finite range of views gets considered in the policy-making circles of most, if not all, states. But it is precisely because of the growing disparity between the strategic estimates that such flawed political decision-making structures produce and the realities that modern warfare creates that the shocks on existing social systems have increased throughout this century.[7]

But the consensus that exists in nations prior to their plunging into wars has never been a purely upper- and middle-class phenomenon, and this fact has profoundly affected socialism's evolution and role in this century. The history of the socialist parties after 1914 revealed that whatever initial consensus they shared with the ruling parties did not prevent their other priorities and interests from eventually undermining it; yet it is also clear that their increasing alienation could not stop the war. The seeming support of the working classes for war was due in part to the weakness of the socialist parties themselves, and especially to their leaders' long-established ambitions and their psychology of acquiescence identical to that of many middle-class elements who also initially sustained a war that subsequently they too were to regard as tragic. Later accounts of this period that assert the existence of a consensus or hegemonic domination of working-class values confuse a very great element of sheer apathy or passivity with nominal approval, much less strong enthusiasm, for qualitatively they are very different both in origin and potential social consequences. Societies do not normally constantly test the basic consensus among classes within it, the cost of which in terms of conflict would be unpredictably great, but usually evoke varying degrees of acquiescence for as long as prevalent policies do not impose a great toll on one or another class. Whatever individuals' personal distastes, their conformity is all the more imperative and likely because the dominant institutions have myriad ways of oppressing them, ranging from unemployment to prison.

Whether socially conditioned conceptions of rationality predictably favor warlike policies, or hegemonic preindustrial notions weigh on the alleged national psyche, or none of these, the fact remains that all social orders are naturally weighted to reinforce a ruling party's priorities for a certain minimal yet crucial amount of time. People, in a word, are not instinctively rebels, but one should not confuse their passivity or the absence of resistance with their granting positive, enthusiastic, or, much less, unconditional approval to a policy or doctrine.

In order to anticipate a social system's possible future tensions or conflicts, apathy or unwillingness to take great risks must always be distinguished from true consensus and hegemony, for these two sets of attitudes potentially can produce very different social dynamics. In this sense the crises of the established ruling classes and the working classes are both aspects of the same problem. For the very existence of a relatively superficial consensus for, or nominal hegemony of, a system's values makes it that much easier for it to embark on policies dangerous to all of its initial supporters, who have confidence in the nation's material and moral ability to wage war successfully when in fact it possesses scarcely more than its desires and misconceptions merged into a grand strategy. When their social costs become so great that internal conflicts of varying degrees of intensity arise, there emerge those upheavals that form so central a part of the political history of this century. It is the very absence of real discussion of social goals and functions within nations, and the conviction that the system can operate successfully in wartime, that increases the likelihood of its making errors that endanger public and social cohesion and become potentially fatal to the existing order. It is important to comprehend why and how a system coheres and is able to embark on war, but also why and when it can no longer continue with the approval of large sectors of the nation—in a word, to study unity and disunity as aspects of the same experiences.

## The Logic of Credibility

It was countless leaders' unwarranted optimism that they would be free from domestic pressure that made possible their embarking on wars for ephemeral and symbolic reasons, the consequences of which were to prove destructive to tens of millions of people. "Almost one might think the world wished to suffer," Winston Churchill later wrote from the perspective of a former (First World) wartime minister seeking to capture the essential irrationality of Europe's unifying mental fixations. "Certainly men were everywhere eager to dare."[8] Crucial to the dangerous logic of the first and subsequent wars was the deeply rooted belief that the very existence of alliance systems created balances and stability in a world that might otherwise prove dangerously precarious.

That so many alliances in this century have consisted of strong nations linked to weak and unstable ones, making the destiny of the major powers dependent on the behavior and role of fragile states, guaranteed that coalition diplomacy would repeatedly fail to preserve peace. By virtue of the reciprocal obligations each entailed, they were to make war much more likely than if no coalitions whatsoever had existed. The most striking—but in no way unique—example of this was Germany's belief in 1914 that maintaining its alliance with the Austro-Hungarian Empire ultimately outweighed any other consideration, and that should Russia back Serbia and defeat Austria the balance of power in Europe would collapse. Germany, of course, was at the very same time attempting to create or sustain alliances with Turkey, Italy, and nations no less precarious domestically than they were adventurist in their foreign relations. Its expansionist, preemptive war doctrines made the Serbian-Austrian crisis in the summer of 1914 a useful vehicle for applying a more ambitious diplomatic calculus. After 1950, in Vietnam, Central America, and elsewhere, American leaders repeatedly became deeply involved in local conflicts because they believed that the stability of nations and even whole regions was at stake if they did not honor their collective security treaties and bilateral accords with dependent client regimes.

Perhaps the single most recurrent justification that leaders of major powers have evoked for risking wars evolved from their belief that their credibility, which allegedly created fear among potential enemies and thereby constrained their actions, depended on their readiness to use force even when the short-term rationality for violence was very much in doubt. Linked to this credibility fixation was also a widespread conviction that when national prestige in one relatively minor place was challenged then there consequently very well might be a succession of other, even greater defeats in the area—a version of what was later dubbed the "domino theory" in U.S. foreign policy.

In mid-July 1914, Austria's rulers argued that it was imperative to come "to an energetic decision in order to prove its vitality" to Serbia.[9] The ultimate consequence was Europe's mobilization, though in Germany's case the long-ascendant preventive-war faction reinforced the reasoning of both those who always cherished much more ambitious designs and elements who felt strongly that the alliance system required Germany to endorse Austro-Hungarian initiatives whatever their inevitable conclusion. A combination of devotion to their allies and a widespread need to take assertive positions to retain the image of their readiness to defend national interests, combined with their older definitions of their needs and values, caused the major European nations to embark on the first massive bloodletting of this century.

The assumption that the symbolic credibility as well as material foundations of its power required it fatalistically to escalate to maintain the world's fears and perceptions of it caused Japan after 1940 to expand the scope of its East Asian aggressions notwithstanding its acute awareness they would eventually force it into a war with the United States it very well might lose. The Truman Doctrine of 1947 reified the domino theory's premise that the loss of one nation would gravely destabilize those around it, and justified all subsequent applications of American military power. Washington's role in Vietnam after 1962, in turn, was to a great extent the consequence of both its de facto alliance with a venal, unstable client regime upon which its position was increasingly dependent, and the belief, as the American deputy commander in Saigon later put it, that "our credibility worldwide also became an important U.S. interest."[10]

Whatever the variations reflecting specific national characteristics, this century's major warring states have also shared many profound analytic and political premises regarding the meaning, justifications, and consequences of war. The net effect of these astonishingly similar impulses and perceptions has been to leave them all incapable of defining the realities of modern war and politics, or to comprehend the implications that wars might have for their societies and their positions as ruling classes. All decision makers, and those influencing them, operated within the framework of the dominant rulers' consensual values and perceptions, with no place for substantive disagreements that could challenge their most cherished biases. This unanimity characterized all political orders—largely because they all reinforced their systems' premises by excluding all who might dissent from conventional wisdom, but also because the pressures of internal politics often caused them to attempt to solve domestic problems in the international arena. The resulting illusions and oversimplifications conveniently strengthened the political and military elites' preconceptions and interests, and decisively reduced the inhibitions on their formulating highly risky alliance strategies, or articulating dangerous military and foreign-policy doctrines, or, ultimately, embarking on war. And this led to their disregarding clearly obvious facts about the technical nature of modern combat, much less confronting far more analytically subtle but valid notions of war's potential implications for the very future of their societies.

What was most remarkable about the consequences of the major combatants' various syntheses of similar ideas, influences, and pressures was that they all produced a uniformly unrealistic and ultimately irrational common outcome, so that the world's leaders entered wars in this century unprepared for their inevitable consequences—to their peoples, to their ruling classes and social systems, and to the modern historical experience. All were suffused with false expectations, and they had few, if any, notions of the monumental costs in blood and property that their astonishingly casual adventures would demand.

# CHAPTER 2

# False Expectations:
# How Things Go Wrong

The men who began this century's wars invariably substituted those delusions that their domestic political interests and personal ambitions required for realistic assessments of the titanic demands and consequences that modern warfare inevitably creates, and their choices of military strategies far more often than not reflected principally their priorities and constraints at home. By failing to comprehend the true internal political and economic preconditions for waging war, they repeatedly produced those unintended social tensions and structural crises that made profound changes and upheavals within nations rather than relations between them the more significant outcome of international conflicts. To anticipate all those factors that decide the results of war would have required an analytic clarity and honesty that political and military leaders rarely possess, and even when useful knowledge and intelligence existed, precisely because it often revealed unfavorable conditions for attaining victory at acceptable costs, the career-oriented men who run states preferred to ignore it.

Nations embarking upon wars in this century have failed not simply from an abstract viewpoint involving moral behavior or philosophical issues, but also in terms of the material gains and losses and the instability of their own as well as other societies after the fighting ceases. Even less have they ever realized how such internal upheavals, whether among their allies or even within their own country, or among their enemies, might transform the future balance and very purpose of world politics.

War, in essence, has always been an adventure intrinsically beset with surprises and false expectations, its total outcome unpredictable to all those who have engaged in it. For the world's leaders in this century to have focused accurately on war's total environment and actual results, or the vast disjunction between their blithe expectations and reality, would have exposed war as an inherently dangerous enterprise to a nation's longer-term interests—and its rulers as profoundly irrational. This socially sanctioned blindness has invariably made military struggles far different than heads of state initially projected and imagined possible or people expected, profoundly traumatizing countless societies and making war the main motor of social upheaval and change in our era.

## Planning for a Convenient War: World War One

It was as if a universal mind-set, down to the most minute detail, had suffused the tiny coterie that dominated Europe's affairs, and virtually the sole major difference within this elite was the language they spoke. This comprehensive socialization within an overarching web of shared beliefs and perceptions is a persistent fact that we shall encounter repeatedly when fathoming the origins of wars and the ways armies have fought them.

Germany, notwithstanding its expansive ambitions and ideological propensity to a dangerous foreign policy, was no exception to this rule. Until 1910 it projected a modest outlay for a war that it was convinced would be short and, of course, victorious. Only after 1910 did its army's spending increase dramatically, but even then it was only a mere fraction of what was later required. The army's preference until 1911 to maintain the social homogeneity of its officer corps—thereby imposing a limit on its size—reinforced this fiscal bias and allowed the navy to obtain nearly a third of the overall military budget. But while this sum was insufficient to implement its ambitions, it was enough to frighten Great Britain into regarding Germany as the principal menace to its naval supremacy.

Britain, by contrast, planned to rely entirely on her naval power in the event of a European war, maintaining a small army designed principally to police the colonies. It retained complete faith in the efficacy of a naval blockade against Germany, and never seriously considered the strategic implications of the French or Russian armies' inability to contain the Central Powers. In the eight years before 1914, as Prime Minister David Lloyd George later recalled, the entire cabinet devoted "a ridiculously small percentage of its time" to foreign affairs, and knew nothing of the secret military agreements between Russia and France. The crisis in the Balkans was not discussed in the cabinet until "the Friday evening before the final declaration of war by Germany. We were much more concerned with the threat of imminent civil war in the North of Ireland."[1] France's cabinet and parliament were no less indifferent.

Because it was affordable, and military doctrines or diplomatic prognostications existed to rationalize the material constraints each nation's economic capacity or military preparedness imposed, World War One began with its main participants utterly unprepared for what it was to become, and loath to expect a material drain capable of profoundly eroding, if not breaking asunder, their economies. The German army thought a nine-month food supply adequate, even though Germany in the decade before the war imported 20 to 25 percent of its agricultural needs and required about a million seasonal foreign agricultural laborers to help produce the rest. Such optimism was based on sheer self-delusion regarding the length of a war and who would fight it, for the Triple Entente of Britain, France, and Russia in 1913 greatly exceeded the Central Powers in population, the size of their military forces, and shares of world manufacturing output. United, the Entente would not easily lose the war—unless, as Germany believed, military strategy and not economic potential could prove decisive quickly.

Notwithstanding a few well-placed skeptics in England, including Kitchener and Haig, who believed the war might last years rather than months, what all historians have dubbed the "short-war illusion" held sway over nearly all of the key political and military leaders in the nations that were to join it. Indeed, it was the only premise with which the French High Command could successfully justify its insistence upon autonomy from civilian interference. And while the very nature of Europe's political systems and alliances assured that nations could rely on crucial aid from their allies to rationalize their continuing to fight after repeated defeats, and the war would thereby become a protracted, intensive melee, the short-war illusion's optimism was crucial to both the initial causes and later denouement of the war.

In early July 1914 the Germans expected the Austro-Serbian war to last not more than three weeks and to remain localized. Even when it realized that it would involve all the continental powers, Berlin was convinced that the war could not be a long one, and the French shared their view. In both cases this common belief that the war would be quite short because no one could afford a long bloodletting coincided with a certain formal economic rationalism that no more described the conduct of nations than it did the workings of economies. When Italy joined the war in May 1915 on the Entente side, it had no plan to pay its expenses because its leaders were confident the conflict could not last much longer.

Every history of World War One amply documents the tactical and strategic failures of all of the participants' planning and assumptions. The Russians and the French possessed what proved to be utterly insufficient supplies of munitions, rifles, and much more, principally because their military leaders had concluded that the war would be won within six weeks on the basis of two fronts against Germany. German strategic calculations of the war's possible length remained about the same, and their lack of preparations revealed other deficiencies, less glaring on tactical details involving armaments but wholly inadequate for protracted conflict; Germany's profound myopia regarding a long struggle became the fundamental source of its embarking on, and losing, the war against France.

Germany's leaders were unanimous in their belief that they had to avoid a two-front war, for which they simply did not have the resources and manpower to assure victory. The army's real concern in the several years preceding August 1914 was that the rapidly increasing size of Russia's army and economy would by 1917 foredoom any military strategy Germany might adopt. The logic of this reading of the material balance of forces and belief in the crucial role of a successful first-strike offensive convinced the key German generals that a preventive war in 1914 was the only course to avoid possible defeat a few years later, and their perceptions increasingly swayed Germany's civilian leaders' attitudes during the crucial months preceding the outbreak of the war.

Germany's much-examined Schlieffen Plan assumed that a massive deployment of its armies against the French, in a huge encircling movement across Belgium that would wheel around both sides of Paris to return eastward to trap the French army massed defensively in fortified areas near Alsace and Lorraine, would produce France's defeat before Russia could mobilize fully to attack the initially lightly defended areas to the east of Germany. Then railroads were to speed German troops to the Russian front. To avoid a simultaneous two-front war was absolutely essential to Germany's quick victory, and violating Belgian neutrality, or being forced to sustain capricious but indispensable Austro-Hungarian allies certain to provoke Russian entry into war, therefore seemed small prices to pay; for even if Belgium brought Britain into the conflict, German generals believed that its small army would be of no consequence in the short conflict. But the plan was fatally flawed because Germany's army was never big enough to implement it, and its expensive navy was irrelevant to the ground war. While Germany had a great land artillery superiority over the French, its army had insufficient transport for the vast maneuver Schlieffen had projected—including such deficiencies as adequate fodder for its predominantly horse-drawn supplies or even field kitchens to feed its troops. Above all, however, its basic strategy of violating Belgian neutrality and sustaining its alliance with the moribund, adventurist Austro-Hungarian Empire guaranteed it would confront much of the remainder of Europe in warfare, producing the very nightmare of a war on two fronts its leaders had convinced themselves they could—and had to—avoid.

The French were fully aware of Germany's plans and intended to respond with a comparable offensive strategy—the so-called Plan XVII of April 1913—which in a general way was to send the highly mobile, lightly armed French armies north toward the Lorraine-Luxembourg area to separate and defeat the German armies in their center and eliminate the rest quickly thereafter. The French possessed nothing like the highly detailed German operations procedures, which read like a railroad timetable, but instead vaguely assumed that the sheer impact of their bravery and audacity would succeed. They had only, as Marshal Joffre later described it, "a full determination to take the offensive with all my forces assembled," and "both sides were in agreement that only a vigorous offensive could bring success."[2] While the French offensive strategy was guided as much by domestic political considerations as any other factor, there can be little doubt that such doctrines reflected a great consensus prevailing among the military of the major adversaries, none of whom, as Lloyd George later put it, were "averse from putting their theories, plans, and hopes to the test."[3] Britain's generals were no less committed to a "human battlefield" involving aggressive closing with the enemy, expecting their bayonets, steel, and bravery to triumph.[4] Romantic militarist illusions left generals everywhere utterly oblivious to the nature of warfare in the machine age.

Both sides, as a consequence, failed on northern France's vast inhospitable, muddy terrain, and the war became a protracted, terrible event completely different from anything the military leaders of Europe who coveted the conflict had ever imagined.

## The Alliance Imperative

Simultaneous with internal political considerations and a fixation with credibility in causing the war were the explicit and, even more important, implicit alliances to which by 1914 all of the world's major nations, including the United States and Japan, adhered. In the United States' case, its unchallenged hegemony in the Western Hemisphere had depended on British support since the end of the nineteenth century, and Japanese domination of the northeast Asian region was intimately connected to the Anglo-Japanese Treaty of 1902, which linked the two nations' destinies in the area for two decades. Such alliances introduced so many dangerously mercurial complexities into diplomatic and military affairs that their proliferation after the end of the nineteenth century virtually guaranteed war in the not-too-distant future. The efforts to maintain them tied the future of nations to essentially ephemeral yet potentially explosive considerations involving the prestige and sangfroid of their allies, and once wars began, alliances both globalized and protracted them.

The infinitely convoluted geopolitical matrix defining the way nations related to others is well illustrated in the case of Great Britain, which some still think might have remained neutral in the war—at least for a time—had Germany not invaded Belgium and thereby threatened control of the Channel. But Britain believed that, to maintain European stability, it had to preserve France as a barrier to German power and expansion. In July 1914 it feared that if it did not remain loyal to France in a Balkans quarrel in which neither was directly concerned, but which involved initially France's Russian ally, it would face the awesome risk of later being isolated after the existing European and global balance of power was upset. This balance depended to some great measure on the willingness of states to go to war for secondary reasons even, as in the case of Britain's relationship to France and Russia, when they had no formal obligation to do so. Moreover, the continued growth of the German fleet reinforced Britain's anxiety. And despite the Quai d'Orsay's intense desire to mediate the Balkans crisis, France too felt that it could not stand alone and must come to Russia's aid, if required, to sustain its military strategy of confronting Germany on two vast fronts.

No less significant, however, was the fact that although Britain and Russia could cooperate as allies against a common menace in Europe, the British regarded Russia as the single greatest threat to their interests in Persia, Afghanistan, and India; freed from its European preoccupations, Russia might very well turn southward at the expense of Britain. That Russia "may become weary of us and throw us overboard," (even cozy up to Germany!) and "cause us an infinity of annoyance" was always a factor in the British government's desire to keep Russia preoccupied with European affairs.[5] It thus had to assuage Russia's legitimate concern that the Triple Entente was not a durable and comprehensive alliance. In the days before war broke out, London considered that if the Germans were to win the war, Britain alone would confront a Germany dominating all of Europe to the Channel, but that if France and Russia won it by themselves they would be free, and probably eager, to challenge British hegemony from the Mediterranean to India. Either way, England would emerge from the conflict far more vulnerable. Calculations such as these made it inevitable that the British, notwithstanding their efforts to forestall it, would join the war at its inception, if only to control its geopolitical aftermath. Britain's intention to do what was necessary to support its formal or de facto allies, and to ensure its potential enemies' belief that it was ultimately prepared on behalf of "credibility" to go to war, was never based on simple reasoning but rather reflected its more complicated global geopolitical integration of issues. Similar calculations guided the decisions of all the other major contestants in World War One.

Germany's relationship with its allies, above all Austria-Hungary, was no less convoluted. Maintaining Vienna in a solid front against the French-Russian alliance was absolutely essential for the Schlieffen Plan's success, for the Austro-Hungarian army was to hold the Russians at bay for the few weeks the Germans thought they needed to implement the strategy and then redirect their forces to the Russian front. But the Austro-German Treaty of 1879 to fight Russia together was quite imprecise, and in the spring of 1914, Austria's preoccupation with Serbia and Slav nationalism revealed to Berlin that its ally was both irresponsible and weak. What the Germans feared most was that the Viennese leaders might make overtures to Russia to solve their dilemmas, thereby both completely destroying Berlin's grand military and diplomatic plans for guiding European affairs and also initiating the dissolution of the Austro-Hungarian Empire in a piecemeal fashion. Were it not to assert its prestige against Serbia, Berlin reasoned, the already declining Austria would "hardly count . . . any longer as a really Great Power," and the Russians would establish an intolerable indirect hegemony in the Balkans. When the crisis in Serbia erupted, Germany's leaders were most concerned about the "political rehabilitation" of the empire, and they bent every effort to persuade the vacillating Austrian rulers to make no concessions, thereby saving the empire from the centrifugal nationalist passions it contained.[6] While Germany initially both preferred and expected that the Austrian attack on Serbia would not evolve into a European war, it knew that whether this would prove true depended entirely on Russia's decision to come to the aid of the Serbs when Austria declared war upon them. Once Russian intervention seemed unavoidable, Berlin accepted the inevitability of a general war—one that it was convinced, in any case, had best begin sooner rather than later.

Since Germany believed that the credibility and the very existence of the Austro-Hungarian Empire was crucial to maintaining its own power and plans, when the Serbs at the end of July acceded to what Germany considered "a capitulation of the most humiliating kind," forcing it to admit privately that "every cause for war has vanished," the Germans nonetheless insisted upon an Austrian occupation of Serbia so that "it [Austria] receive a visible *satisfaction d'honneur*," in effect restoring the credibility of its only crucial ally.[7] Germany thereby linked its designs and role in Europe to the fate of weak powers—Austria-Hungary first of all, but also, in lesser ways, Turkey, Rumania, and Italy. Its goals, for some of its key leaders, involved the creation of a central European sphere of influence as part of a vast regional bloc capable of dealing to its west with the Anglo-Saxon system and to its east with Russia and the putative Slav menace. Berlin's other open-ended ambitions and Teutonic supremacist views reflected the grandiose, if not megalomaniac aspirations of various factions among its ruling class. All of these factors served to convince the Triple Entente that a confrontation with Germany was unavoidable.

Once Europe's powers were locked into alliances that each perceived as crucial to its military security, diplomacy had little role to play as "credibility"—either in the form of giving reassurance to friends that they could be relied upon, or to enemies that they should be feared—defined the decisions of the major states and led inexorably to war. Military strategy, in the case of Germany, bound it to the fate of the Austro-Hungarian Empire so that it could implement its grand strategy toward France and Russia in succession; the Russians committed themselves to an intrinsically precarious offensive against German lines to foil the Schlieffen Plan and bog Germany down on two fronts. And the virtually identical offensive military doctrine and preparations of the major belligerents required them to mobilize their armies first and to strike instantly, precluding any serious role for diplomacy. Too many uncontrollable variables and complex considerations made military conflict inevitable, but the very existence of alliances meant that its members would make the maximum number of enemies possible and that wars would encompass far more territory and people than ever before. They would also last much longer by virtue of the fact that each member of an alliance would judge its own weaknesses not on their own terms but in relationship to the potential of its allies—and thereby persist in fighting on despite growing sacrifices of its human and economic resources. When all of the labyrinthine geopolitical tensions within each alliance and considerations of internal politics merged in mid-1914, then mankind's fate was sealed and on August 4 began the bloodiest conflict the world had ever known.

## World War Two

Although the exceedingly precarious German and Japanese decisions that led to World War Two superficially possess haphazard, incremental aspects, the conflict's origins must in the last analysis be attributed to the pervasive fact that each nation's leaders possessed a profoundly dangerous vision that sought to create a restructured regional order they believed to be both desirable and inevitable. What makes their projects appear so capricious was their initial belief that they might attain their goals without risking a general, protracted war. Distinguishing the war's seemingly immediate causes from the aggressor nations' underlying objectives, values, and premises has been a major challenge to historians, for random, even unpredictable factors also shaped profoundly the war's form, timing, and outcome. But notwithstanding the decisive importance of Hitler and of Japan's war party, the fundamental conditions and political ideologies that made possible their very existence as serious candidates to lead their nations must also be traced back decades before they took power and undertook to conquer Europe and Asia. For Hitler's and Japan's most extreme militarists' calculations also shared a very great deal in common with the facile self-deluding manner by which the leaders of nations until then had viewed the nature and prospects of modern wars. When considered in the context of a tradition of convenient myopia and rationalization, the origins of World War Two were very much the logic of an intellectual process that has pervaded this entire century and also explains the genesis of wars throughout it in the hands of men who, superficially at least, appeared infinitely more rational and humane than Adolf Hitler.

## Hitler's Road to War

Historians share a general consensus on Hitler's broad premises when calculating war and peace, as well as his objectives, and their disagreements on the specific aspects of Hitler's reasoning are largely a result of the bewildering diversity of his statements and comments. But what is clear to all is that until the autumn of 1941, as his close aide Albert Speer later described it, Hitler based his projected "politics on short wars with long stretches of quiet in between."[8] This demanded relatively small, brief, but intensive blitzkriegs against isolated enemies but, above all, the avoidance of a war of attrition on two fronts such as World War One had become despite Germany's leaders plans to avert it. Such conflicts presupposed military preparations sufficient only to overwhelm hapless lone nations without overly taxing Germany's relatively finite economic resources. By definition, this necessitated a reliance on highly mobile armor, firepower and shock troops, airpower and, most important, exploiting the element of surprise. Hitler initially intended to avert a total war, at the very least until Germany had economically digested its victories against Czechoslovakia, Poland, and the Soviet Union. In essence, Hitler outlined a convenient, quite trouble-free vision of Nazi expansion, predicated not only on the validity of his grand military strategy but also on disunited enemies possessing all of the many weaknesses he quite casually, often with little if any knowledge, attributed to them.

In the last analysis, the blitzkrieg doctrine was an elaborate rationalization for Hitler's domestic priorities and the belief that he could avoid the traumatic strains that the First World War had imposed on German society and still gain his foreign objectives. Like Germany's leaders before 1914, he too believed that military policy could be adapted to domestic imperatives.

Hitler appeared not to have a coherent war plan because, as Speer described him, "he always wanted to have everything at once," and he mixed short- and long-range objectives with his sense of the possibilities of the given moment to improvise in attaining his overall goals, goals that were explicit but had neither predetermined means nor a timetable for implementation.[9] Hitler sought to empty large parts of eastern Europe to create *Lebensraum* for Germany's broadly defined Aryan population within the boundaries of a greatly expanded *Reich*, and although some historians have claimed he projected his plan for a vast new state to be launched as early as 1943–45, others have fixed his target a decade later. Either way, he surely believed that it would have to be attained within his lifetime and that he alone could accomplish the mission—and he feared he might die before its fulfillment. Hitler was therefore a gambler, prone to audacity, improvisations, and risks, but in the short run he hoped to conquer adjoining states and thereby acquire the greater raw-materials base he needed for later expansion. His spectacular successes in the Saar, Austria, and Czechoslovakia before 1939 only confirmed his commitment to a blitzkrieg strategy to master Europe.

When Hitler attacked Poland on September 1, 1939, he and his principal advisers believed that France, and certainly England, notwithstanding their pledges to Poland, would, as with Czechoslovakia, most probably remain passive, and that war with the British was not likely before Germany was ready to start it. The war in Poland more than vindicated his faith in his blitzkrieg strategy, and the Poles surrendered on October 6, but London and Paris declared war, compelling him to change his timetable. Hitler had in any case thought that a war with France and Britain about a year after the defeat of Poland was desirable, and with the Hitler-Stalin Pact as insurance against opposition from the USSR and the danger of a two-front war, he turned west earlier than he had planned and before the accelerating Anglo-French military buildup could alter the existing balance of forces. Unquestionably, however, a full-scale war in Europe was something for which Hitler was not yet ready, and although he either ignored them or they kept their opinions to themselves, a few of his generals and admirals thought that war with Britain was premature and would last a very long time.

But Hitler hoped to fight his new enemies as he had his old, employing brief, mobile, massive, and relatively inexpensive campaigns, and his spectacular success against the French in May and June 1940 removed whatever doubts existed among his traditionalist senior officers, who with few exceptions enthusiastically endorsed the June 1941 attack against the USSR. Militarily, it was vastly more precarious than anything Hitler had ever attempted, and the Soviet Union's ability to resist became the single most important factor in determining the war's military outcome.

Hitler expected to defeat Britain, or compel it to concede to his demands, with air and sea power, which required time and resources to build. Hitler always dismissed the Soviet Union as a house of cards militarily, yet after the Hitler-Stalin Pact he was forced to exchange precious raw materials for Russian oil and wheat, and so in July 1940 he decided next to conquer the USSR the following year and integrate its economy before returning to what he supposed to be the more formidable task of defeating Britain. While he allocated five months to the campaign, many of his generals, impressed with Soviet failures during its 1940 war with Finland, thought less time would suffice, and told the Japanese that victory would come within three months. On the assumption that they alone would remain to administer the defeated colossus, the Nazi leadership provided only one-fifth of the German regular forces with winter clothing, and the German army set off with few, if any, reliable maps. The rest is well known: Germany was again enmeshed in a two-front war and Hitler's fantasies were smashed.

Until the Soviet counterattack against the Nazi army at the end of November 1941, Germany had proceeded in its conquest of Europe with only a relatively minimal mobilization of its manpower and resources. In the summer of 1939 its stockpile of strategic materials was adequate only for several months of intensive combat, its tank output was below Britain's and half of France's, while its aircraft production was only equal to Britain's. It had less than six weeks' reserves of munitions when it attacked Poland and major shortages appeared immediately. Civilian consumption and house building in 1939 were at 1929 levels or higher, and when the war began Hitler refused to trim his grandiose construction projects. Per capita civilian consumption in 1942 was still five percent higher than 1934. In autumn of 1939, Germany's share of industrial output devoted to armaments was less than France's. Even in 1941 a higher proportion of Britain's gross national product went to war purposes. Given Hitler's ambitions, the real balance of forces, and the far greater scale of its later arms output, Germany's war effort until late 1941 remained lackadaisical.

Hitler's extraordinary optimism regarding the war's duration and the weakness of his enemies made his army's condition precarious from the very inception of the conflict. Germany's coal supplies lagged with a serious freight-car shortage, and by the spring of 1940 it was only Hitler's audacity and the superior cohesion and discipline of the German army, combined with the deplorable morale and leadership of its French adversaries, that prevented a decisive Nazi defeat. France had 4,000 armored vehicles to confront Germany's attack, half of them modern. Germany deployed 2,500 tanks, not more than 1,000 of which were modern. And apart from the fact that the Allies had significantly more divisions than the Germans, the Nazi air force was only marginally superior to that of the combined Anglo-French, who were on their way to producing far more and better planes when fighting began. Logistically and materially, there was no reason for Germany to win so much so quickly. Hitler's fatal mistake was to assume he could send a haphazardly supplied, indifferently equipped army into Russia, where half of its divisions were dependent exclusively on horses for transport—requiring immense amounts of fodder—and at least two-thirds of its tanks were obsolete or made principally for training, and much inferior to the Soviet T-34 tank.

Hitler's refusal to consider World War Two a total war until two years after its inception, and then only halfheartedly, gave the British, Americans, and Russians a decisive respite during which to mobilize their vast industrial power. With continuing high levels of civilian spending, imported foreign labor became the mainstay of expanded German efforts, increasing ten times from May 1939 to May 1941—not to mention exactions from conquered nations. Suffice it to say here (details are in Chapter 9), Speer accurately described Hitler's policy on the welfare of Germany's civilians as an effort "to keep the morale of the people in the best possible state by concessions. Hitler and the majority of his political followers belonged to the generation who as soldiers had witnessed the Revolution of November 1918 and had never forgotten it. In private Hitler indicated that after the experience of 1918 one could not be cautious enough."[10] Hitler, in brief, preferred courting defeat abroad to revolution at home, thereby transferring by far the greater part of the war's traumatizing social, political, and human costs to other nations.

There was an inherent incoherence in Hitler's means and ends for establishing a thousand-year *Reich* ruling Europe and perhaps large parts of the world, and his assumption that he could pursue an astonishingly ambitious military policy without sacrificing his largely unconstrained domestic objectives, which would have risked alienating his population, only added to the intrinsic madness of the colossal project. The notion that attaining *Lebensraum* in eastern Europe required the defeat of the reluctant British and French caused him to globalize the war, and seek to gain all of his main goals at once, and his capricious decision to make the conquest of Russia a prerequisite for then defeating England endangered his basic military strategy of fighting on one front at a time. But Hitler's fatal misreading of the tasks involved in fighting the Red Army was not based on a special irrationality, because the British and French also shared his contempt for Soviet military power, and had Hitler chosen not to collaborate with it but had attempted first to destroy the USSR, Great Britain and France may not have declared war so quickly—if at all.

As it was, Hitler invaded the Soviet Union with open-ended territorial objectives for his army but also with the conviction that he would have to go all the way to defeat communism and, more vaguely, later recycle the USSR's vast expanses into a new German empire located in still dimly defined borders. In this sense there was no territorial limit imposed on his offensive, either in the short or long run, for Nazism was inherently expansive and it had no confidence in attaining its aims by forming and keeping compromising alliances with other states to whose interests Germany would have to defer. This meant a constant escalation of Nazi military efforts to fulfill its grandiose goals, and hence the inevitable later escalation of its extermination policy, which in the autumn of 1939 was intended principally for Poland's ruling class but subsequently greatly enlarged to include Jews, Gypsies, average Poles, and many others after Hitler's initial design for expelling the Jews from Europe proved unrealistic.

Nazi expectations before 1941 were therefore a composite of their megalomaniac wishes, which the appeasement policies of all those nations that were later compelled to fight Germany helped greatly to define, plus the specific cultural phobias of traditional German chauvinism and its later Nazi mutation's fantastic aspirations and readiness to risk everything abroad, but nothing domestically, to attain them. A coherent military strategy was impossible in this context, for Germany ended by engaging in a war on two major and several minor fronts simultaneously, even though more cautious timing and serious domestic mobilization might very well have produced a victory for it that would have totally transformed Europe and, over time, much of the world, for generations.

### The Allied Strategy

Britain and France based their joint strategy for fighting Germany on a number of crucial but erroneous assumptions, the most important being that they could fight a protracted defensive war in the West and gain sufficient time to bring the superiority of their combined industry and manpower to bear. And they both believed that Germany's military preparations were far more advanced than their own, and that they must make a massive effort to catch up. The two Allies intended the war to last longer than Germany desired or could afford, but it was also supposed to be short enough to permit them both to rebuild their own peacetime economies reasonably quickly. And while they were ready to go to war for Poland, they had no confidence in the Polish army, and Britain was unwilling to give it any significant amount of matériel or money. Unlike in World War One, the British and French expected to fight the war on one front, and even immediately after the Nazis attacked the Soviet Union, they both dismissed the possibility of that nation playing a role; their official assumption was that in no more than six weeks Germany would cripple all effective Russian resistance.

Germany, in fact, was far less prepared than the British believed, but at the war's outset this illusion provoked the British to mobilize their economy to far exceed German output of airplanes and, by the end of 1940, tanks and munitions also. Britain's basic premises during the late 1930s was that sea power would only play a defensive role, as it unexpectedly had from

1914 to 1918, but that it could at least impose a costly blockade on Germany. The bombing of Germany and erosion within its empire were eventually to bring Hitler to his knees, before England became bankrupt. Britain decided to build costly heavy bombers able to drop over three times greater tonnages than existing aircraft, and its leaders expected strategic airpower rather than its army to play the decisive role in the war. But this assumption proved largely invalid, and from June 1939 to June 1945 the British had to increase the size of their armed forces by over 1,000 percent, to 5 million persons, and the war took far longer than they either foresaw or could afford. The conflict became primarily a land war, and thereby gave the USSR a critical, preeminent role—defining to a great degree the political outcome of the war in eastern and central Europe. The British failed to anticipate any of this.

But notwithstanding the British and American agreement on mobilizing their superior economic power over time, the Allies constantly argued on how, where, and when to defeat Germany. In late 1943 an economically desperate London planned to end the war before 1945, but the U.S. refused to accept its strategies for quickly concluding the conflict. Whatever the initial massive errors in Britain's calculations, luck and Germany's own decisive mistakes redeemed them. Notwithstanding their incompetence on crucial matters, the British managed to finesse their way victoriously through the war for reasons largely beyond their control.[11]

The fact that the French shared the largely erroneous British view that German war preparations were far ahead of their own also stimulated them to accelerate their rearmament. In fact, in terms of actual divisions ready to implement the joint Allied defensive strategy, the Allies (including Holland and Belgium) had about a million soldiers more than Germany. French tanks outnumbered Germany's (their monthly tank output by the last half of 1939 greatly exceeded their enemy's), and while Hitler's air force was far superior, its psychological impact was much greater than its purely destructive capacity. France's war effort was only slightly behind Germany's, and had there been time might have exceeded it. Its problems were not principally material but involved strategy and leadership, which were fatally deficient in ways that France's leaders and the British government failed totally to understand or anticipate.

The French in 1939 were unreservedly committed to a strategy of defense. Hitler, not wishing to play into French hands at great cost to his army and economy, simply searched for their weaknesses. The large French army was strung out thinly in fixed positions along its northern and eastern borders, operating according to prearranged plans and oblivious to the meaning of the Nazi commitment to a blitzkrieg strategy. It repeatedly ignored advance warnings giving accurate details of the German attack on May 10, 1940. The French command's radio network was primitive and it required an average of two days before new orders were implemented.

Apart from its wholly irrelevant strategic concept, France's major problem was profound demoralization, principally among its leaders, and a bankrupt alliance policy. Until September 1939 most of its military leaders, particularly the air force, thought the nation was wholly unprepared for conflict, its justification for war unconvincing. France declared war on Germany for attacking Poland, whom the French had never planned to support militarily even though they had cynically pledged to do so. Many of France's leaders saw the war as either unnecessary or premature. In the nine months after war was formally declared but before Hitler attacked, the morale of bored soldiers waiting passively on the defense lines plummeted: alcoholism became far more widespread, and their looting of evacuated villages on the border reflected their deep malaise. When the Germans concentrated forty-five divisions against the nine divisions defending the Ardennes, the added weight of their airpower was sufficient to cause the entire French army to capsize over the next six weeks even though the French had in 1914 done far more with much less. The French failed to comprehend the Nazi strategy or their own grave weaknesses, and the result was fatal.[12]

### Japan's Destiny in Asia

In the Far East the process that led to Japan's protracted war with China, and eventually with the United States, was but a mirror image of the causes, moods, and choices that had guided European states since the turn of the century. And like them in July 1914, or Hitler later, the Japanese anticipated that their steps to impose their political and economic hegemony in North China in the summer of 1937 would be nothing more than a brief, relatively localized, and quite cost-free affair—precisely as their annexation of Manchuria in 1931 had been. What began as the "China Incident" was to terminate as World War Two in Asia, an event that was to traumatize the entire vast region and completely transform it politically.

Whatever the significant differences over timing, rhetoric, and tactics, the Japanese political elite and the army and navy after 1932 shared an officially defined, broad consensus that Japan should be hegemonic in East Asia, and that this required it to convince the United States and, to a lesser extent, the USSR to accept the still unspecified strategic, political, and economic consequences of Japanese mastery over the immense area. Such a goal implied, at the very least, control over China, naval predominance in the western Pacific, and the ability to defeat the Red Army if necessary. There were significant disagreements within the decision-making groups that ruled Japan on how and when to achieve these ambitious goals, but repression precluded challenges to their authority from democratic elements, which had been weak even during the best of times. In 1935 and especially February 1936, bombings and assassinations of senior government and military officials who thwarted the ultrahawks in the army reminded the rulers of the domestic difficulties they might face should they seek to thwart the imperialist mission; but not even the navy, which in 1935 had opposed further expansion in China, if only for pragmatic reasons, questioned the ultimate objective of Japan's control over Asia and the use of force to attain it.

The Marco Polo Bridge clash between Japanese and Chinese forces on July 7, 1937, outside Peking, allowed the hawks to test whether the Chiang Kai-shek Nationalist government would acquiesce to Japan's grand design for it to become a puppet regime, and it was Chiang's resistance that led to the extension of the invasion to Shanghai the following month and then to the coastal cities—committing Tokyo to the first major step toward creating an "East Asian bloc." Japan was now at war with Nationalist China, but it expected that soldiers whom they regarded as racial inferiors would either capitulate or be easily defeated. But the army gave its invading forces insufficient munitions and treated the entire China Incident as a minor challenge to be quickly and cheaply settled within a few months, anticipating that a satellite regime would rule at Japan's behest. They were utterly surprised by the actual sequence of events. For the Chinese refused to surrender. And rather than modify its objectives, Japan increased them, believing that they too would be easy to achieve.

By the following May, Japan's leaders realized that the war in China would take longer and cost far more than planned, and they took what they believed would be the military steps necessary to conclude it, but Chiang abandoned the coastal region and moved inland in the hope of consolidating power in the vast western regions. The conflict was now stalemated and Japan had 1 million troops locked into a hopeless war that it had first supposed, as the army minister had predicted in July 1937, "could be ended within a month."[13]

The essence of Japan's dilemma was that the profound imperialist consensus that united its leaders made them, like Hitler, prone to escalate their objectives whenever it seemed expedient, though in fact they too had insufficient means to attain them. It was because of the costly China quagmire, not the basic imperialist concept itself, that the navy was to urge a modicum of caution during 1940 and 1941. Yet unlike in Germany, the very existence of powerful factions tended to create pressures from officer elements drunk with small victories and whose fanatical militarist credo romantically threw all caution to the winds. Its incredibly ambitious military and political goals and heady chauvinist obsessions left Japan open to profound adventurism, and the China impasse only intensified its rulers' quite irrational militarist reasoning that the best way to overcome obstacles was to expand even further.

The key turning point in Japan's policy came in May 1940, when the Germans advanced into France and Holland, leaving the colonial systems in Southeast Asia defenseless. On September 27, 1940, Japan signed the Tripartite Pact with Germany and Italy, eliminating the obstacles to Japan taking all of Southeast Asia. Its major military factions immediately debated where first to strike, concocting a justification for taking the southern part of French Indochina. One argument was that bases there would allow the war against China to be prosecuted more effectively; another, that Indochina would give Japan a jumping point for taking Malaya and, above all, the Dutch East Indies. It could then integrate the region's vast raw-materials potential to emerge far stronger in the future struggle against China and, even more important, the United States. But when the Nazis attacked the Soviet Union, others urged that Siberia be annexed first. Yet all agreed that the imperatives of Japan's situation required escalation, ostensibly to redeem its dilemmas in China, compensate for its grave raw-materials weaknesses, and attain its grandiose ambitions for all of Asia at the same time.

What had begun as a local, short-term expansion was now transformed into the immense Asia theater of World War Two, as desperate as anything Hitler had undertaken and no less the inevitable logic of a nationalist, militarist dream of hegemony that merged a contempt for other peoples with a fatal ignorance of what modern warfare had become.

It was a measure of the Japanese leadership's irrationality that it embarked on a course virtually certain to produce war with America before Japan attained its goals in China. In 1936 they calculated that Japan could win a war if it fought only one western power, and it might stalemate two, but it would be defeated were it to fight the U.S., Britain, and the USSR together—by far the most likely prospect after June 1941. But given their shared, essentially mystical faith in Japan's destiny, the tempting prizes in Southeast Asia, and their fear of becoming "a third-class nation" otherwise, the Japanese leaders merged an unwarranted optimism and a desperate need for raw materials to rationalize engaging in a strategy that led ineluctably to their decision in 1941 to attack the United States.[14]

War with America was to be principally the navy's responsibility, and although the navy thwarted those who advocated fighting the USSR first, it could not prevail on the government to win the war in China before embarking on a far greater gamble; and so, by September 1940 the navy unhappily agreed to support expansion toward Southeast Asia—with its great risk of confrontation with the U.S.—fully conscious Japan could not defeat its enemy in protracted conflict. Japan's leaders by this time possessed an accurate projection of the nation's long-term deficiencies in industrial output and its gravely inadequate access to oil should the war go on for more than a year. The navy in the summer of 1940 estimated it could fight effectively for about a year with its existing oil reserves, and were the U.S. to opt for a long war, as seemed most likely, its position would quickly deteriorate thereafter. Japan initiated a war with America with only a four-month reserve of iron ore, and a nine-month supply of bauxite, on hand.

But whatever its pessimism and realism, when Washington on July 26, 1941, imposed a total blockade on oil sales to Japan, the navy endorsed the basic principle of imperialism. Japan first struck southward and, in December, attacked the U.S., expecting to rapidly create a more self-contained raw-materials bloc. Japan's leaders now wistfully hoped that they might fight well long enough—the navy now predicted it could do so for two years—to convince the Americans to accede quickly to the Japanese-dominated status quo in East Asia. As a consequence, Japan's leaders initially did not even trouble during 1941 to enlarge their industrial base for making war. But victory in this limited sense depended greatly not only on whether the Japanese could inflict major damage on the U.S. at the inception of the conflict and occupy strategic points—both of which they did—but also on the Americans obligingly deciding for a "quick showdown" militarily while Japan was relatively stronger than its enemy and before the U.S.—with an economy ten times larger than Japan's—could rearm massively.[15]

Few thought this likely. A profound pessimism and fatalism suffused the Japanese leadership's estimates during the weeks before their assault on Pearl Harbor. Their merger of adventurism, a mystical, romantic fatalism, and profound imperialist ambition overcame their astonishingly accurate clarity regarding the facts, driving them further in the grave direction that they embarked upon with their attempt to conquer China. In a century of vast irrationality that has caused so much human suffering, this mixture was surely one of the most bizarre instances of folly.

## Consensus and the Limits of Intelligence

Why have most, if not all, of the men who who have defined the fate of the world and the greater part of its people throughout this century been unable to foresee the obviously enormous cost and self-destructive implications of their policies? With the exception of Japan in 1941, all sides—whether rational democrats with humane pretensions or cynical and mad totalitarians—have initiated wars full of illusions and false expectations as to their future course, and the point is less that their actions were just or unjust but simply that they were counterproductive in terms of the attainment of their objectives. They not only failed to achieve these in the majority of instances, but they left their own nations politically and socially traumatized, thereby making possible revolutions from both the Left and the Right that otherwise would surely never have occurred.

Crucial to fathoming the cause of the ruling class's endemic, systematic myopia is the similarity of the formal and informal methods by which key decision makers are selected and molded in all nations, regardless of their political structures. Such socialization processes are never based on abstract and objective rationality or norms of merit, but unrelentingly weed out very early in their careers those individuals who are likely to treat information as a neutral, rational means to clarify and help formulate policies that have yet to be sharply defined—to ask, thereby, uncomfortable, critical questions about basic issues that interfere with the predetermined assumptions, goals, and interests of a class-dominated system and the men who run it. At the levels that count, there are rarely, if ever, dissidents within ruling classes who can—or choose to—alter policies before they become irrational or self-destructive.

The socialization process of leaders in every modern state is monolithically loyal to the consensus that both defines and binds its dominating class, and whether or not it is ruthless, it is always highly effective. Germany after 1870 easily imposed a homogeneous authoritarian, militarist ideology on a large middle-class constituency that was incorporated into both the politically reliable civil service and the army. And the majority of the key executives in foreign and defense affairs in the U.S. since 1945 have been graduates of banal, often low-status institutions rather than Ivy League universities; but their behavior has been identical to that of the products of elite schools. While some nations, such as Japan before 1941, had factions that disputed issues of timing or the direction of aggression, none questioned the basic premise of imperialism or the use of military force to advance it—or, indeed, the ultimate prerogative of the cabinet and the emperor finally to determine policies. What is most crucial to explain in every nation is continuity in programs and the premises that lead to their repetition, often even after they have patently failed. The United States' consistent pursuit of counterinsurgency warfare after 1947—ranging from supplying aid to proxies to the use of its own troops—notwithstanding its frequent political or military defeats, has never been challenged within key decision-making circles. While one may focus, as elsewhere, on bureaucratic disagreements about procedural aspects over executing a strategy, the essence of the decision-making process of modern nations remains the large measure of consensus itself rather than the normal relatively petty bureaucratic differences among those who implement policies on how best to apply them.

An objective, disinterested "intellectual" rationality to guide a nation's interests has never existed, nor will it emerge in the future. Abstract technical criteria, which Weberian theorists point to with the implication that ability counts most in forming modern organizational structures, become immeasurably less important than careerism and ambition, which is the decisive distinguishing factor that projects people into power. For there are far more men who possess talent and qualifications than there are important posts. Social or family connections by themselves cannot explain success, though in many cases they have been important, but in few countries do the well-born attain high rank without the requisite motivations and ambitions. And it is precisely the factor of careerism and ambition that produces a monolithic consensus among a nation's leaders, nearly all of whom unquestioningly make or endorse the unchallenged grave errors that lead to wars. Such men relate only to each other, adopting the norms and biases of the system in which decision makers are formed, operate, and use intelligence. Their criterion of success reflects overwhelmingly, if not wholly, their ability to operate and prosper—in a word, to be given jobs—within a given organizational system entirely on its own terms, whether nominally democratic or a one-man dictatorship, reasonably rational or quite insane. That the society as a whole is usually far worse off in the medium or long run because of policies subordinated to the ambitions and ignorance of personalities and cliques is irrelevant to aspiring leaders; to them, improvising and confidently rising is much more crucial. The extent to which ideologies truly motivate them can be easily judged by the political careers that former senior Nazi, fascist, or Communist officials and leaders have chosen to play throughout this century—and their one-time opponents' acceptance of their somersaults.

Every nation encourages sycophancy and loyalty among potential decision makers, but also among the vastly greater number who serve them. This may range, on the one extreme, from Hitler's surrounding himself with fawning careerists who unfailingly told him what he wished to hear, to Lyndon Johnson before 1968, when some of the men who advised him protected their positions by carefully keeping to themselves their profound doubts about policies they thought would prove disastrous—and never under any circumstance revealed them to the public. That a political player must be loyal to the tiny elite he is working with in order to prosper is axiomatic in the guidance of foreign affairs.

A mere handful of men lead nations into wars: the views of not more than a dozen men counted in Germany in 1914. Beneath such a minute directorate, those whose opinions are taken seriously or who are experts will be consulted. While organized social-science research in recent decades has increasingly transformed the giving of such advice into a profession of varying degrees of importance in many nations, the process of relying on the opinions and insights of allegedly wise advisers has always been with us. But successful consultants very often self-confidently produce advice or information that only further obfuscates comprehension in order to keep the flow of money or ego-aggrandizing attention coming in their direction. And even if such nominal experts are talented and not merely arrogant, and not simply politically well placed and in a position to obtain contracts for predetermined policy-oriented advice, they are the least likely to be independent. Among military officers, careerism invariably reinforces their tendency to report accomplishments rather than failures to their superiors, for they are judged professionally by the ostensible results they can promise or produce. Military establishments add, although usually no more than civilians, to the building of illusions and myths about realities and the consequences of war. The most significant aspect of intelligence has been the astonishingly great extent to which those paid to produce it distorted it or the rulers of nations ignored that part that did not justify their misconceived and dangerous preconceptions and policies.

For all these reasons, when choices involving war and peace were being made, the men who counted most remained both insulated from—and immune to—accurate estimates of military, economic, and political conditions. Hence the consistency of rulers' grave misjudgments regarding the consequences of their decisions to go to war.[16]

How a nation's political agenda and preferences persistently and irrationally color its interpretation of information of a more limited strategic nature is a standard, well-known aspect of how leaders react to information. If information contradicts official biases, those who provide it are ignored. One such instance was the dissenting French colonel in 1912 who predicted the next war would be long and exhausting for the very reasons that occurred. And while the French knew the details of the Schlieffen Plan years before the war, they discounted wholly its premises in order to justify their own offensive strategy—and were unprepared for the German attack. Even Schlieffen himself foresaw the crucial weaknesses in his strategy, but preferred to ignore them. The French General Staff, on the other hand, seeking to rationalize its commitment to the doctrine of the offensive with which it had sought to control the politicians before the war, not only grossly reduced the number of German troops they predicted France would confront but persisted in deceiving itself with this illusion throughout August 1914—a major cause of the debacle that followed. The German General Staff, for its part, in July 1914 prepared for war believing that England would not participate in it, notwithstanding the fact that since December 1912 the British had warned the Germans that they would stand by Russia and France. But Germany, sharing the czar's illusions regarding

Russian power, entered the war on the assumption that Russia rather than France posed the greater overall menace to it. And the czar ignored a lone conservative adviser who warned him in early 1914 that Russia was ill-prepared for what would become a protracted war with Germany, and that social revolution would be its outcome. In 1916 the Germans refused to accept a captured prisoner's detailed account of the imminent Somme offensive. All sides in 1914 were both ready and, in at least a few cases, anxious for a brief and cheap war, and each was convinced they would never be better able to fight, and so they distorted palpably self-evident military information and realities to justify what were purely political decisions.[17]

The subsequent decades in no way altered the propensity of all nations to substitute their preconceptions, ideological biases, and desires for realistic assessments. The British government before 1938 refused to take seriously its intelligence reports on Nazi rearmament, and even forbade discussions within the military of its most menacing aspects. But once having reversed its appeasement policy, it then grossly exaggerated Germany's weapons-procurement policy in order to justify what proved to be far greater British efforts than those Hitler had mounted. The French received detailed and accurate information on the time and location of the German offensive planned for May 10, 1940, but, because of bureaucratic rivalry among their generals and sheer stupidity, paid no attention to it. The way both the Soviets' later allies and enemies perceived the USSR's military potential was crucial before the outbreak of World War Two in defining Anglo-French and Nazi diplomacy and perceptions. At the end of 1938 the French decided that the Red Army would be a negligible factor in the next war. But in the summer of 1939, when tens of thousands of Soviet and Japanese troops battled for months over the disputed Khalkhin-Gol region on the Manchurian border, the Red Army's combined tank-troop forces defeated the Japanese decisively. Yet both the Germans, who had virtually no serious information on the Red Army before June 1941, and the British, who gave the Soviet Union six weeks against the Nazis, ignored entirely its capacity to become the war's leading tank producer. They judged its potential on the basis of its poor—but exceptional—performance against the Finns in 1940 and, above all, were influenced by their ideological disdain for Communists. Stalin's insistence, solely because he desired to avoid a war with Germany, that the irrefutable data on Hitler's Barbarossa Plan that his intelligence began to deliver after March 20, 1941, was false, was the ultimate example of a refusal to abandon convenient strategic assumptions and the political premises they required; it came precariously close to enabling Hitler to win World War Two. And Japan's attack on Pearl Harbor would not have surprised the U.S. had Washington both believed and responded to the authoritative information it possessed.

But while Japan's attack on Pearl Harbor is one of the best-known cases, by World War Two, in addition to the problem of preconceptions defining facts, the sheer quantity of information available to Allied intelligence services threatened to overwhelm them. National intelligence establishments during the 1950s became huge, and with growing size and cost came declining utility. By the time the United States embarked on the Vietnam War, the system's quantitative explosion was creating decisive qualitative problems throughout its entire information organization.

In Korea in October 1950, or Vietnam fifteen years later, America's incapacity to confront unpleasant facts was no less profound. In Vietnam, utilizing purportedly the most sophisticated planning techniques that U.S. big business and the Harvard Business School had perfected, it immediately lost both control and track of the war's costs, information that it had to have to forestall the later political backlash that proved decisive. Notwithstanding the CIA's increasingly pessimistic analyses after 1964 on the status and prospects of the Vietnam War, the vast majority of key decision makers ignored them until the United States' stunning defeat in the 1968 Tet Offensive—which all the available facts made wholly predictable not just regarding its timing but also its scope—left them no alternative but to face reality. In Angola in 1975, solely because Henry Kissinger wished to reassert America's global credibility after its Vietnam defeat, the U.S. plunged covertly into a bloody but losing civil war and kept it alive for over fifteen years with precious little initial knowledge of whom it was supporting.

Apart from the the use of clinching selective numbers to reinforce a hawkish Vietnam policy, which Walt W. Rostow found useful when swaying Robert McNamara's empiricist predilections or an insecure President Johnson, the sheer amount of information alone guaranteed that decision makers would ignore nearly all of it. Those producing the data tailored it with an eye to what their superiors wished—even demanded—to hear. Policy makers routinely utilized whatever information reinforced their preconceptions and bureaucratic interests. By early 1967, about a thousand pages of captured Communist documents were being translated daily. No one who actually determined Vietnam policy and required information on the war could conceivably follow it by scanning the daily intelligence output, and none did. Much of the analysis of the data simply distorted reality or was irrelevant. More to the point was the fact, as former CIA Director William Colby later admitted, that the Communists were broadcasting and printing openly their far more significant basic strategy. What was known from public sources, another former CIA director, Admiral Stansfield Turner, subsequently confessed, was usually far more important than the secret data that cost the CIA vast sums to obtain.[18]

To varying degrees, the men who have embarked on wars in this century repeatedly, almost exclusively, substituted their interests, desires, and preconceptions for accurate assessments of the most likely possibilities once they began. Most assumed conflicts would be fought conveniently in the ways they preferred and for which their intellectual and social backgrounds and deeply inculcated myopic visions of reality had prepared them. The result was that they learned very little, if anything, from repeated failures. As we shall later see in greater detail, technology and firepower hypnotized and fascinated politicians and generals before wars and shaped their projections of their length and costs, but experience profoundly deceived them and inevitably destroyed their neat plans.

Wars in this century have been the outcome of not only inherited economic or geopolitical structural forces and nationalism, but also of leaders' military strategies and assumptions about the nature, conduct, and risks of armed conflict in exceedingly complex institutional and historical contexts. Combining all these elements with increasingly destructive technology, modern wars have always successively become qualitatively distinctive phenomena which, of course, interact in crucial ways with social and structural legacies but also profoundly transcend them to produce essentially new social, political, and economic challenges for future generations to confront. It is the very unpredictability of such changes, each one different from those of past wars, that has caused the very processes of war to defy planning or control, become nonrational organizationally, and irrationally self-destructive in social and class terms. They have blighted our century in countless, terrible ways.

Ultimately, the world in this century has marched into its increasingly destructive major wars with no safeguards against the irrationality of its doctrines and objectives or against the gravely dysfunctional but relentless political and class needs—both domestic and foreign—of the major aggressors. What was called intelligence became part of an ideologically and politically self-reinforcing system, which complex or often elegant rhetoric buttressed but that repeatedly eliminated any sane, restraining impulses that nominally nonauthoritarian nations still had the latent capacity to consider. Rationality was not the essence of the system but rather its antithesis, and what was deemed "intelligence" became a justification of the propensity of nations to commit fatal errors that only intensified their illusions and false expectations and made wars vastly more costly, both humanly and materially, as the century advanced.

# CHAPTER 3

# Officers: The Eclipse of Warrior Castes

The extent to which officers make and guide conflicts involves issues that are fundamental to comprehending both the nature of war in this century and the class and political structures that have produced professional warriors. To perceive the evolving functions and social attributes of military leaders, and the degree to which they have created distinctive martial values and cultures, illuminates not only how and why wars begin but, above all, how they are organized, fought, and often end. Such insight explains, as well, the radically changing role of officers in the social and class systems of the principal nations that have engaged in this century's major conflicts, and how modern technology has increasingly marginalized them.

The positions of officers during peacetime reveal best their relationship to a nation's social and political class structure. Officer corps have then assumed exclusive, often castelike functions that have included everything from providing socially respectable and leisurely occupations to sons of rural elites that had no more challenging or interesting ways to devote their lives, to safeguarding ruling classes from their domestic challengers. Innumerable writers have pointed to the deepening tensions between officers as integral members of traditional class and social elites, whose essentially ceremonial peacetime activities bore scant relationship to the demands of modern warfare, and increasingly sophisticated military technologies that have necessitated the recruitment of personnel with very different skills and education, thus presumably eroding the social and class cohesion of modern officer corps since the turn of this century.

The degree to which military doctrines, strategies, and preparations were—and even remain—the product not of formal and neutral technical criteria but of the ideologies, culture, and interests of officer classes and factions within them is vital to understanding how relevant "science" as opposed to an atavistic warrior ethos has been to the conduct of war in our times. This relationship also impinges on the tension between the domestic class as opposed to external military functions of armies in many industrial nations. Were the quasi-feudal, privileged origins of the officers *the* crucial source of their political and military perceptions and advice, or did a transcendent military culture or bureaucratic imperative also influence ambitious officers from middle-class, bourgeois origins? Can, in brief, officers play anything else but a class and political role, if only as an aspect of advancing their own personal and service interests, or avoid reflecting the specific values and beliefs always inherent in the profession of warrior? Have they been equipped to help their nations not simply to embark on conflicts but also to prosecute them by "rational" criteria that minimize war's profound internal political and social dislocations?

## The European Officer's World Before 1914

The profession of military officer in the principal European countries during the nineteenth century combined, to varying degrees, social functions and play with martial pretensions, and the English experience was in certain ways both the most extreme and persistent. But while the British officer corps was a preeminent bastion of conservatism, it was also far less ideologically pretentious than its European peers and it had no serious desire to influence political power. British society was entirely stable and no challenge from the masses existed to which officers might respond. To be an officer was to be a sportsman, to join clubs, know how to drink, to dress, and to play according to strictly defined norms; otherwise, the military was conceived principally in terms of maintaining control over the colonies with a small elite army possessing high morale, and an unrivaled navy prepared to defend the home island and project British power throughout the empire.

The army was the place that the peers, gentry, and officers sent their sons, and in 1914 two-thirds of Britain's generals and 56 percent of its colonels were descended from such fathers—only a small fractional drop from the end of the nineteenth century. In 1914, two-thirds of them came from rural areas—even more than in 1899—so that the military had become the place where the rural elite installed sons unable to succeed in the far more demanding urban world. Nearly all officers bought their posts throughout the nineteenth century, and while the purchase system was nominally abolished by the end of the century, until 1914 there still remained decisive financial and social barriers to becoming an officer. Most officer slots required a private income of an amount that increased very significantly with the social prestige and mandatory expenses of the regiment in which they served. It was the regiment, which merged the attributes of the private club with the pecking hierarchy of the public school, to which the officer gave his principal loyalty, for it incorporated his entire social life. Intensely devoted to his peers, disdainful of unreceived wisdom and abstractions, the British officer was above all a gentleman and his military role was quite secondary. If on the one hand he was the least intellectually able officer in Europe, such intense socialization on a peer-group rather than a professional, technical basis produced on the other hand a great deal of mindless personal courage and readiness to sacrifice for his fellows for intangible moral reasons. The British officer was therefore also the least dangerous of any in Europe to the constituted political and social structure, of which he was wholly a part.

Advancement to the very highest ranks in such a tradition-bound officer corps came principally from social contacts and patronage from the royal family and its entourage. Personal ties and loyalty counted far more than competence, so that Britain's industrial skills, save for the navy, largely bypassed its military. Officers belonged to clientelist structures whose members were intensely devoted to one another whatever their faults, and their contented, traditional world remained remarkably static until 1914, but even the trauma of the subsequent years was to affect them far less than those in any other major European nation.[1]

The German officer corps changed more than the British after 1900, but at its higher levels it remained largely the aristocracy's exclusive domain. The German officer corps' class structure was as complicated as its functions, which were social, military, and political at one and the same time. While technically more adaptive than the British army, since it took far more seriously the role of war in expanding German power on the Continent, the demands of warfare still played far less of a role for it than for the French officer corps, and it is quite erroneous to treat the German military as an evolving professional and technocratic organization governed by objective norms. Unlike the British, the officer corps was preeminently the dominating political force, a vehicle for the interests of the aristocracy and Prussia, and its pretensions to influence national policy ultimately were to transcend the existence of the monarchial political structure that awarded it privileges and had kept Germany authoritarian until 1918.

When forced to choose between social homogeneity and military effectiveness, the German army strongly preferred the former, but it did not completely neglect efficiency either. To focus on the decline of aristocrats among Prussian officers from 65 percent in 1860 to 30 percent in 1913 ignores entirely the social unity that persisted at the decisive higher levels. If 96 percent of those promoted to brigadier general before 1871 were from the nobility, the 58 percent appointed in the decade ending 1914 still left the higher officer corps firmly in the nobility's hands. And of these noblemen almost half were of the old elite dating its titles to before 1400. As for the so-called bourgeois generals, one in five married a noble woman and another three in ten married daughters of career officers. One in six was the son of an aristocratic mother. In a world in which social and personal contacts became more important the higher the rank, princes advanced more quickly than knights, old nobility than new. Field marshals were the most likely to have titles from families ennobled before 1400, and from 1866 to 1914, 83 percent of the general-staff generals—the most important posts in the army—were nobles when appointed and 8 percent were entitled later.

As in the British army, the branch an officer went into required varying amounts of private income, and social prestige and the location of a unit meant that until 1914 those with the most money and titles joined the guard units of the cavalry located in big cities—with all the meretricious variations of status such a hierarchic structure created. Aristocrats did not enter the technical services, which they considered undignified, but they commanded the army. Yet they required men who were able to master technical problems, and reluctantly absorbed them into the lower officer levels, where their skills proved indispensable to their elite superiors. Fear of social dilution slowed this process of absorbing sons of the bourgeoisie, notwithstanding the eminently valid argument of some officers after 1900 that welcoming them strengthened the alliance of the army and the middle class. By 1911, when over much opposition the general staff decided that its war-making ambitions demanded a much larger army with more officers, it consented to lower the barriers further. But it refused to raise educational standards that would have excluded young nobles without high school diplomas qualifying them to enter university. While sons of the comfortable middle and upper-middle classes—with the exception of Jews and Social Democrats—were permitted to fulfill indispensable technical and organizational duties, the nobility assiduously retained its hegemony over the army's political as well as military power, with all that implied for the future of German society and politics.

The German middle class, in both the army and the civil service, was constantly tested and socialized to accept the norms and interests of the status quo, and those who did not, never advanced very far. Bourgeois officers were every bit as loyal as aristocrats, they fully respected Prussia's domination over the German Empire and the constituted political order, and their assumptions about warfare and how to fight it were indistinguishable from those of the nobility. For Germany's rulers after 1900 the real question was how large an army they required in light of their ambitions in Europe as opposed to the far less demanding potential domestic requirement of a military capable of implementing its legal right, which it acquired in 1851, to eliminate all civil liberties and arrest opponents of the regime—Social Democrats above all. Those Junkers who argued against enlarging the army until 1911 not only had a dread of merchants' sons wrecking the officer corps' homogeneity but they were often also concerned that their special tax status would be sacrificed to pay for it. The German military remained divided on its external, as opposed to internal, priorities, or how to structure the army to be better able to cope with Russia as well as the burgeoning Social Democratic party, but its officers' social origins was not the cause of its differences. After 1911 the military resolved its tensions and opted for an offensive strategy in Europe that also forced it to increase the size of the military gradually by 210,000 soldiers, the vast bulk of them during 1914.[2]

The Russian officer corps after its 1870s reforms evolved in a manner similar to that of the German army: a rapidly rising share from the middle class, the introduction of certain technical criteria for recruitment, but a persistence of the old nobility's hegemony in crucial ways. Senior officers were paid far too little to survive without private incomes, which also tilted the higher levels heavily to the rich nobility. And like Germany and Britain, they chose the cavalry and artillery, while infantry officers were drawn mainly from the lower middle class and the gentry; by 1902 nearly one-quarter of the new infantry officers came from the peasantry. Nobles who wished to become officers were exempted from those qualifications required of sons of other classes, and they pursued traditional aristocratic pastimes and were largely indolent and inefficient. An attempt to reform the higher ranks after 1883 with the creation of a General Staff Academy only consolidated the dominance of those who had the money that academy members required. A relatively open recruitment system coexisted alongside the traditional structure as the czars attempted to prepare the army for modern warfare, but the reforms largely failed and in 1914, 51 percent of all officers still came from the nobility. Even so, given the preponderance of Russia's agrarian sector, officers from poorer peasant backgrounds were necessarily far more common than elsewhere.

As in Britain and Germany, Russia's monarchs also selected the most senior officers for personal or political reasons, and notwithstanding a promotion system based largely on seniority, the high command was even more a political instrument because the czars wished to forestall the emergence of a coalition of senior officers sufficiently cohesive to mount a coup.

To keep them off-balance politically, the top czarist officers were distinctive in Europe and drawn heavily from the descendants of non-Russian national minorities—especially Balts and Poles—and they commanded a majority of the Russian armies in 1914. In the last analysis, neither technocratic nor the more usual traditional class explanations can account wholly for the composition of the men who ran the Russian army. But just as the German officers remained unified in the face of threats from socialists within the nation, Russia's officers became czarism's final recourse for retaining power, and ultimately a large fraction of them later fought the Bolsheviks.[3]

In varying ways, then, the officers corps of the principal antagonists that embarked on war in 1914, save the French, were linked decisively to the ruling-class structures, reflecting their tensions and contradictions as well as providing many of their sons with careers. The Austro-Hungarian army presented a variation insofar as the nobility after the 1870s disdained to allow its sons to become officers, and only roughly a quarter of the graduates of the elite Vienna Military Academy in the four decades before 1914 were from noble (mainly minor at that) backgrounds. Sons of officers and civil servants, a solidly conservative class, comprised the great majority, and while the larger part of these attended military and cadet schools before reaching the academy, their training did not prevent the Austrian army from being the most incompetent in Europe after 1914.

But the French exception means that to truly comprehend the nature, role, and function of officers we must look well beyond the social origins and roles of officers and ask some fundamental questions regarding their subjective perceptions and ethos as well as objective constraints. It demands too a more nuanced effort to differentiate causes and effects in the emergence of officer-corps roles, the extensive manner in which class influences coexisted with what was a profound military value system prevalent among all of them, and the way in which technology did (or did not) influence its development.

The French officer corps, alone in Europe, was effectively separated from the nobility and selected largely from men who passed rigorously impersonal competitive examinations to become part of a military mandarinate. And precisely because of the absence of class ties with a ruling or powerful nobility, as well as an arrogance that elitist meritocracy encourages everywhere, in no country was the military to challenge civilian authority so profoundly, so often, and for so long as in France. In brief, officers' class origins and functions were crucial and causal in some nations but not all, and given other fundamental similarities between the French and other officer corps immediately before and during wars, we are obliged also to examine common military cultures that reinforce, coexist with, but ultimately also often exist independently of broader class identities or interests. For the issue remains whether the modern officers corps has been most dangerous because of its social ties with civilian power or because of its bellicose value systems and the overriding perceptions that a transcendent, unifying ideology has inculcated in all of them—or combinations of these factors.

Founded in 1794 and 1803 respectively, the École Polytechnique and the Saint-Cyr military academy provided the army with superbly trained artillery and engineering officers and, in Saint-Cyr's case, the senior officers of the infantry. But the very ablest *polytechniciens* entered the highest ranks of the civil service, so that the school's influence extended into the entire state apparatus. Later, other military schools expanded this elitist preparatory system, and a majority of Saint-Cyr and Polytechnique students by the end of the century were on scholarships. Sons of civil servants and officers—largely products of the same system themselves—were given preference over sons of other occupations, so that a very distinct and related meritocracy emerged to administer, to a great extent, the army as well as the government.

Several trends mitigated somewhat this mandarinate's hegemony within the army. During the Third Republic more noblemen entered the officer corps, so that in 1885 they comprised 38 percent of the cavalry officers, but they shunned the other services and a third of them resigned before passing the captain's grade. Moreover, the frequency of French wars and colonial expeditions throughout the nineteenth century required that many qualified sons of peasants and workers be allowed to rise through the ranks, so that the lower officers were relatively more democratized than their seniors. Well into the twentieth century, the continuing combination of recruitment from below and selection by exams caused the French officer corps to remain distinctive in terms of its social origins. But its strategic and technological ideas were indistinguishable from those of the other major armies and shared all of their inherent liabilities, while domestically it became a far graver threat to the political authorities than any other army in Europe.

Politically as well, the French army's role remained reactionary. It was politicized profoundly after the Commune of 1871, and attracted to those autocratic concepts of order and society that made it heavily Bonapartist or monarchist and caused it to support Marshal MacMahon in leading France out of the disgrace of having lost a war with Germany in 1871; its rightist penchant endured, and it subsequently endorsed Vichy and then de Gaulle. The Dreyfus affair in 1898 deeply divided the army and, with little success from 1905 to 1912, it resisted republican efforts to reduce its power, only to attempt to bypass civilian authority after the war began. Religious attitudes were far more important than social origins in explaining its internal divisions, and its superior technical training did not alter the fact that it still propounded a nearly fatally irrelevant military strategy of the offensive, one concocted principally to advance the army's institutional interests against its domestic detractors.[4]

The many differing, simultaneous, and often contradictory roles officers have historically played require a nuanced assessment of their functions. Protection of a nation from attack or making war effectively are among its tasks, indisputably central to every officer corps's definition of its responsibilities; but its position as a social stratum or pillar of a class order based on social exclusiveness has always existed in partial tension with its military duties. But the way and manner that armies were also potentially and in fact instruments of internal social and political control—often far transcending the mere protection of the nobility's social and political privileges—is also a reality that we must confront when assessing the relationship of armies to domestic political power in most nations (but by no means all) in this century. And notwithstanding the risks of facile generalities, the vast majority of European officers in 1914 shared a common cultural heritage and attitudes, from which evolved similar assumptions about the merits and nature of warfare, or the primacy of heroism and morale as opposed to technology and firepower.

In the last analysis, what was decisive about the officers of Europe before 1914 was less their aristocratic origins (the importance of which depends on the context and the time) but their shared vision of the world, their mutual beliefs in a hegemonic militarist culture and its values, and their intimate relationship to societies that were authoritarian or, at best, conservative. And while other factors also motivated them, the vast majority of those officers who made military policy accepted certain values regarding the virtues of arms as a calling, the importance of "character" and the readiness for great sacrifices as a vital, even decisive factor in warfare, and the necessity of patriotism as an overriding national commitment transcending presumably parochial class interests. It is irrelevant to label such unswerving attitudes as neofeudal or preindustrial, because they existed in tandem with a growing, if only self-serving, commitment to mobilize technology and industry in the service of the military. That group interests mediated the choice of specific strategies and enemies that military leaders propounded or projected meant only that, like countless other power blocs in any nation, what was self-serving also defined what they thought best for a nation.[5] Again, to repeat a crucial point, the technocratic bourgeois French officers, the British gentlemen, and the Junker nobility all regarded the world and warfare in essentially the same fashion and were to fight the First

World War in largely the same way—and all were wholly unprepared to cope with the vast challenges that August 1914 initiated.


## 1914–1920: The Transformation of Europe's Officers

The carnage of the First World War exposed all the weaknesses of Europe's officers corps: their blindness to the destructive nature of combat, the futility of their astonishingly similar strategies and assumptions about the war's duration, and their incapacity to fight victoriously. Mass death of immense, unimaginable dimensions, and not reflection, forced them all—technical specialists as well as princes—to confront how irrelevant modern war had made them, how chimerical their expectations of triumph had become.

The British officers corps changed less than those of the other major nations, notwithstanding the frightful losses its mindlessly brave officers suffered, often after making certain their dress appearance on the front lines conformed perfectly to the ceremonial criteria that their sporting days had inculcated in them. Desperately in need of enlarging a junior officer corps able to lead the men in the trenches, at first the army greatly expanded its training schools to accept thousands of public school graduates who, save for their less aristocratic class background, were in most crucial ways similar to the traditional prewar officers in speech and thought. This meant, also, that the highly personalized, obedient senior-officer system linked to the aristocracy, with its rigidly hierarchic way of working, remained unchallenged.

Since the younger officers trained in the prewar manner were killed off only marginally less quickly than new ones could be produced, and the officer class grew eightfold during the war, by 1917 the appointment of officers from the ranks or with temporary commissions expanded to account for half of the total number of second lieutenants created during the war. Britain's wartime army-officer system adapted at the lower levels, but otherwise it still resembled the prewar structure, with its emphasis on personal contacts.

The German War Ministry, expecting the war to be over quickly, even during the period of army expansion after 1912 refused to open the officer ranks to the less well born or to abolish the right of high school graduates—which is to say, the sons of the prosperous—to serve only one year in the event of mobilization. Both the real and potential officer and soldier base for the German army was therefore far, possibly decisively, smaller than it might have been, while the French vastly increased their officer reserves after 1905 to compensate for Germany's much larger population. The French lost 22 percent of their officers during the war but recruited so many others that by late 1918 the officer corps was more than double its

August 1914 size, not counting temporary junior-officer positions given to troops advanced from the ranks. Still, *polytechniciens* and Saint-Cyr graduates at the senior level guided the army throughout its torment.

Germany's dilemma was that in a protracted war there was no way to maintain rigid prewar standards of exclusion and still fight on with a vastly larger army. Like the British, the German army's junior officers were filled with heroic ardor and got killed off far too quickly. The actual war experience profoundly surprised Germany's leaders, and they improvised by doubling the size of the prewar officer corps during 1914–18 and increasing the number of reserve officers at least eight times. It was principally these reserve officers, most of whom had only six weeks' training, who manned the front lines, but unlike the French, the general staff refused to promote outstanding noncommissioned officers from among those in the ranks who had shown leadership talent. For this would have greatly diluted the officers' class exclusiveness. During the war the nobility accounted for six of the seven field marshals, eleven of the fifteen colonel generals, and twenty of the twenty-nine infantry generals. In the end, vast improvisations notwithstanding, the nobility remained in charge of the army.

The senior Russian officer corps, like those of the other European states, resembled the prewar structure until the Bolshevik Revolution eliminated it, but its junior-officer system was very early transformed—with dire consequences. Russia's army mobilized over 15 million men during the war, far more than any other, partly to substitute numbers for lack of equipment, but also because of monumental casualties. Although existing figures on officers vary greatly, they probably lost about 60,000 men—principally junior officers—in the first year of the war. Since the officer schools could only replace from fewer than one-third to slightly more than half such losses, much less meet new needs, the traditional officer structure immediately broke down. There was a grave shortage of officers throughout the war, and if one deducts those who had the connections to obtain posts away from the front, the shortfall was even larger.

At first the Russian command tried to fill its needs by sending educated soldiers to officer training, but this did not suffice and so educational standards were reduced greatly and it moved massive numbers of literate peasants and workers into junior posts. At the same time, noncommissioned officers from the ranks were appointed wholesale but were denied traditional officer privileges. It is probable that at least half, and perhaps many more, of the junior officers commissioned during the war were products of such expedient measures. Only the naval officers retained their prewar aristocratic character. So while Russia's officer corps remained superficially intact at the top, it was transformed far more extensively than any other in Europe, and a critical portion of the lower-ranking leadership of both of the revolutions of 1917 came from the vast mass of déclassé, discontented officers and noncommissioned officers whom aristocrats had assigned to the most dangerous posts.[6]

The relationship of the senior officers to the civilian components of the ruling classes, and their pretensions to be able to manage warfare not only strategically but also in all its economic dimensions, is a central theme in the French, German, and British war-organization experiences, which I detail in the next chapter. In those nations it soon became patently obvious that wherever the military claimed omniscience and profoundly challenged civilian authority it was in fact incapable of organizing the material preconditions of military success—indeed, that its incompetence could easily lose the war. Germany's generals, by virtue of their personal relations with Prussia and the monarchy, which was politically much more institutionalized than elsewhere, most easily assumed a major responsibility for running its war economy. But in the end even those of its senior officers recruited from the middle class, who became much more prominent, lacked the skills necessary to extract the essential minimum the military needed from the economy, and all the officers did was to serve as a decisive element in the rightist class coalition that traumatized Germany's population as well as its soldiers and brought the nation to the threshold of revolution in 1918—in the process unwittingly destroying the monarchy and Prussian domination.

Britain's senior officers had social power and prestige, and their pretensions lasted only as long as they did not threaten to lose the war or bankrupt the nation. Their incompetence and purely informal power led much more quickly than elsewhere to their relinquishing control over the war organization. And the relative cohesion of its officers at all levels and the insularity of the nation spared it the grave trials its allies underwent. In France, however, the most technocratic military leadership of all far exceeded senior officers elsewhere in ignoring constitutional constraints, establishing a direct link between its authoritarian Bonapartist pretensions of the past and its rejection of the democratic Third Republic after 1940. When the French government evacuated Paris for Bordeaux at the beginning of the war, it remained there until Marshal Joffre invited it back at the end of the year. Until mid-1916, when Joffre's increasingly obvious stupidity and arrogance became too dangerous to tolerate any longer, the military dominated France's war effort.

In brief, it was not the aristocratic origins of military leaders per se that made them so dangerous, but rather their domestic political roles and, above all, the fact that nothing in their technical qualifications, however much they had sought to upgrade them with a putative scientific mastery of warfare, permitted them to forestall military disasters. The ideology that caused the German nobility and the French bourgeois to perceive warfare in identical terms and make the same errors evolved from the fact that they shared a common militarist culture, with all its premises about human nature, behavior, social values, and priorities. The military nobility linked to royalty contributed much to this collective ideology, but officers' ideas were never wholly dependent upon monarchism, as very similar doctrines in France, the United States, and innumerable nations have shown since 1914. For this reason the social origins of officers often remains relevant but never decisive for comprehending the nature of armies, the visions of those leading them, or modern warfare.

As the technological and economic requirements of warfare mounted, they placed far greater claims on the skills of officers and the resources of societies. And while the military's expertise grew in absolute terms, often very significantly, it nonetheless still fell increasingly behind armaments' escalating technological demands and the multidimensional complexity of war's many strains upon traditional societies, which weakened in the twentieth century and thereby opened the door to political upheavals in more and more nations and regions.

That nations at war are ultimately no stronger than the resources and cohesion of their economic, political, and social institutions rather than their armaments emerged after 1914 to define the relationships between officers and soldiers as well as the impact of the war upon officers themselves. The most extreme case, naturally, was Russia, whose rulers had improvidently flooded the junior office corps with reluctant young members of the intelligentsia in the chimerical hope that they would serve willingly as cannon fodder.

Such relatively educated Russian officers were initially prowar but included many who had long been antimonarchist. They played two crucial roles. The first was their contact with the traditional noble officers, who regarded them as expendable inferiors best sent to the front lines to lead peasants whom they considered barbaric. Since the nobility had connections, they dominated the rear services, where malingering, relative luxury, and corruption abounded. From the beginning their rapport with new junior officers was tense, and it consistently worsened. The officers in most intimate contact with the troops became increasingly demoralized and quickly lost their respect and awe for their superiors.

The new young officers' second function followed inevitably from their contacts with their troops. In the navy, aristocrats still filled the officer corps, and here the rapport between the ranks and their superiors was always bitter and explains why bolshevism and anarchism were far more powerful among sailors than soldiers. Those traditional army officers in charge of the front regarded the average soldier as scarcely more than a dumb beast incapable of fighting properly, and the more and more alienated, poorly trained and equipped troops responded by listening to their new junior officers' complaints and ideas, their criticisms of the czarist system, and their proposals for reform. In effect, the radicalized junior officers served as a crucial transmission belt for the mounting revolutionary sentiment that was to bear fruit in 1917.

None of the other armies was wracked so profoundly as the Russian. Seventy-five percent of the Austro-Hungarian army's officers spoke German, and only a quarter of the soldiers, but while the gap between officers and men was vast and large sections of the troops evaporated toward the war's end, the ranks did not revolt. British officers held the poorer urban working-class soldiers in obvious disdain. Yet notwithstanding the immense differences in values and speech, and a persistent officer desire to communicate his rank via dress, soldiers respected most junior officers if only because of their readiness to share hardships and lead them into battle. An even greater void, in fact, existed between the lower regimental officers and their superiors far behind their lines whose aloofness and luxurious lifestyles increased with rank and became legendary. Generals rarely witnessed the battles they plotted and treated strategy as an abstract exercise in which the monumental loss of lives seemed inevitable.[7]

## The Erosion of the Officers' World After 1918

The war severely disrupted the lives of countless officers and soldiers throughout Europe and created profound status tensions, leaving an antidemocratic virus to fester within the weak, war-torn nations. Marginalized officers were crucial to the rise of fascism as well as the conservative riposte to the emergence of the Left in the wake of the war's social, economic, and ideological effects. The loss of social unity and coherence—or at least the myth of it—that the eclipse of monarchial, neofeudal conservative institutions entailed produced a discontent among them that was profoundly nostalgic; and the emergence of veterans' organizations helped to generate a comradeship that found conservative and often reactionary expressions in many countries. In searching for an explanation of the vast experience and defeat they had undergone, the new rightists no longer turned abroad but looked at home for causes, and enemies who personified them—liberal democrats and, above all, leftists of all tendencies and Jews. The civil wars within Europe's nations that before 1914 appeared so remote now seemed to be a very real menace in a significant number of them.

Germany, in fact, enthusiastically welcomed back its veterans, and those who had skills reintegrated fairly quickly, but many unemployed school dropouts and disoriented officers gravitated to the club-wielding Free Corps and the ultranationalist parties—including the Nazis—that offered them both status and diverse visions of an antidemocratic future. The army as an institution, while publicly more discreet, could not accept both the defeat that its failed ambitions had produced and its elimination from the central position in the Prussian-monarchial system that had ruled, and ruined, Germany. The senior officers refused consistently to defend the republican system against the challenges that antiparliamentarian reactionary former officers and soldiers posed, and they helped to create and then tolerated the diverse officer-soldier groups that later sought to overthrow the Weimar Republic. The army's senior officers retained what they defined as an overriding political, as opposed to military, mission, and politics became their principal obsession.

In Italy, inflation marginalized former junior officers, who were far less able than workers to cope economically. And a working class that had initially opposed the war and, along with peasants, seemed ready to take power through direct actions, treated them with open hostility. By 1921, when the Fascists were immeasurably larger than the German Right, 57 percent of its members were former servicemen. In Rumania veterans of the war, particularly those in universities, became the first fascists, with anti-Semitism as one of their principal appeals. In eastern Europe generally, officers remained traditional reactionaries, but diverse new fascist movements began to emerge around an anti-Semitic consensus that supplemented the Right's traditional appeals, and officers eventually were to lead it.[8]

### 1939–1945: The Eclipse

In a world changing so quickly technologically, politically, and in so many other ways, the traditional officer corps formed in the relatively static pre-1914 environment were incapable of surviving in their original forms. There was no single pattern explaining events in all nations, each of whose specific characteristics demand close attention. But the officers' conservative, even reactionary, political and social functions remained paramount, and in several instances even grew, wherever the other sectors of the ruling classes lacked both an independent capacity and will to maintain their unquestioned domination over the masses. Italy, Germany, Japan, and France are good examples of this. But in crucial ways, notwithstanding very uneven temporary trends in various nations, both changing politics and technology after World War One combined generally to erode the decisive roles that officers had played historically in guiding Europe's destiny both before and during wars. A somewhat shifting pattern in the social origins of officers after 1918 reduced the relative importance that elite family background had once assumed, but accelerating postwar technical developments left the military no better off in its abilities to direct modern warfare than it had been at the turn of the century. Although the officer corps' military ethos and culture, with all it implied for the function of the state and political priorities, emerged as strong as it had been before, it too failed to compensate for the perceptible decline in the military's power—save possibly in France, and certainly in Japan.

The British case was most instructive on how thoroughly a ruling elite's castelike values and style could socialize outsiders admitted to institutions traditionally reserved for its sons. After 1919 the sons of "gentlemen" entering the elite military academies dropped significantly even though the sons of officers (themselves descended mainly from upper-class families) rose appreciably, so that in 1930 the majority of aspiring officers in these schools came from military backgrounds and the overall figures on class origins were similar to 1914. During World War Two the British attempted to substitute a more objective system for what was clearly a preferential selection system, but the new criteria also imposed skills that the sons of the educated middle classes were most likely to possess, and even in 1961 one-third of all entrants to the top military academies were graduates of the elite public schools. More significant was the fact that the officer corps quickly socialized grammar school men so completely that they became indistinguishable from public school products, so that Britain's officer corps—like its political institutions—retained important vestiges of its original aristocratic caste system longer than any other nation.

In Japan the army was increasingly politicized, and its extremist factions, with their total contempt for democracy, successfully devoted their principal energies during the 1930s to dissolving the nation's superficial parliamentary trappings and involving it in wars it was certain to lose. Its ideological rationale, with its cult of national unity and power and disdain for pragmatic adjustment to the commercial world, had its equivalents among officers in Italy, Germany, and elsewhere who were also tired of flaccid discussions that challenged their right to define their nations' social goals and values—and access to their budgets. In France the leaders of the army regarded with utter contempt and horror the Third Republic's divisive politics and the accession of the Socialists to power after 1935 with Communist support, and they moved irresistibly toward the authoritarian concepts of state supremacy and an imposed social unity that culminated in Vichy. Like their German counterparts, they rejected the very notion of mass legitimacy as the precondition of a political order.[9]

The German case revealed that officers' political commitments and the militarist culture inherent in the profession were far more consequential as an index to their possible behavior than data on their fathers' backgrounds. As with the British, after 1918 an increasing proportion of those entering the German officer corps were themselves the sons of officers, comprising at least one-third of the total 1921-to-1934 sample but rising to over one-half by 1930. The officers' value system was intrinsically, and profoundly, militarist and their ideology had for some decades already begun to transcend the aristocracy's role in initiating and sustaining bellicosity in those nations where the nobility had been so important. A distinctive military ethos and bias persisted among all German officers by definition, and it was neither professional nor technical, if by that one means deference to the weight of objective technological, professional, and modernizing criteria that compel revisions in traditional concepts and modes of conduct. It was an ideological system that posited absolute norms of personal conduct and heroism, aligned officers against political democracy when governments failed to share its military and foreign-affairs priorities, and resisted most of the secular, modernizing trends of the twentieth century.

From the mid-nineteenth century until 1944 the nobility in the officer corps believed that it possessed a higher mission to define Germany's political future, and after 1918 this fixation caused it to reject the parliamentary compromise embodied in the Weimar Republic even though it collaborated with the republican succession after November 1918 in order better to control it and prevent the radical Left from making a revolution. For a decade important sections of the army's leadership regarded with sympathy the putschists and right-wing forces that emerged to keep parliamentary politics unstable. After 1929, Hitler exploited the army's rejection of majoritarianism as well as its desire to rebuild its forces in order to obtain crucial aid from it to assist his rise to power, only in the end to turn on and radically transform the entire military. If the nobility constituted a smaller proportion of the younger officers, they still retained nearly a quarter of the entire officer corps in 1932, and a third of the generals. More important politically was the old Prussian guards' hold over the army command until early 1938.

The German army's leaders provided Hitler with indispensable backing at crucial moments, especially after the summer of 1932, fully expecting to control him when he acceded to office. Hitler's seduction of them warranted their optimism, and after he employed the S.S. in June 1934 to wipe out the Ernst Röhm faction within the Nazi party (to which Röhm's paramilitary S.A. was a rival), it indeed appeared that the army and Hitler would cooperate harmoniously on rearmament and foreign-policy goals. But from August 1934 on, all soldiers had to take a personal oath to Hitler, and he began to flood the junior-officer ranks with commoners whose careers depended on him, and who were ready to serve the führer loyally. At the same time, his great expansion of the S.S. gave him alternative sources of military power to counterbalance the army in case of a showdown. Until the beginning of 1938, when Hitler took over the supreme command and brought the army under his total control, the army and the Nazis had existed essentially as coequals. Hitler's subsequent spectacular territorial gains eliminated the remaining serious opposition among traditionalist officers and, save for a handful, they collaborated eagerly after 1939.

Hitler's vast expansion of the army socially diluted the officer corps, culminating during the war with the massive promotion of noncommissioned officers and those in the ranks whose battlefield performances warranted it. Such officers, of largely working- and lower-middle-class origins, were closer to their men, on one hand, but their subsequent advancement came far more slowly than those from upper-middle-class and officer families who had the requisite manners and formal education for the higher posts. The Wehrmacht now promoted genuine Nazis as generals in preference to new party members, and they all obeyed Hitler's whims unquestioningly. In 1943 the nobility accounted for only 18 percent of the four highest ranks in the army, even though their share of the crucial rank of field marshal had risen since 1932. Because of ineptitude, opportunism, and a persistent fatal ambivalence emerging from their shared common enemies both at home and abroad, the German officer corps fully endorsed Hitler's mad disdain for reality and supported his overall war strategy. Only after it was far too late did some regret their wholesale capitulation, and in their failed assassination attempt against Hitler on July 20, 1944, a relatively small group of noble officers sought to redeem their tragic compromise.[10]

### The Marginalized Officers

After 1945 the United States officer corps was the only one involved in wars on a sustained basis, for Washington alone had both the ambition and the military establishment to undo or forestall the emergence of very diverse but powerful radical, nationalist, and Marxist-Leninist movements and states. Major local wars in Korea and Vietnam, and countless interventions or threats of force elsewhere, left it with continuous challenges beyond those faced by officers of France, the Soviet Union, or smaller nations.

The Americans experienced a relentless and fast-paced transformation of military technology that increasingly ordained the contemporary officer corps to the unique position of playing a crucial yet less and less commanding role in the use of infinitely more destructive and complex weapons. But modern armies—the U.S. above all—facing qualitatively different contexts and threats in the Third World, still operated within traditional intellectual and strategic premises and institutional boundaries. The inadequacy of military strategies characteristic of both world wars became even more of a problem as the sheer size and diversity of the battlefields or potential combat areas on which armies were deployed made arms more inappropriate than ever in coping permanently with the unique and constantly changing political and social causes of conflicts in the Third World.

The American-way-of-war was more developed than those of other nations in degree but not in kind, as vastly more powerful and complex military technologies spread to a growing number of states capable of producing their own weaponry or, what was even more menacing, buying it on the world arms market that burgeoned enormously after 1950. In essence, the pattern in modern war of substituting firepower and technology for manpower approached its ultimate culmination, with 36 percent of the U.S. Army consisting of combat troops in World War Two but only 22 percent by the end of the Vietnam War. During the Vietnam War the amount of munitions employed for every year that one soldier was exposed to combat was twenty-six times more intensive than in the Second World War. The increased cost of tactical aviation illustrates this trend, and the F-4 fighter, which became operational in 1961, cost ten to twenty times more (in constant dollars) than World War Two fighters, while by 1973–75 they were at least thirty-five times more expensive. But apart from modern warfare's immensely greater cost and destructiveness was the concomitant fact that the high technology inherent in such trends forced officers into a dependence on civilians to a far greater extent than ever before.

The growth in military outlays and technology within the framework of a traditional officer corps, with its mental baggage and parochial group loyalties, resulted in an ongoing struggle within the U.S. after 1947 to rationalize the military services. The officers fought for their own interests and funding but nonetheless increasingly had to find civilian allies not only to protect them but to help them cope with weapons that they understood less and less. Successive Defense Department reorganizations expanded the civilian roles in the Pentagon, and the three military services were compelled to turn to universities, specialized research institutes, and industry for virtually all of their basic and applied military research. High technology "civilianized" the huge military establishment but also revealed that rather than there being a coherent national military strategy with some inherent technological justification for it, there were, just as in Europe before 1914, only military factions and their civilian allies, each with rival bureaucratic and economic interests in promoting specific strategies and weapons.

It was this merger of officers with the civilians who largely controlled the greatest military power ever assembled that revealed how dangerous and increasingly irrelevant arms and the strategic pretensions growing out of them had become in the twentieth century. The world was shaped far more by political and economic forces than militarists of all stripes could dare to admit when justifying their rapidly increasing budgets. In this context the officer corps became increasingly irrelevant to the guidance of warfare and capable only of intensifying those strategic chimeras that civilian experts and their political superiors propounded for their own reasons. But the growing, obsessive conflicts among the military branches only conformed to the traditions of intraservice rivalries that had beset all the major powers since the turn of the century and frequently made their competing strategic doctrines scarcely more than palpably inconsistent rationalizations for their conflicting ambitions and the illusions of political leaders.

The Vietnam War, the longest conflict of this century and the largest after 1945, revealed how strategic failures, false expectations, the careerism of officers, the naive reliance on weapons and technology, and all of the fatal flaws among officers and politicians that had made warfare so bloody and protracted after 1914 still defined war in practice as opposed to theory in the latter half of this century. The Kennedy and Johnson administrations believed that they could win the Vietnam War relatively quickly by refining and applying counterinsurgency-war doctrine, intended to be a politically palatable alternative to conventional wars that would also later allow the U.S. to cope decisively and economically with guerrilla movements elsewhere in the Third World. But the civilian leaders and the three services soon abandoned the crucial political-warfare dimension of counterinsurgency to rely principally on firepower and air mobility based on the helicopter. They still believed their years of preparation for war against conventional armies in Europe could also be applied in Vietnam; but the fact that Washington's only political alternatives to the Communists were both endemically venal and incompetent also compelled them to depend on massive firepower. The war was therefore fought very badly, at an immeasurably huge cost both to Vietnam's population and U.S. taxpayers, and in a manner that, domestically, made it the most politically destabilizing and alienating event in modern American history.

American military technology in Vietnam remained firmly locked to the military services, who often applied it in an uncoordinated manner to suit their own doctrines. There were four basic tactical air forces working at one time—in an unusually inefficient and sometimes conflicting fashion. Logistics remained poorly organized, wasteful, and often chaotic. In the end, overwhelmed by the challenges, yet resolved to aid their careers and services, officers at all levels produced false, illusory, or irrelevant data on "body counts" and bomb tonnages dropped on alleged military targets to argue that they were winning the war. This pattern of universal deception emerging from a combination of military careerism and genuine strategic blindness persisted until America's final defeat. Washington's leaders demanded good news and got it from men whose personal ambitions became their principal concern, although many of those leaders knew that the U.S. command in Saigon was constantly deceiving them—and often itself as well.

Long after the Vietnam War the problems of coordination and interservice competition that beset the American military remained to plague it, diminishing its ability to manage increasingly sophisticated weapons systems. Its internal budgeting and strategies remained conflicting, and during the abortive Iran rescue mission of April 1980, service rivalries were responsible for producing complete disaster. Even during the invasion of Grenada in October 1983, the services had no joint land commander, suffered from poorly integrated army-navy fire support and the frequent inability of army and navy units to communicate with each other—and much else. Problems such as these did not appear so prominent during the Gulf War only because in Saddam Hussein the U.S. encountered perhaps the most inept military leader of this century, but significant technological failures and profound interservice conflicts emerged then also.[11]

The diminution of the key role of the aristocracy among officers in a number of countries failed to alter the manner in which military leaders related to the world and the societies around them The deeper logic of militarism, which the aristocracy had helped to transmit in its purest form, scarcely depended on the numbers of nobles who were officers, and even where no nobility existed—as in the United States—militarist ideology drew upon a conservative martial analysis that the major powers universally accepted by 1914; it explains why all the nations of Europe made comparable errors. Officers were integral members of class systems they defended in those nations where it was politically necessary to do so, and in the case of Germany after 1932 their ostensible role in protecting the nation against the outside world became their principal justification for helping greatly to impose a tyrannical political structure. If some officer corps increasingly assumed a technocratic and professional guise, this was only a pretension, and it scarcely concealed their principal conservative domestic priorities. The military's constant penchant everywhere for developing contrived and constraining national security doctrines to defend itself against budget slashes and its opponents' political attacks belied its proclamations of neutrality or professional objectivity. For war's technical basis grew far more quickly than the capacity of even the ablest officers to understand and administer it. Science and technology never altered the military's visions of its international role or its fundamental tasks even as warfare became infinitely more destructive and the rationale for it had no sane basis. Clausewitz's notion that a "science" of strategy and war could be articulated remained pure ideology concealing the preconceived agenda of those who alleged this was what they were doing.

The world after 1914 saw how the huge and constantly increasing disparity between strategic ideas and technology could create unimaginable human and social calamities. Everything essential since then has remained static save firepower: the same blindness to the vast potential domestic consequences of protracted combat; the identical self-seeking concern with service and personal interests when advocating strategies; the same incapacity to deal with all of the social and political dimensions of war. Before

1914 officers could evoke the full range of heroic nationalist appeals or martial values to help get nations into conflicts, although after 1918 civilians remained quite firmly in charge of the crucial decisions leading to them. But it was the inability of both generals and politicians to confine wars in scope, duration, or intensity that increasingly bedeviled militarists of all backgrounds as warfare became far more destructive than anyone with power ever imagined—or their social systems could afford.

# CHAPTER 4

# War Organization:
# The Dilemma of Managing
# Modern War

The way a nation organizes itself during wartime reflects the nature of its entire social system and those forces, ranging from its class structure to its intellectual processes, that define its institutional life and influence its values. To articulate a meaningful strategic theory, or to comprehend war as the central event that has marked so great a part of our century's history, necessitates our grasping the decisive significance of the way existing class and social forms have actually responded to wars and fought them; and this is true even when a war organization is largely an ad hoc adaptive mechanism intended only to meet the immediate physical needs of both combat and society. Whether a state at war will experience victory or defeat is inextricably bound, often decisively, to the way it prepares for the awesome tasks before it, not just in defining a winning strategy but in locating and producing the huge resources necessary to implement whatever plans it has as well as to sustain the commitment and morale of its people. To comprehend the manner in which war organizations have evolved and functioned throughout this century is to confront not only the relative social importance of industrialists or bankers but also to measure the adequacies of all those who have led conflicts between nations.

Questions such as these also are central to dominant contemporary social science theories, with their pretensions to being able to define orderly bureaucratic explanations of where modern civilization has been and where it is going. They are also crucial to understanding the political and military plans and strategies of the heads of so many states—past, present, and future—who have sought to ready nations for wars and their immense consequences. How they actually confronted reality once the heat of battle began to mount is an issue of monumental significance both to the outcome of wars and to the entire modern historical experience.

## 1914–1918: Business Manages War

The nations that so casually marched into the First World War immediately encountered the titanic disparity between their plans and the struggle's insatiable and complex economic and logistical demands. The German General Staff had earlier developed a railroad department to cope with logistical challenges of fighting on two fronts, but its intense desire to maintain the elitist social purity of its officers meant it could not improve its technical skills sufficiently. On balance, its failures to plan for reality far exceeded its creativity, and the Krupp firm, with its intimate contacts with the monarchy, virtually restricted the German army's choice of artillery to those it wished to sell, leaving it with less modern weapons—at the same time exporting half of the Krupp output to foreigners, including potential enemies. Although the Germans had railroads to assist the incredibly ambitious Schlieffen Plan's need for rapid mobility, they lacked sufficient trucks and forage for horses to move huge quantities of munitions and food from trains to the front.

The British and French suffered from comparable problems and shortages. These included a crisis in civilian-military relations for well over a year after the war began as the generals tried initially to hide their incompetence by demanding unquestioned authority to guide the war in the manner they deemed best. Indeed, it quickly became obvious that Europe's entire officer corps could not alone create the organizationally complex systems essential to integrating technology, economic resources, and armies to make war efficiently. Generals could be crucial in starting conflicts, yet they were ill prepared in domains vital to sustaining modern war, which gravely diminished the social and caste pretensions of officers while making victory more elusive than ever. But the largely civilian war managers who assumed innumerable crucial responsibilities tailored arms policies and technology to meet the definitions and material interests of the dominant social stratum from which they were recruited and expected to return. Military technology in modern warfare never transcends the social systems from which it emerges, nor can it establish autonomous or socially neutral industrial and military imperatives that provide objective norms as to how nations should fight.[1]

War and war organizations, as much as any factor in this century, have determined the relationship of the state to the economy both during wartime and thereafter, significantly affecting the distribution of economic power and creating crucial precedents for governments' roles in guiding and dealing with economies. In most nations the impulse to accomplish urgent material tasks in the most expeditious manner the organizational and ideological structure of the society permits has irresistibly overridden the initial planning schemes that their military leaderships articulated. And once wars became matters of protracted attrition in which material forces would obviously decide the outcome, generals, whether willing or not, in most cases made way for the domination of businessmen and financiers over the industrial sector. Whatever exceptions to this broad, general trend occurred did not alter the fact that during the First World War sections of the ruling-class structure articulated the forms and priorities for making war, thereby creating the model for business-state relations which, with some variations, has increasingly characterized most industrial nations throughout this entire century.

Prewar divisions within the business community itself initially hobbled the emergence of war organizations during 1914–18. These were principally divergences between large firms in capital-intensive industrial sectors seeking voluntary coordination among their peers or even politically sanctioned cartels to regulate the market, and the more competitive labor-intensive economic branches that smaller companies dominated. No ideological consensus among businessmen on the role of competition and the economic integration of industrial capitalism existed, then or today. But those who were, in effect, against competition and for regulation of their own industrial sectors, either with or without the state's legal sanction enforcing its rules, rarely transcended their purely functional attitudes to articulate a comprehensive theory of "organized," "regulated," or "political" capitalism as an alternative to the folklore of markets and competition. Such disputes among capitalists over the state's role in the economy have distinguished the complex and often superficially paradoxical relationship of a capitalist economy to the state in most industrialized nations throughout this entire century.

The war merely provided a critical arena for such differences to continue. And notwithstanding mainly temporary exceptions, war organizations, whether informally or in terms of official structures with legal powers at their command, or both, generally strengthened those who advocated integrating industrial capitalism and the state. This pattern, which deepened the de facto, if not the conscious, synthesis of larger capital-intensive firms and the state, occurred not only because existing power alignments reinforced them but also because it was the most practical and quickest way to obtain military resources with which to fight. In this context ideology often played a secondary role. Indeed, the very imperatives of the war itself and the mechanisms created to pursue it modified entire areas of the economy that had once been insulated against political interference, unintentionally producing dynamic interactions that would not be so easily reversed once the war ended. As long as control of political power represented another means of deciding the outcome of economic rivalries between large and small business, the forms and purposes of war organizations were predestined to erode unity among the many capitalists in every industrial economy.

The most articulate efforts to merge the state and industrial constituencies during the First World War occurred in the United States and Germany, which even before the war had strategic industrial groups, which a few firms dominated, eager to create what were (with certain variations) politically sanctioned industrial cartels able to regulate output and prices. Although the armies of both nations initially undertook the principal responsibility for the war economy, they each quickly found themselves unable to cope with the huge magnitude of the task. Within the German General Staff itself, more technically able officers from middle-class backgrounds soon assumed disproportionately greater responsibilities, while industrialists and managers drawn mainly from heavy and capital-intensive industries, precisely the men most in favor of cartels regulating their economic sectors, immediately played a decisive role in all war organizations. That Walter Rathenau, former head of German General Electric (AEG) and a Jew, was largely in charge of the allocation of raw materials, thereby defining both who would perform crucial duties in the war and how, is an example of how functional criteria handed down by a dominant economic elite shaped the organizational forms within which the war was prosecuted. Although these arrangements and the growth of cartels, mergers, and industrial regulation profoundly alienated smaller German business elements and the middle class and seriously damaged their interests, such integration between the political structure and sections of industry was also ultimately far less efficient than it had to be to meet the war's vast material demands; more significant was the fact that big business was able to advance its relative power in German society at war.

The American army, like the traditional Prussian officers, initially regarded civilian mobilization bodies as a threat. But by July 1917, with the creation of the War Industries Board, businessmen controlled the various tiers of all the war procurement organizations, operating both formally and informally through trade association leaders—usually from the biggest companies in that field—and key executives and bankers from the more advanced, principally anticompetitive corporations and banks who had well before the war favored a synthesis of private and public power.

The French case was but another example of this pattern of the most powerful manufacturers running war organizations at the crucial levels affecting their industries. Even before the war, Marshal Joffre, who was the virtual dictator of France during the war's opening months, had for years favored relying on the private sector to solve munitions-supply problems. From the inception of the war, the state both informally and formally worked through the Comité des Forges, which the major metal firms dominated, to solve its problems with arms production, and the Comité was given the power both to import metals and distribute arms contracts on behalf of the state, which funded it. Variations of this consortium principle were applied in innumerable other fields, making each sector virtually self-regulating while enjoying governmental sanctions. The often intimate personal ties between the higher levels of the state bureaucracy dealing with war and the private sectors, and the way the former allowed the Comité freedom to define the interests of all sides or encouraged big business in yet other domains, led to a synthesis of private and public power rivaling both Germany's and the United States'; and this fostered a growing desire among big businessmen for statist solutions to their future economic problems.

British efforts in 1914–18 characteristically abjured ideological justifications, and while few businessmen were attracted to the *dirigisme* that inspired their French or American peers, when Lloyd George in 1915 shattered the prerogatives and, even more, the arrogant pretensions of the War Office and generals, they were assigned a crucial role in the largely successful effort to overcome bottlenecks in arms and munitions production.

The Russian government, utterly disorganized from the inception of the war, in the summer of 1915 initiated a weak effort to create four councils to mobilize the entire economy, also working informally with special war-industries committees, so that a controversial transfer of its authority to the metals industry gave the latter freedom to organize matters to suit its own interests and needs. Nothing, however, could undo the basic miasma that czarist Russia fell into almost immediately, and the chaos in its war organization merely reflected this fact.

Whatever the articulated justifications for their actions, however, or the prewar context that shaped wartime command decisions, war organizations during 1914–18 emerged within the framework of class domination, at least in the sense that strategic sectors of industry and finance essentially controlled them and imposed their priorities and interests on them accordingly. Notwithstanding a large consensus for war among Europe's businessmen before 1914, the moment the question of how to organize war economies arose, their inherent differences and conflicting objectives moved to the fore. Business mastery over the material foundations of war was based not on its capacity to administer according to rational, bureaucratic criteria but was merely the consequence of its decisive political power, which the endemic incapacity of the officer class to manage modern wars only reinforced. In such a vacuum it was entirely predictable that the war would be far more significant as a means of capital accumulation and organizing economies to satisfy the interests of strategic constituencies than as a way of implementing impersonal, efficient, and disinterested norms. Most who maximized their own gains never contemplated that there might be a conflict between their profits and a larger national interest—successful businessmen simply do not pose such questions, nor do capitalist ethics encourage them. But the selflessness that official rhetoric evoked to motivate the masses, the higher patriotism called upon to justify the carnage and destruction on which states embarked, remained an ideological pretense that explains nothing about how wars were actually managed and who gained or lost the most from them.[2]

### Accumulating Power and Capital

Numerous class factions found the war organizations' syntheses of state and private power during 1914–18 quite acceptable, and the military generally settled for its weapons and the freedom to determine how to use them. Capitalists wanted profits and the ability to organize production as it best suited their needs; they sought to control the marketplace for functional reasons and did not covet power for its own sake, although the prewar experiences and ideas among many of the most important industrialists certainly produced designs, many still in gestation, for the integration of politics and economics that were profoundly to influence interwar social thought and policy in the United States, Germany, and France, among others. State bureaucrats and politicians wished to be consulted, but most felt they had an affinity with the military or capitalists and never perceived themselves as serious rivals for the control of power or policy. On the whole, this accommodation of diverse objectives prevailed before 1917 within the Central Powers, when it became increasingly precarious, and for the duration of the war in Britain, France, and America. And precisely because the arrangement satisfied the major social constituencies in those three nations, it established key precedents to be imitated in the future.

But the very process of war itself also initiated objective changes, many of them quite unintended, which affected various interests in very different ways, and these crucial dynamics are integral to any deeper understanding of economic development in this century. Whatever the consensus among social and business groups on overall means and objectives, in practice they did not receive the same benefits when the state distributed huge contracts or allocated economic incentives. Despite the political power of the diverse economic and social constituencies before and during the war, at the end of the conflict their relative influence and affluence was often quite different than it had been at the inception. War organizations in most nations accelerated such changes. They also assured that as the inevitable wartime-generated technological innovations emerged, their development and production would be channeled through existing big businesses, placing them in charge of entirely new fields that began to transform the very nature of industrial activity in a number of nations. This trend greatly increased in importance over the century.

Strategic business and industrial groups made very large gains from the war, but because of cheap credits, subsidies, and a simple lack of adequate data, the full extent of this accumulation of capital is only partly documented. Profits of *all* German joint-stock companies in 1913–14 were 1.6 billion marks, or 10 percent of total capital, and 2.2 billion in 1917–18, or 13.7 percent of capital, but such general data tells us little about the firms most directly involved in war production. Companies in metal manufacturing, taken together, increased their net earnings more than three times between 1912 and 1918. Profits of munitions companies more than quadrupled between 1913 and 1916, and their dividends in the latter year were 23 percent. In France, munitions firms resisted making capital investments employing new technology lest they be stuck with excess production facilities at the end of the war, and so the state provided capital advances at subsidy rates—a crucial process in economic development that other nations were also to repeat, then and later. At other times French steel companies successfully blocked the creation of state-funded plants that they could not control. Given the prices received during the war, French munitions and arms makers probably did at least as well as their German colleagues, though their respective war organizations pampered both. But French war profiteers were notorious for concealing their most sensitive information from inquisitive tax collectors, who did not even have the right to examine company accounts, and an income tax initiated in 1916 was largely ignored. British pretax profits in engineering, shipbuilding, and coal and iron were 32 percent higher in mid-1916 than before the war, and government efforts to tax excess profits led to the usual sort of tax evasion that hid real gains—which we can only impute. Many new fortunes were made, and between 1911–13 and 1926–28 the number of Englishmen worth over £100,000 doubled.

Whatever the original intentions of the war organizers, who scarcely considered these issues at all, the First World War inevitably altered the relative economic significance of various industrial sectors as well as the individuals who owned and managed them. A nation's wartime needs impersonally dictated the directions of economic growth and profit in ways totally different from the peacetime market, thereby laying the foundations for politically assisted entrepreneurial changes that defined both short- and long-term economic development and change—and the nature of power insofar as political and ideological processes interacted with wealth. The war also allowed those industrialists who advocated using state power for conservative regulation of the economic system to give vent to ideas, some predating 1914, that later shaped key interwar economies in crisis. Wars create winners and losers, not only among social classes—which is the subject of later chapters—but also within them, and these became exceedingly significant. The immediate political consequences of such changes certainly bitterly divided the German entrepreneurial classes, especially alienating a portion of those among the traditional economic groups that the war had bypassed—with later far-reaching implications for the emergence of Nazism.

Notwithstanding its relatively smaller scale than its awful sequel, all of the issues that arose during the First World War—the ability of the military to organize the crucial economic and logistical sinews essential for protracted wars, the nature and autonomy of war organizations, the impact of the state on economic developments—defined the nature of war organizations and their economic and class consequences for the remainder of this century. Real institutions and power profoundly mediated the entire process of war-making, confounding the expectations and plans of generals and strategists before the event itself.[3]

## 1920–1945: Consolidating Big-Business Control

The First World War revealed that whatever the military's pretensions to lead nations at war, nowhere did it have the capacity to resolve the most crucial organizational and economic problems once the war began and to overcome shortcomings that were the consequences of the universal failure of their military strategies. The mechanization and protraction of warfare inexorably forced the military to depend on those components of the business community who could produce the sinews of war, so that the trend in civil-military relations in the industrial capitalist nations after 1918 led virtually everywhere to the increasing ascendancy of civilians—above all, businessmen and financiers—over generals. Officers never again claimed to possess the skills and knowledge needed to justify the hegemony most of them had demanded during the opening phases of World World One.

In the United States, during the entire interwar period the various military services and the War Department established formal ties with businessmen possessing indispensable skills and contacts, and those recruited from giant firms dominated all vital sectors of the war-mobilization machinery that existed before 1939. Even in Japan, where the military's influence over the key decisions leading to war or peace was far greater during 1937–41 than in any other major country, and it unquestionably fought for mastery over the nation's basic policy even when it was disunited internally, it had a cooperative relationship with the giant *zaibatsu* holding companies that dominated industry and finance, and there was an exchange of personnel in both directions. When it came to economic affairs and questions of production, most Japanese senior officers appreciated how dependent they were on expertise other than their own.

In Germany's case, the senior officers, above all Field Marshal President von Hindenburg, supported Hitler at that crucial point after November 1932 when he needed their legitimacy and influence with the traditional elite to generate the decisive impetus that would install him in office without a parliamentary majority. In return, they expected that Germany would rearm and they would become coequals with the Nazis and regain much of the power they had lost after 1918. But while they shared an antidemocratic, authoritarian philosophy, and both were expansionists ready to play on each other's ambitions, Hitler also believed that the army was the only force seriously able to challenge him, and by the spring of 1938 he had imposed his absolute control over the entire war-making bureaucracy, replacing most of the Prussian elite in decisive positions with completely loyal officers. He thereby created a nominally "professional" military, at least in the limited sense that it was both unwilling and unable to continue to meddle in politics or defy him.

By the time World War Two began, therefore, the contraction of the officers' control of the commanding levels of war organizations that began after 1915 was far advanced virtually everywhere except Japan, where the situation was more complex but still mirrored the world pattern. In the industrial capitalist world, militarism and warfare now essentially reflected those nonmilitary institutions, ideologies, and political and economic social forces whose leaders pretended to have the skills and resources to attain the triumph in war that generals did not, and were in a position both to make the crucial decisions regarding it and then to lead wars in ways conforming to their specific interests and values. Save in Japan, the military as a caste had become essentially defensive, even, to a crucial extent, in terms of its military doctrine, and in the process it abdicated much or all of its strategic organizational position to each nation's civilian political regime and the economic constraints it imposed.

Precisely because the Japanese military had far more influence than any officer corps among the warring nations at the inception of the conflict, its diminution under the pressure of circumstances is the most interesting example of civil-military relations during World War Two, revealing the dominant power of capitalism whenever the state challenged its interests and autonomy. For although the dominant officers could define Japan's grand objectives before the war, no sooner had they sought to implement them than they had also to confront the deep divisions within their own ranks over who should obtain vital production, not to mention traditional symbolic jealousies, a fractured governmental administration, and rivalries between firms and economic sectors. Moreover, the military discredited itself completely when it became clear it had erred disastrously both in predicting and preparing for only a brief war that was supposed to end with a negotiated peace. In such a context, when the army in mid-1940 attempted to impose its control over the economy at the expense of the men who historically led the *zaibatsus* and the key trade and economic associations, the most important capitalists, who since at least 1940 had advocated government sanctions for their voluntary alliances, resisted. This issue dominated elite politics and was a critical factor in the rise and fall of cabinets until late 1941, when major agreements were made establishing nominal political control over cartels and the economy, which in practice allowed the *zaibatsus* to direct the various key economic sectors in the name of the state. As the war went from bad to worse for them, the archmilitarists in the Tojo cabinet simply acceded to the reality that they could not guide the economy, and so the heads of the largest business interests gradually increased their power for the remainder of the war. By spring 1943, as the officers watched, the *zaibatsus* were essentially running the entire war economy.

While the creation of the United States' war organization never demanded the same drastic demotion of the power and pretensions of the military, in principle it was remarkably comparable to the Japanese structure both in form and consequence, responsive to the priorities of a similar social stratum, and had identical effects on the economic structure. Building on the interwar precedent of business-military cooperation, in 1939 a commission under big-business domination proposed a war organization comprised of hundreds of commodity committees, favorable tax and profit standards, and a minimum role for the military. When its successor, the War Production Board (WPB), was established in January 1942, it essentially followed these recommendations, and representatives of giant firms or trade associations dictated those policies affecting their sectors. The military gained back the right to at least define what it required, but thereafter civilian-controlled agencies decided virtually everything else, including production priorities and levels. Some one thousand key WPB personnel were business executives whom their corporations rather than the government paid, and virtually every account treats the WPB and its successor as essentially an extension of the largest firms in the business community, with the military playing a secondary role.[4]

### The Nazi Synthesis

As a result of the titanic scale of Hitler's ambition and the failure of his blitzkrieg strategy to attain its military objectives quickly with a minimum of internal mobilization and sacrifice, the Nazi war organization became an immensely complex, precarious balancing act that sought to achieve very contradictory political and economic goals simultaneously. The Nazi experience reveals how small a role impersonal, rational standards and organizations play in a life-or-death wartime context. For in Germany political criteria that operated nowhere else created competing economic empires that were linked to rival Nazi leaders spread throughout Germany and occupied Europe; these empires, however, managed to coexist with strategic business protection of their profits and power. Such an arrangement collectively hobbled Nazi war efforts decisively.

The paramount but scarcely exclusive fact regarding the Nazi war machine was that the administration of power resided in basically arbitrary and changing congeries of self-serving men and organizations under Hitler's absolute domination. Although he understood that much more coordination was essential to produce the equipment necessary for war, Hitler was unwilling to centralize economic, political, and military power so that it was both fundamentally rational and predictable but also much more efficient. Ultimately, power resided less in institutions than in individuals who had Hitler's sanction and support, thereby sharing the authority inherent in his charisma. For political reasons Hitler chose to encourage economic decentralization, both to retain the loyalty of those key personalities whom he favored but also to prevent the emergence of any concentration of power strong enough to challenge his authority. Although some have ascribed Hitler's policies to his personal weakness or poor administrative talents rather than Machiavellianism, the logic in his actions and life history before 1941 warrants a more cynical interpretation, even though it was the results rather than the intent of his actions that remain the most crucial for any assessment of the nature of the Nazi war organization. Even assuming Hitler was a weak economic planner, he was unquestionably a genius at calculating how successfully to attain and protect his personal power, which was, after all, his principal concern, and to which he merely subordinated economic decisions. The press and radio remained under the tight control of his closest, most responsive cronies.

Hitler's blitzkrieg theory was very accurately predicated on Germany's hopelessly inferior material basis for waging protracted warfare, even if all the organizational inefficiencies and economic prerogatives of his political allies were abolished; he preferred to bleed occupied Europe rather than the German people. A fundamental reason for the Nazi war organization's centrifugal organizational tendencies was Hitler's conviction that ultimately he could not trust the German masses and that they must never again be subjected to the intense deprivations they experienced during 1916–18, and this reinforced the power of the Nazi *gauleiters* who administered the nation's regions with a remarkable degree of autonomy and were generally inclined to insulate their populations as well as their private luxuries against federal agencies seeking to mobilize labor and economic resources for the war. This meant, also, that Nazi labor policy was articulated principally for political rather than economic reasons, and therefore it was left with authorities that shared Hitler's priorities, thereby precluding those more draconian measures that Germany's desperate military situation might have warranted as "rational" after 1942.

Hitler's reorganization of the military was merely one key aspect of his cunning strategy to retain ultimate power in his charismatic hands, and the state, the Nazi party, and his bevy of key lieutenants coexisted in what was the deliberately encouraged, constantly changing structure of influence and decision making that incessant rivalries and jurisdictional disputes engendered. If superficially the Nazi system appears organizationally chaotic, by Hitler's criteria it was entirely rational: it left him in a central position of absolute, unrivaled control, around which all men and institutions orbited as he remained the conclusive fount of authority. The major consequence of this master strategy, which produced absolute ideological unity and, at times, some intensified but finally insufficient efforts to coordinate economic resources more efficiently when Germany began to lose the war, was a highly fractionated and inherently conflicting administrative and political structure within Germany but especially in nations it conquered, where the basic rules of the occupation had yet to be defined and the existence of huge amounts of booty encouraged competition between men and agencies who were already natural rivals.

The fact that Hitler did not choose to fight a "total war" was not a sign of his incompetence in administrative or economic matters but of his belief that politics was more important than economic "rationality," and this entailed preventing internal social discontent and preserving his loyalist allies at the crucial levers of power. Civilian production continued to a far higher extent and far longer than either the military or key economic leaders, such as Albert Speer, thought desirable. Hence there were at least ten independent war-mobilization organizations seeking to utilize an altogether insufficient amount of resources, and they spent a great deal more time competing with each other than being useful; while other warring nations had diverse agencies, none had so many, so poorly integrated.

But the German war organization nonetheless also possessed specific important class characteristics similar to those existing in other nations. Whatever his ultimate contradictions, Hitler also had a palpable desire to increase his war organization's efficiency as long as it was not at the decisive expense of his political priorities, and this dimension of his fatally flawed strategy is associated most with the work of Speer, who in February 1942 became minister of armaments and war production. Indeed, had Hitler attempted less, the nationalist elite opposition to him may have been far stronger and their attack on his life may have come earlier than July 1944.

Speer's powers were formidable, and he wholly shared Hitler's determination to keep the military establishment out of war production. As a result, the German military had less control over arms production than was the case in virtually any of the other major warring nations. Although Speer later complained that ultimately he failed to overcome many of the local and Nazi fiefdoms or wrangling agencies and their sustained objections to his efforts, there was nonetheless a dramatic growth in German armaments production after 1941, for which Speer has been assigned much of the credit. But Speer, at Hitler's express suggestion in February 1942, merely transferred much of the functional responsibility for production and planning to the businessmen who commanded the committees or organizations that controlled specific industries, and who both before and especially after 1933 had sought to integrate the major industrial sectors. The creation of communities of interest, cartels, and the like was a strategy that he and major sectors of German industry were also ready to extend to the occupied nations, and this they attempted to do in spite of the countless obstacles that competing economic bodies, the S.S., and the army created. Speer sought to centralize the allocation of resources to assist the various industrial sectors that technocrats and businessmen managed in accordance with overall priorities, and much of his effort was channeled through them. But he failed to control the labor force sufficiently, and this proved crucial. While he went as far as anyone possibly could have, given Hitler's organizational and political system, the growth of armaments was to an imponderable degree a result of Hitler's policy of allowing the business community to play a decisive role, and it is here alone that Germany's war organization began to resemble significantly those of other nations.

Germany's businessmen, precisely like their counterparts everywhere, acted to protect their own specific interests, and such class consciousness was the exact opposite of disinterested patriotism, rationalizing for optimal efficiency, or making war organizations technocratically autonomous. That the business groups and firms for which we have adequate information did not behave selflessly to aid the war effort scarcely makes them anti-Nazi, since all wars—and domestic political policies as well—have been mediated in all the participating nations through class processes and interests; capitalists everywhere, even when they nominally adhere to ideologies that proclaim objectives that might conflict with profit, by definition have a transcendent desire to make money. German industry no more sabotaged the Nazi war effort by pursuing its own self-aggrandizement than Americans or Japanese undermined their own causes, for the loss of some hypothetical greater level of efficiency that they all might have attained had business abjured higher profits has encumbered all warring nations throughout the twentieth century.

This natural capitalist instinct for gain caused German business to exploit the many opportunities that the Nazi occupation of Europe created, so that I.G. Farben, the most notable but only one of many firms and banks, extended its direct and indirect control into fields in which it was interested in order to eliminate competition, obtain rights over raw materials, or simply purchase foreign companies at bargain prices, usually citing military necessity or Nazi objectives as sanctions. The coal industry integrated its French and Belgian counterparts as junior partners into a highly organized community of interest they had all striven for years to attain—aspects of which reemerged in 1950 in the Schuman Plan. Both I. G. Farben and the coal industry used large numbers of slave laborers to increase their production, many of whom perished in the process, later of course claiming they had not favored exploiting them. But at the very best, they amorally sought to maximize their profits and they conformed to Nazi labor practices lest they lose their economic monopolies. Privately, big businessmen complained bitterly about Nazi economic policies and whenever possible (which, it turned out, was often) they consistently did what was best for themselves, taking war orders when they could use them or, as in the case of the coal industry, dragging their feet on expansion and lowering significantly the amount of vital energy available to the Nazi war effort solely to attain the industry's own objectives. But whatever their specific differences with the regime, various businessmen were indeed attracted to many aspects of its policies and the power it offered them, and utilized those plans to help themselves and to make the most of countless opportunities the Nazi program opened both at home and in conquered Europe. Although this remains a far cry from attributing the real origins of Nazi wartime economic policies to capitalists, their role was always cooperative, and at operational levels businessmen managed much of the war economy.[5]

**The Economic Gains of the War**
The consequences of World War Two to the accumulation of economic power closely resembled the 1914–18 experience. Even though militarist officers and nationalist fanatics played the critical roles in causing the war, once it began, capitalists in most countries again defined the specific forms that various national war efforts would take, and this they did not to attain some transcendent state interest but to satisfy their very specific company desires for profit and—for sectors of German and Japanese business—also for various stabilizing arrangements for the future organization of industry. But at the same time, the war's vast technological innovations and the massive use of government money to accelerate the production of priority goods produced a demand in the undefeated nations that began to alter the composition of industrial activity during and after World War Two far more than it had during 1914–18. Although the war economy operated within a class framework and for class ends, it nonetheless also affected the functions of that class profoundly and began to pave the way to major technical innovations that were greatly to restructure modern industry.

In many advanced nations during the Second World War, the tendency of the state sector to increase its share of total employment, tax revenues, and the like was already integral to the nature of world capitalism as a political as well as economic phenomenon, and for governmental funding and guidance to grow during the war was the logical consequence of a far older secular trend in global economic development. Notwithstanding the great diversity of state initiatives, which often were the consequence of pressures from capitalist interests, they overwhelmingly resulted in greater private utilization of political power for acquisitive ends, ranging (apart from more banal short-term profit taking) from the use of public capital for private interests to governmental approbation for major organizational changes within the economy. The archrivals Japan and the U.S. reveal how universal the pattern of the state's role in capital accumulation during wars had become, and they remain prototypical of an international trend that the war greatly intensified.

In Japan, big-business domination of specific war agencies dealing with their sectors allowed the giant *zaibatsu* firms to increase further their control over the private sector through state-sanctioned and -promoted mergers (nominally to encourage productivity), extensive use of government capital for these and other purposes, and similar measures. Mergers absorbed 1,354 industrial firms in 1941–43 alone, and even more before the war ended. By the war's conclusion, the four largest *zaibatsus'* industrial assets were nearly ten times their 1935 holdings, while their banking affiliates also greatly increased the concentration of financial resources in their hands. Given the historic government use of its capital to encourage privately owned economic development and to exclude foreign interests, it was predictable that the *zaibatsus* would employ large amounts of state funds to enlarge their power. No less important for the future of the Japanese economy was the profound shift in industry from 1932 to 1942 from light (textiles, foodstuffs, clothing, etc.) to much more sophisticated heavy industry and economic activities, the latter growing from 38 percent of industrial output in 1930 to 73 percent in 1942—so that the war and state policy both helped significantly to create the structural basis for what Japan is today. The army after 1940 attempted to restrict the huge profits industry made off the war, which ran about 13 percent on invested capital during 1941–42, but in 1944 profits were still nearly 11 percent, and for big business the war, in addition to allowing it to consolidate its commanding economic power and expand into crucial new technological domains, became an immensely profitable event.

Experience in the United States paralleled that of Japan in crucial ways, as businessmen acted on acquisitive premises that universally unite them during war or peace. Although private capital provided nearly all wartime funding of new plant and equipment during 1914–18, the American business community now insisted that the government finance most of the expansion—ostensibly because the new industrial capacity would be idle after the war. Such state-provided accumulation of capital was gigantic. In 1939 the entire current U.S. manufacturing plant had cost about $40 billion to construct, and by June 1945 about $26 billion in new plant and equipment had been added to it. About two-thirds of this new sum came directly from federal funds, and while it nominally comprised one-quarter of all manufacturing capital in existence, in fact it constituted a significantly larger share of industry's most efficient sector; and only 25 corporations utilized half of the government-owned facilities, General Motors being the largest. Over three-quarters of this new plant was in fact usable after 1945 and sold as "war surplus" at bargain rates, and 250 corporations acquired 70 percent, or more than their prewar share of U.S. plant capacity—representing a major permanent transfer of public capital to big-business hands. The effect was a powerful surge in the concentration of all manufacturing assets held by corporations with over $50 million, from 37 percent of the national total in 1934 to 49 percent by 1942—and this pattern was to continue. In addition, new amortization laws allowed corporations to deduct certain costs against income, reducing their net wartime taxable income by nearly $10 billion and greatly increasing profits. Such loopholes became crucial because of the $175 billion in prime contracts the WPB issued from June 1940 to September 1944, two-thirds went to a mere 100 corporations, with 10 of them obtaining 30 percent of the total. In effect, as in most of the unoccupied nations engaged in the war, the state's economic role as a sponsor of the accumulation of capital altered the very structure of the American corporate economy, especially accelerating the trend toward greater consolidation of economic power in the hands of firms able to cope with the war and its military aftermath.[6]

## The Postwar Experience

The two world wars created war organizations with a distinctive class leadership and function in most of the industrial nations, and these often profoundly defined how capital and profit would be accumulated, in the process altering the industrial composition of national economies. Such patterns only intensified after 1945 within those nations that continued to arm. And given the exponential technological changes in armaments, which vastly increased in complexity and costs, both the people and companies who seemed qualified to deal with such matters played a far greater role than ever in modern war organizations. Military officers became even less influential, as both class processes and technology virtually eliminated any autonomous military alternative, whether intellectual or organizational, to wars that reflected the economic and class structures from which they emerged. Strategies after 1945 were increasingly capital-intensive, as intricate, costly, and destructive as arms makers could devise, and it was within such overriding constraints that officers articulated ways to make future wars.

Nowhere was this more the case than in the U.S., which became the preeminent, unrivaled military power technologically, and more dependent than ever on the business system to direct its martial efforts. And given its bitter interservice rivalries, which in the late 1940s traumatized the American military as the navy and air force fought viciously for a share of the budget, at the highest levels military power became the administrative domain of civilians recruited overwhelmingly from the leading corporate law firms and finance, plus some industrialists. Hundreds of advisory groups drawn from specific industries guided the government on issues that directly affected their own profits, and private corporations by the mid-1950s had become crucial to all aspects of the Pentagon's advanced-weapons developments. During the Korean War nearly 1,000 people worked full-time without compensation in defense agencies, and many of them shaped policies affecting the profits of the corporations that paid their salaries. The services hired large numbers of civilians to supervise their procurement operations, most of them with private business backgrounds; these civilians made up nearly half the services' purchasing staffs by the late 1950s. By 1959 the seventy-two largest military contractors had hired over 1,400 retired officers, essentially to sell arms to their former colleagues—so that the military structure was more than ever integrally merged with arms firms and the separation between public and private interests was more opaque than it had ever been. In such a technological and organizational context, military officers functioned within a socioeconomic order that imposed its distinctive class rationality and interests upon them as well as their strategies.

This integration of a political authority commanding vast financial resources with the industrial sector producing arms was so intense and sustained that it inevitably affected the structure of economic development in the U.S., further shifting real economic power to the military industries in ways that determined national political and social priorities and consequently which class interests benefited. Although this entire process was initially unplanned, resulting largely from the logic of compounded short-term improvisations, after 1949 it became the ineluctable consequence of a frenetic arms race that further increased the state's economic functions and pushed it in directions that directly aided high-technology and aerospace industries.

The United States armed in a manner that merely applied the principles that had guided war organizations in most nations in this century, suspending yet once again the practices and norms ostensibly integral to the operation of "free market" economics to enrich specific interests with immense capital transfers and guaranteed high profits. Evoking national security and patriotism to forge the consensus essential to a permanent arms race, weapons makers refused to work for profits other economic sectors deemed normal. The various military services gave their contractors huge capital resources in the form of complete industrial facilities, interest-free loans, or the right to retain as exclusive patents the inventions created with government monies, to name only a few ways private interests defined and exploited the state's relationship to war preparations. Cost-plus contracts, in which a firm received an agreed-upon fee, eliminated risks entirely. Competitive military-contract awards covered barely a tenth of the Pentagon's procurement by the end of the 1960s, and the one hundred large companies that received two-thirds to three-quarters of its awards annually could not help but prosper and grow in importance within the economy. Their profits were very large by civilian-goods standards—with 15 to 25 percent deemed normal—but often hidden. Between 1958 and 1966 the Minuteman missile program returned 43 percent annually on investment, and in one case where 8 percent cost-plus profits had been negotiated, the U.S. Tax Court found that in reality 612 and 802 percent profits had been made over two years.

In effect, the enormous transfer of public wealth to corporate hands that World War Two inaugurated only continued, and enabled the largest American corporations after 1945 to obtain the plant essential for expanding into military goods on a highly profitable, virtually no-risk basis. The one hundred biggest manufacturing companies when the war ended had by 1963 increased their share of the total value of the output of all manufacturing from 22 to 33 percent. The two hundred largest companies shared 41 percent of the total value of manufacturing in 1963 compared to 30 percent in 1947, and military contractors accounted for almost all of this growth.[7]

The idea that a nation's war organizations could transcend the influence of dominant elites and factions in the power structure to attain a more disinterested, efficient, and autonomous bureaucratic way of managing war efforts has proved nothing more than an illusion. The very nature of modern war, with its unexpected traumas, has defied any form of real planning because leaders embarking on war have invariably done so with relative impunity and invariably substitute their desires—based to a crucial degree on their wildly optimistic definitions of their own economic and social resources—for a realistic assessment of the true material balance of forces. Virtually all war organizations, with the partial exception of Nazi Germany, have reflected a class hierarchy that was able to solve routine immediate problems, even if very costly, but whose ultimate logic and motives were oblivious both to a disinterested rationality that optimized a nation's ability to engage in the war and to the war's monumental negative consequences upon the societies involved. The dim boundary between private and public power that had characterized most war organizations everywhere before the outbreak of conflicts quickly led to a functional, complete merger of the two, destroying the myth of the state as somehow independent of the class structure. In the process, industrialists and capitalists often employed large amounts of state capital for private profit and used the political system to restructure the economy in directions many of them had long desired. To a remarkable degree, notwithstanding the way wars have increased the power of socialist movements, many strategically placed capitalist groups in both defeated and victorious nations have emerged from conflicts better equipped to cope with more advanced technology and industrial developments, and also relatively stronger in their relationships to their potential rivals within ruling circles—above all the military and smaller industrialists.

The improvisations that followed the outbreak of every war emerged within existing power and class arrangements that ultimately defined the principal forms of each state's organization for meeting wars' titanic economic and material demands. Nowhere was a rational, coherent, and effective war organization in place at the outbreak of conflicts, for the military everywhere consistently proved incapable of dealing with the technical and organizational challenges involved, a fact that increasingly marginalized them until they no longer played the crucial roles they had assumed in Europe prior to 1914; every country's responses were the subject of intense rivalries among economic constituencies as to who would provide the huge quantities of material needed—and profit in the process. The result has been that throughout this century industrial capitalist nations have profoundly mediated wars, and their strategies for fighting them, through class processes.

# PART TWO

# Transforming People, Societies, and Politics

# CHAPTER 5

# World War One:
# The Impact on European
# Society

The First World War had a far greater influence on Europe's social structure, economy, and human and demographic existence than any other event since at least the French Revolution, and it initiated those objective changes that were to alter profoundly the Continent's subjective consciousness and politics after 1917. Given the war's very uneven effects, we must consider its consequences in all their diversity, ranging from those that were catastrophic and decisive, as in the case of Russia, to those that were merely very important, as in Great Britain. Yet no European nation emerged unscathed from the experience as wartime conditions interacted with Europe's many long-standing social and economic problems and tensions to accelerate the crises confronting most of its people in ways that would have appeared inconceivable before 1914.

Defining and coming to grips with such specific objective factors and their material impact is an essential precondition for comprehending both their subsequent general political and intellectual repercussions and, indeed, how traumatic events described initially with exceedingly dry data have produced change in this century. For the people's responses to the war directly shaped the war's principal political and ideological outcomes, transforming significant portions of many traditionally quiescent populations into social actors, at least temporarily, and continued to shape much of Europe's historical experiences in subsequent decades. These great wartime alterations were at their inception the outcome of human and economic phenomena that can be defined in terms of numbers—good, bad, indifferent, and all banal in the deepest human sense—and notwithstanding their many limits, portend the suffering, alienation, and upheavals that inevitably followed from those phenomena. If they are a mere preface and by themselves can never explain events sufficiently, they nonetheless remain necessary to fully comprehend those events. For whether the war's dominant political outcomes emerged in radicalized leftist forms or reactionary and rightist movements that were essentially a conservative response to the Left, they were all reflections of the intense dissolution of traditional social and political orders that inevitably followed from the orgy of slaughter.

## The Economic Costs to the People

The overwhelming majority of Europe's politicians expected and prepared for a short war, and none anticipated the potentially enormous social price and political costs of what was preordained to become an exhausting, debilitating conflict. They planned no extraordinary production or consumption measures, and when all of their assumptions quickly proved erroneous, the living conditions, welfare, and total existence of their subjects were increasingly affected. But until the beginning of 1915 the leaders of both sides hesitated fully to mobilize their economies for the vastly greater costs and material demands that static trench warfare was imposing, and so their populations were temporarily spared the greatest economic sacrifices— though the human loss of sons, husbands, and fathers were huge from the inception. As vast numbers of young peasants were taken into armies, the amount of land under cultivation decreased rapidly in most countries; total European grain production was to decline by one-third over the next four years. Europe's normally crucial international trade was gravely disrupted and, except in Great Britain and France, was wholly incapable of compensating for such cataclysmic economic problems. This also meant that the side with the greatest economic power would be best able to survive and redeem, albeit in a haphazard, often precipitous way, its initial monumental failures in planning to "win," at least in the traditional military meaning, a protracted war of attrition. Ironically, once the nominally victorious Allies finally introduced policies to compensate for past miscalculations, they were to suffer the greatest immediate political consequences when the Bolshevik Revolution occurred.

Estimating the larger economic costs of the war requires nuanced assessments of the population's experiences in specific nations, including careful breakdowns of the changing composition of the labor force, the impact of inflation on the urban class structure, and the relative position of the rural populations. But aggregate data on the overall status of a country, while a useful preliminary index of well-being, conceal the often large discrepancies inherent in all figures on average living standards—requiring greater attention to such inequalities later in this chapter. And while it is worth reiterating that economic descriptions are by no means a sufficient explanation, the extent to which each nation suffered in terms of material deprivation and inflation during the war is a quite accurate gauge of its mass opinion and subsequent political development, both toward the end of the war itself and then over the following two decades.

### Great Britain

Great Britain suffered the least in the war because it possessed an impressive fleet and the financial capacity to import much of what it needed, and while the government kept inflation down to a far lower rate than any of the belligerents, there were significant price increases. The quality of its food fell, and meat consumption declined, but caloric intake was sustained, civilian life expectancy actually rose, and clothing standards maintained. By late 1917 shortages of sugar, potatoes, and coal produced the first queues, but compared to the remainder of Europe, there was no great penury.

Within this broad context, some fared worse than others. Most children improved their diets, but white-collar workers, the elderly, and those on fixed incomes were less able to keep up with inflation. Wages generally lagged behind the rising cost of living during the war itself, so that there was an approximately 10-to-20 percent decline in real income during the 1915–18 period, but this loss was wiped out in 1919 and real income rose sharply over the next decade. The vital disparities within such averages will become clear later in this chapter.

### France

France's problems were far greater than Britain's because the Germans seized the 6 percent of the total agricultural land that was, by far, the most productive in wheat, sugar beets, and oats. The massive draft of peasants, which reduced the rural male work force by about two-thirds, further depleted output, and the area under cultivation shrank significantly—well over half for sugar beets. Declining yields followed, but 1917 was by far the worst year for wheat and rye. Despite these difficulties, because of imports and a fairly rigorous control of the price of heavily subsidized flour, French consumers fared far better than they might have otherwise. Food rationing was not initiated until 1918, although coal rationing began a year earlier.

Notwithstanding its relative successes compared to the rest of the Continent, the French government began to lose control over prices, especially in the spring of 1917, and was compelled to import large quantities of meat. Real income fell gradually by about one-tenth until the end of 1916, but declined more rapidly thereafter so that at the war's end it *averaged* about one-quarter below 1914. While France was far better off than its enemies, much less Russia, after a sustained period of scrounging, the population's health standards fell below prewar levels.

Save for its population in the ten northern *départements* that the Germans occupied in whole or part, compared to World War One's impact on the rest of the Continent (much less its position in 1944), civilian France emerged from the war relatively unscathed. But in the occupied areas of France and all of Belgium, the Germans sought to live off the land as much as possible. By 1915 the larger occupied French cities were suffering from acute shortages, with widespread malnutrition and a doubling of the mortality rate. Belgium fared even worse, and only famine relief toward the end of the war enabled it to avert a calamity.[1]

### Italy

Of all the nations in the Entente that were not extensively invaded, Italy suffered the most economically. Aspiring to a major status in Europe, yet relying upon a wholly inadequate tax structure, Italy had the highest rate of inflation of any member of the alliance. Italy could not afford a war it had only opportunistically entered in May 1915 expecting that its conclusion was imminent and that it could obtain spoils painlessly. Fiscally, Italy borrowed from its population and allies to weather its vast deficits, but even so it was never able to obtain sufficient coal and wheat imports to keep its economy on an even keel. The war caused severe dislocations in vital energy imports and food distribution, and the real income of industrial workers began falling sharply so that by 1918 it was only 65 percent of the 1913 level. But farm wages dropped even more, despite the fact that the draft caused the number of men in agriculture to decline by over half in just four years.

In the short run, Italy emerged from the war in 1918 far weaker economically than it had been at its inception. Whether it could survive the political consequences that would inevitably follow in the wake of the trauma remained very much an open question.

### Germany

Wartime conditions in Germany caused its working class to suffer far more than any other in western Europe or Italy. Once its leaders realized that the war would not be short or its extraordinary demands met from existing reserves, they attempted to mobilize the economy to provide the army with the vast supplies that trench warfare required. This they did more capably than any of their enemies, but from an economic base considerably smaller than that available to the Entente powers, especially after the United States joined the war. Germany simply could not afford a protracted, static war, and when its leaders chose to fight it, they also unwittingly staked the political order's fate on their gamble.

The results appeared in the relative deprivation of the civilian population, and the sudden large increase in direct noncombat-related mortality rates confirms this penury. Germans endured far more than any of their enemies, save the Russians. The agricultural sector was gravely neglected: fertilizer output plummeted, farm labor was conscripted, and draft animals were sold to the army. Imports, normally one-fifth of Germany's grain supply for human and animal needs, a quarter of its milk, and 40 percent of its meat requirements, fell drastically. As in the rest of Europe, 1917 was a poor harvest year, but even in 1918 Germany's rye output was 66 percent of 1913, wheat was 57 percent, and potatoes 56 percent. Employment in the textile and clothing industries fell by over half by 1918, and a severe coal shortage hobbled output and civilian energy needs for most of the war. Notwithstanding the vast increase in war goods, the general index of all industrial production in Germany during the last three years of the war was slightly below three-quarters of the 1913 level. Efforts to create a viable fiscal basis for the extraordinary war effort largely failed, and by 1919 prices were over three times the 1913 level.

While the magnitude of Germany's decline is subject to statistical debates, what remains unquestionable is the downward trend in the population's welfare. The best estimate of real *weekly* wages fails to take into account that Germans worked longer hours at the end of the war than in 1914; on this basis, by the end of the war, average real wages fell 35 percent below prewar levels. Workers in war industries fared better than those producing civilian goods, of course, but the downward trend was universal. Salaried labor, not included in this figure, experienced an even greater drop. But data on living conditions reveal a far greater decline than such approximations imply.

Rationing began in early 1915 and soon covered most foodstuffs purchased legally; there was, as in most of Europe, a thriving black market for those few with the money to take advantage of it. The legally permitted quantities for most basic foods were progressively reduced, except for potatoes and sugar. By the end of 1918 the targeted meat ration was 12 percent of peacetime consumption, flour 48 percent, and vegetable fats 17 percent. In 1917 the caloric value of the official ration was approximately one-half of normal for workers, and laborers in strenuous jobs who were allocated extra food were in reality the worst off in terms of meeting their minimum health standards. By 1918 only one-sixth of the rationed calories from animal foodstuffs could in fact be purchased from the legal markets.[2]

### The Austro-Hungarian Empire
But if the crisis in living standards in Germany was critical, its allies in the Austro-Hungarian Empire suffered far more, notwithstanding the fact that the empire as a whole had been a food-exporting region. Its leaders, like all

others, expected a short war. Not only did combat within its borders, the huge draft, and war preparations cause overall grain production in 1918 to plummet by over one-third of the prewar level, but Hungary retained its greatly reduced output for itself. This situation affected the urban areas, especially Vienna, most of all.

Rationing in the empire began about the same time as in Germany, but established much lower norms, though in fact in both nations what the state allowed always greatly exceeded what was in fact available. The struggle to survive the war became bitter, and the vast majority fared poorly. The most conspicuous problem was bread, which by the end of 1914 was being diluted with barley, potatoes, and corn flour. The proportion of corn in flour eventually reached 80 percent in Vienna but only 10 percent in Pest, the county that included Budapest.

Whatever its statistical problems, data on real income in Vienna and the Hungarian cities justifies the conclusion that there was a catastrophic decline in living standards. By July 1918, the real income of five occupations in Vienna dependent on weekly wages had fallen by over 80 percent! More aggregate data on Hungarian blue-collar workers reveal that between 1913–14 and 1918 their real incomes dropped by about half, but by two-thirds for white-collar employees and civil servants. Foraging for food and fuel became an increasingly time-consuming aspect of human existence, especially after 1915, and children were more and more compelled to supplement family incomes in whatever way they could. Starvation and famine confronted the Austro-Hungarian Empire. "The population of the capital is hungry," a Budapest journalist wrote in July 1918; "they stand in line for hours for bread. . . ."[3]

### Russia

Given the already impoverished prewar state of its urban working class, the nature of its political leadership, and the extensive but inappropriate economic resources available to it, that Russia should immediately prove unable to cope with wartime scarcities was entirely predictable. Urban labor barely subsisted before the war, spending most of its income on food and living, shoddily dressed, in wretched housing. Its real income had remained stable during the seven years before 1914, and was extremely vulnerable to any shocks to the economy. The Russian war economy had no prewar fiscal base on which to expand, for taxes were both unjust and wholly inadequate for the urgent tasks at hand. Since direct taxes would principally hurt the regime's most ardent supporters, its rulers resorted to war loans that brought in far less than needed to avoid inflationary measures.

Whether Russia could survive a protracted war intact with so many initial liabilities depended greatly, but not wholly, on the status of the peasantry and food supplies. Despite the huge conscription of younger peasants and the expropriation of large numbers of draft animals, an agrarian sector that had been overpopulated in peacetime was still able to produce surplus grain, so that even in 1917 there was probably more grain than demand for it—at least hypothetically. But in practice the peasants who produced the larger part of the grain surplus had neither the will nor the ability to deliver it to consumers, especially after 1915, when there was very little they could buy with money. Many began to cut back on grain output and shifted to subsistence foods, reducing cultivated acreage, feeding more grain to animals, and hoarding. Some large landowners found that selling or renting their land was now more profitable; significant numbers of agricultural laborers and poor peasants began to move to the cities, where the need for labor and nominal wages appeared high. But a major reason for the agrarian sector's failure to deliver food was that the rail system, although large (and growing), was extremely inefficient; it existed in the wrong places and was unable to service the needs of both the army and the cities. As a result, the cities suffered the most from the war's impact on all the factors of production, although on paper urban output appeared impressive. And it was in the cities that the potential threats to the political order remained the greatest.

All of the war's dislocations produced critical shortages, interminable queuing, and a rampant inflation that was the worst in any of the major warring nations. While the available data are not entirely consistent, the most conservative estimate is that while prices about doubled during 1914–16, in 1917 they more than tripled—making for an overall sevenfold increase during wartime. Other calculations suggest that wartime prices preceding the Bolshevik Revolution were ten times greater than at the beginning of the war. In this context, while estimates of the real income of workers and others differ, it is certain their living standards fell greatly, especially after mid-1916. More important, given the existing impoverished prewar condition of the urban proletariat, any decrease could only aggravate discontent among those already suffering from an acute scarcity of housing, which the large migration to the city had exacerbated further. Some industries, such as war-related metalworking, maintained or even slightly increased real incomes over 1913, if only because of longer hours of work, but if one takes all industrial workers, monthly real incomes slipped gradually by nearly a fifth through 1916, and in 1917 they tumbled to under one-half of the 1913 level. But relative to their prewar status, white-collar workers and civil servants suffered the greatest real decline of all.[4]

Within a few short years the war profoundly affected large sections of Europe's working class and peasantry in ways that deprived them of much of their gains over the preceding decades and brought a significant portion to the verge of hunger and extreme deprivation. Nowhere were the people as a whole as well off in war as they had been during peace. Marx's theory of increasing immiserization of the proletariat had been relatively glacial or even erroneous until then, but the war suddenly undermined the material welfare of the masses in ways for which there was no precedent in modern European history, taking away from countless millions of them the material incentives to remain committed or, at the worst, acquiescent to ruling classes that had so blithely led them into the conflict's interminable economic maelstrom.

## Mobilizing People for War

Because all of the warring nations in the summer of 1914 assumed that their existing arms and supplies would largely suffice, it was inevitable that they would also confront identical problems. Not until well into 1915 did their leaders begin to adapt seriously to the reality that they were locked in a protracted war of indefinite length, one consuming unprecedented numbers of men and matériel; they now began drastically to reallocate their economic and human resources to enable the fighting to continue.

The magnitude of these changes, the immediate economic consequences of which were reflected in living standards, deeply affected the lives of the people. The social and class structure was subjected to intense pressures which, in greatly varying ways, eventually altered every aspect of the politics, social mores, demography, and human organization of the major states. Coming to grips with some of these basic changes is a prerequisite for comprehending the subsequent evolution of much of Europe.

The most serious problem that Britain, Germany, and France shared by 1916 was insufficient manpower for the seemingly insatiable military and economic tasks they all now confronted. Military leaders and those in charge of producing arms disputed—often bitterly—how to distribute the limited numbers of men available. The mere fact that the French armaments industry had 45,000 workers when the war began but about 2 million when it ended is a measure of the dimensions of the problems each of the belligerents had to resolve as they poured seemingly endless streams of shells on each other. Ultimately, all three nations concluded that very large numbers of skilled men already in the army, or eligible for induction, were more useful in war production than in trenches. By 1918 the French had placed over a half-million such men in factories, and by the summer of 1918 the Germans about 2.4 million. Germany introduced compulsory conscription of all males seventeen to sixty years old, in November 1916, and while this solved the problem of labor mobility, it still could not generate enough manpower to win the war. After late 1914 the British attempted to retain skilled workers in arms-related industries and took measures to keep eager recruiters away from them. How to place men in the most useful positions preoccupied and divided Britain well after Parliament in May 1916 enacted compulsory universal military conscription. The government also sought to draft civilian men for work in war factories, and notwithstanding successful union resistance, it persistently tried to pass laws to that effect. Its problem, ultimately, was that the military services claimed as many men as possible to compensate for the enormous numbers being killed and wounded in France—and the absence of unanimity prevented a coherent common policy as long as there was a shortage of available male bodies.

In the process of confronting the economic imperatives that war imposed, all of the contestants reorganized their industrial sectors in favor of war production in very much the same manner and essentially made the same choices on how best to utilize manpower. Workers in war industries in Italy grew from 20 to 64 percent of the industrial labor force during the war, and from 24 to 76 percent in Russia. Employment in the German war sector increased 44 percent from 1913 to 1918, and the decline in civilian activity was almost as great. Those employed in agriculture, textiles, and clothing, or as domestics, fell both in absolute numbers and as a proportion of overall employment in most of the warring nations. Over two-thirds of the males in French agriculture were absorbed into the army, about one-third of whom were either killed or too seriously wounded ever to work again.[5]

### Working Women
Wartime changes in the occupational and income structure and the nature of the working class were linked very considerably to the altered status of women in the belligerent nations. For as the single most important stimulant of economic and demographic changes, war in this century has increasingly incorporated women into the generally lower-paid sectors of the work force, including the white-collar class. It is simple to define the magnitude of these changes statistically; much more complex is how women workers, and their relationship to family incomes, affect the problems that the working class faces during wartime crises. And no less important is the question of how permanent the wartime changes in the status of women became, and its legacies for the future.

The wartime position of women in Germany, France, and Britain was remarkably similar in crucial regards. The number of women employed in industry and mining increased about 40 percent in Germany between 1907 and 1916, about 36 percent in Britain from July 1914 to July 1918, and 29 percent for France in all domains of economic activity from 1914 to July 1917, when it began slowly to decline. But the reality that many women in peasant and working-class households were already in the labor force complicates any analysis, for by transferring into war-related industries they could not produce significant changes in the class structure. Moreover, many women, confronted with the extra burdens of child rearing and also obligated to spend much more time queuing in shops while their husbands were at war, were unable to become wage workers. German arms manufacturers preferred to hire women who already had experience in civilian industries, and employers in all nations paid women at standards well below wages for men with equivalent skills, denying them fringe benefits whenever possible. Compulsorily insured women workers in Germany in the four years after June 1914 grew only 17 percent—less than half the actual total increase in women's jobs. If women in British industry closed the pay gap somewhat, in the immediate postwar era they still earned only slightly more than half of what men in similar occupational categories were receiving. In Germany too employers paid women somewhat less exploitively than during peacetime to attract them into the labor market, but the bonus was strictly temporary, and while the decline was not quite as great as for men, their real incomes also fell substantially. The over 3.2 million French women already employed in agriculture when the war began had always worked and they were able to sustain production to a significant extent. Many were the wives of soldiers, and since all soldiers' wives received generous allowances, they had little incentive to seek nonfarm employment.

In a word, women in Germany, France, and England played parallel roles and confronted comparable problems during the war. As they entered the labor market in unprecedented numbers, they found increased rather than diminished gender-based wage differentials among workers. But since it also meant temporarily greater family incomes for a large portion of the working class, it enabled many to survive inflation, scarcity, and falling real incomes with less suffering than they might otherwise have experienced— a factor that unquestionably mitigated to some degree the economic causes of workers' anger and the eventual inclination of some to protest. Whether this measure of relief reduced the political challenges to Europe's social orders is impossible to determine, since a significant number faced unprecedented public hostility in any case. Conversely, by mobilizing women, the leaders of the belligerents could also protract the war and human suffering, thereby further increasing the public's alienation.

One can estimate the data on the role of women in the war economies in various ways, yet it will only nuance but not alter the basic conclusion that while the growth in the number of working women was very significant, it was still not as crucial as has often been supposed, and it failed to compensate for the far greater losses of men. It surely did not greatly alter the status of women in the economies or societies of the warring nations; rather, they became a source of cheaper and more easily exploited labor.[6]

## The War and the Class and Social Structure

The First World War, like all wars, affected the warring nations' class and economic systems very unequally, but nowhere (except England) did the destruction, population movements, and scarcities allow the prewar social order to remain unscathed. In some countries, the war telescoped processes of change already underway to create prerevolutionary situations, and if only Russia succumbed to revolution during the war itself, much of central Europe and Italy emerged from its traumatic impact teetering on the abyss of total social and political upheaval. But the war's multiple institutional (as opposed to psychological and intellectual) dimensions sometimes shifted significant wealth, resources, privileges, and power away from the prewar middle and upper classes, not only creating new elites and power brokers as rivals to the prewar ruling coalitions but radicalizing a section of the latter's relationship to the political structure and their vision of the direction in which they wished society to move. Given the war's profound impact on all of the aspects of Europe's social structures, by the time it ended the issue was no longer whether it would change the political and social face of the Continent but only how extensive and deep that transformation would be.

Notwithstanding some significant exceptions, in most of Europe the erosion of living conditions affected those on the land the least and, relative to their prewar status, the urban white-collar and middle classes and *rentiers* dependent on fixed incomes and salaries suffered the most economically. While the war touched every one of the major prewar classes negatively in some important way, not all were affected to the same degree, and components within each benefited significantly. Obviously, those living in the country ate better—often far better—than those in cities. Indeed, while many hitherto marginalized and impoverished peasants remained poor, and virtually everywhere provided a disproportionately greater share of the cannon fodder for the trenches, an unprecedented number also gained and thereby were able to challenge some landowners' dominant positions. Much of Europe had to cope with the speculators in food who prospered immensely off of black markets that flaunted existing laws and conventional norms of decency and who incorporated a significant sector of the agrarian population in what the large majority of the people regarded as dishonorable business.

France's experience is perhaps the best against which to measure those of other nations. About 3.7 million peasants went into the military, leaving the rural areas with an acute labor shortage and dependent on old men, women, and children to sustain output. Inflation seriously hurt big landowners normally dependent on fertilizers and equipment, and while their labor costs did not mount as quickly, the scarcity of agricultural workers by 1920 pushed their wages up at least twice as fast as for urban occupations. Apart from comfortable government allowances to the wives of peasants in the army, and higher prices for their output, a significant portion of farmers leaked goods to the black market and personal rural food consumption also mounted. Prosperity reached the countryside in ways unknown before. Rural France accepted and supported the war more unreservedly than all other classes because, in the last analysis, it gained much more from it than those in the cities. Inflation and increased liquidity allowed many peasants to pay off fixed mortgages and to buy large quantities of land—much of which would have remained untilled anyway—immediately after the war. In Italy, on the other hand, the labor shortage was much less acute and landless laborers who chose to remain in the countryside did far worse than industrial workers. Although food was not as scarce as in the urban areas, many simply abandoned rural hardships for those of the cities, with their immense demand for workers, and some landowners were even ready to sell parts of their property.

In the Austro-Hungarian Empire the situation was more complex, but the countryside was spared the miseries confronting the food-deficient cities, and the richer peasants and landowners gained very significantly from what may have been Europe's largest black-market economy. The majority of Hungarians in rural areas were landless laborers or poor peasants, of course, but there were many fewer of them by virtue of wartime conscription, and the daily struggle to survive affected them far less than, say, Viennese. The rural elite, working with speculators and sharks, prospered amply amid the sea of suffering.

Germany was far better organized, with the entire agricultural system nominally under comprehensive control, and so corruption did not permeate the economy so deeply. The labor-scarce rural population, deprived of many of its horses and unable to buy or afford fertilizers, often refused to cooperate with the official system, and some peasants began to abandon the land to work in war industries. But a significant portion used food, particularly potatoes, for fodder and hoarded wheat and other vital foodstuffs, selling increasing amounts to black-market speculators.

Even in Russia the condition of the peasantry, though difficult, was very different from that of people in the cities, and notwithstanding their problems, some also made substantial gains. The war gravely affected a land system in transition since the 1906 reforms, designed to increase the numbers of peasant landowners. And because the vast draft of peasants into the army and the requisition of draft animals also hurt the large landowners, many were ready to sell off land or rent cheaply to a new peasant bourgeoisie that began to emerge.

In general, poorer Russian peasants were able to adjust to the war-imposed difficulties in transport and supplies by returning to subsistence agriculture, withholding food from the market when it was possible to ship it, or often simply going to work in cities to earn funds with which they hoped later to buy cheapening land. For the first several years, their sale of animals to the government made their assets more liquid than they had ever been. But they could purchase little with cash, and so peasants increasingly consumed and hoarded much more of what they produced, in part because the war ended the legal production of vodka. With time, especially as the transport system failed, they reduced the acreage they cultivated and fed increasing amounts of produce to their animals. In 1917 the bulk of the successful harvest remained on the farms.[7]

### The Crisis of the Middle Class

The European urban middle and white-collar classes and *rentiers* had lived comfortably before the war, and were generally pillars of political and social stability, but their dependence on fixed incomes and salaries exposed them to the war's economic vicissitudes more than any other group. The magnitude of their difficulties varied by nation, but in general they underwent a sustained period of economic tension and anxiety which, while having a significant economic effect on them, altered their once secure political and ideological visions of the world even more profoundly. The complex problem of assessing this class's fate involves, above all, looking at mobility within the more privileged, affluent classes and determining its specific, changing membership rather than at the nature of income and wealth at any fixed time regardless of the identities of those possessing it. The changes that occurred within Europe's traditional higher-income classes are meaningful only to comprehend these elements' relationship to each other—that is, intraclass mobility—for the wealthiest classes' traditional economic position vis-à-vis the masses remained essentially static. If all one does is look only at the broadest relations between the rich and others, most of Europe's economies reemerged in more or less the same form that they had assumed before the war.

The distribution of wealth and power is exceedingly difficult to document even during peacetime, and while the data that exists on such changes in war-torn Europe is often impressionistic and haphazard, many contemporaries both felt and perceived that the war had altered in significant, sometimes basic ways the prewar dominant classes' hegemony, but especially the middle classes' standing and role. Whatever the accuracy of specific theses on the magnitude of such changes, it is certain that the war—like all wars before it—gave men who were enterprising and unscrupulous opportunities to profit from dislocations and scarcity, to carve out important places for themselves in the economic structures and elites of many European nations. No social order can experience prolonged war without all the forms of power within it being altered in some serious, possibly crucial, fashion.

The war also allowed many established industrialists, in addition to speculators, to make large and sometimes extraordinary profits, and comprehending the taxation systems' impact on all those who gained depends upon the accuracy of reported income and the state's ability and will to tax both real and declared revenues. In Germany, Italy, and France the wartime and immediate postwar tax systems were lax and evasion widespread, and inflation further thwarted Germany's efforts to collect war profits. England was much more rigorous, but the concentration of wealth in the hands of its wealthiest 1 percent was much greater than in France and therefore made tax collection simpler; the distribution of income in Britain became somewhat more equal as a result of the war, but this change hardly affected the ownership of real wealth. Notwithstanding a heavier wartime toll on both of them, the richest tenth of Britain and 15 percent of France emerged from the war in virtually the same privileged position they had been in before it.

But whether the very small but statistically ascendant class in those nations for which we have data comprised the same people and groups as before the war, and how the population of Europe's nations perceived the wartime social and economic system, its gainers and losers, are important matters to resolve. Was there, in effect, an important turnover within the existing elites, and was there a tendency toward equalization within the existing class structures, even if only a sharing of deprivation that a putative "proletarianization" of the middle classes created? A nuanced response to these issues leaves us with a complex yet comprehensive description of social realities among the rich and comfortable.

One aspect of the war that greatly complicates, and often obscures, the depth and importance of wartime changes in Europe's class structure was the emergence in most countries of a stratum of high-living consumers, all the more conspicuous because wartime scarcities and the economic crisis delegitimatized the right, so to speak, of the prewar rich to live ostentatiously and spend freely. The phenomenon of the nouveaux riches basking visibly in affluence, as manifested in the consumption of black-market goods, appeared everywhere, including in the midst of the worst miseries of Hungary. They were linked especially to war profiteering and the black market, and scandalized the public in Italy, France, and Germany. Cafés and restaurants in Paris and elsewhere in France boomed, and the luxury trade flourished openly as "society" in wartime continued to play its habitual games as publicly as possible. Germany's spas and resorts were full, and the emergence of heavily made-up women who were seen at assorted bacchanals profoundly shocked many. But whether this ostentatious breed represented an altogether new force in the economic structure, or simply consisted of the strategically placed small businessmen who profited handsomely in Britain and much of Europe, enterprising landowners who capitalized on their access to food, or riffraff as opposed to those who were well off or wealthy before, is less clear. How great a shift in the control of each nation's wealth occurred beyond the normal circulation integral to the very process of economic development remains debatable; but there is no doubt that a socially significant equalization of wealth did not occur in those nations for which data exist. A highly stratified class society persisted in all of Europe except Russia; the debate is only over whether the same individuals dominated it, and whether the prewar elites profited sufficiently to retain their relative economic and social positions. They certainly did with the war-related industries, but as always occurs at times of great economic fluidity, they also had to make space for newcomers.[8]

What is far better understood and socially significant is who lost most from the war economically, both in absolute terms and in ways that profoundly affected their status and subsequent political behavior. While most students of the war correctly assume that Europe's middle classes and white-collar occupations dependent on salaries and fixed sources of income fared very badly, thereby making them receptive to the reactionary postwar political currents, this generalization must be nuanced and, in a few places, rejected. For many blue-collar workers did as badly or worse, and while their relative deprivation was not so great since they had always been straitened, nothing like homogenized societies with less class differentiation emerged anywhere in Europe. Britain and Russia offer two extremes within which to position most of the rest of Europe.

Britain's experience was the simplest to understand. While its agrarian elite was deeply affected, the war left industrialists and businessmen at least as strong as ever in the social hierarchy, and it was this overall system of class and status, altered in important ways but still wholly hierarchical, that survived along with a remarkably unchanged distribution of income and wealth. Class distinctions in consumer spending persisted despite the lower amounts of better-grade foods available to everybody. The income differences between the major occupational categories shifted during the war to the advantage of unskilled workers, foremen, lower professionals, and managers, and fell somewhat for higher professionals, clerical, skilled, and semiskilled workers—but over the next two decades the earlier inequities returned, and the relationship of occupation and income still left the prewar class structure essentially where it had been. In Russia, on the other hand, the numerically small but strategic white-collar and clerical class after 1914 suffered far more than blue-collar labor, though in absolute wages in 1917 it was still on the average almost twice as well off as industrial workers. This relative decline in income and the lowered status it brought helped to drive many fixed-income employees into the various wings of the opposition in 1917. In France and Italy, to cite less catastrophic examples, the lower middle class on fixed incomes suffered the most: office workers, civil servants, small *rentiers*, and the petite bourgeoisie in general. They emerged from the war under growing economic pressure, the material gap between them and many industrial workers declining quickly.

In Germany's case, aspects of the experiences elsewhere merged to create another variation in the overall European pattern, one that ultimately was to prove the most dangerous. As in Russia, the middle class's position dropped furthest compared to its prewar standing, and it suffered a severe drop in status relative to the working class as their economic rank moved closer to each other even as the standard of living of workers dropped generally. Unquestionably, the bourgeoisie that had supported the war, and which inflation and scarcities were now increasingly destroying as a class, was angry during the war itself, though its problems then were still small compared to the impact of the 1920s' inflation on many of them. Whatever the talk of their "proletarianization," such a condition was something they feared far more than they experienced, and as their anxieties mounted, they spent their meager incomes to preserve the status they thought essential to their dignity and identity. Precisely because the middle classes had more clothing and goods to begin with, they could retain their essential symbolic class trappings, but the working class by necessity spent more of its resources on food, and the middle class on rent and education. In one sense the gap between the middle and working classes diminished significantly if all one does is measure incomes, but notwithstanding that both lived increasingly badly, ultimately the prewar class structure reemerged after the war.

One cannot overemphasize the war's impact on the middle class, especially those sections of it linked to land and real estate, which relatively— although not absolutely—suffered the most everywhere. The political significance of this decline became clear as the affected groups later moved to the Right and made Fascist and Nazi triumphs possible. For while the unequal prewar distribution of economic power remained essentially intact at the end of the war, it was precarious sufficiently long to produce the fears eroding the self-assurance of many of the members of the prewar middle class, a portion of whom were indeed losing their economic resources, and it was this sense of insecurity and hostility toward the masses that was to have such monumental consequences.[9]

## Numbers

Numbers mock our powers of description and they trivialize the human condition. But as a preface to understanding the European people's great outcry against the war, and the subsequent political, social, and intellectual breakdown of the traditional European, and then world, order, figures remain both utilitarian and necessary as a starting point, and in our age we are addicted to them. For the war's human and social costs—the hunger, exile, and deaths—were titanic, and without historical precedent however one measures them.

Notwithstanding the often general and not entirely consistent data available, there is no doubt whatsoever that the war was monumentally destructive. First, there were the military deaths, which numbered roughly 10 million killed among the warring nations, plus about 3 million presumed dead. There are never census takers in wartime and so some estimates are somewhat lower, others higher, but 13 million is the general magnitude of military deaths, and a million or two either way does not alter the meaning of such colossal slaughter.

In absolute terms, Germany suffered the greatest losses—about 1.8 million killed—and probably had the most wounded (4.2 million). As a proportion of the total men mobilized, Germany also experienced the highest losses, though France was close behind it. But relative to the size of the entire population, which was anywhere from 17 to 25 million more in Germany (depending on the bases of calculation), France lost more men than any nation save possibly Hungary. Of every 1,000 inhabitants, France mobilized 168 and lost 34, while Germany mobilized 154 and lost 30. Britain mobilized 125 and lost 16. But if one takes military dead per 1,000 of all men aged twenty to forty-five, France lost 182 and Germany 155, with Britain 88 and the United States 3. By this measure Hungary suffered most with 187, and Austria slightly more than Germany. If one calculates the percentage of those mobilized who were killed and the percentage of the active population dead or missing, France again comes first, Germany second, and Britain's dead as a percentage of those mobilized exceeded Russia's. Indeed, Russia lost slightly less than Britain by both these criteria. For while Russia's army of 15.5 million was far larger than any other, its huge losses were well below France's and Germany's as a share because its troops refused to fight, and it quit the war one year before its allies.[10]

Civilian deaths are much more difficult to calculate, although the estimate of about 13 million dead is quite credible. Apart from those killed and wounded in the course of battles, it is certain that civilian mortality rates rose sharply in those nations undergoing the worst food and fuel shortages, even ignoring the catastrophic 1918 Spanish flu epidemic, which was fatal to a great degree because a significant proportion of those many millions who died in it were already weakened from poor diet and a lack of fuel— which lowered their resistance greatly. Germany alone experienced about 300,000 above-normal civilian deaths during the war. But while the war's complex indirect demographic consequences make precise estimates difficult, France unquestionably suffered more than Germany insofar as its prewar birthrate was not even two-thirds of Germany's and its mortality rate was higher. France could less afford its war deaths, and with a surplus of over 1 million women between twenty and thirty-nine years old in 1921, both the number of children below five years and their share of the population fell dramatically. Germany's excess of women in this category was even greater, and the decline in young children even more so, but its capacity to revive its army remained far larger than France's. France's population in 1920 was nearly 3 million less than in 1913.[11]

Apart from human losses, past and future, the warring powers were left with huge debts and massive physical damage. Britain's public debt grew elevenfold from 1913 to 1919, France's sevenfold, and Germany's forty-fold—although adjustments for inflation reduce the extent of these increases considerably. The actual damage to property in all of Europe is impossible to estimate with any degree of reliability, yet it must have been gigantic given the fairly accurate measures of losses we have. To take one reliable example, in France's ten conquered northern *départements*, containing 16 percent of the prewar population, 56 percent of the inhabitants fled the region, and of the 1.2 million buildings in this area, more than three-quarters were destroyed or severely affected in the course of the war. Combat touched directly over half of the cultivable soil, which was often ruined and even sterilized. The German occupation of the area began brutally, but soon moderated, and they relied extensively on the existing municipal authorities for routine administrative tasks until the end of the war. Fraternization commenced quickly, was widespread, and permitted. But the German forces' nominally civilized policies disappeared during planned retreats. Then trees were cut to block roads, wells poisoned, and many buildings destroyed or mined. Later the French fixed their losses from damage at 34 billion prewar francs, or the size of the entire prewar public debt.

Several other indices of Europe's torment broaden our understanding of the outcome of the war. Obviously, by accelerating the pace of industrialization and attracting labor to the cities, the occupational structure was significantly altered, and rural depopulation accelerated to a greater extent than otherwise would have occurred. France is a good example. Many of those who arrived in cities were refugees. But France sought also to attract foreign labor to compensate for its massive losses of men, and it became the world's second-largest recipient of migrants; in many European cities there were serious housing crises, and primitive accommodations became far more common. In Russia's case, by 1916, 6 million new persons had crammed into its cities.

These vast migrations and the general decline in living standards, along with direct war losses, created the conditions in which disease could subsequently inflict a heavy toll on Europe's population. The experience with exanthematic typhus is indicative. It began on the Galician and Turkish fronts, and refugees and war prisoners spread it so that by 1916 the number of reported cases was twice normal, quickly extending throughout the region but especially to Russia. About 9 million cases were reported there alone, and reliable estimates fix at least 1.5 million dead by 1920. Other diseases took the lives of about another half-million Russians. The total excess mortality from all causes in Russia from 1914 to 1923 was about 12 million persons, less than a quarter of whom died as a result of direct wounds.

After 1918 a huge population movement throughout Europe displaced the lives of countless millions as people acted to save their own lives or were forced to move as a result of treaties such as those signed at Lausanne in 1923. Refugees from Russia to the rest of Europe and the Far East have been estimated at anywhere from 900,000 to 3 million, with the figure of 2 million being most likely. About a million Germans left areas given to Poland and France at the Paris Peace Conference; about a half-million Hungarians returned to postwar Hungary; and nearly a million Poles moved to the formerly German part of Poland. The Lausanne Treaty ordered 1.2 million Greeks out of Turkey and 400,000 Turks from Greece. Many millions—no one knows precisely how many—were uprooted and compelled to begin life anew. In this situation, disease and death flourished—along with the hatred and bitterness that would soon transform Europe's politics.[12]

Cold figures will never explain war's true material or human damage, much less express the torment that afflicted great parts of Europe. But the Continent's trial by fire touched unprecedented numbers of people simultaneously, on a scale no one, whether leaders or led, had ever imagined possible, and the whole process quickly became irreversible. Such unrelenting suffering—crudely measured here in numerical terms—penetrated the perceptions, thoughts, and desires of Europe's population, who were now incorporated into the vast, sustained, and deepening mobilization of societies that increasingly controlled the lives of civilians as well as soldiers. The continuous deaths and maiming of sons, husbands, brothers, and neighbors increased the pressures upon countless millions to think about fundamental social issues, issues involving war and peace, justice and oppression, and their rulers' or leaders' wisdom or folly, in ways that had never before seemed possible or required. Daily deprivations—the lack of foods, the need to work longer and harder, or the absence of life's simple amenities—reinforced the necessity of people to reflect and make judgments, for they could no longer sublimate or avoid the consequences of apathy or indifference without paying a constantly growing, intolerable price for passivity and acquiescence.

As the numbers were translated into feelings and consciousness, as suffering and tragedy turned to bitterness and anger, Europe's masses began to change profoundly—and the century would never again be the same.

# CHAPTER 6

# World War One:
# Transforming Europe's People

When Europe's rulers embarked so casually upon war, few among them even remotely imagined the compounding difficulties and challenges they would encounter. Within only a few years the war's enormously diverse and irreversible economic, social, and ideological consequences began to accumulate and transcend the rulers' ability to emerge unscathed from the deepening trauma, and although many of the dominant elites were not replaced before the war's end, their new problems soon reappeared to confront them in yet other grave ways. Eventually, the very survival of a large portion of the traditional social order was at stake.

European society's mounting crises before 1918 were the outcome of innumerable economic, intellectual, and political forces, many of which predated the war but now were far more acute, but they all merged to undermine profoundly the existing verities and institutions, as well as the men who either propounded or led them in most nations. Although no single factor or event can either capture or explain the full magnitude of all of the dilemmas the nations at war faced or the reasons for them, after mid-1917 the deepening alienation among the masses and insecurity among the leaders defined the decisive political context of the war's outcome.

The First World War from its inception produced suffering as well as changes that inexorably were to affect the consciousness of Europe's people, their politics and commitments, and numbers cannot adequately capture this reality. At best, such data create both a utilitarian and an essential context for assessing the many ways that bread lines, long hours of toil, the death and maiming of loved ones, and all of the experiences that cold statistics seek to aggregate reached into the minds and hearts of an unprecedented number of frustrated, increasingly skeptical, and suffering people—people who for some decades had been relatively passive politi-cally—to alter their perceptions of politics and society as well as their social roles within it. This transformation intensified as the war ceased to be the promised, relatively painless conflict of a few months' duration and became an extended bloodletting that involved immeasurable pain for civilians as well as soldiers, population displacements, penury, and hunger in increas-ingly large regions—a war leading to the immediate or eventual breakdown of long-standing political and social orders.

The war was a traumatic social experience for much of Europe, civilians and soldiers alike, and it did not take long for the fact that it would be pro-tracted to begin to erode seriously the commitment of many of those liber-als and socialists who had supported it in France, Germany, or Russia, for nearly all of them had assumed that, like the Franco-Prussian War of 1870–71, it would be over quickly. It was this near-universal expectation of a short war that allowed the socialist parties to abandon so easily their nom-inal internationalism to vote the credits necessary for the Continent's peo-ples to slaughter one another. Their dilemma was that as the war's eco-nomic consequences acutely affected the working class, their historic fatal compromise left them in an increasingly precarious position and made pos-sible the later Leninist challenge to the putative unity of socialism because the Communists alone unequivocally opposed the war. It was the war's irre-sistibly mounting economic and social impact rather than socialist agitators that began to change the European peoples' political beliefs and conduct in differing ways—ranging from relatively moderate agitation in Britain to rev-olutionary upheaval in Russia. Although socialist parties seemed poised to take power in only a few nations, in many of them they became qualita-tively much more important political forces than they had ever been. Coping with the revitalized Left later demanded new responses on the part of the ruling classes—responses which were to emerge in their most extreme form in fascist movements.

## Controlling Labor, Trade Unions, and Strikes

Socialism's leaders and their followers soon had to confront the inherent contradiction between their endorsements of the war and their inability to tolerate the mounting impositions and daily material hardships that it entailed for a constantly growing share of the working class. This challenge intensified the longer the war lasted, and it affected all of the warring countries in varying ways. The quandary that united France, Germany, and Britain was that they all had entered the war with only enough munitions and matériel to fight briefly, and their need to utilize a finite labor supply to mobilize both sufficient arms output and soldiers increasingly required them to attempt to control the lives of male labor, thereby militarizing it in significant ways. All were compelled to exempt skilled labor or "loan" already mobilized qualified manpower to arms plants, and Britain also prevented a large number from being recruited into the military or, after 1916, drafted. In early 1917, ministerial control of the munitions industry locked large numbers of French workers into factories in ways that left them powerless. The German government restrained labor mobility after the fall of 1916 because a significant portion of the workers had quit their jobs to obtain higher wages—a freedom that hurt the key war industries. By late 1918 well over 2 million German men who were soldiers or eligible for the draft were employed in essential industries. And about 640,000 skilled Russians fit for (or even already in) the army were sent to work in war plants. Such a policy of restricting and conscripting labor circumscribed the working class's freedom to change employers, and those among them who were formally in the military service or subject to it feared being sent to the army should they express normal grievances or displease their bosses.

Data in the preceding chapter on declining real wages and living standards in Europe are relevant principally to the condition of workers who in most nations had lost much of their prewar liberty to move or attempt to ameliorate their economic position. In the inflationary context that prevailed in most of Europe, ministerial diktats on hours of labor and wage rates or compulsory arbitration gravely affected the largely urban proletariat. Acute housing shortages in many cities, and a lack of clothing and sanitary facilities, further eroded working-class morale. While such trends varied in each country, in the aggregate the war created a parallel set of radicalizing influences in much of Europe. In Russia and Austria, which were extreme cases, the most pressing problems were the lack of essential foods, and hunger, especially in the cities after late 1916. In Germany the reduction of bread rations in the spring of 1917 occurred while those who profited from the war were seen by workers to be living ostentatiously, and most urban dwellers believed that farmers were withholding grain or feeding it to their animals. British labor increasingly complained bitterly, especially about the cost of living and the quasi prohibition of liquor that was introduced throughout the Anglo-Saxon world. In France the pattern was the same, as wage increases failed to keep pace with inflation.

The efforts of various governments to create a disciplined labor force and maximize war output immediately encountered problems inherent in the demographic transformation of cities and the expansion of factories. Such sudden and depersonalizing changes also created new social tensions and dynamics both for the traditional ruling classes and the trade unions. The vast influx of youth and women, many from rural backgrounds, made effective union organization along customary lines far more difficult, altering the very nature of the working class in significant ways. In Germany, elements of the middle class were disturbed by the "terrific sense of their own importance" of the great number of saucy predraft-age boys absorbed into the economy.[1] The proportion of French women in the labor force grew from 32 to 40 percent between the outbreak of war and the end of 1917. In Russia quickening industrialization before the war had attracted large numbers of rural youth to Petrograd's factories—possibly more than a majority in metalworking alone even by 1914—and when urban workers were subjected to wartime deprivations, they were in fact to a critical degree an already displaced and alienated body of relatively younger men, ripe for Bolshevik appeals and more susceptible than traditional, older workers to acting aggressively. Huge, essentially political strikes centered in Petrograd during the first half of 1914 brought such marginalized, potentially dynamic elements onto the streets, greatly augmenting the Bolsheviks' strength even before the outbreak of war.

Changes such as these in the social and mental composition of the European working class altered labor organizations in various ways, even if they did not entirely unhinge the prewar order. The first effect in France was for the membership of the Confédération Générale du Travail (CGT) in 1915 to drop to one-sixth of its 1913 level, but as the strike movement gathered impetus, it also brought 550,000 new members to the union by 1918, when it far exceeded its prewar strength. The French Socialist Party, by comparison, lost over two-thirds of its 1914 membership by late 1918, and despite gaining back more than that by 1919, it remained vulnerable to an eventual serious challenge from the Communists. More than in any other nation, Britain's unions had militantly resisted state policies, and its workers also emerged from the war relatively better off. Union membership mushroomed during the war, doubling its prewar size to more than 8 million in 1920. Hungarian trade-union membership increased almost sevenfold between 1913 and 1918. As the war upset the prewar world to its very roots, the labor movement in much of Europe became far stronger than it had ever been before. After 1916 a much more critical context for debate and action on the Left began to emerge to polarize political dialogue in various countries and to create new social visions; and while some were more radical than others, all tended to make trade unionism and socialism significantly more articulate and aggressive than they had been since the war's inception.

Considering the war's deepening hardships, it was inevitable that

Europe's workers express their frustrations and anger in the form of increasing numbers of strikes, but it is essential to assess the stoppages realistically in each nation, for both their strengths and their social limitations. Yet given the issues of life and death involved, from the viewpoint of Europe's war managers an extensive strike movement represented a potential threat to the very outcome of the war, so that the numbers involved in the walkouts were crucial even if they generally failed to reach prewar levels. That strikes in most nations were overwhelmingly economic in origin until 1918 did not alter the fact that often grave unintended military—and thereby political—consequences were intrinsic to the very act of attempting to obtain more bread or fewer working hours.

More strikes occurred in Britain during the war than in any other warring nation, except Russia, exceeding 1913 levels even as a share of industrial employment, which also grew considerably during the war. That Britain was among the least radical countries politically reinforces the fact that there was no necessary correlation between the working class's economic militancy and its politics. Over four times as many days were lost in strikes in Britain during the 1915–18 period than in Germany, and about 20 times as many as in Austria. All of the warring nations except Britain experienced very few strikes in the period through 1915, and grievances were purely economic. Wartime strikes in Italy dropped to about half of the 1913 level, which was exceeded only in 1919. Compared to the 1909–13 average, the number of days lost in strikes in France during 1915–16 was a tiny fraction, but in 1917 they shot up to about half of the immediate prewar norms. In 1917 there were five times as many strike days lost in Germany as in the preceding year, and far more than in 1912 or 1913. By 1916 lesser trade-union–led actions that culminated short of work stoppages involved far greater numbers of German workers than before the war, and the following year their number doubled. Russia's strikes, which had been very numerous but largely political from 1905 to 1914, in 1915–16 were still below prewar levels, but now became overwhelmingly economic in nature—and in the end they proved far more dangerous to a nation at war. Most crucial was the fact that after 1915 walkouts in Europe increased significantly among the nominally prowar working class, and that their frequency was linked directly to the cost of living, food supplies, and, especially in Britain, resistance to government controls. That they initially had no political, much less revolutionary, motives was far less significant than the objective effects of their actions on the ability of nations to make war or on the credibility of various factions within national ruling classes who began to advocate diplomatic alternatives to the protracted stalemate. Abstractly, workers accepted the prowar policies of their union leaders but could scarcely tolerate living with their effects; some were often hungry, and many more were increasingly alienated. Strikes therefore became qualitatively as well as quantitatively the most visible of many symptoms of an extremely complex process of change that the war's deprivations were imposing on Europe's laborers. But each national experience had a specific character in terms of its eventual political implications, for despite the fact that—except for Britain and Germany—there were still fewer strikes during the war than before it, they now counted far more.

The German and Austrian strikes illustrate how decisive national differences and their consequences could be. Between 1915 and 1917 the number of people involved in walkouts in both nations increased dramatically, but in both places, notwithstanding some important exceptions, their goals initially remained largely economic. Street demonstrations against scarcities and inequities, mainly involving women and youth, also increased after 1915, with the organized workers only marginally involved in them. Because the principal leaders of the German SPD and unions endorsed wartime labor controls in the hope of both influencing them and retaining their own power, and the German military in charge of the economy sought thereby to co-opt the workers, those strikes that occurred were at least partially successful. But in an inflationary economy that irresistibly absorbed labor for the army, the official socialists' gains were at best temporary, and as the number of strikes that had an economic basis grew many times over, dissident socialists began to include political demands as well—and it was they who increasingly led the strikes. In Austria, however, the official Social Democrats not only supported and led much more militant workers' strikes and protests—which began earlier than those in Germany—but also the spontaneous councils that workers formed, thereby avoiding those schisms within the Left that in Germany were eventually sufficient to produce a strong Communist party and to destroy German Social Democracy's subsequent ability to respond to future challenges with a united organization.[2]

## Radicalizing the Working Class

What all Europeans shared was their need to respond to the mounting economic and personal deprivations that the war imposed upon them; of course, nearly all of these people had endorsed a short, glorious conflict that they supposed would ask very little of patriots. As the masses paid the required price for their folly, both conventional wisdom and inhibitions began to erode. Notwithstanding this shifting mood in much of Europe before 1919, except for Russia the working class as a whole did not yet reach, or even approach, a conscious breaking point in its toleration of the existing social orders. Some among them did begin to challenge the status quo in ways previously thought inconceivable—indeed, that were scarcely even imagined either by socialist theoreticians or their enemies. Inexorably, if unevenly, there were countless events and changes, most small, but all signs of the times, that confirmed that there was a general, if elliptical movement among many of Europe's workers to identify politically with what can only best be subsumed under the broad rubric of the Left. Above all, there was their involvement in diverse forms of action whose practical effects in a number of nations were to undermine existing rulers.

Although the European masses at this initial point in its development generally failed to endorse a coherent ideological or political alternative to the dominant social systems, their actions nonetheless entailed an unprecedented rejection of the prevailing social orders and functionally opposed the existing ruling classes' politics, institutions, and pretensions. And it was the objective consequences of the workers' growing militancy rather than their usually inchoate ideas that most threatened large parts of Europe's status quo at its moment of greatest weakness. Even more important for future politics, the war left what were to prove profound residues of bitter memories and deeply critical attitudes among large sections of both the working and middle classes that later created new political objectives among those who initially appeared to have emerged from the terrible slaughter still largely integrated in existing societies. But to capture their growing alienation and class consciousness, and the reasons that impelled their radicalization, requires an exploration of those many processes of change that over the subsequent two decades were again to traumatize a weakened Europe—and the world.

### Germany

The German experience was certainly among the most important for understanding how the now inexorable growth of radical values, action, and politics was to alter Europe. Although the majority Social Democratic and trade union leadership rationalized their initial support for war precisely because the nation's rulers had promised it would be short, their instinctively patriotic endorsement of militarism was revealed well before the war and was the cause of its vote in 1913 to expand the army. But once the war dragged on, it was not merely falling living standards that radicalized Germany's working class.

The nature of factory work itself was greatly altered, partially because a new and less skilled industrial proletariat diminished the role and status of craft workers who initially had been the earliest supporters of the unions and the SPD and later also provided the radicals with many of their most effective agitators, but principally because wartime discipline created a profoundly alienating work environment. Prewar conditions provided significantly more security and stability, with pensions and benefits for workers who remained with one employer. Wartime controls over the use and allocation of labor compelled many workers to change jobs, and even abandon the kinds of tasks they knew best, greatly depersonalizing the labor process.

And the ability of employers to discipline many workers by threatening them with military induction, and to have the commanders of local military districts actually do so, further militarized the factories. But in addition to such unprecedented changes in the shops and the endless wartime hardships, the fact that workers constantly saw that sacrifices were not being shared equally, and that an affluent elite of war profiteers existed, greatly compounded the working class's alienation—an alienation that the traditional union and SPD leadership initially preferred to ignore rather than redirect.

The union and SPD leaders by 1914 were principally conservative and usually upwardly mobile, self-educated workers now transformed into personally ambitious managers of huge and affluent bureaucracies, and until the summer of 1917 they were receptive to the blandishments that the military offered labor as a part of a concerted effort to gain their cooperation. When the war began, the SPD and union leaders endorsed the government's proclamation of a *Burgfriede*—a civil peace—that obligated them to accept the state's final power to determine all crucial economic policies. But their influence was increasingly undermined as the war greatly eroded the unions' membership and, even worse, compelled many lower-level functionaries to return to the factories or go into the army. Indeed, the state's ability to compel them to cast off their suits became a vital means of disciplining the minority of union and SPD officials who shared or responded to the workers' moods.

The German war industry, under military pressure, made a number of tactical concessions to workers in the hope of gaining their complete acquiescence, but they did so within the framework of a disciplined, hierarchic system that failed to gain the enthusiasm of most workers or to defend their economic positions adequately. This effort at co-opting and integrating the rank-and-file working class into the social order essentially failed from its inception. The SPD's membership in 1917 was less than a quarter of its 1914 level, and its unions in 1917 had well under a half of their 1913 numbers—a decline that the military draft of its members does not wholly explain since the non-SPD unions did not fare so badly. By the end of 1915 at least some of the unions' most conservative leaders realized that the prolongation of wartime hardships would produce strikes. Implicit in this awareness was the union and SPD leaderships' need both to satisfy the demands of the state and to control strike movements and workers' discontent simultaneously in order to preserve their own position as a powerful functional stratum providing stability to the status quo. In reality, the working class's leaders were momentarily in a unique position to use their still-significant, if eroding, credibility both among the proletariat and the traditional ruling class to mediate the imminent profound social crisis whose roots the protracted bloodletting was feeding.

Their ability to succeed in this difficult task over the next five years was due principally to the fact that while Germany's workers were very angry and increasingly alienated, the vast majority were not yet revolutionary. Their wrath surfaced most dramatically in the vast, largely spontaneous spring 1917 strikes, involving 300,000 workers in Berlin alone, in response to reduced bread rations. By then the union leaders understood perfectly well that the war-weary working class had begun to change and was becoming increasingly politicized, that their own roles were in danger of being supplanted, and that they had both to contain and lead labor. To do so required them to maneuver agilely between industrialists, generals, and state leaders, with whom they were essentially allied, and a deeply alienated working class they nominally represented and whose potential for overthrowing the existing system still remained to be tested. The consequences of their effort to normalize and maintain a state and political order in the process of increasingly rapid dissolution was to affect German history profoundly.[3]

### France and Great Britain

The public mood in France and Britain paralleled that in Germany through 1917; all shared the common enigma of a large majority of workers objecting to deprivations but not rejecting outright the war that was the source of their discontent. In France the workers expected a short war, but ultimately they remained sufficiently patriotic to support a long one, though with mounting reservations. As in Germany, the CGT leaders risked losing members because of their opposition to key strikes, and after early 1917 there was a growing wave of discontent for them both to cope with and, if possible, control. This they managed to accomplish, but most French civilians did not pay the same price as the Germans as a whole, and their alienation was in no way comparable. France seemingly emerged from the war as stable as when it had entered.

Britain's trade union and Labour leaders unquestionably had more influence on their government's policies than their German peers, and from the inception they were more prowar than their members. Like politicians of all hues everywhere, many Labour leaders were ambitious careerists, and while they remained committed to operating within the existing power structure, they adroitly reconciled themselves with their constituencies when, as they increasingly were prone to do, the latter ignored their officers. Neither the pacifist nor the revolutionary movements gained many adherents among workers, and the somewhat greater fiscal sacrifices that the British ruling class (unlike those in Germany and France) made to support the war intensified social solidarity. But many ordinary Englishmen increasingly refused to accept the war effort docilely.

The most significant pressure weighing on the British labor movement, apart from real income and food issues that were far less grave than in

Germany, was the conscription of labor for civilian employment as well as military service—a policy that was rational for total war but which would have militarized the labor force as in Germany. Although they supported the war without reservation through 1915, the workers' leaders deplored conscription as the regimentation and dehumanization of labor. It was not until early 1918 that the government was able to enact the conscription law it wanted, but it was hardly enforced. Meanwhile, beginning in the spring of 1917, it was the conscription issue, with wage and hours issues tagged on to it, that made possible the emergence of unofficial "shop stewards" movements in many factories, with massive wildcat strikes during May. Like their German equivalents, the official union leaders, many of them consummate tacticians, were able adroitly to maintain control of events and preserve good relations both with workers far more prone to strike than those in any other nation and with the war government. Many workers supported the stewards movement and repeated or long work stoppages only because it was in their self-interest, which they defended far more ardently and effectively than did any other labor movement in western Europe. Such pragmatism did not, however, greatly alter their opinions on issues of war and peace; with some variations, labor was class-conscious as well as patriotic until the end of the war. But as good unionists they also could defend their turf, and as their militancy increased, they repeatedly and seriously impeded the government's plans.[4]

Seemingly impersonal ideological and political arguments failed to convince Europe's working class, and strikes began because of the increasing daily privations the war imposed, trying the patience of much of European labor and radicalizing their opinions. The workers who had at first endorsed the war initially became alienated from the ruling classes' goals mainly because of economic reasons. The war's costs to the hegemony and future stability of the various European social and political orders mounted with the loss of physical well-being, husbands, or sons, and with the destruction of the wealth of nations in unheard quantities. Although the war's impact varied greatly by nation, what was certain was that Europe would never be the same again, and that the overall consequences of its vast bloodletting would prove decisive to world history for the remainder of the twentieth century.

## Public Opinion and the Consequences of the War

Although the crisis of European civilization initially did not galvanize radically new or systematic political and intellectual responses in every nation, critical ideas and attitudes that transcended the prewar legacies nonetheless began to emerge in differing degrees throughout the Continent. More important still was that there now existed a widespread readiness, even a need, to act, creating an essential but far-from-sufficient precondition for transforming politics and ideology. Various conditions and events—hunger, the war's transformation of the class structure, the disciplining of the labor force, and much else—moved growing numbers of people to behave in ways that eroded their nations' war efforts. Functionally, if unintentionally, they became nonconformists. But at every step of the way Europe was beset with contradictions inherent in the often huge disparity between radical action and realities, on one hand, and the people's persistent if critical endorsement of the war and their confused vision of their own relationship to society on the other. Theory and analysis lagged far behind events, and on the Left the justification of the conduct of parties in or close to power (whether Leninist or Social Democratic), or the vindication of the absolute truth of various Marxist scriptures, became the socialist intellectuals' main preoccupation; after 1917 and for the remainder of this century, they failed to develop a profound or effectual analytic tradition that could explain and help to confront modern historical dynamics adequately.

Europe's established social order therefore changed not as part of a coherent, well-defined response to the war's trauma but because of the quickly altering objective economic and political positions of vital classes or strata in society. Usually such constituencies modified their ideas slowly and in stages, principally because of the mounting pressures of circumstances, including those compulsions the masses imposed upon their nominal leaders, but in some nations the alternatives that the Right as well as the Left were then articulating also played a role. Although there are other examples, nowhere is this better seen than in the overall position of Europe's middle classes, especially those white-collar workers (and particularly civil servants), small *rentiers*, and some shopkeepers, who had few, if any, unions or organizational structures to help them adapt to inflation. Only a small portion of them could even conceive of striking, if only because many performed no strategic economic tasks upon which society was immediately dependent. While the whole of Europe was affected in some way, it was the middle class that during the war suffered the most economically, relative to its prewar condition. In France, Germany, Italy, and elsewhere, this fact was to prove of enormous political significance in the future.

The German middle class was especially vulnerable during the war, but even before the conflict began, important elements of the middle class had come to fear the industrialization of society and the burgeoning cities and their seemingly discontented, politically demanding working classes—with all that that implied in regard to their own already ambiguous status and power. The important and costly status symbols that in the past had always differentiated salaried clerks, technicians, or civil servants from the urban proletariat reinforced an intensely conscious self-esteem that was essential to minimize the middle class's concern over its future. The war threatened to take their nominal prestige away by closing partially, though far from wholly, the income gap between blue- and white-collar labor. Distinctive consumption patterns kept symbolic barriers up somewhat, and the middle class still had a stock of consumer goods from before the war, but there was no question that the marginalization of the middle class that began during the war was an economic trend that persisted and eroded its basic economic position in society over the next fifteen years. The middle class also strongly supported the war in the belief that in addition to being short it would not disturb their daily existence. By 1918 a considerable portion of them had begun to focus their anger on the working class which, despite its losses of real income, suffered no shift in status. But the important differentiation inherent in the middle class's amorphous nature as an inclusive social stratum also produced a small but significant minority that developed a democratic and humanist vision of the war's decisive role in causing their malaise, or sought to work through SPD-oriented white-collar unions to improve their positions; by 1918, as well, many clerks and civil servants were also ready to accept, or at least tolerate, the changes that angry soldiers and workers were to impose upon the political structure.

But notwithstanding their momentary radicalization or even the participation of many white-collar employees in the strike wave that swept Germany over the next several years, by far the greater part remained deeply anxious about their future as marginalized and dispossessed people. This soon made them, along with small businessmen and self-employed artisans, susceptible to reactionary populist appeals that evoked preindustrial values and excoriated both big businessmen who had paid them so poorly during the war as well as workers threatening to become their equals. It was this large and growing body, along with socially insecure white-collar and civil-service employees, that also during the last year of the war and over the next decade increasingly supported the antisocialist conservative, anti-Semitic, and ultranationalist parties and organizations that began to burgeon after 1918 and were to culminate in the triumph of the Nazi party.

Although this transformed middle class, especially the Protestants in small towns and rural areas within it, later proved to be the most crucial political force to emerge from the war, the social and economic processes that traumatized the objective position of this class, and its subsequent decisive political impact, were scarcely confined to Germany. The war's political effects on the Continent's middle classes as a whole were to prove at least as significant as its consequences for the working classes, about which we know much more. Comparable developments in Italy at the same time were later important in providing the new and growing Fascist movement with a large petit bourgeois following, particularly among civil servants. In France the increasing marginalization of the middle class affected its immediate concern about the length of the war and the conflict's raison d'être, and while it did not actively oppose the war, it was also more eager than any other class to see it settled. This reason alone momentarily made Woodrow Wilson its hero when he articulated principles to end the war with which no Continental regime readily agreed. Later they supported Vichy not merely for its anti-Left stance but because it alone was committed to avoiding another protracted bloodletting.[5]

But whatever the reason, as the war dragged on, an increasing proportion of the population questioned their governments' dogged persistence in continuing it. In some nations, such as Russia and Italy, the people had entered the war reluctantly at best, and their later readiness to oppose it was deeply rooted in this reality. As some of Russia's most acute military leaders later admitted, the peasant never understood the reasons for the war and obeyed the call to duty because obedience was a habit and he had no way of escaping. The intelligentsia and bourgeoisie from the inception sought in vast numbers to evade the army, but above all to avoid the front.

The Italian public and many politicians were unique in Europe in terms of being overwhelmingly opposed to entering the war, and only those few intellectuals who laid the doctrinal groundwork for the later emergence of Fascist notions of power and heroism advocated a war for its own sake. Premier Antonio Salandra had genuinely convinced himself and a coalition of monarchists, the army, and conservatives that in the spring of 1915 they could join what was to be a short war, exploit the opportunity to impose control over rising mass protests, and redirect the attention of a press preoccupied with domestic issues—a scenario he accepted largely because for his internal political purposes it was a convenient one to believe. More to the point was Salandra's belief that Italy had to enter the war soon to obtain some of its spoils, especially from Turkey.

It was in this context that the war's economic consequences produced social disorder sufficient to frighten the nation's conservatives over the next years into welcoming Fascism. The Socialist party majority leadership, while ostensibly antiwar, equivocated and resolved neither to support nor oppose the war—which amounted to no stance at all—and until 1917 a moderate leadership controlled the Party. During the spring of that year, largely spontaneous protests over inflation in the north also turned into antiwar demonstrations, and at the end of August a series of peace demonstrations in Turin led to bread riots over which troops armed with tanks and machine guns reimposed order at the cost of 41 lives and over 800 arrests.

But it was the enormous defeat of the Italian army at Caporetto the following October, involving the retreat of 350,000 men in total disorder, plus
almost 300,000 captured, that solidified much of the population's political
attitudes. From this point on, an adroit Socialist leadership evoked both a
reformist and revolutionary program, generating much more rhetoric to
maintain Party unity than it intended ever to put into practice. Yet for all
its contradictions, the Party was still far more militant than the other
European socialists, and it succeeded in the November 1919 elections in
making the Socialists Italy's largest party. The Socialist membership
quadrupled from 1914 to 1919, as did its union, the CGL, which enrolled
over 2 million members. After the 1920 local elections, it administered
about two thousand local governments and twenty-six of the sixty-nine
provinces. While its proclamations unquestionably frightened the traditional rulers, the Party itself had been sufficiently vacillating that it would
not necessarily be taken at its word; it was in fact the profound shift in public opinion under the pressure of economic crisis and war, accelerating a
process of radicalization that had begun before 1915, that was the root
cause of the traditional order's problem. Within a few short years the
nation's historic ruling and middle classes took revenge and preempted the
growing risks of both parliamentarianism and mass action that the war had
created in the form of a deeply dissatisfied population, installing the tiny
Fascist minority in power.[6]

### The Dilemma of Public Opinion

Politically, the fact that the French, German, and Italian socialist parties
were all suffering from grave internal contradictions produced a historic
vacuum that was to prove fatal to world socialism. In practice, the workers
of most nations increasingly refused to accept passively the growing physical burdens the war imposed upon them, and even if many did not articulate an antiwar position, they acted in ways—strikes being the most important—that hindered the ability of their nations to win the war. In a word,
most accepted the war abstractly, even if critically, for a significant duration, but gradually rejected its consequences in fact, and this was, practi-
cally speaking, an antiwar stance. Such an inherently ambiguous position
was scarcely likely to compel their largely opportunistic leaders to act decisively, and because the socialist parties and unions provided insufficient, if
any, leadership to antiwar sentiment within their nations, they produced a
fatal vacuum in European and world socialism that Lenin and the Soviet
Communist party easily filled. There was no consistency or coherence in
Lenin's mercurial concepts on the nature of the party and the road to
power, much less the form of a socialist society, and in this domain he was
no less a pure opportunist than the social democrats, tailoring his position
to the potential of the moment in order to grasp power. But Lenin was

virtually the only European socialist leader who unequivocally damned the war and the imperialist claims of all nations, and it was the purity of this opposition alone that attracted a sufficient core of adherents to allow the permanent, historic schism to emerge within the world socialist movement that preordained it to political impotence in innumerable countries for at least two decades. For in every nation of Europe there were growing numbers of intellectuals and workers who deplored the disparity between their class needs and actions, and the equivocation of the traditional socialist forces in the face of Europe's monumental folly. If the Communists were not the sole alternative they turned to after 1917, they were surely the only permanent one.

The Italian Socialists took a stand against the war and the annexation of territory but refused to oppose the war aggressively inside or outside of the parliament, and the government knew that it could proceed with little risk. The French and German socialists ostensibly held the same war aims but they could not agree on the form of the peace, and the SPD believed it had been forced into an essential, defensive war against czarism. The SPD thought it was not France's prerogative to demand the end of German monarchy and militarism, and it refused to endorse a plebiscite for Alsace-Lorraine but simply urged the restoration of the prewar status quo—which meant Germany would keep that territory. And while Karl Liebknecht was the only Socialist to vote against war credits in December 1914, two months later in the famous "Junius" pamphlet that he, Rosa Luxemburg, and Franz Mehring published, they argued the wholly irrelevant position that "victory or defeat of either of the two war groups would be equally disastrous," advocating instead a vague "international revolutionary action of the proletariat" that could not be described in concrete terms, had no practical meaning in suggesting specific positions or efforts within nations, and allowed the SPD's minority to play a passive role and yet feel ideologically purified.[7] They ignored Germany's role as aggressor and the unequal culpability of the two sides, and they did not urge that Germany withdraw from Belgium immediately. They could produce phrases but not define a plausible political strategy, much less an alternative to Lenin's simple appeal for revolutionary defeatism against one's own government, and they remained irrelevant, hated by the majority of their party, the German Right and, later, the Bolsheviks.

Essentially, the socialist parties responded equivocally to the growing nonconformity of the workers, who did not see the point of suffering placidly but were not able or willing to condemn the war as the origins of their problems, and it was this failure that allowed the Bolsheviks to attain power in Russia and produced the fatal schism in international socialism. The German majority SPD in the summer of 1917, together with other parties, endorsed a "peace of understanding," but they insisted they would also fight on—which meant that their war aims had been purified but that they would also do everything necessary to sustain the war.[8] Later, throughout 1918, when the desire of the people for peace had become overwhelming, the majority SPD and its unions expressed a recognition of why spontaneous strikes and mass opposition were occurring, but they never explicitly supported or condemned them, setting the stage for their subsequent historic effort to gain control over protest in order to mediate between the old order and the masses—a role I detail in Chapter 8.

Opposition to the war in France was much more muted, expressing itself in lassitude and occasional strikes, ebbing and mounting with reports from the battlefields. The war had begun as a sort of grand *fête*, one intended to be glorious and quickly terminated. The fact that the *union sacrée* the parliament created also suspended political debate on basic political and economic issues was not significant, since there was in any case no formal opposition willing to challenge the government. Although France went through the war more united than it had been in at least a century, it did not prevent support from fluctuating significantly. While one must accept Jean-Jacques Becker's superbly documented conclusion that a "very large majority" of the people approved of the war until the end, he also shows important modifications of that support—lethargy and dismay, and increasing complaints.[9] Like their counterparts elsewhere, the urban working class refused to acquiesce to deteriorating living conditions, and unconditional prowar sentiment was mainly rural. After the great military losses in the spring of 1917, public opinion was largely for an undefined peace, and the number of those who sought peace through victory fell dramatically by September. Morale in a majority of the *départements* in spring 1917 was mediocre or poor, and Becker's description of a mood of "patriotic gloom" and "resigned weariness" through early 1918 is accurate.[10] The population, to a growing degree, supported the war abstractly but also increasingly wanted it terminated—although not at any price. Victories during 1918 alleviated this mood significantly, but by then more and more workers had begun to try to ameliorate their conditions, and the dormant CGT—which now abandoned its wartime inhibitions—nearly tripled its 1918 strength to approach 1.5 million in mid-1920. At the same time, a profound revulsion began to set in among a growing number of intellectuals regarding the sheer irrationality of the entire experience. Even in a nation where the desire for glory had always evoked the public's passion, the war lost its heroic aura.

The attitude of Britain's people, especially workers, followed the same trajectory as French opinion. They too were fatigued, but they also acted more than any other West European working class to improve their immediate economic status; they too responded favorably to victories and by late 1918 were also distinctly patriotic in their feelings. Nonetheless, the Labour party, in tune with the underlying mood, for the first time declared its ultimate goal to be socialism.

Once the war became stalemated and total war imposed a monumental burden on both Europe's economies and populations, it was transformed also into a test of the viability of each of the combatant's social system, its resilience and constraints, as well as its economic resources and military prowess. In a word, nations ready to gamble on attaining military victory under acute economic, political, and psychological circumstances that none had anticipated might also provoke revolutionary upheaval. Protracted war corroded the political legitimacy and social cohesion of many of the states involved in it, exposing the social roles and goals of major classes of each of them to unprecedented tensions and revealing a breaking point among the population that few of their leaders and the masses themselves had ever suspected existed. And such social consequences could decisively affect both the political outcome and the military results of the war.

The First World War was a material as well as a mental catalyst in the warring states, evoking innumerable tensions and contradictions within nations. The war compelled countless millions of Europeans to depart from the routines and habits of their daily existence, and to question, at first hesitantly but then with mounting disenchantment, their conformity to traditional values and icons. Such disillusionment affected warring nations very differently, of course, but by early 1917 the processes of destabilization were well advanced in much of Europe, producing increasingly grave economic, social, and political problems for its leaders to resolve. This was all the more true because the Continent's democratic institutions were nonexistent, partial, or still fragile, and their ability to weather the profound crises the war created for them became questionable the moment the conflict passed from being a brief one to a painfully extended one. Whether immediately or over the next decades, authoritarian and repressive movements and regimes became the war's dominant legacy.

All of Europe's key social forces had to resolve the innumerable dilemmas inherent in their commitment to their class interests as opposed to the ostensible transcendent goals of the nation in crisis. After three years of terribly bloody conflict a great part of Europe was increasingly troubled, profoundly altered materially, and many prewar political and intellectual verities were losing their ability to constrain people's daily behavior or win their habitual assent to a larger consensus. And while the traditional political orders became unsettled in varying degrees, no visions of alternatives did or even could emerge to offer stability or to provide a new direction for nations or classes within them that could re-create the political and social cohesion that had existed before the war. The status quo was losing its legitimacy or fatally eroding its organizational capacity to persist in many nations, and events themselves were transcending most of Europe's ability to emerge from the war with the relative unity or permanence that had been its major characteristic before the conflagration began. Although it required the experiences of the next twenty years to confirm to skeptics that this process of dissolution was the dominant fact of modern history, by 1918 the phenomenon itself was irreversible.

# CHAPTER 7

# Soldiers and the Crisis of World War One

States and social orders that have appeared reasonably viable economically and politically, and that have possessed loyal and cohesive officer corps, have been vulnerable to crises whenever they could no longer unhesitatingly rely upon their ordinary soldiers not only to fulfill their superiors' orders on battlefields regardless of the consequences to themselves, but also to turn their guns against their own countrymen if need be. Few of Europe's leaders before 1914 had imagined it would be necessary to mobilize such enormous numbers for so long a period, but protracted war required vast quantities of men, principally draftees, and as the armed forces grew ever larger, the potential significance of the relationship of huge armies to their own societies and the maintenance of existing political systems increased with them. And although the dilemmas—and threats—that mass armies posed existed throughout the Continent by mid-1917, their potential for producing social upheavals was greater the farther east they were located.

Soldiers were selected principally for their utility in making war, and no one in 1914 thought it essential to consider their fidelity to the state and those who ruled it. They were obligated as citizens to fight and, if necessary, to die to defeat their nation's enemies, all the while remaining obedient to those leaders and the ruling classes who had so blithely embarked upon the war. And they were supposed to do so without concern for their own families or their class needs as the sons of peasants and workers. But soldiers are members of social, class, and family networks, with diverse interests and commitments, and as the war dragged on, these ties became increasingly important, decisively so in some of the warring countries. To the extent that the tension between these opposing obligations mounted, or soldiers began to refuse to march unquestioningly to their possible deaths, those nations that could count least on the undivided fealty of their troops confronted an increasingly serious dilemma that influenced their ability to fight—or even to remain in the war. By 1917 it was more and more clear that the nature and evolving loyalties of armies and the men in them might profoundly affect the war's political outcome not just during the struggle itself but in future decades as well. If Europe's leaders did not necessarily have to calculate their ability to rely upon their own armies, they had at least to estimate what they might expect from those of their allies and enemies.

The nature of the soldiery in the diverse armies, their social and economic origins, and the impact of the war upon their personal positions and that of their families therefore becomes crucial to the history of this war as well as all subsequent ones. The relation of the loyalty and roles of armies to the very capacity of nations to make war, and to avoid social and political upheavals in the process, first emerged during the 1914–18 period as a permanent issue in this century. The war's inextricable effects on their beliefs and behavior is integral to our comprehending not only the transformation of the objectives of states but also the outcome of battles and, later, the very future of European politics and social movements both on the Right and Left. For the war's violence was total, involving every aspect of social systems down to their very roots, and their leaders' initial assumption that the relentless conflict could be fought without considering the implications of such trauma on the men in the trenches was one of their greatest miscalculations.

## Who Serves? The Social and Class Composition of Armies

Once the conflict became unlimited both in scale and time, the warring nations shared common problems, and their responses were often similar. Their identical challenge was how best to utilize their finite manpower to satisfy the increasingly insatiable needs of both the military and war production. The warring states' ability to draft men did not alter their need to choose constantly between civilian and war demands; their vast common losses—1.1 million casualties for the British, Germans, and French in the 1916 battle of the Somme alone—left them all undersupplied with men to sustain their humanly voracious strategies. And among all the combatants the ordinary soldiers were drawn disproportionately from the poor, the unskilled, and the peasantry; those who were unable to avoid serving on the front lines and had the least to gain by doing so were thereby called upon to make the greatest sacrifices. All of these essentially class factors combined irresistibly to erode, to greatly varying degrees, the loyalties of armies.

Prewar British soldiers were drawn largely from the unemployed and unskilled working class in industrial and mining centers, and most arrived in the army poorly fed, physically unfit, and badly in need of remedial diets. Reliance on the machine gun presumably compensated for the fact that most English soldiers could not shoot well, and the mechanization of combat was to some degree an adaptation of all modern armies to the lack of skills in the mass of troops. During the war itself the British and Russian armies had to adjust to this reality, and the American army also was drawn disproportionately from immigrants, blacks, illiterates, and the poorly educated.

But even where the recruits were far better nourished, as in Germany and France, troops came unequally from the poorer sectors of every country. This was above all the case because the warring nations increasingly granted deferments to skilled laborers in war plants. By 1917, as Germany's existing supply of fresh cannon fodder dropped precipitously, its draft-exempt manpower pool greatly exceeded the number conscripted. None of the combatants by that year had a sufficient supply of men to continue the conflict much longer in the humanly and financially destructive manner that modern warfare now demanded, and all of them had to release already inducted men to return to arms production. Even France, which in its own fashion had the most democratic army in Europe prior to the war, also created an army whose class character was unmistakable. The French permitted many fewer exemptions before 1914 than the Germans, who assigned a special status to high school graduates and others. Eighty-three percent of the men who were eligible for the draft in France in 1913 were inducted, as opposed to 53 percent in Germany. Above all, France put peasants in the trenches well in excess of their share of the population. Forty-one percent of its male working population was in agriculture in 1910 but 45 percent of the army in 1914 was drawn from it, and during the war they were more likely to be killed than soldiers mobilized from other major occupational backgrounds. Industrial workers in France were disproportionately large in the army as well, while public service and transport employees were greatly underrepresented. An even more unequal pattern existed in Austria-Hungary. In Italy, on the other hand, agriculture before 1914 absorbed 55 percent of the working population but only 46 percent of the conscripts were peasants or rural workers, but they were assigned mainly to the infantry and their death toll was double the rate for those who came from industry or services.[1]

The situation in Russia was the most extreme of all. Obviously, the precise nature and opinion of Europe's soldiers was of great significance to the outcome of the war, and even more to postwar political movements and moods, but only in Russia was the character of the army the decisive factor in bringing about the revolution—even though, obviously, the upheaval was also intimately related to a spectrum of other important causes, not the least of which was that Russia's productive base was simply unable simultaneously to sustain a huge army, fight a protracted war, and satisfy the civilian sector. But as the Russian experience proved, when an army ceases to respect the existing hierarchy and refuses to fight, the permanence of its ruling class becomes very doubtful.

Russia mobilized over 15 million men during the war, in large part because it did not possess the guns and firepower essential to winning on the battlefield. Those who were drafted were weak, not only socially, insofar as the peasantry contributed the vast majority, but also physically and medically. The single most important factor defining the army's social composition was the existence of an exemption system that allowed at least 48 percent of conscription-age men, including the healthiest, best educated, and skilled, to stay home. Among the excused, to a degree larger than in any other warring nation, were the sons of a ruling class that preferred to have peasants confront the great wartime dangers and which naively expected them to remain loyal to a society that both oppressed them and cavalierly exposed them to death.

Educated men received exemptions or special status within the Russian army well before 1914. "Domestic conditions," such as being the only earner in a family, was the major reason for such releases, but this was a badly abused category. Deferments for certain occupations led countless numbers of healthy men to seek out such jobs, although industry in fact needed them. But while the Russian army was large in absolute numbers, it still amounted to a far smaller proportion of the eligible male population than the French or German. Given its great losses and insufficient equipment, as well as its mobilization system, the Russian army by 1917 had almost no manpower reserves with which to sustain the war in the humanly costly fashion it had fought it until then.

The result, therefore, was that at least 75 percent of the Russian army was comprised of peasants at the beginning of the war, and it was over one-half illiterate—and both of these proportions probably increased sharply by 1917, especially among front-line soldiers. As the British military attaché in Moscow, who often toured the fronts, later noted, "The Russian peasant population is essentially pacific and the least Imperialistic in the world. It never understood why it fought."[2] Self-mutilation among soldiers to get out of the army was not uncommon, and alcoholism was rampant. But basically the peasant soldier was unable to identify with the nation's cause, and bitter experience in the conflict and unremitting abuse from haughty superiors greatly intensified the overwhelming alienation that most of them felt regarding their position in the world and the war itself.

From the beginning of the war, the very existence of peasant majorities in many of Europe's armies created problems between officers and the ranks, and they were by no means confined to the Russian army even though tension was most extreme there. There was no way that noble and educated officers could coexist easily with their underlings anywhere, and in the Austro-Hungarian army, where over three-quarters of the officers were German, they could scarcely even communicate with the vast majority of the soldiers, who spoke many other languages. The gulf between officers and men in the British army before the war had been insuperable, but wartime conditions and the death of many regular officers helped greatly to close it—although it often reasserted itself in petty, irritating ways. Junior French officers and troops, by contrast, related to each other far better.

But the distances between the common soldiers and the officers of most warring nations were principally informal and based on custom, though binding nonetheless. In the Russian army, however, the demeaning inferior status of the soldier was detailed in written regulations, ranging from his exclusion from first- and second-class restaurants, his inability to receive newspapers or books without permission, and much else. From the inception of the war there were countless degrading incidents that grew out of the officers' overt contempt for peasants-in-arms. Artillery officers often refused to provide infantry with support simply because they did not think their lives worth the shells or the risk of losing guns. Examples of commanding officers remaining safely so far behind the lines as to be useless are legion. Beating troops was a common occurrence, and some were charged for meals that were supposed to be free. Officers' utter disdain for their men—notwithstanding wartime changes in the social origins of many of them—set the stage for the March 1917 Revolution, when soldiers began to kill especially arrogant officers and demonstrators shot those heading proczarist troops because they knew their subordinates were not likely to react. But of this, more later.

The one redeeming aspect of the heavy preponderance of peasants in European armies was the fact that their wives and dependents could survive the wartime shortages and inflation significantly more easily than those in towns. French peasants were exceptional in that they prospered and their sons and husbands in the army had little to worry about. Substantial government payments further augmented their increased earnings, and both of these factors helped greatly to sustain rural France's strong support for the war. In Germany, however, soldiers had ample cause for concern because state subventions to soldiers' wives ostensibly calculated only their food needs, and even these increasingly lagged behind the rising cost of living. Clothing and rent were not provided for at all, and a soldier's death meant a lifetime of penury for war widows and their families. As a result, their families' circumstances and future were a cause of mounting anxiety for German soldiers, and this issue became a special focus of protest over wartime conditions within Germany itself—especially among soldiers' wives and widows. Russia treated its soldiers' wives as badly as Germany did, but most lived in rural areas and could survive. For the approximately one-fifth in cities, however, the situation was far more difficult, and pensions provided only for food—and most inadequately at that. This issue was a catalyst in alienating and radicalizing rank-and-file Russian and German soldiers.[3]

## Morale and Soldiers' Responses to the War

While very few of Europe's leaders expected or prepared for a long war, absolutely none of them anticipated trench warfare. The First World War became, ultimately, a test between rival economies and societies, and their comparative industrial and manpower potentials and social cohesion, and its ceaseless surprises compelled the adversaries to confront many identical problems. But while their initial responses were often very similar, their resources for coping with the protracted war's overwhelming impositions were very unequal. What differed most decisively, however, and eventually had a critical influence on how well and how long each nation fought, were the human, individual reactions of the common soldiers in the various armies to the interminable horrors to which their leaders constantly exposed them, and how the conflagration shaped their views of politics and society as well as their roles as soldiers.

The fatal German decision to abandon movement and mobility and turn the war into one of static trenches "was chosen purely and simply as being the lesser evil," as the then head of its general staff later wrote, and "under the stern pressure of necessity."[4] And most important, this was the inevitable logic of the initial German strategy's refusal to acknowledge that the changed nature of military technology favored defense rather than offensive campaigns. The Germans simply did not possess the manpower and matériel to attain their grandiose but quite chimerical objectives, and once the war was stalemated in the fall of 1914, they preferred to dig in and hold their gains with their limited manpower rather than give up captured territory and shorten their front in the hope that they could later resume offensive operations against sections of the French-British lines. This decision, to repeat a crucial point, predetermined the outcome of the war, which now depended on the relative industrial and manpower capacities of the enemies over the long run. The utterly surprised French and British leaders also could not grasp the implications that trench warfare had for both their weapons and their strategies until well after the facts were plain for all to see, and while they too made repeated, compounded errors, their combined resources better enabled them to survive them.

The basic fact was that the advent of long-range, accurate rifles, and especially the machine gun—a mechanized, industrial instrument of death enabling one soldier to fire forty times as many bullets in a minute as a rifle-man—created a preponderant, decisive advantage for the defenders of positions. And while the British and French, even more than the Germans, believed that intensive firepower could open the way to significant offensive operations, artillery never neutralized the superiority of the dug-in, relatively untrained foot soldiers who were protected with easily installed barbed wire and armed with rifles, machine guns, and, above all, shovels capable of repairing the great but temporary damage that artillery inflicted upon static lines. Countless times on the western front, machine guns cut down vast numbers of attacking soldiers, especially French and British, when they charged after long, often astonishing heavy artillery barrages that, as in the third battle of Ypres (Passchendaele) consumed an average of nearly five tons of shells for every linear yard of front. Indeed, while intensive artillery barrages could destroy defensive lines easily enough during the first several years of the war, artillery was immensely costly and required huge supporting production and logistical operations, and after 1916 increasingly decentralized German defense lines reduced its efficacy. More important, in churning up battlefields in the hope of destroying enemies, artillery helped greatly to produce the everlasting, ubiquitous mud that time and again paralyzed both sides.

In such a context, where the immensely greater firepower deluging the fronts neutralized each side's deeply flawed strategy and the war appeared to have no end, soldiers with identical social backgrounds on both sides shared not only common searing daily experiences, but their personal responses were often remarkably similar. A repeated sense of chaos and absurdity was one of them, as when French artillery poured shells into their own lines, or when a significant fraction of Russia's soldiers were sent to the front lines without rifles and compelled to take those of their fallen comrades. The recurring universal confusion, poor coordination, and miscalculations on battlefields using increasingly destructive munitions emerges as a central theme in all accounts of the war, one integral to the very event and the existences of the men called upon to fight and die. With it, for most soldiers, came terror, fear, and confusion—in extreme cases dubbed "shell shock" and "war neurosis"—in which the soldier lost control of his nervous system, beginning most commonly with a violent pounding of the heart, an intensely nervous stomach, then trembling and a cold sweat, a weakening of the legs, and, ultimately, for a minority, a loss of control over their urination and bowels.

For traumatized soldiers on both sides of the western front, encased in humid, filthy, rat- and lice-infested narrow trenches for months and years on end, bored and constantly insecure because of the imminence of battle and death, flight, uncontrollable weeping, a loss of hearing, and failure to obey orders were some of their many common reactions to the terror and fear. Increasingly, the soldiers who overcame their dread and fought, as most ultimately did in a fashion, did so out of resignation, even habit in due course, and not because of some abstract sense of responsibility to the nation's cause—the alternatives to obedience were even more daunting, their consequences unknown, and soldiers had loyalties to the men in their own immediate group because they were friends and they also had to survive the war together. In most cases, at least during the first several years of the war, they did their duty regardless of the fate of those who preceded them. Although fear constrained the ability of many of them to function effectively as infantry riflemen, the wholesale bullets of the machine gun— the war's most efficient killer—compensated for their mounting human weaknesses.

The eastern front was not, of course, so static or bogged down in trenches, but since the peasants were unhappy about going to war and had no illusions to begin with, their morale was low from the inception, and the fact that not many who began fighting in 1914 managed to survive unharmed two years later deepened their anxieties profoundly. Much the same was true for the Italian army, which was underequipped, fought poorly, and became demoralized within a few months after joining the war. It too was spared trench warfare as known in France.

The British, French, and Germans entered the war in a superior state of morale, although the British alone could rely exclusively on volunteers until 1916. And while British troops, for personal and social reasons, probably had a deeper loyalty to their battalion for the duration of the war than French or German troops to their units, their attachments stopped there and they regarded officers of other army sections, if not their own, as more arrogant and oppressive than, say, the French *poilu* found his.

The British soldier's basic experience in France revolved around the terrifying reality that 13 percent of those sent there were killed and 36 percent were wounded. Gunshots, principally from machine guns, accounted for about four-fifths of these casualties. Confined to trenches and idle much of the time, they were repeatedly assured that artillery would defeat the enemy, which by 1916 they could scarcely believe. In the battle of the Somme, which began in late June 1916, the British dropped over 1.5 million shells (21,000 tons) on German positions, though many shells went off prematurely and destroyed their gun crews, fell on British lines, or failed to explode. Food supplies on the front lines were short or exhausted before July 1, when the British infantry charged out of their trenches hoping to take German emplacements that had supposedly been blown to pieces. But although many soldiers in them were stunned, most of the German positions remained intact, and their machine guns mowed down wave after wave of Tommies—21,000 killed and twice that number wounded that day alone, but over a million killed and wounded on all sides for the entire battle, which terminated about where it had begun.

French troop morale had initially been high, and less arrogant officers, relatively frequent home leaves, and good food sustained it until the accumulated weight of time, compounded military failures, and manpower losses by late 1916 had gravely eroded it. Like the British, the French relied heavily upon artillery, and they repeatedly suffered from their own shells falling upon their own men, poor organization, and the inability of their officers to find a way to destroy German barbed wire and machine guns before sending soldiers across fields to confront them. No later than 1917, France no longer had the manpower reserves to fight the war in the way it had until then.

The impasse and decline in the Anglo-French armies was, in a more acute way, repeated among German soldiers, who fully expected, and had been trained for, a war of movement. In late 1914 they found themselves, as a sensitive German officer, Rudolf Binding, wrote in his diary, "imprisoned by the soft, sticky mud." Long periods without activity led to intense boredom and a weakening of discipline, and among officers "to nervousness. . . . They lose confidence—they know too much about the shortcomings of their own troops."[5] Recruits after 1915 were hastily trained and inferior to those already in the army, and the growing massive levy of men only accelerated this decline. By 1916 the Germans suffered from a severe manpower shortage, their reserves on the western front were reaching a critical point, and they were unable to replace the loss of large numbers of their best officers. As the war dragged on, trench life became the norm, soldiers were subjected to unrelieved boredom under deteriorating conditions, fewer breaks, and much poorer food than their enemies ate, and then unbelievably terrible days and then weeks of exposure to artillery barrages that growing Anglo-French resources rained upon them. Living in filth in the sometimes trembling earth, with the constant danger of walls capsizing upon them, and cut off from rear lines for long periods—such sustained exposure to imminent death and execrable conditions tested German soldiers to their limits. During 1916 they were increasingly reluctant to leave their trenches to attack, and while General Erich Ludendorff may have exaggerated when in hindsight he described his army in that year as "absolutely exhausted," it was surely not far from that state.[6] Although its losses were smaller than those of the British and French, Germany in the battle of the Somme lost about half a million of its most valuable men, killed and wounded, including many of its ablest officers, and the battle probably was the major turning point in German troop morale. For the first time in the war they began to desert.

Germany's leaders compensated for their ebbing strength in February and March 1917 by carefully withdrawing their front lines and consolidating in new, better defended positions, thereby only postponing the inevitable and protracting the common soldier's misery—which proved to be a grave error. From late 1917 onward, soldiers were aware that the fighting strength of their battalions was falling precipitously, for replacements for casualties no longer existed, and the men became increasingly listless. On the eastern front German forces were comprised largely of middle-aged men who were the antithesis of soldiers. By the summer of 1918 the German troops in France maintained only a semblance of discipline, if that, as they retreated before Entente offensives. Even younger officers now acknowledged the futility of their actions, and soldiers for the first time began to disobey them openly.[7]

## Soldiers' Responses

The First World War was a total conflict, and while it is not difficult to comprehend its overall military, economic, and political context, it is far more daunting to come to grips with the crucial and profound effects it had on the soldiers involved in it every day of their lives. This elusive dimension of war can never be interpreted merely as a banal, mechanistic affair in which men performed their duties because obedience in every society is both a habit and an obligation, much less explained as a patriotic commitment to a struggle that sustained their exposure to frightful deprivation and suffering. Nor were the battlefields simply a prelude to soldiers' involvement in crises in the political orders of states, or revolution—though for Germany and Russia they eventually became that, and elsewhere they profoundly influenced, for better or worse, the postwar political experiences of many nations. There were great differences between the wartime responses and roles of soldiers in, say, Italy as opposed to those in Britain, but in no army did soldiers merely perform as they were supposed to in the manuals of war or their superiors' calculations.

Soldiers sought to survive in countless fashions (attempts to quantify this are meaningless) to save their humanity as well as their lives, and as the daily boredom and trauma stretched over months and then years, they adapted increasingly in ways that were significant, and sometimes crucial, to the later history of the war and its political aftermath. It was less soldiers' rebellion—though in some places it later assumed that form also—than the great variety of their responses to the pressures that discipline and destruction imposed upon them that emerges as so interesting and important.

Some of these reactions were of little consequence, while others were more significant to the course of the war; and to repeat an essential point, the experiences of various nations differed greatly insofar as the unanticipated and undesired behavior of soldiers was concerned. Collectively, however, soldiers' daily interactions with the war were crucial to the event itself because, like the strategies and expectations of the war's leaders, armies too broke down—for they were made of men rather than machines. Ironically, at various times the common suffering caused many soldiers on all sides to personalize their images of each other. The human, social, and political culture many brought with them caused them to reject the demonization of their adversaries that all of their leaders constantly encouraged.

The information we have on battlefield accommodations between Germans and their French and British enemies facing them in trenches, often less than just a hundred meters from each other, is scarcely systematic, but the many accounts and anecdotes on such informal truces that exist warrant our serious attention. According to the regulations and their senior officers, the men in the trenches were to harass and attempt to destroy the enemy at all times, but apparently there were countless occasions, often daily, when soldiers recognized quite explicitly that they were all human beings trapped in relentless torment, with the same needs and desire to live and, increasingly, to see the war end. The first reports of such détentes began after Christmas 1914, when local truces between British and German soldiers in some places lasted as long as five days. In various places they fraternized, even playing soccer, singing, and talking together. Despite an order against such fraternization, it occurred again in significant areas over the following two years, and at least two British officers who failed to stop it were court-martialed. Bavarians and Silesians were allegedly far more willing than Prussians to live-and-let-live with their nominal enemies.

Once this pattern of accommodations began, it was apparently extended to the long lulls between offensives, when soldiers were then once again obligated to attempt to kill each other. French soldiers too, while supposedly more ferocious, by 1915 joined their English allies in making tacit accords with the Germans in trenches facing them (above all where the lines were so close that their artillery could not complicate their lives), touching especially on relations during mealtimes, when soldiers were using toilets, or had to obtain water. Sensitive French soldiers' accounts of their emotions, and their hatred of the bestiality of the war, reveal that many of them regarded Germans as people—and victims—exactly like themselves, and that they were not prepared to destroy them in cold blood at any time, but only when they were ordered to do so or felt they had to kill or be killed.[8]

Discipline, in a word, broke down in countless ways everywhere as soldiers sought to save their lives, or their humanity, or simply proved to be men who did not belong in armies whose leaders sought total control of their consciences and behavior.

## The Dissolution of Armies

The disintegration of the Russian, German, and Austro-Hungarian armies was soon to have a profound effect on Europe's political history. That years in the trenches, killing and being shot at, would also deeply affect the ideas, behavior patterns, and readiness to act of those soldiers even from nominally more stable nations graphically revealed how war ineluctably influenced so many of those who shared in it directly—and the potential problems and legacies that were to be transmitted to yet other nations in the future.

The most serious reflection of the dissolution of armies involved outright desertion. The Italian army experienced the best-known case, but it was scarcely the only one. Italy entered the war in May 1915, long after it had any rational reason to nurture expectations about its being a short one, and the army's morale immediately reflected its leaders' miscalculations. The army was comprised largely of peasants and southerners incapable of adapting to the front in the northern mountains or to the unrelenting arrogance of their officers, who believed they could control the ranks with the strictest discipline, including granting few leaves of absence. The desertion rate rose dramatically, and while the numbers depend on definitional standards, the monthly desertion rate from the inception of the war until the period *before* the Caporetto debacle in October 1917 increased more than eightfold. About 350,000 Italian soldiers, or 6 percent of the total, were tried for military crimes during the war, and 4,028 received the death penalty. Notwithstanding the fact that most of these fled first, the army claimed that 359 soldiers were executed in 1917, over twice the 1916 figure, and altogether 750 were shot during the war. But there are no accurate data on local summary executions, which were probably much more numerous. While the Socialist antiwar and pacifist opinion that had dominated public opinion from the war's inception also influenced soldiers, their behavior was largely the consequence of their officers' draconian policies, and in March and July 1917 there were two serious mutinies in local units. Before October 1917, summary executions of soldiers increased significantly in an attempt to reverse the deepening rot. Caporetto merely revealed how totally demoralized the army had become: 40,000 were killed or wounded, but almost 300,000 men surrendered, while about 350,000 more retreated without their arms—and many of these simply went home. Subsequent political events were to reveal how gravely the war had alienated Italy's former soldiers.

The British army also had significant disciplinary problems, which it attempted to obscure, and as it absorbed all of the nation's eligible men, it had to increase its ratio of military police to soldiers elevenfold. During the six years after the war's inception, its courts-martial processed over 300,000 cases, over 3,000 men were condemned to death—mainly for desertion—and over 300 actually killed. The desertion rate during 1914–18 was almost twice that during 1939–45. As the war dragged on, the army regarded the growing number of surrenders, especially during battles, as often simply a hidden form of desertion, and it deplored the press's treatment of prisoners of war as heroes.

Some of Britain's worst difficulties arose when criminal elements who deserted from the army in France continued to ply their vices around bases there, in the process interacting with increasingly disgruntled British soldiers, who were paid far less than Dominion or French troops and often were compelled to spend their leaves in penury, bored and alienated by invidious comparisons. Many objected also to their officers' abusive conduct, especially when contrasted to the French. What they disliked most was the army's brutalizing regulations and routines. At the end of September 1917 all these factors and people combined when some thousands of Tommies—possibly as many as 10,000—in the Étaples region rioted for several days and smashed much of the town, immobilizing about 100,000 soldiers in the process. If in the end most of them were quickly shipped to the front, there was no doubt that the war had already gravely corroded the esprit of the army of the one nation that had resorted to conscription much later than any other and whose population's reputation for prudence and conservatism was unequaled.

While the vast majority of British troops contained their frustrations and anger during the war itself, their demobilization strikes and riots immediately after the Armistice were a more accurate measure of their true feelings after four years in the trenches. Soldiers now wanted to be demobilized quickly, but meanwhile they demanded better food and conditions, and they opposed being sent to Russia as part of Britain's intervention against the Bolsheviks. In early January 1919, there were three troop demonstrations, ranging from 2,000 men in Dover to 10,000 in Surrey, and strikes and "mutinies" involving 2,000 men each occurred in Shoreham and Calais. In early March 1919, Canadian troops at Ryl rioted, and 5 men were killed, 23 wounded, and much of their camp put to the torch. At least four more "khaki riots" occurred during spring 1919, and in one case 400 men were arrested.[9]

Germany's army also increasingly conscripted men less likely to become good soldiers, and even early in the war German officers noted that their troops, like those across the lines, more and more hesitated to leave their trenches when ordered to charge and face great risks of death or injury. Entering into local tacit truces was but another expression of the fact that, while like the French and British they too would ultimately obey their superiors, they also did not want to die. But until about mid-1918, Germany had fewer serious problems than its enemies, a phenomenon that will be discussed in more detail later.

The French experience with the consequences of its army's morale revealed that the combination of the long years in trenches, the unbearable loss of lives that their generals' failing strategies produced, and the radicalization of soldiers' perception could all merge to produce major challenges to those who sought to protract the war—but also that ultimately the army's leaders could cope with such immediate challenges.

The French army's morale began to decline seriously after mid-1916, when significant acts of indiscipline became more frequent because of the combined weight of the soldiers' deteriorating personal conditions—the dirt, inadequate clothing, and such—the repeated examples of chaos and lack of coordination between the artillery and infantry, their officers' incompetence if not cowardice in remaining safely behind the lines in all-too-many cases, and the realization following the ignominious failure of the combined Anglo-French offensive in April 1917 that there was no end to the war in sight. Indeed, many concluded that the Germans were stronger. After the April debacle an increasing number of soldiers were willing to defend their lines but not to go on the offensive and submit to wholesale massacres, and this was also the position of nearly all of the protesters over the following months.

Rumors of vast troop losses during the spring (and they were large indeed), a general collapse of confidence in the senior officers, the absence of normal leaves, and the example of the Russian troop mutinies during the March Revolution all merged in various ways to produce a series of soldiers' demonstrations that caused British Field Marshal Haig to fear that the "*awful* state of the French troops" might very well affect the entire battlefield—and the war.[10] Between May 20 and June 10, 1917, up to 40,000 troops on or near the front lines engaged in a series of 250 to 300 demonstrations, most of them with fewer than 100 soldiers (but one involving 2,000 men), that created a grave crisis of confidence among the army's leaders and greatly interfered with, if they did not halt, the operations of half the French divisions on the western front. But despite antiwar and socialist tracts that a few soldiers printed, and which provoked hysteria among some generals, more sober officers concluded that the soldiers were scarcely revolutionary but simply expressing their grievances and responding to military defeats. They were soon proved correct—at least insofar as this one brief series of events was concerned.

But to make certain the crisis was not repeated, the army quickly penalized 3,427 soldiers: 554 were sentenced to death, 1,381 to heavy sentences, and 1,492 to lesser ones. Although 51 were actually killed, and half of the others were given lighter sentences, both sides had made their point. Over the coming months the army reduced some of the futile offensive operations that had so capriciously snuffed out the lives of countless *poilus*, and it also ameliorated their living conditions. By November 1917 the army believed that morale had been restored along with discipline, but it admitted that many soldiers remained sullen, and not until early 1918 did its leaders feel that the situation had returned to normal.

We know enough about the soldiers' feelings, thoughts, anxieties, and deepening alienation while in the trenches to understand that in countless small ways they objected and disobeyed, dissented and even protested, but that they also, in sufficient numbers to protract the event, continued to fight and die. From their leaders' viewpoint, however, their efficiency as fighting units declined more and more, and after the war many soldiers expressed their bitterness politically; comprehending their position and reactions is just as essential to understanding the totality of war as figures on munitions and such. For the wartime experience produced a subculture, and in some places an incipient counterculture, of dissidence. The outcome of any war is, to a great degree, ultimately measurable only in political terms—a matter of the larger results it creates, ranging from the beliefs and desires of the masses to the ability of ruling elites to respond to them. And politics is rarely the result of the orderly, ritualized procedures that most political theories focus on, just as economic events never spring full-blown from the ideas and plans in the heads of men or from the unimpeded putative laws of economics that both Marxist and bourgeois thinkers have expounded.

When Europe's generals and political leaders embarked upon their great adventure, their military strategies ignored entirely the many ways by which ordinary soldiers might decisively affect both the military and political outcome of the war. That men in uniforms had minds of their own or were sensitive to suffering and deprivation, much less were not instinctive killers, remained an unthinkable and unfathomable possibility; yet now the unimaginable was becoming reality, and few of the Continent's rulers understood its implications to their grandiose, carefully crafted military and political visions.

# CHAPTER 8

# World War One and the Emergence of the Left

Europe's soldiers responded first to the realities in the trenches, to the lice and shortages of food, the wasted lives and chaotic scenes of warfare. Virtually none had begun as rebels. On the contrary, when the war began they were either patriots committed to their nation's war goals or, at the most, simply apathetic. To varying degrees, their common experiences on battlefields simultaneously transformed a significant fraction of them into radically different social actors in at least four of the warring nations—men who were no longer willing to sacrifice unquestioningly for their leaders' objectives—and although very few were initially prepared to overthrow those who ruled them, their priorities in their own lives changed dramatically from a concern principally for the country's needs and objectives to those affecting themselves, their families, and their social class. It was this gradual yet irresistible transformation of soldiers' commitments and loyalties that was to alter profoundly the very nature of the war in much of Europe and to challenge the geopolitical logic shaping the decisions of the men who ran the affairs of states.

The leaders of each of the Continent's nations had to be able to rely on their soldiers' and military's unequivocal loyalty if the continuity and perhaps even the very existence of their government were to be maintained. The troops' refusal to obey their superiors totally and blindly was their most subversive act, despite the politically inchoate mood that most were in as late as 1918, for it was a condition that made them dangerous even if they were not necessarily political radicals, and it opened an abyss full of uncertainties. Obviously, soldiers were not the only key social force, but they remained capable of being crucial, and throughout the last eighteen months of the war the question arose as to how, or to whom, soldiers would respond in giving vent to their deepening alienation and disenchantment with traditional rulers and their folklore and values. Until the relationship between the masses of increasingly disgruntled troops and those who sought to direct their future roles was resolved, the political fate of much of Europe hung in the balance.

No one in 1914 had even remotely conceived that such dangers could arise, but long wars, to repeat a vital point, taking their vast toll on the daily existences of the people, produce a mounting political and ideological price for social structures and their elites to pay. Indeed, European Marxist and socialist theorists and their conceptions of a "normal" capitalism and political environment, with its progressive and rational social context, completely failed to anticipate the monumental changes and challenges that battles and armies would compel them to confront. Now a qualitatively new situation was emerging, and all the latent social tensions within peacetime societies were brought to a head under the mounting pressure of suffering and pain. Several nations, such as Britain, traversed the experience with remarkably few difficulties. In the short run, France seemed also to have emerged without serious legacies; Italy appeared much more doubtful. But in Russia, Hungary, and Germany the very survival of their social and political systems were put to the test, and in all three, soldiers' desires and actions became decisive.

## The Russian Soldier Leaves the War: Prelude to the Bolshevik Revolution

The vast majority of Russian peasants who were forced into the army had never been promising soldiers, but as the war dragged on and their numbers and defeats mounted, their morale plummeted. By the end of 1915 over four-fifths of the professional officers in the front infantry divisions had been killed, wounded, or transferred, and along with casualties and unusually high surrenders—another way to desert—before 1917 combat regiments had required up to eight and ten massive infusions of new men to sustain their strength. The loss of over 90 percent of the original troops in combat units was the rule. The government's manpower reserves reached a critical point in late 1916 because monthly casualties and prisoner losses from August 1914 until then had averaged nearly 400,000 a month, not to mention numerous deserters, who often created serious disorders behind the fronts.

In late 1916, with the breakdown in the general economy and a rampant inflation that caused peasants to withhold grain and meat as long as possible, the army's food supplies were depleted and its rations were reduced sharply. During the fall of 1916 there were at least a dozen mutinies among troops ordered to mount offensives, involving at least a regiment in no less than eight of the fourteen Russian armies. By 1917 the Russian army was terminally ill, unable to continue the war, and its soldiers were exhausted—and in an increasingly rebellious mood.

In light of the magnitude of the war and the inability of Russia to sustain the economic and human costs it imposed, political disintegration leading to a revolution became increasingly likely, but those who had originally designed and led the war suffered from an endemic myopia that made them incapable of anticipating the dangers they faced. Although none of their enemies could—or did—foresee the revolution's precise initial form either, the subsequent refusal of the leaders of the March 1917 Revolution, and even many key Bolsheviks, to acknowledge the primary importance of the army's profound war fatigue made Lenin's subsequent triumph, if far from predictable, at least comprehensible.* For there existed one, and only one, consensus among Russia's soldiers: they wanted peace and they wanted to go home. The future of Russia essentially hinged upon this single issue.

The army was disintegrating and demoralized when the March Revolution began. And although its leaders soon eliminated the czarist regime, they also made what proved the fatal error of attempting to stem and reverse the army's collapse in the hope of keeping it in the war. While comprehension of the revolution necessarily demands our paying close attention to the troops in and around Petrograd who were to trigger the crucial chain of events, no less essential is perceiving the way soldiers elsewhere acted out their desires and simply deserted. For even if they were not on the scene in Petrograd as direct actors, indirectly their disobedience and mood meant that the army could not continue the war and that this overriding reality would also doom those who overthrew czarism if they resisted it. Stated another way, if the chain of largely spontaneous events that caused about 25,000 activist soldiers in Petrograd to mutiny and join protests had not occurred in March, Russia would have left the war anyway, and those who sought to remain in it would have been eliminated in one manner or another. Such an upheaval would have happened not only because of the soldiers' morale but also because of the absence of most of those material prerequisites for fighting successfully. For the first time in the war, during the post–March 1917 period far more soldiers—over 200,000—surrendered

---

*All Russian dates prior to 1918 are based on the Julian calendar, which the Bolsheviks abolished and whose dates are thirteen days earlier than those of the universal Gregorian calendar.

to their enemies than were killed or wounded; in effect, they deserted. Many more simply went home. The army itself estimated that 100,000 to 150,000 deserted in March 1917 alone, and although some may have later returned to their units, they still would not fight. There were at least 700,000 desertions from January through August 1917. Of the roughly 6 million men allegedly in the Russian army in 1917, neither the czar nor Kerensky after him could get them to do battle willingly, if at all.[1]

The Bolsheviks themselves responded haphazardly to these realities but they scarcely created them, and when they occurred they were as surprised as all the other parties. For one thing, until Lenin's return to Russia in April many key Bolsheviks wavered on the war. The Bolshevik-controlled Military Organization in the army and navy had only 26,000 members in July 1917, mostly very recent recruits who were still only superficially Bolsheviks and who, doctrinally, merely reflected a far more deeply felt, and growing, consensus among the ranks that the war must end soon. Lenin's genius was his capacity to exploit this defeatist mood and to build a strategy around it to attain power—and later, of course, to reconstruct the army to cope with domestic rather than foreign enemies.

Meanwhile, the events in Petrograd in March 1917 simply reflected the larger character and trends in the army until then. Of the minimum of 160,000 soldiers in the region, most were poorly trained and miserably fed peasants, older reservists, and wounded or ill veterans from the front. There was a huge gulf between them and their officers, whom they detested. When food riots and strikes began on February 23, there were enough disciplined and loyal czarist troops to shoot at crowds, but when on the evening of the twenty-sixth a section of the Volinsky regiment decided to kill their commander and join the civilian protesters, it became highly probable that other regiments would also mutiny. From this point onward many officers feared for their lives, especially if they dared to order their men to risk theirs. Troops willing to defend the government were now far outnumbered by those who were ready to attack it; but notwithstanding the latter, the vast majority of Petrograd's soldiers at the inception simply stepped aside and remained passive toward both antagonists. Significantly, local Bolsheviks at first thought the mutineers doomed to failure, but like all the other socialists, they too quickly endorsed the wholly spontaneous maelstrom that none of them had imagined possible. The Romanov dynasty fell on March 3.[2]

By its very nature, a movement seeking to mount a successful revolution, as opposed to a coup or putsch, must be able to relate to a very wide mass base spread throughout the nation, must not only to be able eventually to take hold of the reins of power and administer a society rather than letting it by default remain in the hands of traditional rulers, but also to be able to overcome possible setbacks, such as arrests and defeats, in specific areas. No less essential, it must in some manner be capable of mobilizing and channeling the energies and enthusiasm of a very large number of people who desire profoundly, even if for very diverse reasons, to replace the existing society. It was the wartime experience rather than any party, the Bolsheviks included, that created these decisive human and organizational prerequisites for revolt.

Indeed, while no one party can claim responsibility for leading the revolution, what all parties shared during the crucial days of March 1917 was an eagerness to end the czarist regime and supplant it with one that was nominally democratic. During this heady period no other consensus emerged among the vast number of Petrograd's workers' and soldiers' groups, few of which operated in a conventional organizational manner. But some of them were more durable than others, notwithstanding the fact that their spokesmen often changed constantly, and they goaded the more visible political personalities, lest they hesitate, toward profound innovations in the way Russia—its army, its politics, its land system, and more—had functioned until then. Comprehending these mass-base councils—soviets—is essential to making a linkage between the war and the people's response to it, for it was from them, to repeat a crucial point, rather than from parties and politicians, that the principal force of change emerged.

The idea of the soviets dated back to the aborted 1905 revolution, when it was articulated as a forum for channeling mass participation without allowing it to become chaotic and anarchic, but also to prevent power from remaining exclusively with the traditional political order's organisms and personalities. Well before 1917, socialists in many nations had also discussed the notion of workers' councils. Apart from providing a convenient platform for the enormous numbers of people who now sought to be heard and to apply pressure for reform, they had the advantage of not being associated with the inherited political structure—which after the czar's overthrow still existed in the form of the Duma—and of being capable of acting in defense of the masses' interests against it. During the first days of the soviet's existence in Petrograd, beginning in a hall with about 250 often shouting, excited delegates who represented a very disparate collection of soldiers' and workers' groups, or sometimes scarcely more than themselves, with many people coming and going at all times, it worked both with and independently of the Duma; but elsewhere and later the role of the soviets was usually very different. The soviets' initial strength was their relatively open structure, a spontaneity and formlessness that could easily absorb vast angry numbers with grievances and who were ready to act, and their decentralized nature. And although soviets came into existence everywhere after the end of February—in the military, in factories and villages—all that they did was provide a formal justification for bringing together and focusing to some greater degree the efforts of committees, councils, and meetings that began spontaneously to convene, debate, break up, re-form, and manage to function one way or another.

But the soviets' weakness was their inchoate, flexible nature and the fact that, while they paralleled and tried to advise the Duma and formal political organs, they did not for many months seek to supplement its jurisdiction over political decisions, much less to replace it, until the Bolsheviks and their allies constituted a majority in the soviets. The Bolshevik party regarded the soviet structure not as an end in itself but merely as a vehicle for reaching the masses and seizing political power—and then eliminating altogether the soviets' democratic roles. Moreover, since the very concept of committees of mass representation specified no limits in terms of the numbers and size essential for effective democracy, their inherently fissiparous, unstructured character allowed those seeking to guide events—the Bolsheviks above all—simply to create parallel new bodies whenever they could not immediately control existing soviets. The soviet system, in a word, by its very ambiguous nature, which had given it its initial force as a vehicle of mass mobilization, as well as its fear of falling into the trap of traditional parliamentarianism, was soon unable to avoid floundering on the shoals intrinsic to both conventional politics and parties and its own organizational contradictions. It never articulated a coherent system of representation that combined its democratic functions and potential while guarding against drifting toward a cacophony of positions and tendencies that could easily be exploited or become self-destructive.

The March Revolution, led by centrists as well as socialists under Alexander Kerensky, also had to accommodate to the existence of soviets emerging everywhere, and for some months it did this partially in response to overwhelming pressures and the threats of force from them but also in the hope of channeling and later exploiting their sheer momentum, scope, and power. When in the heat of the events in Petrograd and under pressure from the soldiers gathered there it issued its order number one on March 1, 1917, for the reorganization of the entire army, it legitimized the process of disintegration already well advanced among soldiers and thereby also intensified it. Apart from abolishing all invidious controls that officers had imposed on soldiers, it encouraged the formation of local committees and ended by transferring the ultimate control over arms to them. Although the prowar government quickly tried to modify the order significantly, the basic harm was done and discipline within the army plummeted. Before March, soldiers had increasingly refused to attack their enemies; but subsequently their ability and very willingness to fight was always in grave doubt.

Order number one, even after major revisions, left intact committees representing soldiers because the traditional army leaders hoped also to utilize them to restrain the increasingly unruly troops. This "committee class" became crucial to sustaining the political upheaval within the army, and assumed decisive importance, for it was comprised of relatively few peasants but rather was drawn mainly from conscripted members of the "intelligentsia." It contained many white-collar workers, professionals, a disproportionate number of Jews, former students, and the like; they were highly literate and generally interested in national political developments. Many initially supported the Socialist Revolutionaries, but some already were Bolsheviks, and as the latter became more influential among the troops, the army committees gave them a potentially crucial vehicle for controlling the military.[3]

But action among the soldiers was significant ultimately because it paralleled and then interacted with activities among workers in cities and the peasantry, for they shared fundamental problems and some crucial social attributes. The mass of soldiers came from the peasantry, but many of the urban workers that they were being called upon to discipline had arrived fairly recently from the rural areas and they were younger, often poorly adjusted to the increasingly miserable urban life-style, and inclined principally to activism—and consequently also attracted to anarchist and Bolshevik ideas. Lenin, indeed, shortly before the war, had worried that their "maximalist" propensity to mount ill-conceived strikes might embarrass or jeopardize the Bolsheviks' position. But it was crucial during the decisive March events that the soldiers and urban workers had so much in common socially as well as in the way that they all were increasingly hungry together. Such bonds became indissoluble at the vital moment.

The war's economic pressures on workers—declining real income, inflation, food shortages, and the like—sustained the process of radicalization among them, and the sharp erosion of the economy after March 1917 accelerated it. In the days preceding the revolution many workers had reached the point of desperation and favored decisive action—although they were not yet able to define it coherently. Well before they could control the central trade-union structure, the Bolshevik demand for outright worker control enabled them to influence such angry activist proletarians, enabling the Party to dominate the Petrograd factory committees no later than June.

Because the urban and rural economies were breaking down more or less in tandem, given the worsening conditions within the army and the lower and middle classes, all that the Bolsheviks had to do was support the most extreme workers', soldiers', and peasants' demands, which the Mensheviks would not or could not do, not merely because they were part of a coalition government and favored the continuation of the war, but because they disagreed with many of them in principle. The Mensheviks refused to endorse the eight-hour day for workers, and their failures in this and similar regards weakened labor support for them. And the peasants, isolated and relatively protected from possible reprisals, were much more prone to violence than were the workers. Free from the accountability of power, the Bolsheviks tailored their program to the exigencies of the struggle to gain strength. Their public position on land was unique and simple—free distribution to the peasants—though like the future control of the factories, Lenin planned later to impose the Party's domination over both land and industry once it conquered the state. The war's corroding impact penetrated all of Russia, profoundly affecting the peasantry and the working and middle classes, and the Bolsheviks could take no credit for producing the overall situation they now sought to capitalize upon. They had not organized the countless committees of rebellious soldiers and striking workers, much less been able to mobilize peasants who were confiscating land—and it was these social actors who produced the initial impetus that led to two successive revolutions. The Bolsheviks would have been unable to create such forces even if they had themselves been united sufficiently—which they were not. At most, they had sought repeatedly to recast their program opportunistically, usually under pressure from Lenin, to exploit the potential inherent in the larger dynamics of social dissolution and alienation already far advanced before Lenin's return to Russia on April 3, 1917.[4]

It was the czarist regime, with its capricious institutions founded on an obscurantist ideology and venal, incompetent leaders, that under the pressure of the searing war galvanized the masses to action in ways that no one, including the Bolsheviks, had ever dreamed possible.

## Germany: The Challenge to the Old Order

Events in Germany after early 1918 reflected the striking contradiction between soldiers' and workers' increasingly aggressive daily resistance to continuously deteriorating wartime conditions and the deeply rooted endemic deference to authority that extended not only to the traditional SPD and union leaders but, ultimately, to the greater part of the masses themselves. As the Wilhelmine regime's grave failures and contradictions mounted with defeats on the battlefields, the stunning challenge to its authority that occurred during 1917–18 saw both militant socialists as well as conservative SPD and union leaders merging paradoxical elements of tragedy and farce in their ideas and actions.

Workers' participation in strikes increased sharply during 1917, even as compared to the prewar years, and while most stoppages were economic in nature, the split of the Independent Social Democratic party (USPD) from the SPD in January 1917, provided an umbrella for diverse, quite conflicting antiwar tendencies, also causing a growth in politically motivated walkouts that challenged the state's war policies. USPD membership soon nearly equaled the SPD's, making it a force for both the SPD and the government to reckon with. The January 28, 1918, strike in Berlin, involving approximately 400,000 people, was the USPD's most successful initiative up to that time; while it also presented immediate demands touching upon food supplies, the strike concentrated principally on political issues, calling for mass strikes and worker participation in negotiations to impose a peace without annexations upon the world's rulers. It also advocated the "drastic democratization of the entire state organism in Germany."[5] The SPD's leaders initially opposed the strike but then reversed themselves, hoping to dominate it and retain their hold over the workers, particularly after similar demonstrations spread to other cities. But within days the army suppressed the protest movement, arresting several key leaders and drafting many more.

The January strike was significant because it revealed much concerning the future and of the likely behavior of the key actors in it. The SPD leadership pursued its traditionally cautious line, mediating between workers—a majority of whom were still, if only grudgingly, loyal to them—and the state organs. The army showed both a resolute willingness to act and the ability to do so; and whether this would remain the case in the future was important but not necessarily decisive. Without an even more extreme radicalization and spontaneous mass actions among troops or the public that led one or the other—or both—to act or to create altogether new organizations, in effect the future of Germany depended largely on the ability of the Independents to challenge the SPD's integrationist policies and to redirect a dramatic but nonetheless still hesitant shift among the soldiers and workers toward truly socialist politics and ideas. Having broken with the past to a remarkable degree, the question was how far Germany's dissidents would or could go.

The behavior of the SPD and the army was far less incongruous than that of the Independents or the small groups that split from it, especially the Spartacists under Karl Liebknecht, Rosa Luxemburg, and Franz Mehring, for what the SPD and the army would do was quite predictable. But when dealing with practical issues of action rather than articulating critiques of a reformist SPD whose hold on the workers' allegiance they challenged, the Independents and Spartacists suffered from fatal ambiguities. Intellectuals rather than tacticians, the SPD's leftist critics opposed the war from 1915 on but refused to accept the notion of Germany's—or anyone's—defeat in it. Whatever its merits on grounds of principle, their stance was irrelevant in practical terms because a world revolution to end the war, which they advocated, was scarcely more than a dream and they repeatedly confused their desires with realities. Rather than advocating an unequivocal position that involved a rupture—risky at best—with existing political practices and mechanisms, both the Independents and those to their left who tried to influence the USPD's position repeatedly found that at crucial points that demanded specific, timely, and clear alternatives to the SPD's policies, they were unable to present them. They were themselves often internally divided on crucial issues, which they discussed inordinately, and like many radical intellectuals, they related to politics mainly for existential reasons.

Notwithstanding a growing influence among soldiers and workers, the Independents persisted in asserting that they would operate only in a "constitutional" fashion, even in late 1918 when the entire German political system was in legal transition from a quasi-authoritarian monarchy and a new order that for a brief moment was genuinely, even legally, open to radically new definitions and institutions—at least if there were those willing to take the risks in attempting to impose them. Indeed, once the war issue was behind them, many Independents were indistinguishable from the SPD, and they were neither prepared for the events during the unstable, decisive weeks of late 1918 nor attracted to the prospects for radical change that suddenly became possible. And unlike Lenin, who craved power and repeatedly subordinated his strategy and political positions to obtain it, the essentially small groups on the Left, comprised mostly of intellectuals dissatisfied with Social Democracy and the status quo, sought to make decentralization and a lack of coordination into an antibureaucratic virtue, which usually made it incapable of timely, effective action; in practice, it placed principles above success at crucial junctures. Many of the Left's critical failures immediately after the summer of 1918 must, to a crucial degree, be attributed to the fact that the USPD was both unimaginative and indecisive—and hence impotent. The SPD and the army were therefore to have sufficient room for maneuvering when confronting those millions who had no capable leaders but, momentarily at least, were prepared to accept genuine alternatives to bankrupt traditional politics.[6]

### The Soldiers' Protest and the Restoration

As the war ended in retreat and defeat, the soldiers presented the wartime leaders with their single most serious challenge when their cohesion, views, and relationship to the working class from whom so many were drawn became an open question. The very existence of the social system depended on the discipline of the army, for there were no powerful mediating, inhibiting institutions, like the SPD in relation to the civilian working class, to help the generals control rebellious elements.

Both the SPD and the Independents nonetheless could claim a growing influence among soldiers, and in the fall of 1917 they began to organize large numbers of wounded veterans into associations that, on the whole, proved to be politically militant. Sailors, however, had become radicalized even earlier, and a mutiny in March 1917 was brutally suppressed. Even more important than leftist proselytizing was the profound demoralization that infected countless front soldiers who had come to detest the existing bourgeois society and generals who had sent them off to war to suffer and die—and who after the failure of the spring 1918 German offensive would refuse a negotiated end to the war that would spare the men in the ranks further losses. It was the war rather than often opaque socialist doctrines that radicalized the troops, who from August 1918 began to surrender in large numbers, simply return home, or create councils far more extensive than those that existed among the workers. As Europe's once most powerful army began to disintegrate, its soldiers' behavior threatened to end the war. The army's leaders feared mass desertions before Christmas, and their anxieties reached a fever pitch when at the end of October sailors on warships based at Kiel refused to obey orders, leading to arrests, violence involving about 40,000 partly armed soldiers, sailors, and workers, and a soldiers' and sailors' council takeover of Kiel on November 4. The Kiel upheaval stimulated the formation of soldiers' and workers' councils throughout Germany. For an extremely brief period, the streets of many cities were the scene of continuous meetings and demonstrations unlike any ever seen before, with the very future of the status quo seemingly in doubt, not the least because by October 1918 most of the population intensely desired peace, and this fact alone increased the ability of the Left to take power without resistance from the momentarily indecisive and war-weary upper and middle classes. It was clear, if nothing else was, that Germany could no longer continue the war.

In fact, whether Germany might have had a far more fundamental change in its political and social system at this moment in time, if not a revolution in the Russian sense, was linked to the basic issue of whether the mood in late 1918 reflected some permanent radical transformation of mass opinion and goals or an essentially temporary deep war weariness that produced a military mutiny and mass strikes with objectives capable of being co-opted. And just as crucial was whether the conservative political forces on the scene—including the SPD—which were still credible and retained organizational and ideological power, in every meaning of that term, were capable of utilizing it for essentially traditional, nonradical purposes, thereby leaving intact a social order that resembled in decisive (even if not all) ways the prewar system.[7]

The dramatic events of the following weeks must be analyzed with these questions in the forefront, for the majority of the SPD's leaders changed very little, and they regarded themselves not as agents of social transformation but as system managers representing the working class's interests (as they defined them) within the existing society, notwithstanding certain reforms they wished to see introduced. The army's chiefs believed they had much more to lose than the SPD hierarchy, and at this critical point in Germany's history they consciously calculated that only the traditional socialist leaders could prevent the nation from falling prey to more radical forces, which they identified principally with the soldiers' councils that were springing up everywhere and organizing demonstrations.

On November 9, when the kaiser abdicated under duress, a new republic was declared and Friedrich Ebert, one of the SPD's most conservative leaders, became its first chancellor. His authority for the new office, however, derived only from the fact that the acting regent had bestowed it upon him in the belief that he alone could employ the SPD to head off bolshevism. Ebert had personally preferred a constitutional monarchy to a republic. In a legal sense, Ebert's prerogatives represented a minor change in the traditional order, not its abolition. That night General Wilhelm Groener, head of the Supreme Command, phoned Ebert and reached a basic understanding: Ebert pledged to reinforce the army's efforts to prevent anarchy and bolshevism, and together they would deal with the councils in a friendly spirit as long as they did not challenge normal state functions or representatives and constitutional power as the next National Assembly was to define it. In return, the new government would support the existing officer hierarchy and help it maintain discipline both within its own ranks and in society at large.

The so-called Ebert-Groener deal is usually treated as a turning point in civil-military relations, an accord between two precarious institutions about to flounder to save each other, but it was scarcely so grandiose, and it was arranged in a few minutes. Several socialists to the left of the SPD also believed there was nothing exceptional about the pact, and approved it, for until late December the Independents nominally held as many ministries in the transitional all-socialist government as did the SPD. Groener himself had for several years been very close to the SPD leaders in all matters affecting military production, and they considered him their friend—and their compact a continuation of an institutional and social collaboration to which the SPD's leaders had long been psychologically committed. Groener knew that Ebert and his wing of the party were instinctively conservative and not likely to bend to the radicals, and that they surely would never abolish the army per se. On the contrary, the generals made the crucial decision to work with the SPD's leaders to sustain a republic that the army tolerated temporarily only out of necessity. Once it controlled political power, the SPD had no need for the councils, which it had never encouraged and which were mostly SPD-dominated in any case. In effect, the SPD leaders were so habituated to working with the heads of the traditional order, whom they admired and hoped to imitate, that this accord was essentially just one more step in a long history—and several days later the SPD and major industrialists also reached an agreement conceived in the same collaborative spirit.

Getting the councils in line proved relatively easy precisely because the

SPD had managed to retain the loyalty of a large proportion of the active workers and soldiers, who wanted major political changes, and especially reform of the army, but not a basic revolution. Even the Kiel council within several days fell under the personal control of Gustav Noske, an ardently pro-officer Social Democrat who soon emerged as the single most important defender of the prewar military hierarchy. Soldiers' councils were immediately defined as advisory bodies, committed to strict military discipline, and the dissident soldiers supported such a policy because they saw it as the fastest way to bring troops back from the fronts. This return, along with abundant celebrations to welcome soldiers back, assuaged even if it did not altogether eliminate the soldiers' bitterness. As the army demobilized, the soldiers' councils began dissolving with it, removing the single most powerful threat, if not the only one, to the generals and the traditional ruling class.[8]

The problem in evaluating the events of the next two months is to distinguish substance from the extravagant rhetoric that abounded. This is all the more difficult because throughout this period countless assorted strikes and demonstrations, none of which alone seriously threatened those in power but added to a collective sense of disorder and imminent change throughout the country, continued to issue countless militant declarations. But until elections for a National Assembly could be held, the state in fact was in a constitutional limbo and articulating the future shape of power became a crucial exercise, relevant to the great issues of the next political structure that had yet to be resolved. Militants in Berlin could claim that a German Socialist Republic existed under the ultimate authority of workers' and soldiers' councils, but the councils that existed were spontaneously self-generated bodies structured in every form imaginable, in some places bitter rivals struggling with each other for mastery over local governments, and the extent to which they represented more than themselves was often uncertain. In reality, all of the groups to the left of the SPD were still attempting to formulate their political stances, and their leaders frequently shifted positions or joined other organizations. Even the most radical had conceded that life must go on until they could meet and regularize these ambiguities. More important, however, was the fact that as long as the SPD dominated both the state and the councils it would remain the ultimate arbiter of power—and the SPD simply waited until it could discreetly abolish the councils.

On November 22, the executive of the Berlin councils agreed that the existing local administrative authorities who accepted their power in principle should be allowed to continue to run governments, with area councils merely providing them guidance in ways that were left unspecified. While the councils claimed the right to intervene in matters of general policy, the civil service that had run local and provincial administrations for years largely continued to do so with their approval. The army disintegrated, but the state apparatus remained quite intact. On December 16 a national congress of councils met to provide form, legitimacy, and direction to the entire movement, and the delegates there revealed that the soldiers' councils now accounted for less than a fifth of the representatives. The SPD comprised three-fifths of the delegates and with aplomb proceeded to abolish all the councils' pretensions to political mastery, calling for elections for a National Assembly on January 19; all future political authority would devolve from it. In effect, the councils' claims to real authority—a responsibility they had never quite grasped—were rescinded and bourgeois parliamentarianism was to prevail over a still vague socialist alternative then in gestation. When the Independents, completely isolated, boycotted the election for the central council, the SPD had absolute mastery over it.

But the SPD and the Independents did indeed agree that a major reform of the officer corps was essential. Ebert, however, ignored their demand because he was relying upon the army to sustain the republic. The army, predictably, deplored the idea and key officers threatened to resign—or worse yet, warned they would use loyal forces to resist changes—and when a group of Spartacists, rejecting the advice of Rosa Luxemburg and Karl Liebknecht, their nominal leaders, managed to incite a group of disgruntled marines into taking over Ebert's office on December 23, Ebert again turned to the army to save him. But the first soldiers the army sent to evict the dissidents either refused to shoot or even joined them—and the army was profoundly embarrassed. Groener then obtained the appointment of Noske, whose ability to disarm the Kiel council had impressed the generals deeply, as minister of national defense. Noske believed that the time to use force to handle the Spartacists, and those who sought to imitate them, had come.

By December 1918 many, perhaps most, of the army's remaining soldiers had become deeply infected with socialist, antiwar viruses, and officers could no longer predict their behavior in the event of internal conflicts. Worse yet, the very presence of so many unreliable armed troops obviously now posed a grave menace to the existing political structure and the army's future as an institution. Since it was disintegrating in many places anyway, the Supreme Command decided to completely reorganize the military by creating volunteer units drawn from former junior officers and elite troopers from the front lines who relished combat as a way of life, cadets and nationalist students who regretted having missed action in the war, and the like—absolutely reliable, tough, reactionary men to replace the tainted veterans. Few had working-class origins, and most hated the new republic. A "Free Corps" (*Freikorps*) of volunteer formations thus came into being, one paid for by the national and provincial governments but under the complete control of the Supreme Command. Ebert approved the idea and Noske enthusiastically supported it, and although nominally abolished in May 1920, parts of it survived several more years on private donations. Eventually somewhere between 200,000 and 400,000 men passed through the ranks of a force that ideologically and psychologically closely resembled the later Nazis—who subsequently attracted many former Free Corps members into their fold. In March 1919 the corps legally became the basis of the new German army, but those units that chose not to enter it continued with the help of wealthy business and landowning groups, forming quasi-private armies that in some cases merged into the rightist world of antidemocratic conspirators.

With Noske's and Ebert's permission, the army used the Free Corps first during mid-January 1919 to take over the Spartacist-held buildings in Berlin. And although Liebknecht and Luxemburg had strongly opposed the Spartacist policy of rebellion to take power, the army's leaders still considered them dangerous and so the Free Corps murdered them. Then on January 19 the SPD and the Independents together received 46 percent of the vote, far more than the 35 percent the SPD had received in 1912. From this time onward the national government simply ignored the existence of the councils, which disappeared quickly and quietly in most places. But in Bremen, Mülheim, Halle, and elsewhere the Free Corps bloodied and eliminated its remaining strongholds. And during the first half of March, after the newly founded Communist party encouraged remnants of the radical soldiers' groups in Berlin to stage what proved a pathetic grab for power, Noske used the Free Corps to suppress them without mercy, including orders to shoot on the spot anyone bearing arms. Between 1,200 to 1,500 people died in the process.[9]

The Bavarian government under Kurt Eisner, an Independent, had managed to unite the two principal socialist parties and a peasant party for several months, but while it was at the same time also precariously linked with the councils, in fact it only nominally retained the trappings of power in the region. After Eisner was assassinated on February 21, 1919, this fragile alliance tottered along until an exotic mélange of adventurers and undisciplined Communists on April 7 established a "Soviet republic" in Munich, and the Berlin government and Eisner's successors in late April sent the Free Corps to capture the city. Ten hostages in the Munich group's hands were shot and 68 Free Corps soldiers killed in the several days of fighting, but at least 1,000 leftists were subsequently murdered. The Social Democrats came back to power for ten more months, but the traditionally conservative province now became the spawning ground of reaction, giving birth to the German Workers' party in January 1919, which Adolf Hitler soon joined and helped turn into the Nazi party the following year.

By late 1919 the Free Corps was the single most decisive factor in restraining the Left in Germany. But apart from retaining the old army leadership in a strategic position to guide the nation's politics after its defeat in war and the loss of control over its own soldiers, the Free Corps's very existence confirmed that the war had broken the army and transformed the values and goals of a countless number of men who lived through it, and that traditional ruling forces could no longer rely upon "normal" integrative institutions to protect the constituted economic and class order. They required radically new mechanisms to discipline the people; Nazism was the logical culmination of this imperative, and those who created it over the next years were largely formed in this period, and they were the legitimate bearers of the wartime counterrevolutionary legacy.[10]

### The Demise of the German Left

The failure of socialism in Germany can be attributed to both the nature and relevance of the radical options to the SPD as well as to public opinion, for the traditional institutions could not have survived had both these factors been against them. The mere fact that it had to create a special private army such as the Free Corps and could not trust its own soldiers revealed how far the army had disintegrated; and without an army, the preservation of the social structure that had provided the old order with its ultimate support was, at least for a short but crucial period, problematic.

The leftist opposition to the SPD posed no real challenge. Once the war ended, many of those who had joined the USPD believed that it no longer had a distinctive political role to play, and after it peaked at 750,000 members in 1919, most eventually rejoined the SPD. A majority of the Spartacists helped to establish the Communist party at the beginning of January 1919, ignoring the advice of their former leaders that they were embarking on disastrous putschist adventures and cutting their ties to other militant workers' groups. Fractiousness constantly bedeviled the new socialist parties and groups, and although disunity was not the only fatal cause of the Left's repeated inability to challenge conservative rule, it surely contributed greatly to its endemic failures. Obviously, the SPD's conservative leaders were more powerful and had greater backing, especially among skilled workers, than their detractors, and their refusal to challenge the existing state bureaucracy in late 1918 cannot obscure the reality that the SPD leadership simply did not desire to do so. In effect, the SPD remained firmly in the hands of those who, having reached the top of a vast political and union bureaucracy, refused to stake what they had gained by employing state power to implement the Party's socialist objectives.

As in all societies in our era, the political personality of those who rose to lead existing structures was preeminently pragmatic, geared to the main chance for maximizing their own individual success, and not prone to risking what had already been gained for some abstract creed. Indeed, such principles often, if not usually, were mere organizing mechanisms to gain the support of true believers, and the long history of men who abandoned ideals upon arriving in power, and who in the end acted as if they believed in nothing save what they gained personally from office, can only be explained to some great degree as an aspect of a political process integral to the modern historical experience. Socialist politics was for many (often most) of those leaders engaged in it an avenue of social mobility, a way out of the drudgery and penury of daily working-class existence. If the spokesmen of other ideological persuasions also exploited politics as vehicles for their own advancement, this did not alter the fact that the rhetoric of class struggle has had precious little to do with the behavior of those proclaiming it, and that even if deception—whether conscious or otherwise—has not been the exclusive characteristic of the socialist political experience, it has surely been an integral aspect of it. During the critical days of late 1918, when so much seemed to be and was in fact possible, Germany was no exception to the rule, and its destiny became the responsibility of stolid, conservative SPD functionaries.

In reality, the majority of the SPD and trade-union leaders had, before the war, reached a tacit consensus with Germany's rulers regarding their relationship to existing authority and their share in managing power, and wartime collaboration formalized and intensified their role as an integral part of the status quo. To preserve it made sense from their viewpoint, and notwithstanding the chaotic events of late 1918 and the beginnings of an unequal schism in its ranks, the usually large (even if barely a majority) working-class support for the conservative SPD leadership also reaffirmed the masses' ultimate willingness to continue collaboration with the established regime. The people got what they voted for, and their spokesmen had good reason to believe that the war's effects were both transitional and relatively superficial and had not altered the proletariat's basic acceptance of traditional social, economic, and political power. The fact remained that the bulk of those workers who suffered and lost most in the war returned, even if unenthusiastically, to the SPD, and for a time the troubled nation appeared to have averted the worst dangers from the Left, or disorder, in the transition from the Prussian-dominated monarchy to a nominal republicanism. If this renewed consensus momentarily seemed to have solved Germany's problems, in truth it merely postponed them until a time when the entire Left was both unable and unwilling to prevent its own total destruction.

The war left important residues of frustration and anger in Germany after 1918, but ultimately far less among workers than among significant middle-class elements that had suffered the greatest decline in income and status and feared that their position and power in society, along with their social values and nationalist addictions, were being marginalized. The image of the SPD and union leaders collaborating during and after the war with the army and big industrialists to manage the nation, even for the purposes of protecting it from unruly proletarians, was one many good burghers could not abide. Although the monarchy, the military, and the SPD had partially bypassed the middle class, the latter remained integral to the nation's political future—whatever it might be.

How best to define war's impact is never solely a matter of the working class's position and responses but increasingly those of the middle and upper classes as well, and it was here that the First World War affected Germany's future most deeply. In 1919 the form and direction of middle-class anger was difficult to predict, and the reactionary German National People's party in January 1919 obtained only 10 percent of the vote. Few imagined then that the Nazis would eventually gain the support of the large majority of the lower-middle class and that their power would increase so greatly. And reflecting the middle class's profound anxiety over the wartime experience, when the Nazis embarked on war after 1938, they fully appreciated the way that suffering during 1914–18 had radicalized the working class and soldiers, if only momentarily, and had led the social order to the brink of what appeared to them a revolution; they vowed never again to expose Germany to such hardships or to take such grave risks.[11]

## The Upheavals in Austria and Hungary

All of the warring states in central Europe and Italy suffered during the war, and in both Austria and Hungary, as in Germany, the collapse of the monarchy produced transitional authorities and required a basic reconstruction of the political system, thereby forcing key decisions upon its successors. Also, in both nations the questions of borders and national claims were left unresolved, and nationalism profoundly bedeviled political developments and the responses and roles of the Left.

The problem in Austria was complicated by the fact that the Viennese population had suffered from shortages far more than had the German urban working class, and if this radicalized it in certain ways, it nonetheless still failed to produce a revolutionary class consciousness. The working class remained solidly behind the Social Democrats, and increasing strikes and mass demonstrations at the end of the war and during the weeks that followed it did not alter that fact. While the SPD's leaders had also disagreed over the war, unlike in Germany they never experienced a serious split, and once the war ended they were far abler than their German equivalents to cope with a multitude of issues. Most important, they immediately created and dominated the new army when the old one, plagued by desertions and scavenging, disintegrated. And there was no threat from the Right because the majority of the ministers of the government created on October 30, 1918, were from the bourgeois parties, and that government lasted until June 1920. Although workers' councils and soldiers' councils existed for a time, the Social Democrats dominated them also. In the February 1919 elections the SPD received 69 of the 159 seats in the National Assembly, making it the largest single party.

The Austrian events reflected the precarious political balance of power inherent in the deep divisions between the peasants, who favored the republic but feared socialist Vienna and were willing to secede if necessary, and the urban SPD, which could not govern without their cooperation. Moreover, all of the parties in the new government favored annexing German-speaking portions of Czechoslovakia and Moravia, and they called upon the victors to allow Austria to merge with the new German republic. Until these fragile tensions and ambitions touching the internal political equilibrium as well as the map of central Europe were resolved, Austria continued without a grave crisis for over a decade. But it remained in suspense, and it was far from stable.[12]

Notwithstanding the Left's sheer ineptitude, from March 21 to August 1, 1919, the creation of the Hungarian Soviet Republic produced the most dramatic events in central Europe after mid-1918. And it was all the more ominous because nationalism was the decisive cause of the trauma there, and it therefore impinged upon the peace and stability of the entire region.

The Hungarian tragedy was also bizarre because by 1918 the country did in fact have a profound social basis for a revolution. During the war itself the drop in workers' real income, especially that of civil servants and white-collar workers, was far greater than that in any other belligerent nation, and it profoundly eroded support for the monarchy. The hardships and near famine in Hungary had by 1918 produced a radicalized trade-union movement nearly seven times its prewar size, and from January 1918 to February 1919 it experienced a further fivefold increase. More important yet, 60 percent of the entire population was engaged in agriculture, and of these about two-thirds (or over one-third of the entire nation) were ruthlessly exploited poor peasants and landless agricultural workers or estate servants. Economically and socially, Hungary was one of Europe's most backward countries.

Hungary's political breakdown in October 1918 occurred in part because the status quo was economically fragile, but also because the existing political system was moribund and a growing vacuum remained to be filled.

During October the Social Democrats were too divided to agree upon a strategy, notwithstanding the dissolution of the army, the creation of soldiers' councils, and demonstrations and outbreaks that on the eighteenth led to a police attack on a crowd in Budapest in which three were killed and fifty-five wounded. With the army's disintegration and support for the protesters from soldiers, an essential pillar of the traditional regime crumbled. In what was an omen of things to come, at this point the police, and then the key civil servants', merchants', and manufacturers' groups, decided to switch to what they believed would be the winning side of the National Council headed by Count Mihály Károlyi, a liberal with mild socialist sympathies who many conservatives hoped would be better able to prevent the victorious Entente from imposing punitive peace terms on Hungary. In effect, as Károlyi later concluded, at a time when he was trying to persuade Archduke Joseph to become king of the new nation, spontaneous mass actions rather than the opposition's political decisions forced the government to hand power to his council on October 31. Surprised and even dismayed by the turn of events, a weak and confused coalition consisting of Social Democrats and several small liberal parties assumed power when it had least expected it, and it was not prepared to rule.

The Communists by themselves could never have produced the events leading to the creation of the Soviet Republic, notwithstanding that after October 1917 the Bolshevik influence among workers had grown because of the peace issue, and the new party also included former prisoners of war in the Soviet Union and urban intelligentsia, many of whom were Jews in a country where anti-Semitism was popular. But the Károlyi government was ineffectual, unstable, and incapable of coping with burgeoning workers' and soldiers' councils, and its inaction on agrarian reform led to landless laborers taking possession of royal lands in some places. As the workers' and soldiers' councils became more powerful and economic conditions deteriorated, the Social Democrats moved to the left, and the crucial traditional institutional bastions of state power superficially followed the tide. Although the Communist leadership was jailed and their journals banned at the end of February 1919 after they led bloody attacks against two newspapers, the government continued to weaken.[13]

Just as the police had earlier backed Károlyi when he appeared about to win, in Budapest they switched to the side of the soldiers' council on March 13 just as strikes threatened to paralyze all the cities. Other senior state officials, including the public prosecutors, also saw that the revolutionaries might triumph, and most ended by participating in two revolutions and, after the repression, the counterrevolution also. The sheer opportunism of these elements became a source of strength to the radicals while they were winning, but when the tides of fortune changed, they were equally prepared to turn on their temporary allies. Self-serving behavior and corruption along with dogmatism and ignorance plagued Hungary increasingly as it embarked on its great experiment in revolution. But the state bureaucracy cannot merely be dismissed as opportunist, because during March 1919 the most radical political coalition was also the most nationalist.

Notwithstanding oppressive domestic social conditions, on balance the 1919 Hungarian revolution was due as much as anything to the fact that Czechoslovakia, Yugoslavia, and especially Rumania, all on the victorious side in the war, advanced extensive border claims against Hungary, and at the end of 1918 all three began to occupy its territory. When on March 20 the Allies insisted that Hungarian troops immediately abandon a region of several thousand square miles facing Rumania, they triggered the downfall of the Károlyi government two days later. As their enemies invaded on three fronts, including with French aid in the south, Hungarian nationalists concluded almost unanimously that only the Soviet Red Army, which was then defeating the combined Allied armies along with their domestic proxies, could stop foreign annexations. On March 21 the Communists, who were utterly surprised and unprepared to fill the enormous political and military void, were released from prison and merged into an ostensibly united Socialist party including the Social Democrats, with the latter retaining seventeen ministries, including the nominally most important, to the Communists' fourteen. The key exception was Béla Kun, who was assigned what turned out to be the utterly futile task of obtaining aid from distant Communist Russia on behalf of the Hungarian Soviet Republic and the dictatorship of the proletariat. Kun, while certainly the single most important leader of this period and a devout Communist of Jewish origin, nonetheless depended for his power on a far broader base than the divided party, which was an incongruous collection of instant converts, many of whom were incompetent and corrupt. At the end of March 1919 a broad national consensus, including the bourgeoisie, existed to mobilize the nation to defend its borders. The Communists did not seize power; a bankrupt regime, combined with foreign annexationist pressures, virtually pushed them into it, and they were not any more prepared politically or administratively than their predecessors to cope with the immense responsibility.

Many senior Allied officials, even though they mounted a blockade intended to starve Hungary into replacing the soviets with a government acceptable to themselves, acknowledged that the Communists' power depended mainly on their roles as defenders of the nation's territorial integrity. Had the Rumanians not occupied vast regions, including sections where many of the most radical peasants lived, the Soviet Republic would have lasted, at the most, a few weeks. The Communists largely dominated the new regime and immediately introduced a far-reaching nationalization and draconian economic measures, including death penalties. And while on

April 3 the new power nationalized medium and large landholdings, it bitterly disappointed the poor peasantry, which in many regions had begun to take the land, by refusing to redistribute it; instead—and here the former Social Democrats mostly agreed—they planned to create state farms and cooperatives. The economy quickly disintegrated and the ensuing inflation was among the worst of this century. The regime's policies of brutal terror immediately alienated most of those workers and peasants who since the preceding fall had supported basic social changes. But despite the republic's failure to consolidate its strength among the masses, as long as the choice was between defense of the homeland and antibolshevism, it could persist. Major Red Army victories during May kept the population placid, even if discontented. Before June, there had been no significant counter-revolutionary plots and efforts, but by then the main officers of the Red Army, comprised largely of conservatives from the old order who served for purely nationalist reasons (and some of whom were later to fight against the USSR during World War Two), began to plot the overthrow of the Soviet Republic. But successive defeats preempted their schemes, and the revolution ended as it had begun. In July the army began to disintegrate, and on August 1, Kun fled and his government was overthrown. The Rumanians entered Budapest three days later, to the welcome of many aristocrats, and proceeded to loot the city. A White Terror led by Admiral Miklós Horthy and those who had earlier ruled Hungary for generations—one far bloodier than the brutal red one that had preceded it—then reinstalled most of the prewar social and economic elites and subsequently led the nation into an alliance with Nazi Germany. At least 5,000 liberals and leftists were executed, 75,000 jailed, and over 100,000 escaped to exile.[14]

The Hungarian experience revealed how flammable an admixture of wartime deprivations, nationalist grievances, and inherited inequities could become in challenging a reactionary society. As elsewhere in Europe, the collapse of the army's morale and discipline temporarily undermined the traditional rulers' ability to continue in the face of a foreign invasion and the nationalist resurgence it provoked. Independently of each other, none of these factors would have produced anything like the profound trauma Hungary was to experience. What was surely the most bizarre event in central Europe during this period was possible in large part, although not exclusively, because of the reluctance of anti-Bolsheviks to oppose the strange mélange of rhetoric-prone opportunists and sectarians who came to power as a result of the desire of desperate nationalists to use them to save Hungary's territorial integrity. The revolution's demise would have eventually occurred anyway, but the Hungarian Soviet Republic's utterly counterproductive sectarian adventurism, cynicism, and incompetence led it to behave both savagely and ignorantly, preordaining it to a quick defeat in the hands of an utterly discredited but now resurrected ruling class.

## Italy: Crisis and Reaction

Italy emerged from World War One with more economic problems than any of the other victorious nations, except Russia, and in the aftermath of grave wartime legacies it plunged into a social and political crisis without which the triumph of Fascism would have been impossible. Domestic grain output after the war fell dramatically below 1911–13 norms, partially because at least half of the more than 1 million men killed or permanently disabled came from the rural areas. Vital imports of foodstuffs and coal fell precipitously as the fiscal structure began to break down under a budget deficit that in 1918–19 was roughly a hundred times the prewar level. From the end of 1918 to the end of 1920 the lira fell to less than a quarter of its earlier value against the dollar, and prices between 1918 and 1921 nearly doubled. With over 600,000 war refugees crowding into northern cities, mass emigration, Italy's historic safety valve for domestic difficulties, became impossible because both the United States and Argentina ceased to accept unlimited numbers.

Yet however serious Italy's overall economic malaise, one statistic revealed a major shift in the economic balance in favor of a working class that was ready to struggle to attain equity. In 1918 the real wages of the industrial working class had fallen to 65 percent of the prewar level, but by 1921 they had more than doubled the 1918 figure and were 27 percent higher than in 1913. There is, of course, much more to such numbers insofar as unemployment and other issues are concerned, but whatever the contingencies, the fact remains that the general trend was unquestionably clear. By virtue of its militancy in going on strike and its support of the Left, the working class was at least partially able to insulate itself economically—and it had every incentive to continue on such a course. In the spring of 1919 the centrist-liberal government enacted an eight-hour day for industry, and it was in principle also committed to a transformation of the highly inequitable land system.

Quite apart from the searing political and ideological impact that the war had upon the industrial and rural masses, especially the former soldiers among them, their militancy had an unimpeachable economic justification. This reality imposed a fundamental context within which Italian society and politics, both on the Right and the Left, evolved until those who were losing most turned against the very institution of democracy.

The postwar strike wave and the growth of unions reflected this upsurge in mass activity and consciousness. Before the war, industrial and service workers struck often enough, but in 1919 the number on strike exceeded the prewar peak by about 300 percent, and in 1920 it was one-quarter greater than in 1919. But it was in agriculture—which before the war employed twice as many people as industry—that the biggest changes occurred, because the large mass of agricultural laborers who comprised the majority of the nation's farm population had for years remained relatively conservative and docile. In 1919, both in response to the government's vague wartime pledges favoring land reform and also because of the many veterans whom the war experience had made far less deferential toward their masters, agricultural strikes involved twice as many workers as the pre-war high, but over six times the 1913 level, and in 1920 twice as many agricultural employees struck as in 1919. In all, 2.3 million workers went on strike in 1920, and now nearly half of them were in the rural sector—an unprecedented trend that threatened the very fabric of rural Italy and the small elite that had dominated it for generations. Supplementing formal strikes, there were also riots and direct actions to protest food prices and hoarding, and in the summer of 1919 these too became widespread. Among rural workers, some sought to implement the government's promises by occupying and dividing large estates—actions that received wide attention. Throughout Italy, especially in rural areas, there was constant agitation, much of it spontaneous and involving large numbers of radicalized ex-soldiers. While violence against local elites was talked about much more than practiced, it too increased. And the state's introduction of agrarian-reform measures and partial legalization of land seizures after September 1919 further encouraged poor farm laborers and peasants to take yet more.

Union membership reflected this transformation. Membership in the Socialist-controlled General Confederation of Labor (CGL) increased five-fold in the year after the end of the war, and then nearly doubled by the end of 1920, to reach over 2,000,000. More important yet was the emergence of the Catholic Church–sponsored union, the Italian Confederation of Workers (CIL), which was created in 1918 and grew to a total of 1,160,000 principally rural workers in 1920. The Catholics competed aggressively with the Socialists for the loyalty of the masses, often by being more militant, and their Popular party, the predecessor of the post-1944 Christian Democrats, sought their votes, while priests endorsed the once-cautious, conservative rural poor seeking to attain justice through strikes and land seizures. The Popular party's legislative efforts to legalize land reform frightened the landowners and were opposed by the Socialists. But Popular internal divisions and the Church's own doubts meant its role often remained ambiguous, save insofar as it was strongly anti-Socialist and also stood for opposition to the coalition of largely secular elements which for decades had managed Italy's political structure for the monarchy and the upper and middle classes.[15]

Such social conflict in fields and factories occurred in a context of constitutional political instability and change that accompanied the growth of the Socialist party along with that of the diffuse but antigovernment Popular party. The Socialist party itself quadrupled its membership between 1913 and 1919, to over 200,000, but it remained enigmatic about its real political goals and strategy partially because that helped to maintain internal unity but also because many of its leaders were genuinely perplexed about how to relate to complex mass initiatives and moods. The dual-track policy the Socialists pursued was essentially one many Italians also favored, and to a crucial degree their equivocation and seemingly inconsistent line reflected also a population's unwillingness to sacrifice either electoral politics or extraparliamentary action.

During the war that the Socialists nominally condemned, some of its leaders had openly encouraged soldiers to pursue a defeatist role, yet the party as a whole neatly skirted real opposition or support for the conflict by calling for a peace with reconciliation among warring states. But thanks to the militant atmosphere prevalent among the people, a maximalist faction gained control of the Socialists in September 1918, committing the party to the ultimate creation of a dictatorship of the proletariat attained through the use of violence rather than a constitutional political order, and it attempted unsuccessfully to affiliate with the Communist International. It also rejected collaboration with other parties. Socialist economic demands were no less far-reaching. At the same time, however, the Party managed to pursue an essentially schizophrenic practice of continuing in electoral politics, and in 1919 its newspaper deplored food seizures and increasingly frequent direct actions. But while it never reconciled the profound contradiction between maximalism and parliamentarianism, much less decided seriously how it intended to impose a dictatorship, the Socialist party did manage to prevent still more radical parties, including the Moscow-backed Communists, from seducing the vast bulk of its membership. It also profoundly frightened the men who had dominated Italy's politics and society for generations

Italy in 1919 was unquestionably on the verge of revolution, partially because of past and present economic grievances but also because of the people's intense hatred of the existing society after it had caused them to sacrifice so much blood and goods for a vain cause. The masses both expected and desired comprehensive changes, and the violence and mobilizations then spreading throughout the nation were without equal elsewhere in Europe for such a sustained period. But the Socialists both did not know how to lead this turmoil nor were they ready to take great risks to learn, and instead concluded that the dynamics of the social mood and events would continue to tilt the balance further in their favor and justify their procrastinating policy of neither reform nor revolution—and when the revolution came from the Right, they were passively impotent. In reality, rather than guiding them, they followed the tide of anger and action among the masses.

The Italian electoral system was changed to proportional representation in 1919, replacing the durable prewar administrations with a succession of five governments in three years. In the November 1919 elections the Socialists won 1,835,00 votes, twice their 1913 vote, but the number of seats they held in the Chamber of Deputies tripled, to 156, making them the nation's largest party. The Popular party gained 100 seats, giving the two together a majority. But although the two parties refused to cooperate, all future governments needed one or the other's support to govern—and hence electoral democracy condemned the nation to instability. It was both the success of the Socialists in the parliamentary field and their reliance simultaneously on mass actions to create a more favorable power balance that predetermined the end, because either way the nation's traditional rulers were destined to defeat. The Popular policy also blocked the reemergence of the old-fashioned, stable clientelist politics so familiar to the traditional ruling elites. In the 1920 local elections the Socialist strength grew and they won a majority in 2,022 communes, 24 percent of the total, while the Popular party gained almost as many. The Socialists ran twenty-six of the sixty-nine provinces. For a party that nominally eschewed parliamentarianism, it was doing well enough to hope that the ballot box would, indeed, install it in power.

During the first half of 1920 this intense animation continued without resolution, and while the Socialists bided their time and industrialists, large landowners, and the increasingly anxious middle class began to turn to the Fascists for a solution to their basic dilemma, the extraparliamentary experience in the countryside and factories culminated in the September 1920 strikes. On August 30, as a result of an unresolved wage dispute, Alfa Romeo in Milan locked out its workers and the unions ordered not just a general strike in hundreds of metal-industry factories but their occupation and the maintenance of production for as long as possible. Over 400,000 workers responded, and especially in Genoa, Turin, and Milan they occupied the key factories, which they prepared to defend. Milan was a Socialist city, and the national government felt too weak to evict the workers. In fact, the unstable Liberal government under Giovanni Giolitti was at this time trying to convince the Socialists to enter its coalition to avert immediate civil war, and it was eager to avoid draconian measures. Indeed, Giolitti even later presented a bill that would have made concessions to the workers' demands for factory councils. But the majority of the Party's leaders resolved not to become reformists.

In this period, also, while the factories were occupied and many workers were at a fever pitch of revolutionary ardor and preparing arms to defend them, the very same Socialist leaders met with the CGL and decided it was not the moment to attempt to transform the extensive, but regionally isolated, factory occupations into a revolution. On September 25, after Giolitti forced most of the industrialists to accept a wage increase and some

form of factory councils, the unhappy strikers began to abandon the factories. In effect, the Socialists decided to be neither for nor against reform
and revolution but sought instead to preserve their options on both alternatives—leaving them with only a rich phraseology useful for various ceremonial occasions but not for reality.[16]

The principal immediate outcome of the September 1920 strike was
a palpable working-class decline of faith in the Socialists, who lost a half-
million votes in the May 1921 elections. From late 1920 on, the working
class increasingly ignored Socialist and CGL efforts to lead them, since it
was clear that those two groups did not know where they wanted to go,
much less how to get there; however, consistent with the masses' own contradictions, even as late as the final 1924 elections the Socialist and
Communist vote combined was still over 1 million. But if the politicians'
impotence had been all too obvious for at least four years, the fact
remained that the people themselves had shown remarkably radical, anti-
Establishment initiatives, and it was they who had dragged both the
Socialist and Popular parties toward a complete reversal of the social and
economic system upon which the industrialists, the landowners, and the
middle class based their power. It was by no means certain that the
Socialists would always suffer from their fascination with rhetoric and fatal
indecisiveness, but it was plain to the nation's traditional rulers that the
parliamentary system was no longer manageable. Nor was mass protest
acceptable any longer, for it had lasted too long and gone too far.
Intensifying their capacity to dissent had been the war's main legacy in
shaping peasants' and workers' responses to the conditions and the world
they lived in. The transformation of so many former soldiers into militant
agitators and activists left an insoluble, durable problem so long as the state
tolerated them. Even if they had no capable leaders, discontented and
alienated people would always recall that their struggles after 1918 had
been economically successful, their dignity and self-esteem had grown
immeasurably—and they might renew their agitation.

In November 1919, Benito Mussolini's Fascists ran only in Milan and they
received 4,795 votes. The Fascists had 40,000 members in all of Italy at that
time, mainly in northern cities. Initially, Mussolini had attracted a floating
band of frustrated syndicalists, prowar Socialists like himself, and literary,
student, and bohemian adherents of the Fascist cult of violence, personal
sacrifice, and the deed. Many had been in the elite *arditi* combat units and
were now at loose ends as to their future, but all were addicted to violence;
most were sheer opportunists. But what most characterized the Fascist
rank-and-file membership by 1921 was the fact that 57 percent had been in
the military, nearly all volunteers as opposed to the far greater mass of

Socialist-oriented draftees; their military predilections were far more of an influence on their decision to join than the fact that 40 percent were from the agricultural and urban working class. Some had been common-law criminals who went into the army after the 1915 amnesty; others were former officers who wanted to continue in the paramilitary Fascist structure, or middle-class men whom the postwar inflation had ruined.

It is difficult to categorize the Fascists ideologically because ultimately they themselves hesitated to resolve this question, and Mussolini cynically and eclectically searched for a platform that would allow him to acquire power for its own sake; they had nostrums for all political tendencies, and even offered to cooperate with the September 1920 strikers. They eschewed complex ideas, notwithstanding the fact that they talked superficially about syndicalist and ultranationalist doctrines to which Mussolini and some of his key allies had once adhered. Above all they created a cult of action, in part for its own sake but also one others defined for them during their crucial gestation period. From the beginning, the Fascists received funds from industrialists, and during his first crucial years in power Mussolini followed big-business and middle-class advice on economic policies. After the Party came to power, its leadership was comprised overwhelmingly of upper- and middle-class elements: a handful of aristocrats, many lawyers, independent professionals, bankers, landowners, industrialists, professors, and the like. In 1919 they were a minor group, seemingly with absolutely no future, and even on November 16, 1922, when Mussolini became head of the government by an overwhelming majority vote in the Chamber of Deputies, his own party held only 35 of the 535 seats in that body. For two years the Fascists operated as part of a bloc in the chamber rather than ruling it unilaterally. It was only in early 1925 that they threw over the parliamentary facade and created a totalitarian regime.

Mussolini's meteoric rise reflected the decision of growing elements of the traditional ruling class, especially industrialists, large and medium landowners, and major parts of the middle class, to resist all of the effects of the breakdown of Italian society that their war had generated: the land seizures, the strikes, the elections that critics of property won, and much else. It was in this context that men who earlier had been Liberals and Republicans created common anti-Socialist voting blocs with the Fascists in local elections after 1920, and the Fascists in their first stage of power, like the Nazis a decade later, became the political spearhead on which the traditional forces of conservative order relied to cope with the seeming menace from the Left. At first the Fascists and bands of former soldiers close to them offered their services to big landowners eager to bully peasants claiming land under the new agrarian-reform laws or simply occupying it, and soon industrialists, who as an organization in March 1920 went on record demanding that the government provide order, also sought their aid. But during 1921, as the police and political authorities increasingly stood aside, the Fascists attacked labor-union halls and Socialist offices, and systematically smashed the Left's organizational structure and intimidated the people who led it. In early 1922 they began to occupy major cities with strong Socialist bases, including Milan and Genoa. Cautious estimates claim that about seven hundred premises belonging to the urban and rural unions or Socialists were wrecked in 1921 alone, with 166 killed and about 500 injured. Other figures are much higher, reaching over 1,500 deaths at Fascist and police hands by October 1921.

Whatever the exact numbers, this policy of terror produced a vast increase in Fascist activists, including many former members of the traditional parties who wanted to share in the Fascist ascendancy. From late 1919 to March 1921, Fascist membership doubled to 80,000, but by August 1921 it was 222,000, and 322,000 in May 1922. Mussolini provided the landowners and industrialists what the state could not or, in the case of Socialist-Popular administrations, would not: the muscle to beat down leftist militants. By 1922 the leaders of the army were largely pro-Fascist because they too were anti-Socialist, and in this manner Mussolini won their support as well as that of many senior state officials and policemen concerned that the Socialists might replace them also. Feeble working-class resistance could scarcely cope with the combination of the Fascists with large parts of the traditional Center-Right parties and the civil authority, and while many maximalist Socialist leaders generalized on this reality to advocate worker and peasant passivity until the Fascists had less power, once again their ingenuity with theory led merely to inaction and an absence of any practice—whether reformist or revolutionary—in a highly fluid environment that the new rightist coalition could shape as they wished as long as they had no challenges.

What this broad coalition of traditional politicians and the economically dominant classes objected to was not only the Left's extraparliamentary roles but also its legal political successes, for the Socialists, essentially responding to the masses' actions and desires rather than initiating and guiding them, threatened the coalition's hegemony equally in both domains. Had they pursued either strategy consistently rather than vacillating between the two, the Left may have been considerably more successful, although even this was by no means certain, since those who had the most to lose showed themselves to be willing to do everything necessary to keep the Socialists from power, including abolishing democracy. For even had strikers and landless laborers not been a menace, the electoral system also posed innumerable dangers, and that was reason enough for the liberals and democrats of prewar days, as well as capitalists, landowners, and the middle class, to discard the institutional legacies of decades of stable parliamentarianism and to support the systematic Fascist suppression of political freedom for the next twenty years.[17]

## Lenin's Road to Power

Every leftist party seeking to attain profound or revolutionary social change must confront the innumerable choices emerging from the often vast differences that exist between itself and the masses whose active participation is crucial if power in some form is to be achieved. During "normal" times, when people are generally apathetic or indifferent toward politics, socialist parties, even if they did not, like the Bolsheviks, articulate an elaborate theory of the party as the indispensable leader of the masses, nonetheless assumed that they would at some future historic juncture perform irreplaceable leadership functions. To believe otherwise would have negated a vital reason for the very existence of organizations as ongoing entities attempting to provide continuity at all times, and to this extent at least all socialist parties have been elitist insofar as the term implies an essential guiding role for their group.

The historic problem for every socialist party, and this was very much the case for the Bolsheviks at the beginning of 1917, is that although it always possesses a usually explicit vision of its own ideal organizational form and structure as well as its immediate political objectives and principles, when the possibility of actually attaining power arises it must decide how far it wishes to modify its original notions of the party's structure and goals, and its conception of the ideal road to power, to relate to and channel existing upsurges of mass political consciousness, including the unpredicted, diverse forms it usually assumes. In essence, to what extent does the "vanguard" party follow the proletariat at least as much as lead it along a predetermined path? And how do parties, particularly those that are Bolshevik, radically alter their practices, if not their theories, concerning their internal party structures in order to enroll large numbers of people regardless of whether they had been molded according to some preconceived image of ideological and organizational discipline, thereby transforming the elitist party into a mass party?

Even in times of crisis, revolutions are rarely expected, and the March Revolution utterly astonished everyone: the czar and his allies at home and abroad as well as the entire socialist opposition. Lenin's oft-quoted prognosis of January 1917 that "we, the elder generation, will possibly not live to see the decisive battles of this approaching revolution," merely reflected a unanimous consensus.[18] "Not one party was prepared for the great overturn," a Menshevik leader admitted—and so all parties were compelled to improvise hastily in constantly changing, unpredictable circumstances.[19] And the same myopia that had prevented virtually everyone from predicting the revolution also kept them from accurately estimating the dynamics of the larger events and trends around them, facts that all of their decisions and actions had to take into account if they were to succeed. Lenin's triumph was certainly due not to the fact that he was omniscient but that he made fewer critical mistakes than anyone else, including the majority of other Bolsheviks, less because he fully understood the nature of the crisis in Russia than that his inflexible dogmatism on the war, combined with his pragmatic readiness to exploit existing organizational constraints to make tactical compromises on the road to grasping total power, were better suited to making the most of the opportunities that existed.

The Russian masses' consciousness and readiness to act only intensified as the war continued to make grave demands on their lives and the czar's successors failed to make peace. One can only understand the events of 1917 within this larger framework, for the institutional, mental, and social processes that had led to March made the subsequent Bolshevik Revolution, if not inevitable, at least very possible. That the provisional government initially had little authority anywhere in Russia, including even Petrograd, and that the workers and soldiers were far more responsive to their soviets than to the new state, was less crucial than the Menshevik refusal and inability to cope with—or even to acknowledge in the decisive case of the war itself—those events and forces that had brought it to power. The new regime was for modernizing the political structure while leaving the economic system largely unaltered while it continued the war. It was, from the inception, fatally incapable of reversing those war-induced dynamics that were inexorably to lead to further upheavals.

As Russia's economic crisis intensified, during the spring the whole transport structure collapsed, and the government in July considered it catastrophic. This only aggravated the already-failing food distribution system, increased inflation, and caused strikes to mount as the economy became increasingly paralyzed. In the rural areas land seizures grew dramatically after February because of the nearly total disappearance of central administrative authorities and the new government's failure to enact promised reforms quickly. Spontaneous peasant-elected autonomous town and village committees, in which former soldiers were heavily represented, removed the rural folks' traditional fear of the state, and they increasingly embarked on a collision course with it. In June 1917 there were ten times as many land seizures and confiscations of hay, trees, and the like than in March. The peasants during 1917 were far more radical than the urban working class, and much more willing to engage in violent direct action.

Soldiers encouraged this increasingly radical mood and action after

February, and as I noted earlier, their desertion rate during 1917 rose dramatically, while the decline in discipline among those remaining in the army made it virtually useless for domestic police purposes. The troops wanted most of all to go home—to be done with the war—and it was on this basis, with their food rations falling, that the army's very existence became increasingly dangerous to the provisional government throughout 1917. Even if the Bolsheviks were unable to organize them extensively, the soldiers' sympathy for the Bolshevik position on the war increased with the months, and it became clear no later than June that the troops would not fight as their officers ordered them to; indeed, it was obvious they might even shift extensively to the Bolshevik side if they believed this was the only way to end the war. Lenin alone fully understood the decisive significance of the mood within the army, and he made leaving the war the single most important issue in confronting both Kerensky's regime and the other leaders of his party.

Uniting all these changes in mood and opinion in ways that ultimately were to work in favor of the Bolsheviks throughout 1917 was the profound alteration in the manner in which countless ordinary folk defined their own role in the world and their ability to make a real difference in how it works. The rare experience of self-confidence in oneself and mankind's potential that springs forth in many places and times during periods of great instability and seeming promise profoundly touched a sufficiently important sector of the Russian people to make the role of the masses potentially decisive. And this often euphoric sense of individual freedom was a vital precondition to activism, for without it militancy and its grave risks possessed little justification. There was now a liberation not only from the inhibitions of old ideas but also from a fear of the prerevolutionary machinery of repression. "The streets were full of an atmosphere of exaltation and vague optimism," Bernard Pares, the (London) *Times'* Russian correspondent and adviser to the British government recalled: ". . . perhaps everything was possible, but one was not yet quite certain how far one could go. There were marvellous street placards. Every imaginable idea or fad was advertised."[20]

Events were to prove that while Lenin appreciated those larger factors and forces constraining the decisions of Russia's political leaders far better than anyone, crucial aspects of them also frightened him, for he was neither an anarchist nor a democrat, and he sought to channel the masses' desires, enthusiasm, and potential strength in order to attain power. Momentarily, the soviets permitted him to do this. He also believed the mighty people must be subordinated—ruthlessly, if necessary—once the Bolshevik party, under his ultimate tutelage, consolidated control. His essential problem during 1917 was that, just as the population's opinions and moods were increasingly more radical than those of the provisional government, thereby leaving his party closer to the public, they might also easily get out of hand

and pose grave risks to his successful seizure of power. How best to lead and to follow the masses became the principal challenge facing Lenin during 1917.

Lenin had been in exile for nearly a decade before his return to Russia in April 1917, but well before then he had confronted similar dilemmas. Before the outbreak of war in 1914 he was concerned that the young undisciplined workers then leading the great wave of strikes would raise too many unattainable demands and become adventurist. But his concern about his fellow Bolsheviks equaled his fear of the proletariat leaping ahead of the Party. Organizationally, the Party had been decimated in the several years before the March Revolution. Of its 240 key leaders, 45 were in exile in February 1917, and 73 were inactive or in Siberia. Most of the remainder had gone underground, but about half of these had been arrested at least once because police agents had completely infiltrated their ranks. More important, those who were still active had lost a good deal of their old militancy, and they scarcely could define the implications of the entire war experience for Russian society, much less a revolutionary response to it; during this critical period, as well as even earlier, again to quote Trotsky, "all the leaders of the party at all the most important moments stood to the *right* of Lenin." Worse yet, even including Lenin, "the party also lagged behind the revolutionary dynamic. . . . The most revolutionary party which human history until this time has ever known was nevertheless caught unawares by the events of history."[21] The masses stayed well ahead of it at virtually every point.

But if the Party's organizational structure was seriously impaired, its organizational theory was totally irrelevant to the real conditions in Russia. Lenin's dominating prestige within the Bolsheviks was based originally on his concept of a party comprised of a general staff of carefully selected leaders, fully disciplined and capable of covert activity, with the working class itself serving as the intermediary force under the Party's tight guidance in leading the vast mass of peasants. This neat triangular image was essentially military, and made the Bolsheviks the instrument of the revolutionary intellectuals, who in a predictable, quite orderly and controlled manner were to create the dictatorship of the proletariat.

Lenin in his early theorizing left little room for spontaneous events, and he scarcely anticipated the metamorphosis of his fellow leaders into mainly wavering, even tame strategists when the war broke out and the March Revolution followed directly from it. From 1914 on, Lenin was unable to convince many of his senior colleagues to support his September 1914 theses on the war, which called for the downfall of czarist chauvinism and implied, even if he did not say it as explicitly as he had during the 1904–5 war with Japan, that the Bolsheviks advocated only Russia's loss. Lenin preferred that the socialists of all the warring nations press for the collapse of their own governments and transform the imperialist war into many civil wars. But the five Bolsheviks in the Duma in August 1914, like their German counterparts with the sole exception of Liebknecht, did not vote against war credits but instead abstained because they refused to take a stand that singled out Russia as a villain in the deluge. Like Mehring and his small circle, they favored the simultaneous failure of all the warring nations, but this ideal solution provided parties no basis for action given the realities dominating each nation. The Bolshevik leadership within the country rejected the notion that Russia's defeat alone was to be desired, and when Lenin returned home in April 1917 he too avoided calling for it but instead confined himself entirely to urging that Russia leave the war immediately.

In fact, during the first months of 1917 the Bolsheviks in Russia, whatever their ultimate goals, "intended for an indefinite time to play the part of loyal opposition," as Trotsky aptly put it.[22] Not only did many Bolshevik leaders advocate electing representatives to the provisional government, but most urged both soldiers and workers to restore production and even order. Even more shocking, the older Bolshevik leaders, who controlled the daily *Pravda*, called upon the soldiers to resist German offensives. Their position was for immediate peace negotiations among all warring states—which by then was a view that many European social democrats also endorsed. While this prevarication partially reflected their response to the dominant reality that even in June 1917 the Bolsheviks comprised scarcely more than one-eighth of the All-Russian Congress of Soviets, and that during the post-March mass euphoria they remained disinclined to assume too sectarian a stance, the principal reason for it was that the Party's traditional leadership at no time before then had accepted Lenin's unequivocal opposition to the war.

Lenin was therefore very much isolated from his old comrades both before and after he returned to Russia, and had the Bolsheviks truly operated as the disciplined prewar elitist party he himself had originally designed, he would have remained impotent. But the Bolsheviks were in the process of changing fundamentally from an elitist to a mass party, and this fact presented Lenin with both opportunities and dangers. The nature of the Party after February altered dramatically in terms of numbers as well as in its social and intellectual composition. For a brief but crucial period it became a relatively tolerant, open movement, one both eager and able to channel much of the people's revolutionary energy. In February there had been only 2,000 Bolsheviks in Petrograd, but in April there were 16,000, and by late June twice that, not to mention also about 6,000 soldiers in local Bolshevik military organizations by June. Throughout the nation the

Bolsheviks grew from 20,000 members in March to 260,000 in October. Most of these new recruits were a far cry from an elitist, theoretically sophisticated intelligentsia; now they were ebullient, younger class-conscious workers and soldiers who became Bolsheviks because the Party offered the most radical answers at a moment when they seemed most relevant. Few had a real knowledge of Marxist classics—to them revolution meant action on streets and in factories. Working through them, Lenin could frequently, but not always, outflank the cautious old elite nominally in command of the Party because militancy was what the new members most desired. Lenin, in a word, was much more attuned to the masses' moods than the other Bolshevik leaders.

The Party had hardly screened the new members' views. Most of them failed to conform to the disciplined role and deep knowledge that Lenin had much earlier argued was a prerequisite for every serious revolutionary, and they were constantly threatening to get out of his control or, equally dangerous, simply quit the Bolshevik organizations when they objected to the Party's positions or actions—or lack of them. Lenin sought to use the new members to impose his mastery over the older ones, yet also not to let their demands bind him.[23]

Lenin's dilemma, which was subsequently also to confront many Communist parties, was that his elitist organizational theory was based on the premise that in the long run only a highly literate intelligentsia was permanently concerned about politics and profound social change. It ignored entirely the brief but historically decisive moments when large masses of people, in response to overwhelming events bearing upon them, developed a deep political consciousness and moved without the guidance of aspiring Communist leaders; and the Party's doctrines failed to explain what had to be done in such a context to remain ahead of the masses and to guide them. In 1917 Lenin understood this challenge, and in his quest for power he chose to ignore both his theory and those who had believed in it the longest.

But Lenin never intended that such relatively democratic functional bodies as the soviets, which were initially the only structures capable of exploiting the huge potential for mass mobilization that sprang up suddenly, should last any longer than it took him to again control the Party and the potential rival leadership cadres within it and run them precisely as he thought best, without concern for mass parties, soviets, or even an elitist central committee. The Bolsheviks developed an organizational theory appropriate for a clandestine party struggling under repressive conditions to attain power, but it was totally unprepared for a situation in which the Party became in fact a huge association with virtually open enrollment, much less the circumstances it faced after victory was attained. Lenin never reflected upon what emerged as the practice under his leadership, and would remain that of his successors for over sixty years, in which one man (or, much later, a tiny coterie of power brokers operating clientelist machines) ran the Soviet Union with no concern for the desires of the people, whom he—or they—dominated and mobilized along organizational lines that both protected and maximized their personal power. The result was the emergence of a fragile state, one based on fear and virtually devoid of broad legitimacy, that was much later to disintegrate completely even without serious opposition.

When Lenin returned to Russia, it was largely to the new Party members that he directed his efforts. The one concession he made to the old leaders in his famous "April Theses" was that the Party would not attempt, at least for the moment, to seize power by force, thereby repudiating his long-standing advocacy of civil war. As for Russia's defeat in the war, which earlier he had favored as a lesser evil, he merely ignored the topic. In June, Lenin even denounced the idea of a separate peace treaty between Russia and Germany, but he unequivocally insisted that the Party not support the government or its war effort in any way. But Lenin's ambiguity, which he calculated would avoid alienating many workers who were against both the war and defeat, nonetheless horrified many of his old comrades who still favored a defense of the nation. By using his new allies in the Party and threatening to resign and create a rival body if his position were rejected, Lenin was able to cajole the Bolsheviks into endorsing his modified stance.

Yet Lenin was less fortunate in controlling the radical workers' and soldiers' enthusiastic but provocative actions, and by July, when he went into hiding for over three months, they threatened to doom all of his plans and hopes. Until then, as economic conditions continued to deteriorate and strikes became more frequent, many workers and soldiers in Petrograd, including most of the novice Bolsheviks, decided for themselves that power should be transferred from the provisional government to the soviets, which, however, were still firmly in Menshevik and Socialist Revolutionary (S.R.) hands. Lenin considered the idea both provocative and pointless and strongly denounced it as adventurist, but decisions increasingly moved to a constantly changing outdoor congress of the masses in the streets, where anarchists prodded a melee of deserters from the army, strikers, and a flotsam of humanity. Their militancy was fueled by the fact that the Kerensky government, believing that the troops would fight, now wished to mount an offensive against the German lines, thereby angering the soldiers, who more than ever wanted the war over with and for the first time began to respond seriously to the Bolshevik appeals. Whatever the immediate setbacks for the Bolsheviks during the summer, this shift among the troops was of decisive importance.

By June both the Bolshevik party's sheer size as well as the people in it were in fact also threatening Lenin's ability to control it, especially its Petrograd branches, and when they planned a demonstration on June 22 to demand the transfer of power to the soviets, Lenin barely managed to stop it. An officially sanctioned and tranquil demonstration a week later drew some 400,000 people, but the most radical Bolshevik and anarchist slogans dominated it. On July 3, however, while Lenin was on vacation, forces loyal to Kerensky fired upon a group of demonstrators and Kronstadt sailors in Petrograd; for two days the city was subjected to rioting and looting as soldiers who had refused to go to the front joined the chaotic fray and about 400 people were killed or wounded. Lenin arrived to discourage the crowds, and while the Party called upon the demonstrators to disband, it also declared that their views would eventually prevail. Although the event revealed the great gap between the Party and the population, the government blamed the Bolsheviks for turmoil for which, at least at the highest levels, it had no responsibility whatsoever.

The July upheaval demoralized many rank-and-file activists and Party members, who had joined in the riots on their own, but Party organizations among workers remained intact; within the army the Bolsheviks were hurt badly. The government chose the moment to crack down strongly on all of the radicals, at the same time forming a new cabinet. Who, if anyone, would lead the masses was now in doubt because many Bolshevik leaders went underground. Lenin remained hidden until October 24, but he believed the Party had been damaged very badly and was so discouraged that he advocated staying underground "seriously and for a long time."[24] From Lenin's viewpoint the judgment was accurate because he was not in control of the Party's mass organization, which by virtue of its size and social character had ceased being "Leninist," and he could not visualize a revolution without the Party firmly in his hands. Worse yet, even the old Bolsheviks on the central committee met without him and severely diluted their commitment to his "April Theses," leaving so many questions unanswered that it was no longer clear where many of his old comrades were heading. In reality, Lenin, like the new Kerensky regime, failed during July to comprehend fully the social forces and people that would determine whether the provisional government could remain in command much longer, or how its own internal political contradictions might decisively affect events.

The Bolsheviks, shaken and deeply divided, ceased even to pretend to lead; they now essentially followed the masses' initiatives. They did so while the sheer momentum that the war had produced in traumatizing vast numbers of civilians as well as soldiers and in altering profoundly their vision of their world and what they demanded of it, as well as what they would do to attain it, sustained new waves of radicalization and protests. As long as the

Kerensky government insisted on continuing the war, there was no way a denouement could be averted, and although in July it could count on the loyalty of a sufficient number of soldiers to weather the crisis, time worked irresistibly against it. Lenin and the Bolsheviks did not create this situation nor could they, as they had attempted in July, control it. By September, desertions had completely demoralized the army, and a large majority of the remaining soldiers were either vaguely pro-Bolshevik or neutral. By itself this change may not have been sufficient, but given the context in the cities, the authorities nominally in power had to be able to call upon loyal troops or they would inevitably perish. But whatever else they felt, the vast majority of Russia's people wanted the war ended—and ultimately only the Bolsheviks were prepared to support their insistent demands for peace.

The Bolshevik eclipse did not last long precisely because the society and power within it was so unstable, but their resurrection was greatly assisted by the opera buffa in the form of the "Kornilov affair." As the commander in chief of the army, Kornilov and many of the key generals wished to eliminate the role of the soviets within the military and resurrect the conventional army, and at the end of August the commander ineptly revealed his plans, which would have demoted Kerensky and effectively constituted a coup d'état. Moreover, he selected incompetent officers to seize Petrograd, and they all failed him. The most obvious result of the abortive coup was that Kerensky no longer had senior officers on whom he could rely. More challenging for him, however, was the fact that in the days leading up to the demise of Kornilov's farce, the Bolsheviks chose in deed, if not in word, to rally strongly to the defense of Kerensky by forming units of "Red Guards" from among workers, and when the danger ended a part of them remained intact. Lenin himself briefly abandoned an absolutely intransigent position on behalf of a more modest demand that a new Menshevik–Socialist Revolutionary government transfer political power to the soviets, pledging that the Bolsheviks would work politically, and peacefully, within the soviets, where indeed they were becoming much more successful in winning elections. If after the seemingly profound July reverses Lenin had become much more cautious, this phase was not to last long because in fact there had been a major shift in the balance of military and political forces away from the increasingly isolated and impotent Kerensky regime. In mid-September, Lenin called for what amounted to an immediate insurrection, and on September 15 the Party central committee almost unanimously repudiated him; after scourging it with unprecedented invective, Lenin offered to resign from the committee.

Lenin circumscribed the central committee during October as he had earlier by mobilizing the new Bolsheviks against the old, and because of the restless mood among the former, he was able to push the committee on October 10 to accept the principle of an uprising and seizure of power as soon as possible—contingent, however, on its being feasible. Obviously, Russia had been in a revolutionary mood since March, and such feelings were more intense in October than at any time since then, for the Kerensky regime and army were disintegrating. Even so, only eight of the nineteen Party districts said they were ready to begin fighting immediately, and there were serious reservations among many in the ranks about the arms available, the status of potential fighters, and much else. The Bolsheviks again hesitated.

Kerensky knew of these inconclusive debates, and at least partly in response to them made the fatal decision during the second week of October to send the larger part of the Petrograd troops, many of whom had earlier been loyal to him, out of the city and to the front, thereby removing a potential danger from his midst. With this gesture he made his defeat inevitable, for most of the soldiers refused to go, endorsing the Petrograd soviet or declaring their neutrality in the imminent struggle between it and the government. But until midnight on October 23–24 the Bolsheviks still remained incapable of putting together an organization adequate for an uprising, and they did not feel strong enough to claim and hold power in their own name alone. It was Kerensky's decision to attempt to mobilize loyal troops from outside Petrograd and bring them into the city, thereby forcing the Bolsheviks either to act, finally, or face severe repression, that compelled them to move. Even then the central committee voted not for an uprising but for a consolidation of forces to defend the meeting of the congress of soviets scheduled to open October 25, which would have included non-Bolsheviks and thereby be able to declare a new government and provide it with greater legitimacy than a purely Bolshevik-staged revolution would have done. In effect, they planned to justify their actions as a defense against counterrevolution.

Kerensky, meanwhile, demanded his parliament's approval for putting down a Bolshevik uprising which, while being planned nonetheless remained stalled. Lenin, still outside the city until October 24, watched the posturing and inaction on both sides and appealed to the lower Party organs to ignore the central committee and move decisively before the soviet congress met. After Kerensky received reports that the garrisons in Petrograd would side with the Bolsheviks, on the morning of October 25 he left town hoping to mobilize loyal troops on the front to keep the Bolsheviks, then engaged in light movements against virtually no opposition, from taking power. He was never to return.[25]

World War One created profound, often irreversible, economic, social, and political crises in much of Europe, deeply affecting and then transforming the political consciousness of countless millions of people who remained outside organizational structures, with their possibilities for control and guidance, and who related only to each other as crowds—masses that were relatively inarticulate at the inception, but for a brief but crucial historical moment were intensely hostile to those leaders and political values who had led them into a war that cost the Continent so much blood and suffering. Their sudden emergence as potential actors was the dominant political reality throughout a large part of Europe, creating an autonomous but perhaps decisive constituency for the leftist parties to relate to if they could or would—above all in Germany, Russia, and Italy, the three important nations the war was to affect most profoundly. Could rigid, highly structured parties and their often dogmatic leaders transcend their complex and elitist inherited doctrines and organizational legacies to interact with the masses, who were scarcely doctrinally sophisticated, and retain their ideological identities, and did such parties have any possibilities of success if they refused to take such risks?

If comparable dilemmas were to reappear constantly elsewhere for the remainder of the twentieth century for Social Democratic and, especially, Communist parties, the tension in the revolutionary party between leading and following was the fundamental political issue for the Bolsheviks. But in comprehending how all parties resolved it, we must consider not only their capacity to adapt to challenges but also the nature of their rivals for power and the resistance they confronted, as well as the unpredictable but nonetheless crucial opportunities that emerged for them at decisive but fleeting junctures when they ineptly neither led nor followed the masses but confronted impasses in their struggles to attain power. Such an understanding must also take serious account of the people's real moods, their intensity and durability, and the possibilities such combinations of factors created. In Russia the masses wanted basic changes, and the Bolsheviks temporarily adapted to their state of mind and organizational forms, following or, as in the case of the soviets, participating in them in order later to exploit and control the forces of change. In Germany the SPD's leaders correctly perceived the decisive limits of the people's desires and remained able to guide and inhibit them in traditional ways—which by repeated votes the workers endorsed—and they won a respite, only to be physically liquidated later. In Italy the Socialists didn't so much follow or lead the huge opposition but stood aside, waiting for it to define a clear course, and they were soon crushed.

When Europe's leaders unleashed the dragons of war in 1914, they had no prevision whatsoever of its possible grave, even fatal, consequences for the future of their political and ideological world. If the parties on the Left had to confront the daunting and crucial task of defining an organization and articulating an ideology capable of channeling vast social forces in a way that truly altered social reality, those in power had also to cope with the fundamental implications of the collapse of their armies and the dissipation of the illusions and bonds that had kept soldiers loyal to existing regimes. The political traumatization of troops along with the war's economic, intellectual, and physical impact on vast sections of Europe's middle classes quickly also produced, in a number of forms, a resurgence of irrational nationalist forces with nominally anti-elitist, populist ideologies; these were to spawn a variety of fascist movements that briefly seemed poised to challenge the prewar dominance of aristocrats, capitalists, and historic elites.

In this context, as those who had lost most materially in the war began to prefer stability to the unpredictably dangerous vagaries of open politics, Europe's fragile, often young, parliamentarian systems were gravely threatened. Outside of Russia the principal challenge confronting traditional rulers was less the threat from the Left than the task of imposing their influence over atavistic rightists, an interaction that was profoundly to define the next decades of Europe's history—twenty-five years later culminating in the Second World War and creating another historic opportunity for the diverse forces of the Left.

The First World War fundamentally altered the political universe of the modern world in crucial and unprecedented ways, yet the awesome problems of political and social organization, of traditional as well as radical ideologies, of economics, and much else that beset Europe from 1914 to 1919 remained also to confront the next generation.

# CHAPTER 9

# World War Two and
# European Life and Society

The two decades following World War One provided no lasting respite for a profoundly disturbed Europe, which witnessed the creation of strongly reactionary, anti-Semitic, and nationalist movements dedicated to reversing many of the long war's political and social consequences. The new fascist parties incorporated those parts of the prewar reactionary political legacies and ideological folklore that were valuable to them, amplifying them with populist economic strategies designed to win the masses away from the anticapitalist appeals of a Left that had briefly caused the Continent's historically dominant classes and elites great trepidation. But the very existence of the Soviet Union established a crucial focus for the the resurgent Right's alarmist appeals, and gave it credibility among many who earlier had believed that a formal parliamentarianism was a plausible way of organizing their national polity so long as it did not endanger their economic and class interests.

Although the fear of the Left receded during the 1920s, the political impact of the Great Depression on much of the European working class greatly renewed dread of it in those nations that had not yet succumbed to the many varieties of right-wing authoritarianism, and the Spanish Civil War and the creation of a Popular Front in France magnified the horror of socialism among dominant social classes and elements. The interlude between these two monumental wars is not a topic of this book, but suffice it to say that for all of the political, economic, but also technological reasons and causes already familiar to the reader, many of them the products of the impact of the First World War but others directly related to the very origins of that conflict, a much larger portion of humanity was drawn into the next conflagration—which was to become truly global. The cycle of war's traumatic effects on people's lives, the subsequent inevitable transformation of their ideas about themselves, their society, and the world, along with the emergence of a renewed and greatly expanded Left to challenge established social orders throughout the earth, began anew.

## Planning for War: Things Come Apart

### Hitler's Calculations

All wars are preordained to create surprises among those who unleash them, for they perceive goals far more clearly than the obstacles to their attainment. Hitler's objectives were, at the very least, grandiose; in their most extreme form he talked of mastery over all of Europe and, subsequently, domination of the world, but he had no precise timetable for his megalomaniac plans, and he always left vague the precise manner in which the Nazis would organize and colonize the European *Lebensraum* they conquered. But Hitler was deeply conscious of the fact that Germany's straitened material resources for military expansion first required control of Austrian and Czech agricultural output to enable his next move, whatever it was, to succeed. This he accomplished by 1939. Although Hitler's ultimate aims were clear, his blueprint for gaining them, as many historians have correctly noted, was the product of constant improvisations, and these changed with a frequency that disturbed many of his military advisers, who, because of their traditional obsession with data on arms production, at first overrated the power of Germany's potential adversaries—especially the French.

Hitler initially sought to avoid total war, much less a war on two fronts. He saw both as a threat to Germany's domestic stability and social peace as well as too formidable for its existing material resources, and so he refused to prepare for such conflicts and the nation was at the beginning ill equipped for all-out war. Hitler's fantasy was that he could fight convenient wars sequentially, at the time and place of his choosing: a series of short, intermittent blitzkrieg offensives in small, limited conflicts that made the most of strategic initiatives utilizing a very finite military machine. He believed that he would not have to impose a sustained burden on Germany's limited economy and that his enemies would be as disunited and dilatory as he required. Each conquest and the economic integration of the victimized nations was supposed to augment Germany's capacity to continue the long succession of triumphs. This meant that events had to correspond exactly to Hitler's desires, and until the spring of 1941 they indeed conformed to his fundamental premises about how to fight a war and organize German society to win it, thereby further encouraging his incredibly ambitious hegemonic dreams.

Hitler was quite confident that his attack on Poland in September 1939 would not immediately bring Britain—nor France—into the war, notwithstanding their treaties to defend each other, and his economic mobilization plans predicated a brief, limited war. Germany possessed less than a six-month reserve of the most crucial raw materials when the Second World War began, and it was immediately compelled to rely heavily upon imported foreign labor to free Germans for the army and keep up with rising demands. But Hitler also believed before his strike against Poland that war with Britain and France was inevitable, yet he feared they would seek to avoid fighting until 1945, when their combined military power would purportedly far exceed Germany's, and so he prepared in October 1939 to move west before their intensive rearmament shifted the balance of power. From a purely material viewpoint, his reasoning was correct. Hitler therefore embarked on what was an immensely precarious general war with an operational calculus that was hastily improvised, failed to provide either military or economic coordination over the German war effort, and would surely have soon been disastrous had the French, Poles, and English not been far more disunited and weak than either Hitler or his many initially skeptical generals could imagine. Most important of all, he entered the conflict with a wage and domestic social policy, including sustained consumer-goods production, calculated to keep the working class tranquil, if not happy, and the regime maintained living standards for as long as possible.

Hitler, in a word, determined not to create a total war economy, and he succeeded to an astonishing degree. Although the Nazi occupation policies toward each of the defeated nations depended greatly on racial theories as well as the specific bureaucratic politics of the German war organization in each country, in general it was the Nazi intention—even at the risk of losing after Hitler's original military calculations utterly failed—to transfer, to the degree possible, the war's human and economic costs to all of the conquered nations, so that the German people would be spared the shocks that had unravelled their society in 1918. This crucial objective's significance cannot be stressed too strongly or too often, for it explains to a critical degree the total impact of the war on Europe and, above all, its traumatizing human and political consequences.[1]

The astonishing German triumphs over Poland and France vindicated Hitler's short-war, low-mobilization strategy and increased Nazi reliance on ad hoc war-making that exploited chance opportunities and reinforced their profoundly chauvinist and racist disdain for their enemies. His penchant for substituting his desires for reality caused Hitler to dismiss uncomfortable facts when it came to dealing with his nominal alliance with Stalin in August 1939, a pact that freed him to invade Poland but obligated giving the Russians essential war goods in exchange for vital raw materials—an exchange that by spring of 1940 Hitler considered onerous. When in July of that year Hitler instructed his generals to begin studying "Barbarossa," the invasion of the USSR, his mind was made up and his sycophantic aides reinforced his preconceptions.

When Barbarossa was given final approval in December 1940, Germany's territorial objectives remained vague—but immense at the very least—and while five months were allocated for the war with Russia, Hitler was confident that the Red Army would disintegrate and he would capture Leningrad within three weeks. He left unresolved how and where the war was to end. His principal officers denigrated the Soviet military potential and were no less optimistic that a blitzkrieg would triumph in a matter of weeks in a vast region for which, in fact, they had few accurate maps. Britain's and France's leaders also shared Hitler's scorn for Stalin's army. Hitler and his officers ordered no significant increase in armaments production, and even slightly lowered the level of munitions output from its 1940 peak. Germany sent a smaller air force against the USSR than it had used in 1940 in western Europe. But by the end of 1941 its army in Russia was freezing, its transport collapsing, its tanks increasingly immobilized, and it was locked in a calamitous struggle in which it was to suffer monumental, decisive losses that alone denied Hitler victory in World War Two. Only in 1943 did the Nazis begin to make the efforts necessary to stave off defeat, and while their tank, artillery, and aviation output by 1944 increased three or four times over 1942, far outstripping Britain, it was nonetheless still further than ever behind the combined Allied output, even when the significant amounts they milked from the occupied nations are added to Nazi resources.

Barbarossa was a case of wishes wholly tailoring a basic strategic judgment, in this case a most fatal one, since Hitler initially comprehended that he needed a quick end to the war on the Continent if he were then either to defeat Britain or, more likely, compel it to accept a peace on German terms. He realized that if the war lasted into 1942 it would be very long and that the United States' inevitable entry would tip the balance of military power against Germany. The blitzkrieg strategy was the result of Nazi domestic priorities defining military tactics, but it had succeeded brilliantly wherever Hitler's Continental enemies were either weak or demoralized, and he assumed that the USSR was both. His misplaced confidence now transformed the European war into a protracted conflict on two fronts, for which Germany was ill prepared and ultimately unwilling to pay the terrible price for victory save insofar as it could extract the essential supplies and labor it required from the nations it conquered.[2]

### The Allies Plan the War

Just as Hitler hoped to fight a short war of high mobility and relatively low costs, the British, French, and American governments sought to prolong the conflict long enough to bring their combined industrial and economic weight to bear. Germany could no more win such a struggle after 1940 than it could in 1915.

The ironies that grave miscalculations played in this conflict were scarcely confined to Germany. Stalin's reward for his unscrupulous pact with Hitler was a surprise attack, and he came within a hairsbreadth of defeat. The British planned to protract the war longer than Germany could afford, eventually aiming at victory by the fall of 1944, only to have the Americans lengthen it well past the time London thought both prudent and essential, so that they emerged from the war virtually bankrupt and well down the road to becoming a marginal world power. Moreover, all of the Allies were convinced that Germany had mobilized a formidable war economy long before 1939, and they failed to comprehend that the blitzkrieg strategy was in fact calculated to forestall draconian militarization. So the British, in compensating for their negligence in preparing for war prior to 1939, actually quickly made up for a greatly exaggerated Nazi arms buildup. By 1940, precisely because Germany wanted to fight inexpensive wars, British output of aircraft, armored vehicles, and trucks greatly exceeded Germany's, and in 1941 that lead grew and spread to other critical military weapons. In 1942, Britain's military spending as a share of the government's budget was twice that of Germany's.

Yet it was the technical nature of Britain's rearmament that was most striking, for the Nazi commitment to a quick, cheap victory discouraged their developing sophisticated or attritional weapons, which required both time and money, and it was precisely in this domain that the Americans and, especially, the British, sought to gain the decisive advantage. In September 1939, General Bernard Montgomery believed the British army was "totally unfit to fight a first class war on the continent . . . ," a view that persisted among Britain's leaders until the war was almost over, for they were wholly unwilling once more to pay the cost in lives that the First World War had exacted.[3] Britain therefore emphasized a reliance on sea power and, above all, a strategic air offensive, for which they developed heavy bombers that far exceeded the carrying capacity of German aviation. The British persistently, often irrationally, believed in the decisive advantages of strategic bombing, claiming, as Churchill told Stalin in August 1942, that England "would pay our way by bombing Germany," although it was even by then obvious that strategic bombing was far less effective militarily than had been originally supposed, and that it also created profoundly dangerous consequences that greatly augmented the barbarism of modern warfare.[4]

The United States shared much of the British illusion regarding strategic bombing and the use of increasingly expensive systems of delivering firepower, having fallen under the hypnotic sway of what a Pentagon analyst later dubbed "maximum technological substitution" for manpower—a trend that was already the principal attribute of twentieth-century warfare.[5] But the Americans could also afford conventional land warfare, and their protraction of the war beyond the time the English desired produced bitter conflicts between them on questions of grand strategy. But the problem that both confronted was that strategic bombing, at best, prolonged a war and was inherently slow—a fact that only intensified Germany's need to exploit conquered Europe in order to continue fighting without abandoning its domestic priorities. At worst, strategic bombing was essentially a costly failure militarily, and generated a degree of barbarism and random death among noncombatants that far exceeded anything known prior to World War Two. No later than the end of 1940 the British realized that their original plan to destroy only oil and transport facilities was not succeeding, and that their bombs were either not sufficiently destructive or they missed their targets; moreover, three-quarters of each month the intended targets were not visible at night, which was when most British bombers operated after April 1940. In July 1941 they initiated area bombing designed to ruin morale and destroy essentially urban civilian areas. By the end of the war the vast bulk of Anglo-American bombing was virtually "blind," intended for general urban rather than specific military targets— and, as we shall see, it inflicted astonishingly little damage on the latter but killed hundreds of thousands of civilians and wounded or made refugees of many millions more.

The U.S. simply adopted British reasoning and procedures, which were irrefutable once one accepted the basic assumption that strategic bombing warranted a high commitment of money and manpower and could succeed militarily on its own terms, but it also carried airpower's logic to its ultimate conclusion. Prior to the invasion of Normandy in June 1944, Britain's leaders sought to stop or forestall the massive bombing of French rail yards, which they thought might produce many more victims than the British suffered from German raids on England. As many as 160,000 Frenchmen could be killed or wounded, they argued, but American planners dismissed their concerns. Indeed, French railroad workers played an especially prominent role in the Resistance and were now being designated as prime targets, and even though the estimates of projected deaths were reduced greatly, the British still objected strongly to even 16,000 allies killed or seriously injured. But the Americans prevailed. "Terrible things are being done," Churchill wrote to Anthony Eden at the end of May—yet they were the inexorable logic of a strategic concept the British had designed and that now had passed out of their control.[6]

For the British as well as the Germans, the war had become one of frustrated expectations and profoundly disturbing surprises—as all wars are and forever will be—that inevitably led all sides to draconian escalation.

## The German Response

The failure of Barbarossa compelled Hitler and his key advisers to reconsider their simplistic strategy, for by the end of 1941 the nature of the war had altered completely and his sanguine expectations were now proven to be patently illusory. Their responses, however, comprised a strange combination of bureaucratic inertia and the protection of vested interests, continued myopia, and serious efforts to resolve the urgent material problems of the war—impulses that to varying degrees neutralized one another. The Nazi war machinery and effort is therefore not easy to fathom, and no rational economic (as opposed to political) explanation of it can be formulated because the incremental, ad hoc manner in which it emerged defied institutional rationality; what is clear, however, was its consistent human and political consequences for the European population, who suffered terribly.

Since Hitler and his closest advisers never really trusted the German masses and did not want them to pay in sweat and blood the price that total war might exact, lest it provoke a repetition of the upheavals of 1918, civilian output was maintained until 1944, and much of the prewar Nazi labor mobilization policy remained intact. "The German leaders were not disposed to make sacrifices themselves or to ask sacrifices of the people," Albert Speer later complained.[7] Hitler wanted to have everything at once, he concluded: civilian goods, military equipment, grandiose monuments, and much else, and he thereby became an obstruction to a rationalized war effort—which Speer attempted to organize. His regional *gauleiters* fought to insulate the many territories they administered, with all their vested interests. Above all, Hitler confused facts or ignored those that undermined his key preconceptions, and made crucial decisions in utter ignorance and often without consulting his abler generals. He declared war on the United States on December 11, 1941, without asking the army's opinion, and he always retained a frivolous attitude toward American power.

The Nazis' economic antidote for the consequences of their refusal to impose hardships on Germans comparable to those of 1914–18 was to escalate the barbarism they inflicted on conquered Europe. Hitler no later than November 1941 embraced the principle of integrating the Continent's labor force into the war effort, and over the winter, when he realized the war would not be a short one, the program for extracting the maximum possible from Europe's people and economic resources was greatly intensified. It was in this context, and to some vital degree for these material reasons rather than exclusively racist ideological proclivities (which merely legitimized and reinforced economic necessities), that the Nazis traumatized Europe's people, unleashing a level of terror and brutality unknown in modern history.

There was no detailed Nazi master blueprint for administering Europe after they conquered it, and recent scholarship rightfully assigns more weight to its improvised and ad hoc nature in specific places. But whatever variations or lapses in total repression and exploitation that occurred, there is also no doubt that the Nazis possessed a general vision of what they would do with the vanquished nations. Once it became clear the war would take far more time and resources than Hitler had anticipated, it was virtually certain that Germany's needs would make its occupation policies increasingly repressive.

Apart from hazy Nazi plans for creating *Lebensraum* for the German people in eastern Europe, which implied the removal of the non-Aryan population either by mass expulsions or killings, and the need to exploit the occupied countries for the war, there was also an equally indefinite Nazi vision of a postwar integrated European economy: a "New Order" with a customs union, a more rationalized industrial structure that avoided competitive waste and imposed an efficient division of labor, and a common market. Since Hitler was anxious that the army not gain total control over the conquered nations, chiefs of civil administrations, some of whom were senior Nazi party functionaries or responsible to powerful interests at home, existed alongside the military authorities. Independent police organizations paralleled each other, and the S.S. penetrated various nations only by stages. There was, therefore, generally a calculated tension and often open rivalries between numerous German civil and military agencies, with their competing claims and jurisdictions, but even where they strove to create bureaucratic fiefdoms, many soon realized that their own staffs' paucity of personnel and knowledge required them to rely heavily on existing local ruling political and economic authorities, including the police. All local laws that did not contradict Nazi regulations remained in force.

Ironically, the army was more prepared to work with traditional local elites to install a pragmatic functioning administration; the S.S. and Nazis in the diplomatic service were far more inclined for ideological reasons to give indigenous fascists significant responsibilities, for which they were poorly equipped. And it was precisely the fissiparous, competitive nature of the German occupation regimes, their internal tensions, their inexperience, and the fear of many of its leaders of being shipped off to the eastern front if they failed as administrators, that gave the vanquished elites and entrepreneurs leverage to manipulate their new masters—and even profit from them. In western Europe, in any case, the Nazis intended to be less repressive than in the east, notwithstanding vague plans eventually to annex and merge substantial areas of Belgium, France, and Holland into a greater *Reich*.[8]

Denmark excepted, Nazi policies toward occupied Europe incorporated quite different degrees of repression within an overall policy of exploiting people and resources thoroughly; from the inception in eastern Europe, they intended for racist reasons to utterly destroy existing social systems and crucial sectors of the local populations, eventually to kill or exile them. In western Europe the Germans sought immediately to drain the economies for their own needs, repression being more a means than an end in itself. But the timing and form these goals took in each nation depended to some extent on a variety of factors, including haphazard ones, and the pressures that the war imposed. These war-induced necessities caused the Nazis in western Europe to cross the line into barbarism and engage in policies of deprivation that produced mass suffering and death in ways that they originally had never intended.

Denmark alone was spared the worst horrors until late 1943 because of a split within the local S.S. and a military administration composed until late 1942 of pragmatic officers who were loath to crack down on the people. The Danes held a genuinely free election in March 1943, in which they voted over 90 percent for democratic parties (including Social Democrats), and shortly thereafter local German officials successfully sabotaged Berlin's long-delayed efforts to round up the Jewish population. While Denmark was unique, it highlighted the fact that if senior German officials sought to mitigate the worst Nazi measures, the results could be quite significant for some time, and also that the Germans in charge of occupation regimes were indeed frequently seriously divided. The military governors of both France and Belgium actively favored the conservative German officers' attempt on Hitler's life in July 1944 and were arrested at that time.

After Denmark, Belgium was the least traumatized of the occupied nations, in part because German organizations there often had mutually conflicting economic goals, and especially because of the military governor, General Alexander von Falkenhausen, a conservative aristocrat who attempted to forestall as much as possible the more irrational Nazi racial and political goals. Moreover, since his military administration never had more than 1,000 Germans with which to guide the nation, he had by necessity to rely on Belgians—which gave them some leverage in deciding how (and for whom) the nation would be organized. Falkenhausen, to quote an authoritative critical account of Belgium during the war, "was without doubt the most humane and essentially decent head of any nazi occupation government."[9] But even he could not resist the centralizing economic edicts coming from Berlin, which intensified the pillage of the nation. Although the Belgians had the consolation of newspapers that could print some real news until 1943, or universities that still functioned fairly normally in most fields, in 1943 they nonetheless also had to send 29 percent of their total output to Germany—and even more if other transfers are calculated.

In France, whose northern industrial *départements* were run from Brussels, the struggles among competing German organizations and interests also allowed some Frenchmen to take advantage of the sometimes large interstices in the occupier's administration, and the Vichy-run south was insulated from the occupation until the end of 1942. The German ambassador, whose wife was French, was a nominal Francophile whom Berlin distrusted, notwithstanding his strong Nazi credentials, and he unquestionably made life easier for *certain* Frenchmen—albeit a small minority.

Such variations in the way Nazis went about their terrible business were significant even in Poland, though their explicit goal was eventually to destroy Warsaw and its population and settle it with a small number of Germans. The German occupation agencies in Poland, however, were at least as embroiled in rivalries as those in western Europe, also reducing their overall repressive efficiency to a degree that allowed *some* Poles to gain time and sustenance. Moreover, there were major pockets of corruption among the Germans, and this too aided a small number of Poles. Nonetheless, as everyone knows and as we shall see later in greater detail, the Nazi rule in Poland was genocidal in the aggregate, however many loopholes existed to favor a small minority. There was a decisive difference between Nazi policies in eastern and western Europe, whatever the superficial similarities in German organizational politics in each place. For a Nazi occupation policy existed, if defined only in terms of ultimate objectives and racial doctrine, and it began with the very different degrees of brutality planned for the two major geographic regions, growing worse everywhere as Germany began to lose the war.

In brief, if administratively the Nazi occupation of Europe was never a model of institutional rationality or efficiency, it nonetheless accomplished—albeit not as well as it might have—one fundamental objective: to mobilize prodigious amounts of goods and labor. Had the Nazis not been able to ravage the Continent thoroughly, the war would have ended much earlier; their only alternative to pillage was a breakdown in the German army comparable to that of 1918 or, less likely but still possible, far more open domestic opposition to the war.

### Exploiting Europe
The Nazis expected the conquered nations to provide considerably more foodstuffs than they were able to obtain, but they still marshaled huge quantities. Their grain, meat, fats, potato, and sugar imports from eastern

and southeastern Europe increased three to over five times from 1937 to 1942–43, and in the latter year meat imports from this devastated area alone equaled 25 percent of German domestic production. Food imports from western Europe also grew substantially, although not by the same factor, so that by 1942–43 over one-quarter of all of Germany's food was imported; this does not include the food consumption of millions of Germans in the occupying forces, or significant amounts of food they personally delivered to their families in Germany.

Even though it took considerably more food from Russia before then, by 1943, France was Germany's single largest source of plunder. But the French also had crucial raw materials and manufacturing facilities to exploit, and the Nazis seized at least 155 billion (1938) francs' worth of booty—most of it military, transport, and communications equipment. That it intended bleeding France is clear both from our knowledge of German plans and from the actual results, which became increasingly devastating. Like the Belgians and others, the French were required to pay Nazi occupation costs—fixed at 400 million francs daily in their case—and no matter what exchange rate is utilized, France after 1940 gave far more than the real occupation expenses, so that a surplus equivalent to about 2 to 4 percent of the entire German gross national product accrued annually as a profit from French payments alone. Depending again on the exchange rates employed, France in 1943 and 1944 provided Germany anywhere from 24 to 37 percent of the equivalent of its national income or total products available in 1938. Total French output for Germany increased sevenfold between 1940 and 1943, and by 1943 Germany was utilizing at least 40 percent of France's total existing resources. But by 1943 Belgium, Holland, and the other occupied nations' combined trade deficits with Germany probably more than exceeded France's. And the per capita burden of occupation taxes the Germans imposed in Greece was five times the French level. The conquered nations, in sum, in 1942–43 paid for about 40 percent of Nazi war costs, heavily underwriting Hitler's efforts to maintain Germany's living standards, and sustaining his war at a far higher level than otherwise would have been possible.

While there were innumerable dimensions of the Nazi exploitation of Europe essential to its war effort, some technically impossible to assess accurately, there can be no question that the use of foreign civilian workers and prisoners of war in Germany itself was crucial both to its capacity to make war and to the eventual emergence of resistance among the captive peoples. Foreign labor constituted under 1 percent of the labor force in Germany in 1939, but 21 percent (7.5 million persons) in September 1944. Of these, 1.8 million were prisoners of war. Frenchmen were the largest single component in this massive body, but there were almost as many Russians, and together they comprised about 3 million persons—well over one-third of the total.

At the beginning of the war, some foreign labor went to Germany voluntarily, often to escape unemployment at home, and significant numbers of Dutch and Belgian workers who lived near the borders commuted to Germany daily and are not included among the 7.5 million. Also ignored are those who worked for German military construction firms in France—by late 1942 about 108,000 Dutchmen fell in both these categories. Many volunteers were pushed into making such choices, however, because they were denied unemployment compensation if they refused work abroad, and after May 1942 the Nazis began to aggressively ship forced labor to Germany, causing many to volunteer first. Most, however, were drafted against their wills, especially after 1941.

The problem for the Nazis was that foreign laborers in Germany were less productive than German workers; the French were the best of the lot, the Dutch and Danes being extremely inefficient. While French workers were more productive in Germany than in France, this was largely due to the poor state of French industry, and many skilled Belgian coal miners were employed against their will in marginal tasks in the *Reich*. In the spring of 1943, purely for reasons of efficiency, a deeply divided German bureaucracy agreed to bring fewer forced workers to Germany, especially skilled labor, and instead attempted to raise productivity in western Europe. By that time, however, the fate of captive labor was too well known and many men disappeared to avoid deportation; a portion of them eventually became part of the organized Resistance.[10]

## The Impact on the People

### Germany

There was a monumental disparity in the war's impact on Europe's people; the difference was between life and death, between perturbed but essentially still normal living conditions for many and the edge of the abyss of destruction for countless others. The worst suffering was in the Jewish ghettos, next came the Greek cities, and then the Dutch cities from late 1944 on. On the Continent, however, German civilians endured far less than those in any other nation, and Hitler's objective of insulating them from the war's overwhelming pain was successful in terms of food, notwithstanding the enormous dislocations and death that Anglo-American bombing produced. The Nazis thereby transferred most of the war's countless hardships to the ultimately "victorious" people of Europe as well as to their own allies, and the war's grave political and social, as well as catastrophic human consequences quite predictably reflected this pervasive reality.

Hitler and most of his inner circle simply refused to condone a major reduction in civilian consumption until the war was almost over, but even then made significant exceptions. When, in early 1942, Albert Speer was given what proved a limited power over the war economy, he discovered that only 37.5 percent of Germany's crude steel production was going into the war effort—a full 9 percent less than during the First World War. He attempted to reverse the policy against employing more women, but met a stone wall of resistance from his superiors, and in fact the payments to soldiers' wives were so high that they had scant incentive to work. He could not even do much about the 1.4 million women employed as domestic servants, or over 100,000 Ukrainian women also cleaning German homes. In 1942 civilian production was 95 percent of the 1938 level (Britain's was 79 percent by contrast) and still 93 percent two years later. But imports made up for much, if not all, of this slight decline. The drop in consumer goods and services per capita in Germany from 1938 to 1944 may have exceeded Britain's 16 percent decrease somewhat, but principally because of conditions in the last two years of the war.

Hitler insisted upon the continuation of civilian output, extending even to cosmetics, but in February 1943, aware that its troops' immense sacrifices could no longer quietly be juxtaposed against luxuries at home, a hesitant Nazi leadership publicly endorsed a "total war" effort involving a more abstemious life-style for the privileged—and then proceeded to create ample loopholes so that the Nazi elite and those who profited from the war could continue much as before. Even a year later, as the war began to destroy the ostentatiously affluent idyll the Nazi rulers had enjoyed, many elite members still savored their little pleasures, or voyaged to Vienna for sumptuousness in the grand tradition.

The usual statistical measures do not tell the full story of the black-market economy or of the food and goods that family members brought home from occupied nations, much less reveal the inequalities among consumers that all averages conceal. As in every country of Europe, peasants supplied the black market, and with time it became a major factor in nutrition. Even ignoring these caveats, it is nonetheless clear that the Nazi social policy largely attained its material and, above all, political goals. Real weekly net income in German industry in 1942 peaked at 24 percent higher than 1932, and even in 1944 it was 19 percent above 1932. Among the European nations, British real income alone grew during the final years of the war, but it had been stable or had fallen after 1932, and the German working class was unique in enjoying long-term growth and a significant degree of prosperity. The Nazis also managed to keep prices fairly constant—far more so than Britain and the United States at the same time, and certainly as compared to the vertiginous German experience from 1913 through 1918.

The Nazi labor policy revealed how small a burden Hitler chose to impose on the German people, especially the middle and upper classes, when compared to the Nazi practices in the rest of Europe. For both ideological reasons and to increase the birth rate, women were encouraged to leave the labor market after 1933, and although the German male civilian labor force dropped by nearly 11 million from 1939 through 1944, the number of employed women remained virtually constant over the same period. Huge numbers of men were given draft exemptions—5 million in early 1942—to sustain the economy, and of the 830,000 men in the Waffen-S.S. in March 1945, only 40 percent were German nationals. Not until January 1943 did legislation for the total mobilization of labor even exist, and it was never fully applied, particularly to women.

Hours of work differed considerably in various industries, especially for skilled workers in war plants, but the overall average for male workers in all industries, which had been 46.8 hours per week in 1929, was 49.6 hours in 1939 and 51.6 in 1941. By 1944 the average had fallen to 51.2 hours because factories had been destroyed or there were raw materials shortages, and British men were working three hours more. Taking the hours of men and women combined, however, in 1944 they worked the same length as in 1938, and 1.5 hours less than in 1941. The far longer time that foreign labor in Germany spent, not to mention their welfare, was an altogether different matter—the appalling death rate among them is well known. But notwithstanding its significant co-optive efforts, over the last years of the war the Nazis also enforced disciplinary rules among German workers much more rigorously to maintain or increase productivity; arrests for avoidance of work increased by over half from 1941 to early 1944, and by July 1944 at least 87,000 workers had been imprisoned for violating work norms. Anyone uttering anything hinting of defeatism could be punished also, including by death—and many were, especially after 1943.

German food output during the war is only a partial indication of civilian consumption, but unlike in 1914–18 it did not collapse catastrophically and, above all, the Nazis also imported vast amounts from conquered nations. In 1943 the German grain harvest was 88 percent of that of 1939, and not until 1943–44 did potato production fall dramatically, although still far less than it had during World War One. Estimates of food consumption must be confined to rations as opposed to real intakes, for the latter included both private imports and the black market, neither of which can be quantified accurately. Although a significant drop in meat and fats lowered the quality of German food rations between 1938 and 1942, the average caloric consumption remained much higher than in 1914–18. Still, German food rations, even in 1944 when the food system was worst off, were 83 percent of normal for all adult males but much higher for nearly all of the other categories, and by far the highest on the Continent and comparable only to Britain's. France's ration, by comparison, was only 47 percent of normal for adult males. But many German workers also had access to nonrationed food, and the League of Nations estimated that in 1944 the daily caloric intake of workers was actually slightly higher than it had been before the war. Even allowing for inadequacies in the data, the relative well-being of Germany compared to the rest of Europe remains undeniable. Excluding Poland and the USSR, occupied Europe's rationed food supply (measured by the calorific value of standard rations, excluding private imports) was 66 percent of Germany's in 1941 and 75 percent in 1944; Poland's was far lower. "The German people ought not to do any griping," Goebbels reflected in February 1942; "they still have a standard of living that is impossible in any other country of Europe, whether in the war or not."[11]

## Belgium

Although the Belgian people ostensibly suffered less than most of the population of the conquered nations of Europe or of Germany's allies, and certainly far less than the French or the Dutch, they still underwent a torment that traumatized a significant fraction of the population. Their experience was complex, but also terrible.

It is quite misleading to look only at existing statistics, for ultimately they cannot explain much about the convoluted nature of the occupation or the Belgian responses to it. The nominal Belgian rations do not tell a great deal; by 1944 they were lower than the Dutch rations but much higher than the French. In any event, they were insufficient to sustain healthy life even if they could be purchased, which was often not the case. Production of the main cereals remained fairly stable during the war, but potatoes fell by a third immediately, and meat by two-thirds in 1944. The nation's plight would have immediately been grave were it not for the fact that the Germans in Brussels also administered the two food-rich French *départements* of Nord and Pas-de-Calais, which supplied most of Belgium's large cereal imports as well as providing ingenious Belgian black marketeers a larger arena for peculations and partially compensated for the rapacious Nazi procurement policies.

The black-market economy was probably more important in Belgium than in any other nation in Europe, and impressionistic accounts of the wartime economy and living standards are more informative than the statistics usually offered. The black market, however, was at first largely an effective German method for pillaging the economy and shipping consumer goods home. But it quickly also prevented them from maximizing Belgium's potential as a war economy, and from this viewpoint it was irrational. We will see later how the black market forced the worst aspects of human behavior to come to the fore on a mass scale, but throughout the war there were far fewer queues to obtain food in Belgium than in France. While speculators and wholesale black marketeers emerged to organize the nominally illegal traffic, and then to acquire substantial real estate holdings at bargain prices, the still-significant peasantry as a whole, as everywhere, contributed more goods to the black market and prospered more than any other broad class from the war. Apart from eating normally themselves, their relatives (as in most other countries) also had access to significant amounts of food. In very unequal ways, black-market consumption involved nearly the entire nation and reduced the prospect of general starvation—but for many this was scarcely sufficient to prevent hunger or to neutralize the effects of German policies.

The Germans took their huge monthly occupation levy and bought whatever they desired at black-market prices, thereby creating rampant inflation and, in effect, institutionalizing the black market. Vast amounts of consumer and luxury goods went to Germany in this fashion, and German agencies competed with each other for finite quantities, thereby also diverting Belgian efforts from militarily crucial industries into consumer wares. It did not take long for industry to begin to decline, and workers fell into deepening poverty, notwithstanding the access some had to the black market or to farmers. The coal industry was most crucial to Nazi war efforts, but its output fell dramatically in 1942 as miners began working for farmers part-time or quit mining altogether. And the lack of coal hobbled steel and other basic industries. By 1944, with their caloric intake at least 20 to 30 percent below prewar diets, most workers no longer had the stamina to produce; food shortages reached crisis proportions for the working class and the economy was operating at least one-third below prewar levels. While Belgium was better off than France, and the most privileged sector of it had access to many luxuries, a large portion of the nation was subjected to the same intense privations that ravaged most of western Europe.[12]

### France

The overriding reality confronting the French after May 1940 was that the Nazis installed a competitive, wasteful administrative structure devoted to exploiting the country intensively, not only to feed the Wehrmacht occupiers but also to provide for one-third of its food needs elsewhere, even while depriving France access to its two food-rich *départements* bordering Belgium. The initial German-occupied zone—which was expanded to include the remainder of the country after November 1942—had a majority of the prewar farmers and agricultural output, and 64 percent of the entire population. Allied bombing and the invasion of June 1944 further disrupted transport, and the area subjected to destruction in World War Two was at least twice as large as that during 1914–18.

France's farmers lacked fertilizers and equipment, and using 1938 as a base of 100, all agricultural production fell to 76 in 1941, 71 in 1944, and 64 in 1945. Meat declined much more than crops, but in 1944 the latter were one-fifth below the 1938 level—and from all this the Germans exacted their needs. Industrial production by 1941 fell to 65 percent of the 1938 level, and it slid consistently to 41 percent in 1944.

While theoretical rations are a very rough gauge of reality, in 1944 the adult male's ration was 47 percent of his requirements, or almost half the German norm, and for all French consumers it was 1,135 calories daily in 1944 compared to 2,000 in Germany. In 1944 this ration was only 18 percent of the prewar consumption level for meat, 31 percent for fat, and 70 percent for bread. The drop in real food intake, unquestionably the steepest in western Europe, is much more difficult to estimate, but amounted to at least one-third on the average. Meat consumption went from 41 kilos per person in 1938 to 16 in 1944, sugar from 24 to 10, potatoes from 415 to 196, and milk products from 241 liters to 139. But averages mean little in the French context, except to highlight the fact that the population as a whole was receiving far less food than it required; regional and class differences, as throughout all of Europe, are crucial to comprehending what really happened.

While declining output and German exactions preordained food deficits, the breakdown of transport to a critical extent determined which cities and regions suffered most. Cities in areas of agricultural surplus that were unable to ship to their prewar markets were far better supplied than any others. Shortages in Paris and Toulouse often reached crisis proportions, and Dijon, Lyon, Marseille, Montpellier, Nancy, Orléans, and Reims were worse off than Bordeaux, Limoges, Rennes, Rouen, Lille, and Clermont-Ferrand, which even had occasional food gluts. Eventually, the relationship of geography to production and transport showed up in mortality rates, which declined or remained stable in most *départements* with a food surplus but rose sharply in industrial cities. Ironically, in the wealthy *arrondissements* of Paris the mortality rate rose far more sharply than among the poor during the winter months because the rich could not heat their much larger apartments with the scanty uniform fuel ration.

While data on prices and real incomes are less than adequate, some essential trends are clear. By 1941 prices for foodstuffs had increased more than 50 percent on the whole, but the price of potatoes had more than doubled. By 1944 they cost about triple the 1939 amount, but the cost of services rose much more slowly. Workers in war industries that produced for the Nazis were better paid than others; laborers spent more of their budgets for food, and if their wives were not employed their basic food costs consumed nearly all of their income, or in some cases even exceeded it. The real income of the average Parisian worker with a family of four in 1941–43 was at least one-third lower than in 1938.

Coping with this monumental shortage produced winners and losers and polarized French society, radically altering personal behavior and the relationship of countless individuals to their communities. The peasantry, marginalized economically before the war and slowly disappearing, immediately assumed a crucial role in the economy, and initially various Resistance organizations urged them not to make food deliveries to the German and Vichy authorities. Peasants unquestionably sent or gave food to their urban relations and friends, and as much as 10 to 15 percent of their total output may have been distributed this way. More important, however, they consumed about two-fifths of their total output (meats especially), up from one-fifth of a larger prewar output but still considerably more in absolute terms. Estimates of the amounts they channeled into the official distribution system vary, but a small part of their meat went into it, much more butter and pulses, but probably 60 to 90 percent of all food products remained outside the rationing structure, depending on the item, and this portion supplied German exactions and the approximately one-fifth of the total food output that the black market handled. In 1943–44, over one-third of French meat production was shipped to Germany, about double the 1941–42 share. The peasants, especially those favored with access to urban markets, were the only class to emerge from the war better off as a whole than when it began; many of them behaved as both benefactors and exploiters, but in some cases they were principally one or the other. Very similar patterns appeared in other nations.[13]

The occupation immediately spawned a stratum of entrepreneurs, many of them food wholesalers before the war and in contact with producers as well as with access to transport, who began to take advantage of the potential windfalls, and the Nazis preferred to work through them. In time, the black market attracted countless others, ranging from outright criminals to individuals with helpful relatives in the nearby countryside. And although there were black marketeers who functioned on a large scale and made fortunes, the demand was so extensive that plenty of small entrepreneurs seeking essentially to make their own straitened condition more bearable also trafficked. At the highest level, Germans often played a crucial role with documents, goods to sell, transport, and the like, and their corruption or sanction was essential for the major black-market operators. Germany spent at least 95 billion francs in the black market; half came from soldiers, but the remainder from German procurement agencies rounding up luxuries for consumption in Germany. But in July 1943 nearly all of Paris complained of food shortages, and over two-thirds of the city by necessity used the black market to supplement their rations, which were utterly inadequate for survival, while a far smaller proportion obtained real luxuries. With a black market so vast, it was inevitable that thievery would increase dramatically, ranging from a seventy-year-old woman stealing a veal chop to men digging up a farmer's potatoes to criminal riffraff entering the trade. Between 1938 and 1942 convictions for theft increased more than three times. After D-Day in June 1944, the black market in American cigarettes, C-rations, and gasoline reached what the U.S. Army described as "the proportions of big business," and scarcities kept it alive until 1946.[14]

### The Netherlands

Despite onerous German taxation, the Dutch economy until 1944 was affected far less than the French, and rationing provided a higher share of human needs than in Belgium. Even in 1944, workers' diets, while somewhat below prewar standards, were still among the highest in occupied Europe. Until 1944, Dutch agriculture had managed fairly well, increasing potato production significantly to compensate for a sharp drop in meat output. But industrial output in 1943 fell to 63 percent of the 1940 high, and plummeted to 41 percent for the whole of 1944.

During the final months of 1944, as the Germans prepared to defend, and then retreated from, the country, they opened dikes and flooded huge areas in the process, confiscating most of the transport, and the Dutch economy broke down in ways unprecedented in western Europe. The creation of the first real black market did little to relieve the crisis. The regime introduced three different regional rationing systems in November 1944, and the northeast suffered the least. The west was allotted 1,120 calories a day, but the following February the ration was cut by half to a true starvation level. The southern region began with 690 calories, but it was the first to be liberated. Meanwhile, the urban belt from Amsterdam to Rotterdam starved, and although estimates differ, the famine probably resulted in 25,000 or more deaths in Amsterdam alone. By any criterion, the consequences were catastrophic.[15]

In southern and eastern Europe the Nazis felt no restraints whatsoever, and the enormous suffering they imposed was the direct consequence of both their racist objectives and their avaricious needs. In western Europe they were both rapacious and inefficiently organized, but the immense damage they inflicted was less intentional than simply the unavoidable consequences of their greed and stupidity, which ineluctably spread calamities in its wake; in the case of Holland, it was their military desperation alone that caused them to abandon their remaining inhibitions on criminal behavior in a manner unprecedented in the region.

### Italy

The Germans did not occupy Italy until Mussolini was overthrown on July 25, 1943, by which time the nation's economy was declining, only to be traumatized when Axis and Allied armies battled to near the center of the nation, with the food-rich north remaining in Nazi and Fascist hands until the war was virtually over. The amount of rationed food, which provided a modicum of assurance to everyone, was greater than in Poland in terms of percentage of normal prewar consumption, but actually lower in absolute quantities—for the Poles had eaten more. Prewar Italy had been a large food importer, and until 1942–43 juggled its food production in nonmeats and fats to sustain consumption, but although the quantities of available meats and fats dropped by over half during the last two years of the war, the other foods on hand were still close to normal; average consumption levels in Italy until the Allied invasion in August 1943 fell only 6 percent. In effect, Italy's basic problems resulted principally from the combat's effects on the distribution system and its creation of a growing refugee problem rather than from an actual lack of adequate food production.

The wartime distribution system in Italy as elsewhere therefore increasingly depended on personal contacts and the black market. At the beginning of 1944 there was a great deal more food in the Nazi-held north than in the Anglo-American–controlled south (where 200,000 refugees existed in the U.S.-controlled area alone by spring 1944) even though Italy's industrial production—largely located in the north—had plummeted so that in 1944 it was nearly one-third of what it had been in 1940, and the following year close to a quarter. American planners greatly underestimated the gravity of the transport breakdown their invasion would cause; there were gluts and grave shortages simultaneously. In Naples, for example, they found that "the lower and middle classes . . . are not far from starvation," and the medical consequences of malnutrition began to endanger the Allied armies, forcing them to import relief supplies to cope with hunger and to stamp out typhus and venereal diseases.[16] But the distribution experience was also very similar to that in France or Belgium: rural Italy ate as well as before the war, or better, and in late 1943 it held back nearly two-fifths of the remaining food from the legal distribution system. A significant portion of it ended up in the hands of relatives and friends in cities, but about 15 percent of all agricultural production at the end of 1943 went into the black market one way or another.

When combat caused the entire Italian food system to break down, spiraling inflation resulted. From 1941 to 1944, prices increased nearly ninefold, and then doubled again in 1945. The real wages of industrial workers in 1944 were one-quarter of those in 1941, and even less the following year. The food crisis was essentially an urban problem, for cities relied upon the black market for one-third of their food; by the winter and spring of 1944 massive Allied imports provided rations to over four-fifths of those in the liberated areas, especially those in the cities and towns, who obtained at least half their food from Allied-supplied stocks. The spring 1944 harvests greatly alleviated shortages, save in the large cities, where the black market remained crucial. But most of the nation still remained under Nazi rule, and suffered.[17]

## Greece

Further to the east in Europe, the war's human impact became increasingly terrible, and the agony deepened. The very notion of qualitatively greater tragedy is scarcely permissible, because those who experienced the brunt of the war in France or Holland felt unprecedented torment, but in Greece and Poland the sheer numbers were proportionately far greater, and Poland underwent the ultimate inhumanity.

Greece's anguish was principally the outcome of the Italian, German, and then Bulgarian invasions, but its own black marketeers exploited their fellow countrymen in ways that drastically compounded the effects of Nazi policies. Prewar Greece imported about two-fifths of its wheat, and this it essentially lost. By 1941 its grain harvest was more than one-quarter below the 1934–38 average, and in 1943 it fell to half of the prewar level. Notwithstanding German exactions, however, there often were sufficient fruits and vegetables—which mitigated somewhat the grim basic-foods shortages. While, as elsewhere, the breakdown of the transport system meant that areas with food surpluses usually could not ship them to where they were most needed, Bulgaria also retained the substantial excess grain output in the area it occupied.

The Nazi authorities immediately imposed what was probably the highest per capita occupation tax in Europe, and Greece's officials responded by printing money. By November 1941 the number of drachmas in circulation was 4.6 times greater than in December 1939, 21 times by September 1942, 114 times more by August 1943, and anywhere from 6,500 to 50,000 times larger by June 1944—producing the worst inflation of any occupied European nation. Hyperinflation wiped out much of the real income of employed workers, not to mention the significant numbers who were unemployed, destroyed all bank savings, and profoundly affected much of the middle class.

The immediate consequence of these factors was mass starvation, principally in the Athens region and the Aegean Islands. Approximately 360,000 of Greece's 7.2 million 1940 population died of hunger during the war, comprising over half the nation's total human losses, most of them during the winter 1941–42 famine. The death rate, which drove countless urbanites to rural areas and helped prepare the way for the Resistance, stunned the Nazis in 1942 into allowing the resumption of significant imports—including even German grain stocks—to raise domestic consumption. Greece and Belgium were the only two occupied nations to maintain net imports, albeit small ones, of grain, fats, and meats from Germany during the war. The Nazis even agreed to pay back their troop requisitions in the form of other sources of calories, which ended by being twice what they took. But Greece's black market was far more developed than those in most other captured nations, and it was to remain crucial much longer. Utterly ruthless speculators gravely compounded the nation's calamities, making fortunes from their control over supplies, which they frequently kept off the market in expectation of rising prices. A significant portion of the prewar elite and wealthier classes were compelled to liquidate much of their property in order to buy food on the black market; as in the rest of Europe, peasants were better able to survive, and a significant portion even prospered. Indeed, after the German defeats in North Africa in November 1942, with the threat of their being driven from Greece, food hoarders dumped their stocks on the market and for some months prices actually fell or stabilized—only to resume their heady climb the following summer.[18]

## Poland
The Nazis always intended to extract as much from Poland's economy as they required, without any concern whatsoever for the long-term consequences. Indeed, exploiting it was also one way of fulfilling their ultimate design for destroying the Polish elite and intelligentsia, particularly those in cities. But unlike in most of western Europe, the war left Polish agriculture quite intact: Polish rye production during 1940–44 was comparable to that of the mid-1930s, excepting bumper years, and potato harvests were greater than before the war, as was sugar beet production. Since there were no food shortages at home, the German collection agencies enforced the grain quotas laxly the first year, and actually shipped more grain to Poland in 1939–40 than they removed; during the first two years they exported only about a tenth of the grain they gathered. Thereafter, the quotas were 90 percent collected, and while in 1942–43 about half of it was sent to Germany, its troops on the eastern front probably consumed the greater part of wartime-commandeered grain and meat. But the Nazis also diverted a portion of it into the black market. The Nazis milked Poland mainly during 1942–44, yet their total grain acquisitions in the four years beginning in 1940 were only about 12 percent of the nation's total production of rye and wheat, not to mention barley and oats. They were principally eager to obtain meat and fats, and did so even though they took more from far smaller Holland and over seven times as much from France. For the Germans had plenty of grain at home and ample sources until the war was virtually over, and this fact alone prevented an even greater Polish disaster.

Poland's problems were complicated because its prewar cereal and potato consumption was the highest per capita in Europe, and so its rations were a smaller share of the normal national diet than anywhere save France. Until early 1941, ration cards for non-Jews and Jews were identical, but thereafter Jewish allowances excluded meat and declined to about half the food value of provisions to non-Jews until the beginning of 1943, when rations for Jews not working for the Germans were abolished. More important, after 1941 Jews virtually ceased to have access to black-market food suppliers.

Daily caloric standards per person varied by age, sex, and the like, and while authorized rations were gravely deficient, even in 1943–44—Jews always apart—they were still higher than in France and Italy. Indeed, Polish allotments were considerably greater in absolute terms in 1944 than in 1943. But most people supplemented their quotas through the black market, which may have greatly exceeded rations as a source of food. Poland's catastrophic death rate, which ranked first in Europe, was principally the result of the Nazi decision to liquidate Poles and Jews through means other than starvation—which by itself would have killed incomparably fewer people.

The Polish experience during World War Two, like that in every other European nation, cannot be interpreted as uniform for all the people. In 1930, 66 percent of Poland's working population was employed in agriculture, and the Nazis believed this proportion was about the same in 1943. There can be no doubt that Nazi economic measures worked to the advantage of most peasants, especially those close to urban areas: food prices increased faster than others, debts to Jews were canceled, inflation wiped away many other obligations, and most compulsory food deliveries were postponed. Rural people began to eat more, and especially to drink more homemade wheat and potato alcohol. City dwellers came to them with whatever they had to trade for food: jewelry, household goods of every sort, and the like. Tension between the city and rural folk deepened, for the latter always retained a superior negotiating position and generally exploited it.

Virtually everyone participated in the black market in some fashion, for survival depended upon it, and the Nazis utilized it—as in Belgium and France—as a basic institutional mechanism for attaining very diverse objectives. Competing German agencies, as well as the Wehrmacht, attempted to procure essential goods or perhaps supplement their budgetary resources; also active were Germans who corruptly and illegally sought to gain private fortunes. Corruption was deeply endemic in the economy in all of its aspects. Germans channeled goods into the black market and aided it in various ways, in March 1942 authorizing those seeking food to travel between the cities and countryside to obtain nominally illegal supplies. For a price, virtually anything could be purchased. Germans and Poles alike used the black market systematically, continuously, and massively in ways that were convenient or necessary. Some Poles made fortunes, many millions died, but a great number of peasants also emerged from the war better off than when they had entered it.[19]

The basic goal of the Nazi food policy in Europe was to sustain the German civilian standard of living at prewar norms for as long as possible, and it succeeded. Within this overarching principle, however, there were obviously major differences in the Nazi strategies toward various countries, but in practice most of the nations experienced a great deal in common, and this determined to a crucial extent who would eat or starve throughout the Continent. Many German occupation and procurement authorities acted functionally rather than ideologically in mobilizing and exploiting conquered states, whether this involved food or the procurement of industrial products, raw materials, or taxes; the informal systems to obtain goods useful for the Nazi war effort or the German people's well-being sometimes also mitigated rationing's hardships. When the policy to liquidate large numbers of people for racial reasons was implemented after 1941, the control of food was a tool in this genocidal effort but it was far less important than outright murder and forced labor.

Those not designated for destruction suffered not only from the consequences of short rations but from the results of the European peasantry's mastery over decisive amounts of foodstuffs, their own black marketeers' total lack of social responsibility, and the basic fact that class relations, including innovative forms of exploitation in the hands of new people, defined who would eat—and how well. Throughout Europe the breakdown of transportation or the location of battle lines often had a significant influence on how all of these factors would play themselves out. To a considerable extent, the problems of food distribution in practice transcended initial Nazi objectives, which were carried out in a general, principally nonspecific manner and remained the core of the European peoples' grave difficulties but nonetheless must also be assessed in the larger, more complex context I have outlined here.

Europe's peasants showed great solidarity with their families and friends, but a large part of them were also ready to exploit the black market at the very same time. While data remains rudimentary, they probably allocated approximately equal resources to acting as saviors and as villains during the Continent's long night of terror and suffering. At a personal level, the war affected rural Europeans far less than it did the urban population, above all the working class. City and town dwellers ultimately condemned the Nazis for their misery, and rightly so, but they knew from constant experience that some of their own countrymen were also to blame for many of their misfortunes—and they could not forget everything they had seen and experienced.

## The War's General Consequences

### Migration and Population Redistribution

The calamity of war in Europe included, but also went far beyond, the obviously critical question of food. Given the Nazis' apocalyptic racial objectives and their massive reliance on forced labor, the destructive scope and duration of the war as it spread over vast areas, and the political settlements when the war ended, it was both predictable and inevitable that enormous numbers of civilians would be driven or uprooted from their homes and move to distant, essentially strange new regions. This vast wartime migration was accompanied by grave food shortages, disease, and impoverishment—suffering on a scale unprecedented in modern history.

It is impossible to describe the profundity and magnitude of this tragic upheaval, and the few examples that follow can be extended indefinitely. Between September 1939 and early 1943, at least 30 million Europeans were deported or fled from where they lived. This figure comprises 110,000 Rumanians pushed out of Bulgaria in 1941, 1.5 million Jews who succeeded in escaping Nazi-held Europe, 10 to 12 million Soviet citizens fleeing the German advances—and countless others. It includes the consequences of Nazi and Soviet territorial changes at the inception of the war but *not* of those the victorious Allies later imposed on the vanquished states. That an additional 28 million people lived in areas ceded to other nations only added to the subsequent pressures that displaced vast numbers. These titanic figures of victims of the conflict stagger the imagination, but are only the best existing estimates. For most of the people living under myriad threats of being forced to quit their homes, their very existences had become profoundly impermanent and this searing reality had monumental implications for their ideas and actions.

Two examples illustrate the nature of this cataclysm. When the Nazis entered Poland in 1939, they annexed 103,000 square kilometers, a significant part of which had been German before 1919. They drove about 1.65 million non-Jewish Poles out of the area, and replaced them with a much smaller number of *Volksdeutsche* who had settled in eastern Europe over earlier generations and had, to a large extent, assimilated with the local cultures. In France the exodus from the cities in May and June 1940 began after 2 million Belgian refugees poured across the northern border to escape the Nazi advance, generating a profound panic among Frenchmen that the Germans would destroy their cities—as they had Warsaw. The cities on the Belgian border virtually emptied, and a mass of people carrying their few possessions in carts or on bicycles, in autos for some, or often only on foot, moved toward the Paris region. The French government neither anticipated nor condoned the flight, but did nothing to prevent it from turning into a chaotic mass that blocked roads and quickly immobilized a large part of the French army. Millions of Parisians caught the fever and began to join it. Since no food had been put aside for such a wholly unexpected crisis, many of the pitiful, demoralized, and fearful refugees began looting abandoned houses and stealing, increasing the anarchy. As the people mixed with the army, Nazi planes began to attack their columns, compounding the panic.

A cautious estimate of the numbers of French who became refugees in

May and June of 1940, excluding those who stayed within their own *département* or went to their families, is about 6 million persons. By October over half this number had returned to their homes, and their lives slowly returned to what was now deemed normal under the occupation. The French exodus as a whole was largely temporary, save for nearly a half-million who remained in the Vichy-controlled area for the duration of the war. After 1941, about 1 million Frenchmen evacuated the Atlantic coastal areas.

Far more traumatic was the Nazi policy, which was essentially an incremental response to their failure to win the war, of bringing forced labor to Germany, which began initially with prisoners of war but soon spread to include civilians—at the beginning, mainly Poles. But the death rate among captured soldiers was 58 percent for Soviets, and the actual number of prisoners and laborers taken to Germany was much higher than the 7.5 million foreign workers in Germany in September 1944, for millions had also died there. By 1943, in addition, about 2 million more non-German civilians and soldiers worked for the Nazis elsewhere, mostly under compulsion, in countries other than their own. From 1.3 to 1.5 million Poles were sent to Germany, 85 percent as forced labor. A cascade of similar data for Holland, France, and many other countries only reinforces the basic point: Europe was being profoundly uprooted.

When the war ended, it was the Germans' turn to become refugees. There was a series of human tides, some overlapping. Millions of them fled the advance of the Red Army with whatever possessions they could carry, and from 1944 to 1947, 6 million Germans evacuated the German territory ceded to Poland. About 2.7 million ethnic Germans left Czechoslovakia for Germany or Austria in 1945–46. About 4 million crossed from the Soviet-occupied zone of Germany to West Germany, one-third of whose population in 1950 were born elsewhere. Here too the figures are repetitive, but they reinforce the conclusion that victors and vanquished alike were displaced to varying degrees, and the lives of those swept up in the maelstrom were profoundly affected. Together, the numbers were staggering, and without historical precedent.[20]

### Material Losses

The war's material destruction was terrible and awesome, but it is far more difficult to measure in statistical terms because criteria of economic values and real costs are inherently debatable; calculations on the costs of all wars vary greatly, and World War Two is no exception. The mere fact that in the four decades after 1945 the vanquished nations became much more powerful economically than they had been in 1938 is proof that physical devastation alone cannot destroy all of the factors that produce economic strength. The Nazis made the decision not to fight a war too taxing to their population lest they court rebellion, and they shifted the war's burdens to conquered Europe as much as possible. The triumphant nations chose or were forced to pay the economic price of victory and in the end their people, save in the United States, emerged poorer than the routed aggressors.

Throughout the war both Britain and the U.S. were heavily committed to strategic bombing, yet they remained unable to organize their air forces in ways that allowed airpower to paralyze the Nazi economy decisively. Germany's reliance on the industrial production of conquered nations offered it a partial way around its difficulties, but its own war economy peaked in the summer of 1944, and its railroad system was considerably more efficient in 1943 than in 1938. In 1945, Germany's machine-tool inventory was far larger than it had been in 1938, and it greatly exceeded any other European nation's stock—even rivaling that of the U.S. Hitler's initial refusal to mobilize his nation's people and economy to a greater extent was unquestionably far more significant than Allied bombing in causing him to lose the war.

The costs of America's strategic bombing attack on Germany included 40,000 dead U.S. airmen, 6,000 lost planes, and $43 billion in outlays, and by 1944 the notion that airpower could by itself attain decisive strategic goals had few adherents among American military leaders. The British lost even more planes and lives. By 1944, well over one-half of the bomb tonnage in Germany was being dropped on built up urban areas rather than on defined military targets, destroying housing and civilian lives with increasing frequency. The English, at least as much as the Americans, believed that there was literally nothing potentially decisive to do with this immensely expensive airpower save attack civilian objectives. The logic of this fixation culminated in the British air staff in August 1944 initiating preparations to break German morale by destroying entire cities, and the English provided 800 of the 1,400 sorties that set out to wreck Dresden and its population during February 13–15, 1945. At least 35,000 people were killed in that raid, and similar efforts subsequently followed elsewhere. The Nazis, and then finally the Anglo-Americans, fought the war in a manner intended to inflict unprecedented damage on enemy civilian lives and property. By May 1945, the Anglo-American air assault had killed a minimum of 300,000 German civilians, only about a third of the number British planners had counted upon.

While incontestably accurate information on the war's damage to capital stock does not exist, the best index remains the information already presented in this chapter. Wealth poured into Germany from all of vanquished Europe. The war used up a huge proportion of the Allies' national incomes, which were lost to productive functions and, worse yet, later allocated to sustain the incredibly wasteful postwar arms race. Britain permanently lost most of the profits of its crucial prewar export trade, sold over

£1.1 billion in overseas capital assets, accumulated £2.8 billion in new external debts on which interest and principal had to be paid, and even before 1945 was attempting to confront these new burdens as well as renew its depleted capital equipment. By 1943 Belgium, considered the least affected nation in Europe, was directly transferring 29 percent of its existing industrial output to Germany at essentially confiscatory prices, and an additional amount indirectly. But to this cost we must add the impact of Nazi measures that sharply reduced overall economic activity—also a direct cost to Belgian capital stock.

Certainly, the cost to France cannot be measured easily, but the lost income from Nazi policies and the impact of the war (in 1943–44, industrial output was less than half of that in 1938)—confiscatory taxes and food removals, the exploitation of labor at near-starvation wage rates, outright removal of booty to Germany, and much else—all made the war's deprivations huge. The proportion of total French production that Germany obtained during 1941–44 at confiscatory rates was at least 20 percent of the national output. Wartime German occupation taxes alone amounted to 862 billion francs. Official French estimates fix German war damages at 1.6 trillion 1938 francs, destruction from combat accounting for a quarter of that sum. The railroad system was over half wrecked.[21]

The sheer magnitude of the war's economic toll mocks attempts to estimate it, but it was enormous in France and throughout Europe, and left the prewar social orders gravely weakened and vulnerable to challenges as never before.

**Loss of Lives**
If the Second World War's vast economic costs cannot be precisely assessed, its monumental cost to lives remains all too clear, notwithstanding the fact that even here the figures are only approximate and vary considerably. This is especially the case because Stalin in 1946 grossly minimized the Soviet Union's losses at 7 million total dead for the war, while some recent figures fix its fatalities at 13 million soldiers and 7 million civilians. It could scarcely have been less than 17 million, and if one includes excess mortality because of the war's hardships and its impact on family units, a criterion that can be applied to every country, then 20 million Soviet deaths is surely plausible, and possibly even too low.

The number of Jewish civilians killed was initially estimated at 4.5 million, but Adolf Eichmann subsequently claimed the figure to be 6 million; in fact, the Nazis were far more interested in killing than counting. This range, however, is accurate. The majority of them came from Poland, whose total human losses were at least 5.7 million—roughly one-half of whom were Jews. Relative to its prewar population, Poland suffered greater losses of life—about 16 percent—than any European nation. Yugoslavia came next, having lost 1.7 million civilians and soldiers—or 11 percent of its prewar population.

Appraisals of German losses range from about 4 million, 700,000 of whom were civilians, to 6.8 million, but most tend to the lower figure. These amounted to from 6 to 10 percent of the population. As in all nations, there were also the permanently disabled, requiring medical care, and Germany had about 2.7 million, but its death and infant mortality rate for nonmilitary reasons—a reliable measure of its high food and medical standards—rose only slightly during the war.

France's direct war losses are also controversial: 600,000 dead is the smallest estimate. But France's population in 1945 was at least a million lower than in 1938, adjusted for border changes and emigration, and starvation or hunger caused the normal death and infant mortality rates to climb significantly—much more, indeed, than in Italy. Taking this into account, optional calculations fixing French losses as high at 1.45 million for the war are at least partly accurate. About 635,000, including 100,000 Jews, seems the most plausible number for French deaths, but as with other nations, we shall never know for sure. The war also created 585,000 invalids.

There were, of course, many other nations that suffered terribly, and such pain's magnitude cannot be fathomed with numbers. But for Europe as a whole, the direct military and civilian death toll certainly exceeded 30 million by the most cautious criteria, and some have claimed up to 40 million. Such figures are about three times Europe's losses during World War One. If the indirect losses of life the war caused, or the lower birth rate, are calculated, the war's effects on Europe's people were even greater.[22]

The dimensions of this calamity defy words. Europe's suffering was awesome, and beyond measure.

## Soldiers: The New Context

During the First World War, conditions among soldiers of the warring armies became the single most important cause of crises in Europe's social and political systems, and the critical factor in creating the Bolshevik Revolution. A ruling class that cannot rely upon its army is axiomatically precarious, if not foredoomed, and most of the Continent's conservative leaders never forgot this lesson. A crucial difference between the two conflicts was that during the Second World War Europe's armies never escaped the control of their commanders, nor did they somehow affect the war's political or military outcome by undisciplined conduct. But what the political leaders utterly failed to anticipate was the unprecedented emergence of armed civilians in the form of the Resistance movement in its many diverse forms; so that while formal armies ultimately proved manageable, Europe's status quo still had to confront military challenges.

In part, the reason for stability among soldiers was due to the simple fact that the French army capsized almost immediately and the British and American armies were much more dependent on strategies employing technology rather than a fighting infantry, most of which was assigned an active role only during the relatively brief final stages of the conflict. But if soldiers did not play the same role as in 1914–18, they were still human beings propelled into situations of immense danger and tension for which the vast majority of men everywhere are by nature and instinct badly suited, and to which they reacted. This was especially true of the German army, which on the eastern front endured conditions that in certain crucial ways replicated some of the problems that it had experienced in northern France more than two decades earlier.

### The Case of the Allies

The French army was profoundly demoralized from the war's inception, and this fact was reflected in its alcoholism and depredations against French civilians while it waited in static positions for a Nazi invasion that failed to conform to its leaders' expectations. Draft dodging was abnormally high, and after France's surrender only a minute fraction of its forces outside the country volunteered to continue fighting with the Free French. Both the British and the American armies, on the other hand, made a concerted effort to exclude men who had "psychiatric" problems or seemed potential sources of trouble, establishing special units for marginal cases nonetheless deemed fit for service. The U.S. rejected about 700,000 men, one-third of the 2 million turned down, for psychological reasons alone—or a tenth of all those examined.

But such comprehensive weeding notwithstanding, if British, French, and American armies seemed politically more reliable, they nevertheless remained weak stuff for combat dependent on human endurance, thereby increasing the relative importance of the capital-intensive, elitist technological branches of their military establishments. In the French case, their equipment was, in the aggregate, more abundant than, and superior to, the German, and together with the British, Belgians, and Dutch, they had significantly more field divisions. But demoralization was so profound among its ranks, who universally deplored the war as pointless politically as well as predestined to failure militarily, that nothing could save France from catastrophic defeat. Spectacular cases of vastly superior French forces simply bolting upon the appearance of any Germans were common, and while 100,000 French soldiers were killed during the six weeks the Germans took to win the war, 1.9 million were captured during the greatest rout in modern European history.

The American military establishment, it cannot be reiterated too strongly, was designed to win principally through airpower, sea power, and armor, and its numerically huge army was organized in a dehumanizing fashion whose highly negative consequences were only fully appreciated after the war was over. A scant fifth of it was assigned to combat divisions, and not even half of those were in the infantry. Men from very different geographic backgrounds were incorporated into units because they shared a similar technical background, or often just assigned haphazardly, and their officers generally came from and lived in a world apart. Replacement troops frequently had nothing whatsoever in common with their nominal comrades. When a sense of unity developed among front-line units it was usually out of necessity and a mutual dependence in the struggle to survive as well as a distinct resentment, even aggressive contempt, toward those not exposed to repeated dangers. The bulk of the American forces were engaged principally in administrative and logistical functions, with little risk for the vast bulk of them until June 1944—after which the European war lasted only eleven more months.

In the U.S. case, the results were unimpressive. Although its huge air armada bombed foes far more than friends, it was notoriously imprecise and often terrified soldiers in close proximity to German forces. Battlefields have always been chaotic, but serious risks to Allied forces inevitably mounted with the firepower involved. More significant militarily was that the overwhelming majority of combat soldiers were often frightened, their multiple fear symptoms growing with exposure to combat, and these ranged all the way from a violent pounding of the heart to the loss of urinary and bowel control. Apart from heavier alcohol consumption in the Allied armies, there was the more immediate problem that all of these responses produced an exceedingly poor military performance: during a single operation, an estimated 20 to 25 percent of the American infantry forces involved in it actively used their weapons against enemy positions when they had the opportunity to do so—and often much less than that. Most men operated their weapons properly at some point or another during the war, but it was very rarely anything like the approximately 80 percent of them who had the potential of firing and inflicting damage at any one time. The Allied armies, in a word, were mediocre or worse in the traditional military definition of the term, but succeeded because modern war had become highly industrialized and their side alone possessed the economic prerequisites for fighting it.

If the result was the absence of any of the crises that plagued Allied armies during World War One, and men were rarely called upon to exist under sustained deprivation or perform as they had then, soldiers still had astonishingly scant political commitments. Indeed, that soldiers did their best to survive physically, and avoided as much as possible their nominal task of killing enemies for the sake only of destroying them, or scarcely possessed any strong political views on war and peace, is now conventional wisdom. In the much-studied American case, by the end of the war the large majority of enlisted men shared a comprehensive disdain for the army, the wartime experience had deeply alienated them, and they questioned the entire undertaking. Their attitude toward Hitler was abysmally confused in the case of half of those stationed in Germany, and a majority of soldiers had a more positive opinion of the Germans than of the French. "Bullshit" was the term combat veterans employed most when confronted with ideal-istic explanations of the war.[23] What the typical soldier wanted most after May 1945 was to get out of the army. As for politics, Americans who entered the military thought like the vast majority of their countrymen, and it was to be expected that they should leave it retaining such inchoate beliefs.

### The Question of the German Army

In the case of Germany's soldiers, the environment in which they fought and their history were utterly different, the stakes far greater because their radicalization by 1918 had triggered the collapse of an empire, its army, and momentarily brought the nation to the verge of profound social change. Moreover, Hitler's military strategy relied far less than his enemies' on mas-sive airpower and armor, and on the eastern front the failure of what was intended to be a brief mobile war left millions of German soldiers con-fronting conditions on a vast, decentralized battleground that in many cru-cial ways resembled those of 1914–18. With the virtually unanimous endorsement of his generals, Hitler sent 3 million men into the USSR in June 1941 equipped for one decisive offensive, utterly confident that the war would be over before winter and that their casualties would not exceed 275,000. But the army had no transportation reserves and was completely unprepared for the Red Army's wholly predictable destruction of existing roads and railways, so the "transportation disaster" that soon occurred stunned Hitler and his entourage.[24] The Germans quickly became much more dependent on horse-drawn wagons, many of them stolen from Polish peasants, and only one-fifth of the units managed entirely without them. Yet even horses were inadequate, and they were difficult to feed. The still-small S.S. units apart, the Nazi leaders assumed that only a fifth of their manpower would remain in the USSR the following winter and were pre-pared to do so. "Deaths owing to freezing," Goebbels wrote in his diary in January 1942, "are an especially important factor . . . ," and German soldiers were reduced to stealing warm clothing from the vanquished people, imme-diately initiating a sanctioned policy of unlimited oppression and looting that greatly accelerated the official policy of genocide.[25] By the end of 1941, German casualties were three times the anticipated number, and the army was unable to carry much of the arms and supplies it needed into the com-bat zones.

Until 1945 at least three-quarters of Germany's armed forces fought on the eastern front under conditions of extreme hardship comparable to those of the First World War, or worse. The enormous German losses reflected their relative lack of technology for making war and their dependence on manpower. Thirteen million men were mobilized into all of the German armed forces by September 1944, and nearly 5 million more by the end of the war. Thirty percent of them were killed or incapacitated by September 1944, and by the war's end at least 3.5 million died.

That the German army did not undergo the same process of personal and political radicalization that had occurred a quarter-century earlier is surely the most significant aspect of the relationship of Europe's armies to their political masters throughout World War Two. Man for man, the German army was rated 20 to 30 percent more effective than the British or American army for the duration of the war, and this figure was unquestionably higher in the east. Although the most ideologically motivated men volunteered for the Waffen-S.S., which older Prussian officers feared was becoming "the embryo of a National Socialist army of the future" that would eventually displace them, even with its spectacular growth the S.S. by the end of the war was a scant one-seventh of the size of the regular army, and that partly because its superior living conditions attracted volunteers (many of whom were not born in Germany).[26] The very highest ranks of the military remained firmly elitist, and the broadening of the social bases of lower-level officers was too insignificant to account for the army's cohesion. More important was the fact that German officers mixed with enlisted men far more than was the case in most Allied armies, were more likely to lead them into battle, and died in combat in greater proportions than those they called upon to follow them. Yet such reasons also do not explain why a huge number of men exposed to terrifying hardships for a duration almost as long as the First World War behaved so very differently than their fathers.

German soldiers unquestionably were subjected to intensive ideological efforts, especially after 1943, just as they had earlier been exposed to a school system that sought to inculcate Nazi values. But the fact that the Nazis attempted to politicize the rank and file is scarcely proof that they attained their goal. The notion that the frightful living conditions on the eastern front worked to justify racist notions and ease the way for Nazi propaganda is simply implausible, since comparable trials in 1914–18 had moved soldiers to indiscipline and radicalism. What we know about soldiers everywhere is that even if it does not lead to radicalism, mounting adversity tends to cause them to regard formal justifications for their sacrifices with increasing cynicism—indeed, political indoctrination has never been truly successful in any army. Whatever the impact of Nazi training, many men still came from the working class and the peasantry, where socialism, religion, and a very great deal else were still highly regarded, and we know that the regime itself, whatever its doctrinal line on such cultural topics as music, discreetly tolerated frequent heterodoxy in daily life in order to be better able to use its iron fist for really important matters. Unquestionably, the Nazis would have liked to create an ideologically homogeneous and motivated army, and they made considerable and increasing efforts in that direction only at that point in the war that it was clear to most Germans that Nazism had produced catastrophe for the nation and was likely to be defeated. Even if there were convincing proof— and there is none—that a certain proportion of the soldiers, or even a majority, accepted Nazi doctrines or became true believers so long as the war was being won, it still could not explain the *total* absence of opposition from many whose elders, under comparable conditions, had changed the course of German history. After all, the Nazi adventure in the east was subjecting soldiers daily to unspeakable hardships, the causes of which they could easily perceive and reflect upon. To argue that ideology could have overcome constant experience is to claim that Germans were more stupid than soldiers have ever been anywhere—itself a racist thesis, one all the more difficult to sustain because, Russia excepted, their penchant for indiscipline and radicalism in 1918 was unsurpassed.

As during the First World War, the German army was initially organized largely on regional lines that made its components much more culturally cohesive, and far more unified than any other army. Their junior officers were usually from the same areas, with a relatively unique tradition of being close to their men. Thus, the German army did not at first require ideological motivations, because interpersonal loyalties were more than sufficient to maintain group cohesion and discipline, but as the war eroded lives and disorganized units, an army based on primary groups began to change drastically with it.

After the winter of 1941, morale in the army posed a growing challenge to the Nazi leaders. "Words cannot describe what our soldiers are writing back home from the front," Goebbels noted in January 1942.[27] Although the German army operated as an effective military instrument under terrible conditions, this fact is axiomatic with strong discipline but not necessarily good morale or belief in Nazi dogma. Not all, or even many, freezing and hungry soldiers sent to war unequipped because of their rulers' stupidity will admire those rulers' perspicacity or goals. In reality, the German army was principally made up neither of Nazi fanatics nor of articulate antifascists; rather, they were men seeking to survive personally while under overwhelming military constraints and propelled by a mixture of diverse impulses. Like people everywhere, soldiers were sometimes good or bad, but most often they were neither. Organizational controls kept some in line, and many disliked greatly what they were doing, but like the majority of people in all places, at all times, they did it anyway to avoid immediate difficulties with their peers and superiors. But Nazi leaders had a far better sense of the German soldiery's potential for challenging the system and they resolved that under no circumstances would the terrible dangers of the fall of 1918 ever be repeated. The entire war effort within Germany itself was geared to the need to keep civilians tranquil, and this policy as late as November 1943 succeeded because mass consumption remained relatively high and, as Goebbels assessed it, "partly owing to our good propaganda, but partly also to the severe measures which we have taken against defeatists."[28]

But a carrot-and-stick policy could not be imposed on the army because there were few material baits to give to soldiers on the front lines, although they were permitted to listen to music the regime disliked and free to abuse and rape the local population in eastern Europe in ways strictly forbidden elsewhere. Even assuming the debate over the extent of its ideological mobilization of the army remains inconclusive, what is not the least in doubt is the way the Nazi leadership employed unlimited repression to keep soldiers in line as well as to communicate to potential dissidents the fact that any sign of disobedience would not be tolerated, as essentially it was in 1918.

During the First World War, Germany killed only 48 of its own soldiers, or a tiny fraction of the number the Allies executed within their own ranks. During 1939–40 alone, even before there was the slightest problem with the army, the Nazis sentenced 519 German soldiers to death, the large majority for political reasons. In 1943–44, 4,118 soldiers were sentenced to death, and between 13,000 and 15,000 soldiers were thus "legally" killed during the war for various disciplinary and political reasons; but this figure does not include an unknown number who were merely summarily executed. The Nazis also reinforced this policy of draconian discipline with lesser penalties. In December 1939, 12,853 were tried for various offenses—again long before the army's morale was in any way blemished and repression was far more a warning than a necessity—rising to 44,955 for the month of October 1944. As of mid-1944, 84,346 soldiers had been given over one-year prison sentences, over a quarter of them for very long periods, and 320,000 were sentenced to less than a year imprisonment. This meant that of the 13 million men in the German armed forces from 1939 to September 1944 who were not killed or incapacitated, an astonishingly high 3.4 percent went to prison or were executed.

This policy of unlimited, unrelenting terror against German soldiers meant, simply enough, that whatever their feelings about the war's catastrophes, they would never be permitted to give even the slightest vent to them. By the last months of the war, save for a few Waffen-S.S.–led formations comprised of committed Nazis, the Wehrmacht had become utterly demoralized and unit commanders increasingly ignored Hitler's orders—and according to the official U.S. history, "Hitler's army readily laid down their arms. . . . "[29] Nothing in the behavior of the veterans of Hitler's military after its defeat revealed that more than a very small fraction of it was comprised of Nazi true believers.

## The War and Europe's Class Structure

World War Two, far more than the earlier conflagration, severely affected a larger portion of the Continent and the people in it, and the extent to which it altered the prewar social and class structures in all of their vital dimensions, ranging from occupational and income distribution to the continuity of traditional elites and dominant classes, is important for us to comprehend. Europe's working class, as well, was subjected to all the consequences of the mass draft of male labor into armies, the forced transfer of millions of foreign workers to Germany, and the war's impact on the nature and organization of industry—which shifted dramatically from lighter consumer goods to heavy arms based on high technology. But apart from the occupational structures, it is also crucial to know how the war influenced the existing tax and fiscal systems, and the manner in which inflation and the black market affected the dominating prewar elites' financial power and leverage. How extensive were these changes, and were they permanent? Notwithstanding the paucity of information that has been gathered explicitly to answer all of these crucial if dauntingly broad analytic issues, several generalizations are plausible. But the existing evidence warrants often very different explanations for each nation, ranging from the war's having had little influence on the *objective* institutional aspects of the prewar social orders to its having altered them profoundly.

What did not change significantly was the permanent position of women in the labor force. In Germany, as we have already seen, the Nazis paid the wives of soldiers comfortable family allowances and discouraged women from working. The British, on the contrary, first urged women to enter the labor market and then introduced conscription in stages, and in June 1944, 1.8 million more women were employed in industry—not to mention other economic sectors—than five years earlier, most of them in engineering, doing what was once deemed men's work. But these women were paid much less than male equivalents, their jobs were temporary, many were married to workers then in the military, and rather than transforming the work force in any significant manner, they essentially broadened it for the war's duration.

In every industrialized nation in the war, from Germany and Japan on one hand to France and Britain on the other, there was a major shift in employment from light industry to heavy industry, and from other major economic activities into manufacturing, construction, mining, transport, and communications. But in many of these nations the loss of vast numbers of skilled workers to the armed forces (40 percent of Germany's prewar industrial workers were in the military by mid-1944) pushed male workers with few if any skills into key production jobs, with surprising consequences.

In Germany, as the foreign work force grew to well over one-third of all employed male labor, German male workers were thrust to the top of the factory hierarchy, and of course received much higher compensation. In a word, they momentarily became a relatively privileged working class. In Britain, on the other hand, the existence of huge numbers of unskilled women working alongside men, many of them also with few skills, only increased wage differentials based mainly on sex in the fields of engineering and aircraft, producing male workers of greater status as compared to their positions in prewar factory hierarchies. But when war production was inevitably cut back, unemployment struck hardest those whose pay had increased most, and prewar patterns returned.[30]

In brief, the nature of the wartime work process caused temporary fluctuations in the character and status of labor in various nations but very little, if any, permanent change or improvement in the structural position of the working class in these societies. Lives were altered profoundly, but overwhelmingly for all those reasons linked directly to the Nazi occupation and war mentioned earlier in this chapter and in the next one.

If the war left Europe's traditional working class essentially where it had been before 1939, a much more nuanced conclusion must be drawn for those above them in the prewar economic and social hierarchy. Here two issues are involved: first, whether the prewar class structures of the various war-torn European nations witnessed different constituencies rise to the top of them; and second, if there is evidence of a shift in income and wealth distribution within Great Britain and the United States, the only two warring nations not subjected to the abnormal economic conditions that the German occupation imposed.

Whether there were changes in various national elites depended wholly upon the country, and for each there were three possible alternatives: few or no important variations, temporary modifications, or basic alterations in the prewar pattern of economic control.

Greece and Poland illustrate the extreme examples of a basic, permanent eclipse in traditional national elites. The Nazis essentially destroyed the dominant prewar Polish economic class before the Red Army arrived, targeting educated Poles in preference to others, as well as all Jews; they also subjected the economy to several years of nightmarish trauma during which only audacious survivors, many of them criminals, combined ingenuity and ruthlessness to prosper within the urban economy as it existed, disappearing when the war was over. There was essentially no relationship between what one had before the war and then during it. In the Greek case, the astonishing wartime inflation wiped out the prewar creditors and those holding wealth in the form of paper of any sort, and compelled most of this stratum to liquidate their tangible wealth in order to survive. In effect, they were largely expropriated. Those who succeeded them in this context as speculators and black marketeers were consummately shrewd, wholly immoral, and became the new postwar elite, one able to dominate and prosper from the state's crucial role in Greece's postwar accumulation process.

In France, on the other hand, Nazi-imposed conditions were less cataclysmic and the changes that occurred in the structure of wealth were both minor and essentially temporary, save for those few especially visible industrialists and bankers who were penalized after the war for aggressively supporting Vichy. The problem too was that, as in Belgium, the Nazis employed the black market as a basic instrument of procurement and relied upon important wholesalers. Some of the latter built upon their prewar businesses in distribution and were already quite affluent before 1940, and a number of major suppliers of the black market were clever enough to buy property or art and antiques in the thriving Paris auctions that functioned throughout most of the war. In this form they unostentatiously transferred their wealth into the postwar period, which gave them a basis for joining the higher ranks of the peacetime economy. But whatever their successes, neither in France nor Belgium did they remotely compare to the nouveaux riches in Greece. There were, of course, also riffraff who made large sums, but they generally spent and lost them. Nonetheless, a quarter of the nation dominated most of the French black-market activity and survived well, even luxuriously in the case of a small group. In Belgium, probably even a larger fraction of the people gained from the black market. The peasantry, as everywhere in Europe, certainly fell into the category of temporary winners, but all of these small operators combined were not sufficient to alter significantly the postwar distribution of economic power in France or Belgium, and much the same was true for the largely privileged peasantry elsewhere in Europe. Moreover, notwithstanding the large windfall income to top black-market organizers, in both France and Belgium the prewar industrial and transport structure continued to operate for the Nazis and, in the aggregate, was profitable, and those who controlled it remained an integral part of the economic scene. In essence, economic power in postwar France and Belgium resembled the prewar configuration, notwithstanding the significance of the wartime changes.

Germany represents an example of no basic alterations in the prewar economic structure, and not merely because the victorious Allies penalized only a tiny minority of Nazi party members after the war and eliminated only the most senior Nazis. "Industry pulls the strings," an alienated conservative aristocrat accurately wrote in his diary in October 1940, and although the Nazis largely defined production priorities during the course of the war, after it ended the pre-Nazi businessmen remained completely in control of the nation's economic resources and future.[31] Many Nazi leaders lived sumptuously, but the most acquisitive of them died or disappeared, and while a commerce existed in looted goods from the conquered nations, too many participated in the traffic for it to concentrate and produce major non-Nazi fortunes. The Nazi elite was comprised mainly of men from the petite bourgeoisie or frustrated clerks without talent who by default moved aside as the pre-Nazi economic elite became increasingly important in the organization of the war effort. Hence the social structure remained essentially stable.

While the British and American wartime economies did not have to cope with a serious black market, the war still had to be funded, and both nations relied much more heavily on taxes than they had during the First World War. The result was that those with money—that is, the upper- and middle-income groups—paid much more than ever, and superficially there appeared to be a shift in income distribution in both nations. The fact that during the war those with money had many fewer consumer goods to spend it on reinforced this impression, and along with the relative equality that rationing imposed, the thesis that the war produced economic leveling later became an influential explanation of the consequences of the war for British society and economic power.

The problem is that in both Britain and the United States the effect of higher taxation was to cause the rich to make a much greater effort to avoid it with innumerable legal devices, which became increasingly sophisticated and effective and continued after the war was over, and the wartime decline in the income shares of the rich proved only temporary. Postponed spending led to forced savings, which was much more important among the middle- and upper-income classes, and this was reflected after the war in the perpetuation of the historic inequality of wealth in all of its forms.[32]

In brief, however vast and traumatic the war's impact on the objective position and lives of the people exposed to it directly or, as in Britain and the United States, much more indirectly, it did not upset the basic distribution of economic power in many crucial nations. While its effects cannot be minimized in any of them, and in places like Greece and Poland the war was decisive in recasting the forms of prewar societies at its upper levels, exaggerated views of its consequences to the inherited European social structure also create too many misconceptions, for as the war ended most of the traditional class order had still to be profoundly transformed.

Until the Second World War the people of Europe had never known suffering and torment on such a scale, or been subjected to such intense
deprivation and death. Countless millions of lives were changed profoundly, and with time it became impossible to escape the effects of ferocious combat and the widening net that the Nazis spread. Obviously, as I
have stressed so strongly for its significant implications for each nation's
social system and politics, in no place was the entire population subjected
to the war's rigors in the same manner. As the topics in this chapter illustrate, the objective consequences of the war touched many quite disparate
aspects of human and social existence. The measures of it that are useful,
along with the state of our knowledge, vary greatly in each nation, and the
fate of soldiers or peasants in different countries reveals how strikingly
unequal the war's consequences often were. Yet notwithstanding important nuances, the central fact regarding the war's overall impact is that it
was overwhelmingly pervasive, and completely dominated the lives and
existences of the vast majority of Europeans—the way they ate, worked, or
survived. It was in this context that untold countless people were compelled to think about the world they lived in and the causes of the awesome conditions they were forced to experience—and began to respond in
many diverse and unprecedented ways.

# CHAPTER 10

# European Responses to
# World War Two

The human and political costs of long wars can never be calculated in advance, and those who initiate conflicts as well as the people compelled to experience them never predict the personal or social prices they will have to pay. Political leaders and strategists always prefer clinical, rational visions of warfare, since they have neither the analytic equipment nor human sensibilities essential for grasping warfare's traumatic realities in all their dimensions: the blood, the hunger, the degradation and collapse of personal existences in the course of mass wandering in the elusive quest for safety. None can imagine or define the limits of individual endurance or its political consequences, nor the many ways in which wars will evoke the most extreme antisocial conduct from some determined to survive, yet at the same time create new forms of cooperative activities among men and women bent on resolving their own predicaments as members of social groups and forces. More than any other single factor, the overwhelming and direct consequences of war have shaped the human and political experiences of our century and have become the motor of change within it, creating political and ideological upheavals—revolutions being the most important of them—that otherwise had scant possibility of occurring.

The transformation of the European people's responses as a result of the war's terrible toll evolved over time, both because of the limits of each person's endurance and the unavoidability of choices on the part of millions of people who saw the conflict affecting their very existence and that of future generations. As their consciousness and perceptions of their own positions in society evolved, it also altered the kinds of changes that populations thought were essential both to mete out justice to those who had created their suffering and to prevent more agonies in the future. But their behavior and thought reflected not only the existential factors involving their most immediate personal situations—their daily suffering and ignominy—but also their perceptions of the global balance of forces in the contest between Germany and its enemies, their vision of who was likely to win the war, and its relevance to their action or inaction. As the Nazis began to experience repeated defeats and in their desperation escalated the terror they were inflicting on countless millions, untold Europeans were both compelled and elected to make both difficult and dangerous choices that turned them into actors potentially capable of shaping the war's political outcome.

The political and organizational contexts in which people existed and with which they had to interact were usually profoundly complicated and ambiguous, and initially sufficient to discourage all but a tiny handful from taking any risks whatsoever. Not the least was the fact that regardless of an individual's vision of his or her personal role in an occupied nation, each had also to deal with the probability that occupationally, as a functionary in the government or business, or as a worker whose only significant social role was as a member of a production unit, no one had the power to affect the objective leverage that the Nazis had over the critical institutions in the nations they conquered. Someone might personally oppose the Nazis and resist them in diverse ways outside the workplace, but at the same time be employed in a factory making military goods for the Wehrmacht. Paradoxes like this abounded among men or women considering what their personal roles should be. In very few cases or places were the responses of Europe's peoples to their excruciating dilemmas and conditions ever uncomplicated or categorical, for given the momentous nature of the decisions and the risks of action, the overwhelming mass acted in ways that were rarely simple to describe or understand. There was often no distinct boundary between collaboration and resistance but rather innumerable gradations and nuances from one unequivocal pole of human conduct to the other, within which one must position the vast majority.

## Nazi Occupation Policy

Although Germany's ultimate objectives in western Europe were explicit, its occupation strategy was far from predetermined organizationally, leaving a certain space within which those who were not fascists or pro-Nazi might continue to make significant judgments that affected both their countrymen and themselves without becoming collaborationist in the pejorative sense of that term.

The Nazi mission in eastern Europe was frankly committed from the beginning to the destruction of existing societies and the physical liquidation of their traditional political leadership, and while events frequently affected the timing and methods they employed, Nazi goals themselves were fully articulated. Their administrative experiences in Bohemia, Moravia, and Poland reinforced the Nazis' willingness to rely pragmatically on the conquered western European governments for as many routine functions as possible—including maintaining most local laws. Hitler did not want to see the Wehrmacht deeply involved in civil affairs, and above all he sought to avoid assigning a large number of Germans to managing the defeated nations. The Nazis initially intended that international laws on the administration of occupied nations apply in western Europe, and they certainly did not wish to rely extensively on the usually minute and divided local fascist groups, who had no appropriate skills and could only cause viable states to break down and compound their problems. When the Nazis entered each western European nation, their occupation bureaucracies were complex, often at loggerheads, and still in gestation. To some degree these divisions and the personalities involved in them defined the characteristics that German occupation regimes assumed, even though all adhered scrupulously to the directive to exploit conquered economies ruthlessly; but the precise forms they took depended crucially on the roles that the vanquished local authorities elected to play.[1]

The Nazi occupation authority in France was highly disunited. Its military governor was replaced in 1942 and the S.S. was established about the same time in deference to the army, which did not want responsibility for policing the country. Divisions within the French Right, sections of which had Nazi sponsors, only further encouraged German factionalism. Until 1944 the Vichy regime was not so much fascist as classically authoritarian and, of course, wholly collaborationist because it initially perceived the occupation as an unavoidable, permanent reality even though many of its leaders were less pro-Nazi than anti-British. Although the Nazis could hardly repudiate the local fascists, using them for marginal tasks, they much preferred to work through Pétain and Laval. In Belgium the Nazis concluded even before they invaded that they did not have the manpower to run the country without the aid of the existing state apparatus under the senior civil servants of the Secretaries General. But the Nazis also knew that since 1936 Belgium's key leaders, above all King Leopold, had decided to avoid a repetition of the trauma of 1914–18 and to remain neutral—indeed, to appease Germany when it inevitably reentered Belgium. The Belgian army, in any case, was too small and poorly equipped to resist. In assigning Alexander von Falkenhausen as military governor for most of the war, Berlin made a local elite's accommodationist strategy more likely to succeed in Belgium than in any other country in Europe, for although Falkenhausen was a Prussian who did his job well, he was also less punitive than his peers—and in July 1944 the Nazis arrested him for complicity in the effort to assassinate Hitler.

In The Netherlands the Nazis also hoped to use the existing state machinery, and the Dutch, like the Belgians, initially expected to remain neutral, and in any case planned not to resist an invasion—indeed, the Dutch authorized the state to cooperate with the invaders within the framework of international laws, which in essence they did for the war's duration. But the Nazis had neither an integrated bureaucracy to deal with Holland nor a comprehensive plan for exploiting it, beyond the immediate objective of maintaining an independent nation tied closely to their economy.[2]

But in western Europe the Nazis' relatively benign plans, at least when compared to their intentions and actions in Poland, were the result not only of their own lack of preparation and administrative unity but also of their knowledge that the Continent's three richest countries would not resist—indeed, had embarked for very diverse reasons on policies of collaboration that greatly reduced Germany's need to articulate comprehensive occupation guidelines. This situation allowed Hitler to invest as little manpower in the occupation as possible, and to extract what he needed and wanted from the conquered economies while concentrating on his great military designs elsewhere. In essence, it was a rational strategy that also offered a certain element of predictability to the defeated nations. This was the framework to which western Europeans were compelled to relate—and in which to act.

In Poland, to cite the other extreme in their occupation strategy, the Nazis did not want a collaborationist regime, and early resolved ultimately to eliminate the Polish elite and intelligentsia and all Jews, and their designs were more articulate and far more destructive than in western Europe. Hence there was no question of utilizing the existing state structure, which was formally abolished, but rather of ruling directly. But the Nazis also wished to exploit the economy and people, and to make it possible to use the nation as a base for fighting the war, and so they needed Poles to keep the railroads running, collect foodstuffs, maintain the postal service, and the like, thereby liberating Germans to perform military functions. They therefore created an "auxiliary administration," which at its peak numbered 280,000 Poles and Ukrainians, the majority of whom had worked for the prewar Polish government.[3] But parallel to its de facto government of quiescent Poles, the Nazis allowed corruption to integrate yet other Poles into their occupation structure, creating informal but very practical and important agencies for accomplishing various tasks; such Poles, in return, received favors, if only the ability to live longer. But the German occupation authorities' guidelines shifted capriciously even within the framework of a genocidal grand strategy, which was far less materially productive than the more pragmatic policies in western Europe, and conflicting branches often operated as they thought best. Nazi ideology in Poland was translated into action in the form of mass murder unparalleled in modern history, although even here the Nazi need to utilize portions of the local community unquestionably spared some. Individual Poles were compelled to deal with such utter unpredictability and vicissitudes, their very existence being constantly at stake.

## Responding to the Occupation: Collaboration

The Nazi occupation of Europe was fraught with constant dilemmas, choices, and paradoxes for all those living in the shadow of the ruthless military colossus, and the vast majority resolved them initially by attempting to endure. The ambiguities and ironies of this totally dominating reality evolved directly from the need of the initially tiny minority seeking to resist in some manner also to exploit and become symbiotic upon the existing state and economic machinery in order to act more effectively. To attempt to paralyze the political or economic institutions that the Nazis utilized risked the nearly certain likelihood of terrible failure and retribution as well as the loss of access to organizations that had become useful, even essential, to both the occupiers and their enemies. In brief, there might be "administrative resistance" within mechanisms that routinely also helped the Nazis to extract resources for their war effort. What objectively looked like collaboration to some might in intent be the reverse, and merely a reflection of the functional symbiosis between two diametrically opposed forces using the same "legal" system for totally different purposes.[4]

How could one tell when "administrative resistance" occurred? From the outside, it was impossible to plumb the motives of those involved, and in reality the issue of whether individuals were collaborators or resisters (or, far more likely, neither), frequently boiled down purely to their intentions, since in practice both usually did the same things. Indeed, except in a few cases, mainly involving social relations with the Germans, even today one cannot facilely judge the conduct and reasoning of those whose actions had no visible consequences save to themselves, which is to say the large majority of people, whose social roles or intentions are for practical purposes invisible when they act alone.

Both Belgian and Dutch officials argued later that they sought under dire circumstances to attain the least evil by extracting the best arrangement possible from the Nazis. Such claims were neither proof nor disproof of "administrative resistance," but they did assume that protecting their own national business interests was synonymous with the larger public's welfare, which, given the class origins and social biases of the men involved, was a natural premise. But the Nazis had no problem whatsoever with such a posture because it still produced the goods they desired. Had their own disunity and conflicting interests not so incapacitated them, the Nazis would have obtained even more from Belgian and Dutch compliance. Setting motives aside, all of the occupied nations in western Europe collaborated at a material level, willingly or unwillingly, depending on the intentions and goals of the specific organizations or people involved. Some firms or police departments did more than they were compelled to because they saw gain in it, while others did less. The former unquestionably must be deemed collaborators notwithstanding their reasons, if only because some actions must also be assessed in terms of their consequences rather than merely their intentions lest we destroy those basic norms that create essential barriers to individual conduct that is functionally antisocial. By necessity one can only raise the profoundly ambiguous issue of collaboration most clearly when dealing with important government and business officials.

Moreover, at the war's inception no one could foresee what the final occupation system would look like. To those living in a conquered nation the choice was not one of simple collaboration with what appeared an unavoidable, permanent reality, but of a pragmatic accommodation that many believed might even shape its ultimate character and make it less onerous. And since the true inspiration of people's behavior was known only to themselves, from the very inception the Nazis got what they wanted. In reality, the decisions the vast majority had to make were often not very difficult: what the Nazis initially required was that most men and women continue to work and live more or less as they had before the war; for those contemplating refusal or resigning from government, the personal inconveniences might, at worst, be fatal, but rarely inconsequential. But even if one refused to collaborate, or adapt, or whatever they chose to call it, until well into 1942, the leaders of both Belgium and Holland believed for understandable reasons that the war was lost, that life had to go on, and that people had to be given the best ways available to survive under such monumental constraints. Only a tiny handful of officials opted to play no part whatsoever in such a profoundly equivocal game.

Exploiting the obvious fact that no clear delineation was possible between collaborators and resisters in the vast majority of cases, after the war many who were principally the former in fact as well as in intent could plausibly claim that they were simply living examples of such paradoxes but that their own motives were always those of resistants. But beyond the very real, profound ambiguity in fathoming the true designs of a certain number of people, and the near impossibility of ignoring opportunism among them in so many cases, nowhere did the Nazi occupation enter a political and economic void in which individuals with existential problems made clear choices that were simple for someone later to decipher. All of the occupied nations also had political traditions, economic constituencies, and parties with specific objectives and interests, and these interacted with the invaders in quite explicit ways that in hindsight made collaboration for many seem logical as well as inevitable. For them the Nazi occupation was both a challenge and a chance, and cooperation with it also offered some a means of implementing economic and social goals they had long sought.

## Vichy France

French conservatism's complex attitudes and ambitious aims had long preceded the Nazi triumph in Germany. Some were visceral: such as the bourgeoisie who detested secular republican ideals and the Popular Front under Leon Blum, a Jew, or who looked askance at parliamentarianism's creation of persistent disorder in a nation where unions often struck for higher wages. The notion of a moral order that was Catholic, abstemious in its private mores and which idealized the family, or of a France based on the folkloric rhythm of the peasantry and small towns as opposed to industrial cities with their radicals, Jews, Masons, and immigrants—all of the nostalgic ingredients of a mythologized antimodernist and essentially middle-class society deeply suffused the thought of much of the nation's more affluent population, and this vision in no way depended on the German presence. Associated with it were corporatist notions for reorganizing the economy in a less competitive, ostensibly more humane fashion. All of this sentimentality, articulated in literary forms and reflected as well in a philistinism based on hatreds, converged especially among veterans of the First World War in a cult of adulation for Marshal Philippe Pétain, whom they believed could deliver France from the iniquity that secular republicanism had visited upon it since allegedly great men had been dethroned from politics in the late nineteenth century.

Ideologically, these independent traditional currents and impulses found expression in the Vichy regime. Vichy determined its authoritarian, anti-Semitic political and social agenda autonomously, and it wished to cooperate with the Nazis, partially because the French assumed that the Nazis would win the war and create a permanent order in Europe, but also because Vichy's leaders recognized that many of their goals were mutually compatible and they hoped to seize the opportunity to implement them. But what the Nazis wanted most from France was identical to what it sought also in Belgium and Holland, where the origins and motives of the governments were entirely different: maximum economic resources with the lowest possible expenditure of German manpower to obtain them. For the pragmatic chief Nazis, what France did internally after that was generally not their affair.[5]

The Vichy regime obtained the support of virtually the entire administrative apparatus of the prewar political system, and only 80 of the 569 members of the National Assembly voted against its accord with Germany on July 10, 1940, with over three-quarters of the Socialists also endorsing it. The senior government bureaucracy therefore could loyally continue its duties with equanimity until the war was virtually over; nearly all diplomats stayed at their posts, and local governments also fell entirely into line. The Germans had only about 10,000 of their own men to perform police duties, and depended heavily on at least 100,000 French police to round up Communists, recalcitrants, Jews, and to maintain public order. Until the end of 1942 the Nazis felt the French police performed these tasks in an exemplary fashion, essentially because their goals were identical, especially in catching Communists. In the fall of 1942 the Vichy authorities balked at collecting Frenchmen to be sent as forced labor to Germany, but at the beginning of the new year Pierre Laval ordered his police to cooperate fully. In northern France, the mine owners' ability to use the local police encouraged them to crush the unions, a process which the local Socialists abetted in order to destroy the Communists—thereby enabling the Communists later to replace them entirely.

If opinions and subjective motives can be debated, concrete actions cannot, and in both intent and effect Vichy and its business supporters aided the Nazi war machine in the numerous ways already outlined in the preceding chapter. At a more abstract level, many large industrialists also favored a continuation of the prewar cartel movement's efforts to organize a rationalized pan-European economic structure based on a common market, politically sanctioned cartels, and those measures that many powerful German interests also advocated in the form of the Nazi "New Order" for Europe. Important adherents of an integrated, rationalized European economy also could be found among Belgian and Dutch businessmen, and although corporatist ideologies reinforced this emerging consensus—which later helped to produce the European Economic Community—the basic impulse behind it was a widespread belief among Europe's big businessmen that restricting competition would increase profits. They adhered to these crucial objectives before, during, and after the war. Cooperating with German firms on common projects was therefore based on a more abstract rationale along with the concrete desire to make profits. At the same time, setting aside their voluntary justifications and genuine desires to collaborate, there was never any doubt that the Nazis were going to exploit whatever part of western Europe's industrial potential they coveted regardless of the wishes of its owners, even if they had to confiscate it or ship it back to

Germany; during sharp negotiating sessions the German's often proposed draconian terms, as if they held all the cards, and Europe's defeated capitalists usually had to succumb to them.

But the more technologically advanced sectors of French business were eagerly collaborationist. They sought to sell bauxite and iron to Germany at the highest possible price, and one month after the armistice was signed, Renault and major industrial and financial interests took the initiative to integrate themselves into every phase of the Nazi aeronautics efforts. From 1941 to 1944 the French built 5,622 new planes for Germany and repaired or added motors to three times as many. The entire munitions and locomotives industries willingly geared to Nazi needs, and by spring 1942, 845,000 French workers were making munitions or constructing Nazi airfields and fortifications in France. Building Nazi defenses in France exempted men from being sent to Germany, and many more preferred this option throughout the war than escaped to the maquis. When France's total contribution to the Nazi war economy is calculated, one finds that 8 to 9 million French men and women were employed at the task of providing it.[6]

There were also pure opportunists of various stripes. Since they were so conspicuous, the mostly theretofore obscure mediocrities who under German sponsorship became the lions of the Parisian literary and film world are the best known; many were the protégés of assorted Nazi officials assigned the task of managing aspects of the country's life, and there was no shortage of the usual banal intrigues among them to gain an enviable post ruling over culture from a comfortable Paris office.

Parisians sought, above all, to return to their city's magical existence and the Nazis consciously made it very easy for them to do so. For several months the fate that befell France depressed most of its people, making them listless regarding a defeat that appeared to be permanent. Yet they still had to live, and by autumn of 1940 everything interesting in Paris had reopened: theaters, museums, restaurants, and all the schools (with the obsessive problem of planning la rentrée for parents), and one could quickly return to sitting at one's favorite café while browsing through a daily paper, of which there were nine by 1942. Street names were left untouched. True, there was a food problem for all but the elite, and Jewish or Communist faces disappeared quickly enough, but Parisians did not—indeed, for both physical and psychological reasons could not—repudiate their charmed lives. In November 1940 a group of students paraded in protest and over a hundred were taken away: thereafter there were no more public manifestations until the summer of 1944, and not a single German was killed until 1942. For all the rest there were familiar consolations to keep their minds off the Nazis. The race tracks reopened in October 1940, and by 1942 the number of spectators in Paris's theaters and cinemas exceeded prewar levels. By then there were 600 periodicals of all types being published, and 220 films were produced during the occupation. While much of the population disliked this state of affairs, and their acquiescence was purely the result of necessity, it was in this setting—still eminently comfortable for many— that they had to confront the war.[7]

Objectively and subjectively, Vichy France collaborated with Nazi Germany to a greater extent than any other nation, and it is idle to apportion the causes to an ideological consensus, necessity, or greed, for in most cases various (though changing) degrees of each existed in tandem. Evolving from France's quintessentially traditionalist and nationalist conservative classes and social elements, Vichy's fatal collaboration with foreign occupiers ironically transformed it and its supporters into an antinational force, polarizing political life so that those who opposed the Nazis could alone claim the mantle of nationalism and patriotism. And since the Vichy compromise with foreign domination tarnished the nation's ruling class profoundly, only the Communists were to emerge from the war with a synthesis of class and nationalist claims that had overwhelming legitimacy in the eyes of vast numbers of Frenchmen. It was in this context that the issue of who collaborated, as well as how and why, was soon to become the dominant issue of French political life.

## Belgium

The Belgian experience with collaboration was far more complex than the French, and those who ran the nation had completely different motives than the unabashedly reactionary Vichy leaders. The mass panic that followed the relatively peaceful Nazi entry, involving up to 4 million people abandoning their homes, reinforced the whole nation's subsequent desire to sustain as normal an existence as possible. At the same time, the official government fled to London, leaving the Secretaries General (the most senior civil servants) behind to continue to run the state if possible. Both the Belgian ruling class and the majority of the people wanted neither to collaborate nor to resist (to varying degrees they managed to do both simultaneously) but to avoid the war's hardships at almost any price—and this they accomplished better than anyone else in Europe. With some notable exceptions, in place of ideology they consciously articulated a belief in the pragmatism of pursuing policies that would attain the least evil, which only made their behavior more convoluted. They did what the Nazis demanded, especially if they could profit from it, but they also attempted to protect themselves as much as possible. The notion of choosing lesser evils, precarious at best, became virtually the official ideology, and certainly the most common explanation after the war of the motives of those in power; but the inherent ambiguity of such an approach allowed the definition of what was in reality truly immoral to be bent to serve various interests.

The Germans were ready to work through the Secretaries General, the police under their command, and the leadership of the existing economic structures because this involved fewer of their personnel and they simply had no practical alternative to doing so; indeed, their own internal differences on how to use Belgian resources often created a vacuum that only Belgian authorities could fill. There was a constant tension but also a trade-off between the Secretaries General and the invaders, and while the latter gave the bureaucrats some autonomy, they also obligated them to follow German rules when ordered to do so. On the few occasions when the Secretaries General threatened to resign, the Nazis backed down because they realized they could never replace them with their own people, and while the Belgian police were far less cooperative than the French, particularly in handing over men who refused forced labor in Germany, they nonetheless maintained a degree of order the occupiers appreciated. This alone increased the popularity of the Secretaries Generals by mid-1943 with a public that had often excoriated it for what it considered excessive collaboration.

Whatever the Belgian pretensions of social solidarity, there were also countless smugglers, frauds, and black marketeers—for which the nation justly became famous. The principal motive of the vast majority of such people, which encompassed much of the population if small operators are included, was purely and simply to survive the rigors of the war as well as possible—a quite small portion wanted to enrich themselves, but even most of these imposed limits of how far they would go to do so. Only 1,514 of the 52,400 persons charged after the war with economic collaboration were convicted of especially shameless crimes; but 53,000 were convicted of collaboration in all of its many forms (170 times more than during 1914–18!), over half of them for bearing arms for the Nazis—most of them on the eastern front. The Germans paid them well, but many were Flemish nationalists who were true ideological allies of the Nazis. They too produced barriers to possible opposition to Nazi demands.

Just as a large portion of the nation engaged in the black market to eat, prosper, or both, so too did the industrialists and financial leaders make exceptions to the original program that the most important of them—the so-called Galopin committee—drew up after July 1940, to neither collaborate nor resist completely but rather to try to attain a compromise between the extremes that inflicted the least damage possible on the economy and the people. When this elite reached their decision, the government-in-exile secretly approved it, but their goal always assumed that some industries would do more than others, and in practice it was inherently impossible to implement. What Germany needed most—coal—it received in much smaller amounts than it might have largely because German agencies, including Ruhr producers who wanted to sell their own coal, gravely hobbled Belgian production. Belgian industry and finance made a far greater effort to adapt its complex strategy to produce considerably more for Germany than the Nazis, with their chaotic economic policies, permitted them to do, and the economy declined considerably more than many Belgian business leaders desired. In fact, Belgian business leaders hoped to strike a number of permanent bargains with German interests, similar to those some French industrialists also sought. For decades key sectors of Belgian industry, steel being the most important, had belonged to international cartels, and the concept of an integrated, regulated European economic community always attracted them—and this involved cooperation with German producers.

Striking a balance between noncooperation and economic integration that would later allow them to absolve themselves of collaboration was inherently impossible: Belgian big business wanted to sell and make profit, and it did so, but never with the unabashed eagerness of their French peers. The Galopin committee's initial summer 1941 target for industrial exports to Germany was exceeded by double within half a year, and the volume of German purchases of industrial products increased until early 1944, when it reached at least two-thirds to three-quarters of all Belgian industrial output. Belgian industry was geared to fill Nazi orders almost exclusively. Indeed, its leaders would have gladly sold more had the Germans commanded it and kept economic disorder from lowering productivity after 1942.

Admittedly, Belgium's business and financial leadership acted not out of any ideological preference but only because they pragmatically sought to protect their own profits and economic position. Their policy was self-serving but also hedged its bets regarding the ultimate outcome of the war. But its net effect, notwithstanding the convoluted motives that were revealed later, was a functional collaborationism that defined the basic relationship between Belgium and its conquerors for most of the war.[8]

### The Netherlands
The Dutch experience with collaboration was no less ambivalent than the Belgian and paralleled it in many crucial ways. The Dutch government as early as 1937 concluded that real military resistance to a German invasion was futile, and although the governing cabinet planned to go into exile along with the monarchy, it also instructed the Secretaries General to remain at their posts along with their entire staffs and continue to run the state according to the applicable international legal codes for conquered nations. It did, however, stipulate that under no circumstances could the bureaucracy accept the installation of a government of Dutch Nazis. With this one condition, the Secretaries General offered to cooperate with the Nazi administration under Reich Commissioner Arthur Seyss-Inquart, and

some secretaries both in word and deed revealed their readiness to interpret their original mandate to Germany's advantage. Unlike some of his
peers in Belgium, Seyss-Inquart was a true Nazi, one of only twenty-four
men later executed as war criminals, yet he accepted the secretaries' offer,
assured them they could criticize policies before they were adopted and
resign without recrimination, but also that he expected them to implement them loyally.

In fact, the two sides needed each other for purely pragmatic reasons.
The Nazis had neither the plans nor the personnel to run Holland, and their
agencies there, as in most places, were often at cross purposes with one
another; and while they were friendly to the Dutch Nazis, the NSB
(*Nationaal-Socialistische Beweging*), initially they regarded them as incapable of fulfilling key responsibilities. But the pillars of the Dutch
Establishment at first believed that Germany would win the war and this, for
better or worse, required them to adapt to reality. Moreover, the Nazis
deemed the Dutch to be Aryans and had vague plans eventually to annex
Holland. But even more important than this combination of Nazi and
Dutch elite perceptions and goals was the fact that the Germans got a great
deal of functional cooperation from most of the population for the better
part of the war despite its indifference or hostility toward Nazi and fascist
ideology. That 51,000 Dutchmen (far more than in Belgium) joined
German military units, 17,000 of whom were in the S.S., or that at least
120,000 Dutch were charged with collaboration after the war, did not alter
the fact that the local Nazis were divided, maintained poor relations with
the S.S., and were woefully deficient in those skills essential to Germany if
it were to fully exploit Holland's potential. Even though the Nazis ended
their relatively permissive occupation phase in the spring of 1941 and initiated a ruthless crackdown on the population, it was not until the fall of 1943,
months after their policy toward the public was stiffened even further, that
they replaced most of the mayors of the key cities with NSB members—but
even then they could not dispense with those beneath them.

Indeed, the complexity of the mutually opportunistic relationship
between the Nazis and the Dutch mandarinate was revealed in the remarkable career of the most important of the secretaries, Hans Max Hirschfeld,
who was in charge of trade, industry, agriculture, and water transport.
Hirschfeld was Jewish and remained at his posts throughout the war, after
which he was dismissed from the civil service "with honor" and soon given
other vital government assignments. His obedience to the occupation was
shown when in 1943 he signed the ordinance (the proper official had
refused!) allowing the Nazis to round up recalcitrant men who refused
labor service in Germany, but he also strongly opposed the occupation's
anti-Semitic decrees. He believed that economic chaos had to be avoided
at all cost lest society be destroyed in the process, and this caused him to

do much more to forestall and then control the black market than anyone else in Europe was able to accomplish—a fact which meant that until late 1944, Holland's food problem remained far less grave than any other country's. But while both the Nazis and the traditional Dutch elite pursued their self-serving and cynical objectives pragmatically, the Nazis got by far the better of the bargain.

Dutch exports to Germany between 1938 and 1943 increased more than threefold, even though Dutch industrial production fell by more than a third during the same period and their imports dropped. By 1941–42 over a quarter of all Dutch industrial output, and half of it by 1944, was going to Germany, the larger part of it in the form of military orders—which Dutch businessmen sought out and gained a reputation of filling much better than the French or Belgians. Their profits, as a consequence, were very high. And until spring 1943 the Dutch police, including a large majority of those in Amsterdam, did whatever the Nazis demanded in rounding up Jews and Communists, for which they assumed the principal responsibility. To refuse risked trial before an S.S. court. Given such success in those economic and political areas most important to them, key German officials could overlook the lesser ways by which the Dutch bureaucracy also simultaneously served its other interests, including—when the Nazi defeat seemed inevitable—the Resistance.[9]

### The Polish Torment

The nuances and complexities in fathoming and making judgments on the relationship between the Nazi occupiers and those who administered the governmental and economic institutions they sought to utilize are so problematic in western Europe because the personal risks for anyone in a senior post who hesitated or refused to participate in Nazi plans involved their careers and fortunes, or the material welfare of their families, but their lives were not often at stake. Organizations as such had few choices, for the Nazis had both the power and the will to utilize them, but those who headed them were dispensable and there were always people eager, and generally able, to replace them. Concerning those in less exalted positions, until 1943 even workers or farmers, who were essentially anonymous and whom the Nazis disregarded outside their roles in institutions (of which they were but small cogs), could also usually choose courses that spared them the hazards of destruction.

Moral judgments regarding the conduct of people facing such predicaments are possible, and to the degree that the context in which men and women exist is nonlethal, they become less and less problematic. For in a world full of crises constantly threatening to undermine, erode, and destroy rational values and social organizations, moral judgments regarding the objective consequences of individual action or inaction are not only possible and far easier, but are obligatory insofar as preserving minimal norms for necessary individual reactions to evil and oppression become a prerequisite for the continuity of civilized human behavior and life itself, above all in situations that intrinsically require often difficult or even dangerous personal choices. Although not everyone can or even should play a heroic role, the perpetuation and attainment of rational human values and institutions depends very heavily upon the existence of a sufficient number of foolhardy and selfless idealists prepared at a cost to their own material and physical welfare to inhibit or resist institutional oppression and stimulate needed social changes, for if only egoists and opportunists peopled the world, then chaos would quickly replace human civilization in the positive meaning of that term. After 1942 a very small number of west Europeans began to confront such issues and take what actions their values demanded.

For those living every day in eastern Europe's vortex of total oppression, where the risks of death were overwhelming, each individual was required to adopt altogether distinctive criteria for personal conduct when survival became the principal objective of his or her life. The measure of acceptable or ideal human behavior, if not theoretically for moral philosophers reflecting comfortably after the events then at least in reality, became radically more problematic in those situations where everyone's choices of action were tantamount to decisions involving life or nearly certain death. Once we comprehend the irreversible predicaments that millions on the verge of destruction confronted, the standards for praise and condemnation become far more difficult, notwithstanding the need to maintain a socially responsible basis for judging individual conduct in the face of evil. The very notion of people acting in a minimally socially responsible manner implicitly precludes the prospect of instant death for those behaving with a modicum of decency. In western Europe such risks existed but were not the inviolable rule, but in Poland they were: one could easily die any day in countless ways, and for reasons that were often wholly capricious—nearly 6 million Poles perished and the imminence of death became integral to existence. Even today, after nearly a century of barbarism and war, there are simply no sufficiently nuanced and sensitive moral criteria for facilely evaluating human comportment in the midst of cataclysms.

It was the existence of such cataclysmic options that profoundly affected the relationship of Poles to the Nazi-managed government, which employed about 280,000 of them. The Nazis ignored entirely The Hague conventions on occupied countries that they nominally respected in western Europe, but collaborators and members of the Polish Home Army alike were eager to work in the Nazi regime, for only in that manner could one markedly improve one's chances of survival or, in many instances, assist the Resistance. There were upwards of 1 million genuine collaborators by the summer of 1944, according to Nazi estimates, not including the many Poles among the 100,000 prewar residents of Poland who claimed to be Germans by blood.

Wartime Poland was a nightmare. Blackmailing Jews in hiding or secret Resistance members became widespread. Banditry, much less ordinary thievery, became an increasingly common and ultimately widespread fact of existence that far transcended servicing the black market or the corruption endemic in maintaining it. All of these activities were simply basic forms of survival for those determined to live at any price. Indeed, banditry assumed ostensibly patriotic shapes also, although the population itself could never tell the difference, and it extended the grave problems of living in urban areas to the far more affluent countryside. Disputes between underground organizations or over property, or personal and even family squabbles were resolved when someone sent an anonymous denunciation to the Nazi police—which occurred in at least hundreds of cases. Profound and growing social disintegration and social anarchy produced all the other symptoms associated with violence; alcoholism was the most common by far, but occult practices also flourished in diverse forms: the belief in millennial rumors, fortune-telling, astrology, and the like. Criminal behavior, usually for personal but sometimes for social ends, became pervasive.

In effect, Poland's social organization, and the human bonds and obligations upon which a normal society is based, disintegrated to such an extent that widespread collaboration became integral to the antisocial context which suffused the nation. The population was to an extraordinary degree desocialized and reduced to the most private existences as individuals and their families sought ways to survive. The systemic corruption built into the economy and daily existence reinforced this destruction of a sense of community and social solidarity among much of the population. This insensitivity to each other was also an inevitable concomitant of the large majority of Poles' profound anti-Semitism and indifference, if not initial sympathy among many toward the Nazi persecution of the Jews—which eventually moderated to mere neutrality when the Poles realized that the Nazis were committing genocide. Although there was absolutely nothing that the Poles in their adversity could safely do to prevent it, the fact remains that much Jewish property fell into the hands of many of them, few of whom welcomed any changes that might require them to return it.

Both Jews and Poles suffered a common tragedy in the large areas of Poland where ethnic Ukrainians and White Russians were dominant. The bulk of the latter were farmhands who, like people everywhere, were victims caught in the maelstrom of war: they might become Red Army soldiers or partisans, or be suspected of being enemies and killed; or they could volunteer to become menial auxiliaries of the initially victorious German army, and possibly live. Not many had political convictions but merely wanted to survive the war in the face of the Nazi colossus. Most detested the Poles, who had persecuted all of its minorities for decades. Some unquestionably accepted Nazi arms to murder at least 60,000 of their Polish neighbors, or to avenge themselves against Polish partisans who slaughtered entire Ukrainian villages. When the Nazis began to use some of them as concentration-camp guards or policemen, the Ukrainians or White Russians who volunteered for the Nazi-created auxiliaries were the inevitable deadly products of the intense nationalist prejudices and violence that had inspired Poland's rulers until then. The Nazis recruited almost a half-million of these support forces by the summer of 1942, only about one-fifth of whom lived in Poland itself, and then lost track of their growth, which may have reached as high as 1.2 million the following year. They helped to kill countless numbers of Jews, Poles, and their own countrymen.[10]

This profoundly destructive transformation of human attitudes and behavior in the face of imminent death affected even the Jewish community, whose manpower the Nazis sought to use for the time- and labor-consuming tasks of the Holocaust in much the same way that they also attempted elsewhere to employ Europe's people and economy to extend their own resources. The Nazi-sponsored *Judenräte*—Jewish councils— grew out of the prewar organizations that had for generations dealt with the outside political authorities on behalf of the Jewish community, although the Nazis established them anew in the USSR; 43 percent of the members of the *Judenrat* had been active in Jewish councils and organizations before the war, principally as Zionists. The *Judenrat's* major assignment was to list and deliver Jews for "resettlement." Many Jewish leaders heroically refused the Nazi demands that they share the *Judenrat's* work and died for it, but thousands agreed, and some even volunteered. Many of them, vainly in the case of four-fifths, hoped to save their families and themselves thereby. Some treated their *Judenrat* roles as simply a means of prospering; a few were very corrupt. At first many of them handed over lists of the old, the very young, and the sick, but during the great harvest of lives in Lodz and Warsaw in 1942 the *Judenrat* names became more "democratic." In 1942 the councils worked too slowly for the Nazis, who supplemented them with their own forces, but the majority of the *Judenräte* also opposed resistance and did much to discourage it.

The Nazis unquestionably would have destroyed the Jewish community without the aid of the *Judenräte*, although they would have been less efficient and lives may have been overlooked or spared thereby, and no one doubts that the vast majority of its members detested the unenviable positions into which they had fallen. But the *Judenräte* needed their own staffs to fulfill their tasks, and in Warsaw they had about 6,000 employees, over one-third as police—all but 100 of whom were essentially unpaid volunteers. A majority of the Jewish policemen had been merchants and artisans by trade, and the Nazis preferred to hire refugees with no close ties to the local community. A small portion of them were Resistance members seeking to exploit the police forces, and some of the police attempted to maintain good relations with the underground, which meant they could perform useful tasks at various times. Two-fifths of the police were members of Zionist parties, among whom the Revisionists (who before the war had evolved a quasi-fascist ideology and wore brown shirts) composed almost a half of this excrescence of the human condition in extreme distress. But all were uniformly detested and feared by those over whom they ruled with mounting arrogance. They normally had wooden or rubber clubs, but during the Vilna roundup of October 1942 the Nazis entrusted them with guns. Notwithstanding exceptions, as a whole these volunteer police exploited fully the potential for corruption inherent in their control over the fates of people; many lived very well, they were key figures in the smuggling trade, and they became reliable collaborators with the Nazis in their demonic project to destroy all Jews.[11]

## Attentisme and Public Opinion

Collaboration was widespread everywhere in occupied Europe, above all among the small group of prewar business and government leaders whose decisions had always compelled the masses to conform to their policies. But independently of the overwhelming constraints others imposed on their opposition, Europe's people felt beaten and demoralized, and what very little defiance there was at the inception went virtually unrecorded. Collaboration unquestionably harnessed much of the Continent's economic resources and manpower to the Nazi war effort, and so long as Hitler succeeded, the willingness of countless millions to tolerate such a course persisted in spite of the war's mounting costs to the occupied peoples in terms of lives lost or recast, and of hunger and want. However much they disliked the Nazi cause, Europe's people obeyed their orders, and at least two years passed before significant exceptions arose.

The motives for collaboration varied so radically—from the weight of a sense of overwhelming defeatism, to sheer terror and oppression, to a genuine preference for fascist solutions, and much else—that simplistic explanations remain misleading. Poland revealed how the Nazis ultimately defined almost completely the parameters of possible behavior, disintegrating the very fabric of social life and organization in the course of imposing total terror. Vichy France favored the defeat of the USSR and Great Britain, aligning a traditional, eminently respectable, and reactionary ruling class with Hitler for reasons that principally reflected their free choice. In

Belgium and Holland, notwithstanding the earlier-mentioned fascination among big-business and financial elements for an integrated European economy akin to the Nazi "New Order," the basic influence guiding the traditional leaders of both nations' collaboration was their belief during 1940–41 that the Nazis had won the war and that they had to prepare to live as well as possible with the calamity. By comparing the Belgians and Dutch to the French we can better assess how many fewer compromises the former made than they might have, and these should not be minimized. But in all three nations the pillars of the business community operated as normally as possible, and while very few could have kept their factories from operating, many sought also to profit.

The transition from collaboration to "attentisme," which involves people conforming in their daily conduct but also beginning to withdraw the moral or political support they once gave a regime, while at the same time passively waiting for it to be replaced, is a stance inherently too ambiguous to measure or even describe precisely. There were many who always subjectively disliked, even detested, the Nazi-dominated status quo and yet aided it greatly in many functional ways for diverse reasons, including for some a belief that only by working with an authority could they mitigate its evils. Attentisme is a transitional phase between support and opposition to a ruling power, inspired by anything from a wholly opportunistic urge to be on the winning side, whichever it is, to a critical posture as yet incapable of finding expression in personal behavior. It is less an individual endorsement of a new political option than a mental retraction of toleration or support for an old one. For many it leads no further, for others it is a stage before becoming a part of the opposition when the risks are no longer so overwhelmingly dangerous. The politics of withdrawal and survival can remain politics nonetheless, because beneath the external posture of caution there frequently exists a set of residual attitudes, including perceptions of reality, which are often an intermediate stance fully capable of later being organized at the right time if the leadership or proper context arises. Forces and events inevitably affect people and produce a latent, potentially radicalized consciousness among many of those who have lost the material preconditions for survival or are exhausted. By itself inconclusive, attentisme among the masses is an interval pregnant with potential.

But in social terms and certainly at least in the short run, the practical consequences of individuals' behavior immeasurably outweighs the often opaque meaning of their subjective feelings, which are in the last analysis proper topics for psychologists or intellectual historians rather than social analysts. These dilemmas are significant almost entirely among powerful men whose actions are always infinitely more visible, have calculable consequences, and are later subjected to the scrutiny of historians or, in some cases, postwar courts dealing with collaboration. From this viewpoint there is relatively little difficulty in assessing the role that traditional European leaders played in facilitating the Nazi war machine's desire and need to integrate the conquered nations' economic structures: they all greatly eased Hitler's tasks. If the motives of those who led Belgium and Holland were very different at the inception, and they operated with the endorsements of regimes that sustained prewar legitimacy rather than, as in the case of Vichy, seeking to overthrow it, from the Nazi viewpoint the practical effect was the same.

Save in the case of true Vichyites, or those who enriched themselves during the war by sacrificing the interests and lives of those around them for reasons that had nothing to do with their personal survival or of those dependent upon them, it becomes increasingly difficult to employ moral criteria or opinions as the risks of action increase and the issue of life and death becomes integral to understanding the absence of resistance in its many diverse forms. Indeed, moral and ethical judgments are much more problematic than purely instrumental ones regarding the relative social and human costs of tolerating evil forces as they evolve from their inception to their denouement. When judging the failure of people to act, it is impossible to dismiss the Nazi willingness to kill or the extent to which they did so for reasons that were racist, political, and merely capricious. But in practical fact the more philosophical issues of collaboration and resistance, or that nebulous intermediate stage of attentisme that can be an aspect of both of these stages or stand alone as a wholly autonomous stance in its own right, can usefully be dismissed when analyzing the vast majority of people, the consequences of whose actions as individuals have meaning almost entirely to themselves and their own tiny circle.

At this level of anonymity and functional inconsequentiality when opposition remains unorganized, few had real choices in daily existence: most people in cities had to work every day, to search for food constantly, to cope with the increasingly time-consuming ennui of daily existence under occupation. To say they should have made choices, as ideally they should have or at least we might prefer they did, ignores such essential routine distractions as well as the huge organizations ready to destroy them the instant they got out of hand. A fixation on daily life in the context of terror and the very real obligations it imposes is illuminating, particularly in telling us why changes do not occur and why profoundly evil systems remain unchallenged for as long as they do. It especially accounts for, even if it cannot ultimately exonerate, passive human behavior, the privatization of lives, and the desocialization of the masses.

Such insight, however, does not adequately explain significant change insofar as it involves those men and women who at certain rare but historically decisive times in this century have in fact initiated it: for on exceptional occasions, among a fraction of the people, there *are* basic transformations that traditional decision makers do not initiate, and usually oppose, and which begin with those who either choose to or must drop their routine and challenge society as it has been or is becoming. Such departures rarely have the potential at their inception for evolving into revolutions, but they do undermine the hegemony and tranquility of those who have ruled, driving them in turn to draconian solutions that in the short run are likely to prevail over mass discontent or opposition. Obviously, the way (and the reason why) the masses' consciousness and mode of expressing itself evolves or is organized is crucial, as 1914–18 revealed, and later we will return to this issue in the World War Two context. But the problem here is really to explain the origins of basic social movements that challenge existing social or political systems to create innovating causes or forces that sometimes succeed but more likely fail—of social dynamics rather than stasis. Such issues subsume the main currents of this century's experiences with change, about which we still know far too little.

When, how, and why the European masses' perceptions and desires began gradually and at times imperceptibly to shift is a matter of prime significance. Although when the war began people in most nations related to society and each other with intense personalism and lethargy, by 1945 a greater proportion of Europe's population had become politicized than at any time in this century. This fundamental transformation of political attitudes and goals, this process of resocialization, became the essential precondition for the emergence of Resistance movements; but its significance far transcended it because it left a persistent legacy of political attitudes that by the end of the war, and then afterward, shaped European politics long after the Resistance disappeared in most nations as a potential armed threat to the existing political and class structures. This radicalization very greatly exceeded the willingness of people to become true resisters, and occurred even though the vast majority of Europeans also had increasingly to cope with overwhelming daily concerns. What changed was the context in which they defined the world they lived in, their estimates of the relevance of alternatives, and for some—always a small minority—their conceptions of their own roles as social actors.

World War Two, with its vast firepower and mobility, and the immense economic dislocations inherent in blitzkrieg doctrine, Allied strategic bombing, and the mass mobilization of populations, absorbed civilians to an extent that was technically impossible during 1914–18. Nazi goals and methods made civilians victims as never before. That the war's ultimate political outcome under these circumstances would be defined as much by its impact on individuals—their loyalties and needs—as on the final positions of armies was inevitable as the war became a social process as well as a purely military conflict. Reality's impact caused inherited legacies and beliefs to disintegrate, to free the minds, if not the behavior, of many from the relatively pervasive prewar consensus on politics and the institutional forms that society should ideally assume. Traditional wisdom became fragile, and it was questioned in ways that had never before occurred. And given the class nature of the occupation regimes and the very different responses of social constituencies to the Nazi onslaught, it was also inevitable that those whom the Nazis never consulted, and whose lives and roles remained invisible when they functioned as obscure individuals, should redefine their attitudes toward the dominant prewar class—especially where it was so profoundly compromised as collaborators.

How the war affected the political development and ideas of the people of various nations depended on several factors, which united to produce quite different experiences and had a very uneven impact in each of them. All of these causal elements interacted at the same time, and to focus on them singly is convenient for purposes of explanation even though true comprehension requires that they be treated as unique combinations appropriate to the distinctive characteristics of every country and to the men and women within them.

First was the extent to which a nation suffered economically and militarily, and peoples' lives thereby affected. Obviously, by creating a survivalist mentality and antisocial relations, intense deprivation and the risk of death could produce a total preoccupation with the details of living and a profound pessimism and despair at one time, or an incentive for hatred at another. The least hungry were also the least estranged insofar as this material source of ideological alienation was concerned. But suffering could alter political perceptions, or provoke action in one context but stifle it in yet another.

Nazi repression was a constraint everywhere, but far more decisive in, say, Germany or Poland than in Belgium. One could very easily get killed or go to prison, and fear inhibited communication—and certainly actual deeds. Repression was an immensely effective deterrent to action on the whole, but when it became overwhelming and indiscriminate, it caused some who had previously sought to survive by remaining passive to question whether it made much difference how they behaved, and to conclude that they were safer in the illegal world than in the "legal." An individual had to worry about his own fate but also that of his family, who needed him or who might be held culpable for his conduct. But if repression retarded most collective forms of expression, it could never prevent disaffection and hatred from finding other outlets sooner or later, and it provoked some to action.

No less crucial to the relevance of people's growing hostility toward the Nazis and their surrogates, and whether there was any plausible hope for change, was the real balance of military and political forces in the war itself. When it appeared the Nazis were certain to triumph, then countless tens of millions saw their alienation as a cause of depression and helplessness, for the future seemed bleak whatever they thought or did, and they regarded public expressions of opposition as both dangerous and futile. But the military course of the war prompted the emergence of hostility and a pre-Resistance mentality, even if people were unwilling to embark on activities that endangered themselves at a hopeless moment. In a word, they responded far more eagerly to a cause that was increasingly likely to succeed than one that seemed quixotic, and this perception, linked with the others, was crucial to both political thought and the willingness of a fraction of each nation to both consider and take action that might, at the very least, reverse the war's legacies and possibly achieve necessary vengeance and justice in the future.

### Germany

Given the extent of the terror the Nazis imposed in Germany against all opponents, particularly Social Democrats and Communists, and the elaborate structure they perfected for reporting dissent, repression defined the outer limits on public opinion even though it by no means explains much of the support the regime obtained. In the period immediately after Hitler acceded to power in 1933, over 100,000 persons were arrested, many of them tortured and killed, and countless others were fired from their jobs. The head of the S.S. concentration camps after 1934, who had been in a psychiatric hospital only a year earlier, automatically imposed death sentences for the inmates' most trivial political gestures. Although there were small informal groups of former Social Democrats and Communists who had known each other before the Nazi reign and who still met or communicated secretly, for all practical purposes by 1937 the pre-Nazi Left was mercilessly and successfully obliterated save as a remembrance, the consequences of which appeared harmless until the war was almost over. But the Nazis closely monitored working-class opinion until the war ended, mainly to sustain labor discipline. Mounting arrests of workers for breaches of discipline intimidated those few tempted to resist, as did the nearly sixfold increase in executions between 1940 and 1943—reaching 5,336 in the latter year. Repression was integral to the system, especially against the working class, and by 1941–43 only a minute fraction of those incarcerated were deemed to be political criminals.

As in the rest of Europe, terror and success combined to generate a vast number of the usual opportunists able to prosper in any regime regardless of its nature. They included some former trade unionists who preferred infiltrating the purely ceremonial Nazi labor front to passivity. Only about 5 percent of the Nazi party members in early 1935 had belonged to it before the September 1930 election, when its triumph seemed imminent, and only one-third joined before Hitler came to power. As the war was ending, many of them tried in diverse ways to redeem themselves so that they might avoid retribution.

But neither opportunism nor terror can fully explain the impact of Hitler and his foreign and domestic policies on the public until about June 1941. Full employment and rising real wages after 1936 were gains that all workers desired, and these benefits persisted, albeit along with normal grievances about working conditions. Subsequently, what one social observer has called "nationalism and *embourgeoisement*" tied labor to the regime's destiny.[12] And while much of the population feared war in 1939, a very large portion—half the working class in one estimate, more in others—for a quite brief but significant time became euphoric over the succession of easy conquests in Poland and France. Their principal anxiety was not whether the war was unjust—for the broad masses, including many former leftists, were happy with victories—but that it would become protracted and ultimately might fail. Hitler and his program became genuinely popular, and this support was no longer based principally on the clout that accompanied his carrot; Detlev J. K. Peukert's argument that this conversion of many of those who had voted against Hitler was in large part material seduction by 1941 is well taken. They disliked pogroms, but anti-Semitism itself had deep, historic roots in German political culture and most people endorsed the principle if not the practice. Hitler's personal approval and charisma far transcended that of the Nazi party, which was increasingly disdained as being a haven for corrupt opportunists; Ian Kershaw has argued convincingly that "the great majority" of Germans admired Hitler in 1939, and that many millions retained their heroic fixation on him until the summer of 1944.[13]

Far more public opposition to Nazi policies came from the Catholic Church than from the working class, though even here it remained manageable because the Church's parishioners, especially among the thriving peasantry in Bavaria, shared a consensus on many crucial Nazi policies. Its bishops opposed euthanasia and resisted many of Hitler's measures after his anti-Catholic campaign began in late 1941. The honeymoon between the German public and the Nazis ended in June 1941 with the attack on the USSR, the failure of the winter campaign, and the terrible long lists of dead sons and brothers that kept arriving. The Allied bombing campaign deepened their pessimism, and defeat at Stalingrad during January 1943 shocked the people, even though many, possibly a majority, until mid-1944 retained a belief in eventual victory. By spring 1943 the Nazi leadership privately acknowledged the decline of morale and the emergence of deep defeatism among elite social groups whose enthusiasm or tolerance it could not afford to lose, and one of the reasons it forwent the strict application of its new decrees against their indulgent living was its fear of intensifying their pessimism. While the use of clout against workers increased, notwithstanding the fact that the workers' motives were rarely political, the middle class was coddled because it remained the regime's ultimate bastion of support.

For the working class, submission accompanied their deepening alienation; they neither could nor did become rebellious or organize politically lest they go to prison or die for it. As in the past, if a worker mocked Nazis in a joke, he did it privately and only to intimate acquaintances. Whatever they had felt about the war at its inception, they now perceived themselves as small cogs in a giant machine—helpless to do anything. Workers were more likely than before to attack British plutocracy in public than Communism, while other classes did the reverse. Although what are now described as "everyday forms of resistance"—oaths, cynical comments, malingering, "non-Nazi" behavior—existed among the masses, especially younger people, such inherently elusive and unmeasurable symbolic gestures and nonconformist behavior by themselves in no way threatened the regime. The personalism and escape to private, isolated worlds that profoundly defined the daily life of so many critical and war-weary people also affected the way they related to each other, and while it made them somewhat less pliable for Nazi purposes, it also kept individuals from behaving politically, which required communication. If the Nazis disliked any form of conduct, they merely dragged its perpetrators off to fates that were all too apparent to potential critics.

What those tiny remnants of Social Democracy and Communism who survived could and did do was secretly to keep intact their identities, ideas, and beliefs. When the war ended, the old activists, along with new working-class elements, immediately reproduced the entire prewar structure of unions and traditional parties throughout Germany. They reemerged as large as ever, especially where the Left had been strongest before the war, and for a period many were vaguely radicalized in ways that reflected their long nightmare—in the process challenging Germany's traditionally dominant social classes, who now asserted they had never really been pro-Hitler.[14]

### Belgium and The Netherlands
The Dutch people initially believed that the Nazis had won the war, and therefore considered public opposition to be futile. While this pessimistic view persisted until about the end of 1942, the Dutch still keenly disliked those who collaborated with Nazis, and street brawls between NSB and leftist bands were not infrequent in the period immediately after the German

invasion, while the great bulk of the population listened to the Dutch radio-in-exile and made small but visible patriotic gestures. Nazi permissiveness ended in February 1941 after organized groups of young Jews, working principally with the Communists, fought and badly bloodied NSB thugs sent into Amsterdam's Jewish area to harass them. The Nazis arrested 425 Jews. At the end of the month the Communists called a one-day strike to protest the abuse of Jews, managing to bring out many of the shipyard and metalworkers and sufficient others to paralyze much of the city. In the immediate aftermath the Nazis arrested and deported at least 1,000 strikers—most of whom never returned.

While this moving and unique gesture of solidarity reflected Dutch mass opinion, it was also plain that the Nazis had the will to prevail, and this intensified the public's dejection as well as its hatred. When in April 1943 the Nazis ordered former Dutch soldiers they had released from internment to return to captivity, about 1 million people went on strike, with serious economic consequences, but the Nazis immediately shot sixty and rounded up many protesters. Hatred of the Nazis and collaborators increased, but so too did the costs of opposition. But Dutch policemen, who until then had obeyed the Nazis loyally, both in response to the obvious mood of the people and the growing prospects of Hitler's defeat, began to lose their traditional efficiency in fulfilling German orders. Even the railroad workers, whose union leaders had declared loyalty to the Nazi regime after May 1940 and who impersonally and efficiently shipped over 400,000 labor conscripts and 112,000 Jews to Germany, saw the handwriting on the wall and in September 1944 went on strike at the behest of the Allied Supreme Command—although they successfully insisted on receiving their pay plus overtime and a Christmas bonus.

In both Belgium and Holland the prewar ministers had departed for England—much to the people's displeasure in the Belgian case—and those they authorized to remain collaborated to a degree that left the public stupefied and passive. During the first months many Belgians even welcomed the German presence because even though the great majority deplored their victory, they assumed that it was a foregone reality that had to be accepted fatalistically; and at least it ended the intense insecurity of being a potential battlefield or unable to plan one's life. For well over two years after the invasion, the universities remained essentially untouched and the large bulk of students worried principally about their courses. Not until March 1943, when the Nazis began to draft many male students for labor, did student apathy end. But countless Belgians tried first to pursue normal existences, and believed that they could adapt successfully to a situation it was futile to resist.

Onerous German demands imposed a mounting toll that quickly eroded the Belgian public's initial aspiration to survive with their lives essentially unchanged, and since the Secretaries General were instrumental in implementing the occupation's goals, most people believed it had become collaborationist, a view that grew until about the spring of 1943, when its opposition to the draconian Nazi forced-labor edicts gained it considerable respect. It was no longer conventional wisdom by the latter part of 1942, especially among workers and peasants, that Germany would inevitably be victorious, and those who were truly pro-German became a small minority. Although the public was overwhelmingly against violent resistance it was also far more opposed to helping repress it in any way. Even when food supplies increased, and ingenuity helped overcome many material difficulties, hatred for the Nazis mounted, and now most people believed that Germany would be defeated—a perception that greatly increased respect for the Soviet Union. By early 1944 the population's anger was directed less toward Germans, for most saw the regular Wehrmacht soldier (as opposed to the S.S.) as an essentially decent and oppressed soul, than toward collaborators; the Belgians even showed a certain respect toward General von Falkenhausen, whose removal in the summer of 1944 distressed many of them. The Belgian public survived on fraud to a greater extent and more successfully than others in western Europe, but it always reproached the greatly increasing banditry and violence, whatever the personal or political reason for it. Although by 1944 it hated collaborators most, at the same time many feared that civil war could follow Nazi domination.[15]

### France

French defeatism before the German invasion unquestionably facilitated Vichy's emergence, and in various ways it profoundly influenced the public's views and behavior during the war itself. While the weight of events, from Nazi exactions to Allied victories, affected mass opinion significantly over the course of time, prewar legacies remained crucial also—and no analysis that ignores both can do justice to the complexity of French ideas during the war or the class society that produced them. French opinion varied on the issue of its relationship to Germany far more than that in any other conquered nation, and what one keen observer of the period calls France's "mental baggage" was in reality the inherited perceptions of diverse classes living insulated existences that greatly affected their reactions to all aspects of social experience, politics included. While it was largely the provincial practicing-Catholic petite bourgeoisie and peasants who gave Vichy its large mass base, industrialists and financiers also supported it, along with the rarefied heights of Paris's "milieu politico-salonnard," and these groups provided it with influence and power.[16]

Their idol was Marshal Pétain, who like Hitler remained far more popular, far longer, than the political constituencies backing him, and who revealed the irresistible lure that military demigods have always held for so many Frenchmen. Pétain provided the regime legitimacy long after it otherwise had utterly dissipated it, and even in the spring of 1944 Pétain still could mobilize adoring crowds to hear him inveigh on behalf of the synthesis of the mythologized cult of the nation, God, and human personality upon which Vichy was constructed. Many of those who favored the Allies still harbored the belief that in the end Pétain would emerge as venerated as he had been a quarter-century earlier. And a large majority opposed the severe sentence later imposed upon him or, indeed, any punishment whatsoever.

At first, opposition to the war came from the Left as well as the traditional Right. Former soldiers especially were against it, and there was simply none of the irrational yet indispensable rabid enthusiasm of 1914 to be found anywhere. Without being pro-Nazi, many peasants and bourgeois refused to repeat the protracted suffering of 1914–18. The Communists opposed preparedness, Socialist pacifists were vocal in their party, and the notion of dealing with the Germans pragmatically seemed less reprehensible than the bloody options. The consensus for collaboration was far greater than the power of those against it, and whatever else its opinions on Vichy or de Gaulle, the French public as late as 1944 was overwhelmingly opposed to violence for any reason. As we shall see, this meant that before June 1944 only a tiny minority took tangible steps to resist in ways that affected the Nazis or Vichy materially, and a small minority provided the Resistance with a responsive audience. Similar attitudes also affected Vichy's paramilitary forces in much the same way. The great majority of people were too busy with their daily problems to oppose anyone actively. But however French opinion toward the war evolved within all of these complex constraints, evolve it did.

The first year of the Nazi occupation found France utterly apathetic and exhausted, the Resistance and even its passive sympathizers too minuscule to be measured accurately. Hitler's invasion of the Soviet Union galvanized the Communist party, but its lack of propaganda impact on the general population rivaled Vichy's. British broadcasts kept even isolated provinces aware of major military events, and we possess considerable detail on the state of opinion in various *départements*. By late 1942 not more than one-third of France remained loyal to Vichy, and far more favored an Allied victory. Vichy, as a nominal state, could still mobilize its armed *milice* to cope with dissidence and resistance, and while the *milice* was about as large as the active Resistance in early 1944, its membership in some areas existed mainly on paper—to be in the *milice* was to avoid forced labor service. But if both are reflections of what Frenchmen did, neither is an accurate gauge of how they felt, for the worlds of thought and action are very distinct domains.

As in the case of the million Dutch workers who struck in April 1943

against forcing labor service on former soldiers, in France it was the introduction of compulsory labor—*service du travail obligatoire* (STO)—in
February 1943 that galvanized uncommitted or pro-Vichy public opinion
and alienated it from Vichy to an unparalleled extent. It was far more
important than Nazi economic exactions, which affected Vichy's rural
strongholds the least, if at all, while the STO reached everywhere equally.
By mid-1943 most of France was against Vichy, and the regime knew it.
And by November 1944 a great section of the French public had undergone
a far-reaching shift in its attitudes, and three-fifths of it believed that the
Soviet Union was making the most important contribution to defeating the
Nazis. How far such sentiments might shape postwar political life was a
fundamental challenge for France—and its allies.[17]

## The Emergence of the Resistance

The Nazis fought the Second World War in a manner that affected the
lives of the Continent's civilians more profoundly than any conflict in its
history, thereby making them central to the political and military outcome
of the war in a manner that the leaders of the warring nations had utterly
failed to anticipate. The intensity of the suffering and repression, its capri-
ciousness and frequent unavoidability, and the growing hope of aid from
the outside eventually transformed a pre-Resistance context and mentality
by 1944 into an environment in which many more people than ever were
ready and willing, or simply increasingly obliged, to become a part of the
widespread phenomenon that had no precedent in Europe—the
Resistance. Even where relatively few participated in it directly, the
Resistance's real and potential impact remained great, perhaps even decisive, in many nations; even more significant, the Resistance shaped the
ideas and aspirations of a far greater but inactive group that supported its
actions and goals. It was this pervasive transformation of opinion that produced the most lasting political consequences.

The often highly diverse organizations, movements, and people that
comprised the Resistance in each country had fundamental, even decisive,
effects both on the future of internal politics and on their nation's role in
international affairs, and this was immediately obvious to everyone within
each of them as well as to the outside powers. Although the dominant
French Resistance was qualitatively different ideologically from the Polish,
the fact remains that the very existence of the Resistance in both of these
extreme cases posed identical political challenges to the specific members
of the anti-Nazi alliance whose troops were scheduled to invade each of
these states.

People joined the Resistance for many reasons, and the argument of some writers that its permanent leaders were unusually strong, independent, and selfless characters—all with heroic, charismatic qualities that are all too rare at any time—is neither a sufficient causal explanation nor inconsistent with the fact that most Resistance organizations everywhere had a very distinctive social and class composition. Many Resistance leaders did indeed possess remarkable "spiritual" or existential motives, and while this did not keep them from also being highly political or even paramilitary extensions of Allied armies, it was by itself not the basis of growth; such attributes tended to characterize, above all, the nonleftist Resistance organizations.[18]

Excessive emphasis on personalities and their traits begs the question of why certain class constituencies joined the Resistance in much greater numbers than others, while collaborators too had specific social and class features. For it was precisely the social and class nature of various Resistance organizations, their political and ideological visions and the potential for civil and class conflict they implied, that made them so fraught with implications for the future of various European nations as well as the international power balance axiomatically linked to internal politics. Resistance movements grew because of the pressures the Nazis imposed on people and social groups, the individuals' views of the relative personal risks of activism as opposed to passivity over time, especially as the chances of Allied victory mounted, and the weight of group identification and its importance to cooperative modes of survival. From the beginning of the war politically and morally conscious leaders necessarily functioned within the parameters such larger constraints and opportunities imposed—they might manipulate but they could not transcend them.

Protracted total war also gravely challenges in innumerable ways the social systems of each nation involved in the struggle, their structural and ideological cohesion, and the loyalty of the people in each of them to the ruling party's official doctrine and political legitimacy—not the least during World War Two because the governing classes of many nations collaborated with the Nazis and thereby lost their nationalist cachet. Hence the emergence of the specter, to a degree otherwise unimaginable in 1939, of basic social transformation, even revolution, in the wake of resistance. By late 1943 it was an obvious question, especially in light of the growing Resistance organizations with their resolute and partially armed members, whether Europe would again experience a wave of threatened and real changes comparable both to those of 1917–19 and proportionate to this war's far greater human and institutional impact.

Europe's Resistance movements began as disparate, minute groups, and in many places the role of highly disciplined and motivated personalities or pure idealists was often not crucial, or even present. The gamut of organizational forms and experiences, sometimes in the same nation, ran from the highly localized and spontaneous to tightly organized Allied intelligence operations. Such radically differing organizational forms had obvious implications for the Resistance's possible military functions, especially for the Allied armies, but their latent political dangers everywhere were proportionate to the extent that increasingly large and armed autonomous local forces did—or might—define their own agenda for political action and change in the areas they controlled. In some countries this threat was to become far more crucial than in others, but by no later than mid-1944 such potential challenges were widespread. Regularizing and disciplining the diverse Resistance forces in various nations became a major issue for all the Allies; it was central to the Resistance's capacity as a military force but, above all, to its social and political roles the moment the Nazis decamped and left a vacuum of power that neither Allied armies nor discredited collaborationist or anemic exile governments could fill. Indeed, the political outcome of the Second World War to a very considerable degree depended on the resolution of this fundamental matter.

## Italy

The origins and character of the Italian Resistance were considerably more complicated than anywhere in Europe because politically and militarily Italy passed from being an ally of Germany until September 1943 to being its enemy the following month. The German army entered Italy in force in July 1943, and the nation was a battlefield south of Rome until June 1944, when the city was conquered; thereafter, the Allied armies pushed only as far as the area just south of Pisa and Florence. Meanwhile, in the Nazi-occupied north, with loyal Fascist remnants and German might as support, Mussolini created a new regime. In such a context, Resistance groups spread throughout a vast area and reflected crucial differences in their social composition and organizational structures as well as in their functions and options.

There was no Resistance movement of any consequence in Italy in 1942, and when the Communists in early 1943 decided to create partisan units, the Party had, at most, 5,000 members. Not until after the autumn of 1943, when the Allied invasion wholly transformed the political and military context, were they in a position to implement their Resistance policy. Such externally initiated changes, rather than the decisions of anti-Fascist people or parties, were the principal and decisive reasons the Resistance appeared in its crucial earliest phases, not just in Italy but everywhere in Europe after 1941. This is not to say that the conscious efforts of assorted organized groups, of which the Communist-led partisans emerged as the single most important but by no means the only one, can or should be dismissed; but the Resistance also arose out of local, autonomous, or spontaneous forces. Comprehending that such a nuanced, complex interrelationship existed is not only essential to understanding the movement's strengths and weaknesses, but also its ultimate dangers both to the Anglo-American armies and the Communist leaders who found themselves linked to a mass movement that frequently appeared about to escape their control.

Profound attentisme among anti-Fascists plagued the Resistance's growth until mid-1943, and the Anglo-American invasion of the mainland reinforced the belief among many Italians that liberation would come soon no matter what they did. In mid-1942 only a small minority—under a fifth—of those whom the Fascist political police arrested were charged with belonging to hostile organizations, and at the beginning of 1943 it was still well under one-third, only to leap to two-thirds of a far larger number by spring. During the summer of 1943 a major part of the Italian army, understandably encouraged by the conflicting political claims of Mussolini, rival dissident Fascists, and the Allies, abandoned their arms and went home. Until 1943, it is essential to recall, economic conditions in Italy were straitened but scarcely, as in other European nations, a stimulant to action. For all of the above reasons, to quote an official Communist history, "the earliest manifestations of the Resistance Movement had been almost entirely spontaneous."[19] The most visible proof of this was the Naples uprising at the end of September 1943, when the whole city—hungry, believing liberation imminent, and with access to important quantities of abandoned arms—successfully battled the Nazis for control of the city.

There were, therefore, two Italys for the duration of the war, and in the fall of 1943 Mussolini began to draft men born between 1920 and 1925 for the army he hoped to re-create, and those born in the preceding decade were subject to the labor draft, including possible deportation to Germany (where about 40,000 were in fact sent). Men of these age cohorts could no longer escape the war, and the price of passivity was now potentially greater than that of activism. Virtually all of the partisans fell into these age categories. At the end of 1943 there were, at the most, 10,000 partisans in the various formations, not including a few thousand escaped or liberated Allied prisoners of war. They were poorly equipped, some did scarcely more than stay out of harm's way, and many were the sons of the regions in which they were based.

In class terms, depending on the area and the political group nominally in charge of it, partisan formations were recruited largely from the working class and the poorer peasantry—the origins of half of its members in the Piedmont, where artisans added over a tenth and students somewhat less. But men were far more likely to join a partisan group because it was close by than for any other criterion, including its politics. The leadership cadres, especially where peasants formed a larger share of the formations, were more likely drawn from clerical, technical, and commercial occupations; elsewhere, workers played key roles. Partisans existed everywhere behind

German lines, but especially in the industrial areas of the center and north of the country. Their numbers varied with time and place, but on the whole it was clear that precisely those classes whom the Fascists had muzzled after 1921 were in command of the biggest part of the armed Resistance and that the basic tensions in Italian society that had existed before Mussolini were very likely to reemerge.

Estimates of the share of the Communist-led *Garibaldini* differ quite dramatically, but certainly they were no less than about half of the partisans by the summer of 1944, and two-fifths thereafter. British officials believed they were predominant. But the Action party, a fragile alliance of intellectuals vaguely more radical than the Communists, led approximately one-fourth of the groups, and there were smaller political forces as well. Former officers also created bands, which at most never exceeded a quarter of those north of Florence at any time. Part of these groups did little more than avoid Nazi or Fascist impositions until liberation, others were very active. In 1943 they were essentially on the defensive, as was the rest of the anti-Fascist movement located in the cities.

Appraisals of the size or political control of the partisans, urban anti-Fascist forces, and sympathizers, as everywhere, are only approximate because their membership fluctuated, depending on the political climate, military campaigns, repression, and the arms available. By the summer of 1944 there were about 82,000 partisans, a tenfold growth in seven months but still slightly smaller than the Fascist National Republican Guard. The Nazis did not pay much attention to partisan units until April 1944, but in the fall of 1944 they aimed their fury at them after allegedly losing 7,000 to 8,000 killed or captured and nearly 30,000 wounded over a three-month period. At least six German divisions then sought to destroy the partisans, treating them as outlaws with no protection under international law. And since in some areas the partisans took over large regions and declared them entirely liberated, after June 1944 often behaving like classic armies rather than decentralized guerrilla units, they offered the Nazis vulnerable targets.

The results were frightful, not the least because the partisans lost many of their best members and thereby were weakened far more than was necessary. Estimates of partisans killed—many of them during this period—range from the official figure of 45,000 to 72,500, but in either case it was a large fraction of the core membership, and much greater among Communist-led units than others. But by February 1945 the partisans had grown back to about 100,000 in all political groupings, with another 50,000 joining during the last two months of the war. By then, as well, about a half-million others also aided them materially. Later the Italian government generously estimated that about 300,000 persons had served as partisans at some time, 66,000 of whom were killed or wounded, while 125,000 soldiers became "patriots" by switching to the Allies at the appropriate moment.[20]

If these figures measured the size of the Italian Resistance adequately, they would be very pessimistic indeed, because combined they involve under 2 percent of the nation. But they leave out the role of the working class, principally in northern cities, and are a wholly unreliable index of public opinion, including among those who did nothing whatsoever throughout the epic struggles. The Communists (PCI) sought to lead strikes in the northern cities, which increased dramatically in early 1943 when the Party was still tiny. In terms of sheer numbers, however, it is clear that when 21,000 people walked off their jobs, as in Turin on March 5, 1943, the agitation of fewer than 100 PCI members in the affected factories cannot explain why they did so. There existed an immense potential of residual radical anger, a combination of the memory of what the working class had been two decades earlier as well as a detestation of current hardships, and the PCI sought eagerly to guide a militancy that both preceded and far transcended anything it might urge or do. By the end of 1943 it was better able to claim a crucial catalytic role when strikes broke out in Turin, Genoa, and elsewhere. But Communist efforts were based on cooperating with other anti-Fascist groups, and in March 1944 these all united to produce strikes in the major northern cities lasting up to eight days and involving about a half-million workers who presented explicitly political as well as economic demands in the face of Fascist and Nazi forces. In many regards these strike movements were far more visible and politically significant in their impact on the masses than the partisan activities. Until the fall of 1944, they certainly did at least as much to impair the war effort—and strikes continued throughout the last year of the war.[21]

Italy had not experienced such mass activity since the prelude to Mussolini's ascent to power. But now the middle classes were utterly discredited and impotent, outside the northern cities there were armed partisan bands waiting to enter, and the Anglo-American armies were mired south of Florence. Given such a combination, what might happen?

### Poland

The Nazis' uninhibitedly murderous policy in Poland made the nation's Resistance far less an instrument of opposition than a means of survival. The Resistance in western and southern Europe was to a very large degree a rational response of men seeking to escape the forced-labor draft, while the prospect of Allied victory further stimulated its growth. But Nazi terror in Poland was from its inception overwhelming and capricious, and the means of evading it far more limited than elsewhere: one could collaborate or resist, but the results were very much the same, above all for Jews, the intelligentsia, former officers, and government officials.

Given the total lack of predictability and the imminent dangers in the cities, the risk of joining the Resistance was not much greater than if one did nothing. What underground organizations provided its members was a community and a social context for facing an environment suffused with constant dangers—a base to which one might refer when making difficult decisions, contacts who helped each other materially in the desperate struggle for survival, and access to psychological reassurance during the long epic of human calamities, degradation, and barbarism. Within an inherently irrational, chaotic environment, as Jan Tomasz Gross has so sensitively captured it in his classic account of Polish society during wartime, being a part of the Resistance in one manner or another was for countless urban dwellers the only form of rational behavior available.

It is impossible to estimate the size of the organized Resistance that emerged. Resistance organizations created many illegal social and political groups that were never really designed either to subvert or to fight the Nazis. The Home Army, the largest of a number of armed groups and ostensibly an official branch of the government-in-exile, claimed 350,000 members in 1943, but during the Warsaw uprising in August 1944, which it undertook despite orders to the contrary from London, it fielded 44,000 mostly unarmed men—and four times that number of Poles were killed. It never controlled some of its units, and with a frequency that probably exceeded the problem in Italy or Greece, it was not uncommon for some of them to survive through robbery and banditry. The formal underground youth groups claimed only about 25,000 members, small by even Greek standards.

At one level, the core of the Resistance was highly structured and organized, and included an underground government complete with its own police, a regular biweekly, its own school system with 25,000 students in 1943–44, and the like. But its organizational charts notwithstanding, the Resistance was surely also very disunited at crucial points, not merely for political reasons but also because many former army officers and politicians took it upon themselves to create their own bodies—each with its own structure that duplicated the work of many others. Poland, for example, had at least 1,400 illegal publications, notwithstanding the dangers to everyone associated with them; this was considerably more than in France and Holland, with their far larger combined population. Everything proliferated, including political parties (there were about twenty-five leftist parties alone operating in March 1944!), because, ultimately, overorganization became a means of putative social adaptation in a context where real opposition was futile.

The Resistance also attempted to infiltrate the Nazi-controlled government that Poles staffed. Like everyone and everything in Poland during the reign of human anarchy the Nazis created, a very great deal the Resistance did was ambiguous, even debatable, not only in relationship to the Jews, whom they essentially abandoned to their own devices, but to each other.

The Nazis destroyed everyone who got in their way—and many more. In this terrible context, the real meaning of the Resistance was profoundly enigmatic, more so in Poland than in any other nation in Europe, and Gross is correct in calling "the underground . . . not primarily an anti-German conspiracy but rather a substitute for Polish society. . . ."[22] Most of those who joined it were far less interested in resisting than in surviving, if possible with human dignity.

The Nazis imposed an unprecedentedly dreadful toll on every aspect of Polish life and society, and also on its spirit. The vacuum they left was enormous, and who would fill it, and how, was in 1944 very much an open question.

### France

The moral and political depression that hung over France in the first year after the Nazi conquest was so profound and universal that few people regarded opposition to Vichy and Germany as feasible, and even sympathy for it was almost nonexistent: for the Nazis appeared to have won the war. Some military officers escaped overseas, with de Gaulle as their leader, and a relative handful remained in France in contact with the Free French, or stood ready to act when and if an opportune moment to do so arose. They were not adventurers, then or later. The Communist party was outlawed and 30,000 of its members were arrested in both zones by May 1941, and so it organized an underground preoccupied at first only with its own survival, and it was in this sense alone that it remained active as a clandestine party. Its later exegeses exonerating its convoluted role during this period notwithstanding, the Communists were essentially neutralists. After the Hitler-Stalin Pact the Party condemned military preparedness and was anti-war, proclaiming enemies at home to be its principal concern. It was certainly anti-Hitler, but that by itself was not sufficient to prevent a number of its best members from quitting; a few created minuscule independent Resistance cells, generally over the opposition of the Party. Many more Communists simply became disillusioned and joined the great majority of apathetic Frenchmen.

Once Hitler invaded the USSR in June 1941, the Communists became the most visible organizers of Resistance, creating the *Francs-Tireurs et Partisans* (FTP) as the principal rival to the Gaullists, whom they soon outgrew. The FTP strongly attacked the passive Gaullist strategic doctrine of waiting for foreign arms or an Allied invasion, and its militant posture won it a small number of adherents, principally from among younger, impatient workers who were, at least initially, mostly non-Communists. But its own notion that at a critical moment there should be a national insurrection was really also a doctrine of delay, and its rhetoric greatly outdistanced its action.

As in Italy and elsewhere, until the spring of 1943—by which time a great deal had changed within France, circumstances were pushing many into the Resistance, and it was clear the Nazis would lose the war—the FTP remained very small even though it was the largest of the "fighting" groups; in fact, it did very little fighting until mid-1944. There was also a considerable Gaullist structure in France by 1943, and by then a significant number of Vichy collaborators who recognized that the war was lost, discreetly began to contact it. The intellectual Resistance grew as well, at least as measured by the paper it produced, and then there was the maquis, discussed below. The Communists' principal strength was the working class, which had economic grievances that it periodically vented both spontaneously and otherwise. Given the nearly total demise of the Socialists, many of whom collaborated (they expelled two-thirds of their National Assembly members for it), the unrivaled Communists could suffuse class issues with those involving acts of disobedience to emerge as the internal Resistance's most important component and the only serious alternative to the Gaullists, most of whom remained abroad until June 1944.

France experienced many forms of small work stoppages and a few large, damaging strikes. In the Nord and Pas-de-Calais *départements*, in October 1943 at least 39,000 miners struck, and notwithstanding arrests and deportation for some, they partially won their demands for higher wages. The Communists led the working class, which in turn provided the Resistance everywhere with most of the people upon whom it could rely, especially among the strategic railroad workers. Arrests in the Pas-de-Calais and Nord were overwhelmingly political in character during 1941–44, and miners alone accounted for 47 percent of those detained. Other blue-collar workers comprised another 29 percent, and the unemployed 12 percent—88 percent combined.

Even in rural *départements*, workers were greatly overrepresented, as were artisans and shopkeepers. In Ille-et-Vilaine in Brittany, peasants and agricultural workers comprised 52 percent of the labor force but only 7 percent of the organized Resistance, while railroad workers comprised less than 1 percent of the labor force but 13 percent of the Resistance. Nearly four-fifths of the blue-collar workers, and almost one-half of the other resistants, were in Communist-organized groups. Members of the lower ranks of the police and *gendarmerie* were also very active, for some as atonement for having collaborated during Vichy's fat years, but they joined non-Communist organizations.[23]

The Resistance in France, as in much of Europe, grew rapidly not only because of Allied victories by 1943 but especially because the intensified Nazi labor mobilization made it far more difficult for conformists or attentistes to avoid paying a huge personal price. The Nazis preferred the more productive French labor for use in Germany, and from 1940 onward demanded over 1.5 million workers—and actually obtained half that number. At first the occupations asked Vichy to round the men up, but its initially voluntary recruitment methods proved insufficient, and so the Nazis imposed harsher measures, which culminated in February 1943, as elsewhere in Europe, with a labor draft—the STO.

While the STO was compulsory, certain peasants, railroad workers, miners, policemen (including volunteers for Vichy's militia), and those building fortifications for the Nazis in France, were exempted. One could also attempt to circumvent it by disappearing in a city, or perhaps move somewhere with a new identity and seek to live normally. Far more men chose jobs requiring collaboration to joining the maquis. Large wooded, mountainous regions big enough to hide in existed mainly in the center and south of France, and by October 1943 only about 15,000 men had opted for this course, and were *maquisards*, but within five months the number had at least doubled.

The first *maquisards* practiced civil disobedience by escaping from forced labor and few were interested in the Resistance. Notwithstanding the catalytic role that fugitive foreign workers and prisoners of war initially played in some places, their bands were overwhelmingly spontaneous, haphazard creations, or gangs in the case of many, without any common denominator save the cause of their internal exile and their collective need to find ways of surviving in remote areas. Most chose their own leaders, few of whom knew anything about military matters, they had almost no arms, and in the beginning most hoped to wait peacefully for the end of the war—and a significant minority managed that feat. Some were pure adventurers, many returned to their homes rather than face the winters or prepare to fight, and it was quite common for *maquisards* to compel farmers to provide food, or to rob them.

Imposing some control over the maquis was a major challenge for both the internal Resistance (which at first regarded it with great skepticism), de Gaulle, and the Allies, and the effort began in April 1943. Militarily, much of the maquis was useless, and it remained underarmed and poorly trained and disciplined despite some Allied air drops and training personnel sent to organize it. It was easily infiltrated and compromised. *Maquisards* rarely won organized battles, and usually were defeated when German forces sought them out. There was little Allied strategic incentive to arm or train them all to fight in the peripheral territory they inhabited, but some had a certain utility for specific tasks of sabotage or subversion. Most of the arms the maquis received from the Allies came during the second quarter of 1944 and were intended to divert Germans from the Normandy invasion. But as the men who were interested purely in surviving peacefully dropped away and the maquis's ranks grew and became more promising, it was finally largely transformed into a branch of the Resistance; yet a considerable number of *maquisards* knew nothing about the organizations their leaders tied them to, and sometimes not even their names. Potentially, however, an armed maquis that was politically motivated might control the politics of large regions when Vichy and the Nazis were defeated, and that too was a major reason for the Allies to attempt to rein it in. In the southwest, for example, many of the men who had fled initially to escape the STO soon became Communists. For while the maquis began largely as an ad hoc and marginal response to the Nazis, in 1944 no one could be certain that it would remain so.[24]

The problem of the maquis was paralleled by de Gaulle's even more pressing and challenging need to impose his control over the other Resistance organizations in France, principally the FTP, and I have detailed this inordinately Byzantine story elsewhere. There were valid military reasons for coordination: Resistance groups were not only becoming private political armies but in some areas they were often incompetent and irresponsible in their behavior, and their national leaders scarcely controlled them. The Gaullists feared indiscipline, if not anarchy, in some localities when the war ended. Nominally, a Council of National Resistance (CNR) was created as a coordinating body in May 1943, and de Gaulle employed his ostensible leverage over Anglo-American arms drops to obtain putative agreements from the FTP and others in order to control their actions; but while he had his problems with the British, his relations with the Americans were marked by gross deceit and mutual recriminations throughout the entire war. Truly reliable control over the Communists eluded de Gaulle's grasp until he entered Paris in late August 1944, by which time he had cunningly arranged that a thoroughly compromised police department, which had efficiently delivered countless Jews and Communists to the Nazis and was desperate to redeem itself, serve as his political security force and help him outflank and betray both the Americans and the FTP.

Until August 1944, whatever the form its national leaders wished to impose upon it, the Resistance in practice remained highly decentralized and invariably followed the desires of local leaders and members. Moreover, it was extremely loosely organized, and many of its members were unsuited for disciplined conspiratorial work. Its attacks were often premature, poorly prepared, and unnecessarily cost many attackers their lives, often provoking reprisals that hurt—and alienated—local communities. Worse yet, Gestapo agents infiltrated many Resistance groups, or its members were compromised in the course of time, a reality that repeatedly frustrated large-scale operations. Local Resistance activities nonetheless increased greatly from mid-1943 onward, but the ultimate limit on most of them was a lack of arms. The FTP in particular advocated immediate action, but it obtained most of its paltry supply of weapons by stealing them and it was unable to put doctrine into practice to the extent it desired. Its most effective activities, by far, were sabotage and slowdowns, particularly among railroad workers. De Gaulle's agents and the British promised the FTP arms but they usually failed to deliver them. That over half of the Allied arms dropped into France during the war arrived just before or during the Anglo-American and Free French invasion, minimized the dangers that an independent Resistance might pose. When the Paris uprising began in mid-August 1944, the local Resistance had only 1,800 assorted guns to use against the two German divisions in the city alone.[25]

Notwithstanding all these difficulties, the Resistance grew and by mid-1944 retained a potential role in French life and politics that no one at the time underrated. How large was the Resistance, and who was in it? There is no definitive answer to this question, a fact that by itself made the Resistance's future place loom so ominously large. For in reality (and this was just as true for members of Vichy's *milice*), many people maintained a nominal, often extremely peripheral, contact with various Resistance groups, some purely to protect themselves later from charges of collaboration. There were many hundreds of Resistance publications over the course of the war, and even reading one was an illegal act of defiance—but also, by itself, totally harmless.

In October 1943 the FTP, the most important of the Resistance organizations, believed it had 12,000 people on whom it could rely in all of France, but this was probably a generous estimate. In any case, many of the early resisters were killed or arrested, and at least 40,000 people lost their lives because of their Resistance activities. In some areas, the pre-June 1944 Resistance groups claimed memberships very substantially larger than they really had, in part because many people had merely told someone that they could be relied upon at the right time, and in any case there simply were no weapons available for most who were indeed ready to act. Those who aided resistants in innumerable ways, from giving food or hiding someone, can never be counted, and some of these were politically neutral. In the Cantal, to cite one estimate, there were ten identifiable sympathizers for every active resister. The combined Resistance in the Limousin region alleged it had over 20,000 members in August 1944, but it could arm far fewer than that number, and many had rallied only at the last moment. The total Resistance structure in Paris in July 1944 claimed 35,523 members, even though over 100,000 had demonstrated that Bastille Day in the face of German guns. Allied authorities in London believed that at the end of May 1944 there were, including the maquis, 10,000 men and women in all of France armed to fight more than one day in a serious manner, but 40,000 with arms of some sort. Other estimates generally corroborate these figures. Another 60,000 were in groups in contact with London, 350,000 unarmed persons were in yet other formations (principally Communists), and an equal number existed on whom these might call upon in some way. There were 800,000 workers in unions, mainly Communist-controlled, able to disrupt strategic points. Combined with yet others, the Allies assumed that roughly 3 million people, or approximately one-tenth of the nation's adults, might in some manner be useful to their effort. Although this number was far too small to defeat the Nazis, it was certainly large enough, if unified and led properly, to impose political control over much of France. Later about 170,000 people were awarded active veteran status for their Resistance work, but after the liberation of Paris in August 1944, there was a spectacular surge of members in the Resistance's component groups. This too was to be anticipated.[26]

France had as many heroes as the other occupied nations, but far fewer than the number who later proclaimed their own feats. The fact remains that the vast majority of Europe's people spent their time every day surviving and adapting to the boundaries that others imposed upon their existence. But ultimately the question of quantities of visible members and the extent of a nation's bravery is irrelevant to the reemergence of a socialist tradition that had been significant before the war but, even more important, to the transformation that occurred in the minds of otherwise passive persons who had never before thought of themselves as bitter enemies of the Establishment—in this case one that had actively collaborated. What political loyalties did they now share, and what kind of society did they wish to see emerge from the war? There are not many courageous men and women at any time or place in this or any century, but fundamental changes become possible at crucial historical junctures, and have occurred frequently enough without heroes to define the main contours of modern history.

In the summer of 1944 what the French people wanted and would do remained very much an open question.

### Belgium and The Netherlands
In both Belgium and The Netherlands the Resistance remained proportionately far weaker than in France, in part because daily hardships were much less onerous, but principally because there was no blatantly collaborationist and reactionary regime, such as Vichy, on which to wreak revenge. Both governments could claim their legitimacy, though in fact they collaborated functionally while also managing to a significant degree to insulate their populations from material suffering. Vichy was quintessentially a class regime that traumatized the working class; in Belgium, unions and business leaders cooperated in many domains, and in Holland class conflicts also subsided.

In Belgium as in France, the Communist party preached an ultramilitant line and attracted some younger activists, and although the local Socialist leaders abolished the party and its major leaders collaborated, its parliamentary wing fled to London and kept it alive. The Communists, who in 1939 gained 5 percent of the vote against the Socialists' 30 percent, led the country's first major strike of 60,000 in the Liège region in May 1941 and immediately emerged as the motivating force in the Resistance. They replaced the Socialists as the working class's favored party during the war, and whether they would continue in that role afterward was very much an open question.

The Communists created an active Resistance group in Holland also, but in terms of size and especially daily infractions of Nazi regulations, the Calvinist and Catholic organizations were much more important, especially in hiding people and saving lives. Their motives were essentially spiritual, their work humanitarian. The Dutch Resistance was never unified. But in both Belgium and Holland the Resistance was for most of the war quite small in proportion to that of other nations, and its motives and objectives were less radical. The Dutch did not mind reading an illegal paper or listening to banned radio programs, and while many or even most were hostile toward the Nazis, before June 1944 the entire Dutch Resistance had fewer than 1,200 full-time members left—although the Nazis killed about 10,000 Dutch citizens for Resistance activities during the entire war. They murdered about the same number of Belgians, nearly one-third of them for their role in producing the approximately 650 underground papers. French losses were proportionately larger. Adjusting the degree of general Resistance involvement for the size of the population, it is likely that Belgium was half as active as France, and Holland was certainly no more resistant than Belgium save for its remarkable April 1943 strike, which involved nearly a fifth of all adults. Still, such figures on who was willing to take risks reveal little about the public's thoughts or desires.

The principal Nazi error in both Holland and Belgium, as throughout Europe, was to attempt to draft younger men for labor, including work in Germany. Otherwise, dissidence in both these nations would have been far smaller. The STO did not immediately lead to resistance but, as in France, refusal to obey orders—which was a precondition for it. The labor draft in Belgium began in November 1942, and although it also included exemptions, about two-thirds of those who were eligible simply became illegal, even creating a small maquis in the Ardennes. No single measure affected Belgium so profoundly, and it traumatized and increasingly radicalized young workers who had to stay on the run for the war's duration.

In Holland the Nazis used ostensibly "voluntary" methods of obtaining labor for Germany from 1940 on, and while they attained a fair degree of success, workers could also return home; at the end of 1942, there were about 350,000 in Germany. When the Nazis attempted in April 1943 to recall all demobilized Dutch soldiers for labor service, triggering by far the most massive wartime strike in all of Europe, they also tried to round up students and eighteen-year olds. The result was the same as everywhere: massive noncompliance (reaching 70 percent among university students), men in hiding, and a population called upon to take risks to protect them against raids and arrests. As elsewhere, significant Resistance began at this time, and both it and the Nazis became fiercer in the ways they opposed each other—affecting the Resistance's treatment of the many collaborators as well. Passivity was now more dangerous than resistance, and as the war went from bad to worse for the Nazis, they became increasingly repressive.

In Belgium all of these factors, including increased sentencing of resisters to death, combined in 1943 to intensify Resistance reprisals against collaborators. Indeed, for all practical purposes there had been no significant armed opposition until then. In this context of gravely mounting violence, it was widely believed (especially by conservative elements whose own records were far from unsullied) that Belgium was heading toward civil war and that the Communists would take power when the Nazis departed. It was a fear, in addition, that the London government-in-exile shared, in part because Communist leaders discussed the need for popular communes—in effect, soviets—after the Nazis left but before the legal government returned. In September 1943, as a consequence, officials in London had their banking and business contacts in Belgium loan money to a Resistance fund that could be used to build up a small group run by ex-officers, and to create ways of keeping the desperate labor evaders, who were providing the Resistance with the muscles it badly needed, away from the Communist-controlled *Front de l'Indépendance*. Such a fund would also allow the many rich businessmen who had profited from the war, and who were vulnerable to charges of collaboration, to reestablish their patriotic bona fides. The fund grew to about 180 million BF, and the numerically dominant Front received only 10 million of it, and that only after the Anglo-American armies had landed in France and were close at hand.

Parallel to these events in Belgium, in Holland after 1943, imprisoned Resistance members were executed for their comrades' action, and in the first four months of 1945 many more were killed this way than during the preceding five years. But even as the war was ending, the Nazis concluded that, on balance, "the collaboration of the Dutch departments . . . , apart from a few exceptions, [gave] no cause for complaint."[27]

With Allied troops on Holland's eastern borders after September 1944 and massive starvation in the western region, the confrontation between the Resistance and local profiteers and collaborators became much more violent than at any other time, and far more people became active as victory seemed imminent. Dutch society did not appear nearly so close to civil war as Belgium, but there was nonetheless intense bitterness, and a desire for revenge existed throughout the country.

As the war was ending, both in Belgium and Holland the Resistance movements emerged as strategic, growing forces, legitimate patriotic challengers of tarnished regimes that had done all too much to aid the Nazis. Their influence on the public was growing massively; indeed, no one knew how extensive it was, and their radicalized leadership now constituted a formidable political presence in both nations. More crucial yet, there existed a significant, seemingly mounting public opinion in favor of both revenge and political and social changes that might assert itself in various political or even extraparliamentary ways. In a less acute form, both nations reflected the dominant political and social mood that was influencing most of Europe as it emerged from the terrible long struggle.

## Which Way Europe?

World War Two's political impact was proportionate to its monumental intensity and effects on Europe's people—their daily existences, the unprecedented loss of loved ones, the absence of normal lives and the constant deprivations and tension it imposed in ways and on a scale that the First World War had never equaled. World War Two proved that modern war's political and ideological consequences correspond closely to the inevitable material and psychological damage that its firepower and duration produces, creating repercussions that political leaders and military strategists can never anticipate.

The power of Europe's Resistance movements was purely the outcome of this inevitable reality as well as the existence of a great vacuum that the failure of conventional leaders and their politics created. In most of Europe the prewar ruling classes and dominant parties, having pursued varying degrees of collaborationist policies, sacrificed and lost their nationalist cachet and thereby endangered their purely class interests. The void to be filled was all the more ominous because the non-Communist socialist parties in many nations emerged from the war tainted with the stain of collaboration, and they failed to produce autonomous leaders who could articulate relevant responses to the burning issues each society and its people confronted. Social Democracy was insipid and timid, if not discredited, in much of Europe. Without such profound shortcomings both on the Right and within the traditionally dominant prewar Left, the Communist parties would never have arrived at such a powerful, strategic position, proving once more that it was not the wisdom of Leninist revolutionaries, much less the glacially paced manifestations of Marxist axioms regarding the economy, but rather the folly of old orders that was the origin of the Left's greatest political and ideological successes in the twentieth century. The Left that emerged largely in the form of Communist parties, and Resistance movements they superficially appeared to dominate, synthesized nationalist legitimacy and radical ideologies to increase greatly the political strength and appeal of all those who had opposed the Nazi presence.

The fact that the actual membership of the Resistance was very small everywhere relative to the size of the population did not alter the reality that a decisively significant fraction of the people in most European nations dramatically revised their political perceptions and loyalties, creating an opening to the Left that possessed untold dangers for the defensive, discredited prewar political leaders and their class allies. For there is a fundamental difference between people's radical values and their willingness to make personal commitments that endanger their personal and material security; that there are very few willing heroes to be found at any time or place is not decisive. Indeed, that the wartime events and pressures on individuals compelled many otherwise improbable persons, if only for reasons of survival, to behave in a decisive political fashion in conjunction with others revealed that the very process of war, with its immense impact on all aspects of societies, evoked grave contradictions and tensions within many nations in unpredictable ways that neither socialist or bourgeois theorists had even begun to fathom.

Public opinion, in short, far transcended the size of the actual number of Resistance activists, and ultimately this was a much greater and more durable threat to established orders than the guns in the hands of resistants in 1944. Still, no one could dismiss the strategic potential of a small but nonetheless well-placed armed Resistance existing in Europe's political voids by 1945, for nothing like it had ever occurred. The issue too was whether the countless people whose minds, behavior, and desires the war had affected so profoundly possessed sufficient momentum and the potential to escape from the control of their nominal leaders or, conversely, whether all those who hoped to preserve traditional societies could stop them. Could change after 1944 be both restrained and managed, preventing a repetition of the chain of upheavals that had so dramatically transformed Europe after 1917? For all of these reasons, the issue of the political outcome of the Second World War in Europe in 1944 depended to a crucial extent on how the Communist parties would respond to political, economic, and ideological crises within many traditional European social systems—crises far greater than those of 1917–19, when a revolution had succeeded in one great nation and threatened yet others.

# CHAPTER 11

# European Communism and the Political Consequences of World War Two

The fundamental issue confronting the leaders of Great Britain and the United States at the end of World War Two was the extent to which they could permit its calamitous social and economic repercussions, which had so profoundly altered a growing section of the European people's ideas and aspirations, to define the war's political aftermath and seize the fruits of their military triumph from them. World War Two was much bloodier and more traumatic than the war of 1914–18, gravely affecting the lives of a far greater proportion of Europe's population, and that the magnitude of its social and institutional upheavals might be proportionate to its physical and human impact seemed not merely possible at the end of the war but also very likely. To comprehend why such a transformation ultimately did not occur in southern and western Europe is to fathom the very process of all change, with its potential and limits, in Europe after 1940.

However great the initial obstacles to their finding expression in either words or deeds—their fears of repression, personal distractions, or the heritage of conventional wisdom—by the war's end a very substantial portion of Europe's population had either reaffirmed or developed conscious, critical political attitudes that rejected the traditional approaches to their nations' problems as well as those men who for decades had advocated them. Changing the old orders became a cause that evoked the political enthusiasm and participation of far more people than at any time since at least 1918. Ironically, the impending arrival of victorious Anglo-American military forces that made the issue of social change so immediate to Italians or Greeks at the same time compelled Britain and the United States to decide how far they would tolerate autonomous political developments that affected their interests and objectives. For a brief, fleeting period, it seemed that the avenues for attaining desperately needed social reconstruction and reforms were far more open than they had been in many decades—since, indeed, 1917.

The basic dilemma facing all of the members in the anti-Nazi coalition in 1944—the Resistance movements, the Communists, Stalin and the USSR, the Anglo-American leaders—was whether or not their essentially accidental alliance of mutual necessity borne of a common struggle against the Nazis and fascism could survive the uninhibited evolution of the burgeoning local, autonomous forces of change without shattering in political discord. And while the extent of this risk was linked inextricably to the nature and potential roles of the various national Communist parties, it was also partly dependent upon the character of those individuals who had joined the organizations associated with the opposition—the intensity of their ardor, their options for attaining their goals, and the degree to which Communist party chiefs could maintain control over them.

Were the angry, traumatized men and women—mainly workers and peasants—who joined the Resistance and especially its parties in massive numbers at the first sign of opportunity and success, and were often spread out over large areas in decentralized environments where their freedom to act was relatively far greater, capable of escaping their nominal leaders' discipline and imposing their own agendas and desires? Did a vacuum exist into which recent, often instant converts drawn from Europe's disadvantaged, forgotten peoples might rush, or even be pushed into by a concatenation of objective economic, political, and organizational circumstances—in either case creating a source of profound discord among the members of the wartime alliance? Hitler, for his part, by the end of 1944 came to believe that such a schism would emerge, and that Nazi Germany might exploit it to endure.

Given the innumerable weaknesses and compromises of the prewar elites and forces of tradition, ranging from royalists to Social Democrats, such challenges were anything but abstract; rather, they deeply colored relations between the wartime allies, and they were later to define the whole course of international affairs after the war and create the "Cold War" in Europe—the only region where one can aptly employ that term. In France and Italy most of the bourgeoisie was politically disgraced as collaborationist. In Greece, where a portion of it had collaborated, it remained largely passive, while the small group within the prewar elite that nominally resisted refused to cooperate politically in any manner with the Left until May 1944, by which time the latter controlled much of the nation. Instead,

Greece's former rulers counted upon the British to save them from both the Germans and the radicals. Wherever the Anglo-American armies went, those traditional classes and elements with whom their leaders were most inclined to align themselves were fatally discredited politically and morally, far weaker than at any time in recent history and irreversibly compromised in the face of Resistance forces that were mushrooming to challenge them, movements that now possessed a unique claim to the mantle of nationalist legitimacy. The legacies of all of their accumulated objective political and economic weaknesses, which dated back many decades, left them seemingly impotent at a crucial juncture in Europe's history. That political and social upheavals would follow in the wake of the war, as they had in 1917–19, and that peace would only initiate a new cycle of crises, appeared an imminent danger in 1944.

## Greece: Turning Back Change

The Allied coalition was always a supremely fragile one of mutual convenience and need rather than choice, predestined to fall apart eventually, and the fact that it dissolved after 1945 partly because of a crisis in Greece was scarcely accidental, for nowhere else in Europe were the diverse political, economic, and geographic factors that create change in modern times so beyond the control of the major powers or of the Greek and Soviet Communist parties. Greece remains the best illustration of what at least significant parts of Europe may have become had Britain and the United States lacked the resolve to intervene decisively to save, at least momentarily, fatally compromised and weakened traditional elites. It was also a striking example of Stalin's readiness to sacrifice local radical forces to Soviet national interests rather than conform to Moscow's international pretensions.

The Greek political scene was probably the most labyrinthine in Europe, but the wartime Left existed within the framework of the National Liberation Front (EAM) that the Communist party (KKE) and five other parties created in September 1941. The EAM was by far the largest component of the organized opposition to the Italian and German occupations, and the following April it founded the People's Liberation Army (ELAS). The ELAS developed within a highly decentralized rural power void, one full of sufficient elements of chance and improvisation to elude the KKE's persistent efforts to impose both coherence and control over it. While this context alone would have predestined to failure the KKE leadership's desire to guide rather than follow events, the complex character of that party was itself also a crucial destabilizing factor.

The KKE's core leadership was essentially a loyal Stalinist group that tried its best to conform to what it often had to deduce was Soviet policy, but the Party's tasks grew enormously after 1940 as it expanded from 17,500 members in 1935 to four times that number by 1945, when it comprised 1 percent of the entire nation and became the largest party in Greece. Although the KKE was never comparable to the Italian Communist party, which grew well over three-hundred-fold within a few years to enroll nearly 4 percent of the entire nation, it was nonetheless far from being the well-disciplined, carefully recruited elite of professional revolutionaries who conformed to classic Leninist criteria. While it was concentrated principally in urban areas, where discipline and clandestine methods were far more essential than in the mountains, the KKE 's urban leaders and members were also disunited and periodically escaped the control of its Stalinist leaders. The Party was pro-Soviet in intent, but in practice it was far from being monolithic or so completely under Stalin's thumb as the French and Italian parties, and the Russians knew this. In a word, just as there was a quite obvious and permanent tension between the urban KKE leaders and the ELAS military chiefs in the mountains—and the Party's leadership after 1942 was eager to cooperate in a united front far larger than the EAM alone—there were at various times also much more subtle but nonetheless real strains between the Greek party as a whole and the Kremlin—and these were to emerge frequently enough from 1944 to 1949 to make the KKE unique in Europe.

As in Yugoslavia, where the first armed revolts against the invaders began spontaneously with Serbian bands that united to defend themselves against Croatian fascists, in Greece armed groups formed in the mountains without coordination, discipline, or often any real sense of politics other than hating the occupiers. And also as in Yugoslavia, where Serbs embarked on intercommunal vendettas in many places at the same time that they opposed the Italians and their proxies, the Greek bodies frequently had strong local social links to families, clans, and villages, and these ties often determined why men belonged to one armed party or another—considerations that left indelible, bitter legacies. Some units, however, were created when individuals went to the mountains to escape Axis soldiers; others were composed of former bandits who initially had sought to survive the war's rigors by living off the peasantry. Most of them were extemporaneous, remained close to the areas in which they originated, and an appreciable number possessed an ugly chauvinist character, pitting Greeks, Albanians, and Macedonians against each other in ways that were far more primally tribal and clannish than political, and many of the armed branches in the ELAS and its successor always retained such communalist attributes. They always remained the strongest in areas with ethnic minorities, including among the million and a quarter Greeks repatriated from Turkey after 1922, and where peasants were not so poor as to be unable to spare food or other essentials to sustain guerrillas.

Under Aris Velouchiotis, its most important leader, the ELAS attempted to integrate and control such groups or to destroy them, but Aris himself often acted on his own initiative, and the KKE only reluctantly authorized some of his main military feats. Territoriality therefore became a persistent preoccupation of the ELAS's activities, which caused it to engage in armed conflicts not only with the considerably smaller anti-Nazi Resistance armies—which also tended to dominate their turf for power rather than for political reasons and were as prepared to fight the ELAS as the Axis—but also with Communist-led Macedonian nationalist organizations with secessionist goals that initially operated within the ELAS as separate bodies and were to become increasingly important and eventually to undermine the KKE's nationalist credentials. While the concept of warlordism fails to describe all the dimensions of the guerrillas' activities, it does capture one vital aspect of their functional relationship to potential rivals, the Axis, and even, to some extent, the urban-based KKE.[1]

As in Yugoslavia, the Communists initially sought to build a Resistance army by joining with, and uniting if possible, these diverse constituencies. This genesis of the ELAS in local bands created an inauspicious basis for establishing a disciplined body. It was difficult for the KKE to control such a guerrilla force, which grew from about 12,500 regulars and reserves in the summer of 1943 to about 50,000 by late 1944. A significant portion of them had joined after February 1943, when the Nazis required all 16- to 45-year-old males to register for compulsory labor services, and not more than half of the ELAS's members were active at any given time. Moreover, often charismatic leaders, *capetans*, employed personal and local loyalties much more often than political doctrines to unite many of the disparate bands, and most ELAS members were responsive principally to them. Whatever the formal organizational chart, the numerous *capetans* formed the heart of the ELAS in the mountains; many were political only in the most general sense of that term, and the KKE tolerated their crucial roles strictly out of necessity in what was and remained a relatively informal, undisciplined, and democratic guerrilla army until the ELAS was dissolved. The Party much preferred avoiding violence that would evoke terrible Nazi reprisals, stressing political organization, and the undisciplined *capetans* were a constant challenge to its strategy. And since the local EAM groups avoided any hint of Marxist sectarianism, both respecting and integrating the Greek Orthodox Church and private property and concentrating instead on local grievances, their adherents were never called upon to accept an ideologically rigorous position. As the British admitted, the average EAM or ELAS member was indistinguishable from the followers of the other, much smaller armed anti-Axis groups.

The KKE attempted to centralize and closely integrate the ELAS after the spring of 1943, when a substantial cadre of antimonarchist officers from the prewar army joined it; it assigned nominally powerful political commissars to major units, but they never eliminated the *capetans'* and military leaders' dominant roles, their final control over military matters, or their inclination to oppose (and even fight) the other Greek resistance groups rather than—as the KKE wished—unite with them. For one thing, the KKE's oldest members remained largely in the cities, where they found it easier to recruit, and its commissars in the mountains were mostly unprepared for their tasks. And even in the urban KKE a significant minority faction under Ioannis Ioannidis advocated an orthodox revolution based on the urban proletariat rather than the Party's more benign stance after 1942 in favor of a united front. No one who joined the KKE in this milieu of relative freedom and space ever became a senior leader, and the division between the ELAS and the Party—which was for practical purposes synonymous with the rural as opposed to urban movements—persisted as its fundamental contradiction for the remainder of the decade. Most important, the veteran KKE leaders, especially the dominant group that George Siantos headed as secretary-general, correctly perceived that a coalition dependent on such autonomous elements might escape their control and thereby unhinge the KKE's basic political strategy.[2]

The KKE retained a nominally decisive position in the EAM, never comprising more than one-fifth of its membership, and probably considerably less, but the EAM's program was so general and all-encompassing that there was no ideological barrier to prevent it from becoming a vast mass movement. Aside from resisting the Axis occupation, the EAM opposed the monarchy and favored a democratic government committed to social progress. By late 1944 the EAM claimed to control three-quarters of Greece's territory—comprising one-tenth to one-fifth of the population—and to have 1.5 million members in all its many component sections. Its very diffuseness and size made it impossible for the old-line KKE leaders to establish their hegemony, in part because most Party members were new, unindoctrinated idealists, many of whom remained quite independent, but principally because the sheer lack of communications and the geography militated against a truly disciplined command organization such that Lenin had once imagined both possible and essential.

The EAM's local program introduced a hitherto modernizing political culture of democratic activism and reform to which many, especially women and youth, were attracted. Although these still-modest but long-overdue social and economic reforms in the countryside failed to produce disciplined Party militants, they nonetheless frightened the nation's traditional political and economic elites, which were reactionary, generally monarchist, for the Metaxas dictatorship after 1936, pro-British if not fascist, and opposed to change in whatever shape it assumed. It was less the substance of innovation than its democratic and popular form—which radicalized and politicized countless people and displaced established decision-making constituencies—that both horrified and endangered the pillars of the old system at least as much as the ELAS's men-in-arms.[3]

## Great-Power Relations and Greek Communism

Most of the numerous accounts of the relationship of the Kremlin to the Greek question slight or even ignore the much more significant diplomatic context that had been established throughout eastern and southern Europe well before the oft-described dramatic October 1944 meeting between Stalin and Churchill in Moscow, during which they ostensibly divided the Axis satellites, Greece, and Yugoslavia into spheres of influence. Stalin himself, dating back to his triumph over Trotsky and subsequent ruthless consolidation of power, had always assigned a far higher priority to protecting the USSR's interests as a state, and the Communist International's policies were subordinated to this end. Stalin's absolute control over who should head the various national parties allowed him to impose his contradictory twists and turns upon them as well. He demanded that all Communist parties after June 1941 totally submerge traditional class aims on behalf of creating a united front incorporating any group prepared to fight the Axis, and by late 1942 the Kremlin had begun aggressively (but unsuccessfully) to try to reverse the Yugoslav party's "sectarian" and autonomous line, which eventually enabled the Yugoslav Communists to become the only party in Europe to come to power unaided and laid the basis for the later Tito-Stalin split.

Just as prone to wishful thinking about the permanency of the wartime alliance as he had been about his pact with Hitler, Stalin's abolition of the Comintern in May 1943 was designed to assuage Anglo-American fears of an aggressive postwar communism, but it in no way lessened his efforts to subordinate national Communist parties to Soviet interests. By definition, this required making them much less militant at a crucial point when most of their countless new adherents were being radicalized and were still far from disciplined. It was also a time when Europe's rulers needed a precious respite from leftist ambitions. Stalin, as one former Comintern official later put it, "was certainly prepared to pay a price for the post-war alliance," and this meant dampening any revolutionary fervor that local parties might possess, not just during the war but afterward as well.[4]

This was the context in which the United States and Britain after August 1943 rejected several of Moscow's efforts to employ the Italian surrender negotiations—the first to arise with Hitler's allies—as a precedent for a comprehensive joint political-military commission that would subsequently also deal with Rumania, Hungary, and Bulgaria. Such a body would have given the Russians a real voice in Italian affairs and, conversely, the same power to the Anglo-Americans in Axis territory the Red Army was to conquer. But Washington strongly opposed it, and so purely advisory and powerless surrogate bodies were created as an alternative. By blocking the possibility of a Soviet veto in Italy, the Anglo-Americans gave themselves a free political hand in that country but also revealed to Stalin the decisive political constraints the Americans and British were prepared to impose where their political and strategic interests were involved. Much more important, it confirmed the reality that military conquest rather than negotiations would define the political outcome of the war in Europe.

This crucial "Italian precedent" set the stage for most of the subsequent political developments in Europe and, even more important, in Japan, where the United States excluded everyone, including Britain and China, from real political control over the only other major Axis power. The British quickly developed second thoughts regarding the wisdom of derogating the Russians to ceremonial and impotent roles, but beginning in March 1944 the Russians openly supported a conservative Italy conforming to the initial Anglo-American scheme. It was from this time onward that the USSR, both publicly and privately, repeatedly endorsed Anglo-American political initiatives in those places of prime importance to them, at the same time reiterating its much older line that Communists should participate, even at the cost of their social and political goals, in united fronts to fight Hitler. The following month the Red Army crossed into Rumanian territory, where they fought until an armistice was signed at the end of August 1944. The Russians then explicitly stated that they would apply there exactly those principles the Allied Control Commission for Italy had established. Implicitly, they would also do the same in Bulgaria and Hungary.

It was this larger framework, employing the antecedent the U.S. and Britain had defined while fully conscious of its political implications for the division of Europe, that determined the political outcome of the war in the Axis nations, making military possession 90 percent of the law. Whether Stalin might have taken a position more to the advantage of local Communists under other circumstances is a moot point, although my own estimate is that, after 1942, he would have continued to urge the same united-front policies upon the southern and western European Communists even had no quid pro quo been reached. In any case, the precedents created in the year after the summer of 1943 were far more significant than the famous Stalin-Churchill understanding of October 1944, which merely formalized the fairly comprehensive and consistent geopolitical accommodations of the preceding fifteen months, now extended to nations that had resisted as well as supported Hitler and callously optimized Soviet and Anglo-American interests while suppressing local freedom of political choice throughout much of Europe.

That Stalin was ready long before his encounter with Churchill to go to great lengths to placate British anxieties was revealed in his agreement after May 1944 to link London's support for Soviet policy in Rumania to his acceptance of British plans for Greece. In fact the nations were not comparable: Greece had fought the Axis while Rumania supported Hitler. But Churchill by June 1944 was obsessed with the "slithering to the Left," and he was determined to prevent the bolshevization of Europe that he believed was close, if not imminent, especially in the Balkans.[5] Notwithstanding a persistent American reticence to take up political issues before the war was over, during June, Churchill actively exchanged ideas with Soviet leaders regarding what he at first disingenuously described as a purely trial three-month military arrangement, one essentially too vague to mean much, rather than as an accord to establish spheres of influence—which in fact it was in the process of becoming. The British, especially Churchill, in fact were concocting other geopolitical schemes at this time, and did not hesitate to remind a reluctant Washington that they respected the Monroe Doctrine and its hegemony in the Western Hemisphere. In any case, by the summer of 1944, to repeat a crucial point, the Russians were actively furthering British interests in Greece.

We need not linger on the intricacies and contradictions of British creativity, which, while objecting to Tito and his party's imminent mastery over Yugoslavia, also explored ways to expand it to create a south Balkan bloc capable of becoming a barrier to Russian power. The Russians knew that any accord without U.S. approval meant little, but after delaying over the summer, Stalin agreed to meet an exhausted and ill Churchill, then distraught over the prospect that "Communism raised its head behind the thundering Russian battle-front," to listen to his audacious urging that he help suppress the red menace.[6] By this time it was clear Churchill was wholly inconsistent as to whether Stalin was the danger or the salvation—nor did he reconcile how he could be treated as both at one and the same time.

The genial haggling that occurred between the opportunistic Tory leader and the brutal dictator during mid-October 1944 only revealed Churchill to be frantically deluded both as to the nature of the danger confronting him and to the extent of Stalin's power; Stalin once again emerged from the talks as utterly unprincipled but also quite cynically prepared to humor Churchill. He did not have to be cajoled; in fact, everything crucial involving future Soviet relations to its wartime allies and the Left in Europe and Asia was already as resolved as it could be at the time. Churchill proposed percentage figures that allocated a poorly defined predominance to one or the other side, there was some dickering, and Stalin's approval was based on what Churchill called a temporary arrangement—one the U.S., in any event, refused to endorse. The October meeting has no special significance as to what either Great Britain or the USSR had done in the past or would do in the future, and notwithstanding the very great drama attached to it and the way it subsequently mesmerized both historians and politicians, it remains an inadequate index of the ultimate calculations that each nation was to employ to define their policies in the region and world.[7]

## The Soviet Union and the Greek Communists

Neither Stalin nor Churchill needed to negotiate to define their objectives in Greece, for the former had long since articulated his goal of strengthening Soviet state interests through alliances with capitalist nations. The British, in order to keep Greece out of the hands of the ELAS, as early as September 1943 had prepared for a rapid descent on Athens in the event of a sudden German withdrawal. The British could not accept the EAM's triumph whether it opted for a military or a parliamentary approach, for either path would have led to the nearly certain demise of the prewar political and social classes upon which British hegemony was wholly dependent; and while Churchill sought Stalin's sanction for the force that he had resolved to employ, it was not absolutely essential that he have it.

Britain's problem was that while it alone was ready to intervene militarily to restore something resembling the prewar status quo, ultimately it did not have sufficient economic and military resources to transform a corrupt, cynical elite into a viable, stable political order, and this fundamental dilemma was within several years to produce Europe's first major postwar challenge to the Anglo-American bloc. Meanwhile the Soviet Union helped England in crucial ways to fend off temporarily the threat of the ELAS and the more radical wing of the KKE.

The ELAS began to request Soviet military aid in January 1944, after supplies from Britain were virtually terminated, but it received nothing. Both publicly and privately, during the first half of 1944 the Kremlin endorsed the British-dominated, Cairo-based, Greek government-in-exile's appeals for unity on its terms. The intensity of this commitment was revealed when in early April, after a large part of the exiled Greek military forces in the Middle East went on strike and rioted in favor of a non-monarchist government that would include the EAM (an action even the EAM condemned), the British complained that the Soviet news agency reported the fact that they had put about 10,000 of them in prison camps. Molotov assured them that nothing like it would occur again—and kept the promise. When the EAM hesitated to enter into a government-in-exile that the British sought to patch together after the end of May, Russian officials in Cairo from late June on instructed it to join. But since the radical wing of the KKE and the distant ELAS leadership refused to transfer much of their power to what promised to be a monarchist, conservative government under British domination, the Russians at the end of July sent a mission to the ELAS headquarters in the mountains.

Privately, the Russian mission regarded the motley guerrilla army with disdain, if not horror, and one of them commented to a British officer "that although Russia had no interest in Greece, he was very much puzzled by one thing—why had the British put up with this rabble for so long?"[8] The envoys made it unequivocally clear that the ELAS would never receive aid from the Soviet Union and insisted that they accept the British-sponsored coalition government unconditionally. Although this pill proved extremely disagreeable for much of the ELAS and a part of the KKE Politburo to swallow, since it meant relinquishing a very great deal to join a united front, on August 15 the EAM ignominiously entered the exile-government without any reservations whatsoever. The following month the EAM agreed that the ELAS should soon pass to the control of the new government and that, as in Italy, all military forces would be under Allied—in this case British—command. Considerably later, the Kremlin often cited the Greek and Italian precedents when critics attacked comparable Soviet repression elsewhere.

To project ahead, after relations between the British and ELAS finally led to the bloody month of December 1944, when combat between their forces raged in Athens and elsewhere, the Russians not only kept a discreet but exceedingly obvious silence but also appointed an ambassador to the rump regime the British were fighting to preserve. "I am increasingly impressed . . . ," Churchill wrote on December 11, "with the loyalty with which, under much temptation and very likely pressure, Stalin has kept off Greece."[9] When the horrified KKE leadership attempted to send a Politburo member to Moscow to explain their side of the story, Soviet authorities arrested him in Sofia, Bulgaria, and after three days crudely dispatched him back to the Greek border. On January 13, 1945, the Soviets informed the KKE that they "categorically disapproved" of their policies. At Yalta, Stalin told Churchill "that he had no intention of criticizing British actions" in Greece.[10]

One cannot explain Stalin's behavior simply as cynical realpolitik that the war and Soviet objectives in places closer and more crucial to it warranted; such factors unquestionably played an important role, but it was at least as important that Stalin profoundly mistrusted the distinctive leftist combination that had emerged in Greece—its enthusiasm and creativity, its mass base and local initiative, and all those independent attributes and the lack of total internal discipline that he sought to expunge from Communist parties everywhere in Europe so as better to control them. Even in early 1946, when the wartime alliance was in shambles and the Cold War was replacing it, the KKE's Russian handlers urged them to focus their efforts by taking part in rigged elections as a preferred strategy, one that gave the British-controlled regime a legitimacy it sorely needed. And in September 1947, with the Cold War already intense and Greece the scene of the only armed struggle in Europe, the KKE was conspicuously absent from the founding meeting of the Cominform: their revolutionary course, as unintended as it initially was, was one that Stalin could never sanction. The Yugoslav Communists also interpreted it as an indication of his continuing loyalty to his quid pro quo with Britain.[11]

### Greek Communism's Crises

Prodigious research has gone into examining the KKE's role in the events that led to the murderous fighting that began in Athens during December 1944, which cost about 5,000 lives among combatants alone (not to mention a significantly greater number that both sides killed in reprisals, or helpless civilians caught in the fire) and was the only battle between a Resistance force and an Allied army to occur anywhere in Europe during the Second World War. If the definitive account probably cannot be written, the crucial context remains quite clear. The KKE was never united internally and it never exercised total hegemony over the vast, decentralized EAM and ELAS structure it had helped to organize. At the same time, it faced bitter hostility from Britain that profoundly affected its internal differences and made irrelevant the peaceful options that Siantos and the dominant, but by no means absolute, KKE leaders repeatedly advocated in conformity with the Soviet line on united fronts. The Greek non-Communists, mostly conservatives, many of whom had stained wartime records, emerged from the war greatly weakened but still quite intact and very much in favor of decisive British measures to eliminate the Left once and for all—steps that they themselves were as yet unable to implement but which Churchill was eager to take. With all these factors operating in the decentralized, often chaotic environment prevailing during the last months of 1944, that a major battle erupted is not at all surprising—it would have been even more astonishing if a serious struggle had been avoided entirely. No one side had sufficient power to prevent it, and only the Siantos wing of the KKE and the Russians wished at all costs to avoid a confrontation.

Siantos, in conformity with the Soviet line, had always accepted Britain's intention to keep Greece within its sphere of influence and to remain the ultimate arbiter of its role in the world, but within this framework he hoped the KKE could function as a legal party—itself a radical departure from its prewar status. Siantos's problem had always been with the ELAS, especially Aris and the many who followed his *capetans*, and to a lesser extent with the revolutionary urban-oriented KKE faction centered largely in Athens. While the ELAS had agreed at the end of September 1944 to place its forces under the British, it never did so unreservedly, and many of the ELAS's officers and members, motivated as much by fear as any other factor, were reticent to do so. Britain's most crucial immediate objective was to keep the ELAS out of Athens when or if the Nazis left so that its troops could occupy it, and when the Germans started a lightning withdrawal from the Greek mainland at the beginning of October, the ELAS loyally remained outside the capital, regardless of the fact that there were about 20,000 people within it whose help they could have called upon to take it. The KKE, despite the desire of the nearby ELAS leaders to move into the vacuum, simply called upon all Greeks to maintain public order. Had the KKE or ELAS intended to attain power by force, this was the best, if not only, time to do it easily, but they allowed the British, followed a few days later by the government-in-exile, to enter Athens on October 14. That the KKE Politburo pursued a nonrevolutionary line at such an opportune moment is crucial to understanding that when it later accepted violence as necessary its motives remained essentially defensive.

Given their isolation and the clan and group conflicts in rural areas, some ELAS members refused to hand in all their arms—and many of those who did so soon regretted it. Moreover, the KKE leadership had no power to keep the ELAS under Markos Vafiadis near Thessaloniki from marching into the city before the British arrived. During November, relations between the British and ELAS deteriorated, and although the KKE apparatus under Siantos's control called for maintaining the united-front government and dissolving the ELAS, the KKE was quickly bypassed. For one thing, since late 1943 the British had planned to send troops to Greece rather than trust the ELAS should the Germans withdraw, and Churchill— weeks before the ELAS provided any conceivable justification—was always attracted to a show of force in order to permanently resolve his political problems with the Left. "Having paid the price we have to Russia for freedom of action in Greece," Churchill advised Eden on November 7, "we should not hesitate to use British troops. . . . I hope the Greek Brigade will arrive soon, and will not hesitate to shoot when necessary. . . . I fully expect a clash with E.A.M., and we must not shrink from it. . . ."[12] Churchill's confidence that the ELAS would back away from a sustained or expanded conflict was very much linked to the pledges Stalin had given him, and had the ELAS fanned out to the mountains, a far greater number of Britain's troops would have been tied up chasing it than Churchill could conceivably have afforded either militarily or politically.

But in the fall of 1944 the British comprehended that unless they saved the prewar elites the EAM was very likely to come to power, including by parliamentary means. For one thing, they were very uncertain whether the coalition under George Papandreou they proposed to install in Greece had the capacity to survive without a large armed British presence. The readiness of significant dissident elements in both the ELAS and the KKE to accept Soviet diktats also remained a serious question. A massive exhibition or even use of British power, either to undo any ELAS action or simply to intimidate the ELAS, struck Churchill as highly desirable even when the EAM initially accepted all of the exile-government's onerous political and military conditions. The Nazis understood fully how tensions such as these might produce civil war, and as they departed they left arms dumps for the ELAS to seize.

On November 16 the British commander warned the ELAS of dire consequences if they entered Athens with arms or disobeyed his troops. By then the British—ignoring Papandreou's conciliatory stance—believed that armed clashes were both possible as well as desirable, if not yet probable, not the least because the KKE and ELAS leaders were no longer able to restrain all of their followers. British-controlled troops and airplanes began pouring into the country until they numbered about 23,000 in November and more than twice that by mid-December. At that time, the leadership of the KKE and ELAS understandably discussed options in case of a British attack, which appeared imminent, and while they did not preclude any alternative neither could the various factions unite on a coherent policy. The KKE strongly criticized Aris's meetings and coordination with other ELAS commanders, and he was isolated, but those he represented were a growing force in the Athens region; Siantos continued to issue statements proclaiming the need for unity and tranquility; but within Athens itself an underground responsive to Ioannidis's militant line probably wished to defend itself.

The likelihood that they would have to do so increased greatly as both the British and the feeble Papandreou government they were seeking to sustain brought many rightist troops into the city and imposed royalist control over the army. When on December 1 the British and Papandreou demanded the immediate disarmament of the ELAS and the integration of only a small part of it into a national army the Right was to control, the EAM quit the government the same day. The next day the EAM received permission to hold a protest demonstration at 11:00 A.M. on December 3; it was banned late the night before the event, but began anyway. Shortly after it started, Greek police fired upon the main group, killing about 22 and wounding many more, and the battle of Athens commenced. Churchill had eagerly sought it, and although the ELAS avoided taking the offensive against British troops until December 12, his immediate response was decisive: ". . . do not hesitate to fire at any armed male in Athens who assails the British authority or Greek authority with which we are working. It would be well of course if your commands were reinforced by the authority of some Greek Government, and Papandreou is being told by Leeper to stop and help. *Do not however hesitate to act as if you were in a conquered city where a local rebellion is in progress.*"[13]

The battle of Athens was surely the most bitter experience any national resistance movement was to suffer, and its political implications were understood everywhere in Europe: conservative foreign states—in this case Britain, but later the U.S. as well—would prevent radical leftist forces from coming to power, whether they did so by political or military means. Militarily, the British intervention was decisive, and without it the Greek Right would have been very quickly overwhelmed. Although the American ambassador in Greece was horrified by British intransigence and the way it had alienated so many middle-class Greeks, and the U.S. press and public condemned British brutality, privately Washington backed a beleaguered Churchill unequivocally, even as he was strongly attacked in England. Many, myself included, have detailed the bloody events that followed during December, but from December 8 on, even though they were still in a position to defeat the British and their allies, the Communists made several overtures to end the fighting, and on the twenty-second, at a point when the ELAS controlled about three-quarters of Greece and the British commander warned Churchill that he had only sufficient power to conquer the Athens region, the ELAS offered to disarm in the Athens area and, with Siantos largely in charge, they embarked on public negotiations.

The result was a truce accord on January 11, 1945, in which the ELAS made major concessions on their control of arms. A month later the EAM signed the Varkiza Agreement notwithstanding the arrest of EAM members in the days leading up to it, the public warning of the new prime minister, General Nicholas Plastiras, that the Left could expect severe retribution, and the creation of a National Guard comprised of many with collaborationist records to reinforce the British-backed regime. Under its terms, the ELAS was disbanded, it was to surrender its arms, and the larger part of Greece was transferred to the Athens regime's control. Both the EAM and the KKE were recognized as legal parties, an election and plebiscite on the monarchy were promised within a year, freedom from prosecution and reprisals were assured to most EAM and ELAS members, and the existing bureaucracy was to be purged of collaborators. Contingent on the accord being implemented, the KKE chose to follow the same route as the French and Italian Communist parties.

The Varkiza Agreement, which Ionnis Sophianopoulos negotiated on behalf of the Athens government, was, in his words, "not carried out by subsequent administrations; reactionary elements, active during the Metaxas dictatorship and the enemy occupation, have been kept in key positions in the Civil Service, Army, Police and Gendarmerie."[14] The British and their clients proceeded to impose their draconian control over the nation. They placed prewar royalist officers in command of the army, absorbing monarchist and many former collaborationists to make the military a solid instrument of their cause. Real power in Greece moved to the hands of these promonarchist forces, who operated with relative autonomy. When Plastiras, who was conservative but also mildly republican, objected, they replaced him with a wholly pliable admiral. The Communists had stopped the ELAS, but they could not halt Churchill and the local Right, who now had both the freedom and the force (conceded to them by both the Stalinist wing of the KKE and Stalin himself) to remove any future threats to their power and property.

Athens' rulers had no intention whatsoever of allowing the KKE to use peaceful means to gain power, and like many regimes before them, they fully understood they had to depend upon Britain to cope with the inevitable destabilizing political consequences of their venal domestic policies. Throughout 1945 the repression mounted, and it continued thereafter: random assassinations, arrests, intimidation, and martial law existed outside of Athens until August. Rightist bands freely meted out retribution in many districts, and at the end of the year even a British parliamentary mission estimated that at least 50,000 political victims had been arrested after December 1944, the majority since the Varkiza Agreement, and at the end of 1945 at least 17,000 remained in filthy, crowded prisons. About 25,000 radicals, plus an equal number of minority ethnics, fled to Yugoslavia and Bulgaria to escape persecution.

At the end of May 1945, Nikos Zachariadis returned to Greece and replaced Siantos as head of the KKE. An unimaginative and mediocre Moscow-trained ideologue, he aspired to turn the KKE into a thoroughly disciplined party completely responsive to Soviet guidance, and he made friendship with Britain and recognition of its regional strategic primacy the keystone of the KKE policy. All he asked was that London not interfere in Greek internal politics, and allow the voters rather than the British-backed repression of civil liberties, by then reaching massive dimensions, to determine the nation's future. To prove his reliability, in June, Zachariadis expelled Aris Velouchiotis from the Party as an adventurist and former "Metaxas agent." Aris had opposed the Varkiza Agreement and had fled to the mountains to avoid being killed. Elusive until then, soldiers of the Athens regime were able to track him down quickly; his head was displayed in public. The KKE, which probably informed the government where to locate Aris, had removed the single biggest obstacle to a Stalinist policy and organization that had existed until then.[15]

But despite its Stalinist leadership and Soviet advice, the KKE was to become the only Communist party in southern or western Europe to pose a threat to a state enjoying Anglo-American sponsorship. Its uniqueness was due in part to the fact that the strongly urban-oriented KKE leadership and membership were completely out of touch with largely rural and strongly decentralized organizations and the people in them, and that most of the EAM and ELAS had escaped falling under their total control. Ultimately, however, the Greek Left's originality resulted from the terrible pressures and dilemmas that the British and their proxies imposed upon them: if they accepted the British demands, as the official KKE leaders urged, they would disappear as a political movement and many would go to prison. For when they finally agreed to Britain's terms, the Left's very existence was threatened even more gravely than had it continued to fight.

Given that a very unequal sustained civil war between discredited elements of the old order and the Left had just been narrowly averted, it is no wonder that there arose a growing possibility at the end of World War Two and during its immediate aftermath that repression might compel former ELAS members to defend themselves. That Britain would then intervene to prevent the Left's imminent triumph, thereby internationalizing the political and military consequences of the traditional Greek order's follies, seemed a foregone conclusion. With corruption, vertiginous inflation, and the economy in shambles, England's quandary was obvious: its protégés were incapable of creating a stable economic and political order. So it planned to keep two divisions in Greece until the elections and plebiscite were over—thereby initiating what proved to be a vastly greater and longer foreign intervention into the country's affairs.[16]

## France: The Communists and Order

The French Communist party's growth presented both a promise and a threat to its leadership as well as to the Soviet Union. The Party (PCF) had 328,000 members in 1937 but claimed three times that number in June 1945, and precisely because of this expansion its position became extremely paradoxical. On one hand, the bulk of its members had joined only after the risks of doing so no longer existed. Hence, notwithstanding most of its adherents' youth and militancy, many were also not completely unaware of the hazards of opposition. On the other hand, these enthusiastic new members, as in all mass Communist parties in the world that have experienced comparable growth, lacked much of the discipline that a Leninist party nominally requires. Both of these attributes, from the viewpoint of the Party's chieftans, made them potentially both dangerously adventurist and unreliable at one and the same time. As France emerged from the Nazi yoke in 1944–45, the Party's leaders had to consider both risks.

The Communist party's growth was directly linked to its central role in the Resistance, which gave it the nationalist legitimacy it had lacked after 1919, and a great many of the men and women it attracted for this reason were activists who both desired and expected great social changes. They were the bearers of a burgeoning—even if vaguely defined—radical culture, one that a majority of the population supported during the last months of the war, and one that the Stalinist party had yet to bring under its complete control. It was this sense of anticipation, and the feeling and hope among so many of them that liberation was only the beginning of an ongoing process of national renovation, one in which they would be called upon to use the Resistance's values and goals to purge and transform a decadent old order, that created so many profound anxieties for anti-Communists. This concern was heightened by the fact that Communists were very important in the departmental liberation committees, many of which for weeks and even months filled the sudden large administrative vacuum that the Nazi evacuation and Vichy's demise produced; indeed, they were strongest in the southern, Vichy zone, comprising 35 percent of its departmental committees' membership in a vast region that had few Anglo-American or Free French soldiers to check them. But even in the northern zone, Communists constituted 26 percent of the total of key local liberation committees members, although they dominated some entirely. This also meant Communist participation in, and often control over, the Patriotic Militia (as the FTP was called after October 1944) of many regions where they enjoyed a near monopoly of arms and great prestige. The magnitude of the problems confronting anti-Communists for some critical, anxious months in late 1944 were all linked to the degree of Communist power in various localities as well as the intensity, nature, and potential of the political ideas and motives of those eager, romantic neophytes who proclaimed their loyalty to the Party—and also to the ability and desire of its leaders to channel their followers' goals in ways that posed no challenge to Britain, the United States and, above all, the Gaullists.

Most of these seeming dangers were a result of the decentralization and regionalism that existed during the brief but crucial period after June 1944 during which the traditional forces of order were discredited or literally nonexistent. The greatest danger from local autonomy was the *épuration*— the reprisals—which began the moment that Resistance groups took over an area. These purges reflected not only the balance of forces in specific regions, the ardor and aspirations of the Resistance's local membership and its leadership, but also the extent to which what one American civil-affairs officer described as self-serving "hoodlums and grudgeholders flocked to the colors after the fighting was over."[17] There was in fact a plethora of new armed resisters in many places, some only teenagers or those who simply put on the necessary armbands, and while a certain portion were essentially nonpolitical opportunists, and other former Vichyites seeking to adapt to the new exigencies, many possessed very clear political attitudes. On the whole, Communist-led resistants and workers were disproportionately stronger than other groups, even in many rural areas, and this reality strongly affected the Resistance's actions. Even more important, the most militant Communists rose to the leadership of the FTP. Charles Tillon, its head, consistently opposed the Party's line and later was summarily expelled. Georges Guingouin, the dominant figure in the unusually effective FTP in the Limousin region (which includes three central-western *départements*, had an alleged 20,000 or more persons under its command, and was the most powerful in the country), had disobeyed the Party during the time of the Hitler-Stalin Pact, and it never forgave the "French Tito" for it. Beginning in September 1943, the Politburo unsuccessfully sought to control him. But while those whom the Party earlier or later criticized for lack of discipline played a crucial role in its Resistance movement, it nonetheless also advocated chastising traitors, and its members played an appreciable part in the nominally illegal but extensive purges that occurred during 1944–45.

The extent of summary executions during the *épuration* remains both unknown and incapable of precise measurement. Nearly 7,000 people were legally sentenced to death, but only 770 were actually executed, and over 38,000 of the roughly four times that number who were tried for collaboration were sent to prison or forced labor for some term. But the estimates of those summarily killed range from 4,500 to 68,000, with the most likely being about 10,000.[18] While it simplifies events to claim, as some have, that a civil war was taking place in parts of France by the summer of 1944, it was nonetheless a fact that illegal killings were sufficiently numerous to quite understandably raise the specter of it among many. The *épuration* in various areas created the very real, even imminent risk of local Resistance groups defying the Party's orders from Paris. The implications of such militancy for the relationship of the armed Resistance to the conservative order were perfectly obvious. The principal question at that time was how far it would or could go—and, above all, how to control it.

The *épuration* was most acute in those regions that the organized Resistance liberated by itself, with the majority of executions occurring before victory. Since the Allied thrust toward the German border allowed a portion of the German army to retain pockets in central and central-western France until April 1945 in a line reaching from Royan to Lyons, the Resistance groups—about two-thirds of whom were in the FTP—in the area south of it fought much more than they were called upon to do elsewhere. It was here too that most of the purges occurred, and within that large region the Limousin and Dordogne were the most dangerous places in France for collaborators. Even after the various militia were nominally integrated in the period after September 1944, it was impossible to dissolve it in those places where no adequate regular police force or army existed, or where German troops remained—and so its dissolution was both protracted and uneven. And since some thousands of owners and managers of companies who had collaborated with the Nazis prudently disappeared for a period, workers' committees took over the direction of many factories, especially in Lyon, Marseille, and industrial towns near them. Compounding both these nominal threats were the liberation committees, and while they did not challenge the Gaullist-led government's legitimacy, most Communists thought that the briefly important parallel bodies they had often created and led during mid-1944 should also be given legal status— in effect, that dual power be sanctioned. At the end of August 1944 even Jacques Duclos, who was then the single most important Party leader within France, propounded the ambiguous notion that both the FTP and liberation committees should continue to function.[19]

The fundamental challenge facing Britain, the U.S., and de Gaulle until November was how to contain this potential threat to a still-fragile state and whether the violence against the Vichy collaborationists principally in the less populated south was capable of spreading elsewhere, notwithstanding their efforts to prevent it, and threatening civil war in France.

### Stalin and French Communism

The essential context for comprehending French Communist policy was its leadership's subservience to general Soviet policy. The USSR after June 1941 insisted that Communists everywhere pursue a genuine united-front line because it believed that it was the strategy most likely to help defeat Hitler, and it sternly rebuked any thought of taking power unilaterally. And while Communists could raise social objectives in the course of mobilizing people, these were always regarded as secondary in the larger war effort. For Stalin, the Communist parties in every nation were instrumental forces to be integrated into his overall military campaign.

At the beginning of 1942 the USSR began formal negotiations with de Gaulle's representatives and thereafter maintained cordial relations with him despite the fact that the French party had been highly critical of Gaullism and for five months was obviously extremely distressed with Moscow's acceptance of it. Stalin assured de Gaulle in February 1942 that he would not incite the French to create a Communist regime—a guarantee of noninterference that Molotov reiterated in May—and he was especially eager to have the Free French apply maximum pressure on the British and Americans to open a second front in France as soon as possible. Stalin also unquestionably welcomed the prospect of a strong France—even one led by an anti-Communist nationalist—as a balance to Germany in the postwar era. De Gaulle, for his part, aside from the obviously decisive means Moscow gave him for controlling the PCF, also saw the Soviet Union's friendship as a lever to employ against the U.S., which still recognized Vichy. He warned the Americans that their failure to invade France risked leaving the USSR masters of the entire Continent and that their support for Vichy and refusal to recognize him would only strengthen the Communists.

Once Moscow acknowledged de Gaulle's committee as the leading organ of the French Resistance, the Party submerged its serious objections to him. However disputatiously its leaders within France itself thereafter sought to guard its organizational integrity, the Communists pursued the Soviet policy. By mid-1942 the Party accepted the principle of de Gaulle's supremacy, and he initiated the tortured negotiations that were to lead to the putative integration of the FTP into his Committee of National Liberation (CNL) in May 1943. Because of the bitter Anglo-American dispute over de Gaulle, which allied the U.S. with Vichy for most of the war, the USSR hesitated to recognize the CNL formally until August 1943, after it had Britain's full support, but by then there was scarcely any doubt that de Gaulle would be non-Communist France's principal political leader at the end of the war. De Gaulle fully intended both to use and wholly control the PCF, for which he had contempt as well as anxiety, and from 1942 on he understood clearly that the most effective way to do deal with the Party was through a cooperative Moscow. He now publicly recognized the Party as a stabilizing factor in French politics, an unprecedented concession from so conservative a man and the bourgeois coalition ranged behind him, and assigned it minor posts in his shadow cabinets.

De Gaulle merely bided his time until he could establish his power in France, a goal that the Americans, far more than the Communists, blocked, and upon succeeding, he summarily minimized the aid the PCF had given him. But Stalin, working through Maurice Thorez, loyally backed the general. Thorez had remained in Moscow throughout the war and became the Party's virtual dictator when de Gaulle permitted him to come home at the end of November 1944 upon obtaining assurance that he would remain loyal to the Gaullist-led coalition by then firmly established in Paris. Thorez's presence, de Gaulle believed, "would involve more advantages than drawbacks at the present moment"; he and his close advisers were convinced he was the best Communist leader on the scene, and that "once the Communists adopted preponderance in a parliamentary regime instead of revolution as their goal, society ran far fewer risks."[20] But ultimately de Gaulle's confidence rested less in Thorez himself than in his understanding of Moscow's strategy in France.

Before Thorez returned to France, Stalin acknowledged to him that de Gaulle had dictatorial impulses but reemphasized the need to avoid class conflict and maintain the united front against Hitler. The ever-obedient Thorez had no reticence about such an alliance, and until his return the majority of the PCF's leaders essentially followed his instructions. Their real difficulty until then, apart from the absence of detailed continuous guidance from Thorez (and Moscow!), was that although the Party was essentially deeply committed to the united front it was also in favor of legitimizing the militias and liberation committees, and many of its followers expected and desired considerably more change than it could deliver.

But Stalin's involvement with France extended to questions with international ramifications well beyond de Gaulle and the PCF. Postwar France's relations with Britain and the U.S.—themselves deeply divided over French internal politics and France's potential role when peace came—was of prime significance, and it was linked to the still-implicit larger issue of the Allies' control over politics in those nations their armies conquered—in a word, spheres of influence. The invasion of Italy produced the first precedent regarding this fundamental matter, and while France was nominally an ally, the Vichy regime had enthusiastically collaborated with Germany. Such a Byzantine international context required finesse on Stalin's part, and while it most likely influenced Moscow's initial advice to the PCF, after mid-1943 the problem of the shape of postwar European power was unquestionably the principal factor in determining its French policy—and the policies that the PCF was ultimately to pursue.

The USSR employed the question of Anglo-American jurisdiction in France after the invasion to test the applicability of the Italian precedent in which occupying armies evoked ostensibly military justifications to reserve decisive political powers for themselves. This issue, as in Italy, remained complicated as long as London and Washington could not agree on which local groups to support—in this case, de Gaulle's CNL. They did resolve, however, to inform the Russians that, in effect, they would not be consulted in any way until the British and Americans patched together an accord, which would then be applied notwithstanding Soviet opinions. After D-Day, June 6, 1944, the CNL, which had a nominal if small Communist component, desperately attempted over American objections to have its organization in France recognized as the provisional government. Seeking at the same time to win Soviet endorsement, Moscow informed the French representatives in that city, as American Ambassador W. Averell Harriman recounted it, "that the Soviet Government would take no action vis-à-vis the French at variance with the Anglo-American position"—which in fact had still to be hammered out. "Molotov has told me several times," Harriman reported on July 9, 1944, ". . . that it was the Soviet policy to leave the initiative in French policy to the British and ourselves."[21] Such a carte blanche was certainly not a new policy but merely an extension of Stalin's conviction that it was essentially military possession that would define the political outcome of the war, and that neither London nor Washington would waver from such a policy—even if they protested the Soviet application of it in countries they conquered.

The political consequences of this posture was that Moscow insisted upon the PCF's continued loyalty to its alliance with conservative nationalists, one in which they remained a subservient element. After the liberation of Paris, Tillon recalls, Soviet diplomats reminded the PCF that it must do nothing to oppose de Gaulle's orders or those of the Allies. Such trends certainly reassured key U.S. authorities, especially Eisenhower, who reproached Washington for refusing to give de Gaulle's government de jure recognition even though he had managed to get the Communists "to eschew petty party squabbles in order to speed reconstruction" and was the only person able to create a united, stronger France that would serve as a barrier to the feared Soviet domination of Europe.[22]

## The Party Contains Dissidence

However valid many of the reasons that French Communists later gave for their conservative reinforcement of de Gaulle's power during the crucial year of 1944, none alters the basic fact that it was its leadership's servile commitment since 1921 to following Moscow's orders that explains the origins of basic PCF policy. But to say that Thorez was ultimately in charge should not obscure the significant tensions existing within the PCF leadership or the pressures from distant and virtually autonomous Party units, a mass of still unindoctrinated new members, and a widespread radicalization among them that created a sense of urgency and opportunity at one and the same time. The Party directors in Algiers under André Marty were the least tractable group, but within France itself the FTP's leaders, even though they had only vague notions regarding their organization's future structure and purposes, also objected to transferring the power of command and their limited arms to the Gaullist-controlled French Forces of the Interior (FFI) and government. Despite the Party's support for their demands in the three months before Thorez returned, it was this recalcitrant element, nearly all of whom were later expelled or simply left the Party, that most troubled Thorez in his efforts to pursue Moscow's policy slavishly.

The Moscow–de Gaulle axis had not been easy for most Party members to accept, but it was an overriding constraining reality and they were obligated to conform to it. The initial integration of the FTP into the FFI after much tortured negotiation was more an abstraction than a reality under the occupation: the FTP retained a certain element of functional autonomy even as it acknowledged the FFI's supremacy, and in return it received very few arms. The different components of the Resistance never fully trusted each other nor did they cooperate closely, and this was shown prior to August 1944 when the Communist-dominated FFI in Paris, after bitter argument, formally acceded to the Gaullist representatives' organizational demands and then ignored many of them in practice—only to be ignominiously shunted aside during and after the liberation of Paris. In the end, many Communists complained about the unceremoniously crude way in which the FTP had been dissolved, but they nonetheless submitted to it after September 1944.[23]

When Thorez returned to France, he almost immediately suggested that the Patriotic Militia and the liberation committees should be permitted to coexist with the regular government army and administrative organs only until, in the latter case, elections were held—thereby partially assuaging the militants who, in the aggregate, had led the Party until then. But the Communists also talked of creating a single party with the Socialists, or a common Resistance ticket in future elections, and sought to make themselves look suitably moderate; Thorez quickly ended mentioning the Party's earlier demands for parallel political and military powers. During January 1945 he unequivocally attacked local militia involved in the *épuration* and those extraparliamentary institutions substituting for traditional governmental organizations. The people could express their opinion, he now instructed, but only legal authorities could confiscate property, make arrests, or hand down and execute judgments. To Thorez, national unity to win the war as quickly as possible was the only task before the population, and there could be only one state, one police, and one army. He ordered those Party activists who wished to continue their wartime style of work to terminate what he described as sectarianism. Disarming the militia was greatly accelerated, and while the regular army absorbed many of its members individually, significant groups continued to function; but after January the Party central committee demanded the abolition of all the remaining Patriotic Militia and liberation committees, and the latter disappeared when local elections were held the following April. Thorez now concentrated on exhorting the working class to make greater efforts to restore production.

By August 1944, some PCF leaders were candidly arguing that cooperation with de Gaulle and the restored prewar order should be continued but without "any illusion"; in practice, however, such a compromise initiated the process of integrating the entire Party, dissidents included, into the redeemed capitalist state that de Gaulle and his allies were reconstituting.[24] Since the end of 1943 the Party had intensively lobbied to be incorporated in a provisional war government, and then joined de Gaulle's administration in September 1944 with two of the twenty-one ministers, of whom the erstwhile leftist militant Tillon was one. The fact remains that those who wished to define an alternative to the Moscow-Thorez line, while ambivalent about working with de Gaulle exclusively on his terms, also ultimately agreed to do so, and both they and the Party loyalists developed serious second thoughts about this policy mainly after May 1947, when they were ignominiously thrown out of the coalition government at the United States' behest. All of them were basically solid reformists who required occasional dollops of radical rhetoric to justify their seeming not to be an outright social democratic party, which essentially the Communists had become by 1945. But until de Gaulle quit politics in January 1946, they treated him as the leader of the nation rather than as the savior of the patriotic bourgeoisie, and for sixteen more months they advocated a no-strike policy, maximum production for war, and, subsequently, to rebuild the economy. The PCF's leadership as a whole remained good bourgeois legalists, with Thorez becoming a minister in October 1945. But even after its expulsion it believed that it should be part of the government coalition, and although the Soviets criticized them privately in the fall of 1947 for being too uncritical politically, Moscow had long since explicitly opposed insurrection.

When the Party later tried to exonerate the glaring contradiction between its political behavior in loyally supporting a bourgeois government while remaining ideological Leninists, they sought to claim that they had no arms in 1944 and de Gaulle had hoped to isolate them. But in reality, apart from the fact that in certain areas Communists had both arms and de facto control of local governments, de Gaulle's policy was based on his accurate reading of Moscow's policy combined with his successful strategy of co-opting the PCF and restraining it at the price of a few minor posts. Party spokesmen subsequently asserted that nearly 2 million British and American soldiers in France would have doomed any effort to take power, but while the point may be valid, it is by no means certain. It would have been far more difficult for the Allies to defeat the Nazis and capture a large part of Germany under such conditions, and Eisenhower surely understood this when he refused de Gaulle's request at the end of September 1944 to spare two French divisions from the front immediately so that he could handle the Communists in the vast Toulouse-Limousin area—thereby also increasing de Gaulle's dependence on Moscow and Thorez to cope with possible leftist threats to his authority. The Party's later exculpation that revolutions are not the work of organized minorities is irrelevant—such a notion not only contradicts Leninist theory but there were probably many more Communists in France in late 1944 as a proportion of the nation than there were in Russia in 1917. It was also true that many FFI members, including those that were Communist-led, desired to end their military careers as soon as possible, and had little heart for new adventures. And if a considerable portion of them appeared to be more resistants than radicals, this could not be proven until tested, and later most of them voted Communist year after year.

But while it is unquestionably one thing to desire great changes and another to do something about it, one cannot attribute the Party's inaction to the allegedly underdeveloped status of mass consciousness. Revolutionary politics involves the willingness at crucial points to take risks, and never in recent French history had the Left been so strong or the traditional ruling class so compromised. Such speculations become completely irrelevant not because they are groundless but because even if there had been a revolutionary majority, the PCF would have abjured taking power since Stalin was unalterably opposed to social revolutions in western and southern

Europe; that the Party's leaders, who certainly were the dullest and least able on the Continent, were to remain the most Stalinist of the major European Communist parties was certainly *the* most crucial factor in its behavior during French capitalism's most vulnerable moment in the twentieth century. And, ultimately, de Gaulle and both the United States and Britain understood that a decisive Soviet constraint on French Communism existed—and that they could remain tranquil regarding it while pursuing the war against Hitler, and afterward as well.[25]

## The Italian Dilemma

Political and geographical decentralization and local spontaneity were all crucial to the Italian Resistance and Left's development throughout the period after the Anglo-American invasion in September 1943. Above all, northern Italy remained insulated and under the Nazi yoke until the war was virtually over, and it was the inability of either the Allied armies, the residues of the Fascist order, or the Communist (PCI) and other leftist parties to quickly gain decisive control over the huge region's seemingly autonomous people and accelerating developments that produced critical challenges for all of them. Northern Italy appeared to teeter on the abyss of far-reaching, if not revolutionary, changes long after such possibilities had been resolved south of a line from Pisa to Rimini.

When the Anglo-American authorities and conservative Italian political leaders assessed the situation in northern Italy during 1944–45, an instinctive pessimism suffused their conclusions, shaping their actions accordingly. Apart from the burgeoning strikes, local armed bands, and the like, deep concern among them that such disputatious if not rebellious elements even existed and potentially could move beyond even the PCI's control and play yet more independent roles was a primary calculation in their responses to the dilemmas they confronted. None of the responsible American or English officials believed they could afford to dismiss the Communists' or Socialists' earlier rhetoric and history, and when the PCI proclaimed that it was now a new, fundamentally altered, essentially moderate party, its assurance was hardly sufficient to calm those with a knowledge of the past and concern for the present. After all, the Allied armies were a long way off and the Fascists and Nazi forces were either disintegrating or about to abandon the north to armed groups with what seemed to be extremely diverse political and social characteristics. But even if the Left abjured violence—and this was by no means clear insofar as the Socialists were concerned—there still remained the danger of its attaining power through parliamentary means, and it was possibilities such as these that had caused the ruling classes to turn to Fascism in the early 1920s.

Later, in 1946, the combined Socialist-Communist vote was 40 percent nationally compared to 29 percent in 1921, but in Italy north of Rome the two leftist parties were—and remained—the dominant political force. Sheer prudence dictated that those opposed to it consider the Marxist threat an imminent possibility; they could scarcely afford to do otherwise.[26]

## The Communist Menace

The Resistance and the organized parties within it had been very small, even minute in the case of the Communists, until mid-1943, when they all began to flourish spectacularly, and this fact alone profoundly defined the broader movement's political and ideological coherence and influenced its subsequent behavior. Many joined specific partisan units for initially quite arbitrary reasons—proximity being as important as any—which then became the subsequent basis of their political identities. The Committee of National Liberation (CLN) program for the future remained too general to be translated into an agenda for action; the only tangible goal its member organizations agreed upon was the destruction of Fascism and all of its institutional manifestations, although not on how to accomplish it. But those who became a part of the Resistance in its earliest, most perilous stages were required to break from conventional behavior at great risk to themselves, and however inchoate their visions for the future they were overwhelmingly nonconformists, radicals, and innovators who were far more prepared than others to face hazards on behalf of their ideals. During the crucial months leading to April 1945, persons such as these appeared to be defining political culture and its direction in the northern part of the nation.

The widespread emergence of what can generally be characterized as natural radical actors was distinctive in Italy, also, because the PCI, alone in Europe, had a powerful rival on the Left in the form of the Socialists (PSIUP), under Pietro Nenni, a party whose wartime record was unsullied and which acted as a considerably more uncompromising force in terms of specific demands, calling for abolition of the monarchy and the bourgeois state, a thorough purge of all Fascists, and a workers' republic. By late 1945 the PSIUP had recruited some 700,000 members, and in the June 1946 election its vote was still one-tenth greater than that of the Communists. At the local level the Socialists tended to make the PCI more militant than it otherwise might have been had its leaders been free from their organized pressure. The Communist growth from 5,000 members in June 1943 to 1.7 million scarcely two years later was due to the fact that the Party's leaders simply accommodated, often in an ad hoc manner, to the people's spontaneity. In a matter of only months the PCI went from being an inconsequential but disciplined Leninist sect to a mass party comprised of members whose future conduct was still unpredictable.

This remarkable metamorphosis was the consequence of both a lack of sectarianism among the Party's leadership, who were obligated to submerge their ideological instincts in order to cooperate with other Resistance and Left forces that were virtually their equals, and of sheer opportunism. As we shall see, it was also the logical step for a party committed (contrary to Leninist orthodoxy) to avoiding a nonparliamentary seizure of power. But once the Communists decided to build a mass party designed to become a triumphant electoral machine, they suppressed all ideological and class criteria for membership: there were no barriers for "religious faith or philosophical convictions," and their December 1945 platform defended private property, religious freedom, and the family. Indeed, even former Fascists were openly welcomed.[27] But although it dreamed of becoming a party for all classes, and many members were good Catholics, the overwhelming majority of its members still came from the urban working class and poorer rural elements.

The average Communist was, in brief, far from being a heavily indoctrinated, carefully screened revolutionary, but much more likely to be a part of a local social and human network that shared general political goals—a very personal arrangement that endured all sorts of vicissitudes and caused both the Party and its vote to increase over future years. Such intimate ties cultivated a sentimental attitude toward the PCI's icons, of which the USSR and especially Stalin as a quasi-divine leader were preeminent, but although its literature praised Stalin slavishly, the PCI never imposed absolute ideological discipline on its mass membership. Moreover, the motivation and commitment of the vast majority of those who joined it were an open question. Of its 410,000 members in March 1945, only a quarter of them were in the occupied north—people who had joined the Party when it was dangerous to do so and were incontestably true radicals. Over the next eight months the PCI's national membership quadrupled, and many of its new recruits had the most ephemeral reasons for joining or were opportunists. The belief that power was theirs if the electoral machine was maintained intact was a cement that kept many of these new Communists of dubious provenance united with older members who had shared a common experience in the Resistance or comprehended Leninist scripture. Such a constituency and program lent itself to the construction of a mass party and electoral organization, but ideologically these members were initially weak stuff and untested in terms of reliability and discipline, especially in the north before April 1945. All that remained nominally Leninist in the PCI was the tight elite domination over it, and its vast membership had no effective channels for shaping Party policy; but while it never developed a democratic structure or theory appropriate for its size, the same may be said about most non-Leninist parties, which also remained oligarchical in practice.

Until it could create a coherent, stable political system out of the residues of Fascism and the effects of the war, Italy remained in suspense politically; and while we now fully appreciate the factors of underlying stability that existed in the form of Soviet policy and Communist party leadership, during the heady, precarious days after September 1943 no one could be certain of the future. In large part this was the inevitable consequence of the desire of so many people for revenge and equity and the absence of any force able to control them fully, but the fact that the various political parties often outbid the others for the people's sympathies by catering rhetorically to their radical sentiments also made the north's destiny appear problematic.[28]

### The Soviet Union and the Anglo-American Schism

The Italian imbroglio was complicated after the fall of 1943 not only because of the inherent unpredictability of the role that the people might play; profound Anglo-American rivalries also suffused the specific policies of the Allied Military Government of Occupied Territories (AMGOT). The British and Americans agreed on the desirability of minimizing Soviet influence and preventing the Communists from taking over, but not on how to attain these goals—or much else. Moreover, until the spring of 1944, the Soviet position, as expressed in policies of the PCI, had yet to be made explicit. There are many accounts of this inordinately convoluted period, but several aspects of it need to be emphasized here.

Anglo-American differences produced what later U.S. official histories have described as a "great debate," and it was one that evolved from the British insistence that since their interests in the region were paramount they should define the occupation government's basic policies.[29] The U.S., on the other hand, refused to give up its own objectives, which Roosevelt's efforts to win the Italian-American vote in the November 1944 election greatly complicated, and issues of form and jurisdiction often prevented the two sides from concurring on substance even when they favored the same ends. Italian political factions quickly learned how to play on this division.

London and Washington agreed that the collapse of Fascism could not be allowed to produce a political vacuum into which the Left could enter, and the question of the purge of Fascists in the state organs and control over the Left became inextricably linked issues. Both allies were publicly pledged to "defascistization," but their officers found it was far simpler to leave existing officeholders at their posts, and they quickly concluded that most of them were quite harmless and acceptable nonpolitical conformists or opportunists. Privately, the British opposed a thorough purge (save for a few prominent figures) and planned to use the existing administrative system, including the police—which is precisely what happened. Not only did

American authorities follow their lead, but even the PCI and most of the CLN parties were lukewarm toward the total purge that only the Socialists advocated. The defascistization legislation that both AMGOT and the Italian government issued was full of major escape clauses, and only a handful of very well-known Fascists who did not escape Italy were charged criminally and sentenced. As for the immense group beneath them, large numbers were examined and 1 percent or less were fired from their positions, but they avoided criminal penalties.

While the Allied Military Government claimed exclusive jurisdiction in liberated areas, from the inception it suffered from an acute shortage of civil-affairs officers, which meant that in countless communes the ex-Fascists or their collaborators stayed in office. This, in turn, provoked numerous protests and riots, and while CLN-approved administrations subsequently took over in some places, this only partially altered the situation. Variations of this civil-administration dilemma persisted until the war ended. Former Fascist officials soon began using their power to exploit relief supplies for private gain via the black market and other forms of corruption. In essence, those who had loyally served Fascism for decades, including many who had joined the Party, still dominated the post-Mussolini civil, military, and police systems. The result was what one U.S. officer involved in civil affairs described as a "loss of faith in the liberators" as well as an increasing number of protests and even riots during which recycled Fascist police and carabinieri were used against the people.[30] In a context in which AMGOT initially controlled all publications, the right to hold meetings, and political activity, the prospect of Fascists retaining much of their original power only increased the desire of many leftists to keep whatever weapons they had, presenting everyone else with a grave dilemma.

The Anglo-American split emerged most strongly because Churchill insisted that Marshal Pietro Badoglio and King Victor Emmanuel III, who deposed Mussolini on July 25, 1943, at the behest of the Fascist Grand Council, monarchists, and officers who had all been his loyal supporters for decades, were the sole barrier to "rampant Bolshevism."[31] And while many senior American officials also agreed that self-determination posed major dangers, Badoglio and his reactionary circle were particularly inept and counterproductive, and by early 1944 Washington had concluded that a more effective government would better confront the threat from the Left and that maintaining the monarchy should not, in itself, be a political objective.

This political dispute notwithstanding, the British and Americans agreed completely on a common response to liberated Italy's troubling larger political and social trends. In the areas AMGOT controlled it disarmed and arrested many partisans by putting them in special camps, and beginning in early 1944 it equipped 180,000 former soldiers and *carabinieri* for internal security purposes. The problem of the still-occupied north was far more complicated because it was the historic stronghold of the Left and likely to remain inaccessible until the war was virtually over. Initially, the Committee of National Liberation for Northern Italy (CLNAI) was independent of the CLN in Rome even though the parties in both overlapped, and while the civil occupation authorities sought to make certain that the political dangers the CLNAI might pose were forestalled, Allied generals at the same time endeavored until late 1944 to gain as much as possible militarily from its growing partisan units.[32]

It was in this context of intrigues and struggles for power in Rome that the Soviet Union unexpectedly entered the picture to eliminate some, but surely not all, of the political dangers that British and American officials feared they might confront. The Badoglio administration was eager to remove the numerous onerous conditions the British and Americans had imposed upon it in two armistice accords, for which it needed leverage in the form of Soviet acceptance of its capacity to rule. Any gesture of support from Moscow would presumably not only strengthen the thoroughly compromised and opportunist regime but also reinforce British opposition to the mounting American pressures to replace it. And at least as important, as Badoglio and his conservatives coalition and the British fully realized, the USSR alone had the power to muzzle a Communist party that was initially highly critical of Badoglio and prevented the CLN from participating in the Rome government. Stalin's principal incentive for plunging into the Italian imbroglio was the prospect of getting a much greater Italian participation in the war against the Nazis, but he was also piqued over the exclusion of the USSR from any real voice in Allied management of Italy's present and future role in Europe—an irritation that the Stalin-Churchill understanding the following October removed. It was for this reason that Andrei Vishinsky, the Russian member of the powerless Advisory Council for Italy, headquartered in Algiers, probably indicated to the Badoglio regime in late 1943 that direct diplomatic contacts might be possible, thereby offering Mussolini's former associates a way to resolve several critical challenges in one grand swoop.

In early January 1944, unknown to either the British or the Americans, Badoglio's diplomats took the initiative to begin crucial secret negotiations with the Russians that touched on, along with other topics that soon proved far less significant, the Communists' future role in Italian politics. The Russians contemplated the implications of the package—which explicitly presupposed a cooperative PCI in the future—until March 4, when they told Badoglio they were ready to establish normal diplomatic relations.

Several days later Badoglio's representatives notified the American authorities of the imminent normalization of Italo-Soviet relations, hiding their role in concocting the accord, and the U.S. interpreted subsequent developments as a case of unwarranted Russian interference in Italian affairs. With great ingenuity but little durable effect the Badoglio regime attempted to play on Anglo-American disagreements, and their mutual fear of the growth of Soviet influence, to alter its own legal status in the war.[33]

On March 13, 1944, just as Roosevelt informed Churchill that their inability to garner local political support required that they replace Badoglio and the king, Moscow extended de jure recognition—quickly downgraded to de facto—to the former conqueror of Abyssinia, giving the neo-Fascists in power a new lease on life. Washington was initially very perturbed in principle because it did not want Russia to play any political role whatsoever in the former Axis nation, not the least because it was also reinforcing the British pretensions to a dominant influence in Italy. When discussing the matter with the U.S., the British also objected to Soviet involvement, but it is probably no coincidence that Churchill at this very time endorsed the USSR's claims to the Curzon Line in Poland. Still, both the Americans and the English were soon delighted to learn that "under orders from Moscow" the PCI would join the Badoglio government without conditions.[34] And the Soviets informed the irate American government that it had no reason to complain because Italian politics would soon be unified and the nation could play a much bigger role in the war effort. As the official British diplomatic history of the war observed three decades later, at this point "the Soviet representative on the Italian Advisory Council had been reasonable . . . and the Italian Communist Party, clearly under orders from Moscow, had suddenly given up attacking the monarchy and Marshal Badoglio and was advocating Communist-Catholic cooperation."[35] The Soviet intrusion, however inept, was probably privately welcome in London and had far-reaching consequences for Italy's future.

To make certain the PCI cooperated, on March 28, Palmiro Togliatti, the one foreigner then allegedly closest to the Soviet leadership, returned to Italy to resume control of the Party. There can be no question that the PCI leadership was acting on Moscow's instructions during this crucial period, a point they reiterated privately when the Yugoslavs in 1947 criticized their reformism. Stalin was unequivocally in favor of doing everything to win the war quickly, which meant a united front of all anti-Nazi parties and a much greater Italian war effort, more stress on nationalism and social amity, and an avoidance of sectarian issues that might divide a coalition devoted to these goals. In essence, Stalin hoped that his suppression of class demands and conflicts in various countries would cause the USSR's allies to trust it and cooperate after, as well as during, the war; to accomplish this, Soviet interests had to take exclusive precedence over those of the local Communist parties and their followers. "We do not want revolutions in the West . . . ," former Soviet Foreign Minister Maxim Litvinov assured the American representative on the Italian Advisory Council in September 1944.[36]

Togliatti had often spoken on Radio Moscow, and he was permitted to return to Italy because he was known to accept unreservedly Stalin's line that war-torn European nations had to establish sufficient political stability to assure postwar peace and cooperation between the Allies. This utter loyalty to Soviet direction and the support this in turn gave him was the sole basis for his reestablishing virtually absolute domination over the PCI's leaders within Italy itself, a significant portion of whom favored a much more radical line opposed to collaboration with other parties and wished to see Communist power consolidated by force of arms. Togliatti persuaded some that this was an error, while the others he brought under control by evoking his mandate from Moscow. But unlike other Stalinists, he rarely expelled those who disagreed with him, so that in the long run a far more serious debate occurred within the always-quite-diverse PCI leadership than in any other major Communist party. This relative pluralism was instrumental in the much-later emergence of "Eurocommunism" and the end of Soviet control over the PCI.

In his famous press conference at Salerno on April 1, 1944, Togliatti proclaimed that the Communists would defer the question of the monarchy until the war was over, join the Badoglio government as well as collaborate with the anti-Fascist parties who remained out of it, and work for social and class cooperation in a democratic and parliamentary Italy. He also committed the Communists to the creation of a mass party open to everyone, and implicitly abandoned much of the Leninist organizational scripture. Togliatti's speeches, Badoglio later recalled, "caused a perfect ferment among the other parties as offering a chance of escape from the blind alley into which they had strayed."[37] His undertaking to share power in a united front guided the Party's political strategy for nearly three more years because its partners soon concluded that the Communists acted responsibly and could be trusted. But whatever the initial wartime motives, this alliance persisted long after the war, and the very existence of a tractable PCI confirmed Stalin's acceptance of Italy as being within Britain's or America's sphere of influence.

Still, from Togliatti's viewpoint there were other, even more persuasive reasons for this class-collaborationist line. First, it was certainly most compatible with building a nonsectarian mass party aiming at electoral successes. But, like Gramsci before him, Togliatti was also sincerely convinced that the same middle classes he now proposed to work with had largely turned to Mussolini in the early 1920s when they saw socialism as a real threat to their power, sustaining Fascism for nearly two decades—and that their ostensible devotion to democracy remained tentative. The utter fail-ure of the defascistization program in their hands only confirmed the Right and Center's essential ambiguity toward the Fascist period. If radical extremism seemed imminent, Togliatti believed, then the antisocialist classes would again mobilize to destroy it. According to his reasoning, were the Communist party also to talk or behave like Nenni's Socialists—who in fact were as much addicted to strong Marxist rhetoric as their predecessors had been after 1918—there would be neither a democratic nor a socialist Italy. In a word, Togliatti insisted that just as the Right had ample reason to fear an aggressive militant leftist movement, so the Left had cause to worry about a resurgent authoritarianism, all the more powerful because both the British and the Americans ultimately would support it. Whether either of these threats was false or not is irrelevant; given Italy's past his-tory, both were, with some considerable plausibility, widely feared and explain the behavior of each side.

Once embarked on such a cautious role, Togliatti, who was consum-mately urbane and witty, successfully ingratiated himself with the British and Americans in Rome and with Badoglio and the king, but he horrified many Resistance members in the north and, initially, the CLN parties in the south as well. But later in April the CLN, Communists included, joined the Badoglio cabinet. We need not detail the subsequent political intrigues in the Allied-occupied zone, which were largely the result of the conflict among Anglo-American proxies, but Togliatti was never the source of any of them and the PCI played a cooperative political role as a strictly consti-tutional force until May 1947, when U.S. pressures forced it out of the government.[38]

### Reining in the North

The problem for the British and Americans was not simply whether they could trust Togliatti and the PCI for long, but whether the Party was able materially to assist AMGOT with the daunting challenge of imposing its political and military authority in the areas already liberated and, above all, in the north, where the PCI still remained a more complex, far less disci-plined or united party and was in real or nominal control of about half of the armed men or radicals the Anglo-Americans had yet to deal with.

The mere fact that the CLNAI had a genuinely divided and pluralistic leadership meant that key decisions were debated much more than they had been in France or Greece—and every party in the north was politically under pressure to be militant lest it lose followers to its rivals. More impor-tant, the kinds of people who joined the parties were themselves only par-tially, if at all, disciplined. For Italy was full of angry men and women eager to undo oppression. They had been responsible for the strike wave in the northern industrial cities at the end of 1943, and apart from the tens of thousands who were in the various partisan armies in 1945, countless more were to participate in the April 1945 insurrections in Genoa, Milan, Bologna, and elsewhere. It was far from certain to AMGOT that this mixture of instant Communist and Socialist converts, members of local groups with only the vaguest ties to the organizations they were nominally affiliated with, and people who simply moved to fill in the ever-growing vacuum that Fascism's demise was creating, would be amenable to the elaborate controls that both the Allied Military Government and those politicians in Rome it supported hoped to impose.

During the summer of 1944 the partisans in the occupied north tied down as many as fourteen Axis divisions at one time, and were a significant military asset. The Allies could not, therefore, abandon them lightly, and the CLNAI in return wanted their precious aid along with political recognition, and so both sides maintained a strained interdependence. But the Anglo-American military and political officers profoundly distrusted them, their worst nightmare being a sudden German withdrawal that would permit the CLNAI to occupy the vacuum before friendly troops could arrive, in which case, American officials believed, "a situation not unlike that which exists in Greece today" would recur.[39] Indeed, one of Churchill's strongest arguments for the British offensive in Athens in December 1944 was precisely the need to create an example that would deter radical uprisings that "may spread to Italy" and elsewhere.[40] Disarming and pacifying partisans in the liberated south had been difficult enough, and only partially successful as of the end of 1944, but the problem in the north was compounded because the CLNAI considered itself the legitimate government of the occupied region and after difficult negotiations refused to acknowledge the supremacy of the CLN-backed government in Rome. It was in this profoundly strained political context, in which the only leverage they had was their aid supplies, that General Sir Harold Alexander, the supreme Allied commander in Italy, broadcast an appeal on November 13 to the partisans in the north, never mentioning the CLNAI by name, to cease most of their activities and save their supplies because of the Allies' alleged inability to help them during the winter. As an astute political analyst, Alexander was fully aware that his statement would act as a virtual invitation to a Nazi and Fascist offensive, which predictability occurred and battered the poorly equipped partisans, causing death, defections, and demoralization—and paved the way for the CLNAI's capitulation to Rome.

Throughout this crisis the official PCI tried to put the best face on the Allied pressures, and both the Socialists and the Action party took the most radical position and were quite prepared to create two nations and establish a socialist, republican government in the north once the Germans departed —and later the Socialists won more votes in key regions there. But notwithstanding some important differences among the PCI's leaders in the north, they went along with Togliatti's insistence that national unity and political cooperation was the Party's principal objective. Without the PCI, the northern Left could not proceed alone. The CLNAI's delegates returned to negotiate with AMGOT representatives eager to avoid a repetition of the violence then beginning to wrack Athens and who gladly exploited the partisan weaknesses to the limit. On December 7, in exchange for promises of financial subsidies and material aid, the CLNAI agreed to subordinate itself to the supreme Allied commander, not to appoint a military head of the CLNAI unacceptable to him, to hand over power to the Allied military government when it arrived in the north, and to obey its orders before and after liberation. But until the British threatened a total break, the CLNAI refused to accept the Rome government's political supremacy, and only on December 26 did the Allies obtain written assurance that the Resistance would not present it with a quasi-revolutionary, independent state in the richer half of Italy.

The Anglo-American political authorities never trusted the northern leaders or their followers, accords notwithstanding, and believed that "speed in getting ourselves firmly established is the essential factor: without this there is real danger of extreme Communist elements taking control. . . ."[41] They were convinced that the Left would seize power the moment the Germans departed, and began reducing the supplies they had promised to the Resistance and discouraging the expansion of their forces. It was because of this fear that "prior occupation of this area by Communist-dominated forces might well determine the zones of postwar influence, or even occupation," as Allen Dulles wrote later of his role as head of the U.S. Office of Strategic Services in Bern, that he began his secret negotiations with the Nazi commander in northern Italy.[42] After false starts and bitter recriminations between Stalin and America's leaders concerning the scope of the territory involved, on April 24—eight full days after the CLNAI called for a general uprising to take power—the Germans agreed to remain in their existing positions and surrender their arms only to those forces the Anglo-Americans designated; in a word, they would neither surrender to the CLNAI nor transfer power to it. Until the Anglo-American armies arrived, the Nazis were to "maintain in operation all public utility and essential civilian services," and with the aid of the CLNAI provide for "the general maintenance of law and order."[43] In effect, the Allies attempted to rely on the Nazis to forestall, as best they could, the Resistance's consolidation of total power.

But neither the Germans nor the CLNAI behaved as the Americans expected. German soldiers refused to risk their lives to keep radicals out of power, and their units began to disintegrate. Armed workers during April took over the key northern cities and countless factories—and then relinquished control of them. The CLNAI assumed full command of the entire state apparatus at all levels. Notwithstanding this, American officers felt that their effort to disarm partisans met "with astonishing success," mainly because their commanders maintained sufficient discipline among their forces and cooperated fully.[44] But ignoring the explicit opposition of their leaders, a considerable number of Communist partisans hid their arms and by the end of June 1945 more than a third of their estimated weapons remained in their possession.

Throughout the upper half of Italy many local CLNAI committees, acting independently of their parent organization as well as of AMGOT, drove out Fascists and their appointees and presented the Allies with seemingly troublesome *faits accompli*. The people's intense desire for justice after twenty years of Fascist oppression proved too difficult for both the CLNAI and the Allies to restrain. Most reprisals against Fascists, as in France, were not documented because small groups carried them out on their own initiative, but many who had suffered so long sought revenge, and the most cautious estimate is that several thousand were summarily killed in the north in the spring of 1945. Other projections reach 20,000, but in addition to those executed, tens of thousands were put in prisons for at least brief periods.

All CLNAI decrees and orders were nullified as of the end of May, but the military government quickly found the people and policies the CLNAI established so "sensible and the appointments well chosen" that it pragmatically (as with ex-Fascists) used those that served its objective of consolidating the conservative order.[45] And rather than resisting, by June 1 the Americans in charge concluded that "the CLNAI on the whole has lived up to the agreements made prior to occupation and has cooperated insofar as possible under the pressure exerted by the various political parties within the Committee."[46] Notwithstanding a few local committees that attempted to exert authority, or some unauthorized arms retentions, the Communists emerged at this crucial point in the bourgeoisie's vulnerability to create a united front with it. Nenni challenged the Allies far more than Togliatti did, and was even briefly arrested for making a speech highly critical of them, ostensibly without a permit—all of which later gained the Socialists popular support.

By the time the Allies reined in the CLNAI, the issue of Italy's future was linked to the lingering question of whether the Communists might abandon their cooperation and to the more sensitive and subtle problem of Anglo-American relations. There were important American officials who completely failed to comprehend the Communist political intentions and the decisive manner in which they were stabilizing such a deeply divided, precarious nation, and warned Washington "of an anarchical movement fostered by Moscow to bring Italy within the sphere of Russian influence."[47] The British believed that troops should not be withdrawn entirely from the north until at least the end of 1945 and the creation of police and armed forces adequate for internal security—a position the U.S. endorsed.

In making their decision to prolong a military presence, U.S. officials worried about "violent outbreaks," but they also perceived they had "a long-term interest" that required them not to seem to be "abandoning the Italian peninsula to purely British policy," one which they had bitterly opposed for over two years.[48] Even if it had yet to define a plan for Italy that formally assigned the United States a predominant influence there after the war, Washington's political and economic objectives required that it deny both Britain and the USSR such roles, and given Italy's economic dependence this ultimately necessitated an immeasurably greater American involvement in that nation's affairs than it had ever imagined possible.

## Europe's Destiny: Errors and Illusions

The decision of much of Europe's middle and traditional ruling classes to compromise with Nazi Germany, or actively to support it in the case of Italy and France, greatly weakened the major institutional barriers to the triumph of the forces of change and radical renovation that flourished in the wake of Allied military successes. Millions of new converts believed that only the Left, with its identification with patriotism, could pretend to fill the massive moral, political, and organizational vacuum that the elites' collaboration had created, and the Communists were the principal beneficiaries of this mood. In Greece, France, and Italy, this transformation posed a basic question about the political and economic future of these crucial nations—but elsewhere the war's consequences gave the Left both nationalist legitimacy and those appeals essential to making it far stronger than it had ever been.

The greatest crises during World War One had occurred as a consequence of the actions or disappearance of radicalized or demoralized soldiers, but after 1943 the armies and police forces that had once protected conservative political structures were, if not defunct, at least greatly compromised and immeasurably weakened. For many potentially decisive weeks or even months, in large portions of Europe no credible armed force stood between an organized and often armed Resistance, one drawn mainly from and allied with the working class and poorer peasantry, and its conquest of political and administrative power. Europe's oppressed seemed highly likely to triumph in all or at least major portions of three nations.

It was only the internationalization of such domestic social conflicts, to a far greater extent than during 1918–19, that prevented this unequal power equation from transforming the political map of Europe to a much larger degree than was to occur. That foreign powers after the experiences of 1918–19 would once again attempt to determine the ultimate outcomes of critical national political and ideological struggles and subject them to decisive pressures, with the real balance of political or physical power within each country being neutralized, was virtually inevitable. Although the men and groups that chose to collaborate after 1939 failed to comprehend sufficiently the potential domestic disasters they were courting, there were ample precedents for counterrevolution as their salvation during and after World War One. But what they could not even begin to imagine beforehand—though in due course they grasped it in sufficient time to survive—was that the pervasive internationalization of internal political dynamics during the Second World War, and the very existence of traditional capitalist social systems, might also gain profoundly from the stabilizing role that Bolshevik Russia could play.

The Left too was oblivious of this consummately ironic possibility.

Social dynamics during the two European wars differed greatly in several important ways. Most social mobilization during 1918 occurred within a relatively short span of time and principally in cities; from 1943 well into 1945 it was much more decentralized, involved many more and far better armed and organized people in inaccessible places for substantially longer periods, and was not nearly as vulnerable to the risk of repression from either national armed agencies or foreign military forces. Counterrevolution in 1918–19 was far more feasible than in 1945, when it confronted very substantially greater physical limitations. Suffice it to say, whether or not a mortal danger to Europe's status quo from the Left really existed, it is vital to understand the extent to which the very fear of it shaped Anglo-American wartime military, political, and diplomatic conduct and policy—and how it defined Britain and America's later obsessions and anxieties to produce the Cold War in Europe. The United States and Britain took the Left very seriously and acted accordingly, even long after it was evident that Stalin would attempt to solve their most immediate problems. But apart from trusting his intentions, which they could and usually did do, there still existed the question of whether he was capable of eliminating the inherent dangers that the European Left's diverse organizational forms and physical decentralization created.

Assessing the real potential of Europe's Left after 1943 is far more difficult and enigmatic. While most theories of mass conduct—its origins, timing, and how people can be expected to behave—are inextricably deductive speculations, the historical fact remains that the masses, even if they fail to do so in the vast majority of cases, in various times and places *will and do* act decisively in ways that contain the potential to profoundly change institutions and the course of history. Conservatives, for absolutely valid reasons, prudently behave as if this is always a serious possibility, and just because leftist theoreticians have been unable—in large part because of their fixation on nebulous formulae extracted from Marx or Lenin—to develop a coherent, analytically valid concept of the causes and timing of mass action does not eliminate its potential enormous weight and historical role. Coming to grips with such change is crucial for comprehending the modern historical experience. During wars, with their monumental effects in telescoping peoples' economic and mental condition and aspirations, the masses' actions in defining the political and social outcomes of conflicts becomes integral to a theory of radical change and when it does or does not occur. Obviously, long-term prewar secular trends also play a crucial role in providing a basis for potential crises, and these then also significantly influence various (but far from all) forms they take, but wars ignite and then accelerate and intensify them, transforming them into real challenges as they convince or compel people to behave in ways they are rarely willing or able to do in peacetime.

Ultimately, the issue of precisely when and to what extent radicalized masses are ready to act can never be known in advance. If their condition and desires are sufficiently acute, they will respond intellectually and politically—and eventually behave accordingly. Modern history, and the emergence of the Left as an operational or potentially decisive force at crucial moments, merely reflects this obvious fact. But to intellectualize social dynamics into a formula that considers history predictable and pliable is a chimera, and to demand such insight as a prerequisite for action is to preordain one to apathy. No one can ever be absolutely certain when the opportune moment has arrived, and the willingness and capacity to take chances is an integral aspect of all political action—radical included. Without risks, there can never be success, even though the vast majority of such speculations are destined to failure and their progenitors to frustration, obscurity, or often much worse. One must be born at the right time and at the right place to see or do great things, but also be a great gambler to initiate them. Politics, like warfare, is very often an art form as well as a rational exercise—great clarity and acute judgment are necessary preconditions for success, but an intangible sense of timing is also often essential.

Given the overall balance of forces—physical, political, and ideological—in Greece, Italy, and France after 1943, the Left was closer to attaining dominant power in at least two of these nations than at any time before or since. The vast numbers who entered Communist and other parties were not deeply indoctrinated or disciplined ideologically. They joined both the Resistance and the Communists only after victory was virtually assured, and in the vast majority of cases this imminent success was the essential precondition for their initial heroism. That they would be willing to fight much longer against domestic enemies and former allies was not at all certain. On the other hand, the Communists' real problem was not the possible weaknesses in the masses' commitments made late in the war, which Communist writers later cited to exonerate their parties' passivity at this crucial moment—notwithstanding the reality that the main, if not exclusive reason for their restraint was Stalin's policy.[49] In fact, these people remained members or voted Communist in France and Italy decades after the war ended. The principal challenge confronting Stalin and his anointed leaders was to prevent the enormous numbers who enrolled from acting autonomously of the Party line, which is precisely what they did in Greece when reprisals left them no alternative. For the Communist elites the greatest threat inherent in large memberships under tight elite control was the possibility of losing absolute mastery of their parties' organizations. In France, Thorez regarded autonomy of any nature as a menace to the creation of a finely honed, absolutely responsive political machine—purging countless other leaders and members over the years to maintain complete domination of it for himself and his chosen successors. But in Greece and Italy it was precisely the fact that most new Party and Resistance members were untrained and undisciplined that created the most danger, and in both places greater decentralization and a somewhat less authoritarian leadership style than that of Thorez's resulted in leaving open the future course that the radicalized masses might take. The average Communist in Italy and, especially, Greece, retained a certain capacity for independence and action that neither the British and Americans nor the internal Center-Right ever minimized—nor should we.

Notwithstanding their recent conversions and what proved to be the healthy absence of orthodox Communist doctrine, the European masses' leftist phase was more intense and lasted considerably longer in more nations after 1943 than after 1917. It was quite clear that most Communists were more radical, which is to say less cynical, than their leaders, who simply became Social Democrats in political practice and remained Bolsheviks only in terms of their authoritarian control over vast party machines. After 1918, by contrast, there was no hegemonic, inhibiting party on the Left, and given the traditional parties' and social classes' continuing strengths and viability, they were able to persist as serious political forces and eventually mount counterrevolutionary repression in much of Europe. After 1943 the Communist parties comprised most of the leftist opposition at a time in history when the old orders' power had declined enormously and conservatives believed earnestly, if incorrectly, that they were dependent exclusively on foreign armies to guarantee their survival. Had the Communists not existed, or not played the role of an anodyne for social discontent, then there certainly would have been many more strikes and social conflicts, and quite possibly more truly revolutionary challenges in southern and western Europe than the one in Greece that occurred only because people undergoing brutal repression had both the space and the dire incentive to take matters into their own hands.

But could such a revolutionary movement have taken power given the presence of massive Anglo-American armies? Communist writers have frequently argued that it would have been impossible, and even Nenni said as much in April 1946.[50] But such skeptical judgments entirely disregard the larger context of the war with Germany, the purely military problems involved, as well as the formidable political difficulties that sustained counterrevolutionary wars would have encountered both in England and the U.S.

The British and Americans faced not one but three potential threats in Europe, and had the challenges overlapped each other in time, they would have confronted qualitatively greater difficulties. Had the FTP chosen to impose its political control in central-western France in the summer of 1944, which it was easily able to do there and probably elsewhere as well, the diversion of Anglo-American troops to such vast, hilly spaces to depose it would have—depending on the number of men required—more or less seriously affected the offensive against Hitler's army, which as late as December 1944 was able to drive the Americans back into the Ardennes. A major commitment to fight an inherently time-consuming counterrevolutionary war would have found very little, if any, favor among western generals, and their willingness to do so was certainly not preordained. To delay the offensive against the Nazis risked leaving the Red Army in possession of much more, if not all, of German territory, the consequences of which would have meant far more to Europe's future than the existence of large Communist-controlled zones in rural France.

The British chose to fight in Athens in December 1944 against numerically inferior, poorly equipped guerrillas, who were not defeated but laid down their arms. Had the ELAS decided to retain its territory (which is to say most of Greece) by force of arms, Britain would have had to send in many more than 50,000 troops, again seriously affecting the war against Germany. Had the CLNAI chosen to create a socialist republic in the vast mountainous expanses of northern Italy, the numbers required to suppress it would have been far greater yet, and by itself would have redefined the nature of the war against Germany. Two, much less three, interventions would simply have been quite unmanageable militarily for both the Americans and the British. In a word, there was ample reason to believe that had the armed Left been ready to take power in these three nations it would have succeeded in part, if not entirely, for at least an indefinite period. Its prospects were at least as good as those of the Bolsheviks in Russia in 1917. If it had failed in France, it would have been due principally to the continuing viability of French conservatism mobilized around de Gaulle; elsewhere the traditional ruling classes had neither military resources nor political legitimacy—above all in the north of Italy and most of Greece.

But the political obstacles to transforming the war in Europe into a principally counterrevolutionary effort would have been more formidable than even the military hazards. The Allied intervention in Russia after 1917 was delayed and remained unsuccessful because of, among other things, domestic opposition in the U.S. and Britain. It would have been extremely difficult to persuade the British and American publics that troops sent to Europe were to be diverted to putting down Resistance movements that had earlier fought Hitler; it certainly would not have been palatable to their soldiers, who by the end of 1944 wanted to go home as soon as possible. And since the independent nature of these Resistance forces would have been the political prerequisite of their taking power, they could not have been portrayed as an extension of Soviet Communism; it would not have been easy to convince many people that it was preferable to reinstate ex-Fascists, collaborators, and monarchists in power. In brief, the subsequent Communist rationalization that the existence of Anglo-American armies precluded their taking power merely unconvincingly obfuscates the true reasons for their failures to do so.

Putting aside such military dimensions entirely, what would have occurred throughout Europe after the defeat of the diverse Axis coalition had Joseph Stalin not existed, or if Russia had not been under Communist control? Stated this way, we can better understand the monumental historic implications of Stalin and a disciplined international Communist movement for the survival of much of European capitalism and conservatism after 1944. Indeed, even in eastern Europe radical forces with their own independent priorities may have emerged; above all, a radicalized, unified German socialism insulated from the Cold War's obsessions and much more eager to penalize the historic German ruling class for its alliance with Hitler after 1932 is likely to have arisen and guided that nation's destiny during this crucial period.

That more astute French and Italian conservatives understood the decisive significance of Soviet control over their Communist parties, and quietly but successfully exploited it through direct negotiations, reveals the single most important dimension of the interaction between Stalin, counterrevolution, and the subsequent stability of two of Europe's most economically and strategically crucial nations. The Russians repeatedly assured their allies that they would oppose revolutions in those places most vital to Anglo-American interests. Churchill's 1944 accords with Stalin over Greece only reiterated the fact that the Soviet dictator was ready to provide the decisive and most effective assistance needed to save southern and western Europe from the folly and chicanery of its traditional ruling classes: Stalin would prevent the Communist parties from reaching for power.

The Yugoslav experience, like the Chinese, raised the question of whether Stalin's desires alone would always prove sufficient, and his split with Tito highlighted the existence and potential grave dangers of independent Communists to both Soviet and western interests. Where would the British and Americans have been had there been others like Tito? But if, as the Greek civil war was to reveal, Stalin's power also had its limits, it nonetheless remained sufficient in two major nations to provide bankrupt conservatives with the respite essential to their future. Yet even the Greek Communists took to arms initially much less intent on taking power than on surviving the repressive onslaught against them; had the Right there been less vindictive and willing to risk the perils of parliamentary politics, the Stalinist wing of the KKE would have almost certainly been able to avert the crisis that ensued.

The war's enormous economic, social, human, and intellectual impact therefore produced far less change in western and southern Europe than would otherwise have occurred. It probably remains the greatest irony of this century that the principal political outcome of the First World War in the form of the USSR led to the neutralization of the potentially far more drastic political consequences that were likely to have resulted from the much more destructive conflagration that followed it. The implications of this paradox for world power and the future of the Left were decisive. The larger part of Europe remained capitalist, and no independent socialist nations emerged to create a model that could have strengthened the influence and power of other socialist parties on the Continent. European socialism reached an impasse after 1945.

After a brief flirtation with an autonomous radical line in both Germany and Italy, the social democratic parties were intimidated by the alleged terrors of the Cold War to instinctively return to their bureaucratic, cautious roles and became a constituent part of an anti-Soviet bloc that for the presumed sake of anticommunism sublimated social policy and change to the priorities and exigencies of rearmament and integration into conservative orders. The Communist parties submerged the promises and dynamism of their initial years of growth and created huge electoral machines—with patronage to sustain them—and social institutions, and successfully focused their energies on winning local elections. Between its social democratic and Communist versions, socialism in Europe as the vital political and economic alternative to war, institutional and human irrationality, and social injustice atrophied over the last half of the twentieth century. The concept of internationalism, with all of the visions and enthusiasm that it could evoke, died, and the belief that basic social change was possible perished with it, as nothing comparable emerged to replace the socialist ideal in the masses' hearts and minds. What had once been an inspiring vital force became scarcely more than a utopian desire, and the consequences of the most destructive conflict in European history failed to change the western world's commitment to war as the keystone of its historical experience.

But notwithstanding the respite gained to a decisive degree because of Stalin, the assumptions, forces, and institutions that made wars both possible and inevitable nonetheless continued to define politics throughout much of the globe. For there was no peace after 1945, and most of the world remained deeply troubled.

# CHAPTER 12

# China: War, Society, and Revolution

The Second World War's profound impact upon the entire fabric of Asia's society, economy, and once-dominant colonial systems was largely the outcome of Japan's rapacious goals and the draconian occupation policies that its leaders believed were an essential precondition for victory. Like all nations, Japan sought to pursue its national interests in the traditional narrow definition of that concept, but it also chose to become the champion of a transnational Asian doctrine and movement that was not merely anticolonialist but expounded hatred toward whites, cynically manipulating such concepts both to rationalize and advance its self-serving goals. But although most of Japan's decision-making elite was strongly antiwestern ideologically, they were scarcely less contemptuous of other Asians. On one hand, Japan posed as Asia's savior; on the other, and far more important, it had to quickly and ruthlessly avail itself of the region's resources lest it lose the war, and from the very beginning it was always fully conscious of this necessity. While Japan's simultaneous policies of liberation and exploitation appear contradictory, in practice its rhetoric as Asia's emancipator never interfered in the slightest with the substance of its occupation policies. Japan between 1937 and 1945 bled and wholly transformed Asia, producing monumental consequences for the future of global politics and power that ultimately far exceeded the war's repercussions in Europe.

Japan's quick annexation of Manchuria after 1931 only reinforced expansionist pressures on Tokyo from more junior army officers, Japanese colonists in Manchuria, and ultranationalist elements at home who clamored for a continuation of what promised to be an enticingly easy campaign to conquer North China and broaden the nation's economic base. A pervasive militarist ideology, as well as a justifiable fear among its critics after 1935 of assassination at the hands of right-wing fanatics, reinforced an operational consensus on the principle of the need for continued imperialism, although not its direction and timing, neutralizing any caveats that realists among its leaders posed. But the navy, focusing on the drastically unfavorable military and economic numbers involved, from 1936 until virtually late November 1941 persisted in injecting an element of caution concerning the difficulties of winning a war against the U.S., Britain, and Russia; its reticence, above all, repeatedly defined the direction and form of Japan's policies in Asia once it made the decision to embark on war.

When Japan attacked China in July 1937, its army fully expected to attain its goals within a month. Notwithstanding delays, it stiffened its demands, seeking, in effect, to detach North China from the Kuomintang-led Nationalist government's control and to create an integrated economic bloc that would have vastly increased Japan's economic and raw-materials potential so that in due course all of its Asian ambitions might be realized in spite of any American or British opposition that might arise. But the China "incident" was a fundamental miscalculation, for Chiang Kai-shek, the Kuomintang (KMT) dictator, refused to accept defeat and retreated into China's vast hinterlands. Seeking to limit its unanticipated commitments, Japan, until 1944, held the coastal areas and main axes of communications with about 1 million soldiers, leaving a contested region of up to a hundred miles across the rice-growing areas of central China, periodically entering and sacking it and fighting minor engagements in what essentially became a stabilized war that permitted Japan to redirect its principal efforts elsewhere.

While there was unquestionably an element of irrational fatalism in the way the army and militarists confronted their insuperable dilemmas in China, the European war after 1940 left the entire Asian colonial world essentially undefended and made expansion seem an enticing and seemingly easy way to remedy Japan's acute shortage of those raw materials so essential for winning the war in China, keeping the United States at bay, and constructing an East Asia economic zone under tight Japanese control to service its interests permanently. The convoluted doctrinal rationalizations for these objectives could in no way mask Japan's bald imperialist ambitions. Its leaders' decision to bypass China temporarily and take Southeast Asia in order to strengthen Japan's medium- and long-term military power also meant that the resources and people of the conquered areas had to be speedily and systematically exploited. Their incessant discussions about the supplies of oil, bauxite, nickel, tin, and crude rubber were premised entirely on this crucial assumption, and the raw materials that Japan would acquire became their principal rationale for invading Europe's vulnerable colonies, above all the Dutch East Indies.[1]

Japan's rulers elected for war with the United States over the reservations of the extremely pessimistic navy, and they did not expect to defeat it but rather to create rapidly a self-sufficient East Asian economy that would allow them to stalemate the still-not-mobilized American colossus, whose overwhelming superiority for purposes of protracted war they always acknowledged. The navy, indeed, was the strongest advocate of draining colonial resources without nominal concessions to local nationalist aspirations. Japan's only war aim was to compel Washington to recognize its new sphere of power in East Asia. The strategy failed, and as an initially poor Japan suffered repeated defeats and air raids after 1943, reducing it to a bare subsistence economy, its intensified exactions in its conquered territories helped greatly to produce revolution throughout most of Asia.

Japan's basic dilemma after its China debacle, however, was that while it could ill afford to employ large numbers of troops and resources to administer the vast territories it first coveted and then conquered, its overriding objective of capitalizing on East Asia was scarcely calculated to win it friends among the oppressed peoples of Asia or their anticolonial leaders, who were the objects of its antiwestern preaching. Despite this, save for French Indochina, Japan pragmatically chose to create puppet regimes in the hope of reducing the need to utilize its own men as occupation forces. Tokyo cynically expounded pan-Asian anticolonialist, antiwhite doctrines while locating a mixture of opportunists to run each country, mainly drawn from the existing indigenous elites—the only natural rivals to the still-tiny but potentially crucial leftist forces in most of these nations—and nationalists willing to aid the Japanese in order to obtain a nominal independence. In Indochina, where it sent a remarkably small number of troops, it permitted a carefully circumscribed French administration to remain until the last months of the war, belying Japan's commitment to a rhetorical anticolonialism and revealing its preference for efficiency. In the Philippines it simply continued to utilize *ilustrados* who had collaborated for decades with the Americans. Such starkly glaring inconsistencies were logical because Japan's most important leaders were crude expansionists, with no ideology worthy of the name beyond a primitive xenophobia. Its forced-labor policy in the Dutch East Indies alone took about a half-million lives.

But by virtue of its ruthless milking of the region's resources, it discredited many, though by no means all, of its local collaborators and created a large postwar vacuum in the region's political leadership that was to provide emerging local leftist forces with unprecedented opportunities. Japan's notion of an acceptable administration, as in China in late 1937, was always one that did its bidding both unreservedly and permanently. The stark contradictions between its public ideology and its behavior increased when Japanese trading companies, possessing enormous political leverage, sought to participate in plundering Asia and intensified further the exploitation of the vast area. In practice, there was no basic tension between its policy of despoiling as opposed to co-opting Asia because it always unreservedly chose the former, with dire consequences.

But its systematic pillaging of East Asia's resources reflected the logic of Japan's overriding military strategy, and it provided the principal consensus on which its leaders could agree. Even before they embarked on the war, Japan's rulers believed they must "do our utmost to keep the [Japanese] people tranquil, and particularly to maintain the social order . . . [and] prevent social disorganization. . . ."[2] To the extent that they could extract more from their conquests, this risk of disruption might also be lessened, so that the policy of maximum spoliation served both to make war possible and social disorder within Japan less likely. By 1944 an increasing number of its politicians feared losing the war less than its prolongation, which might provoke revolution at home and their destruction as a social class. The catastrophic, growing shortages of food, fuel, and clothing, they felt, were radicalizing the masses, and might lead, as Foreign Minister Togo Shigenori later put it, "not only to political but to social revolution," one that could imperil the emperor system.[3] "What we have to fear," former Premier Prince Konoye told the emperor in February 1945, "is not so much a defeat as a Communist revolution," and the longer the war's hardships continued, the greater that prospect.[4] Japan sacked Asia ruthlessly because the stakes of not doing so profoundly endangered it both domestically and militarily, and it was in this context that it embarked on the occupation, traumatization, and transformation of Asia.

## The War's Impact on China's Social Order

China's vast size and impotent political leadership had for centuries plagued it with warlordism. Before 1937 it remained disunited among regional fiefdoms, the small Communist Party, and the Nationalist Kuomintang, heir to the legacy of the Sun Yat-sen's 1911 revolution, with its centralizing and antiforeign aspirations. The Japanese invasion quickly exposed China's already fragile political and administrative structures as inherently weak and incapable of absorbing the vast, terrible shocks the conflict imposed upon them. In China, as in every Asian nation, whether the established class systems had the capacity to survive the war immediately became a fundamental issue. Would the struggle's social, economic, and psychological impact allow the prewar orders to continue, and what kind of society could emerge if the trauma changed prevailing land and economic relations profoundly? Was there some way that the thoughts and actions of Asia's peasants, seemingly living a timeless way of life bound over generations to nature's rhythm, might alter and cause the countless millions hidden in vast, isolated expanses to mobilize and behave in radically new ways? What could cause them to act? What were the limits of mass endurance, and how, when, and why would it produce revolt? Given the social and economic legacies, how might the war's effects compound existing class tensions to produce new combinations corrosive of whatever stability remained within Chinese as well as other diverse Asian societies? Would the war, in brief, produce not only political revolutions inherent in the destruction of existing political coteries, but social and economic upheavals as well?

And once the people began to respond to the war's great consequences for their lives, how would the existing Marxist-Leninist parties, with their preconceptions regarding the necessity of a centralized leadership and discipline, function in such vast spaces, where communication was at best extremely difficult, and where the origins and nature and speed of change were so painfully difficult to anticipate? Given the magnitude and character of the structural changes the war was creating, how could Communists mobilize and lead, or would mass movements and their radical class demands circumscribe the parameters within which they had to function? And would their ostensible obedience to the Moscow-controlled Communist International, which after 1935 insisted upon a united front of nearly all classes in the antifascist struggle, define their responses to the growing potential for radical reform that existed throughout Asia, inhibiting their policies and behavior as Stalin had those of nearly all of the European Communist parties? In a word, in China and much of conquered Asia, the central issue for the incipient revolutionary movements was who would lead and who would follow.

All of these questions and their social, political, and human dimensions defined the crucial processes, events, and structures that were to determine the impact and outcome of World War Two in Asia.

## Economics and the Urban Crisis
When the Japanese invaded China's awesome vastness in 1937, they scarcely anticipated the complex challenges they would face or the extent to which the Chinese social order was already experiencing profound economic and political crises. These crises, which the war accelerated, produced sufficient chaos to enable the Communists eventually to fill the huge vacuum that was to emerge. It was this interaction between China's preexisting economic and social problems and the Japanese invasion that was to produce the single most important and durable political upheaval that the world experienced after 1917, and while it is scarcely possible here

to detail the contextual aspects so crucial to the Communist rise to power, several vital points require our attention. For while the war damaged China's economy and population greatly, and its human and material losses were huge in absolute terms, China suffered relatively no more than a number of European nations and less than Poland, the Soviet Union, and others. Its descent into a maelstrom sufficient to bring the Communists to power must be attributed ultimately to the nature of the KMT's Nationalist government, the context within which it operated, and its responses to the war and its aftermath.

All of the abundant data on the war's impact on China are only approximate. As late as 1949, three-quarters of the people lived in rural areas where statistics were usually inaccurate or unobtainable. War-related civilian deaths range in number from 15 million to, more officially, "some twenty-odd millions."[5] A credible estimate of deaths among the military suggests 3.2 million from combat plus a significant but indeterminable portion of up to 8.4 million soldiers who disappeared because of noncombat causes. From 25 to 30 million total deaths seems entirely plausible.

Ultimately, the numbers that accompany descriptions of China's transformation are meaningful only if we also comprehend the dynamics within its society and institutions, their impact on the people's attitudes and actions, and their consequences. This social framework and history was comprised of ingredients, most of them unquantifiable, that merged to produce a revolutionary environment where before it had been exceedingly unlikely. While China's wartime material deficiencies were grave, it is nonetheless also the case that had there been a less venal and incompetent political and organizational leadership, China would have by no means been predestined for Communism; much more likely was that it would have gotten along in the future as it had during preceding decades, which is to say badly, with the eventual outcome impossible to predict.

Measured purely in terms of resources available to it, the war did not ruin China either industrially or agriculturally. While what is termed industry was really about two-thirds handicrafts production, this sector was more resilient and mobile than capital-intensive factories, and although the vast majority of the latter remained in Japanese hands, trade between occupied and "Free" China continued in various, albeit more limited forms, and China's industrial output, notwithstanding annual variations, increased considerably from 1933 on. In 1942 real output exceeded significantly any year since Japan's invasion, then declined slowly during the next two crucial years until 1945, the worst year, when it began to climb sharply.

Even agricultural output was far from disastrous, if only because when the Kuomintang retreated from seven of China's twenty-two provinces it abandoned people but not the best agricultural land to Japan. Free China from 1931 to 1937 accounted for 54 percent of the nation's population but

77 percent of its rice production. Food production fluctuated and on the whole fell, but not calamitously, and given the food potential of its territory, its resources were less straitened than the area under Japanese occupation. Chiang's failure was preeminently political and organizational, and it was reflected in an inflation unique in the entire world during this century.

China's inflation was not as extreme as, say, that of Germany in 1923 or Hungary during 1945–46, but it lasted twelve years, far longer than any other, and it was the reasons for this spiral far more than the absence of resources that explain the distinctive way that the war transformed the nation. While there were important regional differences, and the situation in Japanese-dominated areas was worse, throughout Free China as a whole, prices only tripled from July 1937 to the end of 1939, but by the end of 1941 they were twenty times those of July 1937, 228 times greater by the end of 1943, and about 2,200 times higher when Japan was defeated. Two years later, in June 1947, prices were 36,872 times those of July 1937, and 1,335,000 times greater a year later.[6]

This calamity traumatized every aspect of society, including in vast areas that combat did not affect directly, and it created most, if not all, of the decisive social and human forces of change that I detail below. For it was the Kuomintang's economic policies that played the decisive role in producing the instability and events that ineluctably filtered into the lives of all of China's peasants, soldiers, and urban dwellers, altering them profoundly.

While the KMT government's budget had a substantial deficit before 1937, its revenues always covered the larger part of its expenses and its economy was relatively stable. With the Japanese invasion its expenses greatly exceeded its income, and by 1941 they were ten times its income. Given the inefficiency and corruption in land taxation, in July 1941—on the recommendation of his American advisers—Chiang introduced a land tax paid in sacks of grain, and the following year also imposed compulsory grain sales, equivalent to the amount taxed, at fixed prices which, given inflation, proved confiscatory. These seemingly technical decisions constituted the single most important error Chiang ever made, because they transferred much of the great cost of the war to the poorer peasants, those least able to resist the exactions of the village chieftans charged with collecting the grain and who retained a considerable portion of the proceeds for themselves. What they did not appropriate was further embezzled by others. The government's vast deficits continued, and it borrowed from banks that simply printed money, and inflation consequently made barter the only reliable method of exchange.

China's more traditional urban elements, especially the prewar elite, were ill suited to survive in this context. Many politically crucial, once-affluent families belonged to the gentry that had traditionally provided civil servants, professors, and teachers, and by 1943 people in these occupational categories had lost 80 to 90 percent of their real income when compared to 1937, pushing them to near-starvation conditions. They, their families, and their class had also been the principal creditors and savers before the war, and their holdings became worthless. Hyperinflation everywhere in this century has been an irresistible destroyer of established class structures, ruining them with a speed and thoroughness that revolutionaries could never remotely equal. But while in Europe it drove most of the once comfortable classes toward extreme right-wing alternatives to the status quo, in China the Right was responsible for the chaos and a crucial number of educated and now alienated members of the once-dominant economic strata began to shift toward neutrality in the nation's political struggles, while some became Communists.

The only urban elements capable of prospering in this economic chaos were a small group of politically well-placed entrepreneurs and a largely upstart class of nouveaux riches and speculators, hoarders, and corrupt government officials. They paid almost no taxes on their gains and circumscribed whatever feeble Nationalist efforts were made to control their peculations. Almost none of their money was diverted to productive investments, because even manufacturers by 1943 had lost nearly one-third of their real incomes. Retail merchants, able to adjust prices quickly, managed to improve their condition over prewar levels somewhat, but did no more than survive comfortably. After experiencing a brief surge in their real incomes after the war began, by 1943 industrial workers and urban laborers were earning incomes a quarter to a third lower than in 1937, but the following year they fell appreciably. In contrast, speculators' real income in 1940 was eight times that of 1938, though it fluctuated at a lower level thereafter. Those among them who managed to get American currency and securities made fortunes, and capital flight in dollars to the U.S. alone nearly doubled during the war, although most of it was probably sent to other countries.[7]

This traumatization of strategic urban elements whose toleration, if not active support, was essential for the stability and even the continuation of the Nationalist regime quickly became a fundamental political factor. Urban China on the whole fared relatively worse than the rural population, but the Nationalists' principal support after 1911 had come from cities. To lose this backing was to expose the government to dangers even greater than those the Japanese might create, and to recast completely the domestic political framework in which the Communists operated after 1939. While the urban context proved critical to the triumph of the Communist revolution, in an overwhelmingly rural nation the events in the countryside were decisive, for although the Communists might possibly have won without the factors that transformed the urban populace, they surely would not have been victorious had rural China not been so deeply shaken. And it was the profound economic and social changes in the agrarian sector that had begun well before the war that greatly accelerated their eventual successes among the peasantry.

### The War's Impact on the Peasantry

Rural China, as all of Asia, had an inequitable land system, but for centuries family kinship and village ties produced communities with cooperative economic and social networks that had partly mitigated its worst consequences. In regions with inferior soil or insufficient population, however, the tenure conditions imposed upon poorer peasants were less onerous and land was more equitably distributed. After the turn of the century whatever social insulation against calamity that had existed began to dissolve as a more purely capitalist calculus started to define the investment strategies of landlords with money who were linked, as many were, to merchants and usurers, and who bought land with the sole intention of making it more profitable. In some places new landlords, many of whom had acquired their wealth as officers or illegally, controlled most of the land, displacing the traditional landlords. As the landlord system changed and became less socially integrated, it usually became more exploitive. In the northwest, for example, landowners demanded that tenants switch from grain to the much more lucrative opium cash crop, and food production suffered in an area that already often had too little to eat.

In general, whatever their social origins, the families and clans that dominated most of the economic power at the county and village levels controlled the local political systems as well, greatly facilitating their making certain that taxes and the depredations of warlords, armies, and higher authorities fell upon poor peasants unable to resist them. This remained the case when the Nationalists in 1939 reorganized the local village administrative structure, and then in 1941 assigned it the task of exacting taxes-in-kind from the rural masses.

No less important was the disappearance of accessible land to which discontented peasants could migrate, a change that greatly improved the leverage of landlords in their dealings with tenants. By the 1920s the peasants' security and living conditions in a growing part of China had deteriorated, so that in many sections the population now exceeded the capacity of the land to support it, and farm sizes tended to become smaller. During this decade also, Chinese food imports rose dramatically, in part because of the 1921–22 famine—probably the worst of this century—followed by the Shensi famine in the northwest after 1928. But food production either failed to keep up with population pressures or stagnated before 1937. And during each famine land ownership altered dramatically, increasing absentee landlordism, and the numbers of wealthy and mid-level landowners declined in many areas while those who were poor increased.

There were many regional and local variations and exceptions to this trend and pattern, some quite crucial, but in the aggregate about one-tenth of the landowners possessed at least half of all land, and they usually accounted for most of the marketable surplus production. Over one-half of the farming families in the 1930s were owner-tenants or nonowning tenants renting about 30 percent of the land and subject to the mercies of both the landlord and the market, which tended increasingly to favor the landlords. Half of these in 1934 paid a fixed rental in crops, a little more than a quarter were sharecroppers, and a combined average of 43 percent of their crops went to the landlords. But additional burdens in the form of obligatory labor services, fees to the landlord at New Year, his birthday, and such, or his collection agent's extra charges, were common. Before the outbreak of war, China's land system had been beset with grave difficulties and was undergoing a profound transformation; it was already highly vulnerable when the vast array of cataclysmic wartime problems struck.

The information that exists on rural income after the inception of war suffers decisively not only from deficient data but also from the fact that it is given as an average for all farmers regardless of their size. On this basis, agriculture's real income held up far better than that of the vast majority of those in cities, especially if they were close to urban centers and could supply their special demands, and in 1941 it was allegedly 15 percent higher than in 1937. Even during 1944–46 it was only one-sixth to one-eighth lower than in 1937. More crucial was the fact that the imposition of taxes-in-kind and the compulsory sale of fixed quotas of grain to the government all hit the poor peasantry most heavily, and in addition to his rents to his landlord, the *average* farmer's land tax to the Nationalist government in 1942 was nearly five times higher than before the war. While this accounted for only 8 percent of the total rice and wheat output in 1943–44, there were additional local taxes and they all fell much more heavily on poor subsistence peasants who had no surplus whatsoever to spare. Most important of all, however, was that the war imposed a monumental burden on human lives that must also be taken into account. And it is here that the impressions of a great many observers in China at the time—and our respect for the social and political outcome of the war—deserve more attention than dubious official numbers.[8]

## The Kuomintang Traumatizes China

### The Army, the People, and the War

Making them the principal source of its tax revenues was only one of the many ways the KMT-led Nationalist government traumatized the lives of the poorer peasantry. Most important, it conscripted their sons for the army and paid soldiers so little that they were compelled to live off the land, thereby disorganizing local economies and imposing further incalculable burdens on the peasantry. And it virtually confiscated countless carts and indispensable transport essential to a peasant economy. When all these factors are considered, it becomes clear that the poorer peasants suffered from the war more than any of China's classes, and this fact immeasurably facilitated the Communist takeover of power.

Conscription into the various Nationalist armies was far less a military necessity than a profitable racket that traded in human lives, a subterfuge in which the state was wholly involved, and which thereby alienated most of the nation. At the inception of the war there was only one rifle for every three men in the army, and American advisers in China in 1943 believed that the KMT's military was at least twice as large as could be supported effectively. Chiang Kai-shek initially argued that his basic military strategy in the war was to trade space for time in order to build a modern army to fight Japan, but such an army remained a dream and he soon concluded that his foreign allies would defeat Japan while he consolidated his power within the areas the Nationalists nominally held. There was never a military rationale for his army's size, and scarcely a political one. It was, above all, a very lucrative business for the officers who ran it, and this fact kept many of them committed to Chiang's regime, at least to a sufficient degree so as not to challenge it directly.

The Nationalists assigned quotas for army recruits to provincial governors throughout the war, and eventually about 14 million men were gathered to serve unlimited terms. Where local army units could not round up adequate manpower, they farmed the task out to press gangs who were paid by the head, and both managed to corral or kidnap hapless men drawn almost exclusively from the poorer peasantry. Those with money could buy replacements for their sons or arrange for them to receive exemptions, and during the last years of the war the burden of this system fell increasingly upon the poor in those southwestern provinces that had hitherto been insulated from both the Japanese and Communists. At least two-thirds of the draftees failed to meet minimum health standards, and stronger men tended to be placed in the forces governors retained for their own political purposes.

Conscripts usually walked great distances to their designated units, always guarded and frequently tied together with ropes; sometimes their captors took their clothes at night to prevent them from escaping. Their commanders received lump sums in cash and rations for the number of men they were supposed to have, and if anyone died and it was not reported, they continued to receive the allotment, providing an incentive for neglect and brutality. American experts concluded that their allies found that it was profitable to be under strength. About one-tenth of the draftees, or 1.4 million men, were estimated to have died during the war before they even reached their assigned field divisions. "Conscription comes to the Chinese peasant like famine or flood, only more regularly . . . ," the American commander in China reported in horror, ". . . and claims more victims. Famine, flood, and drought compare with conscription like chicken pox with the plague." All eyewitness American accounts of this army describe the abhorrent "physical condition of the troops dragging along the streets and highways. Their clothes are old, patched, and tattered, but far worse is their physical condition. Obviously they are suffering from every sort of disease and are just able to walk. Occasional stretchers carry those too weak to make even an attempt to walk. It is not unusual to see the occupants of the litters dumped by the side of the road either dead or soon to die. . . . The worst groups are the replacements."[9] Such an utterly demoralized army was incapable of resisting the Japanese, but during the infrequent occasions it did fight, any soldier who received even a minor wound could expect no adequate treatment whatever—with death all too likely. All the more reason to avoid combat!

Precisely because their officers received their allotments even after they disappeared, the fate of at least 9 million of these men has never been explained, and they either deserted or—and this includes a large fraction—died while in the army. Their superiors routinely reduced the draftees' rations of food or money, which in any event by 1942 fell with inflation to roughly one-tenth of its 1937 value. While soldiers supplemented their diets by living off the land, which is to say confiscating it from peasants, by 1945 American doctors concluded that at least 57 percent suffered from one or more nutritional deficiencies. The KMT's Thirteenth Army in March 1945 could not make a short march "without men falling out wholesale and many dying from utter starvation."[10]

This pathetic mass of starving humanity moved like a plague throughout the Nationalist-controlled areas where no Communists had ever been, often stealing without restraint from the peasants, billeting in their homes, and spreading their diseases wherever they stopped. They took food in deficit areas as well, and their officers routinely commandeered peasant carts. If capturing the vast drama and horror of all these factors defies mere words, suffice it to say that the loss of their sons, compounded with the exactions of the Nationalist armies and their traumatization of vast rural areas, combined with the KMT's ruthless tax collections and all of the effects of the Japanese invasion itself, united to produce the explosive mixture that made the subsequent Communist victory virtually inevitable.

China had known famines before, and in the Shensi region about 2.5 million people, nearly one-third of the population, died of starvation from 1928 to 1933. It was to Shensi that the remnants of Mao Tse-tung's defeated Communist armies later repaired after surviving their "Long March." But the situation in China after 1937 worsened greatly. The imposition of far more burdensome taxes drawn from a reduced economic base, the loss of millions of productive men to a parasitic army and the subsequent sharp reduction of food output, and the ravages of Japanese forays all merged to produce catastrophe. Most of the nation had no food reserves for meeting new demands or poor weather.

Given the vagaries inherent in both the war and the climate, the KMT's insistence on collecting all taxes in grain from the peasantry in Honan province after 1941 was to produce famine. Japanese troops surrounded three sides of the region in 1941, and from a half-million to a million KMT troops were stationed in the province. But as important as any factor was the large number of civilian laborers who were conscripted to build military fortifications, forcing food output to drop greatly. Honan's peasants simply could not pay the taxes in grain that the government insisted upon collecting on the basis of a normal year's output—principally to allow local commanders and officials to sell it on the black market. Farmers sold their property and land to rich landlords and officials for absurdly reduced prices to meet taxes and buy food; then, as they were reduced to eating leaves, bark, and even human flesh, many tried to sell their children. Famine affected up to 30 million people, and an estimated 2 to 3 million people migrated from the province while an equivalent number died of starvation.

During 1943–44 a minimum of 1.5 million people died in the Kwangtung province famine, but here too, as in all other comparable areas, the local KMT officials always attempted to obtain the maximum taxes possible as if nothing else mattered, and they invariably made large sums selling the grain on the open market or to the Japanese. For many peasants, such events exhausted their capacity to suffer passively, and they considered the Nationalist armies scarcely better than the Japanese. Poor peasants were conditioned increasingly on the anvil of war and corruption to hate the society that starved them—and this ominous mood preceded by several years the arrival of any significant number of Communist organizers.

What is also certain is that the crisis in Chinese society that during the nineteenth century had initiated significant migrations to escape poverty and war now culminated in uprooting considerably larger masses of people, who were no longer subject to their communities' inhibiting, stabilizing influences and could only lose from the continuance of the status quo. Migration became much more common after 1937, producing men and women who were either to succeed in new contexts or, far more commonly, lose any stake whatsoever in the existing order. Here too data is at best only approximate, but about 15 million persons fled the Japanese-occupied areas, although some estimates claim 25 million. The Japanese were systematically destructive during their offensives, and savage when not on the march, and one can believe their justifiably terrible reputation frightened many into eluding them. To these estimates one must add the incalculable millions who hoped to evade the consequences of KMT economic policies by moving elsewhere. Together, the numbers were staggering whatever they may be exactly, for it is certain that a very large part of a static rural society was being ripped asunder as horrors drove people to take to the roads, producing a mass of potential converts for the Communists and recruits for their eventually victorious armies.[11]

The officers in charge of the Nationalist armies were ambitious and corrupt, and as a leading scholar has phrased it, they spent much of their time "engaged in gambling, whoring, and smuggling."[12] Few of them were the sons of the relatively affluent and educated classes that staffed the officer corps in most nations, for these purchased exemptions. Many kept their families with their units, and even during battles allocated precious transport resources to them. The vast majority stole their soldiers' rations, even after they died, abused them while they were living, and most were inefficient and incompetent. Many sought, if at all possible, to avoid fighting the Japanese (just as they were later to circumvent the Communists), often by reaching tacit and even explicit accords with the invaders to avoid offensive operations—which suited perfectly Japan's mainly passive occupation strategy. Eager to avoid tying up too many men, the Japanese usually preferred to work with local warlords, especially to administer rural areas, and some of these during the war collaborated with every side that could fatten their pockets. Accommodations were the rule because in practice the KMT regarded the astonishingly large trade between Japanese-occupied China and their areas as acceptable, save for a restricted number of items, and strategic raw materials and even American-supplied medicines, along with much else, ended up in Japanese-held zones. The KMT in turn could purchase aviation fuel, and the postal services integrated both zones. Senior Nationalist officers arranged and shared in the great profits from this trade.[13]

### The Nature of Chiang Kai-shek's System

The Nationalist political system was what has been described as a coalition based on "residual warlordism," which Chiang Kai-shek sought to balance so that he could rule over the fragile structure, but it was inherently precarious and he could never rest secure.[14] The generals who controlled about four-fifths of the Nationalist army manpower and ruled huge provinces were autonomously powerful and mainly cynical political manipulators whose loyalty to Chiang often fluctuated with the successes of Japanese military operations. In Shantung, for example, from 1940 to 1943 Chiang's nominal allies responded to Japanese military successes simply by transforming the great majority of the so-called Kuomintang into puppet troops.

Half of those in control of Chiang's principal war zones on the Japanese front had already fought against the KMT or offered to do so. Perhaps a half of all of his commanders obeyed Chiang's orders, but not always the same group each time, and this problem, along with a grave lack of military coordination, persisted throughout the war. Usually linked with local merchants, bankers, and landowning elites in their regions, most warlords were wholly amoral, interested in preserving their personal power and that of their family and allies in their region, and even before 1941 a few who had no option were equally willing to work with the Communists. In Japanese-controlled areas this local ruling class served as puppets to advance their own accounts, often in the same way that they collaborated with Chiang. The class forces committed to preserving Chinese society as then constituted were located within these relatively insulated regional satrapies, but they were not functionally united beyond their own boundaries. Chiang attempted to fill his government's civil bureaucracy as much as possible with men from the two provinces that provided the basis of his power, including his home province, but only half of its senior personnel came from them, and he refused to appoint the few capable and honest generals the Americans identified because they were not loyal to him.

In reality, Chiang was in crucial ways merely a superwarlord presiding over a precarious combination of what U.S. experts later described "as semi-independent provincial governors"; he never commanded an integrated nation or army and he could neither cope with nor afford the war's consequences for China's social and economic structure.[15] He was utterly incapable of appreciating the countless ways in which his quixotic policies were traumatizing China and preparing the way for an astonishingly rapid Communist victory. Chiang perceived his problems as political—linked to warlord politics—rather than military, much less economic and social, and since he fully planned on the U.S. defeating Japan he saw no reason to abandon his preoccupations. Such a stance infuriated the senior American officers in China, and explains General Joseph W. Stilwell's well-known utter contempt for him, for they fully comprehended the fragile nature of the Nationalist military alliance.

It was for all of the above reasons, as well, that 1 million Japanese troops could occupy and exploit a vast part of China against far larger armies.

## Transforming the Chinese Political Mind

Any assessment of China's road to revolution must take into account the nation's vast size and the decentralization inherent both in its spatial and political structure, and the decisive ways in which both encouraged quite diverse political scenarios to evolve. What is certain is that the changing pattern in social and land relations began long before 1938, and the war brought to fruition all of the society's latent weaknesses. The Japanese invasion and the Nationalist mobilization, with their depredations of millions of peasants and the resulting vast suffering, interacted with and greatly accelerated this process.

For numberless peasants, the war ended the physical and mental insulation in which most had lived since time immemorial, forcibly broadening their perceptions of the relationship of their communities to the region and nation, and it imposed an identification with China on many of them. Even if only a small minority, whatever the previous state of their political consciousness or their vision of alternatives, it became obvious to countless people that they could not avoid the consequences of the vast changes occurring around them merely by tending to their own affairs. Even if it was not by itself sufficient, this realization was an essential precondition for breaking out of a traditionalist, conservative environment and taking eventual action. And while this new context cannot wholly explain the causes of the Chinese revolution, it is surely essential to the comprehension of them. The nature and direction of individual and group values and roles in a catastrophic wartime setting reveals the momentum to which the Communists eventually had to relate.

During the two decades before the Japanese invasion, peasants had spontaneously resisted growing economic and social changes and problems. There were no revolts but at least several hundred protests, generally involving taxes and rent issues, occasional riots, and defensive actions to protect local interests and traditional rights. Local notables often incited and led such episodes, and they frequently pitted communities against outsiders seeking to impose onerous burdens and changes upon them. The Communists concentrated on organizing in cities until 1928, and their few attempts to create peasant armies failed entirely. Only after the catastrophic Shensi famine were local Communists, acting on their own initiatives, able to create a successful peasant base, bringing former bandits and warlord soldiers together with radicalized peasants in a purely pragmatic fashion that violated all of the Party's organizational scriptures. If in the narrowest sense there was no direct relationship between early peasant protests and the later Communist forces, in fact both were products of the same larger and heterogeneous patterns of economic, political, and social change and crisis that defined modern China's history and to which an unprecedented number of peasants would respond in one manner or another. But ultimately revolutions occur not because challengers are able to take power but principally because rulers cannot manage that which they possess in ways that will preserve and, if necessary, enlarge their authority. China was vast, inherently decentralized and capable thereby of experiencing a great variety of local changes simultaneously. While warlordism was the historically dominant expression of this potential diversity, the emergence of sometimes quite parochial Communist bodies was another, but by themselves neither was conceivably competent of replacing a fissiparous government before the wartime experience's full effects had penetrated the entire nation.

Those who resisted the Japanese occupation of North China after 1937 may also have opposed a comparable southern Chinese invasion if there had been one at that time, especially if it conscripted and taxed the people as in the rest of the nation. But the fact that it was against foreigners gave nationalism a legitimacy that transcended the local and provincial loyalties and power structures. The very existence of warlord armies, some quite localized, and banditry revealed that isolated peasants had a deeply rooted capacity to take matters into their own hands and did not require Japanese atrocities or Communist organizers to mobilize them. Many of these responses were scarcely radical, seeking only to reverse the imposition of onerous new measures upon specific areas rather than overthrow traditional authority relations, and in the case of banditry they were often antisocial.

The Nationalist policies' draconian impact on the peasantry revealed also that the risks of the Japanese alternative would not dissuade them from acting against oppression from fellow Chinese when it became intolerable. The Kansu province rebellion that began in early 1942 because of grain taxes, labor corvées, and conscription mobilized anywhere from 50,000 to 200,000 men against all outsiders, including the Nationalists. More important than the exact numbers was the support they had from virtually the entire provincial population. In mid-1943, Chiang sent two of his best divisions into Kansu and killed at least 14,000 rebels.

When the crisis in Honan province became calamitous in 1943, the first peasant protests began, to no avail. But the following year peasants attacked and disarmed up to 50,000 soldiers retreating from a Japanese offensive, killing a number of them. As elsewhere, groups of "bandits," often ranging from 200 to 4,000 in size and comprised of draft evaders and army deserters, began increasingly to appear in Honan as peasants chose the risks of illegality over farming, usually just brutally victimizing other poor folk. Among the numerous, diverse protests and uprisings of various sizes against Nationalist exactions that occurred throughout the country after 1942, Communist involvement in them was noted in only a few instances—and even then sometimes simply as part of their alliances with local groups.[16]

While the Communist role in mobilizing such peasant outrage into a coherent political and military force unquestionably became increasingly vital in due course, the legitimacy of the KMT government and its crucial provincial components fell precipitously in the eyes of most of the people as their ruthless exploitation in the hands of their rulers mounted. As the existing Nationalist political order disintegrated, individuals worried infinitely less about the state's problems than their own, causing an articulate minority to begin to support the opposition. This was at least as true in the cities as in rural areas, and urban China played a crucial role, both politically and in providing the Communists with leadership cadres, in bringing down the existing society. What the experience under Chiang revealed was that a corrupt clientelist regime, venal and solely concerned with the consolidation and exploitation of its power, is inherently incapable under wartime conditions of stabilizing or mitigating war's most dangerous consequences, and that it is the interaction of war with all of these factors rather than one element by itself that produces the essential preconditions for revolution. War and the nature of a regime (as in Russia earlier) become integrated issues when the dangerous variables possible from their combination define social reality and deeply penetrate the lives of the people.

Although the Communists provided an alternative program, and vital protection against local and national oppressors' vengeance, one can scarcely attribute the principal cause in making a revolution to them as opposed to the more impersonal changes and policies that the Kuomintang and its allies, and then the Japanese, imposed. The crucial question is not whether the Communists created the revolution but whether China could have emerged from the war, given its myriad grave consequences for every aspect of the society, without some sort of fundamental social and political upheaval after all that had occurred to it both as a result of a foreign invasion and the policies of those who ruled it. For the Communists, the real issue was the extent to which all of these objective conditions and innovations would also circumscribe their choices, and how far they too would have to bend before the realities and constraints that war and the utter collapse of a society were imposing.

## The Communist Road to Power

Many factors played a role in producing the Chinese Communist party's victory, and although scholars have attempted to assign weight and causal importance to each of them, ultimately such exercises are futile because they all intersected in crucial ways as part of a broad, interrelated field of elements; the whole was far greater than the sum of its parts. The wartime environment for the Party ranged from the impact of the Japanese invasion to the dire consequences of the Nationalist armies' functions and conduct in those vast areas the Japanese did not occupy. The highly decentralized political nature of warlordism was not the principal cause of Chiang's inability to respond to the nation's massive social and economic challenges. He rarely thought of doing so under any circumstances, and then only vaguely, with irrelevant nationalist and statist methods that American officials considered fascistic in inspiration. In a vast nation where gangsterism more than any other single explanation describes the nature and purpose of politics, Chiang and his KMT were the most important players; and notwithstanding the fact that their economic policies conditioned events in much of the nation, neither perceived the challenges before them in this broader framework. Rather than attempt to solve the myriad national problems to attain his ultimate nominal ambition to lead a unified country, Chiang preferred to relate to economic and social events in incremental, often erratic ways designed to strengthen his power base in the short run.

The very decentralized nature of Chinese politics and life that made warlordism and localized private armies endemic to the very character of power in much of China also enabled the Communist party to build its strength region by region insofar as it was able to relate to the social and political circumstances in each one, creating military forces as it went along. While in a quite limited way it was able to do so earlier in extremely isolated areas, the wartime context created the prerequisites for it to expand throughout the nation and make its triumph the ineluctable culmination of all the forces the war unleashed. But such necessary preconditions were by no means sufficient for its ultimate victory, and here the Party's responses to countless challenges require close attention, since in the great diversity that was China, its conduct too was often exceedingly variegated. Its formal justifications for it usually followed later. As a Bolshevik party in theory, it assumed that it would lead the masses to revolution, though in fact its doctrine's influence in China was due far less to its capacity to cope with the vast nation's countless difficulties than to the fact that among young radical intellectuals in the early 1920s the Soviet example's influence had few rivals. But the Party in practice led and followed, and it led principally because after its failures in the period up to 1935—which were largely the consequences of its having loyally followed Moscow's advice—it understood that in the last analysis the alternative to tactics that responded flexibly to the peoples' needs, desires, and constraints was total failure and destruction.

The Communist party after the Japanese invasion could legitimately claim to be the leader of a nationalist resistance, and undoubtedly its heroic opposition to the Japanese won it support, especially in the cities. Scholars have debated inconclusively the extent to which rural backing for the Communists reflected the peasantry's desire for protection against local warlords as well as Japanese brutality, or the attainment of greater equity in the land system and redressing rural grievances. But given the greatly increasing physical dangers and insecurity of economic life in many parts of China, there was no conflict between the peasantry's acceptance of Communist leadership in obtaining reforms and its patriotism, and none of these explanations are mutually exclusive. Indeed, the evidence points to all of them as significant, if unequal, causes for the Party's growth. After 1937, whether reaching out to the peasantry or, increasingly with time, people in cities, it attempted to use various combinations of both nationalist and economic or class issues, with whatever stress on each the local context warranted.

By 1935 the Communist party's calamitous military endeavors, culminating in the Long March that cost the lives of over two-thirds of its participants, did not permit it to be anything but pragmatic and opportunist, including in its overall relations with the Nationalist armies and Chiang Kai-shek himself. Mao Tse-tung arrived in late 1935 with the remnants of the march to the Shensi region to build a new base area in what was already the only successful Communist stronghold in China precisely because the local leaders had ignored Maoist military doctrine, accepted warlord and bandit soldiers into their ranks, and been supremely eclectic and pragmatic. The local Party had also begun to introduce radical land reform to win peasant support, treating it, however, as a tool for military mobilization rather than as an end in itself. Whatever the Party leadership's bitter disagreements over theory and practice in the Shensi region, which prevented the local land-reform program from being implemented, events there revealed in broad outline a praxis, if not a theory, that they would follow until final victory. The Party did not choose among a "mass line" of agrarian radicalism, a united-front strategy that integrated more prosperous peasants and rural elites into a political coalition, or an appeal to patriotism, but in most regions employed all three simultaneously, shifting its emphasis to one or the other to adapt to the needs of the time—above all to the threats from the Japanese or the Nationalists. Although nominally committed to engaging in civil war and defense of the nation concurrently, in practice the Communists until 1945 increasingly attempted first to consolidate their strength and pacify potential Chinese enemies. The acquisition of power for its own sake became, and remains, the Party's permanent obsession.

Mao pledged the Party to a united front because, as a consummate Leninist, he feared the spontaneity and dynamism of the poorer masses and he wished above all to discipline and shape them to the Party's grand strategy. The Party therefore always remained deeply committed to a united front based on the "three-thirds" system, which nominally assigned the Party one-third of the posts in local governments, with the remainder going to elected and representative spokesmen of the peasantry, landlords, the bourgeoisie, and others; for since the late 1920s, Mao had regarded the Party's enemies as only a tiny section of the nation, comprising the big landlords and big bourgeoisie but only a fraction of the national bourgeoisie, rich peasants, and small landlords. To neutralize and mobilize the remainder was a tactical problem, and minimizing class conflicts that damaged the Party's interests was crucial to that goal. After the Japanese invasion the Party's demands for a united front won a sufficient response among otherwise anti-Communist Chinese to constrain at least a significant portion of the Nationalist alliance from striking at will against the still vulnerable, scattered Communist forces, gaining them an essential and perhaps decisive respite.[17]

That the Soviet Union in 1935 called for a united front everywhere against Germany and Japan was not crucial to Mao's decisions, since, from this time on, Stalin supported Chiang Kai-shek loyally, as well as Mao's key opponents for leadership within the Party. Mao's interpretation of the united front, in any case, was very different than Stalin's, for he refused to risk or sacrifice the Party's political and military autonomy in any way inimical to its larger interests and survival, and in his hands the policy became a major tactical chord on which he played—sometimes more loudly—along with others; it was not at all what Stalin had in mind or imposed upon most European Communist parties. The united front made sense to Mao in a purely Chinese context in his relations with the Nationalists, and in any case after 1937 he never allowed Moscow to dictate to him on any crucial issue, for he knew that the USSR would sacrifice his Party's interests to advance its own. Mao's differences with Stalin were also the inevitable consequences of his irresistible predilection for a cult of personality and the hegemony over policy that came with it, which required him increasingly to stress the distinctive nature of Chinese communism compared to the Soviet version. By no later than 1943 he audaciously suggested that "the Chinese Communist Party has in its twenty-two years passed through many more great events than any other Party in the world and has had richer experience in the revolutionary struggle," all of which justified the "correctness of Comrade Mao Tse-tung's line" and implicitly challenged Soviet pretensions to hegemony over the world Communist movement.[18]

While the united front, with its nationalist emphasis after 1938, temporarily obtained cooperation in North China for the Communists' anti-Japanese efforts, the ultimate purpose of the policy was to neutralize potential opposition. But it alone could not build the loyalty among the poorer masses so necessary for its military mobilization. Resolving the inherent tension between the united front and the demands of poor peasants produced numerous shifts in Mao's accentuation on one as opposed to the other. Mao, whose diktat was virtually supreme by 1937, preferred to avoid radical land reform after that time, stressing fairly modest rent reductions instead; but much of the peasantry could not be sufficiently motivated around anemic goals, and the very existence of new Party-sponsored, community-based organizational structures repeatedly emboldened them in countless villages to demand, and implement, genuine land redistribution. Higher Party cadres often tried to prevent peasant "leftist excesses," but when lower cadres recruited from the peasantry, and the peasants themselves forced the issue, as they often did, the Party reluctantly acceded because ultimately it needed the rural masses' support far more than strict discipline—which it never could fully impose. Above all else, the war, in addition to worsening the peasants' economic position gravely, created a new vacuum in administrative and political power in many areas and the poorer peasants insisted upon filling a large part of it. And without them, the Party had no military future, for they provided the soldiers and guerrillas.

How to resolve this tension between class objectives, which were democratic and mass-based in character, and the united front, which required a hierarchic, managed party ultimately immune to pressures from below, was the single most enduring dilemma in the Communists' efforts to attain power. The Party's moderate land-reform program had never precisely defined the class nature of "rich" or "middle" peasants, and it often deliberately left the latter with substantial, even decisive power in many villages, if only to maximize food output. But in May 1946, immediately after Chiang mounted a successful offensive and the Communists required more recruits for their depleted army, they returned to a stronger land-reform policy, soon losing control of its implementation to young and poorer peasants, and in 1948 the Party successfully attempted to reverse what was again denigrated as a leftist deviation—again citing the need to maintain food production along with unity.[19]

Communist policy cannot be schematized simply as rural versus urban, or for or against emphasis on the united front, because it responded pragmatically over the long run to the war's immense impact on society, seeking opportunities to extend the Party's influences in a vast context that subsumed everything occurring in China. Mao's initial rural emphasis was the logical result of his desire for physical security, but once he attained the minimum necessary, he could turn his sights elsewhere, not the least because all of the Communist debates over strategy until 1939 were carried on before the Party could adequately assess the inflation's catastrophic impact on the entire nation, above all the cities.

The inflation created countless urban possibilities that had never existed before, and Mao's analysis of the class structure there assumed that the large majority of town dwellers would support the Party or remain neutral toward it. Moreover, after 1937 it was in the cities that nationalist arguments for a united front were most likely to prove most credible and capable of not only neutralizing the KMT's main power base but also of making possible the reformation and expansion of the Party's own leadership structure. But no less important than such new opportunities was the fact that, notwithstanding its strategy's agrarian emphasis or its rapidly growing rural base, the Communists' elitist organizational theory irresistibly infused it with a basically urban orientation.

The Party began as a highly intellectual student movement, and until the KMT-organized massacres in 1927, its 58,000 members, the vast majority of whom disappeared, were overwhelmingly city dwellers. It lost yet more urban cadres in the Long March, and while the Party grew rapidly in the late 1930s, its changed social composition both solved and created problems. All too many were peasants who were excellent organizers of the masses but ideologically thin—and thereby less disciplined and often more radical and difficult to control. After the Japanese invasion a large number of urbanized students with essential, scarce skills arrived and became lower-level political cadres, whose strict discipline and obedience was most desirable. And for several years after 1940, having exploded from 40,000 members in 1937 to 800,000 in 1940, the Party expelled weaker members, ceasing in effect to be an elite organism save at the very highest levels. In general, by the early 1940s about one-quarter of its members had significant urban backgrounds: most having been born or educated in cities. This constituency totally controlled the Party by the late 1940s, when almost the entire central committee came from it, and it provided 99 percent of the high-level and three-quarters of the middle-level cadres. The rural masses existed in a world quite unrelated to that of such officials, many of whom were well-educated, ambitious, and eager to move to the cities after victory.[20]

By the early 1940s, therefore, the Communist organizational and social structure had begun to produce a number of tensions that were in subsequent years to assert themselves in various forms—including the Cultural Revolution. It contained an urban-rural dichotomy based on class and education. While living largely in the countryside, the Party's leadership remained basically urban both in its social composition and its mentality, and as much the instrument of the nation's radicalized intelligentsia as it had been at its founding. Ideologically, it was intrinsically hierarchical, for as a Bolshevik party it was supposed to be a highly integrated, disciplined structure, and this assumed literate, trained members at every level. It also meant that the Party's strategy and goals would reflect far more its urban sectors' priorities and problems than those of the peasants, who provided most of its soldiers and followers.

In the last analysis, Mao's fundamental concept of the Party's form was scarcely an impersonal one; he wanted it to pursue the path he staked out for it, and nothing even in the hierarchical Leninist organizational theory justified the tyrannical personality cult that he increasingly sought to institutionalize. But notwithstanding his desires, before 1949 he could not immediately overcome the centrifugal—and hence democratic as well as vital—Party structure that China's vast size and absence of effective communication made unavoidable. In brief, although the Nationalist regime was deeply divided and full of contradictions, the Communists possessed some crucial ones also, albeit far less serious. Just as space and numbers had defied Chiang Kai-shek, so too did it confront Mao with problems. Mao deplored "localism," but the reality of distances imposed decentralization upon regional parties that often were without contact with the nominal center for long periods, and while in fact these regions had to exercise much initiative to survive and grow, it was a constant challenge to Mao to make certain that a minimum coordination on basic programs and principles existed. Often it did not. Many of these dilemmas in China and the rest of the Bolshevik world are much clearer today now that a vast portion of it has disintegrated, but their existence during the war was also a reality of signal importance.

The crucial question for the men who ran the Communist party was the degree to which they could lead the masses—their self-assigned historic role—or would be compelled to follow them. To the extent that the leadership had managed to infuse the higher Party levels with educated urbanites, they solved part of their difficulties, but far from all of them. But tactically, notwithstanding certain failures and frictions the Party confronted, especially among poor peasant radicals, Mao managed sufficiently to overcome the tensions between the united front and radical change, made the most of the inferior army at his disposal to keep both the Japanese and the KMT at bay, urbanized the Party sufficiently to keep it from becoming too responsive to the imperatives of the nation's vast expanse and the people in it, and much else. As a strategist of power, flexible and adept at pragmatically defining the best tactics available at any given moment, Mao was a rare figure in the twentieth century, and his consummately egotistical qualities that two decades later were to rip China asunder proved successful in the 1940s, but only because of the context. However, as an analyst and theorist Mao's ideas were intellectually crude, often derived, and inconsistent save insofar as he constantly sought to exploit the dynamics of a nation in chaos to attain power. Nowhere in his writings does one find a serious attempt to diagnose China's social processes, their complex institutional bases and contradictions, and the war's impact upon society. Even Stalin's early attempts at social analysis were far superior.

The challenges remaining for the Communists when the war with Japan ended were still awesome. In the summer of 1941 they controlled 8 to 10 million people in an area of 17,400 square miles, and were largely self-sufficient. By mid-1945 their population had grown to 95 million, their territory to almost 400,000 square miles, and their regular army to 910,000 men, but this region comprised the poorest northern areas and only a few cities. Materially, while the Communists were stronger than before, so too was the Nationalist government. The over four-fifths of China nominally in Nationalist hands in 1945 was far richer; Chiang's forces had a regular army three times the size of Mao's, with five times the number of rifles, a near monopoly of artillery, and the only air force in China. No longer confronting the Japanese army, by the end of 1945, Chiang's military also had 113,000 U.S. personnel helping it to move into northern cities it had never before ruled, and it received over $2.8 billion in new American military and economic assistance after the war ended. In addition, the Soviet army helped the KMT to occupy crucial northern cities by early 1946, and provided other assistance. The value of the Japanese industrial and other holdings in China that Chiang thus acquired were conservatively valued at $3.6 billion in 1945 dollars, and the physical quantity of industrial and agricultural goods in areas he controlled increased significantly for two years. "We have never heard it said," the Kuomintang's Ministry of National Defense concluded in a secret 1950 report from Taiwan, "that our military defeat in recent years resulted from a lack of ammunition or an insufficiency of other supplies."[21]

When World War Two ended, therefore, the Communists were still a long way from victory, seriously overextended in crucial areas, and the question was really whether Chiang could now use his far superior physical resources to cope with the economic, organizational, and military problems that had made possible most, if not all, of the Communist successes until then. That he failed to do so was not significantly due to the wisdom of the Communists but to his own profound incompetence and the corrupt nature of the society and state over which he presided. Had this not been the case, the Communists more than likely would not have won the civil war, for the Kuomintang had within its grasp sufficient resources to assuage, if not solve, many of China's critical problems. But because of its intrinsically venal nature, it could not do so, making Mao's task infinitely easier.

The Communists were still very much dependent on the support of the peasantry and adroitly attempted to placate it with minimal but sufficient reform measures. To meet the administrative challenges success brought with it, they also abandoned their purification efforts and recruited members without imposing inhibiting criteria designed to prevent apolitical opportunists from joining. From 736,000 members in 1942 the Party grew to 1.2 million in April 1945 and 2.2 million in January 1947, 3 million the next year, and 4.5 million at the end of 1949, when it was fully installed in power. In effect, the Party itself became another instrument of mass mobilization, opening the door to millions who had never undergone the required period of training and trials once integral to Bolshevik organizational doctrine—and ostensibly the prerequisite for a nominal role in decisions. If the lower Party members were now voiceless, a fact they took for granted, they nonetheless were also privileged, and their Party cards allowed them to advance for reasons often having no relationship to merit or sacrifices. Decision making was in practice—without an organizational doctrine ever being formulated to explain or justify it—confined to a handful of men who had been together since the 1920s and had personal and often clientelist ties.

But after August 1945 the dynamics in China's economy and society that had so traumatized the country over the preceding eight years intensified until no social class or important faction of society remained to defend the Kuomintang system. In the context of a disintegrating social order and an increasingly divided, contentious, and corrupt elite seeking to drive it in many different directions, the still massive inferiority of Communist numbers becomes unimportant. Indeed, after Chiang's military successes in the first part of 1946, the Red Army abandoned the cities it had entered in the wake of Japan's defeat and its regular forces declined by at least a third. Even at the beginning of 1947, when the KMT armies captured the Communist capital of Yenan, Chiang's arms superiority was comparable to his position at the end of the war with Japan. And while the number of his armed followers fell drastically during 1947 and the Communist army grew by 100,000, at the end of that year, the KMT's forces were still nearly twice as large, although they had lost many heavier weapons and the army remained a dispirited mass of humanity. Yet even as late as October 10, 1948, Mao anticipated that fighting would likely continue until mid-1951—and with another kind of enemy with comparable equipment, it very well may have. But Chiang's regime was disintegrating, and barely three months later he resigned as president and shipped China's remaining gold and currency reserves to Formosa.[22] The Communists simply moved into a growing vacuum, sustained far less by soldiers than by the masses' desire for stability and peace at long last.

It was this larger social process and erosion that explains the Communist triumph. Obviously, many of China's structural problems dated from well before Japan's aggression, but the war immeasurably intensified the decay and caused it to produce a grave social, economic, and political illness that might otherwise have lasted much longer. It was Chiang's responses to the war, as well as the nature of the inherently disunited and self-serving, precarious warlord coalition over which he presided, that guaranteed that this combination of factors would fundamentally alter the status quo relatively quickly. The Communist policies toward both the war and the Nationalist system were brilliant only in that after 1935 Mao made no irreversible major error on the long path of accumulating power. He lacked a doctrinaire commitment to specific social forms, and ideology and theory for Mao were scarcely more than homilies and generalities that justified those conclusions that he reached usually by opting for whatever added to the Party's authority and, above all, his own absolute hegemony. In this regard, his enormous flexibility made him a worthy successor of Lenin, whose acumen on the road to victory was unrivalled, and the two men conceived of the organization of socialism largely in terms of their personal abilities to rule over it, thereby laying the foundations for its eventual demise in both nations.

# CHAPTER 13

# War, Revolution, and Reaction
# in Southeast Asia

Japan's invasion of China traumatized a great part of a nation whose culture and decentralized, fragile political structure had historically remained virtually immune to foreign influences, and it was therefore highly likely that distinctive Chinese responses to the war and its consequences would emerge. In Mao Tse-tung's hands, the Communist party interpreted Marxist-Leninist ideology from the perspective of a unique national experience and its traditionalist lore, gradually transforming it into a schismatic doctrine.

While the tactics of the other Asian Marxist-Leninist parties were often similar to those of the Chinese Communists, and it was natural that many of the poor agrarian nations in crisis share comparable trials, their basic strategies varied greatly because imperialism profoundly conditioned the political contexts and ideas operating in each of the colonies at war. Resistance to the Japanese intrusion into Southeast Asia evolved, in large measure, within the dominant framework of anticolonialist movements. And unlike China, in much of the rest of Asia the local leaders' significant exposure to other languages and cultures prepared many of them to respond to their emerging crises in quite different ways. No less important was the fact that the Japanese conquered the colonial Asian nations quickly and utilized relatively small numbers of troops, while in China three major hostile, intact forces maneuvered for years against each other from fairly autonomous regions. The bureaucracies the imperialist powers had constructed to a very important degree also mediated Japan's interaction with the colonies, and it was partially through them that Japan then sought to advance its own interests. These consisted essentially of extracting as quickly as possible the optimum amount of raw materials desperately required for Japan's war against the United States, while at the same time investing a minimum of manpower and resources in the process.

Japan's temporary destruction of European and American imperialist authority, and its own subsequent defeat, greatly facilitated the demand for independence that was so integral to the Communist parties' platforms in the colonies. In China the Communists had nothing comparable to the issue of anticolonialism to add to their economic and political appeals to the masses, and the Nationalists also advocated resistance to the Japanese invasion. But since the war greatly intensified the strain on much of Asia's already fragile inequitable land and economic systems, in both Vietnam and the Philippines it also immediately pushed to the fore class issues of social equality and justice as well as national unity against Japan. Vietnamese and Filipino leftists therefore had to relate to a much wider spectrum of issues and concerns than the Chinese Communists, and such complexities forced them into much more problematic positions—and analogous situations existed in nations in the region I do not discuss here, particularly the Dutch East Indies. Because of the broader and more challenging contexts, and the postwar restoration of the colonial powers' military forces, Asia's anticolonial struggles were to last much longer than China's civil war and to profoundly influence the history of the following decades.

In Vietnam's case the wartime economic crisis was far graver than in the Philippines, and it was sufficient to give the radical opposition the added momentum required to make victory conceivable. In addition, numerous linguistic and physical barriers separated the masses in the Philippines, and they never attained the relative cultural unity that Vietnam's long but contiguous land mass and one dominating language made possible. Yet in both of these nations, the specific nature of the Communist parties also proved crucial. Success would be the result not only of the social, economic, and political dynamics the war unleashed, but would also reflect human wisdom and choices.

## Toward Revolution in Vietnam

When Japan conquered French Indochina in July 1941, most of France was under Nazi occupation and Tokyo was completely free to organize the three Indochinese states in any way compatible with its scarce manpower and rapacious material objectives so that it could continue its offensive toward

the rest of Southeast Asia. The fundamental interests of the French administration and the Japanese were complementary: the French knew they were
far too weak to resist the invaders and they sought primarily to retain purely
nominal legal and economic authority so that no political vacuum would
emerge and their formal sovereignty over Indochina would continue during
and, above all, after the war; Japan wished to act functionally, and it did not
add to its administrative burdens by evoking the rhetorical pretensions to
be leading a selfless pan-Asian crusade that it employed elsewhere. The pro-
Vichy French bureaucracy therefore remained completely in place, ruling
Indochina on behalf of Japan in practice if not in theory.

As a consequence of these overlapping objectives, it was not until March
9, 1945, long after de Gaulle had replaced Vichy, that Japan removed the
French administration, but even then it retained a significant portion of its
mid-level bureaucrats at various tasks; very few Japanese soldiers occupied
Vietnam. A French military force of 12,000 to 20,000 aging Europeans, in
charge of an indigenous army of extremely dubious quality estimated at
anywhere from 38,000 to 79,000, held Indochina for most of the war. The
Japanese employed a far smaller army until the spring of 1945, when both
to replace the French and resist a possible Allied invasion they increased
their manpower throughout Vietnam to around 62,000 men. Until then
they had only about 10,000 men in the crucial Tonkin region in the north,
concentrated almost wholly in the cities and along transportation routes.

To an astonishing degree, the events in Vietnam after 1941 were to
evolve in what was essentially a military vacuum that the French-Japanese
accommodation produced. The inherently unreliable French-led forces
could not be reinforced and they were spread over a vast territory; and the
Japanese never came close to filling this immense void. Vietnam was therefore spared most of the ravages of combat that so traumatized both China
and the Philippines, and it was possible for the Communists to take power
against far less armed resistance than potentially existed elsewhere.
Vietnam's monumental loss of life was not the result of firepower but of
those economic policies that inexorably accompanied Japan's occupation
policies and French implementation of them.[1]

### The Economics of Disaster

The Vichy administration attempted to retain as strong a position in the
economy as possible, managing in ways that allowed it and its politically
influential cronies to profit from foreign commerce organized wholly on
Japanese terms via annual contracts that imposed exact quantities and conditions for the delivery of raw materials. Japan paid for its constantly
mounting purchases and expenses in piastres that the French sold to it in
return for special yen, of which the French could use only a small part
to pay for certain expenses; this arrangement, ultimately, was a form of

confiscation. So the French simply printed money, thereby imposing most of the losses on the Indochinese masses, especially those in Tonkin, although a significant portion of the middle class and once-prosperous landowners also suffered heavily, creating an inflation that favored, above all, those well-connected speculators linked with the biggest French and Chinese interests. From 1939 to the end of 1944 the volume of piastres circulating in all Vietnam increased nearly sevenfold. Fiscally, the system reflected a convoluted political arrangement that eventually could only produce chaos. At the same time, the French decided in 1941 to restore the exceedingly oligarchic village-control system in Tonkin that had been abolished two decades earlier, thereby destabilizing the political structure at the grass-roots level and preparing the way for mass-based local reform movements even before economic pressures did so.

The French initially agreed in 1941 to provide Japan, at predetermined prices, fixed quantities of rice and corn comprising the estimated normal surplus. As American attacks disrupted maritime transportation, the volume of rice, rubber, tin, zinc, tea, and the like exported to Japan fell by 1944 to less than a quarter of 1941 tonnage, but the French continued to apply the rapacious procurement policies that had won them Japanese toleration, storing huge quantities of rice and much else withdrawn from normal local consumption; as the output of commodities fell, these stocks constituted a gold mine for speculators. The Japanese redirected a significant part of the goods earmarked for the homeland to China and other conquered areas where the profits were extremely high, and they supplied the local black market as well. With time, the Japanese only increased their impositions on the French, demanding delivery whatever the consequences, and also insisting that the French give Japan's trading companies a share of the lucrative commerce.

While the French authority was supposed to collect rice for the Japanese at fixed prices from the peasants and landowners proportionate to their landholdings, and the scheme was fairly progressive in theory, in practice it was confiscatory and impoverished a significant portion of the once-affluent peasantry as well as the poor who had no connections with the village oligarchies and could not evade their rice quotas. Two percent of Tonkin's landowners accounted for 40 percent of the rice land, and their production costs for their own output were much less than that of their tenants; some also managed to conceal their holdings. From the beginning, the government paid the peasants considerably less than the market price, but with rampant inflation the gap between the market price and that paid to peasants widened and the forced deliveries became virtual expropriation. More significant was the fact that small rice producers had scant storage facilities and were obligated to sell their rice as it was produced, and they accounted for about a third of the surplus available, while the bulk of it belonged to large landowners and merchants, many of whom possessed warehouses and kept rice off the market to sell at the opportune moment— thereby making sufficient profits to recoup losses from forced sales, or even gain. But those unable to provide the amounts of rice the government demanded had to pay the difference between the market price of the rice they could not deliver and the far smaller payments they would have received, which economically ruined many of those who had no way of escaping the impositions. Tenants, in addition to the compulsory sales, had also to pay rent to their landlords, usually in the form of fixed amounts of rice annually, and the tenants became the scheme's principal, although not exclusive, victims.

Throughout this period, moreover, the French implemented Japanese demands that a significant amount of rice land be converted to produce other commodities, so that the surface devoted to vegetable oils more than quadrupled between 1939 and 1944, cotton acreage increased eightfold, while jute acreage tripled. Production of all other useful raw materials— rubber, wood, and the like—also grew significantly. At the same time, the Japanese began to convert increasing amounts of rice into alcohol to fuel vehicles.

Harvests during 1941, 1942, and 1943 were normal, but even then the taxes were becoming increasingly onerous for the poorer peasants. Moreover, transport between the surplus-producing areas in southern Cochin and poorer Tonkin in the north broke down almost entirely by 1944, in part because of Allied attacks on shipping but also because French officials would not pay the numerous junk operators adequately for their services. The Japanese, on the other hand, found the transport to sell rice abroad. With growing quantities of surplus rice accumulating in the south, in the summer of 1944 three major typhoons destroyed most of the rice crop in the northern coastal areas.

The Japanese collected a million tons of rice each year during 1942 and 1943, and about half that in 1944. In early 1945 they asked for 550,000 tons for the year, all of which was destined for sale in the region, locally at black-market rates, or for their own use. Rice in warehouses accumulated much more quickly than the Japanese could remove it, although some of it was by this time even being burnt directly in power plants in Cochin. When the Japanese finally evicted the French from nominal authority in March, about 500,000 tons of rice paddy was waiting in warehouses to be milled— enough to feed the entire nation normally for about four months. Most was in the south, but considerable amounts remained in the hands of northern speculators as well as the Japanese there. Millions of Vietnamese knew that sufficient rice stocks existed to end the starvation and misery all around them, including their own.[2]

Even during the best years a very significant portion of the Vietnamese peasantry had lived at very close to subsistence levels, but the combination of Japanese exactions, the breakdown of the economy and transport, and the weather made inevitable the catastrophe that was to change completely the course of Vietnamese history. Starvation conditions appeared in Tonkin even in late 1943, and a year later, as the weather turned cold earlier than usual and the shortages spread to northern Annam, the nation's central region, peasants began to eat what were normally animal feeds: rice husks, grasses, and the like. After the summer 1944 typhoons, both the weak political authority and the peasants totally abandoned the already neglected but crucial dike system, adding to the flooding. The Cochin and southern Annam regions, though facing difficulties, were spared the famine. The Tran Trong Kim puppet regime the Japanese had installed after deposing the French could do nothing to cope with the calamity, and events were entirely beyond its control. As peasants in the villages began to starve, many abandoned their homes and attempted to walk to cities to beg, often dying on the way and creating unprecedented scenes of horror. Children were sold or abandoned, and daily removal of corpses from the cities became essential to contain a typhus epidemic. In the countryside the bodies lay everywhere, the survivors too weak to bury them.

Depending on the source's bias, the estimates of the famine's toll vary, but Admiral Jean Decoux, the French governor-general until March 1945 and a principal figure in creating the conditions leading to it, later wrote that the famine caused about 1 million deaths. The Communist leader, Vo Nguyen Giap, concluded that a million died before the spring 1945 harvest, and another million afterward. No one at the time, of course, attempted to gather precise numbers, but 1.5 to 2 million deaths—or about one-fifth of Tonkin's entire population—has become the most accepted estimate among scholars, including those who are strongly anti-Communist. What is certain is that by early 1945 the entire northern half of Vietnam was profoundly traumatized: large parts of the rural areas were depopulated, huge numbers of homeless peasants were wandering aimlessly, and the cities were full of a pitiable mass of desperate humanity.[3]

### The Communists Take Power
As a leading French official at the time subsequently recalled, France had not had significant political problems with the Vietnamese population before early 1945. But once the famine began the people had absolutely nothing more to lose from the overthrow of the colonial system or its legacies. On the contrary, its destruction seemed an essential precondition for their very survival.

The Vietnamese Communist party had been one of many tiny Marxist-Leninist organizations in the colonial world; Moscow largely forgot it, and the French never took it too seriously. Until 1941, when Ho Chi Minh secretly returned to the country after three decades of exile, it had experienced innumerable reverses since mainly students and intellectuals from petit bourgeois and even poor mandarin backgrounds had founded it in 1930.* From its inception, like most Leninist parties it was an organization of the radicalized intelligentsia, and its theoretical elitism reflected this reality. The Comintern removed Ho from leadership in late 1930 because of his emphasis on mobilizing peasants, and he lived obscurely throughout the 1930s. Even long after his return, the Party always retained a curiously irrelevant but ideologically orthodox belief in the crucial political role of the proletariat in a nation that virtually had none.

Until 1941, regional autonomy and frequent dissidence had nearly proved fatal to the Party, and the central committee had often been incapable of imposing strict discipline over the southern organization. Locally initiated insurrections in Annam in 1930–31 and Cochin in the summer of 1940 led to the arrest and decimation of most Party members and followers in those regions. Vast distances and primitive communications plagued the Vietnamese party as they had the Chinese, even within many of the provinces, and discipline remained a constant challenge to its leaders for much of its history—and they repeatedly, even obsessively at times, sought to prevent local "leftist" deviations or hasty, premature actions. Decentralization was a permanent and overriding fact of the Communist party's experience throughout its entire history, and while this pervasive reality greatly augmented its ability to reach people in remote places, thereby creating sources of strength and allowing the masses to articulate the kinds of resistance they believed most effective, it also posed dangers to leaders who sought to define and coordinate local actions with national policies. Initially, the Party remained elitist both out of desire and necessity, but tight organizational control in poor and inherently decentralized nations is invariably a chimera.

In reality, the Communist party fared poorly in the two years after the Japanese invasion. In late 1939 it had embarked on a united-front strategy that aggressively subordinated agrarian-reform issues to a class alliance in the struggle against both the French and the Japanese, and after May 1941, when it created the Vietminh as a united-front umbrella organization, it hoped also to initiate guerrilla warfare. Given its utterly inconsequential size, the Party expected that success would come less from its own efforts, though they were deemed crucial, than from the impact of the war on both the French colonial and Japanese systems. If in this regard the Party was

---

* Ho's pseudonym at this time was Nguyen Ai Quoc. To avoid confusion, I use Ho Chi Minh throughout.

keenly prescient, it still confronted what appeared for several years the insuperable task of surviving and growing within a rapidly changing global context that also constrained its future possibilities.

For two years the Communists attempted to organize armed groups to resist the French and Japanese, less as part of a plan for general insurrection in the near future than as a contingency that might later become more relevant, most likely in conjunction with invading Allied forces. It did this quite ineffectively among ethnic-minority recruits along the vast, desolate northern border with China, and somewhat further south in a mountainous area still a long distance from Hanoi. Such small bands survived as long as the French ignored the Vietminh and failed to send their largely indigenous forces into these abandoned regions, but they had scarcely any modern arms and every French-led foray decimated them. The Vietminh militia in 1944 comprised 812 members, over 300 fewer than in 1943, while the Party itself had only 2,000 to 3,000 members in 1944. At the end of 1944, imitating a Chinese Communist precedent, it modified its depleted military resources to create armed propaganda units, but at their inception these too lacked weapons and their principal function was to protect political-education activities. Both the Party's initial united-front and guerrilla warfare policies had, in essence, failed to produce results even remotely commensurate with the traumatic events that were starting to transform the nation, much less the monumental challenges it was soon to confront.

At the beginning of 1943 the Party also made the decision to attempt to expand its urban following, especially concentrating on winning over youth-group members and scouts in Vichy-sponsored organizations, as well as students and younger intelligentsia like themselves—and to whom they could speak far more effectively than to the often hostile minorities and peasants in the remote countryside. The Party also created cultural fronts, and while its urban efforts fared far better than its rural work, the Party itself and even the Vietminh remained highly elitist. In contrast to China (admittedly a very different context), where in 1944 the Communists had 850,000 members, the Vietnamese party kept its size limited by refusing to recruit freely. Its discipline seemed worth the restriction in numbers because it wanted no repetition of the mass insurrectionary movements that its more independent members had earlier chosen to lead. In 1944 the Party was still very small and weak by any criterion. Few, if any, of its leaders in that year, Ho Chi Minh included, could imagine that victory was imminent.[4]

The famine completely altered the Communist party's role, and was unquestionably the decisive event in Vietnam's modern history. Japan's defeat and France's profound compromise, by themselves, would not have greatly changed the Communists' military prospects, because as weak as these two foreign powers were, without the famine the Vietminh very likely would have remained relatively impotent. What the Party had been unable to do throughout most of the war was to mobilize the mass movement that is a precondition for revolution, and in fact its elitist organization strategy and its united-front emphasis had kept it from appealing to the peasantry—among whom its following had been negligible.

By the spring of 1945 the famine in the northern half of Vietnam had forged an intense mass readiness to rebel, one that is rare in human history anywhere save under comparable conditions. Millions of people lost their otherwise normal fear of defying authority principally because they had infinitely more to lose from apathy or obeisance to laws than from taking matters into their own hands, but also because the small French and Japanese forces and their Vietnamese auxiliaries were either immobilized or indifferent. Nationalism might have entered the picture for some, but for the great majority the issue was reduced simply to food and survival as opposed to the mounting probability of death. Under these circumstances the Vietnamese Communist party's tasks were immeasurably simplified, and by early 1945 it understood that it must immediately relate to this primal mass impulse.

### From March 1945 to the August Revolution

When the Party's central committee met in the second week of March 1945 to chart its future course, its organization was both small and troubled. Many of its key leaders were in prison, and the famine had cost some members their lives and compelled a large portion of them, possibly even a majority, to spend most of their time searching for food. The Party renewed its commitment to the creation of a united front made up essentially of all classes; seeking to bypass the problem of how to reconcile the united front with taking rice from rich peasants and landlords, it strongly implied that peasants should confiscate only the paddy stock that the French and Japanese held—a proscription that starving people could not afford to obey and the Party's activists could not afford to apply. Now the Party even proposed to collaborate with whatever anti-Japanese French Resistance forces emerged in the wake of Japan's formal March 9 takeover of power from France. It also assumed that the remaining Japanese troops would be willing to fight and that the war would probably end relatively soon with Allied armies landing in Indochina. The Party believed that its general insurrection would most likely be dependent on such an invasion, and that it should begin *after* it began; but if the Allies did not come, it expected eventually to mount its own rebellion against Japan. Although how and when all these options were to occur was left unspecified, it was clear that, after the disasters that had followed in the wake of two earlier premature mass uprisings, a cautious Party leadership would be loath to authorize any hasty move. In fact, the central committee believed it was in "the period of pre-insurrection" and completely failed to predict the Allied and Japanese roles, or especially Japan's sudden surrender, over the following five and a half critical months.[5]

Far more significant was the committee's decision to endorse a strategy "to break open the rice stores to avert famine."[6] It was this policy alone, and none other, that allowed it to mobilize the deepening undercurrent of desperation and anger among the people and to harness their profound instinct to survive for the Party's military as well as political objectives— bringing it to power within months in a chaotic, decentralized manner it utterly failed to anticipate. And given the Japanese arrest of most French military personnel at this time, it urged all of its followers to act before the Japanese could install a new administrative and military structure and fill the vacuum of power that now existed in vast regions.

Vietminh and Party activists helped to initiate countless attacks on rice stocks that the Japanese and "reactionaries" held throughout the northern part of the nation, and thanks to the absence of enemy troops in most of the rural areas, the process was crowned with success and critical amounts of food were distributed—encouraging others to follow. Indeed, the lack of any real central political authority caused many village notables and thousands of now leaderless colonial soldiers to remain passive or even to simply transfer their allegiance—and precious weapons—to the Vietminh, or join them outright. Even some smaller landlords, as well as the so-called national bourgeoisie, cooperated with the Communists in the following months, which reinforced the Party's desire to minimize divisive class issues. By the summer of 1945 many members of these classes had suffered greatly from the wartime economic policies, and a significant number of them (and especially their children) supported the Vietminh. While there was some resistance, including from a number of hapless Japanese, the Communists began to install a viable administrative and military structure in rural areas where in fact the old one either no longer existed or which the rapidly changing events had utterly disoriented.

Faced with a choice between anarchy with starvation or the Vietminh, the peasants overwhelmingly chose the latter. As the Party later wrote in its official account, success brought with it a sudden flood of new recruits, and "the number of Viet Minh members increased from some thousand to tens of thousands. . . . The confiscation of paddy stocks by the masses . . . drew millions of people into the revolutionary struggle. . . ."[7] It was under the leadership of these largely instant Vietminh converts—nearly all of whom were anything but ideal Bolsheviks—that the peasantry engaged in political and military activities, which by necessity often fed on each other. Their revolutionary network spread throughout much of the rural north during the spring of 1945, confiscating whatever rice they could find to save lives, including often from wealthier persons initially earmarked to become part of a united front. Meanwhile, drawing on younger men who had first begun with rice-liberation campaigns, the regular Vietminh army in the region north of Hanoi increased tenfold, to about 5,000, from March to August, while roughly 200,000 irregular and militia forces, armed overwhelmingly with primitive weapons at the inception but with increasing numbers of captured French and Japanese arms over time, existed in the vast region extending down to the center of Vietnam.

By late May the Vietminh, in the quite amorphous form it now assumed, controlled most of the north's mountain and plains areas, and in early June it set up its first government in a liberated zone encompassing the remote six northernmost provinces. It had no armed rivals in the north. "The revolution broke out like a whirlwind," Giap later recollected, but it remained essentially rural during its crucial early months, by the end of which time it was able to continue permanently in some form, whatever occurred in the towns and cities.[8] The Vietnamese Revolution in its first, and decisive, stage was essentially an agrarian, peasant-based event, and from this foundation it was able also to triumph in the cities several months later.

The Communists' only modest urban successes before the spring of 1945 had been among youth, and after they had sufficiently consolidated their rural gains, they turned more attention to the cities. When on August 10, Japan offered to surrender to the Allies, its officers and troops decided that the war was over for them and what the Vietminh chose to do was no longer their affair. In fact, the Vietminh had begun as early as June to operate publicly with increasing audacity in Hanoi, Hué, and especially Saigon, in large part because many of the puppet regime's indigenous troops and police understood which way the wind was blowing and sought (successfully in many cases!) to transfer their allegiance; the Vietminh controlled a substantial and rapidly growing section of them well before the Tran Trong Kim regime resigned on August 15. With the French disarmed and some still in Japanese prisons, there was now virtually a complete political void in Vietnam's cities, and most of the existing mass organizations the French and Japanese had created, as well as a crucial portion of the nominal state organs, were in the hands of mainly instant Vietminh converts, countless thousands of whom now surfaced in public.

The news of the Japanese surrender offer reached Vietnam's Communist leaders about August 13, and late that day they commanded their entire political and military organization to embark on a general insurrection to take the cities and disarm the Japanese. The order arrived in Hanoi three days later, but in many areas local Vietminh and the people had already begun to act on their own initiative—indeed, such a process of autonomous local action had been developing since March. There was only one case of Japanese resistance.

The Hanoi uprising began when a relative handful of activists, probably fewer than 100, initiated public demonstrations on August 17 by taking over a huge mass meeting that a few diehards from the Kim regime had convened, and the puppet troops who were supposed to defend it either joined or gave their arms to the Vietminh. Until that point, the Vietminh military strength in Hanoi had comprised about 900 audacious workers and youth, who initially possessed only about seventy motley weapons. Two days later, after a large infusion of mainly unarmed peasants from the countryside reinforced them, they took power in Hanoi without firing a single shot in anger. By August 22 the entire north was in the Vietminh's hands, and the nearly unarmed revolution next took over Hué and Danang in central Vietnam within several days. In Cochin, which had been spared the famine, a Communist-led coalition controlled Saigon on August 25, and then quickly spread effortlessly to the other key regional cities. On August 30, Emperor Bao Dai abdicated the throne, transferring all the symbols of authority to the Vietminh and offering to cooperate with the new government, and on September 2, Ho Chi Minh proclaimed the creation of the Democratic Republic of Vietnam and ended the monarchy and French domination.[9]

Ho understood clearly that the Communists had come to virtually total power by what must have appeared to be a very great measure of astonishing but also accidental fortune, which was not likely to be repeated, and he did not want to dissipate it by applying those criteria that had kept the Party disciplined and pure but tiny. So he leaned heavily toward a united-front strategy that would allow him to consolidate administrative authority, minimize domestic resistance to what were intended to be quite modest reforms, and, above all, resolve the crucial problem of food while fending off the inevitable French return. To be as effective as possible, he eliminated any hint that he and his new government were Communists, beginning by changing the name he'd used since 1930 to Ho Chi Minh. The Party disappeared informally until November 11, 1945, when it proclaimed itself dissolved. "Our Party decided to avoid doing anything that might provoke the enemies of the nation and the class," Giap recounted later. "But they still recognized us."[10] No one spoke in public as a Communist, but rather as a member of the Vietminh, and with emphasis on patriotism and anticolonialism rather than class conflict. Meanwhile, the Party's membership quadrupled to 20,000 in the year after the August Revolution, and rose to 180,000 by the end of 1948. In effect, virtually all able, useful, and nominally committed persons who had shown their mettle in the preceding months were enrolled, and as in all the Leninist nations, a de facto mass party replaced the original model—opening the door to everyone from inexperienced, sincere idealists to opportunists who, like a considerable portion of all those who join all parties everywhere, saw membership as a way to advance themselves. How such a huge and growing body would participate in making decisions, if at all, was to emerge as the enduring legacy—and contradiction—of all comparable Leninist parties.

The Communists sought to resolve at least part of their immediate orga-nizational difficulties by retaining a significant portion of the civil servants who had worked for the earlier regimes—and most were happy to cooper-ate until December 1946, when the Party moved to remote base areas and abandoned the cities to the arriving French. Before then, however, the Communists used the crucial interregnum to build an 80,000-man regular army, plus a huge militia, the successor of which was eventually to defeat both France and the United States in full-scale warfare.

A genuine national consensus existed that the problem of food must be resolved, and it was the Communist ability to use their time in power to accomplish this feat by the spring of 1946 that enabled them easily to neu-tralize the few Vietnamese challengers to their authority (most of whom were localized, sectarian, and had collaborationist records) and to win the endorsement of a large majority of the people and the active assistance of a sufficient number of them to carry on through countless trials for three more decades. But except for some quite modest and unevenly imple-mented rent, interest, and tax reforms for the poor peasantry, and the redis-tribution of French- and collaborationist-owned land, the Party's initial united-front strategy discouraged any fundamental changes in Vietnamese society as it then existed.[11]

The final weeks that witnessed the replacement of the French colonial sys-tem were essentially bloodless, and much of the remaining state mecha-nism was simply transferred to the Communists. Such a profound and rapid change was possible, above all, because the famine compelled a very crucial portion of the rural masses to act to feed themselves, often provid-ing their own leadership when the Vietminh was not on the scene to initi-ate action—and then joining with it in later conflicts. The sequence of Japanese-initiated political events from March through August 1945 pro-duced both an administrative and a military vacuum and left no coherent or sufficiently large authority to cope with the mushrooming, decentralized Vietminh, whose urban triumph came only after the die was cast in the rural areas and the weight of all the preceding months' developments made it a virtual certainty. Yet it is crucial to understand that, even had the Japanese or the French in the cities not been passive or immobilized, they were not likely to win the struggle in a countryside that remained the base of the Communist strength for many years to come.

The occupation of Indochina was anomalous and full of contradictions from its inception. The collaboration between colonialists and invaders, both administratively and in terms of nominal legal authority, was unique for Asia and produced immense economic problems—and, for the Communists, possibilities—that did not appear elsewhere. That such a situation would create the grave political void that emerged was likely because here as elsewhere in Asia, Japan could not invest the manpower to run the colonies directly while imposing policies that served only to traumatize and radicalize them. The French managed to retain control of the Indochinese bureaucratic structure until it was too late for the Japanese to change it significantly, guarding the legal basis for their return only months later, but at a price that was too great for their colonial system to bear either organizationally or in terms of political legitimacy. Moreover, both had managed to compromise a sufficient number of possible indigenous religious and class rivals to the Communists so as to leave the latter a political field essentially devoid of competition—a fact that allowed them to recover from the effects of a number of errors they were to make over the coming months and years.

Initially, the ephemeral Communist military power survived only because both the French and the Japanese or their surrogates were unwilling or unable to use their vastly superior arms, but the Party's increasingly numerous but very poorly armed and trained soldiers were not called upon to do any serious fighting. Without excluding the possible influence of what was essentially their potential for violence rather than their real capabilities, the Communists succeeded by September 1945 because both Japanese wartime economic policies and French collaboration with them caused an economic and social collapse that galvanized the masses to action—indeed, left many of them no option but death. But unlike China and the Philippines, Vietnam did not suffer from combat-inflicted damage.

It somewhat simplifies the experience to state that the French and Japanese policies rather than the Communists made the revolution, but the latter had not made any significant progress before the end of 1944, when in practice they jettisoned most of their inhibiting elitist and Leninist organizational policies and rode behind or on top of the tide of events far more than they led them. Only after August 1945 and the resolution of the vitally fundamental food question did the Communists show a greater flexibility and shrewdness, revealing a sustained ability to capitalize on chance and good luck to make a sufficient number of correct choices to justify their pretensions to lead because they possessed more clarity than myopia—at least relative to the competence of their adversaries.

But although the Vietnamese Revolution in crucial regards appears to have been the consequence of highly unique, if not accidental events, in fact it was no more fortuitous than the war upon which it was wholly symbiotic. War has inevitable grave consequences, and in this case the great potential for revolutionary upheavals was one of them. While the Communist leaders were never wholly in charge, and had a conception of their role that often bore scant or no relationship to the way that massive changes were really occurring, on the whole they did have a sufficient sense of the times, its opportunities, and the tasks essential to consolidating their hold on power. If they lacked the prescience and ideological knowledge they later argued provided the legitimacy for their absolute control of all decisions, they nonetheless made more correct choices than fatal ones.

Still, there were many small Communist parties elsewhere with comparable organizations and leaders in 1945, and none came to power in the manner of the Vietnamese party; this fact alone supports the contention that it was the disintegration of a colonial society in the context of its interaction with the war's impact and pillage that caused the revolution to triumph. One cannot gainsay the ability of the tiny leadership to persevere and reconstitute itself at the appropriate times—itself a major leadership accomplishment—but the Communists scarcely had any tactical and strategic options after the famine wracked rural Vietnam. The purely Leninist organizational theory and structure they cherished until then was less counterproductive than irrelevant in its refusal to trust new leaders emerging from among the masses. When the Party greatly reduced its centralizing objectives and tolerated, even if it never formally acknowledged, the constraints that poor communications placed on its leadership functions, adapting to them pragmatically, it finally created the basis for much more timely responses to the astonishingly rapid changes occurring after March 1945. But this meant that the Party's guidance of the masses, a notion integral to its Leninist pretensions, was increasingly one of selecting between a finite and often very circumscribed set of choices emerging from the war-torn social order it was seeking to replace, and those constraints that the masses themselves, with their uncoordinated behavior and quickly evolving desires, imposed upon its decisions. Such a role didn't so much require special wisdom based on doctrinal understanding, or a tightly organized hierarchical party organizational structure, but common sense as to what was likely to succeed in attaining power. The needs and desires of the masses at a given historical moment, masses who had either to be satisfied, cajoled, or deceived, but could not be ignored by any group wishing to remain credible to them, defined the outer limits of Vietnamese history. That lesson was to be repeated often over the next three decades.

## Restoring the Old Order in the Philippines

When Japan invaded the Philippines in January 1942, it was determined to employ a significant portion of the Filipino political oligarchy with which the United States had worked intimately since 1907. These relatively efficient, if self-serving and frequently corrupt men, had assumed increasing responsibility for the islands' administrative structure and economy, and the U.S. in March 1934 promised the colony nominal independence in ten years. As elsewhere in Asia, Japan's alternative to working through the existing authorities was to embark on the inherently dubious task of creating a new governing system, which would have required assigning a much larger number of its own personnel to the highly decentralized islands, with their numerous distinct languages. Given the opportunistic nature of the men who had worked with the Americans, the Japanese saw no reason to choose this option.

The small Filipino elite comprised a series of regional oligarchies whose political structures have perceptively been described as reciprocity-based compadre and patron-client systems, founded largely on extended families who usually also dominated the economies of specific islands and entered cynically into often transitory coalitions with each other for purposes of national politics. At the top of this structure in 1941 was Manuel L. Quezon, who had presided over what amounted to a one-party dictatorship that had collaborated with the Americans for three decades. Such clientelism reinforced the national pattern of insular parochialism and was in crucial ways organizationally a carbon copy of American machine politics. There was very little formal ideology motivating it, save a rhetorical adherence to what was an implicitly conservative view of politics, society, and the need to maintain the existing hierarchical order. When the Americans captured the islands at the turn of the century, the *ilustrados* (the wealthy traditional families comprising the social and political elite) readily accommodated to them to advance their own interests through the elaborate patronage structure linking economics and politics. In practice—for such ideas and values as they had posed no obstacles—there was no insurmountable barrier to their collaborating with the Japanese to protect their own power and maintain their political machinery. The Filipino elite was neither pro-American nor pro-Japanese during World War Two, and only its pursuit of its self-interest provided coherence to its behavior during the war as well as the decades before and after it.[12]

### The Occupation Regime

Quezon, along with his vice president and a handful of senior officials, retreated with the Americans, but he instructed the bulk of his cabinet, the entire Council of State, and virtually the whole government to remain. It is unquestionable that when senior Filipinos who were told to stay at their posts asked the responsible Americans how they should relate to the Japanese they were advised to continue at their positions and do whatever they were ordered—except take an oath of allegiance to Japan.[13]

Washington's motives at this time were quite straightforward, and its policy toward collaborators when the war ended confirmed that it too wanted the traditional elite, with whom men such as General Douglas MacArthur, the most influential American on Philippine issues, were personally close, to keep their jobs and then continue ruling after the war. The options to such a strategy were too unpredictable, and involved nationalists as well as untested men who might create any number of problems for the U.S. after independence. And it became quickly obvious that the existing elite was the only viable barrier to a leftist movement that had begun to grow significantly in the late 1930s and expanded greatly during the war. For the islands' traditional rulers to resist—and they were overwhelmingly unwilling to embark on that course—would only have led to the destruction of many of them and the likely domination of strongly anti-American nationalists over much of the nation or a dangerous power vacuum at the war's end. Japan's principal collaborators, therefore, could with reasonable confidence expect to gain no matter who lost the war.

Within a month of the Japanese arrival the strategic Filipino officials, and nearly the entire civil administration, began to work for the occupation government. The Japanese proclaimed all the laws in force at the time valid unless changed, and "the executive and judicial institutions shall continue to be effective for the time being. . . . all public officials shall remain in their present posts. . . ."[14] Few Japanese were stationed on isolated islands, such as Leyte, and the existing administrative structure, including the elected governor, continued to run that island as before—only now they were nominally members of a Japanese-created political party. José Laurel, former chief justice of the Supreme Court, became the president of the puppet government. Quezon, before his departure, made Jorge Vargas the mayor of Manila and left him with orders to cooperate with the Japanese, who retained him in that post for two more years—and the U.S. throughout this time appreciated his efforts "toward restraining guerrilla warfare."[15] A handful of ultranationalists sincerely welcomed the Japanese, but they were scarcely useful as state managers, and the important political figures who appeared most enthusiastic publicly and served in the puppet regime, such as Senator Claro M. Recto, while unquestionably nationalists, later produced tortuous apologias for their behavior which only confirmed their endemic opportunism. Self-serving, in effect, explains the motives of the vast majority of those who collaborated, although most preferred to claim they were really acting under American orders and seeking only to mitigate Japan's grave impact on the people.

As everywhere in Asia, Japan's principal objective during the occupation was to minimize its administrative responsibilities and milk the economy intensively, but because of the highly decentralized islands and the growing shortage of shipping, it probably extracted far more, relative to the potential, from Vietnam. The Japanese introduced a special unbacked currency that caused economic chaos favoring speculators, and began to confiscate a large proportion of the existing vehicles, machinery, hardware, and any-thing useful for the war effort. But after stripping many of the islands' mines of equipment, they later brought them back into production. They took over many factories and often installed Japanese managers to run them, while their trading companies gathered coconut oil, copra, and wood products to export to Japan. As in Vietnam, they routinely commandeered all the rice and grain they could, even though the country had been an importer before the war, to supply their own forces and hoard whatever they were unable to send home. Sugar lands were converted to cotton and rice production, and sugar itself was turned into alcohol. In a word, Japan exploited the economy pitilessly, but despite terrible hardships no cata-strophe comparable to Vietnam's famine ravaged the Philippines.

Precisely because the Japanese played a far greater direct role in running the Philippines than they did in Indochina, they were also much more bru-tal. Notwithstanding their pan-Asian ideological doctrines and promise that Filipinos would now "enjoy your own prosperity and culture," they possessed a profoundly racist contempt for the people—who had no effec-tive authority to defend them. The death penalty could be imposed on those "who show hostility" against the Japanese army, "who disturb the minds of the officials and the people," who perform "any action disturbing the economic and financial condition" or were "not careful in words and deeds." Filipinos had to bow to Japanese soldiers, who freely slapped any-one who failed to do so or for whatever reason entered their minds. They were especially savage during occasional forays against guerrillas, when tor-ture, imprisonment, and looting were commonplace occurrences. As in the rest of Asia, women were forced to work in brothels for soldiers. "Offering resistance or committing a hostile act against the Japanese Armed Forces in any manner," its first occupation proclamation read, "leads the whole native land to ashes."[16] Japan's policies in the Philippines therefore resulted in some of the worst atrocities of the war.

### The Economic Impact of the War

Estimating the war's impact on the Philippines poses many more problems than in Vietnam because while the latter suffered a terrible famine it also was spared the Philippines' incredibly destructive combat. The greatest calamity occurred when the Americans returned and fought to regain key islands, which had been relatively unscathed until then. Per capita income in 1946 was less than a half of that in 1938, the 1944–45 crop was 60 per-cent of the average, and 1946 total physical production was slightly more than one-third of 1937. Estimates of the value of property losses range from $1.3 billion to $5 billion, and nearly 300,000 structures were destroyed or damaged. This number includes almost all the significant buildings in Manila, which probably became the most devastated non-Japanese city in

Asia. All such figures should be used critically, but they are the best estimates we have: 91,000 Filipino civilians died from murder, torture, and starvation. This fails, of course, to measure the longer-term physical damage from diseases, malnutrition, or wounds. But notwithstanding the war, the national population from 1937 to 1946 increased by 3 million. The Vietnamese people suffered far more, and even though the Left in the Philippines before the war had made considerably more progress than in Vietnam, revolution occurred only in Vietnam. Yet the war's legacies nonetheless affected the Philippines profoundly for decades.

Before the Philippines became a battleground, however, the population, as everywhere, suffered unevenly. During 1943 the Japanese intensified their foraging in food-rich central Luzon, but life went on fairly normally in those impoverished islands or regions they largely ignored, with barter replacing currency. On Luzon the poorer peasants were better able to adjust than others, since their consumption had always been low, and as landowners fled to the cities, many peasants ceased to pay all or part of their rents. Any peasant—and this would exclude the poorest—able to build a rice surplus found it easy to trade it in the cities for the possessions of the now-hungry affluent classes, and while this redistribution of wealth was probably not as extensive as it was widely believed to be at the time or thereafter, it certainly was not uncommon. But as in all nations during wars, whenever people no longer have access to basic food supplies, most peasants fare much better than city dwellers.

Urban life was much more complicated, especially after the spring of 1943, when the Japanese began to impose compulsory labor demands and the food supply continued to fall—even though a subsistence level of rationed essentials at fixed prices was established to prevent the masses from starving to death as a result of the constant, growing inflation. Manila's class structure has always been highly unequal, but for the one-quarter of the city unemployed in 1943, life was desperate. Moreover, the existence of a war currency encouraged speculation and barter, and rationed goods leaked into the black market. Food smuggled into cities from rural areas also provided some lubrication for it, and stolen, smuggled, or clandestinely produced goods yet more. The Japanese exploited this parallel economy ruthlessly, and helped to sustain it in various ways. Crime and vice were rampant. The bourgeois who were unwilling or unable to root in the rough-and-tumble clandestine economy sold off their possessions and began to sink down in the class hierarchy. Those with connections, above all to the Japanese or the right government officials, or who were ready to abandon their remaining scruples to do whatever was necessary to survive and prosper, flourished. Expensive, well-stocked restaurants and night clubs existed to serve such nouveaux riches, and some of them—especially Chinese merchants, who fared better than anybody in this climate—began to acquire anything useful that Japan's occupation currency could buy before its defeat made the paper worthless. By the time the war ended, a significant number of new landowners had emerged from this element, causing important though far from comprehensive alterations in both the urban and rural class structures.[17]

Filipino politics evolved during the war and thereafter in this traumatic and rapidly changing social and human context, amid suffering, humiliation, deprivation, and violence as well as the traditional ruling class's profound opportunism. For the United States the primary question was whether this already fragile oligarchical political system could survive and reestablish a congenial political and economic regime after independence. For the people the main challenge was to overcome the heritage of exploitation and backwardness that the politically most compromised elites had imposed in the past and hoped to sustain in the future. And the old oligarchy sought to emerge from the war just as firmly in command of the new state as they had been when administering American and Japanese hegemony.

### The Guerrilla Movements

The civil administration that the retreating Americans had fashioned, with all of its assets and liabilities, remained essentially intact and ready for the Japanese to utilize. But throughout the islands, lapses in the traditional corrupt local and regional boss-dominated political machinery allowed the oppressed masses spontaneously to release some of the anger that had accumulated during years of suffering. Many local manifestations of the weakening of the authority and police upon whom prewar power had relied were scarcely more than banditry in nature, but some were indeed political. The result was a complex guerrilla movement that took several distinctive forms, but by the end of the war it left the United States with a major dilemma regarding the preservation of order and the continuity of the society it had established. This putative resistance to Japan embodied, to a great degree, the diversity and egoism of traditional Philippine politics as well as the social discontent that its conservative economic policies had generated over earlier decades.

Autonomous local movements with an unmistakable social character arose as soon as the decline in the police's power became obvious. In central Luzon, what the Communists later denounced as "extreme leftist actions by the people" began in February 1942, or as soon as the disappearance of the traditional state allowed workers, including union activists, to kill at least one prominent planter and wreak a certain amount of havoc before their peers imposed restraint upon them.[18] Even though it was to materialize almost exclusively in central Luzon, the potential for socially significant rural rebellion throughout the islands lingered as a real possibility for the entire war. This was shown on the island of Negros, with its vast sugar plantations worked by seasonal wage labor living in abject poverty, and where the tiny Filipino and Spanish elite that controlled most of the island's land and refineries had maintained a quasi-feudal, ostentatiously luxurious existence. During the latter half of 1942, with the Japanese uninterested in imposing control over most of the island's towns, groups of workers began spontaneously to burn sugar fields and the large planters' elegant haciendas, killing many of them along with their wives and children. The surviving big planters escaped to the major provincial city or Manila before police restored some semblance of order.

More common and widespread, however, essentially because they reflected the precedents that self-serving local political mores had sanctioned for decades, were the guerrilla organizations outside central Luzon. Given the paucity of local police and especially Japanese troops, the freedom inherent in space and insularity, the virtual lack of any ideology motivating its leaders, and the economic pressures wartime conditions imposed, numerous guerrilla groups resembled warlord armies far more than the patriotic resistance forces they usually purported to be.

When the U.S. Army evacuated the islands, they left behind American and Filipino officers with authority to organize guerrillas in various regions, and an estimated 839,000 men were listed as being in such units throughout the course of the war, although in May 1945 the existing forces comprised about 100,000. By contrast, Japanese troops numbered only 64,000 at the beginning of 1942, a figure that quadrupled in 1944 only because of the imminent American invasion. But nine-tenths of these nominal guerrillas existed only on the vast island of Luzon, which included Manila and key towns, making the nature of the resistance there most important. From the very inception of their efforts, the Americans found themselves embroiled in a Byzantine world of rivalry, deceptions, intrigue, and chicanery that deprived the guerrillas of significant military value but gave them a crucial political function in containing the only political guerrilla movement that existed, the Hukbalahap (People's Anti-Japanese Army), or Huks, which was created in March 1942.

Senior American officers believed that the Huks "will probably remain a difficult problem during reoccupation and possibly afterwards," a perception that wholly defined their relations with them.[19] For the guerrilla groups existed principally where the Japanese presence, consistent with the latter's desire to avoid wasting forces, was negligible or nonexistent, and the Japanese had scant incentive to chase down most of them. There were undoubtedly guerrilla forces that inflicted some damage upon the Japanese, but the best organized of them concentrated on gathering intelligence and waiting for a full-scale U.S. invasion rather than on fighting, for which they had insufficient equipment. The backbone of the Japanese presence was the Filipino puppet regime, which the U.S.-sponsored and -supplied guerrillas largely ignored, save when they claimed its property.

There was a surrealistic quality to most of the guerrilla groups with whom the well-informed Americans cooperated. Guerrilla bands existed in almost every province, but there were many dozens, possibly hundreds of them, and each ultimately was an autonomous entity; save on the fairly marginal island of Panay, attempts to get them to cooperate failed and revealed most to be little more than private armies out for booty and survival. As the U.S. intelligence described it in a representative assessment, "Only a few were active. Mixed with these were a large number of bandits. . . ."[20] Lacking money and supplies, many simply took it from the people "and wantonly raped the countryside. For a time all of the groups were discredited by the people."[21] Quite typical was an OSS report describing one of the more enterprising guerrilla groups as "exploited by high ranking army officers and politicians, who made personal profits at the expense of the people. The people were held under control by terror tactics and anyone opposing the army was eliminated."[22]

Many fought each other to establish their jurisdiction over territory and resources, and mutual executions of leaders, including some American officers sucked into the vortex of constant intrigues, were not uncommon. Once one band defeated another, men on the losing side sometimes switched allegiance to Japan. "Because it was getting to be a vicious circle," senior U.S. officers outside the islands occasionally dissolved whole regional organizations and attempted (generally in vain) to reconstruct them. Morale was usually poor, and ". . . crumbles every time the Japanese start a campaign in each particular area." The Japanese often saved themselves the trouble of fighting by offering amnesties, which many guerrillas accepted, and they had little difficulty planting informants where they needed them. But they had little incentive to attack many guerrilla units because, as American intelligence reports described, in some areas "fighting between units over matters of area command almost exceeds any fighting against the Japanese," and in central Luzon one major group that U.S. officers commanded had as "the main mission of the unit . . . fighting the communistic HUKBALAJAPS. . . ."[23]

It was for such diverse reasons as these that many more men purportedly joined the guerrillas than could be counted when the war ended. Some units existed on paper only, their ostensible numbers being far greater than the arms they possessed, and training was usually poor or nonexistent. When pressed by the Japanese and their collaborators on one side or the so-called guerrillas on the other, countless persons pretended to comply with the demands of each and sought to survive as best they could. The guerrilla phenomenon, to a significant degree, was a microcosm of Filipino politics with its personal fiefdoms, and many who cooperated with the Japanese

could in perfectly good faith after the war claim also to have worked intimately with the guerrillas—but for their own accounts, because generally
there was no fundamental conflict between the two sides. The dominant
guerrilla organizations that the U.S. endorsed failed to politicize the people
(which they had neither the desire nor the capacity to do), had no social
content, and their resistance was far more nominal than real. The Filipino
guerrilla movement was therefore quite unique during World War Two,
perhaps in the entire world, and its principal utility to the Americans and
the Filipino elite was that its armed men might be able for some crucial
months at the war's end to plug the temporary political vacuum that
wartime collaboration had produced and that they all feared the Huks
might otherwise fill.

Given its formidable prewar social and economic problems, and the spontaneous violence of the rural poor and the peasants in some of the most
oppressed regions at the war's inception, the Philippines before 1945 was at
least as promising as Indochina as a nation in which the Communists could
flourish. Their failure to do so cannot be wholly attributed to the anti-
radical guerrillas or the Japanese, but reflected also, to a crucial degree, the
nature of the Communist party itself.

Central Luzon itself had begun to experience a major transformation of
its agricultural economy even before the First World War. As in both
China and Vietnam, the changes were but another case of the breakdown
in the traditional socially and economically insulating tenant-landlord relationship as a consequence of new crops and modernization, the shifting
ownership of land from more patronizing, sometimes kin-related landlords
to commercially motivated proprietors, and the impact of fluctuating prices
and the world market on the economic conditions and frequently declining
real income of tenants. The central Luzon sugar industry, with its relatively
high capital investment and demand for seasonal hired labor only, had
begun to supplement and even replace rice production during and after
World War One, attracting land speculators with it. At the same time, the
population pressure on the available land rose greatly, and there was a
widely felt land hunger. The great bulk of the peasants were now merely
tenants, more and more overwhelmed with excessive rents and debts that
forced many of them off the soil, and the region had the highest tenancy
rates in the Philippines. With the insecurity of seasonal work for those
dependent on sugar and with growing poverty there came also peasant
union organizations that outside radical leaders initiated but which nevertheless remained very much under the control of *barrio*—village—activists.
Indeed, frequent and increasingly large peasant protests usually mobilized
far greater numbers of people than actually joined organizations, and when

all the peasant or rural labor protests throughout the Philippines during the 1930s are added together, one sees that nearly two-thirds of them were located in four central Luzon provinces with less than one-tenth of the nation's population.[24]

### The Hukbalahap

The Huk guerrilla movement prospered in this still-unique central Luzon seedbed of peasant radicalism and protest, where it was principally concentrated, but its threat to the Americans and the Filipino elite came less from its actual numbers at any given time than the fact that it alone had a programmatic basis for expansion elsewhere. Even before the Hukbalahap was formed in March 1942, peasants on their own volition had created local armed bodies, at least partially to defend themselves against predatory bandits who moved into the sudden administrative vacuum, and some embarked upon what the Communists (PKP) deplored as leftist extremism. In December 1941 the PKP had called for the creation of a guerrilla force based on a united front, but before the March 1942 meeting some of its most important leaders were arrested; the Huks' founders were really a coalition of peasant activists, many of whom had been in prewar peasant organizations, with sharply differing conceptions of what the main purpose of the movement should be. The PKP was very important in the Huks, but as with every other genuine mass association in Asia, it was very far from comprising the whole of it. Both before and after 1942, the PKP was essentially an urban party and, as we shall see, not completely in control of the Huks because it was itself far from united. While a far higher degree of coordination existed among the Huk groups than among the other guerrilla forces, the Huks contained significant local components emerging from much older peasant groups. Operating in a highly decentralized context, they often decided for themselves how and when to act. Their regional commands were largely autonomous. In a few cases of "anarchistic" behavior or corruption tantamount to banditry, local groups were disciplined and some of their leaders killed.[25] But the peasants who supported the Huks wanted social change, and while the PKP was nominally for reforms also, like all disciplined Communist parties it placed a higher priority on establishing a united front against fascism. It therefore included patriotic landowners and bourgeois elements, and the question of the united front and the nature of the PKP leadership was gravely to trouble the Left in Philippines politics for years.

Meanwhile, the Huks emerged as the best single guerrilla army, and with its social objectives and active political-education program it also became a major, often decisive political force in the large regions within which it operated. By September 1944 it comprised about 10,000 regular forces organized into semi-independent squadrons of 80 to 200 men, plus 10,000 more trained men in reserves and over 10,000 others. Its mass base of committed supporters in the seven provinces in which it was most active numbered at least 500,000. Its principal problem was that it had arms sufficient for only about 5,000 men. But unlike the other guerrilla groups, it was also much more aggressive in confronting Japanese troops or the Philippines Constabulary working with them. It did not collaborate with the other nominally U.S.-controlled guerrillas, with whom it fought repeatedly, and the Americans in charge of such matters ostracized the Huks, especially after 1943, and at no time gave them arms or supplies. Although the Huks were not large in relation to all other guerrilla forces combined, they were far more stable and cohesive than any of them and growing quickly, so that their size was not an adequate indication of their real or potential power. And while they were still restricted to central Luzon, they were well positioned to expand to the rest of Luzon, the nation's largest and most important island, if permitted to operate freely.

As the war ended, the Huk movement had to confront a variety of formidable problems that the Americans and their local allies created, but these were no greater than the challenges facing other Communist parties in Asia that were relatively far weaker militarily and organizationally but yet were to accomplish a great deal more, or even, as in the Vietnamese case, come to power. Without minimizing the significance of externally imposed difficulties, the Huks' main failures resulted principally from the nature of the PKP and the deep divisions within it during the war and thereafter.

A small, highly educated, radicalized segment of the intelligentsia, some of them from well-known elite families, founded the PKP in 1930; one of the founders, Vicente Lava (whose family held key Party posts for decades), possessed a Ph.D. from Columbia University. Given its social composition, and its complete loyalty to whatever line Moscow proclaimed, it was inevitable that the PKP at first stress urban activity and a united front-policy toward "all strata." In December 1941 its program "pledge[d] loyalty" to the United States and its local government.[26] But arrests decimated the PKP's city organization and by early 1942 it had no option but to sacrifice its urban emphasis, at least temporarily, and the urban Party membership declined during the war. Most PKP members working among the Huks in crucial positions were not equipped to propagate Party ideology and they quickly became preoccupied with the imperatives of living in the countryside and organizing resistance—in a word, the environment changed them far more than they altered the deep-seated desires of the peasants supporting the Huks.

With its rigid line and lack of control over its followers, the PKP thus confronted many of the same dilemmas that were bedeviling both the Chinese and the Vietnamese Communists at the same time. The united-front strategy was the first PKP policy to remain largely frozen in "the blueprint stage," as the PKP commander of the Huks, Luis Taruc, later described it.[27] The PKP wanted peasants and landlords to agree on the harvest division, confiscating only the crops of collaborators. But peasants generally saw the matter differently and many preferred to settle prewar grievances while they were in the position to do so. They also largely ignored the PKP's urging that their organizations abandon their direct political control of many villages and share power with landlords. In the spring of 1943 the PKP ordered the Huks to decentralize even further and to go on the defensive after a Japanese offensive battered the guerrillas, but most units, and even Taruc himself, ignored the Party's instructions and it was eventually compelled to retract them.

In brief, the PKP top hierarchy failed to control the Hukbalahap rank-and-file's political and military actions, and the typical Party activist was either incapable or unwilling—or both—to impose its official line. Many PKP members regarded the highly educated professors and those around them as aloof and "cliquish"; this remoteness, plus their desire to implement Moscow's positions strictly, caused the nominal leaders to lose contact with the masses.[28] They lacked a keen appreciation of Filipino rural life, its constraints as well as its possibilities, and their belief even in 1945 that a party with an extremely centralized organizational theory could impose its program in a highly decentralized context became its recipe for the future—and for failure. As a consequence, the Communists emerged from the war divided, confused, and defensive.

### The United States Restores the Old Order

The American army under MacArthur, by contrast, knew precisely what it wanted and resolved no later than 1943 to disarm the Huks and eliminate them as a potential threat to the existing collaborationist government and whatever successor it might designate to replace it. It assigned whatever violence was essential to accomplish this task to guerrilla groups under U.S. influence or control, all of whom had fought the Japanese (if at all!) far less energetically than they did the Huks. The Americans had kept them in reserve mainly for this function.

At the end of December 1944 the U.S. offensive reached central Luzon and the Huks came out in full strength against the Japanese army, capturing or merely walking into many towns and establishing united-front people's councils in most of them—although in the *barrios* the local Huks made few such concessions. Three provinces elected or proclaimed PKP leaders as governors. But as the Americans entered these areas, they appointed their own civilian administrations and removed all Huk-supported officials. Above all, they sought to disarm as many as possible. This sometimes occurred at gunpoint, but also by promising to supply new arms later if old guns were handed in immediately, or by innumerable outright arrests. On February 7, 1945, in the presence of U.S. officers, a guerrilla group arrested a Huk squadron passing through Malolos, and that night massacred at least 109 of them. They then designated the Filipino in charge of the murder as mayor. Exposed as they were, the Huk leadership naively expected the Americans to tolerate them even though there was nothing in the Americans' previous words or actions to sustain such illusions, thus enabling the U.S. forces and their local allies to quickly and easily neutralize a crucial section of the Huks. In late February, U.S. counterintelligence agents arrested Taruc and key members of the Huk general command, put them in solitary confinement, then released them twenty-two days later when at least 30,000 angry peasants descended on the town where they were imprisoned. This repressive general strategy, which MacArthur had formulated and was never challenged in Washington, was not a haphazard decision but reflected a calculated and consistently applied long-term policy.

Over the subsequent months the stunned Huks lost most of their weapons, and the intimidation of peasants and their leaders in rural areas mounted greatly. Because of what Taruc later described as "our united front frame of mind," which persisted until the war with Japan ended only because it was the Soviet policy for all Communist parties, they had not prepared the peasants for reality.[29] The PKP had badly misled them and failed at this crucial juncture in ways that neither the Vietnamese or Chinese Communists ever did. In addition to economic deprivation, the peasants faced far greater political repression than before the war.

Anticipating the proclamation of independence on July 4, 1946, MacArthur sought to reconstruct postwar Filipino politics to correspond well with U.S. interests. By necessity, this meant not penalizing collaborators, except for a few symbolic cases, thereby saving much of the prewar ruling class from political oblivion. Quezon had died during the war, and MacArthur disliked his successor, Sergio Osmeña, who was a typical power-hungry regional political chief. Manuel A. Roxas in prewar days had been president of the Senate and Quezon's consummately ambitious chief rival, as well as a personal friend of MacArthur and other American generals. During the war he had collaborated with the Japanese in the same reluctant, essentially self-serving way as many of his peers, and he was interned when the U.S. forces captured Manila. On April 18, 1945, Roxas was "liberated" from prison but those arrested with him remained a while longer. In this compromised status Roxas became the most pliable important political personality for the Americans to rely upon. "Roxas has indicated by word and deed," the U.S. high commissioner reported, "his desire to follow American pattern of government and retain closest ties with us in all matters. . . ."[30] His brigadier generalship in the army was returned to him, and he was fully exonerated. Every political careerist and member of the elite saw him as both a winner and as someone who would treat collaborators with the utmost tolerance while cracking down even more firmly on the Huks, and with such endorsements he was easily elected in April 1946 to be the new nation's first president. It was Roxas who was to grant amnesty to all accused collaborators, and to wipe the slate clean for the Japanese occupation period. Now the essential prewar political, economic, and social structure was seemingly restored, with the American role almost as pervasive as under colonialism

But the acute social and economic problems of one of the world's poorest nations remained unchanged, and no political means for resolving them existed.

## World War Two in Asia

Any assessment of the principal causes of change in war-torn Asia during World War Two, the immense forces and factors that produced both the Chinese and Vietnamese revolutions, or the absence of a comparable upheaval in the Philippines, must by necessity begin with Japan's impact and objectives. And while specialists have disputed the question of how and why the two revolutions took place, the subject can to be placed in an indispensable perspective simply by speculating as to what might have occurred in East Asia after the defeat of the colonial powers in Europe if Japan had chosen not to move into the resulting immense vacuum, or if it had not attacked North China in 1937.

When put this way, the answer is reasonably uncontroversial; the colonial structures would have emerged weakened but also intact and capable of surviving at least somewhat longer, and China would most likely have remained divided indefinitely among rival warlord-dominated regions; but the economies and social structures of much of East Asia would not have experienced the great catastrophes that produced radicalized peasant populations and traumatized the existing urban societies. It is simply inconceivable in such a context that there would have been a quantum expansion of the Communist parties and armies—or the revolutions that brought them to power so quickly. Such a conclusion in no way implies that there would otherwise have been no significant challenges to the existing colonial structures or the precarious Chinese political order—on the contrary, they were almost certain to occur—but these would would have been devoid of the great force the Communists now were helping to guide against moribund systems, and certainly a far cry from the overwhelming, decisive transformations that took place. But by definition, expansion was meaningless for the Japanese unless they exploited their conquered territory ruthlessly, which they proceeded to do in ways that generated maximum disorder and suffering, thereby eroding the victimized nations' social, class, and economic organizations and greatly increasing all the inherited prewar tensions they contained. In this fundamental sense, Asia's revolutions and political changes were integral to the Japanese war, becoming by far its most enduring and significant legacy.

After Japan embarked upon its campaign of aggression and created the general framework which made the revolutions and crises that followed possible for the first time, the factors leading to Communist victories or, as in the case of the Philippines, defeat, became crucial, and I attach great importance to all of them. But rather than weighting them, it is preferable simply to avert the inconclusive debates over such questions and include all the interacting causes and forces that both in reality and for purposes of analysis seem important, if not equally decisive. Fathoming the full texture of the vast wartime experiences, in any case, defies monocausal or simple speculations, and those who have attempted it have committed faults of omission that more than counterbalance the risks of pluralistic explanations, which also escape a certain exactitude that some find comforting, others schematic .

Obviously, the nature of the regimes in place that were compelled to cope with problems that the war generated was crucial, and in those parts of China that the Japanese army did not reach, they were decisive. Japan cannot be held responsible in any way for creating the Kuomintang's calamitous economic or military policies but only for the context in which they were enacted. Social and political systems everywhere can, and do, tolerate a degree of political turpitude and the protection of factional power and control during normal times without capsizing, and corruption is integral to the political processes of innumerable developed and Third World nations. Indeed, as long as there are no serious challenges, it can serve as an integrative force and co-opt a regime's potential rivals. But when wartime scarcities exist, the institutional price of such exploitation of the political structure can prove decisive when the social and human impact of long wars tests to the limit a population's capacity to tolerate avoidable suffering. Both the Kuomintang and French-Japanese wartime administrations' military and economic policies greatly compounded and extended their populations' suffering, and the people could easily see the inequalities and injustices that prevailed while they were on or over the brink of starvation.

These policies profoundly affected the small but relatively crucial urban sectors, whose ways of life were totally transformed in both nations so that their traditional commitment to preserving the status quo disintegrated in the process. Urban populations, both because of their previous levels of consumption and relative expectations, including even those who were still better off than the peasantry, were less able and willing to absorb the destitution that the war itself and the status quo's policies and practices inflicted upon them so unnecessarily. In China this urban experience and reaction became crucial, and in Vietnam it meant that what was initially a peasant-backed rebellion for physical survival gained vital reinforcement from urban forces, which subsequently provided it with essential administrative talents. In the Philippines, corruption was common also, but while there was much misery and deprivation, and significant human losses, there were no comparable food catastrophes for its rulers to cope with.

Japanese aggression's interaction with venal, self-serving regimes created varying degrees of inflation that greatly altered the urban class structures and thereby radicalized a crucial part of them, helping (along with the merciless pillaging of agriculture) to produce episodes of great famine in two nations and widespread hunger in all of them for much of the war, along with huge population migrations in China and Vietnam. The ensuing transformation of the attitudes of a sufficient proportion of the rural and urban masses made the delegitimization of the values and pretensions of traditional societies and ruling orders sufficiently far-reaching to allow mass mobilization, both under Communist leadership and independently of it, to occur.

Protracted war with such profound social and economic consequences, drawn out in large part because Japan's power proved inadequate to achieve total military victories quickly in the vast spaces it encountered, radically altered the war's significance from that of a struggle between nations' conventional armies into, ultimately, a test of the ability of Asia's traditional political and social systems to endure in the face of civil or anticolonial wars that eventually posed far greater threats to their continuity than Japan's army. As the war's effects increasingly swept up the masses and compelled them to relate to the reality about them, both to survive and to preclude more trauma like it in the future, and as Japan's defeat created both a huge political and administrative void, revolution in Asia became imminently possible. Only the Filipino status quo was to survive this upheaval, but in a seriously impaired form that was to define the history of that nation's next half century.

This galvanization of vast numbers of people, with its articulation of their feelings and opinions, was the war's principal political consequence, and it was to this mass mood that the Communist parties responded. War alone made them serious political forces with great possibilities rather than an isolated and eventually manageable opposition, one no more threatening, say, than many warlords in China. But the Communists' fundamental dilemma was that this metamorphosis of the people and creation of a radical potential was taking place autonomously over vast decentralized spaces and as a response to social and economic realities, and only very incidentally as a result of the parties' activities and education, which according to their scriptures also had a vital role to play.

The disjunction between the parties' highly elitist organizational theory and existing reality was always a profoundly disturbing challenge to them, for in Leninism they had neither a description or theory of actuality to help guide them. In China and Vietnam, and even to a degree in the Philippines, the revolutionary process was the outcome of the collapse of the traditional social orders immeasurably more than of conscious, calculated efforts at overthrowing them, and the basic processes leading to disintegration were quite beyond the ability of Communists to either initiate or arrest. Revolutionary mobilization, for practical purposes, often meant merely moving into a vacuum that war's interaction with moribund societies had created, even though each party was later to claim that its foresight and acumen allowed it to make decisive choices and that the road to power was not so very narrowly circumscribed for it—in effect, that it could and did play an indispensable leadership role. But often they failed even to predict such vast changes because their analytic equipment for doing so was too schematic and deductive, and they chased after and sought to capture great historical epics rather than causing them to occur at their initial crucial stages. To fail to respond to the opportunities available as well as the constraints real choices imposed was to abandon the imminent opportunity to seize power, though the absolutely essential ability to define what these choices really consisted of also demanded a vital degree of crucial acuity—and here the PKP showed itself far less able than the two successful Asian Communist parties.

All three Communist parties were the creations of the radicalized intelligentsia, with their explicit confidence in their own ability to guide the people and later to administer their nations. But since they had to seize the moment, both the Chinese and Vietnamese parties accommodated, at least momentarily, to the real social dynamics transforming their nations, and ultimately they were to become mass parties, but based on organizational doctrines and leadership structures that made no permanent concessions to their vast size as popular movements. There was simply no place in Leninist theory for systematized feedback from the masses as an integral aspect of a party's decision-making process. As inheritors of a Bolshevik organizational doctrine that Lenin had devised in response to czarist political repression at the turn of this century and had defended against Luxemburg and other detractors, their own instinctive elitist pretensions (rooted in their class origins) found the initial centralizing rationale highly congenial, and they returned to it as soon as feasible, thereby creating a huge disjunction between the parties' capricious practice, its mass character, and elitist theory. If in the end they relied on the rule of self-perpetuating politburos or, as under Mao, personality cults for which no conceivable doctrinal justification ever existed in Leninist texts, what is most important was that the men who controlled Communist parties always felt uncomfortable with the mass pressures and movements they were often temporarily forced to heed.

The peasantry as a social and ideological force was ranked in importance below the working class in the Leninist hierarchy, and the proletariat was to impose its leadership over the tillers of soil, even though in Asia there was no genuine proletariat of any consequence and the small parties' memberships designated themselves as serving that decisive class function. Meanwhile, each party allowed those tactics likely to advance it on the road to power to determine its immediate actions, and this often meant acceding to the masses' priorities when agrarian issues involving land and administrative matters were concerned. The Chinese and Vietnamese parties often led by following, generally cajoling and pushing the peasants toward united-front strategies over the years but ultimately making sufficient concessions to pressures from the poorer rural folk to keep them firmly on their side during the crucial periods of the struggle for power. Afterward, they rightly calculated, when there were no challenges from enemies from without and within, they could rectify those deviations from their basic objectives and strategy that had been expedient. In practice, though, their repeated emphasis on the acquisition of power and the tactics essential for it took on a life of its own, and earlier blueprints were blurred or disappeared as the functional consolidation of the successes attained until then increasingly dominated their actions. Both triumphant parties quickly learned that if they sought total control of the forces and directions of change that the masses produced, they could very well fail in the attempt, and that popular pressures might continue without them in forms wholly beyond their influence. They emerged as uncontested leaders precisely because they knew when and how to accommodate to the peoples' demands—in a word, to follow the masses in order later to lead them.

Such flexibility—and success—on the part of the Chinese and Vietnamese parties was possible to some extent because both became essentially independent of Moscow's positions on a variety of issues, the united front being the most important among them. The Chinese party long preceded the Vietnamese in this regard, but notwithstanding certain gestures in the direction of the Comintern, the Vietnamese party basically also defined its own agenda. The latter's united-front strategy after August 1945 was the autonomously generated result of its realization that it had obtained power only as a minuscule party and that given the imperative administrative challenges involved in running a state, and the imminence of a French return, it had also to evoke patriotism in order to consolidate a far larger following and to exploit a transitory national consensus that the

Communists' success in ending the famine warranted their continuing in power.

The dominant Filipino Communist leaders were unique in seeking to conform both psychologically and functionally to the prevalent Soviet line, and they ignored, even more than the Chinese and Vietnamese parties, the dangers confronting them, the mood of the people who were still a part of the mass movement they had nominally led, and the threat of their ortho-doxy to their own internal unity. Those who wished to adapt and concen-trate upon the diffuse but promising reality in the countryside, who ques-tioned the viability of urban activity dependent on running candidates for office, or who were skeptical about giving up their arms, were bypassed at a critical moment of opportunity—one that their later efforts could not re-create. The Filipino Communists were therefore to suffer major strategic defeats as the war ended, and later to split both informally and then in fact.

World War Two caused the breakdown of the stabilizing influences and institutions of China, Vietnam, and the Philippines, as well as elsewhere, and the dominant social classes and strata, their economic power, and the military and political administrative systems essential to their preservation were in varying degrees of disarray, and often utterly shattered. The new mutations that emerged from these great transformations varied in each country, but altogether unprecedented factors existed in all of them in the form of radicalized, activist populations backed by military forces able to confront seriously the vestiges of the traditional social and political systems.

The war produced the first fundamental crisis in Asian politics and power in this century, and ultimately it was to become the single most important, though very far from exclusive, consequence of the terrible global conflagration—encompassing a vast area and much of the world's population. These repercussions endured far longer and proved vastly more challenging to the victors than developments in Europe or elsewhere. What was unique about Asia's upheaval was that the principal political legacy of the First World War in the form of the Soviet Union, even though its efforts to dominate the European Communist parties were vastly more intensive and vital to its definition of its basic interests, now sought also to control events in Asia.

But the two successful Asian revolutions refused in practice, though not formally until much later, to accept Soviet guidance, and this independence proved in due course to be the hallmark of their domestic and foreign poli-cies as well as the precondition for their success. Notwithstanding the deeply irrational anxiety among leaders of the capitalist world that the Soviet role was itself the inspiration of radical challenges to their power, and designed to be subversive, in reality Stalin was far more an advocate of prudence and caution than anything else. He attempted repeatedly to become a constraining, stabilizing factor in the policies of various Asian Communist parties. Seeking only to protect the USSR's own national stake in maintaining the status quo, often for purely geopolitical reasons that made, say, a weak Chinese neighbor under the Kuomintang preferable to a strong one under nominal Marxist-Leninists, or fearing the consequences of affairs in Asia to its far higher priorities in Europe, the Soviet leaders, by their very existence, helped to retard and inhibit various local Asian parties. If its constraining advice was not necessarily a decisive factor in protecting the existing fragile colonies from much greater challenges, the cautious nature of its role remains an absolutely essential fact whose significance can be neither under- or overestimated, but must be judged in the context of all the factors changing each Asian nation during and after World War Two.

But stability could not be achieved in most of Asia, for the forces and conditions that the war unleashed made it unattainable, and any implicit or even formal accords between the United States, its allies, and the USSR became irrelevant to events in many places. The U.S. by itself was to prove unable to preserve the essence of the prewar social systems when it embarked upon that vast, costly enterprise over the coming decades. Ultimately, the Soviet Union had nothing to give or take back in that far greater part of Asia over which it had no influence. For the impact of the First World War on the European colonial powers, and the monumental consequences of its even more terrible sequel on both Europe and Asia, guaranteed that the emerging new global political, military, and economic context would produce continued crises—and wars.

# PART THREE

The United States,
Politics, and Warfare in a
Complex World,
1946–1991:
The Limits of Power

# CHAPTER 14

# Repression, Rebellion, and the Limits of Military Power, 1945–1953

The accumulated institutional, social, and ideological legacies that emerged from World War Two's great traumatic upheavals intersected after 1945 with a vastly more destructive military technology in the hands of American leaders who were eager not only to regulate Europe's affairs but also prepared to confront the crises of colonial societies and the development of yet new, gravely unsettling structural problems in much of the Third World. The result was the era erroneously dubbed the "Cold War" despite the presence of actual war in many parts of the world since 1945.

Explaining the sources of change over the past fifty years demands a serious appreciation of the intensity and depth of the Second World War's increasingly complex institutional and human processes and how they created basic social transformations and challenges both to traditionalist, capitalist nations and to Leninist parties and states. While the perils of apocalyptic assessments should not be minimized, this century's thinkers have for the most part erred far more on the side of optimism, regarding most social systems as rationally functioning, predictable structures and ignoring the central effects of all wars for the modern historical experience. The result has been that their predictions for the future have been inaccurate and their attempts to define rational, humane solutions to problems immeasurably less relevant than if they had adequately acknowledged the profoundly destabilizing historical and political dynamics that have bedeviled the entire century.

However delayed its effects or the complexity of the reasons for them, World War Two radicalized a historically unprecedented fraction of Europe's and Asia's masses and mobilized them into leftist political parties as well as armed organizations. And what with the fragility of the traditional political and social elites, and the fatal compromises so many of them made with diverse forms of fascism and reaction, the Left emerged from the war not only far more powerful but, more important, with a degree of nationalist legitimacy that most of its conservative rivals could no longer claim. That so many revolutionary leaders ultimately became unimaginative functionaries who had no intention of disobeying Stalin's strictures is essentially irrelevant: very few people in 1945 understood the many ways in which the USSR had become a major source of stability in the world. More important, it was the Communist parties' and the Resistance armies' abilities to take power rather than their intentions or Moscow's inhibitions that struck anti-Communist politicians as the crucial challenge facing them.

In many nations, conservatives perceived their task as not merely to block change but to destroy entirely the capacity of those on the Left to defy them in any manner, whether parliamentary or violent. There is a qualitative difference between simply creating obstacles to reform and embarking upon a counterrevolutionary campaign to remove the Left from political life entirely, especially when such curbs obtain active support from foreign powers. These efforts involved not just restoring discredited prewar traditional elites but also containing the monumental political effects of the war on many people as well as the prewar socioeconomic order that had sustained the status quo. The suppression of domestic opposition and elimination of citizens' human and civil rights fundamentally redefines the parameters of the political processes within a society, thereby profoundly circumscribing the opposition parties' political choices in those nations experiencing repression or counterrevolution.

It was the existence of such draconian constraints and the loss of freedom in a number of nations after 1945 that created the principal problem confronting the Left and altered the political landscape in ways that made it appear an armed threat. In a context in which Communist parties loyal to the Soviet line would willingly have acquiesced to being integrated into a peaceful political milieu had they been allowed to do so, the stages by which docile parties were transformed into nominally revolutionary ones were complex and usually elliptical, varying from country to country, but all engendered certain common attributes: most important were the traditional ruling classes' elimination of the ability of Communist parties to continue along the essentially social democratic route that the USSR or their own inclinations preferred. In a word, conservative forces compelled leftists to act defensively or to face extinction, and what were described as revolutionary efforts in nations such as Greece and the Philippines actually began as unwilling and indecisive reactive responses on the part of hitherto unknown men and women.

But the very process of coping with such dilemmas revealed these Communist parties as essentially undisciplined entities often incapable of restraining many of their own members and a significant number of its leaders from taking independent action. In this context of pressure and threats, Communist parties emerged not as totally monolithic organizations under tight Soviet control but rather as complex, sometimes mercurial products of the wartime environment—the reaction of ordinary people to their rulers' outrages and injustices of the past, and the embodiment of their hopes for the future.

Obviously, in many nations Communists were sufficiently docile to spare Stalin anxieties, but where repression circumscribed the options, the fragility inherent in the social composition and hasty formation of a considerable number of parties emerged quite quickly, and these demand a far more nuanced understanding on our part of the character of Leninist organizations and the Left since 1945. From Stalin's viewpoint, all this was a challenge to his hegemony, because the very precariousness of discipline within so many Communist parties also helped greatly to lay the foundation for the subsequent collapse of the entire Soviet-led world system.

## The Greek Civil War:
## Communist Dilemmas and Soviet Hegemony

The repression confronting leftists in Greece after the Varkiza Agreement of February 1945, to refresh the reader, went from bad to worse and the peace accord was never implemented. At least 50,000 EAM supporters were imprisoned and interned during 1945, and beginning in July nearly 16,000 mainly pro-EAM civil servants were dismissed. But apart from intensifying state repression, village clans and families that had collaborated with or opposed the ELAS settled innumerable wartime scores and private political and personal feuds, and small political units now took advantage of official protection. The government did nothing to discourage them. "Up to the end of 1945. . . ," C. M. Woodhouse, the ablest official British expert wrote later, "so far as political labels could be attached to the perpetrators, the blame for bloodshed lay primarily on right-wing forces. . . ."[1]

By the summer of 1945, repression in rural areas was becoming organized and even more violent, contributing to the toll of nearly 1,300 assassinations that would take place by the following spring, and bands of former ELAS supporters began to flee to the mountains "to escape terrorism exercised by the extreme Right"—as a British parliamentary delegation phrased it.[2] But these groups were tiny—generally seven to ten men—and uncoordinated until a year later, equipped mainly with old arms, and as yet without support. Most of them dissolved during the autumn of 1945. Only in Macedonia, which the Athens regime had yet to occupy, did the ELAS remain dominant, largely because significant Slavo-Macedonian separatist forces affiliated with it ignored the KKE's policies entirely. They, especially, continued to complicate Zachiaridis's life for four more years.

It was not only an increasingly concerted policy of repression that was to push Greece to civil war. The economic situation also radicalized countless numbers of people throughout the nation, and to them only a totally new regime seemed a solution to the monumental corruption and venality that persisted unabated after the war ended. The Greek ruling class was surely among the most exploitive and reckless in the world, and foreigners repeatedly wrote about the immense contrast between the life-style of the Athens elite and that of the vast majority of the nation. Supplies sent by the United Nations Relief and Rehabilitation Administration (UNRRA) and others to relieve serious malnutrition and hunger largely entered the black market and enriched corrupt politicians and businessmen linked to them. No effort was made to hide the practice, and scarcely any to conceal its beneficiaries. The British government openly criticized such evils, regarding its aid as useless in this context—and quickly resolved to transfer the bill to Washington, which in turn had no illusions whatsoever about living conditions in Greece or the probity of its future clients.

A handful of speculators ruthlessly manipulated the distribution system at the war's end, producing rampant inflation, and both agricultural and industrial output in 1945 were about a third of prewar levels—reaching 85 and 70 percent, respectively, by the end of 1947. But rising output did not basically alter the economic crisis for the remainder of the decade because of tax avoidance among the rich, their collusion with the political leaders to monopolize imports for their mutual advantage, and gold speculation. More private gold flowed out of Greece by the end of 1946 than the value of all the aid it received from UNRRA. In 1947 the Greek standard of living was the lowest in Europe, well below prewar norms, and urban workers remained close to a subsistence level or below it into the 1950s, partially because of government policies and also because of the huge refugee problem—which I detail later. Rural Greece, by contrast, was better able to adapt to economic difficulties than the urban sector. Given the spiraling inflation that speculators sustained long after actual production ceased to justify scarcity prices, labor troubles were common.[3] All of these trends confirmed that the existing order was failing gravely and that the Left would reemerge in one form or another to replace it if parliamentary processes were permitted to operate.

But a clientelist and especially immoral ruling class prepared to risk its future by bleeding the masses economically is rarely prepared to observe parliamentary niceties. As discussed in chapter 11, the KKE's leadership and most of its members during the war itself emphasized the pursuit of a political route to power based principally on the urban world in which they dwelled, and given the economic realities in cities, such a strategy could be convincingly justified so long as repression did not become overwhelming—which was precisely what began to occur after 1945. Whatever Zachariadis's other faults, which proved decisive, his urban fixation cannot be dismissed as having initially been purely capricious.

Reinforcing the KKE's urban strategy was the condition of the army. Comprised of about 90,000 men at the end of 1946, most of the army's recruits were not soldiers by choice, and they also had hungry families. In the spring of 1944 about half of the exiled Greek army in the Middle East had mutinied in support of the EAM. Based on the Russian experience, the defection of a regime's army was an invitation to seize power, and while this surely reinforced Zachariadis's instincts, the presence of an extensive KKE organization within the legal armed forces was a fact that he understandably could not ignore. The army was seriously demoralized, and in June 1946, when there was a small mutiny and the authorities took steps to control rebellious soldiers and sailors, there were many more EAM and KKE members and sympathizers within the official armed forces than guerrillas outside it. The main KKE leadership sought to keep them there, forbidding the defection of its units or members to the guerrillas and eagerly preserving its cells within the government military as long as possible.

Zachariadis and the Politburo he dominated preferred to pursue an urban strategy within a legal framework, and began to purge much of its quite heterogeneous village organization, but they were less dogmatic on this count than on their stress on succeeding in cities by whatever means necessary and possible. Even though at the beginning of 1946 Soviet advisers urged them to follow the parliamentary route and not to go beyond creating purely self-defense paramilitary units, they decided to boycott the March 1946 elections. Zachariadis never ceased to be devoutly loyal to Stalin, but internal compulsions sometimes caused him to wobble. For the KKE's problems were too complicated simply to choose a policy at random, and Zachariadis's seemingly perpetual indecisiveness reflected intense pressures from sharply differing factions within the KKE, and he essentially began to pursue a dual strategy on the issue of violence. But for two years the KKE attempted to do the impossible and reconcile them, without applying any single option coherently.

The most compelling consideration weighing on the Communist leaders was the growing repression and the fact that by the summer of 1946 up to 2,700 fearful and often demoralized radicals had escaped to the mountains. If the KKE failed to unite and lead them, they would nonetheless remain there and continue to grow rapidly. Most of the population still lived in rural regions, and it was inconceivable for the Party to allow a significant military force based on those escaping repression to emerge (as appeared very likely to occur regardless of its decision) under any other group's auspices. During the latter half of 1945 the KKE hesitantly condoned the existence of strictly defensive groups, but it did not take a clear position in their favor until February 1946, and even then approved only their using the least force possible. While Zachariadis discouraged urban members from fleeing to safety, and most KKE members remained partial to legal methods, the ELAS's former leaders thought differently.[4]

In February 1946 the Politburo still strongly preferred an urban-based route of power, but basically it had yet to opt irreversibly for any strategy, whether peaceful or violent. Not until the following July, after continuous controversy within the Party itself, did it sanction organizing those in the mountains, equipped only with motley arms at this point, into a coherent structure under Markos Vafiadis, a former ELAS leader whom the Politburo always thoroughly mistrusted. But it circumscribed his forces in crucial ways and restricted them to taking only minimal defensive action. The Politburo had yet to waver from its urban fixation—a fact that later caused Vafiadis to complain bitterly that the Party neglected the rural-based armed struggle. While "the result," to quote from a careful assessment of the KKE's convoluted position, "was the inconsistent policy which led the Party stumbling into civil war without any clear idea of where it was going," it nonetheless is a fact that while it could never define a clear, unified strategy, the KKE also had to respond to those options its enemies forced upon it.[5]

While the Athens regime's intensifying suppression resolved the KKE's equivocation to some extent, the Party nonetheless remained doubt-ridden and subject to irreconcilable conflicting pressures throughout this period. The throttling of the opposition and the Left certainly provides the overriding framework within which one must assess the events in Greece; the repression persisted as the source of the domestic turmoil because it drove people to the mountains in desperation. After the United States proclaimed the Truman Doctrine in March 1947 and assumed the military and economic costs that Greece's venal rulers generated, the regime's incentive to find nonviolent, political solutions disappeared, and from the very beginning the U.S. consistently opposed a negotiated peace. The cycle of repression and responses to it increased the scale of violence and eliminated human and civil rights, but the successive rightist regimes clearly initiated the causal chain. Given their corruption and their inability to survive in a democratic political context, and the condition of the economy and the weakness of their army, repression was the Greek authorities' only recourse. American officials nominally supported the demand of basic liberties but at the very same time encouraged a policy of massive forced evacuations in the regions where the rebels were strongest, despite the fact that even a congressional committee that included Richard Nixon in January 1948 believed "that the evils which may result from such a sweeping abrogation of civil liberty may outweigh any possible usefulness. . . ."[6] Only a tenth of the guerrillas, the committee noted, were true Communists; others have claimed this proportion to be one-fifth, still a small minority. Those contemporaries who alleged that the remainder were impressed against their will ignored that they fought too well—indeed, far better than the demoralized official army—for such an argument to explain the reasons for the insurgents' size and successes.

The rising tide of reaction took many forms, from random assassinations to massive arrests and the exiling of tens of thousands to detention camps on the islands. By March 1947 the prison population was double its prewar size, and in excess of 16,000. At the beginning of July 1947 at least 14,000 persons were exiled to detention camps without trial, and the island of Makronisos alone held at least 30,000 people in its camps throughout this period. In December 1947, the government outlawed strikes and permitted the death penalty for violators. The regime admitted executing about 3,100 persons "legally" for all political reasons during 1946–49—though the true number of killings was much higher. At the end of 1947 the authorities arrested the editors of four Liberal journals, even though the Liberals provided critical support to the regime as a minority party within it, and martial law was declared in the Athens region in May 1948 and in the remainder of the country in November. But the fear of repression had long preceded legislation and drove countless persons either to silence or to acts of desperation. By August 1948 even U.S. Secretary of State George C. Marshall warned his embassy in Athens that while they were perfectly legal, "certain Grk policies (particularly regarding executions and strikes) have succeded [sic] in stigmatizing Grk government" and that moderating its draconian measures somewhat was desirable.[7]

Official figures on the magnitude of the terror naturally remain minimal approximations, but the government claimed that during a twenty-six-month period in 1947–49 it held 37,000 military courts-martial (in half of which the defendants were acquitted), to which one must add civil trials and deportations without legal processes. But in mid-1948 there remained about 48,000 semilegal armed right-wing local militia who imposed their brand of justice without any formalities whatsoever. They did the dirtiest work. In June 1950 the State Department claimed that 23,000 political prisoners existed—and this figure was probably too small. The number of deaths from all causes as a result of the civil war is impossible to estimate precisely; the Greek government first alleged 40,000, but Washington's figure was nearly twice that, and other calculations are about 158,000—or about 2 percent of the entire population.

The government's evacuation program, initiated in 1946 but which American advisers urged it to accelerate, affected the greatest number of people, moving them out of areas where guerrillas either functioned or could find material support and recruits. From 19,000 persons in January 1947 it reached 430,000 by the end of the year and at least 706,000 by May 1949—nearly one-fifth of the entire rural population. The vast majority of this group was removed against its will and, predictably, it immediately became apparent that many thousands preferred to stay near their homes as rebels than being deported to some unknown fate elsewhere. In the end, most of this immense mass of deportees landed in cities that already had deplorable living conditions and unemployment, thereby deepening the people's profound resentment against their political masters.[8]

### Armed Struggle and the Soviet Union

The Democratic Army proclaimed at the end of October 1946 could grow quickly in the Greek environment, the limits on it being the very finite quantities of arms—mainly captured and purchased domestically—it had available and the position of the KKE's leadership, the Soviet Union, and the neighboring Communist states of Yugoslavia, Bulgaria, and Albania. With a maximum of 3,000 members in the summer of 1946, it rose to anywhere between 6,000 to 13,500 by the end of the year. By the spring of 1947 it had increased from 13,000 to 18,000, and some have estimated it reached a peak of 23,000 in July 1947 and 26,000 at the end of the year. Doubt about such numbers exists because Athens authorities issued most of them with an eye to justifying larger U.S. military aid and exonerating their army's sustained demoralization and failures during most of the war; one objective observer estimates that as few as 45,000 or 50,000 people, principally from rural origins, served in the Democratic Army from 1946 to 1949, which would have made it considerably smaller at any given point than the above figures indicate. Others claim 100,000, at least. But whatever the case, in the autumn of 1946 it had large pockets in central and southern Greece, and even in Crete, but its main strength was in northern Macedonia and Thrace. By the end of 1947 about three-fifths of its forces were in the north—many of the latter being Slavo-Macedonians who desired autonomy or even independence from Athens. This concentration, to look ahead, was of significant, possibly decisive importance to the Democratic Army's ability to survive with support from across the borders, but it also was increasingly to turn the problem of Macedonian nationalism into an obstacle to a unified Left.

Meanwhile, the KKE leadership remained both disunited and ambivalent about the growing Democratic Army and the regime's closure of political options, and apart from those like Siantos who opposed armed struggle altogether, Zachariadis himself was uncertain how far to pursue it and thereby risk jeopardizing the political alternatives. To him, the existence of an insurgent army initially remained more a lever to pressure the regime into political negotiations than a means of conquering power. In February 1947 the Politburo agreed that the military effort was to receive the Party's main emphasis, but not to the exclusion of pursuing legal alternatives. Not until September did it endorse violence as the sole route to power, principally because by then it had no option to the Athens regime's refusal to consider a political arrangement that would have allowed the KKE and the entire Left to operate freely in the political arena. At the end of 1947, when Vafiadis proclaimed a provisional government of which he was the head, his forces controlled over three-quarters of Greece's territory against a demoralized, infiltrated army that had still to absorb the vast amount of American military aid and advisers that were beginning to arrive.[9]

The Soviet Union never recognized the rebel government in the mountains, nor did the Yugoslavs, Bulgarians, and Albanians, notwithstanding the fact that Greek irredentism and its bellicose territorial claims gave them a major incentive to replace the reactionary administration. Moscow's role until this point had been to counsel defensive moderation, but it essentially remained passive, even indifferent, toward the KKE's objectives, which were still in gestation and which it probably believed would be resolved politically and in a way that averted a crisis. In 1944, Stalin had assigned Greece to Britain's sphere of influence, and notwithstanding the mutual recriminations that followed the onset of the Cold War, his perception of the intensity of Anglo-American interests and motivations made him anxious to avoid any crisis over Greece. And while he did temporarily recall his ambassador to Athens in August 1946, Stalin distanced himself from affairs in that nation, and in autumn 1947 the KKE was not invited to join the newly created Cominform. At the end of 1946 the Soviets let the KKE know that they much preferred their pursuing legal efforts than relying upon armed efforts, which they insisted should remain defensive. Since it was clear from the KKE's dual policy before mid-1947 that it would gladly pursue a parliamentary course if permitted to do so, the Kremlin could safely remain fairly aloof toward the problems there. Stalin initially showed confidence in Zachariadis, but he failed to realize how divisions within the Party and repression were pressuring him to concede, however reluctantly, to a more aggressive strategy. Most important, by about mid-1947 the question of the Greek upheaval had become inextricably tangled with Stalin's relations with Tito, and the USSR from this time onward regarded events in Greece wholly in this context.

The Yugoslav connections with the KKE were exceedingly convoluted, in part because of the divisions within the KKE itself but also because of the tangled Macedonian issue and the fact that the increasingly important Macedonian units in the Democratic Army, who retained a distinct organization, were themselves split among various separatist tendencies (some oriented to Yugoslavia, more toward Bulgaria, others yet in different ways). While the Albanians aided the Democratic Army with some supplies and safe havens to escape from attacks, and the Bulgarians provided mainly safe havens, Yugoslav arms transfers—not to mention training—were considerably larger, even though they may have amounted to only about a tenth of the motley, wholly inadequate arms the rebels possessed. The Yugoslavs were sympathetic to Vafiadis's militant line but not to the other factions. They also retained designs, dating back to World War Two, for a nebulous, potentially vast south Balkan federation under their aegis, including a possible role for Greece, as a logical extension of the federal concept on which the Yugoslav state was formed.

At the end of 1947, this scheme became a clear challenge to Stalin's hegemony in eastern Europe when Tito convinced Georgi Dimitrov, head of Bulgaria's Communists, to support it. When Dimitrov publicly endorsed the principle at the end of January 1948, Stalin exploded and summoned the Yugoslavs and Bulgarians to the famous meetings in the Kremlin in the second week of February. The Bulgarians immediately capsized, but the Yugoslavs did not, and Stalin warned them of their folly and demanded that the Greek civil war, which he deemed an impossible challenge to Anglo-American regional interests, be "rolled up" or "folded up" as quickly as possible.[10] But when the Yugoslavs protested that they had not started the war in Greece and were loath to seal their frontier, Stalin regarded this too as a grave challenge, and the Greek question immediately became a test of discipline within the Cominform, from which, after some stormy months of recriminations and anathemas, Yugoslavia was expelled on June 28.

By no later than January 1948, the civil war evolved in the wholly dominant context of deep divisions among the nominal Communist nations and a profound schism within the KKE itself, not merely regarding the efficacy of armed struggle, which the Athens regime had pushed it into despite its hesitancy, but on how the Party should respond to the Tito-Stalin split. Tito was trapped in an unenviable position between Anglo-American and Soviet hostility, his very control over his nation at stake.

Until this point the war had gone badly for the Athens government's army, despite the fact that it grew to 147,000 better-trained men, a great deal of American equipment (including aviation and napalm) had much improved it, and over 450 Americans advised it at every level. It simply could not cope with Vafiadis's mobile small-unit tactics spread over a vast mountainous region. While the Democratic Army suffered losses, especially after Zachariadis increasingly pressured it after mid–1947 to shift to a static positional strategy that favored Athens's far superior conventional war resources, its enemies were poorly motivated and by the fall of 1948 their morale was lower than usual. The U.S. even then believed that the rebels numbered about 20,000 men and it expected the war to continue indefinitely as a classic guerrilla struggle. Such an assumption made sense because, it is absolutely crucial to recall, the insurgents could have continued fighting without Yugoslavia's aid or access to its territory, and they never came close to losing the war militarily. Even in September 1949 there were still 3,500 of them in Greece and about 16,000 in Albania and Bulgaria. Only in this context does what was to follow become comprehensible.

By the time the Tito-Stalin split reached the point of no return, the United States had become the Athens regime's principal economic and military supporter, and it literally could not have survived without Washington's money. The U.S. mission in Greece itself played a decisive role in every phase of Athens's activities, including the forced evacuation of people in regions where the Democratic Army operated and the suspension of the population's civil liberties. The use of American combat forces along with the military advisers remained a very serious possibility for much of this period. After March 1947, Washington's commitment to Greece was very much involved with the symbolism of the credibility of American power and its ability to suppress nominally Communist challenges to its omnipotent guidance of the events in a nation and, via the new domino theory elaborated at the same time, in the region bordering it. Many American experts fully comprehended that Greece's turmoil was not a premeditated Communist assault on a U.S. client but rather a series of incremental and often inconsistent responses to the repression of leftists—but they now considered this beside the point.

From this time on, whenever the credibility of American power became involved, discomforting facts or the behavior of its proxies were pushed aside for the larger symbolic issues involved, and Greece was the first postwar crisis in which Washington invoked both the domino theory and U.S. credibility as the basis of its policy. Under these circumstances, throughout 1947 and 1948 the U.S. opposed a negotiated end to the conflict, a solution that might have opened the way for the Left to return to politics but that would have prevented America from attaining the symbolic victory that was essential both to its containment doctrine and to establishing its credibility. Stalin therefore had either to capitulate entirely on the question of Greece or risk a serious confrontation in a region where Tito was likely to gain the most from the Democratic Army's victory; after the Berlin blockade began in June 1948, greatly raising the temperature in the Cold War, Stalin resolved to terminate the Greek conflict.

Tito himself was caught between the hammer of Stalin's new hostility—which took an economic as well as a threatening military form—and the inherited anvil of Anglo-American economic boycotts and ostracism. At first deeply committed to the Greek rebellion, he had no option but to take seriously Soviet threats to his survival, the inordinately complex rivalries over Macedonia that threatened to annex the southern part of Yugoslavia, and, above all, the manner in which the deeply divided KKE responded to his schism with the USSR. In June 1948 the KKE central committee, on Zachariadis's orders, secretly condemned Tito and unequivocally endorsed Stalin's policy, but since it needed continuing Yugoslav support, it waited until the following January to make its stance public. It is virtually certain that Tito was aware of it immediately, but in any case his diplomats shortly thereafter informed U.S. officials that Yugoslavia—implicitly in return for American aid—would "liquidate Greek situation as soon as possible" and that the USSR "was not now particularly interested in Greece."[11] Vafiadis had urged the Party to remain neutral in the dispute, and by this time his differences with Zachariadis on military strategy and politics had become overwhelming. Some have claimed that during the summer of 1948 Zachariadis attempted to assassinate Vafiadis, but on November 15, 1948, he fired him as head of the Democratic Army; the Party expelled him, along with other fractious senior leaders, two years later. Yugoslav aid to the Democratic Army began to decline after mid-1948, but Tito kept his borders open to it until July 1949.

Meanwhile, Stalin began to prepare the way for terminating a civil war that might otherwise have continued for a number of years longer and ended with a negotiated compromise, and possibly even a Communist victory. In March 1948 the Kremlin began to hint to the British that the Soviet position on Greece was becoming more accommodating, and in June both Bulgaria and Albania offered to resume diplomatic relations with the Athens regime, sharply reducing their aid to the guerrillas from this time forward. In July, Soviet diplomats proposed direct secret negotiations with Athens on all Greek and regional questions. By this time also the British had begun to convince Washington that they had an overriding mutual interest in supporting Tito, and after the beginning of 1949 speedy progress was made in persuading Tito to terminate his remaining support for the Greek rebels.

The USSR was now far more interested in destroying Tito than in sustaining the tattered illusion of its backing for Greek opposition to a reactionary, oppressive administration. Moreover, the Russians wanted to terminate the dangerous tensions that the Berlin blockade had generated after mid-1948, and in private talks with American diplomats during April 1949, they embarked on a peace offensive, one linked to a public international campaign, that threw in an offer to end the civil war in Greece as a bonus to a settlement on Berlin. But Washington saw no reason to negotiate on Greece, given Tito's precarious position as well as what they knew of the KKE's deep ambivalence and Stalin's utter indifference toward it since World War Two. Instead, it waited for victory to fall into its lap.

On July 10, 1949, Tito publicly responded to the Cominform economic blockade that was threatening his destruction by opening the door to Anglo-American aid, which he knew in principle would soon be forthcoming, and in return closed the borders to rebel forces—just as he had proposed to do a year earlier. But to reiterate an absolutely crucial point, had the KKE chosen to, the significant guerrilla remnants it still commanded could have fought on for years had the Bulgarians and Albanians been willing to assist them in small but crucial ways. On October 9, 1949, conforming to what Zachariadis described as "the Soviet proposals" and trying to blame Tito for the KKE's failures, the slavishly loyal Party leader proclaimed an end to armed struggle and a return to political activity—which, of course, was now wholly impossible.[12] In effect, he surrendered and virtually the entire remaining Communist leadership and activists, joining an estimated 50,000 to 100,000 others, went into exile.

The Greek rebellion, which from its inception had been a reluctant, forced response to a closed political world, oppression, and calamitous economic conditions, was now crushed between the Tito-Stalin conflict on one hand and the combined hostility and power of the Anglo-American and Athens governments on the other. By the time the civil war ended, the Greek regime and the social and political order it represented had not become less corrupt or more viable, or even decisively more powerful militarily. It was saved principally because the Soviet Union's priorities, first in recognizing Britain's hegemony and then in its obsessive desire to destroy Tito and all he stood for as an alternative to Stalinist control over national Communist parties, made the Greek radical movement an expendable pawn in Soviet foreign policy. Had there been no Bolshevik Revolution in 1917, or perchance had it subsequently been spared the phenomenon of Stalinism, then it is more than likely that the Left—in one form or another—would have taken power in Greece after World War Two. Instead, its people continued to experience oppression over two decades.

## The Philippines: Land, Repression, and Resistance

National governments in the Philippines have suffered from the bane of localism since early in this century, and successful politicians have invariably relied upon family-based and clientelist power blocs and island political bosses linked to dominant regional economic interests to weave together reciprocal alliances just strong enough to win power. Because such central governments have been no more stable or unified than the inherently fragile and often shifting, opportunistic elements that have been melded to construct them, massive pork barreling and outright corruption have always been the adhesive maintaining the fiction of a national political system.

The state-based accumulation of capital and economic power that culminated in the Marcos regime from 1966 to 1985 was merely the logic of a political structure with which the United States endowed the Philippines during the colonial period and which persists to this day.

When General Douglas MacArthur in April 1945 liberated Manuel Roxas from prison as an alleged collaborator and positioned him to become president of the newly independent republic, he understood that his docile client would operate according to the traditional invidious procedures of the Filipino political game and that Washington's influence would remain decisive, largely because America was to supply most of the patronage funds, provide the nation's export-led economy guaranteed markets for its agricultural commodities, and retain a privileged economic status as a condition of its granting independence. The option to Roxas, Sergio Osmeña, was simply a rival boss who also played the political game according to these cynical, time-proven rules, and many of his supporters were ready to switch their allegiances if there was gain to be made thereby. Roxas's victory was based upon a fragile alliance that played down the inconvenient issue of collaboration and included most of the factions that had supported Quezon during his long presidency before 1942. For Washington to have made an issue of collaboration would have meant challenging an indigenous power structure that it had created and with which its interests were intimately linked, and no important American conceived of a plausible alternative to the mixture of regionalized power and class domination that the Philippine society embodied.

The war's monumental economic effects, however, made the costs of such a venal political legacy all the more burdensome because it gravely distorted the task of reconstruction in what was normally a desperately poor country. It also accelerated the transformation of the land system and long-standing tenant-landlord relations, especially in central Luzon, where the Huk guerrilla movement had grown partly out of earlier peasant leagues that had sought to mitigate the impact of the increasingly commercial and impersonal land system in that region. But while the poorer peasantry in Luzon was economically worse off at the end of the war, organizationally it was far more potent thanks to the Huks and the network of groups that defended the peasants—of which the Huk movement was an extension. As we saw in the preceding chapter, the U.S. feared the Huks and attempted to disarm them, and both applied and encouraged a tough, repressive policy; but because the land issues that pitted them against landlords remained to traumatize the daily existences of toilers, radicalized peasants did not disappear.

The issue of the Huks immediately merged with the problem of land reform, the local political and power alliances, and, for those on the Left, the viability of congressional politics as opposed to a renewal of armed resistance. At the time that Japan surrendered, land and class grievances gave innumerable peasants an incentive to organize but not yet to rebel, since it was still fairly unclear what political options would emerge. Their military experiences and associations provided them a structure for rebellion that they lacked before the war, but they also had parallel peasant groups that potentially could play a part in a political process if it operated more fairly than the traditional system. Because local political authority, along with the police forces responsive to it alone, remained the near monopoly of the big landlord-political boss alliance that had controlled all aspects of life in so many areas, social conflicts over land immediately involved state power as well, and the employment of state police on behalf of village and town elites precipitated confrontations throughout central Luzon. Certainly, the crisis in the land system and the vestiges of the war made pressures for change both necessary and inevitable. In effect, what the radicalized peasantry—particularly in central Luzon—would do depended on their options for both economic and political reform and the extent of repression, and not even the Communist party's (PKP) initial efforts to become players in the existing political game could reverse the impact of decisions that remained overwhelmingly in the hands of the rich and the mighty.

Such social realities predetermined the Philippines' future in ways neither Roxas nor the PKP could control, bypassing them both. Given the grave wartime economic legacies and the continuous worsening of conditions for tenants, land reform quickly became a bitterly contested issue. At first many peasants joined the National Peasants Union (PKM), created by ex-Huks who had been peasant leaders even before the war; it demanded a 60–40 division of the crops in favor of the peasants, which it nominally obtained at the end of 1945, yet it also attempted to end reprisals against former Huks, who joined it and comprised most of its leaders. But it was one thing to negotiate a more equitable division, another to interpret and have local courts and police enforce it. When in September 1946, Roxas promulgated a tenancy act that provided for a 70–30 crop division between renter and landlord, it contained so many loopholes as to remain largely invalid; threats and violence between landlords and tenants, especially where landowners were unable to leave farming and go into other businesses, were much more likely to define daily experiences in much of rural Luzon.[13]

There was no way that legislation issued in Manila could override the de facto justice system in the *barrios* and towns. Bigger landlords hired armed men to protect their interests, and many private militias helped to make certain that all land-reform legislation remain null and void. Such special police reinforced the merger of private privilege with legal authority, which in many cases was itself but a traditional means by which the advantaged utilized municipal and village governments to become even richer. The guards on personal payrolls were particularly unsavory social misfits, far more prone than regular police to abusive violence, wanton destruction, looting, and rape. Although land reform, the role of private and public police, and repression quickly became the key grievances in central Luzon, throughout 1946 former Huks and PKM members increasingly emphasized repression and the special guards heavily responsible for it. Peasants had the economic compulsion to make demands, and landlords the material incentive to resist them. The result was mounting violence against peasant activists and former Huks—and incipient civil war throughout the region.

Arrests of peasant activists and the destruction of property mounted after mid-1945, principally because of the settling of wartime scores between rival guerrilla groups or collaborators who were now back in power, as well as personal grudges. Although the Huks formally disbanded when the war ended, and its leadership handed over a roster of the names of all of its members to the U.S. Army in the quixotic hope that they would receive veterans benefits, most former Huks, anxious about the culture of violence that permeated so many communities, hid their weapons and it did not take long for the victims to respond; by late 1945 some had begun to do so on their own initiative, both to protect themselves and also to retaliate against perpetrators of violence. In mid-1946 those who fled and created bands in forests or mountains probably numbered roughly 1,000. Apart from the threat of death, the magnitude of which we can only estimate crudely, the growing likelihood of imprisonment without charge or trial for long periods exacerbated the tension. During the months leading up to the April 1946 presidential election, as with all elections since then, the level of violence grew. The PKM claimed that in the two months after the election at least 500 of its members were killed, and three times that were jailed, tortured, or missing.

There can be no doubt that, given the PKP's opposition to armed conflict and a serious split among its leaders regarding the surrender of arms, the reestablishment of groups of former Huks was spontaneous; they were also still purely defensive. Such divisions left the Huk movement at this time profoundly uncertain as to its real goals and the extent to which, in the long run, it wanted to function through legal political mechanisms. The PKM and Huk leaders' ambivalence caused them to enter into negotiations with the new Roxas administration and to offer fewer concessions than the new president demanded but more than some rebels thought prudent. What they asked for was the strict enforcement of existing laws and the abolition of private guards; in return, they proposed to register, but not surrender, their arms. But even while the bargaining was proceeding, violence against the Huks mounted significantly, and on August 24, 1946, two of the three Huks dealing with the government received a warning that the regime was planning to murder them as they returned to Manila; but the third was not reached, and he was killed along with four companions. The Huk movement now went underground, repression against PKM leaders and members greatly increased, and the incipient civil war in central Luzon commenced in earnest and was to last for many years.[14]

### Ambivalent Rebels: The Huks and the Communists

Although massive repression resolved the vacillation among many peasants and former Huks, it was still unable to alter the PKP's emphasis on urban activity and a political united front after it had helped create the Democratic Alliance in July 1945, which it essentially controlled. The Alliance endorsed Osmeña for the presidency on the contrived grounds that he represented the nationalist bourgeoisie and was neither a collaborator nor a U.S. puppet. The PKP also ran Democratic Alliance candidates in the April 1946 elections in the hope of winning the balance of power, with which it could later extract political concessions from Osmeña. But Osmeña's politics and statements reflected his consummate ambition and in reality were scarcely different from those of Roxas; the Alliance, in essence, conformed to the traditional Filipino notion of creating coalitions to attain power. For purposes of justifying its position in Marxist terms, the PKP's leaders argued that they were really trying to create a united front. While such a coalition was then also the position of Communist parties in western Europe responsive to Soviet advice, there is no evidence whatsoever of direct Kremlin involvement in Philippine affairs at any point. If the PKP looked to any foreign party, it was to the Chinese, which via the overseas Chinese community did have a voice on its Politburo, but the Chinese practice, which simultaneously embodied both a united front as well as armed struggle, offered it no clear guidance either.

The PKP's policies reflected its own autonomous priorities as well as contradictions inherent in its class composition. Its leaders remained largely urban both in social origins and orientation, and not until mid-1948 did the majority of them acknowledge the futility of their position. Until then most of the minority among the Party heads who came out of the peasant movement related locally to the reemergent Huks both out of desire and necessity, and they were the men that Roxas's police most sought. But they did so on their own initiative, and some PKP rural members and former Huk officials who were not persecuted never joined the new peasant resistance. While the majority of the PKP's leaders opposed relying on armed struggle, the overwhelming bulk of its members, who numbered roughly 3,000 to 5,000 at the end of 1945, lived in rural areas— and only about 250 in the Manila region. For much of this crucial period in its history, the PKP leadership and rank and file, as in Greece, remained divided along urban-rural lines and pursued radically different strategies: the peasant sector responded overwhelmingly to the reality of repression even as the urban chiefs concentrated on political gamesmanship.

Ironically, in the April elections the Democratic Alliance won six seats, all in central Luzon, in the House of Representatives; in addition, one House and three Senate candidates who shared Alliance views were also elected. While this was not sufficient to parlay the Alliance into the role of a power broker, it was enough to block the passage of a constitutional amendment endorsing the Bell Act, which created free trade with the U.S. and made the Philippine economy heavily dependent on American imports. Its enactment was Washington's precondition for reconstruction aid, with which Roxas planned to consolidate his power. Roxas easily eliminated this obstacle by denying the ten their seats for wholly spurious reasons; the PKP's political line now became a chimera, but since the Party was still loath to admit this, it toiled on for two more years in the cities with very limited success. In 1947 it endorsed four senatorial candidates running on Roxas's ticket, and even in the November 1949 presidential elections it was able to get the Huk organization—of which by then it was a crucial part—to endorse the Nationalist, José Laurel.[15]

But it was in the countryside that the Philippines' principal social problems were located, and even today still largely remain. Over the objections of the PKP leadership, during the summer of 1946 the Huk movement was reconstituted in an ad hoc fashion, and its organization and coordination grew. And precisely because it was principally a response to repression, in effect, self-defense, the PKP's majority leadership considered it weak at its core and less promising than its urban options; in January 1947 it explicitly rejected violence. The PKP's political and legal emphasis, which relegated arms to a defensive expedient, was an ambiguous and quite unrealistic position that it shared with many other Communist parties at this time. For while its rural efforts unquestionably confronted the formidable obstacles and problems that the PKP's leaders identified, their chances of success in cities or via the ballot box remained far worse.

During 1947 the Huks faced the state's wrath and slowly grew in central Luzon, unable to expand significantly elsewhere because its organizers generally refused distant assignments. The Huks' positions therefore reflected the specific land, security, and political conditions prevailing in a crucial but nonetheless finite part of the country, a limit that was to prove fatal to it. For Manila's military and police forces never had to diffuse their resources over a vast terrain, which would have created the same insoluble difficulties they encountered after 1972 when they failed to defeat an initially far smaller but decentralized guerrilla movement. Repressive measures in central and parts of southern Luzon eliminated the Huks' political options, and in March 1948, coinciding with a government offensive, the PKM and the Huks were outlawed. But Roxas died of a heart attack the following month, and his successor, Elpidio Quirino, quickly sought to negotiate an amnesty with Luis Taruc, the Huk leader and a member of the PKP Politburo. The terms agreed upon were sharply disputed, but the barred

Democratic Alliance congressmen were offered their seats in Congress and over 600 Huks and PKM members were promised release from prisons; but the status of land reforms and the Huks' arms, among other contentious matters, were left unresolved, and local police and private guards continued their raids against peasant activists and especially those identified during the amnesty talks. The talks broke down, and fighting intensified.

With all of its possible illusions shattered, in May 1948 the PKP's leadership was replaced and it now endorsed armed struggle as its principal strategy. The Huks by this time had anywhere from 5,000 to 10,000 fighters, but they suffered from a severe shortage of weapons. The core of their immediate grievances remained local repression, which unlike land problems could not be postponed and involved immediate life-and-death issues. Before and after the November 1949 election, which was more corrupt than usual, violence flourished. With increasing conflict, in some regions the landlords moved out and relied upon their paid guards and employees to manage their estates, decreasing food output as well as raising the level of violence. Self-defense, the desire for revenge, and personal ties with other rebels caused Huk ranks to swell to from 11,000 to 15,000 poorly armed people between 1949 and early 1951, roughly equivalent to its optimum strength during World War Two.

Its rapid growth after 1949 produced a degree of premature optimism that misled a significant portion of the PKP and Huk leaders, who believed not only that the U.S. would not intervene sufficiently to save the unusually corrupt Quirino administration and its puppets but that peasants in other regions would also take up arms and impose an intolerable burden on the government's forces. Both assumptions proved incorrect. More important, however, was that, notwithstanding the elitist Leninist basis for their reasoning, there was indeed a certain validity in the older PKP's urban leaders' view that the limited goals of the peasants who supported the Huks provided a weak basis for embarking on a protracted war—which by 1951 the rebellion had to become if it was to have any hope at all for success. Virtually none of the dissidents, including the vast majority of PKP members, knew anything about Marxism-Leninism—in fact, a disturbing number of Huks liked Americans and even valued their employment-creating military installations. Whatever their elaborate schemes for liberated zones or military strategy, the PKP leadership was never able to implement them. Most of its new Politburo also suffered gravely from their backgrounds and latent illusions, for they insisted on remaining in Manila, and on October 18, 1950, the new American-supported secretary of defense, Ramón Magsaysay, arrested the PKP's general secretary, José Lava, two Politburo members, and over a hundred others.[16]

The peasants' first loyalties were to their families and communities, which were being oppressed and had to be defended. They believed in land reform and a moral economy in abstract terms, but concretely they wanted a larger share of the harvests. For a small core of doctrinally equipped leaders to attempt—as some of them wished to do—to even begin to educate such a diffuse force of essentially good sons and daughters of the earth required an infinitely better communications system than the Huks ever possessed. But while repression and abuse had outraged and driven peasants to resistance as a means of both social protest and physical survival, it is nonetheless also misleading to describe them as essentially moderate reformers rather than radicals and revolutionaries. What people are and can or will become is not often the reflection of their initial impulses and desires but rather of their complex interaction with particular social and economic conditions, as well as the choices available to them. Revolutions most often occur despite those involved in them, and revolutionaries are created, not born. How traditionally cautious men and women are transformed into enemies of a society reveals much about the very nature and process of social change and society in our time, and in the Philippines and Greece—and many other nations not considered here—events outstripped the desires of both leaders and followers at every stage of their history.

But the Huks, like any mass movement, also inevitably attracted a cross section of humanity, especially because the physically and economically harsh terrain made its power useful to those simply trying to mitigate life's hardships; conditions drove some to waver from the standards of high morality and discipline Communists nominally expected. Financial accountability was lax, and graft and thefts were not uncommon; excess use of force and random terror occurred more rarely, but there were incidents, including, as during World War Two, some cases of banditry that hurt other peasants—infractions that violated the basic rules for making successful rebellion. A considerable number of Huks wore magic amulets to protect themselves against being killed. The PKP leadership's relationship to the peasant rebellion, in essence, was far less one of guiding it as attempting to capture it and steer its exceedingly decentralized and unwieldy form in a different direction.

In the end, as in Greece, the Party's directorship changed far more than did the stolid but irrepressible masses, sacrificing much of its orthodox doctrines and strategy, and following much more than guiding people. The lesser PKP officers in the provinces understood very well the strengths and weaknesses of their constituency, as did Taruc, and they favored using this knowledge in an attempt to optimize the peasantry's very real power. But the PKP leadership by 1950 had begun to question Taruc's personal and political reliability, notwithstanding that it was itself unable to define and implement practical alternatives, or even to avoid arrest. The Huk movement reached its apex in 1951, when it had anywhere from 1 million to 2 million supporters in a relatively small part of the country, and then began to decline rapidly for a variety of reasons.

The divisions and inconsistencies within the PKP's highest ranks were surely crucial, as was the very nature of the vast majority of the Huk followers and of their grievances. Had the Huk movement been more ably led and somewhat more disciplined after mid-1950, when the U.S. in the aftermath of the Korean War became alarmed over Philippine trends and began to intervene there much more actively, it might have continued its struggle for many more years and possibly dominated major parts of the islands. With minor exceptions, the nation's social and economic conditions changed very little throughout this period and its politicians not only remained corrupt and self-serving but later became even worse. As it was, the U.S. accomplished so much with so little, very quickly, because the Huk movement's strengths in the *barrios* and among the masses, which allowed it to exist and grow notwithstanding the PKP's irrelevancies, were less enduring than its human weaknesses.

The U.S. gave Manila $700 million in the four years after independence in 1946, and most of it was squandered. When Washington quadrupled military aid between fiscal 1950 and 1951, it insisted that Magsaysay alone be put in charge of the aid, not only because it considered him substantially more honest than his peers but also because after October 1950 the CIA, through Colonel Edward Lansdale, managed him. Over the next five years the Philippines nominally received a half-billion dollars in economic and military assistance, but it was really far greater because much of the military aid was grossly undervalued surplus equipment. Even as the CIA mounted a successful effort to make Magsaysay president in November 1953, a number of crucial changes were made in the army. It became more mobile, which improved its military effectiveness, and better paid, making it less abusive and exploitive of peasants. Magsaysay himself was a consummately ambitious pork-barreling politician but also an effective communicator and much more popular with peasants than any of his predecessors. Above all, he disbanded the repressive private guards (who reemerged after the Huks disappeared) and promulgated amnesties for rank-and-file Huks. Minor social services such as credit facilities, clinics, the construction of wells, and even a purely ceremonial land-reform measure also had an effect. These ephemeral efforts lasted only long enough to attain the immediate political objective of defeating the Huks, for the nation's underlying problems remained in place to create new and deeper challenges to the venal ruling oligarchies later.

The cleverly conceived American intervention gathered momentum just at the PKP and Huk leadership were more disunited than usual, this time on how to respond to the rapid attrition within their ranks. Fatigue began to affect many important Huk veterans, who simply dropped out, as well as many of their supporters. Some surrendered, others were driven to remote areas and suffered terrible hardships, or were killed. The urban-based PKP chieftains opposed negotiations but instead advocated the contradictory policies of both protracted warfare and a return to legal tactics. Taruc and most Huk leaders acknowledged that the loss of mass support made fighting futile, and they wanted to end it and negotiate their return to normal society. But in the end they did nothing, profound demoralization set in, and in May 1954, Taruc surrendered. The Huks disintegrated; some small groups struggled to survive mainly to avoid prison, and a few simply became outright bandits and criminals.

Elated with its success, and convinced that the U.S. could freely apply covert tactics and counterinsurgency elsewhere to bypass some of the grave frustrations of limited conventional war that the Korean War had imposed upon its strategic calculations, at the end of 1953, Washington optimistically sent the triumphant Lansdale to Saigon to pursue the same policy in Vietnam. Ironically, by drawing the wrong conclusion from its experience in the Philippines, and by never comprehending the entirely different context into which it was about to plunge, the U.S. paid an infinitely greater price later; and the Philippines after 1970 became the only nation in East Asia where a powerful guerrilla movement was to reemerge in the same social environment that had existed both before and after the Magsaysay period—this time to endure for decades.[17]

The events in both Greece and the Philippines after 1945 further exposed as myth the notion that the Marxist-Leninist party is able to choose its own basic strategy and successfully to lead the masses regardless of the larger constraining social and political context that its adversaries create. By 1946 the disparity between Leninist organizational theory and practice had become enormous, yet both orthodox Communists and their enemies who mobilized the Cold War remained oblivious to reality, if only because it would have required them to react to the sources of international tension very differently than both their interests and cherished illusions demanded. But Greece and the Philippines conveyed a simple lesson relevant to many other nations both then and later: people will inevitably, even if hesitantly at the inception, respond to economic and social injustices and to repression, and Communist parties often had precious little to do with initiating people's actions. At those times they sought to prevent resistance, they frequently succeeded, but they sometimes failed. The forms such mass reactions took (and will take) reflected the physical and human environment in which they developed. But however long it requires, the policies or even the demise of Communist parties cannot always save social orders from their own follies and contradictions. Powerful Communist parties throughout this century remained the products of the breakdowns of traditional societies rather than their causes, notwithstanding the fact that afterward many ceased to be radical politically and ended by aborting the very dynamics of change that had created their social potential. Whatever the Soviet Union's power over them in many places before and after 1945, in a growing number of nations actually experiencing profound social tensions, Moscow's hegemony subsequently began to decline, in large part due to its advocacy of restraint, and to some crucial degree this explains Leninism's eventual demise as a world system. But even more important was the way that the very character of these parties—their eclectic origins, their incremental adaptations, the flaws intrinsic in their ideas, and the opportunistic means their leaders used to remain in power—later also made it possible for so many of them to abandon their nominal values and goals, and ultimately to disintegrate entirely.

The Second World War, of course, compromised and weakened the traditional elites of many nations, and it intensified the innumerable social and economic conflicts and problems that long preceded the war. These ruling classes survived in very great measure, if not wholly, because of the United States' efforts to save them. This internationalization of domestic conflicts was a logical continuation of the pattern of foreign intervention and diplomacy that began at the end of the First World War, and after 1945 the U.S. assumed this task—which it dignified as "containment"—as its principal mission. While it did so also to preserve class structures and their ideologies in ways it deemed essential to safeguarding its own vital economic interests, its mission soon transcended this principal concern, although protecting capitalism continued to play a variable and sometimes decisive role virtually everywhere.

While widespread political instability could easily lure the U.S. into various degrees of intervention, the crucial question still remained as to how well it could cope militarily to redeem a regime dependent upon it, as inevitably it would be called upon to do, when it employed its own military forces. For its successes in Greece and the Philippines were not principally the result of the effectiveness of its military and economic aid, much less the viability of its client states, but rather the internal political contradictions and failures of its enemies. War and its consequences, given the very nature of the world we live in, continued to become increasingly complicated and dangerous, not only militarily but economically and politically as well.

## Korea and the Limits of American Power

Greece and the Philippines disclosed how and why the consequences of armed struggles against traditional orders might be effectively contained, providing some of them with a respite. But more than offsetting such success for the U.S., Korea was to reveal that the very nature of modern war and the technology on which it was based, and the basic criterion of victory and success along with it, was altering fundamentally. Comprehending the complex and contemporaneous experiences in these three nations and their interrelationships required critical reflection, and the question was whether the United States, now the world's preeminent military power, could learn as much as it had to from them. Whether the very scope and ambition of its foreign military policy, which automatically endowed events in one nation with symbolic relevance in a regional and even global setting—"credibility" and the "domino theory" being the two most persistent doctrines in such a geopolitical vision—would necessitate an unwavering readiness on its part to undertake new risks, was an issue of decisive importance. And would its intrinsically flawed, simplistic perception of the nature of Communist parties, their origins and the causes of their actions, and their relationships to the Soviet Union (which might not always be able to prove so helpful to U.S. objectives) continue notwithstanding Stalin's decisive aid on Greece? And perhaps most significant of all, would American leaders, like others throughout the world since the turn of the century, persevere in cherishing fatal illusions regarding the efficacy of their weapons and strategies, especially in winning wars that evolved out of domestic social and political grievances?

Crises in any one state can never be divorced from the far greater diplomatic context and period in which they occur, and the more ambitious the foreign policy of a nation, the more likely it is that such interactions will influence its behavior, for it is in such a grand framework that aspiring hegemonic nations define reality in specific places and judge their responses to it. Even as affairs in Greece, the Philippines, and Korea were unfolding, the U.S. was beginning to embark on a basic review of its foreign and military policies, which produced the crucial background for the virtually exponential transformation of warfare that occurred after 1949 and defined its reactions to the Korean conflict. Until the Soviet explosion of an atomic bomb in August 1949, Washington had complete confidence in its military technology and its ability to cope with any possible challenges within the constraints of a relatively noninflationary annual military budget of about $15 billion. While it often conjured up dangers for an increasingly apathetic public or Congress reticent to appropriate funds, in fact the Truman administration thought a war with the USSR highly unlikely because it believed, for entirely valid reasons, Stalin's military and economic power to be too feeble. Yet what it completely failed to predict was the risk of wars beginning in ways and places that Moscow could not control.

But it was not only the Soviet A-bomb that challenged America's over-confidence; its leaders were convinced that the final Communist triumph in China during 1949 had profoundly altered the balance of power in Asia, and that along with Communist-led guerrillas in Vietnam and a momentum toward the Left in much of Asia, there existed a trend that, if successful, might very well destroy Japan's ability to prosper in Asia without accommodating, if not succumbing, to growing Communist might. Well before the Soviets shattered its strategic military superiority, Washington authorized a comprehensive reassessment of its position and policies in the Far East. Its review committee under Ambassador Philip C. Jessup operated within the Truman administration's fundamental premise that the United States' primary global interests were in Europe and that while its policies and actions in Asia were subordinate to that basic priority, it would also seek to prevent the extension of Asian communism. This meant—among other things—that in Indochina, where France was bogged down and adamant that Germany not rearm until the Vietminh were defeated, the administration chose to help the French win that struggle, a decision it made well before the outbreak of the Korean War and whose consequences later proved monumental.

At the end of 1949, Truman authorized the State and Defense departments to embark on a full-scale review of America's global military and economic objectives, which resulted in the most important of all postwar policy papers, NSC-68 (which remained "Top Secret" until 1975). Both Secretary of State Dean Acheson and the Joint Chiefs of Staff had already concluded that the U.S. must develop the hydrogen bomb to regain a decisive military lead over the USSR, but they could not agree on the cost of a new arms race, which also involved European and German rearmament. The State Department successfully argued that the postwar economic boom was ending and that the recession that had begun in mid-1949 had to be reversed, a goal that "might itself be aided by a build-up of the economic and military strength of the United States and the free world." NSC-68 not only systematically treated the arms race as a Keynesian pump-priming measure for domestic recovery; "perhaps most important," it deplored "indications of a let-down of United States efforts" among the public and Congress. A renewed sense of crisis would presumably neutralize these "doubts" and consequently allow the executive again to obtain "a large measure of sacrifice and discipline . . . of the American people." Since 1946, unifying the nation behind the government's program with the threat of alleged international dangers had become intrinsic to sustaining the domestic support for its military and foreign policies. A renewal of this process would place maximum strain on the USSR, thereby weakening its hold on its satellites, as the administration secretly replaced the containment of Soviet power with a policy of eventually causing "a retraction" to "reduce" it, or a rollback strategy.[18] Meanwhile, the Americans would have to pay far higher taxes to fund an expansion of military power that the review committee on April 14, 1950, projected to cost $35 to $50 billion— or three to four times the fiscal 1949 military outlay.

By early 1950, in effect, America's leaders were out to recast their relationship to the world in a manner that not only presaged crises but even required them to implement their secret rearmament agenda. In both the Philippines and Indochina they had already begun to act with confidence, fully anticipating a much greater effort in both places. When Acheson gave his minutely dissected "defensive perimeter" speech in January 1950, he mentioned neither Korea nor Indochina by name, even though the administration had already made the decision to become far more active in the latter. Local crises, in essence, were originally perceived as mere instruments of the U.S. in attaining its much larger global objectives, as embodied in NSC-68, and how it responded to them initially depended on how it defined the relationship of specific places and problems to achieving American goals in a far broader perspective focused principally on Europe but including Asia as well.

Notwithstanding the Truman administration's earliest articulation of its international aims or the logic of its foreign policy, the Korean War possessed its own momentum and soon evaded not only U.S. control but also that of all the other players involved in the event, above all the USSR and China, who also became its victims rather than its masters. Certainly, on a military level the U.S. was caught utterly unawares by the potential scope and duration of the war, and given its careful prioritization of its global and regional interests before June 1950, it is most probable that if America's leaders could have predicted all of the military and political challenges they were to confront, they would not have intervened in Korea in June 1950. Suffice it to say, while such speculations are moot, the terrible implications of the war to all of its participants are not, and unless we assume that they were all highly irrational and embarked on one of the most destructive wars of all times fully aware of the consequences, it is essential to define a more accurate explanation of how such a calamity could have occurred in the first place. As in every other war in this century, the men who made fatal decisions all suffered from false expectations. Their short-term ulterior motives and goals caused them to take risks when great prudence alone was rational, and they failed to comprehend how the experiences of their last war had no relevance to the Korean conflict and to the fundamental constraints of their technology. But in the case of the U.S. one also has to understand the decision makers and the context in order to understand how such wars become possible. Such an assessment in no way exonerates them, for stupidity in high places has been the bane of modern history and can scarcely be explained away, much less justified. There are totally pervasive consensual standards that make such socially sanctioned ignorance not only merely normal but probable, and they are intended to serve a leadership's class and factional interests, thereby making the institutional values and goals of a system as much a danger as the leaders themselves.

The two Koreans who mattered most, Syngman Rhee and Kim Il Sung, were both, in the end, sufficiently independent of those who initially appeared to be both their sponsors and masters to upset entirely the calculations and desires of their great-power patrons. Rhee sought American support for as long as it suited his purposes, but he openly advocated the reunification of the nation at any cost, and while the U.S. often seemed to be his sovereign, it too, as with innumerable nominal clients later, ultimately became wholly dependent upon him and subject to his blackmail. In 1953 the U.S. was ready to organize a coup against Rhee and, if necessary, kill him. Kim Il Sung cunningly cultivated Soviet backing over the years in order to eliminate his numerous but disunited rivals among the principal founders and leaders of the Korean Communist party. But it is certain—as both the events of the past forty years and newly-opened Soviet archives have only confirmed—that Kim was ultimately his own man, who took the initiative on the most crucial decisions and became increasingly contemptuous of the USSR after he found himself able to exploit the Sino-Soviet dispute to win aid from both sides and push them on to courses neither desired.[19]

### From Civil War to Protracted Conflict
The conflict in Korea in June 1950 was the outcome of an incipient civil war that both Korean sides aggressively encouraged and which culminated in full-scale combat when Kim's forces crossed the 38th parallel on June 25, 1950. After October 1948, Rhee confronted a number of localized rebellions within his army and among peasants, some of which lasted for months on end, and when North Korean soldiers first crossed the 38th parallel on May 3, 1949, two battalions of Republic of Korea (ROK) troops defected to them. For the next year, literally hundreds of small clashes occurred along the parallel. No less important was the continuous political opposition to Rhee within the south itself, so that in the May 30, 1950, elections chiefly rightist opponents of Rhee won an overwhelming majority of the seats in the parliament.

In such a highly unstable political and military environment, Kim Il Sung was probably understandably convinced that he would win less by the force of his arms than by a serious shock causing Rhee's already teetering regime and army simply to disintegrate when he crossed the border, and it was for this reason, and possibly also to preempt pressures that his even more militant rivals among the northern Communists were creating, that his assault on June 25 began when only half of his divisions were fully mobilized. The invasion itself was no surprise to the American government, for on May 10, Seoul officials had announced that one was imminent. But since Rhee and his allies throughout this period were often threatening their own march northward (a risk that unquestionably encouraged Kim to act), no one took their information at face value. No less important was the fact that while the North Koreans enjoyed a temporary weapons lead before June 1950, it would not have been sufficient to win a war against the slightly larger ROK army had the latter been ordered to resist or been motivated to do so. American officials had feared that if the U.S. gave Seoul heavier arms, as the State Department's representative in Japan later wrote, "Rhee promptly would punch northward across the 38th parallel."[20] On May 23, however, the U.S. began receiving its own high-level intelligence predictions of an imminent invasion, even though many close observers of the civil war had long anticipated that it would eventually culminate in just such a large cross-border invasion. By June 19 its evidence for an attack was overwhelming, and all that was missing was the exact time. While Kim Il Sung most likely planned only a strike against the Seoul region with the expectation that Rhee's forces would fall apart within a few days and that he could dictate a peace settlement to Rhee's successors, instead the ROK army retreated, often in good order without offering resistance, opening an enormous vacuum into which Kim's forces could easily enter. Kim cajoled Stalin's support for the venture, and neither of them believed the U.S. would enter the conflict.

The actual events stunned both Stalin and Mao, and immediately upset their general foreign policies. The Russians had walked out of the U.N. Security Council on January 10, 1950, to protest the U.N.'s refusal to seat Communist China, remaining away until August 1. Had they really expected a long struggle in Korea, they almost certainly would have returned to the Council to veto the subsequent U.N. involvement in the Korean War lest they be accused of being treacherous to the North Koreans. Elsewhere, they were still deeply engrossed in their peace campaign to prevent exactly the sort of U.S.-led western military buildup the conflict in Korea made possible. For all of these reasons American scholars with policy-making experience who have studied the matter have exculpated Stalin for ordering the Korean conflict, and Soviet archives have confirmed their view. The Chinese Communists were at that time concentrating troops across from Formosa, prior to an imminent invasion that the American government expected, and disclaimed responsibility for events in Korea. A war there hurt them the most, since it immediately prevented the liberation of the last Chinese province and dramatically altered both China's position and America's role in Asia. Had he known that Kim's June 25 offensive would challenge the U.S. to join the war, it is virtually certain that Mao would have stopped him.[21]

One need not review the steps by which America entered the Korean fray, but one crucial reason was that the Truman administration immediately interpreted it as a test of its willingness to respond to what it labeled Soviet-sponsored aggression: in a word, the credibility of U.S. military power and of its ability to deter future crises like it. Historians have ably documented many other important causes as well, ranging from a desire to employ the tension to attain goals elsewhere—including obtaining congressional approval for NSC-68—to the special role of General MacArthur, the U.S. commander in the Far East, in repeatedly forcing the administration to escalate the war, and they have also shown that there were experts in Washington who understood exactly how and why the Korean conflict was a civil rather than an international war during its initial stage. But what is even more important and incontrovertible is that, like those in so many nations in other places and times, America's leaders utterly failed to comprehend the military costs of the Korean War and its potential for producing domestic political and economic repercussions they had not anticipated. Even more important, they were blind to the ways it might erode the military basis of American power globally.

### Stumbling into Protracted War
The Korean War quickly produced wholly unanticipated challenges that confounded the warring nations' original assumptions concerning the length and intensity of the combat, once more exposing the grave fallibility of elite calculations. In the context of vast spaces and decentralized armies, it disclosed immediately the decisive constraints and contradictions of costly military technology. No less vital, it indicated once again how politics—whether within the U.S. or involving its putative proxy, Syngman Rhee—could gravely complicate the timing and direction of the war in a way that transformed and protracted it. The Korean War in all of its phases was a consummate surprise to the U.S.

Within a month of the war's inception the U.S. Air Force not only established air supremacy but "neutralized" all but one strategic installation contributing to the seemingly relentless and victorious offensive of the North Korean People's Army (NKPA).[22] True, most of the NKPA's logistical support came from outside Korea, and the U.S. Army, Air Force, Navy, and Marines, reflecting their own rival parochial concepts of how modern wars should be fought, immediately were unable to overcome their often sharply differing interservice prejudices, but the potential liabilities of this persistent troubled relationship, which led to each air arm being given separate operation zones rather than being integrated, appeared manageable because America's leaders initially believed that the fight was likely to be very brief.

The United States' epic decision to cross the 38th parallel on October 7,

1950, after having virtually annihilated the hopelessly overextended North Korean army, altered what would otherwise certainly have been a three-month war to restore the status quo at the parallel into a prolonged, inconclusive three-year struggle. This fatal choice produced what by any standard was to become a bloody, massive test of arms and military power, one whose lessons were relevant throughout much of the world and fraught with major implications for America's way of making war. Even more important, it exposed the awesome nature and consequences of modern war and firepower to the peoples of nations engaged in it.

No one who favored what was tantamount to unifying all of Korea by force of arms, with the exception of MacArthur, believed that a major conflict would ensue from crossing the parallel, much less welcomed such a prospect. But almost from the time that it began, and even as Rhee and the U.S. forces in the summer of 1950 were claiming they were close to being driven entirely out of South Korea, dominant opinion in the media, Congress, the Pentagon, and the State Department favored carrying the war north and reunifying the country. That the Republicans would accuse the Truman administration of appeasement were it to refuse to do so was certain. But all the proponents of forcible reunification assumed that neither the USSR nor China would enter the war, the effort would be a short one, and that Rhee's troops would do most of the fighting. It was precisely this great measure of consensus on attaining a political as well as a military victory at no risk that convinced both MacArthur and Rhee, whose objectives were very different from Washington's and whose willingness to take chances was far larger, that they could succeed in forcing the U.S. into situations that carried enormous rewards but equally great dangers.

Rhee had for years hoped to reunify the nation and was preparing to do so, including by force of arms, long before he could count on hundreds of thousands of U.S. and other troops fighting beside him. Not for a moment did he plan to forgo this rare opportunity for success—nor did he. MacArthur wished to roll back Communism in China and prevent its expansion in Asia, but especially to shatter what he believed to be the Truman administration's erroneous preoccupation with Europe as the area most vital to the U.S. And while Truman did not want to be accused of being soft on communism, even more important was the fact that by the end of September 1950 Congress had not yet appropriated the funds necessary to implement NSC-68. Nor had it endorsed his resolve to confront the USSR militarily, principally in Europe, in ways that the administration consciously believed demanded a sustained period of intense tension and fear. During a fairly brief but decisive period, both MacArthur and the White House agreed on tactics but not ends, soon introducing the gravest crisis in civil-military relations since the Civil War. Truman and Acheson, as the latter explained it to Canada's minister of external affairs at the end of July 1950, regarded Korea as "only an incident" in a "very dangerous international" context that ". . . had made it politically possible for the United States to secure congressional and public support for a quick and great increase in defence expenditures. . . ."[23] A swift victory with limited goals would reveal how ephemeral Communist power was; to continue the war only somewhat longer seemed to the administration a small risk compared to its important later benefits in coping with Congress.

Although his forces were technically circumscribed after crossing the parallel, the extent of which the Truman administration subsequently greatly exaggerated, MacArthur also knew that he could exploit Washington's aggressive tactical objectives to enable him to continue to escalate the war and thereby attain his own grandiose goals in the war. They both optimistically assumed that most North Korean troops would not make it back across the parallel, and that Rhee's forces would do most of the quite brief mopping up north of it. Only Rhee's men would fight in the provinces adjacent to China and the USSR, and the U.N. was to stop its offensive if by small chance either intervened. After October 1 the Chinese repeatedly transmitted warnings that they would not remain passive, but while Truman's advisers correctly assumed that Stalin wanted to avoid war at the time, they erroneously concluded that he could constrain China's actions. By the end of October, with the north largely conquered and the administration confident the war would soon end, it chose to dismiss the significance of a massive Chinese troop buildup along the border. The U.S. government had attempted to achieve Korean reunification at a nominal price while simultaneously using what was intended to be a slightly longer conflict as a lever to achieve its basic goals elsewhere and subsequently to devote the greater part of its attention and resources to Europe. Instead, the following month it was embroiled in a war with massive Chinese forces.[24]

### The Dilemma of Limited War
The well-known events of the war itself need no recounting here, save to remind the reader that by June 1951 the ferocious battle between the Communists and the U.S.-led bloc had stabilized roughly where it began— the 38th parallel. In May 1952 there were 908,000 men on the Communist side against nearly 700,000 (293,000 of them Americans) for the U.N. It also became the second-most expensive war the U.S. had ever fought. While the Truman administration never imagined that a conflict of this scope and duration was possible, still less did it expect that its vast superiority of airpower, munitions, and technology would be stalemated. Interservice rivalries were only a minor, if costly and persistent reason for that failure. What the United States had for the first time to confront in Korea

was the limits of technology in attaining both its political and military goals in a highly decentralized Third World context, and the grave ways in which such constraints could impact on its economic and political life to undermine its domestic stability in a significant, and in certain ways decisive, fashion.

While the Americans from the inception always emphasized high firepower rather than combat manpower in the Korean War, by late 1951 their preference for air and artillery instead of bloody ground operations that endangered soldiers became formal doctrine. The combined U.N. air forces dropped 1 million tons of munitions on enemy positions and destroyed at least 118,000 structures. The American-led forces' artillery fired off ten to twenty times the number of Communist rounds during the peak months for both sides, and the U.S. utilized 2.1 million tons of surface-delivered munitions. How this wartime total of 3 million tons, equivalent to 43 percent of the entire tonnage the U.S. utilized during all of World War Two, replaced manpower engaged in classic infantry combat may be defined in terms of tons of munitions exploded per man-year of combat exposure, which during Korea was eight times the World War Two level. War for the U.S. was increasingly based on incredibly destructive and expensive technology and firepower.

Yet this immensely superior firepower, which by necessity devoured the lives and property of countless civilians, failed to translate into military victory. Apart from losing 1,986 aircraft from all causes, the combined U.N. military casualties were over 500,000 compared to over three times that for their enemies. Of the 94,000 dead on the U.N. side, 33,629 were Americans, and three times that number of Americans were wounded. But estimates of civilian deaths are over a million in South Korea and about the same number in the north. Half the southern population lost their homes or became refugees by early 1951, up to 4 million refugees arrived from the north, and 5 million people in the south were on relief when the war ended.[25]

In a virtually static war of positions, the Chinese found cheap ways to stalemate every move the U.S.-led coalition mounted until the spring of 1953, creating a virtually impregnable defense in depth while preserving good morale among its forces. They (far more than their adversaries) constantly constructed fortifications, including large caves, that effectively protected them against firepower. Their use of poor weather and the night in which to fight or to move essential supplies, which were one-tenth of the needs of an American division, foiled airpower. Human porters and animals often substituted for motorized transport. U.S. officers marveled at their skill, ingenuity, and persistence. Their air defenses improved considerably with time, and while they essentially employed positional warfare once the war reached an impasse, they did so with a fluidity that consistently frustrated American explosives. Shovels, dispersion, and darkness, in brief, neutralized a military force spending vastly greater sums on high technology.

By the end of 1952 the United States' dilemma in Korea was twofold. As its military leaders knew, fighting a conventional war on a greater scale within Korea itself was impossible, for the trained manpower and equipment, not to mention the funding, simply did not exist. The alternative of taking the war to China, apart from the enormous risks, also was unrealistic for much the same reasons, and when General and President-elect Eisenhower made his much-vaunted trip to Korea in December 1952 he ruled out escalation.

On the other hand, the usual military targets, such as buildings and bridges, were destroyed within a year, and firebomb raids on Pyongyang began in January 1951. Everything feasible in North Korea, save the Suiho hydroelectric plants, the Toksan irrigation dams north of Pyongyang, and targets on the Chinese and Soviet borders, was destroyed before 1952. General William F. Dean, who was taken prisoner and viewed everything from the ground, recalled that "the city Huichon amazed me. The city I'd seen before—two-storied buildings, a prominent main street—wasn't there any more. . . . I think no important bridge between Pyongyang and Kanggye had been missed and most of the towns were just rubble or snowy open spaces where buildings had been. . . . The little towns, once full of people, were unoccupied shells. The villagers lived in entirely new temporary villages, hidden in canyons. . . ."[26] At the same time, the Communist ability to take countermeasures enabling them to continue to fight effectively neutralized the military consequences of the massive destruction of increasingly civilian resources. For America's leaders, their frustrating need was to redefine airpower's role in a context where there were almost no strategic and economic targets and military installations were decentralized and hidden. Comparable problems had arisen during World War Two, although until August 1945, Allied air- and firepower was far less destructive than in Korea; but the logic was the same, and remains historically the fundamental dilemma in military technology that has inexorably moved it increasingly to make war against civilians and suck them into the vortex of destruction.

America's leaders also believed that the hint of escalating the war was also a crucial political lever to influence Chinese behavior at the cease-fire discussions. But Truman's implied threat on November 30, 1950, to use atomic bombs had the reverse effect; it brought British Prime Minister Clement Attlee rushing to Washington, producing a crisis within the U.S.-led alliance, and thereafter the British played a wary, inhibiting role. The Chinese called Washington's bluff and caused its credibility to sink. But in fact the U.S. had only four atomic bombs in its arsenal in July 1950 and they were being reserved for a possible war in Europe. The Truman administration instead increased its use of artillery and aviation until June 1952, when as a warning to the Chinese of even more dire escalation, it chose to destroy virtually the entire Suiho electric power complex, claiming it was a military objective. In Europe there was outrage, again putting Washington on the defensive politically and further diminishing its credibility. While electrical power played a secondary military role, it was equally clear that the war would continue as usual without it; for it was civilian life that was most gravely affected by the destruction of over 90 percent of North Korea's power capacity at a time that the war's ravages had already ruined its social and health infrastructure and both typhus and smallpox were epidemic.[27]

Airpower was unable to extract political concessions from China, and other than extending the war to China and Manchuria, no new military intimidation was possible, so at the end of 1952, Eisenhower—notwithstanding the dramatic accounts of journalists and historians then and thereafter—was no more ready to escalate the war significantly or to use atomic bombs than he was in Indochina over a year later. Limited wars no longer held out hope for clear victories, and the president and, especially, Secretary of State John Foster Dulles sought desperately to define a new strategic doctrine, soon dubbed "the New Look," which employed the threat to use atomic and then nuclear weapons at a time and place of America's choosing as a last resort should other means fail. But it was never a coherent, integral concept that could be, or ever was, applied in practice. For the fact was that after 1950 Washington suffered, like many powerful and expansive nations before it, from a growing strategic confusion, and combining its material resources to create a victorious synthesis relevant to inordinately complex politics and economics both abroad and at home, as well as the exigencies of combat, remained its obsession from this time on—and it was never to succeed in devising it.

What the new president and especially Dulles did do, however, was to seek to intimidate China in sometimes excruciatingly vague but always ominous ways—ranging from an implied use of atomic bombs against it to explicitly "unleashing" Chiang Kai-shek against the mainland if the truce talks remained stalemated. Atomic missiles were probably moved to Okinawa in the spring of 1953, and contingency plans for every situation were prepared. But options are not policies, and the Eisenhower administration had to resolve an even greater threat in the form of Syngman Rhee. To some extent it dealt with the two sides in tandem, pressuring them both in the hope of ending the protracted war so that escalation, which was inherently dangerous and irrational, would prove unnecessary. In war normal diplomacy is nonexistent and warnings of escalation serve as bargaining levers in dealing with enemies; between Washington and Rhee, however, the situation was scarcely different, and to a significant degree, as it embarked on one of the most convoluted, uncertain periods in postwar American foreign policy, the United States' threats against

China were designed as much to placate its ostensible friend as to frighten its enemy.

Two facts complicated the U.S. position in Korea after Eisenhower came to office. First, the Chinese after September 1952 let it be known that they were ready in principle to negotiate an end to the war, and Washington could deal with them, aware that they shared the common dilemma that the cost of military victory was too high for both sides; given the mutual desire, only the means for implementing it needed to be agreed upon. But any settlement that accepted the existing troop deployments would leave the nation divided around the 38th parallel. For the U.S. this was no major obstacle, for it had already made the crucial point, defined as its basic war aim in January 1951, that any threat on its part to intervene was now credible and that it would check China's ability to "undermine the resistance of non-Communist Asia" without sacrificing its commitment to its higher priorities outside Asia.[28] But for Rhee a negotiated cease-fire represented an abandonment of reunification, for which he had passionately fought since 1945, and which he now hoped to achieve with the aid of the huge foreign military presence. No sooner had armistice talks begun in July 1951 than Rhee made his ambitious objectives clear, and he became so great a menace that in 1952 Washington began to formulate contingency plans for coping with him. When the Eisenhower administration began to pursue the cease-fire negotiations with an ominous earnestness, Rhee incessantly undermined its efforts and produced a sustained crisis in their relations, proving far more troublesome than the Communists. His demand for a march north to reunify Korea at any cost, or his threat to fight on without the U.S., did not panic American officials. But his release of prisoners of war and his creation of new demands on China threatened to scuttle the peace parley unless the Chinese made some significant concessions that solved the United States' problems with a rebellious client eager to keep it mired in the hopeless war.

The U.S. then chose to send clear signals both to the Chinese and to Rhee, but in the latter case it had to confront an intractable ally who was engaging in blackmail but could not, after seven years of U.S. support, be deposed without great embarrassment. In February 1953 the Eisenhower administration refined earlier contingency plans to control Rhee; no later than the end of May, by which time he became the single greatest menace to the imminent ceasefire accord about to be reached and was taking measures to sabotage it, the administration's contingency plans included possible combat with Rhee's forces, replacing him after installing a military government, seizing him and his key officers, and killing him if necessary. At the same time, if he cooperated, the U.S. would provide him massive military and economic aid and give guarantees of assistance in case of a future Communist offensive. But the Americans also subjected the Chinese to rumors of atomic war should they stick to the original negotiated compromises and not allow Washington off the hook with the recalcitrant Rhee. More ominous, beginning May 10, with the truce talks again stalemated, the air force began to bomb the most sensitive targets in the north, while Washington informed China via India that if there was no settlement the war would spread to Manchuria (even though the Joint Chiefs of Staff were not yet prepared to go that far).

The Toksan and Chosan irrigation dams north of Pyongyang were civilian targets essential to rice production. "Humanitarian considerations," according to the official U.S. Army history, "had argued against the bombing. . . .," in a war where such inhibitions had been virtually unknown; ". . . many FEAF officers were troubled by the implications," writes the official air force historian.[29] On May 13 the attacks against the dams began, and "the damage done by the deluge far exceeded the hopes of everyone," the Fifth Air Force reported.[30] It talked of roads, bridges, and rails being wiped away, of course, but above all of vast quantities of rice, the new and primary target, lost. That traditional international canons made war against food taboo is implicitly conceded in the official histories. And although the destruction of rice could not alter the outcome of the war one iota, symbolically it made clear to China that the U.S. was now capable of any war crime. It also revealed that the very logic of frustrating, protracted wars, along with the intrinsic nature of military technology, led inevitably to civilians and the economy sustaining them becoming targets, thereby ripping apart the very fabric of societies in order somehow to obtain military successes that persistently mocked firepower.

America had to cope with the failure of its strategic doctrines, but even more important was the impact of the war on U.S. public opinion and the economy, as well as its distortion of America's global priorities, and all these questions became intertwined. The Truman administration had planned to spend far more to implement NSC-68, and national security expenditures increased from $13 billion in the year ending June 30, 1950, to $50.4 billion in 1953, when Eisenhower took office. Inflation, which had been nominal in the two years before the war, leaped to 7.9 percent in 1951—which shocked the public—while the federal budget deficit reached an abnormal $6.5 billion in Truman's last year. Public opinion reacted negatively to these trends but especially to mounting American casualties, and the war became increasingly unpopular. A large majority had supported the U.S. intervention in July 1950, but by the end of the year Americans had grown more critical, until by October 1952 they were mainly hostile toward it. Eisenhower's election victory was linked directly to these factors and to his pledge to end the war and reduce military spending. The war had become ominously counterproductive politically and economically.

Eisenhower worked within these potentially decisive restraints, and knew that escalating the war would spell doom for his party's political future and undermine his desire to reduce spending and inflation. Threats of unleashing war as part of a search for a new strategic synthesis, the so-called New Look, still evaded the central tension the U.S. now confronted between its virtually universal ambitions and the constraints that the sheer cost of its all-too-fallible weapons systems created. As with all nations before it, the U.S. could easily get into a war; victory was another and far more complex matter. Meanwhile, its initial resolve not to allow its commitments in Korea and Asia to reorient its original international priorities was being gravely eroded; and as the pressure of events elsewhere on this unstable earth weighed upon it, its loss of confidence and lack of a firm, economically and politically affordable basis for coping with challenges all over the world pervaded Washington, producing a fundamental crisis in the strategic doctrine and premises sustaining America's global activism.

### The Enigma of Limited War

The United States' experiences in its ambitious postwar interventions in Greece and the Philippines revealed that it could win significant counter-insurgency conflicts only if its enemies were seriously disunited and their movements were essentially reluctant, defensive responses to domestic repression. That neither countries' insurgents had support or encouragement from the Soviet Union or China abetted the American effort greatly, and in this framework it understandably had no need to question the efficacy of its military technology in a Third World context. Its success was based on a generous measure of good luck, which failed to recur consistently in the future. It planned for wars that were convenient for its overall priorities, the technological mix of resources that emerged from its inter-service rivalries, and its finite budget. Korea proved dramatically that Washington's premises were gravely unrealistic, and its subsequent determination to vindicate the credibility of American military power intensified its sheer frustration in fighting a war against enemies who employed the elements, space, and time successfully to foil it repeatedly, transforming what it intended to be a short, limited interlude into a bloody conflict almost as long as World War Two.

The basic equivalency in power between the earth's richest nation, employing enormous quantities of arms, and one that was immeasurably poorer economically raised fundamental questions regarding the very future of modern warfare, especially after the U.S., with its massive use of munitions against civilians and the infrastructures upon which their existences depended, intensified it qualitatively, displacing a large part of

Korea's population and wrecking most of the north. And Washington's frustrating experiences with Syngman Rhee revealed to it that not all of its clients would be as docile or obliging as those in Greece and the Philippines, and that the political viability of its military efforts, a factor that could have a profound effect on the length and very outcome of a war, might rest principally with political decisions that leaders of other nations made. How often this would again prove true in the future was still to be determined.

The compulsive logic of military technology until 1950 was toward increasing firepower and destruction—exponentially with the invention of the atomic bomb—to compensate for its past failures, greatly increasing its costs financially but, above all, in terms of human suffering. Compared to past wars, after 1945 so-called limited wars were extremely expensive economically, devastating physically, and potentially far more politically destabilizing to a government when there was little or no domestic consensus once they became protracted. In Korea the U.S. had to confront the reality that its technology could not, regardless of the claims of its many advocates, produce victory. And while the political and moral justifications for war that conclude with a durable political victory are already sufficiently contentious, wars become the ultimate folly in which humankind can engage when their success is not only uncertain but increasingly improbable with destructive modern technology.

Like most nations before it, America's distinctive military technology hypnotized it and caused it to describe the nature of reality in terms that justified its procurement and budget decisions but which experience was to mock repeatedly—creating further pressures to increase firepower. What the U.S. did not anticipate, like so many before it, was that its enemies could cheaply adapt to advanced technology in ways that create near equivalencies of real power, foiling all its expectations regarding the length and costs of a conflict. But the Korean War, while raising this challenge for America's leaders, by itself did not cause them to come to rational conclusions and abjure yet more attempts to redefine the nature of U.S. military power in order to reassert it in more potent ways, much less seek to avert new adventures that might once again expose their inability to articulate more effective options. Ironically, as General J. Lawton Collins concluded much later from bitter experience, for all the problems Korea posed to the U.S., wars elsewhere, where the sea did not both protect and expose a nation's flanks on both sides, or where there were jungles and enervating heat, would prove decisively worse.[31]

Notwithstanding the United States' refusal to acknowledge the obvious reality, the Korean experience seriously challenged the viability of wars that relied principally upon high technology and massive firepower, but it also revealed the profound vulnerability of successive administrations in their grave and irreversible dependence both on client regimes and a fickle American public. As the principal world power, and by far the most ready and best able to embark on war, the United States' responses to such primordial dilemmas were to define the nature and extent of conflict and violence in much of the world over the next four decades.

# CHAPTER 15

# Warfare at an Impasse:
# The United States Confronts
# the World, 1954–1991

Every major power embarking upon an offensive war in this century was convinced that it possessed a coherent military doctrine that would surmount often daunting political, economic, and technological challenges to attain victory, for to have assumed that its strategy would accomplish less would have been tantamount to acknowledging the inherent irrationality of its adventure. As the nation most engaged in making war in the latter half of this century, the United States' sustained efforts to produce a unified, effective strategic vision that enabled it to employ its unprecedentedly massive resources to master and guide political and social developments throughout the world after 1949 would have occurred under any circumstance. But with the failure of conventional war in Korea and the Soviet explosion of a hydrogen bomb in August 1953, America's leaders believed that it was more imperative than ever for them to formulate a realistic basis for future action.

The task they confronted was inherently insoluble because, like the major European powers before it, after 1945 the U.S. could not discern the relationship between innumerable specific foreign-policy and military dilemmas—to which it responded instinctively in a usually incremental, ad hoc fashion—and its overall priorities. The men who defined U.S. foreign and military policies developed justifications for them that possessed inherently activist and quite inflexible premises that foredoomed the rational calculations and restrained behavior essential to balancing its real capabilities with its myriad interests. At the same time, the question of military spending obsessed Eisenhower and most of his key economic advisers, who sincerely believed that a growing budget deficit and inflation were profoundly subversive to the fabric of American society and its values. But while its "New Look" doctrine threatening massive retaliation with nuclear weapons promised more destruction for less money and initially allowed the administration to make substantial cuts in the size of the military budget and its share of the gross national product, it still did not produce the solution to America's decisive strategic contradictions.

It was immediately obvious that the United States' dependence on sophisticated weapons aimed at industrial and urban targets in the Soviet Union and elsewhere, as well as its conventional weaponry, could not cheaply or quickly win wars in Third World contexts, if at all. Such local wars usually originated in ways that neither the USSR nor China could control, and threatening them with nuclear cataclysms was simply irrelevant. And the fact that the USSR after the fall of 1949 was also engaged in a technologically advanced and expensive atomic arms race meant that the U.S. could no longer impose a permanent ceiling on its military outlays. Moscow's ability in October 1957 to put an earth satellite in orbit by means of a long-range missile, before the U.S. could do so, simply reinforced the reality, obvious since 1949, that the certainty of mutual destruction in a nuclear war made the Eisenhower administration's massive-retaliation doctrine meaningless, and a grave deterrent to the irresponsible use of American power now existed. The New Look was less a coherent military doctrine than a reflection of Washington's futile postwar efforts to define an effective grand strategy.

No less crucial was the fact that after 1950 the military budget became increasingly important to the health of the American economy, attaining the role of the principal countercyclical economic tool that NSC-68 had planned, and although Republican conservatives strongly objected to the very notion of deficit spending, when forced to choose between fiscal prudence and the costly pretensions of being the world's anticommunist policeman, they invariably chose the latter. Few members of Congress, regardless of their beliefs, could willingly accept the reduction of military expenditures in their own districts lest they be defeated in the next election; and since funding the military was the only expenditure on which a bipartisan consensus existed, economic policy to attain full employment and growth was based, notwithstanding its vastly greater waste, costs, and risks, on arms outlays rather than satisfying social needs directly.

But the very existence of the arms race and weapons generated its own imperatives. Above all, it required fear—what Dulles once described as "a feeling of need in the face of danger" lest "the Free World's efforts . . .

rapidly decline. . . . "[1] Such permanent tension abjured a serious role for diplomacy, which the Eisenhower administration discouraged repeatedly, especially relating to European issues after Stalin died in March 1953 or to Indochina. For sustaining the image of an allegedly omniscient and omnipotent Soviet menace after 1946 had kept both the American Congress and public mobilized behind the expensive, hazardous Cold War. This dependence on terror as a unifying catalyst caused the U.S. to employ—partly cynically but increasingly due also to its own self-mystifying paranoia—the most dubious but utilitarian statistics to create descriptions of Soviet power and intentions that bore scant relationship to reality, eventually leaving both its leaders and experts utterly unprepared for schisms in the Soviet bloc and the subsequent stunning demise of the entire Communist system. These cultivated anxieties also mobilized European nations to join NATO and other alliances, and Washington used them as well to deplore the menace of "neutralism" elsewhere. Fear thereby integrated very diverse countries under the United States' hegemonic direction for several decades, until the inherently fissiparous economic and political qualities of the industrial capitalist nations caused its alliances to unravel, if not disappear altogether.[2] But while both truth and realism became the first victims of such a doctrinal offensive, the consensus it produced within its own ranks did not enable the American-led world order to overcome the profound limits intrinsic in its military and political policies.

### Washington Searches for Options

Rather than accept the lesson of Korea that conventional war was no longer plausible, or the obvious fact that nuclear "deterrence" was far too dangerous, Washington after 1953 compounded its contradictions and confusions, neither augmenting its power at less cost nor discovering a definitive means for coping with events in the Third World without dire risks to itself. Its principal problem, which plagued it both before and after the Korean War, was that whatever its official strategists wrote about the need for a capacity to embark on a limited war to deter a present or future enemy, the U.S. found it exceedingly difficult to define conclusions to a conflict short of military victory, much less to accept negotiated compromises that allowed the enemies of those it supported to operate politically. Precisely because it had an instinctive addiction to triumph that was incompatible with the constraining premises of limited warfare, there always existed a risk that America would escalate what were intended to be finite interventions into protracted conflicts. Such impulses invariably overshadowed its other objectives and priorities, confusing and usually reversing them.

But if the U.S. ultimately could not articulate a comprehensive doctrine that offered an alternative to Armageddon, it did act, if only in ways that generated yet other grave dangers but in the short run seemed to solve some of its pressing immediate challenges. This path of least resistance did indeed succeed temporarily in many places, even though its new techniques of intervention increasingly also impinged upon the "credibility" of American power. Indeed, credibility via the domino theory with which it was invariably associated, symbolically linked the fate of an entire region to events in virtually any one country within it—including those of only minor intrinsic significance to American interests. Credibility was inherently biased against diplomacy and nonintervention; it became a growing obsession that increasingly shaped U.S. calculations and actions after 1950, entangling and ultimately subverting efforts to define a strategy for avoiding another Korean debacle so that in Vietnam credibility, more than any other single motive, was eventually to produce a calamity for two nations as well as stalemate America's military power in ways that in fact made it appear less awesome than ever before. To create the fear that the U.S. would go to the brink of war to attain its goals, which included no further Communist territorial gains, was enshrined in U.S. objectives under the Eisenhower administration, producing an inherently belligerent posture and an open-ended commitment wholly inconsistent with a coherent, regulated diplomatic and military policy. Such a stance was preordained to generate monumental surprises.

The U.S. after Korea believed that it might also avoid the massive employment of its own troops again in Third World contexts by relying upon friendly leaders and their armies to cope with local rebellions (many of them radical but not necessarily Leninist), aiding them with equipment, training, and funds and turning them into proxies of American power. Its concept of a "flexible response" to a Communist menace after the Korean War assigned a crucial role to such local allies, ostensibly making Washington's willingness to use nuclear retaliation at the appropriate time and place more believable. But such a posture immediately created a compulsive American bias to view all governments ready to work with the U. S. in this manner as both legitimate and worth preserving, thereby involving it in the politics of innumerable nations where political instability was a permanent fact of life.

Annual military aid in the form of equipment, advisers, and training to nations in Latin America and Asia quadrupled under Eisenhower, compared to such aid during the Truman years, and the creation of integrative regional military alliances—SEATO and CENTO to begin with—further tied Washington's destiny, and credibility, to that of its proxies. Reliance on the military as the most promising single power group in Third World nations became official policy, although this did not preclude support for other tyrants. Augmenting this dependence on officers was the United States' systematic efforts to improve the ability of local police departments to perform political functions. "Public safety" missions, and equipment, were sent to thirty-eight countries over a seven-year period, and many people were brought from those states to undergo training in the U.S. Even more important was the great expansion of the CIA's covert activities, a supremely flexible mechanism that allowed the U.S. both to intervene in countless ways in innumerable countries and to deny responsibility in case of embarrassment or failure. Its "clandestine service" consisted of 2,800 people by 1952, not including a larger number of contract personnel, but under Eisenhower it almost doubled again to become the CIA's largest budget item. The CIA could attempt virtually anything with impunity, and often did with great success, as in Iran in 1953 and Guatemala in 1954, giving Washington "unconventional" means to become enmeshed, for better or worse, in many more nations.[3]

It was now much simpler for the U.S. to attempt to guide a country's political destiny covertly, and so while a great deal more could be undertaken at far less cost than in the days of conventional armies, this new reality also quickly entangled its definition of the credibility of American power with the fate of innumerable dictators and corruptionists. This very ease caused it to intervene in various ways it might otherwise not have done— ranging from larger military-aid missions, as in the case of the Ngo Dinh Diem regime in South Vietnam after 1954, to sending the fleet armed with nuclear missiles to Lebanon in July 1958. What began as part of an effort to make military responses cheaper as well as more flexible and measured to resolve the contradictions in its strategic doctrines ended by implicating the U.S. in many more potentially dangerous situations, not the least because the stability of its proxies was directly linked to politics and conditions within nations that soldiers and guns could scarcely stabilize. The result was an even greater loss of control over its military and foreign policy because seemingly incremental, nominally small decisions pushed Washington in unintended directions that eventually were to determine its broad preoccupations and interests. For whatever its covert successes, which cannot be minimized even if we know much less than we would like regarding many of them, its deepening fixation with credibility and the sheer magnitude of the U.S. global efforts predestined it to some obvious public failures certain to require it to escalate its involvement in various nations to avert the appearance of impotence.

### The Third World Conundrum
Overt United States military activism in the Third World, defined only as the employment of force without engaging in actual war, also increased greatly after 1949. Public exhibits of Washington's might ranged from using small numbers of men and aircraft in a third of the cases to deploy-

ing strategic nuclear forces in at least 15 of over 215 incidents in the period 1946–75. These intimidating displays of power occurred more and more in the Third World, with a direct Soviet or Chinese presence in less than half of them. But no one in Washington ever attempted to formulate a grand political-military strategy that offered a rational justification for the many hazards inherent in the often mindless actions that successive administrations embarked upon.

To some degree, real or purported crises involving the American military were useful in sustaining the tension crucial to the maintenance of a hegemonic Cold War consensus within the U.S. itself as well as in nations of the alliances it dominated. Apart from such cynical manipulation was the fact that the American leadership system was so internally cohesive and analytically monolithic that it simply did not have the capacity to operate other than in the way it did. Intelligence and political analysis became self-reinforcing, and the outpouring of books and articles after 1955 on military strategy were written by advisers—Henry Kissinger being only the best-known example—whose consuming ambitions even more than their convictions made it inconceivable for them to challenge seriously the illusions and false assumptions of conventional wisdom or the mounting risks the U.S. was taking in the Third World lest they be pegged as nonconformists and destroy their career prospects. There was simply no way that men of power would realistically define the obstacles to attaining America's goals in the world, much less challenge those objectives, and in this regard U.S. leaders merely behaved as politicians and bureaucrats do in virtually all modern political orders.

The U.S. dilemma in the increasingly unstable Third World was due largely to its refusal to accept willingly the nationalist movements and doctrines sweeping the less-developed nations. Indeed, it was the very absence of a significant Communist role in most of the Third World that revealed the growing importance of structural alterations crucial to the U.S. and the conservative role it played to safeguard its principally economic interests. Privately and publicly, America's leaders nonetheless attributed to the Russians a transcendent ability to cause, exploit, or shape events in even the most remote countries. They condemned "extreme nationalism" as an objective Communist tool, in spite of the fact that its leading proponents were often the conservative Latin American or Asian bourgeoisie who advocated it to advance industrialization behind protectionist walls, just as the U.S. had done after 1861. The U.S. positioned itself on the wrong side of the great post-1945 decolonization wave, and it was suspicious and usually opposed to the innumerable liberation movements, taking their anti-imperialist rhetoric at its face value. In a fundamental sense, America's leaders never comprehended the complexity of Soviet motives and behavior

throughout the world or the autonomous genesis of revolutionary move-
ments. On this basis they generally aligned themselves against the main
non-Communist political developments that were altering politics in the
Third World, sustaining colonialism in Africa, intervening covertly in
Guatemala in 1954 and Brazil in 1964 to thwart nationalists, and far more.
Simultaneously, the U.S. also encouraged conservative nationalism in the
Middle East in order to replace British power with its own. If the only consistency that emerges from such diverse efforts is the pursuit of national
interest, the very attempt to make its will and needs felt in so many places
also engendered the growing risk of failure, a loss of credibility and,
inevitably, the escalation of its involvement. It required only one such case
to profoundly test the strategic and political assumptions on which
American power was based and to plunge it into war.

But the United States' fixation was not merely the product of its desire
to maintain hegemony and credibility or of its bureaucratic sclerosis, for its
vital interests also goaded it to attempt to control changes in the Third
World. By the decade of the 1950s the U.S. was importing 48 percent of its
total supply of metals, compared to 5 percent in the 1920s, and the very
health of its economy now depended on crucial supplies from the Third
World. This relationship guaranteed that the U.S. would be confronted
with new challenges that increasingly required it to employ its covert and
overt resources to regulate the affairs of states spread out over vast distances—a process hazarding conflict and war once American troops and
equipment moved onto the scene.

Many indices of growing misery throughout the Third World help us to
comprehend yet other profound changes, which became much more acute
after the 1950s and affected the political environment the U.S. sought to
relate to. Only a few examples here reveal the complexity of the issues, to
which we will return later. In the aggregate, by the 1950s, population in the
Third World was growing faster than new land area devoted to agriculture,
and much more of the latter was being allocated to export crops than to
food for local consumption. By 1950, agricultural production in per capita
terms had fallen sharply in Latin America and Asia compared to 1936, and
in many nations the agricultural labor force was shifting from a relatively
secure permanent status to temporary employment. Countless other indi-
cators reveal that when America's leaders began to apply their military
power and strategy to the world's problems after Korea, they had virtually
no notion of how these and similar trends would create social upheavals
and challenges for them in the future. The New Look and the threat of
massive retaliation were simply irrelevant to such changes, as events in
many nations increasingly transcended both American weapons and the
traditional Communist parties.[4]

## Vietnam and the Testing of American Power *

Vietnam was to become the paramount example of how infinitely complicated the social realities in many Third World nations had become, and how they would inevitably test the many regimes and elites on which Washington was so fatally dependent, and along with them the political foundations on which American foreign policy and military power had come to rest. American leaders always responded to the events and issues in Vietnam in the larger context of their ongoing search for a decisive global strategy relevant to the entire Third World, perceiving Vietnam as just one manifestation of innumerable challenges they confronted throughout the world: the efficacy of limited war, the credibility of American power, the risk of defeat in one nation spreading to those bordering it, and much else. Vietnam was to become the epitome of the postwar crisis of U.S. expansionism and power at a crucial stage of its intensive, frustrating effort to articulate a viable, flexible military and political basis for establishing an international socioeconomic environment congenial to it. Although it was mainly chance that designated Vietnam as the primary arena of trial, by 1960 it was virtually preordained that America would attempt somewhere to attain those vital military successes essential to confirm its credibility lest the compounding failures and dilemmas it had confronted in Korea, Cuba, and elsewhere in the Third World since 1949 undermine the very foundations of the conservative order it was seeking either to establish in some nations or to defend in others.

The structural origins of the crisis in Vietnam also existed in varying forms in much of the Third World, and revealed how social institutions and the people in them made conventional assumptions regarding warfare so irrelevant. As a microcosm of our times, the Vietnam conflict again elucidated the limits of human endurance and the way in which internal strife and war's destructive effects transform the very character of the conflict itself, including its eventual political, human, and social consequences. Both within the U.S. and Vietnam, the war produced dramatically new parameters of social and political as well as physical struggle, thereby frustrating the ability of leaders on all sides to control it. Vietnam once more exposed how unpredictable and terrible war's processes and outcome are— and always will be.

The causal elements that produced conflict in Vietnam existed in many countries, and still do. Although it is impossible to ignore other vital fac-

---

* The reader wishing a more comprehensive account of all aspects of the Vietnam War may consult my *Anatomy of a War: Vietnam, the United States, and the Modern Historical Experience* (New York, 1994).

tors, the single most important issue of the war in the south after 1960 as well as in the entire history of the Vietnamese revolution was land and land-related matters. Before World War Two, land in Cochin was highly inequitably owned and the larger part was rented by tenants who paid land-lords 40 to 60 percent of the output. The landlords also dominated usury, further oppressing the peasantry, with 50 to 70 percent interest annually being typical. While the war itself vastly accelerated the deprivation and insecurity among peasants in the northern half of Vietnam, the agrarian crisis that had begun much earlier provided the Communists with a favorable national environment in which to mobilize countless new followers after 1945. The Party had sought to introduce only minor reforms where it had the ability to do so, for it feared alienating most of the landlords and preferred broad patriotic appeals for a united front behind the anti-French struggle. But it still affected about four-fifths of the peasants in some manner, ranging from lowering rents to 25 percent or even abolishing them in some places, to eliminating the worst abuses of usury and annulling prewar debts.

After the U.S. installed Ngo Dinh Diem in power and created a wholly dependent, artificial new nation in the southern part of Vietnam in mid-1954, Diem instituted his own "reforms," and he imposed a new elite of politically reliable Catholic refugees from the north upon the rural administrative and land structure. As an intensely devout Catholic in an overwhelmingly Buddhist nation, Diem employed religion in ways preordained to polarize the society, in the process reintroducing exploitive land relations and high rents. Simultaneously, Diem persecuted not just Communists but all of the dissident non-Catholic religious sects that flourished in Cochin.

The Party in the north, which defined policy for its southern branch, hoped to have the political accord they had signed with the French at Geneva in June 1954 implemented, and persisted with this line notwithstanding both Diem's and Washington's immediate denunciation of the Geneva Agreement. The northern Party's grave crisis over land issues during 1955–57, its own serious problems in consolidating its economic power, and aid-linked pressures from both China and the USSR to avoid risking a confrontation involving the U.S. caused Ho Chi Minh and his colleagues to insist that southern Party members behave as if the Geneva terms would be fulfilled. The result was that about two-thirds of the southern Party members were killed or arrested over four years, culminating in 1959 with intensified suppression that endangered the lives of all who remained free. Irresistible southern demands to approve armed struggle created a profound tension between the Party in the south and that in the north that threatened to produce, at the very least, yet another southern resistance movement that Hanoi could not control, and possibly a schism. As had been and was to remain the case so often elsewhere, the war that began in the south after 1959 was far more the response of desperate people to repression than the decision of revolutionaries to embark on the seizure of power.

The creation of the National Liberation Front (NLF) in the south in 1960 was the outcome of pressure from southerners upon the ruling Party in the north, which sought to constrain it for several more years. But after Diem's long muzzling, the NLF obtained far greater peasant backing than the Vietminh had earlier been able to mobilize, above all among younger, poorer peasants, so that it possessed a crucial class basis and pursued a "poor peasant" land-reform line for five decisive years, reducing rents, redistributing land, and similar measures. Given the extent of landlessness and oppression, it is no surprise that the NLF's initial support and subsequent persistence was greatest where such conditions had predominated, and notwithstanding the decisive U.S. role in making it possible, the war always possessed characteristics of both a civil and class conflict.[5]

Such a broad social foundation for the fight in the south meant that it would be, like all comparable struggles elsewhere, principally a people's war in terms of its supporters and logistics—resilient and highly decentralized, with a great deal of local autonomy. Indeed, both physically and politically it presented the U.S. with vastly more difficult problems than had the Korean War, not only for these reasons but also because the terrain made concealment so easy. Vietnam, therefore, was a fundamental challenge not only to the succession of political proxies the U.S. had sponsored for twenty years but also to the very premises of its high-technology warfare.

When the United States in 1964 embarked step-by-step to apply enormous quantities of modern arms and the strategic and political assumptions underpinning them, it resolved to transcend the Korean War's frustrating stalemate in order to vindicate the credibility of its military power and political determination. To accomplish this the Pentagon had to discover and apply strategies that could overcome not merely the limits of combat but also neutralize the socioeconomic pressures that made poor peasants ready to fight for their cause, and to produce an effective political-economic alternative to the revolutionary cause. Above all, it hoped to establish a proxy who would not only create a viable social order but also provide most of the manpower essential for the tough, bloody combat that the war entailed. And if Washington was to avert the financial costs and public alienation that the Korean War generated, a premise that was crucial to its post-Korean strategic doctrines, victory would have to be gained relatively rapidly and not require massive numbers of American troops. At least as crucial, the U.S. had to fight the war in such a way that it did not, as has occurred so often throughout this century, produce unanticipated cataclysmic social and institutional consequences within Vietnam that might thereby snatch political success from the hands of the militarily more powerful nation. No advocate of escalation before 1966 grasped the magnitude or even the existence of some of these challenges or ever imagined what the war's eventual outcome would be. And in this they shared precisely all the illusions and false expectations that had preceded all major conflicts in this century. After over a half-century of surprises, the ignorance and myopia of the men who embark upon wars in our times was as great as ever.

### The Organization and Intelligence Impasse

Thousands of books have probed every conceivable dimension of the Vietnam War, but all that need concern us here is the war's relationship to two crucial problems confronting the U.S. as the preeminent world military power in the second half of the twentieth century. First was whether the war answered or compounded America's strategic and political dilemmas that the Korean War had revealed and which successive administrations sought to overcome with new weapons and doctrines; and next was the extent to which the traumatic political, social, and economic consequences of making war themselves defined its final outcome and thereby confounded the military assumptions of politicians and generals.

Certain aspects of the Vietnam War were dramatically different from earlier conflicts, but the organization of the various armed services, and the kinds of justifications they concocted for their bureaucratic autonomy remained much as they have been since World War Two (and continue to this day). Such bitter service-jurisdictional conflicts over emoluments and budgets, which were translated into careers for many, bore no relationship to reality, and often made it impossible after 1964 to judge the true state of the conflict and whether the Americans were losing or winning. They also greatly increased the war's costs.

As in Korea, the U.S. Army, Air Force, Marines, and Navy could not agree on the integrated use of their airpower, notwithstanding the increasingly ambitious organizational schemes and doctrines that emerged after the Korean War and especially after Kennedy's immensely pretentious experts from universities and industry, of whom the Defense Department's Robert McNamara was the most imposing, arrived in Washington with their quasi-magical innovative budgeting conceptions. The tactical aviation components belonging to the various services were assigned separate territories, some overlapping, resolving intraservice conflicts but proving inefficient at crucial moments and much more expensive. The air force, internally divided into strategic and tactical aviation, strenuously fought the army's control over helicopters and a whole variety of planes until April 1966, when it traded away its claims in return for the army's forgoing new fixed-wing aircraft. Even the air force's commands were divided into three distinct units, and nominally overseeing the entire war in Indochina was the navy's Pacific commander in chief in Hawaii, who had been assigned what initially was a small responsibility in February 1962 and subsequently refused to relinquish his central place in the command-and-control organizational chart. It was a fact that rivalry among the services was a pervasive reality around which much else would remain subsidiary, and that they could only fight modern warfare in this context.

The role of intelligence in Vietnam, at least defined as relevant information reported without prejudice, played the same minor part in the Vietnam War that it has for every nation throughout this century—except that there was vastly more of it because of electronic signal technology and the increase in the number and size of intelligence agencies. Indeed, the quantitative growth made the qualitative, analytic aspect of intelligence much more important, but it also consumed a great deal more time and money. There were thirteen intelligence agencies overlapping each other in Vietnam at one time, and in early 1967 the army alone was producing 1,400 pounds of reports daily. This indigestible volume led one Pentagon office to produce what amounted to a synthesizing digest about every six weeks beginning in January 1967. The Joint Chiefs of Staff tried unsuccessfully several times to restrict its circulation because it sometimes was unduly candid, if not pessimistic, regarding the efficacy of the administration's basic military operations and assumptions. The CIA's general assessments of the war, on balance, remained skeptical. Analysts in specialized agencies, such as the Rand Corporation, were even more negative, and some often described the U.S. failures and challenges with candor and accuracy.

The mere fact that it took Washington nine years to conclude that its client, Ngo Dinh Diem, had been predestined to lose the war, requiring the U.S. finally to play a decisive role in his assassination, reveals how immune basic policies and biases were to what had become common knowledge. That there was vastly more information to choose from actually made it easier for those who had prejudged their decisions (or had strong career and personal motives) to use whatever suited their interests and ignore the remainder. Careerism and sheer hucksterism surely played a major, perhaps dominant role as generals and officials issued press releases, covering everything from grand strategy to weekly "body counts," that justified their actions and led to promotions. As compounding falsities and cultivated illusions created a fantasy world that promised imminent success if only Washington would authorize a relatively small increment in effort, escalation followed escalation as the fear of losing the nation's credibility rationalized each denial of what was the increasingly irrefutable truth—that the United States' fundamental military and political premises were both false and failing. To report bad news was also to court probable professional difficulties, and opportunism triumphed: among political leaders and their appointed senior officials exuding calm self-confidence; officers of all ranks;

social-science contractors who in return for more money offered elite academia's insights as a means of triumphing over peasants—and others. Many were cynical bureaucratic game players, whose jobs and incomes were far more significant to them than war and peace and people's lives; a good portion, if not simply stupid, were far less clever than they pretended or considered themselves to be, and they placed their convictions before rational calculations and were inherently unable to do otherwise. The intense socialization of functionaries and political personalties, and their total mental integration into a consensus that qualifies them to compete for a role in administering power, was certainly not unique to the U.S., but rather a political fact of life that has paved the way to compromise, acquiescence, and war everywhere throughout this century. All the worse for them was the fact that they ignored the surprisingly accurate information on the futility of the war that was freely available in official circles for as long as they did; they confronted it, and even then often cautiously, only after the Tet Offensive in February 1968 made it indelibly clear that the war was not only being lost but also had become the most divisive, traumatic, and costly error in the modern American experience—and a profound turning point in the history of the nation.[6]

### The Premises—and Problems—of American Strategy

Vietnam presented America's political leaders with the opportunity either to resolve the accumulated strategic and military problems that emerged from the Korean War and the global arms race, and which the New Look and subsequent limited war thinkers attempted to resolve theoretically, or to compound them gravely. The crisis of military technology that began with World War One was intrinsic in the fact that the inflated claims of strategic doctrines justifying arms had protracted every major war since 1914, and in the process of doing so their monumental nonmilitary consequences—ranging from economic dislocations to the massive destruction of civilian populations and the transformation of their political attitudes and a great deal more besides—had defined the political outcome of conflicts far more than had the positions of armies. Military power became both increasingly indiscriminate and its strategies irrelevant to gaining mastery over enemies in a purely physical sense of that term; and insofar as its pretensions made war seem plausible or, as in the case of the notion of credibility, occasionally essential, it had also become fatally counterproductive. The Vietnam War was but one major milestone in mankind's repeated, futile experience of making wars that profoundly shaped global political and social development in this century in ways ultimately much more dangerous for the war-makers. The illusions American political and military leaders cherished were ones they shared with most of those elsewhere who had earlier embarked upon similar fatal courses. What was unique, however, was the fact that the United States had both the will and the resources to aspire to lead the world longer than any other nation in this century, so that after 1945 it engaged in many more wars than any state in recent times. Whether it also had the capacity to succeed in such a role remained to be proved.

The compounded frustrations, experiences, and concerns of the 1950s strongly influenced the step-by-step American intervention that led to the longest war in its history. In the beginning, Washington attempted to create a viable client regime under Diem, but its failure to do so led to increasing direct American participation, until ultimately at one time about three-quarters of a million of its military personnel were either in Indochina or involved in the war from offshore locations. U.S. leaders hoped to establish the credibility of their military might, prevent a succession of regional defeats that they believed the "loss" of South Vietnam would trigger, articulate new counterinsurgency techniques that could win local conflicts elsewhere as well, and much else. But when dependence on its local proxies to achieve victory became an obvious cul-de-sac and massive numbers of its soldiers poured into Vietnam, the American way-of-war sought to triumph by relying on huge quantities of technology and firepower, either on the field of battle against enemy soldiers and their alleged civilian supporters or by attempting through punitive air strikes to destroy the will of the Democratic Republic of Vietnam (DRV) to support the war in the south.

Several of the American military's own analysts after 1975 diagnosed the fatal assumptions of what one has called the "Army Concept," which allowed tactics and operational successes, employing lavish firepower and the unique mobility that helicopters afforded, to dominate and ultimately define grand strategy—an approach ignoring that there was, at best, only a scant relationship between technology and the outcome of ground combat.[7] Military writers have even cogently criticized the hallowed official presumption that political success would follow from military victory. But however valid such censure, the way the U.S. fought in Vietnam remained essentially a predictable phase in the inexorable escalation in technology and firepower that has repeatedly defined the nature of warfare everywhere throughout our century, irresistibly making civilians and their societies increasingly significant military objectives. Vietnam was the most extreme example of this pattern only because the U.S. had far greater resources to do what many other industrial nations had earlier also attempted.

The decline in the use of infantry and combat manpower as a proportion of armies is a universal pattern. The U.S. military's problem in Vietnam was that enemy fighters could easily hide until the initiative favored them and they could exploit the element of surprise. The principal U.S. strategy was to flush them out in "search and destroy" operations, using the infantry to make contact and then quickly pulling back so that devastating artillery and air-munitions barrages could saturate large areas where battle lines were often nonexistent and where civilians inhabited the terrain. The combat infantryman was primarily a bait, barely a fifth of army manpower at the war's peak, whose role was subordinated to the conviction that the massive use of aviation and artillery would decisively influence the war's strategic balance. A reliable measure of this increasing reliance on technology and firepower is the tons of munitions per man-year of combat exposure: using World War Two as the base of one ton per year of combat, by Korea it had reached eight tons per year, and it was 26 tons per year in Southeast Asia during 1966–71. The U.S. alone used 15 million tons of munitions in Indochina, over twice the quantity it consumed in all of World War Two and five times the Korean War level. Aircraft dropped half of it; in the case of the B-52s, from as high as 30,000 feet. The air force's own estimate was that, in half the instances, B-52s struck where there were no enemies; about 70 percent of all artillery shells were fired for "harassing and interdiction" purposes where there was light or no combat. The results were enormous civilian casualties and damage, the transformation of Vietnamese society, huge outlays for the U.S. taxpayer, and the consequent American military failure to win the war.

The incredibly expensive futurist dimensions of the U.S. military effort are painfully familiar, ranging from people sniffers on computer-coordinated electronic battlefields to extraordinarily complex $15 million aircraft; but the helicopter was the single most important innovation. Although it had been developed for use in Europe, McNamara believed the helicopter to be a decisive weapon in counterinsurgency, allowing highly mobile manpower and firepower to overcome jungle terrain. The army did not share his enthusiasm but was swept along, eventually concluding that its initial skepticism had been correct. Helicopters were costly to run and maintain, they eliminated the element of surprise, and they were vulnerable to ground fire: 4,857 of them were lost during the entire war, considerably more than the 3,500 in use in Vietnam at the mid-1968 peak. Senior officers tended to use them to direct combat, and the army later concluded this had been a serious error since it removed them from battlefield conditions and gravely flawed their judgments. Expensive weaponry and munitions became an even more important component of the war after 1969 as U.S. manpower levels declined.[8]

But the strategically indecisive weapons and equipment used to fight it made the war enormously dear and produced decisive new dilemmas even for the U.S. Leaving aside the war's impact on the balance of political and social forces within Vietnam itself, America's technology had to be efficient in terms of the amount of time it required to attain its military and political goals lest a protracted conflict create economic problems as well as serious opposition among the public at home. Indeed, while a very few

American leaders always feared such potential complications, none ever imagined that the ultimate price of the war would—as had occurred so often with other armies earlier in the century—eventually include the breakdown of the U.S. military establishment in Vietnam in ways that severely affected the nation's ability to continue the conflict. It was the conjunction of all of these successive, decisive challenges that eventually forced the Nixon administration to reduce its presence in Vietnam greatly and ultimately to depend once again on a venal and incompetent client regime to win the war, compelling the U.S., like so many nations before it, to confront the limits of its power in the face of the heavy, unanticipated constraints that wars invariably create.

Economically, the Vietnam War differed fundamentally from the four other wars the U.S. had engaged in since 1898, for all the earlier conflicts had begun when the economy was in recession or still emerging from a period of idle productive capacity. In addition to advancing the nation's political goals, they had created new prosperity, producing neither structural challenges globally nor alienating a major domestic social constituency. But the massive escalation after 1965 began well into the longest sustained period of expansion since 1945, causing the rate of inflation in the latter half of the decade to become three times greater than during the first half, expanding the demand for labor so that the productivity of manufacturing fell dramatically, and weakening the dollar internationally. The Johnson administration was already heavily committed to its "Great Society" reforms, which benefited the poor and black communities most of all, and the question of how to pay for both a war and domestic programs entailed consideration of basic political issues and priorities. To reconcile this tension the president had, at the very least, to manage the budget astutely.

McNamara emerged as the decisive figure in this dilemma, for Johnson trusted him until his fatal mistakes could no longer be undone. But McNamara merely allowed the services to spend whatever they thought they needed, and on March 1, 1965, he issued a "blank check" making it clear "that there is an unlimited appropriation available" for Vietnam, believing, like all his peers at the time, that the war would not last long.[9] As needs exceeded the amount of funds he had budgeted, he merely extracted supplemental appropriations from Congress, and since Johnson considered tax increases politically dangerous, for over two years the president cut spending for the popular Great Society program to help pay for the war. Only in July 1968 was a new tax bill enacted. But notwithstanding his supreme self-confidence, which initially disarmed potential critics, McNamara underestimated the costs of the war for fiscal 1967 by over 100 percent, running up an $11 billion deficit for which reductions in domestic spending hardly sufficed. In fiscal 1968, which began in July 1967, the deficit was well over twice that amount, by which time Johnson had lost all confidence in McNamara, who belatedly concluded about then that the U.S. could no longer expect yet more escalation to achieve victory. These compounded economic factors emerged and interacted with domestic politics and international finance to constrain further escalation, but suffice it to say that the structural inhibitions on American war-making had become decisive, and set the context for a subsequent partial reduction of its role not only in Vietnam but, in certain crucial ways, elsewhere as well. The gap between the nation's vast desires and finite resources, and its obligation to impose priorities on its global objectives in order to attain any of them, was now an obvious and fundamental constraint and a source of domestic conflict and opposition, including from economic elites that since 1914 had consistently supported a vigorous foreign and military policy.

While U.S. leaders had obviously miscalculated the nature of a war against resourceful, determined enemies in jungle terrain, they also gravely misunderstood the costs and complexities of their own way of warfare and the extravagant technological fetishism on which it was premised. Only surrealists can aspire to capture the daunting realities of a high-consumption war providing its soldiers with innumerable imported amenities and utilizing stupendous amounts of equipment and firepower in a highly decentralized, primitive economy. The buildup that was to occur was unprecedented in the history of warfare and the Pentagon purchased everything it desired on a crash basis, cynically charging a great deal not related to the war to the Vietnam account. As an official review later put it, "The zeal and energy and money that went into the effort to equip and supply U.S. forces in Vietnam generated mountainous new procurements, choked supply pipelines, overburdened transportation systems, and for a time caused complete loss of control at depots in Vietnam."[10] Apart from pure waste in terms of useless luxuries and futurist weapons, much of which many industrial nations now deemed essential to modern warfare, the standard solution for equipment lost in the logistics logjam was to order more, speed being more crucial than economy. By the end of 1967 the Pentagon managed to impose some constraints on such extravagant spending, and its logistics control began, in its own words, to be "slowly established."[11]

But the inherent counterproductivity of the entire system was clear: it was militarily inconclusive and so costly that it precipitated grave economic problems at home and internationally. Above all, it transformed the nation the U.S. was seeking to dominate. The problems that the Korean War had created seem relatively small by comparison!

The Johnson administration completely failed to anticipate the war's metamorphosis of public opinion. The United States' foreign-affairs activism after 1898 had been inextricably linked to the American public's acquiescence to, if not enthusiasm for, the policies that successive presidencies defined, but the sustained, growing financial sacrifices they also imposed upon taxpayers after 1946 required stable popular endorsement. Opinion on the Korean War shifted at the end of 1950, but the majority of the people ultimately backed it, especially after Eisenhower was nominated and elected president. That politicians might pay a fatal political price for their military policies was a dramatic and unprecedented development, and a potential inhibitor of vast significance. But the length of the war, the economic and intellectual dislocations it caused, and the repeated dashed hopes that the administration's persistently optimistic prognostications created—with its consequent "credibility gap" in its relationship with its citizens—began to erode support for it, especially among blue-collar, low-income voters without whom the Democrats could not be reelected. By 1967 the proportion of Americans favoring the war began to decline, until by the end of that year opinion was evenly divided. The Tet Offensive in February caused approval to drop sharply, and it continued to fall thereafter until by January 1973 two out of three Americans opposed the war.

Vietnam revealed that profound disunity in American society would accompany protracted war, and that the historic political underdevelopment of the population and the absence of a significant leftist party had nonetheless not eliminated the public's capacity, however inchoate its expressions, to become alienated in ways that might seriously constrain the nation's foreign policy in the future. At this time, as well, a Congress that for two decades had docilely acquiesced to the definitions and demands of successive administrations started to develop a greatly expanded capacity to evaluate and affect foreign policy and budget issues, and began to challenge executive supremacy—culminating in driving Nixon from the White House in August 1974, and much tamer forms thereafter. Like countless millions of Europeans and Asians since 1914, the American people also had a breaking point that patriotic calls to glory could not neutralize.[12]

### The Breakdown of the American Military

While at the inception of the war the administration failed to foresee the loss of popular support, still less the emergence of an articulate and often massive antiwar movement, there were some small precedents for such opposition that could have forewarned them. There were, however, no precedents whatsoever for the breakdown of its military services in Vietnam, which raised the issue of the very viability of the principal instruments of American military power and strategy, particularly the army. The U.S. Army in Vietnam was highly stratified; the officers consisted mainly of career men from middle-class and small-town backgrounds who often used their subordinates in ways that aided their own advancement, or poorly motivated temporary officers, far more interested in survival than heroism, who were either ROTC graduates or selected from the lower ranks after ROTC volunteers declined by two-thirds during the war. Of the approximately 2 million men who served in Vietnam, those from low-income families, blacks, and Hispanics formed a greatly disproportionate share of the combat rifle companies who were sent on the dangerous search-and-destroy missions intended to flush out the enemy so that the skilled air and artillery personnel could saturate them with explosives. It was this group, roughly a fifth of the entire army, that avoided engaging the enemy as much as possible, and attempted, at the very least in 788 confirmed cases during 1969–72 (succeeding in 86 instances), to kill their officers for pushing them too energetically to fight or denying them access to hard drugs. Never before in wartime had the American military experienced so much insubordination or such profound racial tension and frequent riots, much less heroin addiction among 20 percent of its personnel and widespread use of marijuana and alcohol.[13]

Withdrawing the American military force from Vietnam by 1973 gained political respite for Nixon's presidency, and it also reduced the cost of the war in mandatory ways both because of domestic political and economic pressures and the insistence of the other industrial capitalist nations that Washington protect the dollar from further weakening. But rather than resolving the crisis in American strategy, doctrine, and weaponry, Vietnam intensified it profoundly, leaving the "credibility" of its military power far more in doubt than ever before. Not only had weapons failed militarily, but politically and economically they had created irreconcilable dilemmas. But all modern theories of military strategy have totally ignored the simple reality that the skills and motivation of those who are responsible for the dirty tasks of implementing them are fundamental, and that there is no possibility whatsoever of victory when soldiers refuse to perform as expected. No one in the American military or among its civilian strategists had ever imagined the possibility of such an outcome to an effort of this scope. In the end, as the well-groomed politicians and generals who articulated strategies and made grand claims for their weapons became irrelevant and pathetic in wartime, the constraints on those in power were greater than ever, and their conventional wisdom collapsed totally.

### The Structural Causes of America's Defeat
The United States failed in Vietnam not solely because its strategy and the technology to implement it, much less the political and economic institutions on which they were based, were fatally flawed. At least as significant was the fact that in the very process of fighting such a war, massive firepower transformed the basic structure of Vietnamese society in ways that gravely aggravated the already profound organizational and economic

weaknesses of America's dependent regimes in Saigon. Even though the war seriously traumatized the Communist side too, reducing its military capacities, the social and economic impact of the American way-of-war, in common with so many conflicts before it, decisively altered the framework and forces that would determine victory and defeat. The astonishing manner in which the Vietnam War ended revealed how profoundly counterproductive Washington's military arm had become.

The escalation of warfare to destroy or affect civilians in ways that violate constraining "rules of war" increasingly became the norm among all of the major adversaries during World War Two. Notwithstanding the qualitatively and therefore morally distinctive Nazi and Japanese intentions and roles, the Allies consistently transgressed traditional legal and ethical standards concerning civilians and war crimes. The Korean War saw the U.S. take yet one more large step away from the "rules of war." While the Vietnam experience reflected the sheer overwhelming quantity of technology that America's wealth could purchase, both the weaponry itself and its uses were the ineluctable product of the military premises and institutions that have guided much of the "civilized" world since 1914.

Such caveats notwithstanding, the U.S. carried the war against civilians in Vietnam to an extent that only Germany and Japan have surpassed in modern history. Astonishingly superficial putative ethical anti-Communist justifications were concocted to rationalize the United States' behavior, but an additional animus of outright cruelty, especially among airpower advocates, as well as a racist undercurrent, reinforced it. More important, however, was a kind of "amoral" pragmatic conviction among U.S. leaders that America could win the war more quickly if, by utilizing every form of warfare available to it short of nuclear weapons, it emptied vast regions of the population essential to sustaining the enemy. What they did not suspect was that exactly the reverse would occur due to a variety of complex and subtle social, economic, and organizational processes that were easily predictable and today appear starkly obvious. In brief, as has happened so often in the century, nominally good and virtuous men whom conventional wisdom had so mesmerized once again committed consummately evil acts with the gravest human consequences because the system within which they operated made conformity to a dangerously narrow view the rule for decisive periods of time. In this case, such conduct was not only morally reprehensible; pragmatically too it was unjustifiable, save for the careers of individuals concerned.

America's generals and political leaders consciously sanctioned the use of massive firepower in much of Vietnam because, as General William C. Westmoreland put it, "it does deprive the enemy of the population . . . ," from which it recruited soldiers and support.[14] In the vast "free-fire zones," every person was deemed an enemy in fact if not in intent, and the stupendous amounts of unobserved artillery ("H&I" in military slang) and bombs accounted for much of the war's tonnage. Civilians in these zones were deliberately driven away.[15] Search-and-destroy operations applied the free-fire principle in yet another way. Chemical warfare, which the Pentagon privately acknowledged exposed it to war-crimes charges (thereby causing it to attempt to keep the program secret), was one more means of displacing people.

The use of defoliating herbicides in Vietnam began on an experimental basis in August 1961, increasing from 6,000 acres in 1962 to 1.7 million in 1967. Diem initially urged the U.S. to employ it against rice in order to deprive the NLF and its supporters of food, and by 1965, 42 percent of the chemicals fell on food crops, affecting civilians and combatants alike. In 1963, U.S. experts learned that the principal defoliant, Agent Orange, might cause cancer, birth defects, and much else (a fear that was confirmed), but this failed to affect policy in any way. The Americans used defoliants for nine years, spraying 20 percent of all the south's jungles and 36 percent of its mangrove forests—resulting in irrevocable, enormous human and environmental damage. Bulldozing vast areas also caused permanent devastation, and some 3,000 square kilometers, including food crops and water-control systems, were plowed under during the war.

The predictable result of such destruction by these and so many other techniques was the uprooting of a rural society, exactly as the U.S. policy intended. While precise data will never be known, even the Pentagon has conceded that between 700,000 to 1,225,000 civilians were killed and wounded between 1965 and 1972 in South Vietnam, an area with 18 million people in 1970, but U.S. Senate estimates are higher, with deaths comprising anywhere from 195,000 to 415,000 of these totals. Diem claimed to have moved 8.2 million people—about half of the south—into nominally controlled areas by 1962 alone, and successive pacification programs repeatedly forced or drove peasants from their homes. At least half of all peasants, but especially those in NLF-dominated territory, were pushed into refugee camps, where their standard of living dropped by about two-thirds, and they also suffered incalculable psychic losses. In 1960 only 20 percent of South Vietnam's population lived in urban regions, but by 1971, mainly for reasons of physical safety and dire economic necessity, this share had increased to 43 percent—a growth rate five times that for the Third World as a whole.[16]

To some critical extent, therefore, the Communists were cut off from the peasantry in large parts of the nation, and in this sense America's military calculus succeeded brilliantly, but the responsibility for sustaining the distinctive social order that emerged fell entirely on the U.S. and its surrogate, and here the resources necessary for attaining this monumental goal were wholly dependent on economic and political factors over which both had very little, if any, control. The marginalized urban population lived on the sidewalk economy or was unemployed, worked as prostitutes in the case of 200,000 women, and survived precariously in a transitional, artificial cacophonous urban world completely different from their native villages; but the U.S managed effectively to rupture their relationship to the NLF. The personalism and apathy that the imperative to survive instilled quickly produced a deeply alienated population, yet American officials believed that the uprooting of a traditional peasant society in wartime would create an alternative to the Communists. But this assumption totally ignored the fact that alienation in the context of urbanization also generated crucial dangers, providing no legitimacy or stability to a puppet regime unless it had the money and force to placate those now in the cities. It was relatively easy to destroy a nation, but infinitely more difficult to create a viable alternative that could transcend the war's terrible impact on the values and behavior of millions of people in vital locations and positions, much less evoke their loyalties in times of crisis. For the Americans' problem was not whether they could transfer military power to their surrogates, as they had often sought to do elsewhere after 1945, but rather whether they could establish those political, economic, and ideological institutions and forms that are the prerequisite for enduring military successes in the Third World.[17]

It was this vast structural, social, and cultural transformation of a nation that increasingly altered the war after the late 1960s from one that was principally military to a conflict whose outcome would reflect now largely autonomous factors inherent in a gravely flawed social and human organization. That the NLF's means for dealing with the new realities of the nation were altered profoundly was unquestionable. But was this now so decisive? The Americans believed it was, at least to the extent that a significant constriction of the Communist's mass following could become the basis, along with other diplomatic and military measures, for defeating them permanently.

### The Balance of Forces in People's War

In terms of their original strategic assumptions and real power, both the U.S. and the Communists were significantly weaker in 1969 than they had been before the Tet Offensive. The U.S. inflicted massive casualties on the NLF and DRV armies, and it repeatedly escalated its firepower and manpower to compensate for Communist successes until 1968, but its strategy still failed to alter the enemy's will and ability to persist—nor could it afford economically or politically to increase its military commitments. And while the NLF and many of its supporters had either been driven out of much of the countryside or killed, the Pentagon's highly unreliable data on hamlet security said nothing about the loyalties of the peasants that its side claimed to control, and its experts knew that many of them, including those ideologically non- or even anti-Communist, were making accommodations with the remaining NLF structure and often selling it rice.[18]

In the most fundamental sense, the war's future was no longer in the hands of either the U.S. or its enemies, subject to their decisions, desires, and resources. It had lasted so long that it had significantly transformed the basic nature of the contest, greatly reducing the importance of battlefields and armies. The very process and character of the war itself, with its multi-faceted social, cultural, economic, and political dimensions, were moving impersonally to shape the orbit within which the forces that were to determine victory or defeat were increasingly likely to occur.

It is certain that the Communists believed, for reasons that seemed persuasive and logical to them as well as to the Americans, that they were far weaker after the Tet Offensive than before it, and residues of their defeatism persisted until the war ended. The NLF infrastructure and manpower losses after 1968 were enormous, and the Communists' central Tet Offensive objective to rebuild their power in the cities failed abysmally. The marginalized urban masses remained immune to their appeals, and while a substantial minority were attentistes, most of these were of doubtful reliability. For military purposes, the Party was no longer significant in cities, and in many rural areas its stress on physical security did not allow it to operate freely among peasants, many of whom had become apathetic or too traumatized by repeated suffering and repression to dare to make a visible political commitment to anyone—whether the NLF or the Saigon regime. The majority of the peasantry before 1966 had supported the NLF for a variety of reasons, ranging from genuine conviction to conformity to neighborhood and family opinion, but after 1969 most were concerned with their own survival and well-being, which meant adjusting to power realities. With American troop reductions after 1969 and erosion and corruption in the Saigon army, the NLF regained access to at least 60 percent of the Mekong Delta by 1974, and many peasants adapted to the new power balance, including selling rice at premium rates to the NLF, but compared to their roles a decade earlier most remained relatively passive. As for the Communist-led army, it emerged from 1968 so bloodied that it avoided a major battle until the Saigon regime's invasion of Laos in February 1971 compelled it to fight—and to win. And while it attained major tactical successes when its conventional army struck across the 17th parallel in May 1972, its heavy losses and failure to coordinate its military components infused it with a defensive, cautious mentality for nearly three more years.

The Communists appeared to have been weakened in vital ways; even more important, their leaders believed this to be the case. The crucial point is that of all those overwhelming military factors which both the Americans and the Communists thought to be the decisive measures of power, none possessed anything like the significance either attached to them. Neither side, ultimately, comprehended the nature and structure of the war after its initial military impact became translated over time into a test of social systems and social forces which, while they included combat, increasingly transcended it.

The Korean War painfully revealed to the United States how armies that are materially very unequal can become stalemated on battlefields, and in Vietnam it unsuccessfully attempted to respond to that lesson by developing a grand strategy based on massive firepower and high mobility. That the war was too costly and too long merely reiterated the lesson of Korea. Although the U.S. believed after 1964 that its military power would transcend past frustrations, by 1969 it had to confront the relationship of its own credibility and sacrifices to the nature and viability of the client regime it was seeking to keep in power in Vietnam. Would its endorsement of Nguyen Van Thieu and reliance on his policies cause the U.S. to lose the war regardless of the balance of military power, making its power ultimately no greater than the weakest link in a struggle whose character and complexity far transcended the assumptions about it that America's leaders held when they embarked on the fatal adventure? And was Vietnam but one reflection of the unresolvable contradiction inherent in the United States' confrontation with much of the Third World, and its fatal dependence on corrupt clients elsewhere a harbinger of future defeats?

In essence, the Army of the Republic of Vietnam (ARVN) evolved from a style of military organization much closer to Chiang Kai-shek's during World War Two than to the idealized forces that American officers and court strategists considered in their plans and theories concerning Third World armies. Thieu's Byzantine military system was essentially a mechanism for controlling the political structure and, above all, to prevent the army from mounting a coup against him; the American-subsidized economic order was basically a vast fiefdom for guaranteeing the personal fortunes and political loyalties of Thieu and his supporters. With over a million men nominally within its ranks in 1972, and after 1967 with its senior officers selected only for their devotion to Thieu, the ARVN was incapable of fighting seriously, much less with the modern arms the Americans lavished on it but which it could neither service nor operate properly. Between 1965 and 1972 almost 1 million men deserted it, peaking at 132,000 in 1972, reducing the army's combat strength by 30 percent in an average year. Roughly one-quarter of the men ostensibly in its ranks were "ghost soldiers" who had deserted, were dead, or held outside jobs—a status that allowed their officers to pocket their pay and allowances. The social barriers between officers and soldiers were immense and ranged from education to religion, Catholics being especially overrepresented among officers. And since soldiers had to serve until age forty-five, the families of nearly half of them lived with or near them, which meant that the population of wives and children around ARVN bases far exceeded that of the army itself. The United States' proxy was merely another variation of a typical moribund Third World military regime.

Suffice it to say that in January 1975 the ARVN had what on paper appeared to be a crushing numerical lead over the combined Communist forces in the south: over three times the artillery, twice the tanks and armored personnel carriers, 1,400 aircraft against none, a two-to-one advantage in combat troops, and three times the manpower. ARVN fired nine times as many shells at the end of 1974 as the Communists, and had huge munitions stocks and comparatively simple logistical problems. It was not the strength of the miscellaneous Communist forces that was decisive but rather the weakness of Thieu's army in all domains that affect warfare. By 1974 it was disintegrating amid the ravages of inflation and demoralization, ready to capsize before the first significant challenge. Had Hanoi not attacked in March 1975, the war would still have ended in the very near future with economic and political upheavals—the imminence of which even some American official experts predicted—from which the Communists would have emerged victorious after a period of social chaos.

Only such profound social, economic, and ideological decay explains why the ARVN scarcely used the huge supply of arms and training the U.S. had lavished upon it. When the Communist army attacked in the Central Highlands in mid-March 1975 it expected the war in the vast mountainous region to last through the year and perhaps longer, and it was utterly unprepared to win total victory in a conventional war. But the ARVN troops immediately intermingled with their families and the army disintegrated after very brief combat, and the panic that spread throughout the northern half of South Vietnam was wholly unanticipated by anyone. Relative to earlier battles, there was very little fighting, and the ARVN deserted and fell apart in a process that was social, psychological, and organizational—and scarcely military in the narrow, traditional definition of that term. The germs of such a defeat had always been there for anyone to see, but none of the principals in the war had understood the essential factors that caused Saigon's catastrophe, and so the Communists entered a huge territorial void relatively peacefully and wholly unready for the monumental economic and administrative tasks that suddenly were theirs. For them it was the second time since August 1945 that great power and responsibility had fallen in their hands to some critical degree because of a conjunction of decisive objective forces that were largely not a result of their own strategy and efforts.[19]

The Vietnam War was the quintessential conflict in the long history of warfare in our century, one in which the social, economic, and organizational dimensions of wars increasingly overshadowed the purely military to become decisive in determining their outcomes. In such a context, aspects of which now existed in various forms and degrees in many other countries, war in the accepted military sense had become obsolete and no longer capable of producing victory in the conventional meaning of that term. Wars could wreck traditional societies, producing new socioeconomic configurations and problems that were terribly daunting to those seeking to build socialist alternatives, and the people who undertook to do so often failed because of them. But it was clear, as well, after Korea and Vietnam that the U.S. was also incapable of defining a strategy or fighting a war that surmounted the decisive political, social, and economic challenges, both at home and in whatever nation in which it was fighting, that inevitably accompanied conflicts of this magnitude. It might fight to a stalemate, as in Korea, or lose, as in Vietnam, but the victories it coveted by force of arms were now far beyond its ability to attain.

## The Challenge of the Third World After Vietnam

The utter failure of the United States in the longest, costliest, and most divisive war in its history occurred at a point in the world's political and social development at which the U.S. needed more urgently than ever a military strategy capable of preventing radical institutional changes in the Third World, whatever ideological guise they assume. This growing disparity between the magnitude of the task and America's military resources for accomplishing it has been a dominant theme in the history of the past four decades, constantly coloring the news that has penetrated our daily lives and defined the obsessions of political leaders. Precisely because the parameters within which wars now occur have altered so profoundly, it is vital that we comprehend the implications of the changing post-1945 Third World contexts for military conflicts. The collapse of the Communist bloc after 1989 has coincided with growing crises in much of the Third World and the increasing challenges they have presented to American leaders, greatly magnifying their difficulties in regulating international affairs. The fact that politics in large parts of Europe have again become so dangerous and urgent, and the balance of power there has destabilized in ways that challenge both the U.S. and world peace in a manner unimaginable after 1946, has made our globe more complex and precarious than ever before.

The economic, social, and demographic dimensions of the Third World crisis and its relationship to the industrialized nations are all so well known that we need only refresh ourselves briefly regarding those structural factors eroding political and social stability in innumerable countries. Such problems were neither the product of leftists seeking to alter their society—much less linked to the Soviet Union—nor of wars; ironically, it was pre-eminently the U.S., which in the process of furthering its own interests contributed greatly to the economic, social, and demographic forces undermining peace. The fact that conservative orders began to weaken, or even capsize, when there were not always many radicals present to accelerate or exploit the process, created uncontrollable and essentially complex new situations to which the U.S. and other industrial states had now to relate their very imperfect military as well as finite political and economic resources. The 1959 Cuban Revolution was the harbinger of such changes, for both the venal ruling elite and the class that supported it proved unwilling to defend their system from the inherently fragile challenge that Castro's amorphous coalition posed. Only later did Castro's movement radicalize, but by then the U.S., which never would have tolerated a Marxist revolution in the Western Hemisphere at a point it could easily have destroyed it, could not find the means to prevent it from consolidating its power.

Descriptions of the Third World's structural conditions demand caveats regarding the meaning of statistics and averages. Apart from the uneven accuracy of existing data is the fact that great variations between nations and regions make generalizations subject to important contingencies; certainly not all places fared equally badly, and a significant number actually prospered. But such structural challenges to the social classes to which U.S. interests were linked, while troublesome enough immediately after the Second World War, increased qualitatively after the 1960s and by the late 1970s were transforming many places. From the viewpoint of the Americans it was less important that these trends were far from universal than that in a number of countries—far more, indeed, than it could cope with—there existed destabilizing social and political developments that might test, at least in the eyes of its officials, the United States' military resources for controlling them.

Land issues were one crucial index of the epic transformation that was unfolding. In parts of Asia the population grew faster than available land and thereby produced smaller average landholdings, greater numbers of displaced peasants working as hired laborers dependent on seasonal employment, and a vast movement toward Third World cities. Some of these trends were at least partially offset by higher productivity, but the one nation of the region that experienced the most acute land problems, the Philippines, also developed the only significant guerrilla movement. In Latin America the land problem was far more than a case of one sick nation in a region; there was an overall malaise that affected much of the entire continent, above all most of Central America (where 1 or 2 percent of the farms contained half or more of the land), and absolute poverty grew along with it. Average farm size declined along with the changing structure of agriculture, and marginalized small landowners and tenant peasants increasingly became seasonal workers, pushed on to poorer land, or were driven out of agriculture entirely.

Throughout the Third World, it was the growth of agricultural products for export that emerged as the single most important cause of the people's immiserization and displacement; in the quarter-century after 1950 the physical volume of agriculture for export from Africa, Latin America, and Asia more than doubled. This pattern affected Nicaragua and El Salvador profoundly, and the land and human crises there became armed conflicts. Due to the burgeoning U.S. market for its output and "development" loans from the U.S., the World Bank, and the Inter-American Development Bank to build roads and processing facilities that made possible the exploitation of vast areas once devoted to food for local consumption, Central America became the quintessential example of the traumatization of agrarian economies. The transfer of much of the best corn land to cotton for export to multinational corporations operating through local elites began in the 1960s with the Alliance for Progress, quadrupling the value of cotton exports in less than two decades. Cotton alone would not have harmed the peasantry so seriously, but with the burgeoning fast-food industry in the U.S., and its voracious demand for cheap beef, Central America succumbed to intensive U.S. and international bank pressures, uprooting and impoverishing the peasantry more gravely than ever. Cattle raising requires far less labor than cotton farming and it absorbed hitherto isolated areas for grazing. It also demands a local infrastructure too expensive for smaller farmers, and foreign public and private funding was channeled through local oligarches, who profited greatly as beef growing displaced more peasants than any other export boom before it. The quantity of beef exported from Central America rose about two-hundred-fold between 1957 and 1980. The area devoted to food crops increased slowly, due mainly to the opening of marginal, hitherto neglected areas, while the generally superior land allocated to export agriculture more than doubled in the quarter century after 1950, and by the end of this period nearly equaled land devoted to local food needs. To this day Washington advocates such commercialization of the region's agriculture and its integration with the U.S. economy as part of an eventual hemispheric free-trade zone.[20]

In Latin America such trends caused the share of the population living in urban areas to mount from 49 percent in 1960 to 70 percent in 1989. With populations and poverty expanding faster than the economies, important elements of the somewhat modernized, and growing, middle classes began to question the traditional oligarchies' abilities to rule over such complex transitional societies without triggering social explosions, thereby dividing the well-off in some countries into rival camps in ways that undermined the familiar military-oligarchy alliances that had stabilized many nations after 1945. But urbanization notwithstanding, the number of rural poor in developing nations increased by 40 percent in the two decades ending in 1992. Some countries, of course, experienced sufficient economic growth to mitigate such trends, and among them the potential for instability declined significantly. Coping with those who gained little or nothing from this great transformation of the larger part of the world—the displaced inhabitants of shantytowns linked to the vast polluted urban conglomerations rapidly expanding in most of the world's poorest nations, or the scavengers and prostitutes and the dust of the human condition—emerged as a central challenge to those social elites on whose power Washington's influence largely rested.

That such daunting economic problems would be resolved easily or always peaceably seemed unlikely for a variety of decisive reasons, some unrelated to the venal rulers of so many of the Third World's nations. For one thing, the export economies that they sought to develop for their own class interests, and under pressure from international development banks and the U.S., existed in a global context in which commodity prices historically have greatly favored the industrial nations. After 1970 the prices of all nonoil commodities and metals and minerals declined relative to manufactured goods, and Latin America's and Africa's terms-of-trade fell sharply during the 1980s—in part because the development banks continued to encourage the production of export commodities for an already saturated world market.[21]

But such external forces aside, most Third World leaders pursued self-serving policies and accepted inducements from the U.S. and many other industrial nations that necessarily eroded any hope for balanced development and stability. Third World arms expenditures after 1970 grew nearly threefold by 1987, including in regions such as Latin America and Africa generally not at war, and during some years exceeded the economic aid they received. The ruling elites of many nations revealed their true feelings about their own futures by transferring capital to safe havens, an amount of money which by the end of 1990 was equivalent to 55 percent of their total external debt. The Third World's debt to the richer nations continued as a permanent and paralyzing burden, especially since the prices they received for many of their exports declined. Notwithstanding a temporary restructuring of nearly half of it during the 1980s, its total debt stock reached an all-time high of $1.2 trillion in 1991.

As domestic debt piled on foreign debt, in many Third World nations economic problems grew enormously and the ultimate political consequences of the countries' de facto insolvency became increasingly unpredictable. Latin America's average growth rate during 1981–85 was one-tenth of the 1961–70 rate, but in thirteen of the region's twenty-five nations, their economies contracted as nations struggled to meet accumulated internal problems and to cope with external debt demands, capital flight, and foreign investors' repatriated profits. And Latin America's net resources transfer to the world in the period 1980–89 exceeded the inflow of income from all sources by $160 billion, but its external debt still nearly doubled. So that during 1961–70, before the region's ruling classes had both eagerly and under pressure leaped into the foreign-debt trap, only four Latin nations suffered from high inflation, as opposed to ten the following decade and nineteen in 1991! [22]

When figures such as these are translated into human terms, the eventual political and military risks of such structural trends become very obvious. The gross domestic product per capita in constant dollars in all of Latin America increased sharply from 1960 to 1980, largely because of Mexico's and Brazil's rapid growth, yet by 1990 it had fallen to 11 percent below the 1980 level. But such an overall descent, for which there is no precedent, obscures Peru's 28 percent decline over the decade, and much else. Such averages also hide the extremely skewed income distribution. The income share of the wealthiest fifth of Latin America is far greater than in the developed world, where distribution is already highly inequitable. There was no longer any doubt that a vast region's problems were now parlous and defied the industrial capitalist world's repeated gestures to ameliorate it—without, however, sacrificing its privileges of buying cheaply and selling dearly, much less renouncing its accumulated debts. Real wages dropped in most of Latin America after 1980, especially in Brazil, Mexico, Peru, and Argentina. In 1970, about 40 percent of the region's population lived in poverty, and although it declined over the decade the proportion probably increased during the 1980s because of economic stagnation and population growth. But beneath "poverty," and included in it for statistical purposes, is "destitution," so that while 73 percent of Guatemala's population was classed as suffering from poverty in 1986, of these, two-thirds were in fact destitute.[23] Such enduring, recurrent structural problems, ranging from the breakdown of export-oriented economies to the conditions of marginalized peasants eking out an existence, and many others like them in Latin America, Africa, and selected Asian nations, by the 1970s had begun to define the now-familiar human and physical geography in which future political upheavals and warfare could occur.

## The Dilemma of American Political Strategy and Military Power in a World Adrift

How to respond to the inevitable social and political consequences of such deeply rooted objective trends in many nations, without experiencing

another debacle like Vietnam, remained for the U.S. after 1968 a fundamental and growing challenge, but it was one that it had scant hope of
resolving because of its endemic inability either to anticipate or find viable
solutions for the vast bulk of the trends' causes or effects. Long after its
defeat in Vietnam, Washington was still engaged in a quixotic search for a
military doctrine that offered it reasonable assurance of victory in Third
World contexts. The prospect for confrontations and crises in the future
therefore remains virtually as great as ever after Leninism's demise, because
the opposition to the political and social regimes the U.S. seeks to sustain
in so many countries has become increasingly diverse, ranging from conservative nationalist and Islamic movements to the indigenous Left.

A crucial inherent limit of America's intelligence and its ability to comprehend and adapt to the long-term trends shaping the modern world,
remains the dilemmas of insight, analysis, and policy that have also profoundly shaped the decision-making processes of every major state in this
century. The continuity and consensus among leaders have persistently
immunized them from essential information as well as the processes of reason at critical moments, so that intelligence organizations gather data of
tactical rather than strategic utility.

American Establishment experts have often acknowledged that predetermined strategies and desires define their government's crucial perceptions, and that U.S. foreign-policy leaders are incapable of anticipating
major events in order to forestall or avert serious challenges. At an operational level transcending the basic analytic myopia built into the system, by
concentrating principally on obtaining and using secret information the
CIA has often obfuscated crucial main trends that can much more accurately and cheaply be gleaned from public sources—attempting thereby to
preserve a distinctive mystique regarding knowledge that justifies the
Agency's immense expenditures. And because a tiny group of men, sometimes as few as two or three, have monopolized the crucial international-
affairs decisions of successive postwar administrations, they have simply
not had the capacity (ignoring their biases entirely) to cope with or comprehend so many diverse and complex issues simultaneously, so that
neglect and sheer ignorance become far greater factors when crises, including many that were avoidable, descend upon them.[24] And this makes
deductive, symbolic reactions to specific situations, notwithstanding their
possible counterproductivity and dangers, much more probable.

The result of these rigidities has been a growing American inability to
anticipate long-term trends that are inherent in the objective changes
affecting innumerable nations' social and economic organizations, along
with their political and strategic implications for U.S. interests and power.
Washington's responses have increasingly been ill considered and incompetent, partially offsetting the advantages that the demise of Soviet power

might have given the U.S. In the case of the Angolan crisis of 1975, the head of the CIA's operation there subsequently complained that "we were mounting a major covert action to support two Angolan liberation movements about which we had little reliable intelligence," thereby committing U.S. arms and prestige to what remains to this day a terrible, destructive conflict.[25] The Iranian Revolution of 1979, whose consequences have profoundly altered the entire Gulf region and the Middle East, utterly surprised Washington. Solely because he was close to America and purchased huge quantities of its most advanced armaments, it assumed the shah was immune to challenges. Nixon explicitly regarded him as an extension of U.S. power in the region, on whom it was deeply dependent. And so Washington ignored political and economic conditions in Iran, never raising serious questions to the embassy staff, who in turn relied for years principally on the shah's intelligence for its information. When Washington finally confronted the problem, it was already wholly beyond control.

After 1965, Washington's readiness to send its military off to threaten the use of force, increasingly in the Middle East but also in Southeast and East Asia, still remained high—as if the Vietnam experience, with its unexpected loss of control over national priorities, carried no inhibiting lessons. Nixon's siding with Pakistan in its confrontation with India over the secession of Bangladesh in late 1971, notwithstanding his private acknowledgment that the rebels had good reasons for their action or of the grave risks of escalation that might have involved the U.S., was due to the fact that Pakistan was an old ally fighting with American arms while India, although friendly, had Soviet equipment and was neutral. Maintaining the credibility of American power as a deterrent, in the White House's eyes, required it to remain prepared to intervene virtually anywhere but especially to give those Third World tyrants and corruptionists acting as faithful proxies (by providing advisers or even ground forces whenever necessary) its unquestioning loyalty and support. Its fixation with this virtually religious concept as well as the domino theory wholly negated the influence that information and rational insight might have conceivably had. For reasons such as these, Nixon supported Ferdinand Marcos's imposition of martial law in the fall of 1972; similarly, as the CIA station chief recalled, "frustrated by our humiliation in Vietnam, Kissinger was seeking to challenge the Soviets...," and so he "overruled his advisers and refused to seek diplomatic solutions in Angola."[26] The perpetuation of such thinking and action since then has made it impossible to predict where and when America's next crisis would occur, or how long until a conflict of wills would again mire it down.

### Military Doctrine and the Dilemma of American Power

At the very point that world history has altered to make the causes of basic change less the results of wars and their aftermaths than at any time since

1914, the U.S. has been endemically incapable of coping with the subtle, nuanced social and political transformations that now also profoundly shape the modern historical experience. After the failure of counter-insurgency in Vietnam, the American quest for a new and effective strategic synthesis lacked the self-confident optimism that suffused its post-Korean efforts, and the dead hand of earlier frustrations and the strong similarities between the difficulties the U.S. faced in the 1960s and those of two decades later left official strategists somewhat chastened. Moreover, the reality of competing military services, each with distinctive tactics and rival interests that reinforced their doctrines and claims in the struggle for a share of the total military budget, persists unabated as a fundamental, extremely costly aspect of both the definition and application of American military power. During the Iranian hostage rescue debacle in April 1980, the invasion of Grenada in October 1983, or the 1990–91 Gulf War, the lack of coordination and communication, due either to rivalries or some-times the absence of simple equipment, reinforced the reality that given such an inherently schismatic institutional context the prospects for attain-ing an affordable, effective American military doctrine and strategy was no more likely as the century ended than it was after Korea. Such a goal remains as much a chimera for the U.S. as it has been for every other aspir-ing power in the twentieth century.

No less significant was that America's search never occurred in a static context, but even as innumerable decisions were being taken about how to relate to ongoing or new crises in El Salvador, Nicaragua, Angola, Afghanistan, and many other places. Despite its words on paper, in practice Washington's policies once again consisted of incremental, ad hoc responses to specific challenges; operationally, its strategy still remained the sum of its parts. And these ranged from the outright use of troops in Grenada and Panama to obviously public "covert" aid in the form of arms and advisers in Afghanistan, Nicaragua, and elsewhere—and all the varia-tions between. But notwithstanding the glaring contradictions between its efforts to think realistically and its conduct, a number of assumptions have influenced Washington's planning.

In principle, there was virtually an official consensus that unless the American public were willing to support a military effort for as long as it requires to gain victory, the U.S. should avoid making a deep commitment by engaging its own troops; even the political and military goals of any direct intervention had to be both clear and attainable, and the level of American forces employed to achieve it quickly had to be sufficiently large, even massive as in the case of the Gulf War of 1990–91, from the incep-tion. Officially enshrined as national policy in the November 1984 "Weinberger Doctrine," such a stance repeatedly acknowledged the pub-lic's fickleness and the dangers that created, yet the new course left many questions unanswered. Whenever the prospects of employing American forces and risking war arose, the Pentagon and the Joint Chiefs of Staff were now usually far less pugnacious than the White House.[27]

But the Reagan administration believed ardently that confronting communism aggressively was essential lest the operation of the domino theory erode American power and influence, and it quickly sanctified its militancy with a "Reagan Doctrine." Notwithstanding its bellicosity, the doctrine implicitly acknowledged many of the constraints confronting the U.S. that Defense Secretary Caspar Weinberger later articulated by emphasizing means other than the use of U.S. forces to accomplish the basic goal of defeating America's enemies and protecting its friends. In practice, none of its applications of American power were new, including its much greater reliance on especially pernicious covert techniques. Virtually all American strategists since then have urged a reliance upon local allies to serve as proxies, hopefully "pretty-good guys," as one described them, because perfect ones did not exist.[28] No one advocated depending on outright villains, but in Angola and Namibia, to use one of many possible examples, the U.S. nonetheless worked with South Africa's intelligence and clients as the most effective way of attaining its goals. Still, most proponents of aggressive American support for local proxies conceded that if they were to succeed, significant economic, political, and social action would have to complement military efforts, even though few had illusions that the indigenous establishments would cooperate.

But even where there were no "good guys," Washington, with the strong encouragement of the most influential Establishment strategic thinkers, became increasingly committed both in theory and practice to "covert" action that aided "anti-Communist" insurgencies, of which the Iran-Contra scandal was merely the best known of many. The domino theory as a description of how change occurs in the Third World remained conventional wisdom, as did the ultimate willingness to resist threats to U.S. credibility by whatever means required. By 1988 such definitions were no longer justified as being responses to ostensible Soviet-American rivalries; rather, as such analysts put it with much greater candor regarding its own economic needs, "America's ability to defend its interests in the most vital regions" should justify its firm actions.[29]

Finding the means of relating power to reality continued to elude the United States at the end of the twentieth century just as it had eluded European nations much earlier, and it was a predicament for which no solution existed either in theory or practice. This futile search has had many expressions, all marked by theoretical failure, and this is best revealed in two ways: first, in the army's effort to articulate doctrinal coherence for its role in the Third World in a concept of "low-intensity conflict (LIC)," and then in the concurrent U.S. experience with the civil war in El Salvador, which, although only one frustration of many, was probably the one the Pentagon studied most closely and which therefore reveals best how enduring its dilemmas remain.

Advocates of LIC theory immediately confronted the obstacles of selecting nations of sufficient importance to U.S. interests and the absence of a consensus on goals, the levels of necessary violence, and the extent to which military objectives took precedence over social and economic ones. Critics of LIC, most of them within the army itself, pointed out that it was really counterinsurgency under another rubric, and that it had failed in Vietnam and elsewhere and suffered from precisely the same deficiencies. Although the Joint Chiefs of Staff in 1986 nominally approved the LIC concept, within the army itself critics called it a "doctrinal foster home for orphaned warfare concepts" such as had helped to mire the U.S. in Vietnam.[30] Some Pentagon experts, anticipating defeats such as their troops suffered in Mugadishu, Somalia, in late 1993, warned that the doctrine was irrelevant in the urban Third World, which was increasingly becoming the focus of guerrilla activity. After sustained, wilting criticism within its own ranks, LIC for practical purposes became an underfunded, low-priority program, both irrelevant and moribund.

To a critical degree, the resistance to LIC reflected the U.S. Army's bitter experiences in El Salvador, whose civil war had by 1990 lasted a decade and cost the U.S. $6 billion, as well as the fears of some of its officers that cultivating illusions regarding local wars and counterinsurgency would only lead to a repetition of the painfully demoralizing Vietnam debacle. In early 1988 four lieutenant colonels publicly excoriated the El Salvador conflict as an example of a flawed policy whose disparity between execution and comprehension and theory had doomed it to failure from the inception. American troops had not been committed to combat, but the struggle was stalemated and LIC had failed. The population had not supported the regime, on which the U.S. relied, and economic aid had achieved little. Washington had no clear policy objectives, and meanwhile the war had become wholly dependent on large amounts of its money. A Rand Corporation analysis of El Salvador for the Pentagon three years later was even more critical, treating the event as an illustration of the limits of American power in the Third World, a demonstration of how its desire for victory and refusal to make compromises had protracted human suffering; and it cast grave doubts on the new American scheme for fighting such contests elsewhere. The enduring dilemma of sustaining the status quo remained: the regime had not transformed local armed forces that were still integral to a class and crony system, had refused to adopt counterinsurgency tactics, was corrupt and oppressive, had frustrated essential economic reforms, "and the disparity between the rich and poor has grown."[31]

By the end of the century the U.S. could no longer contemplate deliberate nuclear war, and even the original targets of that strategy had ceased to be enemies. Limited and local wars ended in stalemates, producing political and economic crises at home. Covert wars invariably depended upon venal and unstable local allies, were immensely costly, and politically were generally failures. Whether with or without American forces, counter-insurgency was ineffective in military terms and traumatic in every other regard, and was more likely than any other method to produce consequences fatal to U.S. interests. Although engaged in it longer than any other nation in this century, America's grand designs for making war had successively failed, leaving it in an insoluble impasse as the world's sole nation strong enough to absorb the economic, political, and social costs of accumulated defeats and failures yet still unable to avoid more in the future because of its own interests, ambitions, and hubris.

The growing crisis in doctrine and political policy the U.S. confronted after Korea defied all of its efforts to articulate even partial solutions to the impasse and confusion into which it had fallen in much of the Third World. Notwithstanding the collapse of the entire Soviet bloc, the emergence of new challenges elsewhere left it with enduring dilemmas. Its war with Iraq during 1990–91, more than any single event since the Vietnam War, revealed this most dramatically, and reflected the adventurist nature of American political goals in our vastly more complex world, as well as the counterproductivity of the military power on which their attainment was largely dependent.

The U.S. war with Iraq represented the consummate failure of a decade-old political policy in the Gulf, and left a balance of power in the world's richest oil region that was guaranteed to sustain instability in the area—and eventually to embroil America in yet another war. After Ayotollah Khomeini overthrew the shah and the ignominious failure of America's April 1980 raid in Iran to free its hostages, Washington, Saudi Arabia, and Kuwait strongly supported Iraq's invasion of Iran five months later in the belief that Saddam Hussein would annex part of the charismatic Islamic regime's territory and help greatly to contain Iran's position in the area. Beginning with supplying Iraq with fatally optimistic intelligence before the war, thereby encouraging Saddam's adventure, the U.S. role as Iraq's backer was crucial. Since Iraq could not defeat the far larger Iranian state, whose weaknesses it had at first greatly overestimated, the U.S. resolved at least to aid Iraq at critical moments to prevent the regional balance of power from shifting decisively in Iran's favor. It gave Iraq highly classified intelligence throughout the war, permitted arms sales to it, encouraged the Saudis and Kuwait to fund Iraq, and at the end of 1986 reflagged half of Kuwait's tankers and provided U.S. Navy protection for them after Iran threatened to penalize Kuwait for its decisive role in financing the war. During the period from 1982 to 1990, Iraq received over $5 billion in American subsidized and credit-financed food, technology, and industrial products, and in the fall of 1989, over two years after Saddam had killed at least 4,000 of his own rebellious citizens with cyanide and nerve gases, the Bush administration allotted Iraq $1 billion in loan guarantees to buy U.S. food. As Bush reflected in early 1992, "As you may remember in history, there was a lot of support at the time for Iraq as a balance to a much more aggressive Iran under Khomeini. . . . So that was part of the policy of the Reagan administration. I was very proud to support that."[32]

By any criterion, America was Iraq's functional ally and helped it to build a huge army superbly equipped with armor, artillery, missiles, and chemical and biological weapons. In contrast to the United States' and other industrial nations' vast and profitable arms sales to innumerable countries for decades in which there was no concern for the dangers to regional military stability, in this case it had been American political policy for ten years to assist Iraq in order to undermine Iran. That Saddam could also use his overwhelming military might to annex Kuwait in August 1990 was a risk his arms suppliers, including the Kuwaitis and Saudis, had never even contemplated—but with the profusion of advanced arms in so many hands and the transformation of international power relations at the end of the twentieth century, such a prospect (and others like it) were increasingly likely.

From a purely military viewpoint, the American-led offensive against Iraq at the end of 1990 and early 1991 was easily successful, for the ground campaign began only after there were about 700,000 U.S. soldiers, possessing total mastery of the air, against about 183,000 Iraqis. The various U.S. services once again were frequently at loggerheads, even bombing the same targets with their distinctive expensive weaponry, some of which, as with immensely costly missiles and laser-guided bombs, missed their objectives in at least 40 percent of the cases. And contrary to initial Pentagon claims regarding precision accuracy, heavy damage was inflicted upon the civilian infrastructure, and while appraisals of civilians killed during the war itself range from 5,000 to 15,000, a very large part of the population subsequently suffered dire shortages of food and essentials for years, compounding war-caused suffering enormously. An estimated 33,000 civilians died as a result of the war and the Shiite and Kurdish rebellions that followed, and over twice that number died in the six months after the end of hostilities from hunger and from war damage to the health and sanitation infrastructure.[33]

Politically, the 1990–91 Gulf War was a total disaster, an outcome that was entirely predictable and much-discussed before the event itself. It exposed the grave consequences of America's decade-old policy in the crucial region and cast greater doubt than ever on its ability to define a more coherent, realistic political strategy elsewhere, or to identify clients to advance its goals without later turning yesterday's quasi allies into mortal enemies. In light of such extreme gyrations in its diplomatic strategies, anticipating future American behavior with any reasonable assurance was no longer possible because the White House had once again ignored its ostensible priorities and failed utterly to calculate the economic, military, and political costs of a war. Without removing Saddam from office, Iraq's destruction produced the very outcome it had been U.S. policy for over a decade to avert: Iran became the overwhelming power in the incredibly rich Gulf, and a vacuum was created that guaranteed it would remain the principal long-term threat to the interests of the U.S. and its regional allies.

That nuclear weapons and the means for delivering them would in due course become part of the military equation in the area now seemed virtually inevitable.

Rather than solving the United States' problems and creating stability, the collapse of communism and the Soviet Union, which was certainly the most profound revolution in world power since at least 1918, aggravated in crucial ways the challenges America confronted and produced yet new ones.

Notwithstanding its many tensions, the Cold War in Europe after the 1948 Berlin Blockade was brought under a reasonably reliable system of crisis management, with incidents between the two blocs that involved the threat of force declining consistently, and this reality alone made it possible for the U.S. to redirect more and more of its attention from Europe, the region of by far the greatest importance to it, to entangling challenges throughout the Third World. By the time the Reagan Doctrine was formulated, the USSR, as one former senior Washington official described the period, "behaved with a studied prudence," concerned not only with the implicit but vague Sino-American alliance that had threatened it for some years after 1978 but also increasingly distracted by its own myriad ideological, economic, and military problems.[34]

Fundamentally, the existence of the USSR ceased to be a decisive inhibition on Washington shortly after the Cold War in Europe began; Russia's subsequent significance for the U.S. emerged from the growth of military technology and the amounts each side spent on the arms race or on military aid to their respective Third World clients. But by the time the USSR collapsed, there was a growing consensus among American strategic thinkers that the location, nature, and form of the principal difficulties facing the U.S. no longer depended on Soviet support for national liberation movements, which had in any event been far more rhetorical than real for decades, and that it was these many diverse problems that could erode America's vital interests piecemeal because it lacked effective military-political responses to them. As the Bolshevik legacies of the two great world wars began to disintegrate, official strategic circles finally acknowledged that revolutions would occur without Communists and increasingly even without classic guerrillas whom American weapons could target most easily.

Indeed, as the Soviet Communist Party capsized and was even in the process of being outlawed, and the U.S. triumph over it was unimaginably complete, the highest American officials accurately predicated that major dangers were likely to emerge if Moscow's centralizing authority dissolved to the extent of leaving an enormous void in what had been the USSR. In addition, they rightly believed that yet other risks for American power would arise. Rather than being safer, the world that Washington confronted at the end of the twentieth century possessed mounting hazards, ranging from those inherent in the continuous proliferation of weapons of all sorts to the rapid growth of diverse non-Communist movements, from Islamic fundamentalists or the Brazilian Workers party, seeking to replace governments in which the U.S. had major stakes.

The breakdown of the Cold War tension, as Undersecretary of State Lawrence Eagleburger confessed at the end of 1991, meant also loosening the control "of the international system over the behavior of its constituent members," so that "nations will be tempted to go their own way with little regard for the common good. . . ."[35] The U.S. ultimately had to concede that the Soviet Union's stabilizing role since 1945 had been vital to its interests, though none of its analysts ever adequately appreciated the magnitude of its contribution in curbing the Left since 1944, for such insight would have destroyed the very foundations of their world view. In the case of the new status quo in eastern Europe and the former USSR itself, the enormous perils of civil wars and bloody conflicts between new and independent states, which the highest American officials had feared, began to be fulfilled immediately. For the first time since 1945, parts of Europe were again at war. Even the Iraqi invasion of Kuwait itself, a top U.S. planner confessed, was a result of the "international deregulation" that was occurring, for "even at the height of U.S.-Soviet geopolitical competition, the Kremlin could normally be counted upon not to allow the rivalry of clients to escalate to the point that direct U.S.-Soviet confrontation became a possibility," and Iraq had perceived "the Soviet Union was too weak and distracted to do much of anything in the way of restraint." The USSR's "increasingly constructive role" was now ended—everywhere.[36] Conversely, because "we can conduct military operations in the Middle East without worrying about triggering World War III," as a leading Establishment authority put it in September 1990, the only inhibitions on more aggressive American conduct were the inherent difficulties of the task itself and, of course, a domestic public opinion that had opposed a Gulf War until the last moment, shown enthusiasm for it only during its brief period of success, and then voted the president responsible for it out of office.[37]

The demise of communism occurred just as increasingly tense economic rivalries were making the institutional basis of an American-led global alliance more precarious than it had been since 1945, and together they produced forms of "international deregulation" of a bipolar world that Washington, for just reason, truly feared. As David L. Boren, chairman of the U.S. Senate's Intelligence Committee, phrased it, "we've had a strange and symbiotic relationship with the Soviet Union. . . . the decline of the Soviet Union . . . could very well lead to the decline of the United States as well. . . . the European countries, Japan, and others have been willing to follow the lead of the United States over the past few decades. Why? Because they needed us. . . . Will they be willing, in this new environment, to follow the lead of the United States as they were just a few short months ago? I don't think so."[38] Not only states in the former Soviet bloc would go their own way, Eagleburger admitted over a year later and after the conflicts within America's alliance had grown much more acrimonious; "gone, too, is a Soviet threat of such a magnitude as to force the Western democracies to compromise their differences and accommodate each other's interests on a continuing basis."[39] In fact, it became the common assumption among senior political and military leaders, as the Joint Chiefs of Staff phrased it in mid-1991, that there would be "the intensification of intractable conflicts between historical enemies, now fueled by weapons of enormous destructiveness and less constrained by the bipolar Superpower alignments."[40]

As the fear that had ultimately been the U.S.-led alliance's most enduring cement disappeared, the debate within it turned bitterly to rival trade blocs, containing Japan's power in all of its forms, preventing Europe from pursuing an autonomous political and economic strategy on the Continent, or Germany from reemerging dominant over it—and so much else that those both within and outside the world's capitals felt overwhelmed by the sheer complexity and diversity that was revolutionizing, and threatening, international relations at an astonishing speed. That sufficient weaponry existed in so many places to make possible conflicts of every sort, and once again repeat the suffering that has characterized the globe throughout this century, was a reality that mocked both humanity's wisdom as well as the countless justifications its leaders had given in the past for arms and war as a means of protecting and advancing modern civilization.

Whether mankind would continue as it had since 1914, with the prospect of yet more wars of greater devastation than ever, was the most fundamental challenge confronting it at the end of the twentieth century. For what was now beyond doubt were the monumental human, political, and social costs that the world would continue to have to pay if it did not abandon the path toward war on which it had repeatedly marched throughout this century of mechanized, mass destruction.

# CONCLUSION

The world has experienced more suffering in the twentieth century than ever before, and to comprehend it greatly taxes our imaginations. But to fathom how and why our century has been marred so gravely, and to decide whether a very large measure of its torments might have been avoided and, indeed, whether the events of the last eight decades can teach us anything, are essential preconditions for reversing modern civilization's destructive impulses so that mankind can aspire to avert the disasters of both conventional and nuclear wars in the future.

To study history for didactic lessons is always an inherently precarious undertaking, often subjecting us to the intellectual whims and frailties of those who cite it only to legitimate their own prescriptions for the future—making their conclusions far worse than none at all. Our dilemma remains that, notwithstanding its limits, there is no other method than critical, sustained reasoning for confronting the world's past as well as creating a defense against more blindness and folly pursued in the name of truth, of which our age has seen far, far too much. Whatever its constraints—and they are not to be minimized—we can only employ unrelenting and critical analysis if we are ever to overcome the grave erosion in contemporary social thought's ability to assess accurately the world's fate until now and to cope with its future. It is both the illusion and pretension of certainty, or at least sufficiency, on the part of those on the Left as well as the Right, which has given both leaders and led the confidence to embark repeatedly upon courses that were often terribly destructive, and that have inflicted the most damage to social theory and policy in our times.

There is so much about the experience of our age to reconsider, and to explain, and it is so desperately imperative that we escape from the present uneven yet steady descent along the path of war on which mankind has been locked since 1914, that we must not allow the risks of historical didacticism, false logic, and erroneous conclusions deter us from boldly confronting what has gone wrong with this century, lest we enter the next one committing the same errors and suffering from the same fatal delusions.

## The Failure of Leaders

Whatever the legitimacy they claimed because of birth, caste, or class origins and linkages, or their presumed abilities and wisdom to fulfill the responsibilities they held, the fundamental reality in modern history is that those who have led the world's key war-making nations and governments in this century have repeatedly and calamitously misjudged the ultimate consequences of their command decisions, consequences which they rarely, if ever, anticipated. All wars have invariably produced fatal surprises, creating challenges and new environments that quickly transcended anything men of power expected and altered every conflict's nature, meaning, and possible outcome. While the populations of most nations have initially shared a consensus that favored wars before they began, such agreements have frequently proven superficial, and the naive belief of rulers that their public's support would remain intact notwithstanding its suffering has been the origin of their downfall in innumerable instances. The world's leaders and their governments have time after time revealed an ignorance that has cost humanity a price in suffering beyond any measure. Their desires, interests, and illusions have shaped their definitions of reality and justified diplomatic and military policies that produced disasters, only some of which I have described in these pages.

These adventures were often merely responses to domestic political considerations and pressures, ranging from a fear of the masses, as in the case of Germany before both of the world wars, to the illusions and ideologies of both civilian and military advocates of war among all of the major powers before 1914, men who invariably justified it as something splendid—a brief but ennobling digression in the nation's normal drab routine. The ways states planned to fight wars invariably have also reflected some convenient and simplistic assumptions: that mobility would allow a speedy victory, as in the case of both France and Germany in 1914; or as with the United States from 1941 to this day, airpower and technology would prove quickly effective and thereby relatively cheap; and, as we have seen, many other illusions. Modern military strategy has contemplated the kinds of wars nations would prefer to fight given their budgets and overall priorities, the power and choices of those advocating various alternatives, or their experiences with past wars. Real wars have, painfully, been very different.

Theories of rational bureaucratic, organizational, and historical evolution, whether conservative, Marxist, or Weberian, gravely distort much of mankind's past experiences and are far more misleading than insightful. One cannot employ the kinds of neat, orderly generalizations about the coherence of social evolution that dominate much of modern social-science thinking to fathom the consummately self-destructive irresponsibility of leaders playing with the lives of their subjects and gambling on the very future of their social and political orders. The basic misconceptions they share about societies following a predictable cycle or rational organizational norms become, in effect if not intent, what are essentially elegant apologetics for ignorance and, all too often, great evil. The very extent to which the notion of the credibility of a nation, or its supposed need to maintain the inviolability of its alliances, has caused states to join conflicts in which they objectively had only minimal interests, and then escalate their involvement in them upon the first failure of their expectations, by itself is proof of the profound irrationality that has characterized so many of the world's social systems and leaders in this century.

Once wars have begun, completely unforeseen class and structural factors, much more than political and military leaders, have affected the actual ways wars have been fought, and the conflicts have repeatedly confirmed the inability of those who embark upon them to anticipate, much less control, their trajectories or consequences. The atavistic, romantic ideas that inspired officers before 1914 failed to prepare them, whether they were English gentlemen or French meritocrats, for the technical and logistical complexity of protracted conflicts. Even after dominant military cultures ebb, as they have since 1918, and the pretensions of their advocates have become tarnished, officers have been less able than ever to manage conflict, for modern wars in practice have quickly, completely transcended the skills of its most ardent proponents. War organizations —whether those of democratic France and the United States in World War One or totalitarian Germany and Japan a quarter-century later— under capitalism have always been mediated through class processes, and were never rational in a bureaucratic sense of intending merely to advance the nation's war effort in some neutral, classless manner. They have often consisted of mergers of private and public power, in which sectors of technically advanced big business played a crucial role. Such interests made as few sacrifices as possible and generally tailored policies to strengthen their own profit and economic positions at the expense of competition, the public, and the attainment of a maximum war effort at a less onerous price. Ad hoc improvisations and ceaseless surprises are the leitmotif of all societies at war, regardless of whether military or political leaders are in charge of them. And gradually officers, who initially comprised a cohesive caste based on class, social ties, or education, have been marginalized in industrialized nations since 1918 as the logistical and planning mechanics of modern warfare have become the purvey of specialized companies and technicians.

Coming to grips with the nature and attributes of the people who guide nations into and through wars is absolutely crucial, because there is such a remarkable congruence in the experiences of so many countries that their great similarities, notwithstanding the Nazi example, justify far more emphasis than they have received. The very continuity in leadership in the world's major states, including Germany and Japan but even within the Communist nations during and after the Leninist parties' demise, requires a much more comprehensive notion of leadership and politics than those that prevail in conventional wisdom today.

Warring heads of states' military strategies have invariably been syntheses of gravely flawed doctrines of convenience reflecting the society's sanctioned knowledge and desires, which they have rarely (if ever) challenged, and institutional pressures from economic, business, and service lobbies. Whether chosen for reasons of family, caste, merit, political and legal authority, or some combination of these or yet other reasons, executives have all managed to function in an institutional context which has encouraged them to ignore or obfuscate facts that interfere with their perceptions, class or caste bias, and personal interests in retaining power. Precisely because of such an inherent, even unavoidable institutional myopia, options and decisions that are intrinsically dangerous and irrational very often become not merely plausible but the only form of reasoning about war and diplomacy that is possible in official circles. Well-ordered arguments and logic for the illogical, and the consummate irresponsibility of playing with the lives of anonymous people who are either sent off to die or will be engulfed in battles, become the rule for a self-contained leadership that in each nation feeds itself information that in the end reflects its desires, interests, and illusions.

In this context it becomes intrinsically impossible for nations on the verge of war or engaged in it to make truly rational decisions based on a reasonably objective weighing of the consequences and effectiveness of various policy options in attaining goals. Intelligence in the true, neutral construction of that term fails to operate before and frequently during wars insofar as strategic questions are concerned, and its purveyors in all of its forms, including the mainstream press, are highly socialized personnel who share the assumptions of the system in which they operate. False definitions of reality are built into every social order, whose leaders often make disastrous, if not fatal, errors and repeatedly have no adequate safeguard against irrationality.

In the most general, strategic sense, therefore, those who have guided and run the world's warring nations throughout this century have, in varying degrees, been inherently ignorant of what they were doing in terms of both their ability to manage the processes of war as well as insight into the grave consequences of their decisions. There were major differences among leaders, of course, but even the ablest and least authoritarian of them have committed dire errors, and some—such as Hitler—failed most of the time; but the sheer extent of all of their miscalculations and false judgments combined has defined the main contours of modern history. Their ability to remain in power was (and is) due to everything from illusions that their peoples have initially shared for a crucial period—which has left them passive or even supportive until it was too late—to propaganda and repression.

Only those fortunate countries whose economic might favored them, and which could absorb the costs of their mistakes over time, have managed to emerge from wars victorious, a fact that has not prevented some, as in the case of the United States, from subsequently getting into severe difficulties as a result of their exaggerated sense of power. Advocates of change on the Left have scarcely been abler when they have attained authority, for reasons that were infrequently, if ever, of their own making. Their consistent failure to redeem and significantly (as well as permanently) transform societies when in a position to do so is testimony to their analytic inadequacies and the grave, persistent weaknesses of their leadership and organizations. It is this reality that has marginalized both social democracy and communism in innumerable nations since 1914, providing respites throughout the century to capitalist classes and their allies that otherwise would never have survived socialist regimes that implemented even a small fraction of the reforms outlined in their programs.

## The Consequences of Wars and the Nature of the Left

No one can definitively resolve the issue of whether the traditional societies and capitalism in Europe and Asia would have "matured" to crisis levels and been replaced—as Marxism postulated in the case of the capitalist economies—without wars to intensify all of their contradictions. For one thing, Marxists failed to consider the profound importance of international migration in reducing the social pressure from a surplus labor army, and apart from the fact that many of their economic theorems were either incapable of being proven, incomplete, or unclear when not simply incorrect, events prevented them from being tested in the peacetime environment that was always implicit in Marxist theories.

But if the economics can be debated, what remains unquestionable is that the greatest human, social, and economic costs of capitalism and the societies and cultures in which it flourished have been the consequences of the repeated propensity of its leading nations to go to war. And it was this, rather than opaque economic tendencies or laws, that was irresistibly to lead either to capitalism's destruction or to grave instability in innumerable nations throughout this century. For while the masses in Europe, and then Asia as well, in reality overwhelmingly refused to contest its foibles seriously during peacetime, during wars the personal costs of compliance proved far too high for unprecedented portions of them. Capitalism's sustained moral and political associations with wars guaranteed the emergence of a repeated and increasingly determined opposition to it throughout this century.

Just as there has been a profound difference between what the parties of the Left have promised and what they have done since 1914, there has been as great a distance between the causes to which they later attributed the origins of their successes in coming to power and the way they actually succeeded. Grasping both of these crucial dichotomies is vital for comprehending the historical function of the socialist movement—and both its victories and failures. More important, it also suggests that, notwithstanding socialism's monumental political shortcomings in the twentieth century or its utter demoralization and programmatic exhaustion today, movements of ostensible change, whether called "socialist" or something else emerging from the same broad radical and humanistic tradition, will remain politically significant in the future as long as capitalist nations continue the social and institutional follies to which so many have long been addicted. In a word, it is still those who rule nations who make social crises and radical changes possible, and to a very great extent their opponents have been compelled to adapt to the disastrous economic and social legacies they bequeathed them. The end of communism is only the beginning of another epoch in which new forms of conflict and social movements will appear.

Not only Leninists but conservative believers in conspiracy theories have insisted that the Communist role in history has never been passive, for they either argue (as in the case of the Communists) that an elite party must perform an irreplaceable function in creatively leading the masses through the shoals of historical events to attain victory, or that it was principally Bolshevik machinations that brought down otherwise viable societies. The decisive weight that Communist leaders have assigned to their own roles was an essential justification for their own existences and the total obedience they demanded from their followers. The contemporary organizational demise of Communist parties virtually everywhere but Asia, where they have wholly abandoned their original social goals in practice, is itself testimony to their confusion and lack of control in coping with reality. That Communist parties triumphed in the past was ultimately a reflection of the crisis in global politics after 1917, and essentially a protest against the way that the world operated rather than the result of Lenin's acumen. Indeed, after 1928 the USSR acted purely on the basis of its national interests rather than that of its internationalist pretensions, and it did far more to inhibit events wherever it could do so than to encourage further upheavals.

Because the Chinese and Vietnamese Communist parties played a leadership role at crucial moments in what were essentially tactical matters in no way vindicates the basic Leninist theses on the central and implicitly sufficient role of the party, for had Japan not embarked on war in Asia *and* its enemies not been so venal, it is inconceivable that either of these parties would have triumphed. In Russia after 1917, the Leninist doctrine of the party became purely rhetorical for reasons having nothing to do with the fact that no Communist party subsequently acquired control of a state operating literally according to Lenin's prescriptions. Once Lenin in his quest for personal hegemony introduced a one-man dictatorship he abandoned his own early organizational theories and established the cult of the leader as the Soviet Union's informal but dominant system of authority. Most Communist states and parties either imitated him or a tiny elite sought to establish (usually successfully) its self-perpetuating mastery, leaving communism without an explicit operational theory to guide its conduct—a reality that helped greatly to delegitimize its parties and create the basis for their later astonishing demise. The subsequent emergence of Communist parties as vehicles of mass mobilization that recruited vast numbers who had only the vaguest ideological qualifications and no influence whatever over party policies further widened the gap between Bolshevik practice and ideology. Socialists in this century, social democrats included, existed without an intellectual apparatus or analysis adequate to describe their own internal organization or practices as well as the nature of the societies they existed within or the global contexts in which they evolved. Devoid of essential clarity on such fundamental matters, socialists have failed spectacularly until now both to define and implement effective alternatives and political strategies for redeeming the world's problems or the grave inadequacies of capitalist societies.

The history of Communist parties, in essence, was principally one of improvisations and ad hoc responses to situations and opportunities that its enemies created, as in Russia in October 1917, China after 1946, and Vietnam in 1975, often compelling them to rely principally upon armed struggle rather than the preferred political route to attempt to prevent themselves from being destroyed, as in the cases of both Greece and the Philippines. The ability of victorious parties to remain relatively passive and survive until their enemies' failures and contradictions caused them either to disintegrate or created a situation ripe for action was much more useful to leftists than any other quality. With the partial exception of the Bolshevik Revolution, it has far more often been the old order rather than radical parties that has determined the Left's choice of paths to power. All social democratic and even most Bolshevik parties have permitted themselves to be repressed before acknowledging the failure of parliamentarianism. One can never forget the innumerable occasions during this century when antisocialist leaders of nations, including Italy's liberals, have abolished democratic systems because of a ruling class's unwillingness to tolerate pacific leftist political challenges to their follies.

But not all Communist revolutions that have succeeded were led identically, although all benefited enormously from wartime conditions and the social character of their adversaries. The Vietnamese Communists showed a significantly greater tactical ability than any other Asian party, and their repeated tactical successes were by no means merely accidents of time and circumstances that revolutionaries had slight or no role in creating. Their enemies' far greater blunders more than offset their own major errors, but in the end they too abandoned socialism as an economic goal and profoundly undermined their own power in the process. The Cuban Revolution, by contrast, occurred and survived for two crucial years for reasons utterly unrelated to Fidel Castro's abilities, and it was a historically unprecedented accident that Washington never permitted to happen again.

Successful Communist revolutions all share the common attribute of having taken place, to varying degrees, in decentralized nations with rudimentary communications, and while they were often able to survive by virtue of the protection that great spaces provide, they were also incapable—for the very same reasons—of creating truly disciplined, coordinated organizations. Their diversity meant that each national Communist movement adaptively responded to peasant demands at crucial points in their history, frequently in very different ways, and they recruited much larger numbers than would otherwise have occurred had strictly Leninist criteria been applied, producing mass rather than elite parties. Their vitality was to some extent linked to their capacity to work at decisive moments within the parameters the masses designated, above all on land issues, and thereby to organize them so that when a vacuum in their adversaries' camp opened, they were best positioned to fill it—often by improvising in crucial ways. Although formal Leninist theory repudiated the very notion, space also made parties pluralistic for quite brief but important periods, introducing differences especially among locally and regionally based party leaders; some followed mass initiatives, while others in due course sought to control them completely. Significant, if temporary, differences among party leaders in many nations were at times a reality—especially during World War Two—that must be taken into account.

To varying degrees, this tension is a central theme in the history of all of the successful Communist parties because the branch of the socialist movement that was theoretically the most elitist has at the same time been the most decentralized—producing a conflict between theory and practice that it never resolved because Leninism basically feared the democracy which alone might have given communism the ultimate legitimacy and flexibility to adapt and survive in a socialist form beyond the 1980s. Organizationally, the most successful and dominant Communist leaders were purely power-oriented, which only opened the door to unprincipled opportunists who were capable of unlimited flexibility in their conduct and policies and were greatly to help bring about the later peaceful disintegration of the Soviet bloc.

Wars have been the principal mediators between the collapse of the traditional societies and the emergence of powerful radical forces, especially before 1950. Whether coping with food problems or the varied consequences of inflation, challenging rich collaborators with foreign enemies or mobilizing peasants to rectify land grievances, the countless, diverse yet overlapping processes that wars unleash have simultaneously created both crucial opportunities and encumbering liabilities for the Left in this century, and most of the fundamental problems that socialists have faced have grown out of the ironies that this contradictory combination produced. For while war capitalism ended in war socialism in vast areas of the world, it produced intolerable political, economic, and organizational legacies that left it with wrecked economies to repair and caused the negative potential within socialist movements—from Leninism to the "social patriotism" of the SPD—to dominate its conduct. The first experience with socialists in power—in Russia—emerged from the profound disorder czarism left, and in this form communism was inherently eclectic and opportunist in its commitment to retaining power. In essence, it was to a crucial extent a reflection of the social order it superceded, embodying its worst attributes and transforming the existing culture only very superficially and laying the basis for its spectacular fall seventy years later.

The breakdown of capitalist or agrarian societies during war created a context and potential in which socialists had to overcome the legacies of 1914–18 before the forces of reaction—now in the form of diverse fascist parties—emerged also to cope with them. Neither the Communist nor the social democratic parties after 1919 fundamentally adjusted their theory and practice to the new realities of politics and the alternative strategies capitalist nations might pursue in the future, either in relation to one another or in aborting any menaces the Left might pose. Communists became, essentially, obedient vehicles of Stalin's policies until 1941, and social democracy brought about its own marginalization by responding equivocally to the two decades of challenges that terminated in World War

Two. Socialists of all schools, in brief, never frankly acknowledged the irrelevance of so much they had thought and done in order to chart new options more appropriate to the realities of politics and society in this century. Those mass Communist and socialist parties that later emerged from truly popular roots functioned not on the basis of creative theory but on that of dogmatic scripture, and when they came to power it was by virtue of forces they scarcely predicted and under conditions they had failed to anticipate. Neither of the two major branches of socialism after 1917 developed original critical analyses of capitalism, the world, or their own political premises, and they both placed their theoreticians' loyalty to the party above intellectual clarity. They were politically and ideologically wholly exhausted long before the debacle that began to destroy both these movements after the mid-1980s.

This process of decline was greatly accelerated because the very promise of success associated with many of the socialist movements after 1944, whether in or out of power, attracted innumerable individuals who sought to share in the many assets rulership brings—a process that the absence of articulated principles and goals made all the easier. The result was that socialist parties of both tendencies became channels of mobility for all kinds of ambitious opportunists and technocrats, who after 1988 had no inhibitions whatsoever as members of privileged economic and political elites to implement the most conservative strategies for restructuring their economies—many of them cynically retaining authority after most Communist parties were abolished or, in the case of social democrats and nominal Communists, assuming responsibility for reducing the living standards of the masses who had voted or struggled to bring them into power.

For those whom socialism and socialists had challenged throughout the twentieth century, the Left's collapse after 1980 was an utterly unanticipated salvation, just as surprising as the wholly unexpected outcomes of their own monumental follies had been. Had socialism been constituted on a firmer basis, and had the Soviet Union not exercised its inhibiting authority over most of European communism, then Europe after 1944 might well have taken a very different road and presented the United States and Britain with far more serious challenges than they were to confront when the USSR confined its ambitions to establishing a security zone in eastern Europe. As it was, the refusal of French and Italian Communists to reach for power, or the Soviet unwillingness to aid the Greek Left, gave the utterly discredited ruling elites in these three countries a vital respite that was the difference between life and death for the historic social orders in nations that were of immeasurably greater importance to the Anglo-Americans than those in eastern Europe. From the American viewpoint, the worst-case scenarios in Europe would have been for Moscow to pursue policies after 1944 identical to those it advocated in 1918, or for the USSR *not* to have hegemony over all the European Communist parties and for its advice to have been of no consequence. It was the very absence of Stalin's influence in Asia that led to the triumph of Communist power in both China and Vietnam in a context in which the success of either of these parties was possible but far from inevitable, and very well might have been aborted had they obeyed him.

Had Soviet Communism not emerged from the First World War, or had Stalin not guided the USSR in a cautious, state-centered manner, or had the European socialist parties behaved during the First World War in ways that prevented the Communist schisms from occurring, then the political complexion of the world today would be very different. In this sense, the Bolshevik Revolution in Russia in 1917 certainly spared the European continent far more turmoil after 1944 than it actually experienced, and it prevented the emergence of autonomous socialist parties, more radical than social democracy, as potential threats. Revolutions in Asia would have occurred after 1945 whatever the trends in Europe. Aside from what uninhibited leftists in France and Italy may have done, as the experiences in eastern Europe since 1989 have shown, events in that region would have been continuously troublesome, involving important non-Communist leftist as well as nationalist parties in otherwise extremely convoluted and dangerous ethnic and religious disputes, both internally and with their neighbors.

On balance, communism in Russia proved to be a far smaller price than the warring world might have paid had a number of entirely possible events kept Lenin from power, not the least because the system he founded ultimately proved impermanent. What would have been most dangerous for the men whose decisions and influence shape human destiny would have been for existing socialist parties to have learned the lessons of the two wars and brought their actions into reasonable conformity with their aspirations and pretensions to bring about fundamental change in the world. Independent and incapable of being disciplined by a Soviet Union whose only fixed, guiding motivation was its own national interest, socialism's promise or threat—depending on one's viewpoint—then would have remained what it appeared to have been prior to August 1914.

## Summing Up Modern War: Theses

Ironically, notwithstanding the monumental importance of the subject, the strategists who have most justified and abetted war have also articulated the greater part of contemporary explanations and theories regarding them. Their theses have largely consisted of well-ordered models of projected future events that have made various types of conflicts—above all, but certainly not exclusively, the United States' "limited wars" and nominally small interventions since 1954—appear as entirely plausible ways both to resolve differences between states and to protect and advance the nation's interest. But even though the successive escalations during the Vietnam War and the failures of counterinsurgency elsewhere have revealed the fallacies inherent in such doctrines, thinking about war in official circles and among those strategic analysts attached to them, not only in the United States but elsewhere, has remained remarkably impervious to experience. They persist in employing systematic, essentially static arguments to offer logic for the illogical, presenting what is inherently dangerous to humankind not only as rational but even as the only form of reasoning about war and peace that is "serious."

Conventional strategic theories even today continue to ignore the countless past errors in prediction, especially on the decisive importance of war's innumerable economic and political consequences both for a nation fighting outside its own borders and for the invaded state. Even Marxists have failed to weigh how wars greatly accelerate political and economic developments, especially by imposing new organizational forms, imperatives, and constraints on their original theorems, and, like the conservatives, they have largely disregarded the obvious implications that wars' actual events have for their analyses. It is astonishing that at the end of nearly a century of monumental and increasingly unrelenting conflict, that virtually all of the influential currents in social theory should, each in their own fashion, essentially marginalize contemporary history's central political, social, and military experiences. The overwhelmingly static bias in all such thought is toward describing stable systems that operate predictably, by rules if not laws, so that the concepts that have dominated conventional wisdom since at least 1914—whether they were those of defenders of the status quo or its principal critics—have not had an adequate, if any, predictive value.

But even those who acknowledge the central importance of war for social analysis and theory have found it exceedingly difficult to apply their insight systematically, if only because the sheer scope of everything they must incorporate—from culture to demography and politics, and so much else besides—makes the task of defining an adequate synthesis exceedingly daunting. For one thing, studies of specific nations do not necessarily illuminate events elsewhere. Moreover, since wars are regionally, even globally interlocking events that impinge vitally on the life of all the states involved in them, it becomes essential to approach the subject comparatively.

Because doctrines that pretend to offer total explanations have been intellectually soporific until now, a strong case can be made against generating grand syntheses that might again play the same role. Precisely because they purport to decipher virtually everything, or in the case of Marxism also offer a methodology for doing so which has reassured countless thinkers that what they do not presently understand can at least be perceived in the future, comprehensive conceptualizations in practice explain the least and scarcely get us further than simplistic traditional strategic theories. In a world so complex, modes of analysis have to be far richer and more nuanced than they have been until now, and conclusions more contingent. We need integrative efforts desperately because received wisdom tells us far too little about matters that are so urgent. But ultimately we can only generalize on whatever lends itself to such efforts, respecting the individuality of specific historical experiences wherever essential so that theory is systemically open, more permeable, and never allowed to become dogma whose every declaration and proposition—as in the case of much of both Marxist and bourgeois economic theories since the middle of the last century—is subjected to opaque exegetical efforts to unravel hidden truths in order to justify them.

Everything I have written should also be subjected to such caveats, and it is in this sense that I offer the following theses, which integrate many of the events and ideas discussed in this book to provide the reader with a broader conception of the nature of war and its role in shaping the history of the past century.

• The impact of wars on the general processes of change requires that in every country we focus on total social environments. This demands a wholly different framework and method for judging wars, how they occur, and their implications for social systems in coping with every aspect of them—economics being but one important dimension. To forecast the likely ultimate outcome of any conflict, it is at least as vital to analyze decisive war-induced changes within nations as to study the results of battles between them. Wars are to some great extent the products of the dominant economic, social, political, and ideological forces within a state, but also the logical consequences of the definitions and assumptions of military strategies that nations articulate and then apply to international relations. While war interacts with such inherited social and structural legacies, in some states it also accelerates them enormously, creating distinctive and essentially new mutations and forces with which a nation must cope. These changes—nearly all unpredicted and inherently unfathomable before the events themselves—provide the framework for leadership decision making in all of the nations that wars affect the most. Those who rule must now function within a context of unexpected economic, social, and intellectual transformations that demand altogether unique responses that are of grave, often decisive, significance for many of them. In such situations, the possibilities of diplomacy terminating conflicts in ways that create predictable political results decline to the degree that the social processes and disintegration that wars generate make for constant alterations in national, regional, and world orders, thereby defying the efforts of political and military chiefs to stabilize or control them.

The very great extent to which wars in this century have culminated in ways national leaders utterly failed to anticipate is confirmation of the reality that, once the fighting starts, those who begin wars invariably lose control of their decisive aspects. In much of Europe the First World War ended in a riot of disorder and upheaval that wholly surprised the Continent's rulers, leaving bitter reactionary political residues as a necessary by-product of the struggle's duration and effects, legacies that essentially defined war and peace in Europe over the next quarter-century—and thereafter. The Second World War was no exception, especially in Asia, where hunger and deprivation of every imaginable sort transformed the entire vast region politically; and even the crucial element of stability that Stalin created when he inhibited most of the European Communist parties was one his British and American allies utterly failed to predict, and subsequently scarcely comprehended. The leaders of Europe's vast conflagration, of whom Hitler was the most extreme case but hardly alone, did not anticipate the risks and dire consequences of the policies they were pursuing, and as the disparity between their expectations and reality grew ever larger, they all resorted to increasingly violent, destructive remedies for their accumulating frustrations and shortcomings.

Both the Korean and Vietnam wars, as well as many of the United States' counterinsurgency efforts, confirmed once more that modern wars evolve in their own fashion, in response to the inherently messy and unpredictable conditions that fundamentally shape both battlefields and, above all, the societies surrounding them. Even if the United States' "limited wars" did not necessarily wholly alter America's own domestic environment (although Vietnam went further in this direction than any preceding conflict since the Civil War), the encounters' effects upon the nations where they were fought have been not merely overwhelming but, as in the case of Vietnam, decisive in shaping the contest's very outcome. Orderly and nominally military strategies, with all their forecasts, have repeatedly and continually proven to be chimeras, and their advocates, however unintentionally, have been prophets of deceit and disaster incapable of fathoming the real social and military forces and factors that define modern warfare.

• The demographic consequences of wars for nations can be enormous, modifying the social character of countries, which both lose and receive people. They accelerate the emergence of multicultural, mixed societies—especially insofar as the working class and poor are concerned—and dilute and complicate, often decisively, the traditional Marxist model of social change. The revisions of borders in the wake of wars can concoct comparable problems by generating yet additional ethnic rivalries within states to stratify the class structure in ways transcending the people's purely economic roles. Migration accelerates urbanization in some cases; in others, the "surplus labor army" departs for countries and continents in need of toilers. The growth of cities as a result of wartime conditions or internal migration may profoundly affect social stability insofar as it concentrates strategically placed pockets of potential opposition that can articulate social discontent at crucial historical moments, creates nonproductive economic sectors exposed to greater deprivation than peasants, and undermines the capacities of rulers and their economies to feed them.

Such demographic changes scarcely play a role in modern theories of war or society, but they have had inestimable consequences throughout this century, beginning with the congestion of Russian cities before and during World War One that made the Bolshevik mobilization of the new working class feasible and ending with forced depopulation of rural areas as a consequence of American-sponsored counterinsurgencies in Vietnam or, most recently, Central America. Europe's negotiated territorial settlements after 1918, much less the displacement of whole social classes and ethnic groups in the wake of the war, uprooted countless millions of persons, marginalizing many of them economically, leading inevitably to famine in the worst cases, and produced vast residues of discontent and frustrated nationalist claims that have profoundly and terribly colored eastern Europe's politics to this very day.

Profoundly alienated men and women, formed as a consequence of wartime demographic changes, repeatedly played crucial roles in affecting the short- and long-term outcomes of wars and in shaping history. While China and Vietnam during World War Two were the most extreme cases in this century of population displacements and their consequences opening the path to revolutions that otherwise were not likely to happen, variations subsequently occurred elsewhere. People who undergo the trauma of being uprooted do not often emerge from the process as wholly neutral, passive agents whose possible roles can be dismissed from the calculations of those able initially to define and control their lives so profoundly. Greece's forced evacuation of rebellious rural areas after 1946 helped greatly to foster the very revolt it was designed to smother, and to keep it alive. A policy of deliberate massive population removals in Vietnam after 1960 became the single most crucial factor in deciding the war's ultimate outcome, not only because it caused many to join the NLF but also because it produced an artificially urbanized society for which there was no durable, long-term economic or political basis.

• Whenever nations at war undergo great impoverishment and economic trauma, particularly in the form of inflation, it affects the class structure of the previously more affluent, higher-status social strata relatively more than any other, often considerably altering their internal composition while leaving intact the existing distribution of wealth. Such changes cause some sectors of the prewar elites to sink lower in the economic hierarchy and often accelerates the rise of nouveaux riches, many of them successful because of the political connections they enjoy, and it frequently creates tensions within the traditionally dominant class. Insofar as wars offer great possibilities for gains in the form of state contracts and subsidies, particularly in more developed economies, significant fortunes are made, especially by the politically well placed. Capital accumulation during wartime, even though it usually occurs in the hands of those already among the most powerful economically, in some nations increases the concentration of industrial resources in the hands of a small fraction of the population and sharpens class distinctions. At the same time, marginalization often leads to the radicalization of some former members of the elite, ranging from its attraction to Fascism in Italy to communism in China—with all the variations in between.

The First World War's economic impact was very uneven both between and within nations, but in the aggregate it undermined as never before the economic welfare of Europe's people. Britain was affected far less than any other nation, and France adapted in ways that mitigated the war's worst possibilities. But Germany suffered gravely, as did Russia and the Austro-Hungarian Empire, and the subsequent political experiences of these nations roughly reflected the objective economic position of each one of them. Although most peasants throughout much of Europe were able to nourish themselves well, and a significant portion of them even prospered, the bulk of the working and middle classes were poorly positioned to avoid wartime economic tribulations, and for the next quarter-century Italian and German social tensions and rightist politics evolved within the parameters of such wartime legacies, which in Russia led to revolution. After 1917 this century's Right as well as the Left, insofar as they truly challenged the status quos of diverse nations, descended directly from such wartime-induced economic upheavals.

But notwithstanding strains within Europe's class structures, insofar as the ascendant capitalist class was concerned, continuity characterized it more than changes. In Germany, France, Britain, and the United States, those who dominated industrial capitalism before the war largely divided the enormous cornucopia of war contracts. As many salaried and interest-dependent middle-class constituencies declined relative to their prewar positions, and monarchy suffered wherever it had been truly powerful in guiding the affairs of states, or even disappeared, those industrialists and bankers related to military production fattened in the heady wartime economic dynamism.

World War Two was no exception in Europe, although the fate that had earlier befallen Germany was reversed as a consequence of Hitler's successful determination to transfer the war's punitive economic consequences entirely to the Continent's defeated peoples. Peasants once again generally prospered, even in the midst of the unbridled terror that the Nazis imposed upon Poland, and they became integral to a black-market economy that existed to varying degrees in most of the region's economies. But only in Greece did an altogether new economic elite emerge to displace the dominant prewar class, and this largely because it was politically well connected and unusually insensitive to the damage its economic activities imposed upon the population. Europe's middle class suffered after 1943 mainly because it, more than any other large social stratum, not only collaborated but also eagerly endorsed the larger fascist political movement, of which Nazism was only the German manifestation.

On the whole, in most of non-Soviet Europe, the United States, and Japan, the most important pre-1939 industrial capitalists and their bankers accounted for by far the largest part of military production, and their relative power grew everywhere. Unlike the middle classes, they could not be marginalized or treated indifferently, so that after 1945 they once again emerged in most nations as ascendant economically, if not politically, as they had been before 1939. Their functional, if not ideological, collaboration with Nazism or fascism barely diluted their power—save (and that only partially) in France.

• By mobilizing vast numbers of men into armies, a government that does whatever is essential to sustain protracted war in an effort to attain victory also risks provoking deep social trauma and crises, if not revolutionary upheavals. This may particularly be the case if soldiers occupy strategic locations, especially cities. The precise social nature and structure of an army can be decisive to the outcome of a conflict even if rival forces fight relatively little, and a materially far superior army can easily lose a war if its organization is corrupt or its morale low. Insofar as the class differences between officers and soldiers are great, or the plight of soldiers' families a source of deep anxiety and alienation, then the likelihood of a crisis in an army increases.

World War One produced successful or nearly triumphant revolutions, to some great extent, because the collapse and radicalization of the Russian, Hungarian, and German armies ultimately posed a far greater threat to the constituted orders than did the working classes. As discipline deteriorated and armies became less efficient as military units, a subculture of dissidence and defeatism grew up, and variations of such patterns became virtually universal—indeed, integral to all mass armies. That inherently weak armies have also won wars, as in Greece in 1949, is due as much to nonmilitary factors as to any other consideration. Both in China during the late 1940s and Vietnam after 1973, where the sheer size and character of the armies made them counterproductive in military terms and illusory, if not dangerous, as instruments for maintaining the status quo, the Communists' final triumph was intimately linked to the social character and morale of the armies they confronted.

Military disintegration occurs not only because of the social composition of mass armies but is also due to the fact that modern warfare is invariably protracted, testing the devotion and social commitments of its soldiers to the state's goals, as opposed to their families, far more than was earlier the case. But the increasing violence and sheer physical demands that modern warfare's firepower produces also subjects soldiers to untold personal hardships, whether in muddy or freezing trenches or in jungles, and this mounting terror has repeatedly exposed one of contemporary warfare's potentially decisive weak links: the hapless men, mostly drawn from poorer and marginalized social origins, whom officers and military theorists call upon to risk their lives to implement their strategies.

The profound crisis in making war that such realities engender—notwithstanding their often radically different consequences—has persisted from the time that simple Russian peasants after 1914 began to malinger and refuse to fight, to the breakdown of much of the American army in Vietnam, with its assaults on its officers, over a half century later. In between, there have been countless events and episodes affecting most armies, all confirming the lowly soldier's progressive loss of morale and readiness to risk his life for causes with which he identifies less and less. This development, by itself, wholly undermines the military strategies that have dominated conventional wisdom since the nineteenth century.

• The technology and firepower that warfare relies upon has intensified enormously, even exponentially at times, and it has increasingly engulfed far greater sectors of the civilian population and become vastly more destructive of their lives as well as more costly. The growing barbarization of warfare transcends the conscious policy of one state, and notwithstanding the initial profoundly differing intentions of World War Two's adversaries, inhumanity was by no means restricted to the Nazis, and it has become an inherent part of the very nature and logic of military technology in this century no matter who employs it. It was for this reason that democrats dropped vast tonnages of bombs on German and Japanese civilians at the same time that the Nazis were systematically destroying countless millions, and used atomic bombs to obliterate two Japanese cities. Warfare after 1937 has increasingly eliminated the distinction between combatants and others, which essentially was respected during the First World War, and has abolished the existence of safe zones, traumatizing more and more civilians and entire nations. In the process it has also radicalized a great number of civilians and accelerated and intensified the grave social and political crises that traditional ruling classes and their foreign patrons must confront.

The emergence of airpower and the doctrines justifying it inevitably leads to the escalation of the scale and extent of destructive military campaigns during wars. The very existence of combat over vast spaces, combat that often becomes neutralized because of decentralizaton and effective countermeasures, leads incrementally to greater use of firepower against what before 1937 were generally deemed to be civilian or illegal objectives—against people, many of whom are innocents in every sense of the term, and the resources that sustain their daily existences. The Nazis deliberately earmarked specific social and ethnic groups for systematic destruction, but the far more nonideological Japanese came close to attaining much the same quantitative results simply by making war in ways they believed would achieve their material objectives quickly. During the Korean War the United States routinely attacked purely civilian targets, and in Vietnam it eradicated food supplies, forced massive noncombatant populations into controlled areas, and targeted peasants and their property in war zones.

However distinctive the intentions, human life itself in this age of massive conventional firepower has been made completely secondary, and atomic and nuclear weapons strategies now regard it as utterly expendable.

• Warfare's scope not only incorporates and affects much greater numbers of people but it becomes more capital-intensive at the same time, absorbing growing material resources. Because wars, especially those between industrialized nations and those in highly decentralized Third World contexts, are now stalemated more easily and tend to last longer, they also increasingly affect the morale and opinions of the otherwise placid people and constituencies who live in belligerent countries not subject to attack. The economic burdens of protracted, total war have meant that even when war is between nominal unequals, as in Korea and Vietnam, economic strains impose demands even on civilians in distant havens, and tend to transform such conflicts into tests of social systems and especially their political and economic capacities to sustain open-ended, interminable efforts. The fundamental contradiction of modern war since it has become totally mechanized is that it extends combat to many more people than ever before, protracts the length of time it requires, and vastly augments the material price of any effort, so that when its innumerable demographic, human, and social costs are combined its outcome ceases to be predictable. For at least a century, the ahistorical, narrow military factors that traditional official strategists and leaders focus upon to the exclusion of such crucial elements have failed to explain how modern wars evolve in reality.

Precisely because wars have become so much more expensive, and increasingly last much longer than those who initiated them predicted, the measures states take to pay for them affect the war's outcome to the extent that nonmilitary factors are important. Hitler's decision to spare his own population and make occupied Europe bear the war's costs, as much as any single cause, forced men into the Resistance—notwithstanding their deep passivity before the application of compulsory labor rules by early 1943. Japan's decision to extract as many resources as possible from the conquered colonies and China contributed enormously to the successful Chinese and Vietnamese revolutions, and mobilized movements elsewhere that later greatly accelerated the decolonization process.

After 1945 the costs of wars and colonial interventions made them inflationary and unpopular, in the case of the United States eroding the mass and elite support that existed at the inception of both the Korean and Vietnam wars.

• Wars often alter the objective condition and even the nature of the working class in ways that vastly intensify economic influences on their sentiments and objectives. They affect the masses' subjective attitudes, values, and consciousness far more quickly and in a much more visible form than those institutional factors operating on them during peacetime and upon which all, but especially Marxist, theories have concentrated. Wars' traumas produce radicalization, and thereby new and usually unexpected potentials for change, even when they do not cause all of the people to take great personal risks. But when a sufficient number are ready to do so, it is most likely to occur because of the direct or indirect impact of armed conflicts upon them. Although this telescoping may alter their earlier views only temporarily, even their relatively brief periods of social dynamism and development can have consequences of immense significance, creating civil conflicts within nations at the very time they are engaged in international wars. Since a country that is internally paralyzed is much more likely to lose, the outcomes of wars often ultimately reflect the ways social systems function in all domains, and their effectiveness in tests of arms is to some vital extent proportionate to the stability of each nation internally as well as its ability to confront foreign adversaries.

For most nations, political and economic problems during wartime evolve much more rapidly than solutions for them, producing decisive constraints which are inherent in military activity and technology, and to which the world's leaders have remained oblivious. Wars have become total conflicts that increasingly involve people directly—whether as soldiers, forced labor, targets, etc.—and the political price the defenders of traditional orders have been compelled to pay has mounted with the destruction of lives and goods.

As I have repeatedly suggested, the increasing scope and duration of wars have transformed them into inherently unpredictable political contests, both internally and between states, and have determined their conclusions profoundly. Disenchantment with traditional institutions, authorities, and value systems, whether it came slowly or suddenly, has affected countless persons, ranging from Chinese peasants whose villages their own soldiers had pillaged to burghers forced to sell off their luxuries to survive, continuously eroding the status quos of the world throughout this century. Not only was there both the threat and reality of social and armed conflict within nations while the First World War was being fought, but the residues of mass alienation remaining after the fighting ended spawned fascist movements as well as various leftist forces. The traumatization of Europe's middle classes beginning with World War One alone guaranteed that the Right would produce political instability for the next crucial quarter-century; and in Asia, as had been the case to a lesser extent in Russia before 1918, radicalized sectors of once-privileged middle classes led the Communist parties.

There was no linear movement from Right to Left at any time during this century, but only tendencies that were often quite elliptical. Except in Russia, the European Left's protests before 1920 confronted far too many obstacles to succeed, but they galvanized conservative reaction in ways that proved much more significant and enduring, and great but fleeting episodes of spontaneity alone were not a sufficient condition to radically transform that vast region. Peoples' beliefs and desires evolved largely in response to the daily deprivations they experienced in factories or food lines, and to their perception of the war's course—in effect, whether their mounting sacrifices would ultimately culminate in victory or defeat. Growing strikes provided a common denominator for the quite diverse European working class's protests, yet these had a largely economic basis most of the time, although in Russia and Germany political grievances eventually moved to the fore.

The cataclysmic Axis impact on Europe and Asia during World War Two was much more universal and prolonged, and by making the costs of personal neutrality virtually as great as resistance, it compelled many more people to turn against traditional political institutions and values even if they were not initially members of the mobilized opposition. The stages by which the historically unprecedented civilian Resistance emerged in each of Europe's occupied nations corresponded generally to the intensity of repression and the growing consequences of mere attentisme as well as the prospects of Allied victory, but the many ways in which the established conservative leaders collaborated with the Nazis and thereby delegitimized themselves also greatly affected the complex process of radicalization that occurred among the Continent's men and women. Yet notwithstanding the often convoluted manner by which people made difficult personal choices that had untold political implications, the net result was a much more enduring shift in European opinion toward the Left than had occurred after 1917—a legacy that for a time seemed to threaten the political outcome of the war and was subsequently to define Continental politics and diplomacy profoundly. But only in Asia was this cycle of traumatization and mass militancy to prove largely irreversible, fixing the political course of China and Vietnam against the desires and interests of the victorious Allies for forty more years. To comprehend the phases by which the thinking and behavior of Italian workers or Chinese peasants were profoundly altered is also to fathom the often complex nature of those forces changing the world since 1939.

Whatever the exceptions or the Left's shortcomings, wars increasingly made politics in vast parts of the world fluid, unpredictable, and dangerous to those seeking stability and order along with the protection of capitalism as the prevailing system within which the global economy operated. This later produced the Cold War and American interventionism—the principal forces sustaining mankind's organized violence after 1945—and dominated the modern historical experience.

• Leaving aside the exact causes for wars at specific times and places, capitalism, whatever its diverse national forms, cannot escape the principal responsibility for societies whose economies and cultures have engaged in armed conflicts throughout this century. Capitalism has been the only economic form able to incorporate the innumerable varieties of nationalist ideological legacies, many of them dangerously irrational, and provide them all a congenial institutional environment within which to prosper. There is no inherent rationality in the whole panoply of capitalist doctrines but only a fiercely selfish devotion to the protection and growth of economic interests, which operates whether or not primitive, chauvinist concepts also help it to galvanize wars. Certainly the refurbished nineteenth-century theory of an impersonal, decisive marketplace that has today created such a profound consensus among conservatives and former leftists cannot explain capitalism's historical development or actual operations, particularly in its relationship to the state for purposes of capital accumulation and control of markets or the practices of its huge oligopolistic sector. The egotism and avarice its ideology sanctifies creates an ideal setting for the development of values and aspirations condusive to international expansion and, ultimately, conflict. But even when such primitive impulses do not have a major ideological impact, wars occur nonetheless. The nation that has embarked on the most and the longest wars in this century—the United States—is as unencumbered with atavistic ideologies and political institutions as any (although it has nonetheless had some), reiterating the enduring, primary symbiosis between capitalism and war. And it has been war, infinitely more than the domestic operations of capitalism as described in Marx's economic theorems, that has endangered the status quos of the earth. So long as war remains a constant reality or possibility in the modern world, the likelihood of hapless people gravely challenging leaders and groups responsible for them will remain as great in the future as it was seventy years ago.

Given the absence of a political consensus within the United States in favor of spending on civilian programs, its military budget after World War Two became a very crude surrogate for public works or social measures and alone made government deficits possible—thereby sustaining the general economy in a manner that Keynesian theory once assumed that spending for far less dangerous purposes would perform. Without having an explicit alternative model of how to manage capitalism to overcome those historic fluctuations that had earlier preoccupied Keynes and countless other economic thinkers, an incremental, ad hoc economic system for which no articulate rationale was needed came into existence to attempt to solve the contractions that business cycles inevitably create. At various crucial points since 1947, the short-run benefits of arms outlays have also primed the economies of western Europe and Japan, so that aside from the perceived threat that the American-led bloc has attributed to the USSR, a very deep vested interest in the arms race developed that far transcended Washington's purely military justifications for it. This symbiosis between growth and relative prosperity in the capitalist world and preparations for war inevitably also helped greatly to create the context for the subsequent crises of credibility that led to repeated U.S. interventions in the Third World (of which Vietnam was the penultimate example) as well as much less frequent but much more dangerous confrontations with the USSR, such as the 1962 Cuban Missile Crisis. The very existence of military preparations carried with it an inherent propensity for activism, with all of the consummate risks that entailed. In this regard, despite the decline of some of the more irrational turn-of-the-century romantic ideologies, the reasoning of the world's most important leaders at the beginning and the end of this century closely paralleled each other.

The very absence of a politically potent alternative force able both to define and implement peaceful, socially useful options to arms spending in the United States as a means of sustaining prosperity and full employment locked the earth's single most important economy after 1945 into a policy that carried much of the world with it—and thereby defined its central experiences after World War Two. Opportunities for arms control and political détente, all of which would have hastened the inevitable demise of the Leninist nations and prevented the emergence of at least some Communist movements elsewhere, were either rejected or belatedly and halfheartedly implemented long after a time when small gestures in favor of peace could neutralize or reverse the dangerous workings of the international structure.

But a superarmed globe rapidly experiencing generalized nuclear-weapons proliferation was still beset with all the dilemmas of military doctrines and warfare that had undone nations since 1914, and strategy was even less "rational" in the 1990s than it had been much earlier. Could wars be fought at the end of the twentieth century in ways that avoided all of the many grave consequences that had so plagued human existence and upset existing political orders throughout the preceding century? Did the use of means of mass destruction axiomatically entail popular challenges to the leaders and societies that embarked on conflicts so fraught with suffering for the peoples sucked into the maelstrom of violence? Had any military thinker devised a new or better way to make war while sparing the world all the trials it had experienced so often in the past? That there will be continuity between the past and future human history and condition seems, by far, the likeliest prospect for mankind at the present time—a dour vision that only fundamental changes in the way the world operates can alter.

## Facing the Future

We live in a historically unprecedented period of great and virtually universal disillusion with all of the pretensions of socialism, whatever ideological form it takes, and of its capacity to remedy the world's social, economic, and political afflictions. This profound disenchantment and mood of intellectual confusion and depression is occurring not only at a time when the political, military, and economic challenges confronting mankind are monumental but also when the historic alternatives to socialism are less able than ever to cope with them. For socialism's theoretical and political failure is but a reflection of the even greater exhaustion of contemporary social and political thought and strategy throughout the globe. The world Marxist-Leninist regimes' uncritical conversion to capitalist economic dogmas and their most uninhibited practices only confirms, yet again, communism's historic failure to sustain both the theory and practice of socialism, and also that its ability to channel much of humanity's support for the Left since 1917 created a monumental cul-de-sac for the very concept of socialism. Social democracy has long since abandoned the minimum premises inherent in any commitment to social justice and equity, also failing to define a durable alternative program that can serve as a basis for action; instead, whenever elected it has contented itself with managing capitalist economies in ways that accept the legitimacy of the prevailing distribution of wealth and power.

An uncompromisingly candid reconsideration of this historic debacle is absolutely essential if we are to comprehend socialism's relationship to war in the past and future. It is also a necessary precondition for attaining the core objectives that socialists once claimed to be their goal and that remain relevant not just to the creation of a reasonable measure of equity within nations but, above all, to peace and stability between them. There is absolutely no intellectual comfort or clarity to be obtained from respecting inherited doctrines and icons that have failed to provide an adequate basis for either understanding or changing the world we live in, or that only deepen the gap between ideology and reality in ways that intensify the profound demoralization that today permeates the entire Left.

One can exonerate Marx only very partially by saying that he was only a mere man, a product of his times who was incapable of providing a sufficient foundation for such a colossal project as both explaining and transforming the world. It is quite irrelevant that he was able to perceive only the century he lived in as a basis for projecting into the future, or that it was Engels who partly transformed the seminal nature of Marx's work into a cosmology with a universality and unlimited pretension that encouraged subsequent socialist thinkers to believe that they could unfathom the present and future by reading Marxist scriptures exegetically rather than transcending them with original and, if necessary, iconoclastic and irreverent social analyses and criticisms of their own. Marx himself, like so many of his bourgeois contemporaries and predecessors, much too mechanistically viewed history as a cycle of progressive stages leading inexorably to a better future, thereby failing to see social reform and theory as a constant, neverceasing challenge to human intelligence and conduct. Much that was fundamental, ranging from migration to the far more complex nature of capitalism and its relation to the state and politics, or to the role of nationalism, atavism, and war, he simply ignored. Worse yet, the entire Marxist theory of the road to power was painfully imprecise, offering precious few warnings of the parliamentarian pitfalls or the revolutionary upheavals we have actually experienced, much less the problems of ruling-class resistance and reaction. Nor did Marx confront the decisive issue of how socialist parties in office were to fulfill their promises. Above all, he was fatally weak on the question of war, the institutional and social factors that produce it, as well as the even more difficult matter of how both socialist parties and individuals were to relate to such profound evil. This huge void in theory left ample space for the ambitious and unprincipled to rationalize their practices in the most convenient ways possible, producing every form of capitulation and tyranny associated with socialists in power, for there were all too few explicit criteria or taboos against which to measure their actual conduct. Any explanatory theory that cannot anticipate future trends with reasonable accuracy, or illuminate reality with sufficient clarity, is worse than useless if it discourages creative, radical analysis, and the canonization of received Marxist doctrine gravely bedeviled the idealistic and most necessary goals of socialism.

Notwithstanding Marxism's failures, its value in focusing attention on the role of the working class in industrialized nations can never be gainsaid, and had Marxism also overcame its Eurocentric perspectives to consider action among peasants and the poor in the rest of the world, it would have explained far more. What is certain is that throughout this century workers and peasants have behaved most radically in the context of wars, when capitalist or traditional orders were far less able to co-opt or repress their discontent. That Communists mediated and disarmed mass protest for seventy years was due to factors (primarily the failure of the social democratic option to them) quite independent of war itself, and their role proved decisive. It is a myth that there is an innate universal working-class readiness to revolt, for the vast majority of people have abided injustices for as long as it is possible. But that rebellious behavior among workers and peasants has occurred in some places at crucial junctures in modern history (usually when men and women realize that the consequences of inaction are at least as great as those of activism and they can no longer evade their effects) and has been sufficient to transform the very nature of wars to the extent of determining their outcome and subsequent international relations, is also an indisputable fact that demands explanations of why revolts occur, fail, or succeed. That parties and leaders aborted and betrayed the masses in no way mitigates the power or legitimacy of peoples' grievances and feelings, and just as no one predicted the timing or shape of their protests in the past, it is equally likely that they will recur in the future precisely because the forces and experiences that make for change ultimately will transcend the constraints on opposition that have existed until very recently in the form of both communism and social democracy.

The most significant periods of mass radicalism in this century have not required parties to initiate them, but social disintegration, which wars have invariably greatly accelerated. No leftist party by itself ever threatened an existing social system, and socialism's role and destiny has consistently been linked principally to the wartime political crises of capitalism. In the last analysis it was not Lenin who created the Soviet Union but Europe's traditional leaders. Socialism's dilemmas today are far less the consequences of the integrative skills and strength of its adversaries than of its own inability when in power both to cope with existing problems, as in the case of social democracy, or, as with Communists, to establish the social consensus and institutional legitimacy essential to make its governance durable. The future of radical opposition—whether it is designated as socialist or something that conveys the same meaning—still depends principally on the capacity of those who run today's world to behave a very great deal more rationally in the future than they have quite consistently acted since 1914. It is the pluralism and diversity of events over this past century, and the endemic inability of all capitalist nations to keep the peace, that have repeatedly undermined the hegemony of the great powers and will increasingly dominate a world whose future appears more ominous now than it has in at least forty years.

Yet in certain crucial ways the quandaries of socialism today ultimately also remain very distinct from the status and future of capitalism. Apart from the fact that history has come full circle insofar as the restoration of German power, the reemergence of nationalist atavisms in eastern Europe, or the position of Japan in Asia are concerned, there is nothing in the current momentary hegemony of the ideology of market economics in the ex-Communist world and formerly statist Third World nations that can create permanent tranquility. So-called liberal economics caters exclusively to the needs of individuals rather than to common interests and shared group relations in a civil society that imposes essential restraints on people's freedom to exploit and asserts public over private interests. Liberal economics' devotion to personal egotism and avarice as the fundamental basis of social organization has been a persistent source of human misery and societal instability since the school of thought was founded two hundred years ago. Economic liberals have no inherent commitment to political freedom and human rights, and suffer from the stigma of having repeatedly abandoned civil liberties—from installing Mussolini in November 1922 to having voted to give Hitler full powers in March 1933, and innumerable other instances —in order to preserve their individual privileges against the real or imagined claims of a larger community

Indeed, in the final analysis capitalism's proponents have no more of an accurate operational theory of the manner in which economies work in practice than do their critics on the Left, but instead propagate their own mythologies regarding the nature of economics, politics, and power. For notwithstanding the arguments of bourgeois economists since Adam Smith and a virtually universal consensus today, there are no impersonal, purely economic laws functioning anywhere but rather nations pitted against each other, if not continuously then at least sufficiently to produce those conflicts that have often ended in wars; nationalism has always been symbiotic with competitive economic doctrine. Those who argue that war and preparation for it is not necessary to capitalism's existence or prosperity miss the point entirely: it simply has not functioned in any other way in the past and there is nothing in the present to warrant the assumption that the coming decades will be any different. Modern capitalism in every country has always developed in a manner that transcends economics alone and involves complex social, political, and ideological systems linked to dominant class interests. And these have been anything but rational, simple, or predictable, but capable of often very great, even simultaneous, contradictions and mutations that have allowed nations to be pillars of civil liberties and humanism at one time and repressive, intolerant, and destructive at yet others—but always drawing from an ambiguous western cultural and intellectual heritage that sustains many totally contradictory impulses and allows the dragons of war and irrationality to lie dormant until they are yet once again evoked. For all of these persistent reasons, at the end of the twentieth century the world remains fraught with all of the dangers that were endemic in it eighty years ago.

The future of mankind and the very existence of rational civilization and human relations are hostage to this state of affairs, and the morality and desirability of today's dominant social systems are linked directly to the issue of war and peace. Even if the causes of this challenge are not exclusively economic, the fact that capitalism as it exists today is far more multifaceted in its motives and origins than Marxism allowed, retaining legacies of nationalism and atavism along with its acquisitive impulses, in no way mitigates its dilemmas—and ours. And it is this, above all, which will not only perpetuate a radical opposition to capitalism in the future but makes a rational and equitable economic alternative imperative—at a time that the very notion of such a transformation is but an aspiration whose power now rests far less on its own articulate vision for the future than the immense risks to much of humanity if the status quo remains.

Political conflicts will never disappear, nor is there ultimately any way to escape the consequences of political blunders and evil or selfish deeds. Radical opposition will inevitably reemerge as long as the political and economic crises so characteristic of the nations of the world as they now exist continue, poorer people suffer the most from them, and the need to strive for solutions to them remains not just an existential necessity but the precondition of avoiding a twenty-first century in which nuclear weapons abound and are inevitably employed. But this time the Left's efforts must not be wasted, and hopefully it will not have to depend once again on war to swell its ranks.

Such a revival remains conceivable not for positive reasons evolving from the accomplishments of the two historic branches of socialism— quite the contrary. Were not the tasks before civilization such that capitalism remains the principal threat to its future peaceful survival, the socialist movement as an option would be worthy only of a nostalgic burial because it has failed repeatedly to attain its minimum objectives. The usages to which the word "socialism" have been put are so disparate, and make such a mockery of its original dedication to social justice, that the concept has been devalued to a very great measure, evoking well-deserved cynicism from those who still believe in its simpler, broad goals. But the astonishing demise of Communist parties at least wipes the slate clean for a radical renewal on the Left, for they created a decisive obstacle to such a regeneration as long as they existed and were subservient to the Soviet Union's dictates.

Indeed, while the term "socialism" itself would warrant a replacement if a better definition could be devised, the much larger rationalist, internationalist, humanitarian, and radical tradition from which it evolved, and which long preceded Marxism and was ultimately irrevocably committed to the goals of equality and social cooperation both between nations and within them, remains more imperative than ever. The vitality of the still-quite-vague socialist vision of a new economic organization is not that it is the perfect way to structure an economic system but only by far the best given the alternatives, their impact upon human and social forms and, above all else, their consequences for peace and war in the future. The strongest argument for the equitable distribution of wealth and income is not that it maximizes economic incentives and growth, which it probably does not do in the strictly short-term manner that dominant economic thought calculates, but rather that it stabilizes economies and societies in ways that are much more likely to prevent the emergence of atavistic, reactionary, and ultimately materially highly destructive political forces. It is social stability within states that remains the precondition for peace between them, and the loss of mythical capitalist efficiencies to attain those goals is a positive achievement. For the central issue of economics today is civilization's survival, which requires doing whatever increases the chances for peace as opposed to militarism and war.

The difference now is that socialists—or their possible surrogates—can no longer talk of changing the world but must finally do so, and this means that socialist movements must assume radically different forms than they did in their Communist and social democratic versions. We can be done with the fallacies and illusions of total explanations, which Marxism's pretensions encouraged, and the excess neatness and tyranny of analytic ideas that intellectually paralyzed the socialist cause.

This is not the place for blueprints, but suffice it to say that the test of a policy is its results and what it accomplishes in attaining those essential primary goals on which the very existence of much of the world may depend; within this limitation, the exact structure of reforms can and should be altered if results warrant it. Determining the purely economic aims of a renovated socialism is the least difficult aspect of the task, for institutions must remain instrumental and sufficiently flexible to create stable nations in a peaceful world. In the last analysis, how such means and ends are defined are constrained only by a quite simple dedication to being on the side of the oppressed, the disadvantaged, and the people who really work to earn what they spend, whenever the basic criterion of who should gain or lose in a society is applied. In the most basic sense, when the question of "whose side are you on" is asked, this is ultimately the only response to it that makes the entire historic tradition of reform, the improvement of society, and socialism both meaningful and consistent. Such a commitment alone characterizes the dichotomy between the Right and the Left which has been a central if not exclusive focus of the politics of virtually all nations for well over a century—and will remain so. And it complements an equally necessary devotion to the prevention of war.

The much more crucial and difficult issue confronting radical politics is the control of leadership and the political class—to impose foolproof standards and checks on people and the institutions they command that prevent a repetition of opportunism, duplicity, egotism and so much else among them. To make radical political rhetoric credible once more, reining in the representatives of the people and preventing their betrayal of power and the confidence of those who gave them responsibility, is a precondition for which no exceptions can be made. This means controls of every sort, gladly accepting whatever inefficiencies they require because there is no other view of politicians warranted except a skeptical one, and it is much safer to operate on such a pessimistic basis than to give them leeway for repeating the fatal compromises and abuses of authority that have blighted socialism and much else in this century.

Such an approach not only requires new constitutional forms, which are rarely easy to attain in parliamentary systems, but especially innovative party structures that have workable procedures of recall, circumscribed tenure, and discipline, all wholly autonomous of state constitutions, and are imposed upon every leader in ways none may evade. These must deliberately be encumbering and based on the historically justified assumption that leaders as a class can never be uncritically trusted, and that it is far preferable to eliminate good ones prematurely or unjustly than to have to suffer interminably under others. Only the Left imperatively requires such organizational strictures and methods and must, in effect, creatively reinvent both parties and politics in order to attain their goals, since it alone has a self-assigned historic obligation to transform societies to their core. Conservatives can, and do, serve their systems faithfully even if they are personally corrupt.

But not only the definition and role of leadership demand fundamental reformation; so too does the concept of individual responsibility and participation in political and social processes. The vast majority of the world's people have been wholly or relatively indifferent to such institutional trends during peacetime, and even if they have been politically alienated, the large majorities in most nations have remained functionally passive save, in the case of some, for periodic elections of new men to lead them. They have been acquiescent in terms of their obligation to become social actors until mainly war-induced upheavals have pushed or compelled them to, and then it has usually been too little, too reluctantly, and too late. To a degree that we cannot estimate precisely, but certainly far more than in the past, men and women must function during peacetime to attain basic, necessary social and political changes upon which the future of a new and sane politics—and probably of mankind—depends. The commitment to activism is desirable to the maximum extent possible, though in fact it has never existed on any broad institutional basis for sustained periods, and it is by no means obvious or even likely that many people will choose to be permanently involved in extraparliamentary bodies, which must have truly representative mass participation lest they become disruptively counterproductive.

But the basic premise that while society owes everyone a reasonable material minimum, individuals in turn also have a constant duty to weave significant networks of social cooperation and interaction, is no less vital. A dedication to personal participation is also an essential precondition for the control of political leaders, which cannot be attained where there is a large measure of apathy among those who share the same nominal goals. Social responsibility that operates reciprocally between a society and its members has hardly been considered in the general socialist literature, but it remains a precondition for the emergence of a more rational human organization, and above all of truly radical politics based on changing both societies and people—and thereby the world.

It is extremely difficult to write an appropriate conclusion to a long analysis and history of the twentieth century's tragically monumental experiences, much less to avoid a distinctly pessimistic note concerning mankind's future. But there are no easy solutions to the problems of irresponsible, deluded leaders and the classes they represent, or the hesitation of people to reverse the world's folly before they are themselves subjected to its grievous consequences. So much remains to be done—and it is late. While the prospects for essential and sufficient changes appear, and in fact are very uncertain at the present moment, allowing the world's drift since 1914 to reach its inevitable destructive culmination is a course that our natural desire for human survival instinctively rejects; what is undeniable is that those who remain apathetic or despairing will pay, along with future generations, the ultimate price should we fail to reverse it.

But if our expectations for the next generation are to alter radically from what they are at present, then the legacies and defects of the past must be overcome, the lessons learned, and the necessary actions taken. Dispelling the myths of history, dismantling the pretensions of conventional wisdom and of leaders who claim omniscience, and discarding the shibboleths of ideologies that have betrayed their followers are all preconditions for escaping from the fatal illusions and errors that this century has bequeathed to us.

For only then can we even hope to move forward, and to act in the time that we have left to reverse the cycles of wars and human suffering that have formed so great a part of modern history—and to transcend them.

# NOTES

The following citations provide the sources of quotations and information in the paragraphs immediately preceding the note. Complete publication details on them are found in "References."

### Chapter 1. Preparing the World for War

1. These currents of thought are ably discussed in Cairns, 280–85; Travers, 38, 43, 87; Steiner, 154–63; Vagts, 11–13, 192–93; Nef, 404–5; Kitchen, 96–103; Phillips, 83; and V. R. Berghahn in Iggers, 163–67, among others.

2. Joffre, I, 23, 32. See also ibid., 33, 69; Travers, 86–87; Liddell Hart 1938, 39.

3. These ideas are discussed in Fischer 1975, 37–38, 207; Phillips, passim; Cairns, 285; Morley 1984, 238–39; Crowley, 86–87, who stresses the role of ideology; and Shafer, 5–7.

4. Woodward 1967, 53, 140–41; Charteris, 185, passim; Liddell Hart 1938, 32–45; Travers, 87–88; Magnus, 11, 331; Kautsky, 599; Shafer, 11–13; Betts 1977, 185–91, 203.

5. For French war planning, see Williamson, 117–29; Michon, passim; Cairns, 284; Miller 1985, 4, 110–11, 121, 130–31; Snyder, 104–5; Ralston, chap. 7, 353; Millett, I, 85; Ferro 1969, 63–65; Porch, 194, 227; Vagts, 380–81; Kennedy 1985, 147.

6. German calculations are debated in Vagts, 374; Wehler, 30–31; Berghahn, 3, 13–14, 22, 85, 147, 161–68, 204–5; Berghahn in Iggers, 158–62; Fischer 1975, viii–ix, 258, 389ff., 469–70; Fischer 1967, 50–51, 95–96; Gordon, 201–9; Eley, 2–4; Farrar, 5, 38–39.

7. The preceding themes are analyzed in Fischer 1975, chap. 11; Deist, 24; Iggers, 158, 178, passim; Travers, 43–44; Morley 1984, 278–85, 334–35; Palmer 1984, 29.

8. Churchill 1923, 199.

9. Kautsky, 112. See also ibid., 131–32, 261; Fischer 1975, 49–51, 258; Vagts, 367; Kennedy 1985, 18.

10. Palmer 1984, 28. See also Hayne, 291–95, for France's overriding desire in 1914 to maintain its alliance with Russia; for Japan, see Morley 1980, 117–19.

## Chapter 2. False Expectations: How Things Go Wrong

1. Lloyd George, 46, 53–54. See also, for Germany, Fischer 1975, 99–201; Berghahn, 7–9, 85–123, esp. 113ff.; for England, Burk, 7–10; Gooch 1938, 663; for France, Hayne, 57.

2. Joffre, I, 69, 23. For the warring nations' expectations, see Magnus, 284ff.; Ralston, 339, 376; Berghahn, 195–201; Auerbach, 19–20; Kautsky, 131–32, 189; Farrar, 5–7; Porch, 220ff.; Hayne, 271; Bond 1983, 83–85; Stone 1975, 45, 145; Chabod, 22–23; Knox, xxiv; Fischer 1975, 398–99, 469–70, 503; Fischer 1967, 50–55; Gooch 1926, 24, 30, 53; Ritter, passim; Millett, I, 93; Ropp, 208–9; Kennedy 1985, 199–203.

3. Lloyd George, 60.

4. Travers, 67.

5. Gooch 1938, 786. See also ibid., 663, 774–77; Steiner, chaps. 4 and 6; Gooch 1926, 81–82, 120–21, 180, 228–29; for France, see Hayne, 284–95.

6. Kautsky, 131. See also ibid., 112–13; German Comm. of Inquiry, 13; Berghahn, 137; Kennedy 1985, 9. For France's apprehensions of its allies in the Near East and elsewhere, see Hayne, 259–61; Keiger, 89–93, 103–4, 122–23.

7. Kautsky, 273, as in original. See also ibid., 132; Berghahn, 188, 196, passim; Renouvin, 174. Fischer argues that Germany wanted general war from the inception; see Fischer 1967, 30–31, 101; Fischer 1975, 50–51, 207, 393. But Keiger, passim; and esp. Steiner, passim, provide essential balance.

8. Speer, 215.

9. Ibid., 218. See also Weinberg, 19; Cecil, 47–48; Deist, 283–84; Watt 1989, 42–44.

10. Speer, 214. Hitler's preparations are summed up in Klein, 3–5, 77, 184, 232, passim; Carroll, 11–12, 213, passim; Milward 1965, 14, 28–29, 39–45; Cecil, 128–29, 146–47; Homze, passim; Crémieux-Brilhac, II, 347–50.

11. For British planning, see Frankland, 48–51; Ehrman, V, xvi, 24, 50–51; Ehrman, VI, 238–39; Watts 1989, 93, 330–34, 451–52; Parkinson 1973, 262–63, 268; Loewenheim, 235; Matloff, 11, 42.

12. For French planning, see Bidwell 1973, 210–13; Crémieux-Brilhac, II, 347–50, 440–42, 269; Cohen 1990, 201ff., 219–20; Watt 1973, 117–20; Watt 1989, 331–32, 452.

13. Morley 1983, 290. For Japan's plans see ibid., 3–4, 265–69, 280–81, 299–300; Crowley, xvi–ii, 214–15, 234, 244–50, 278–79, 299, 323–42, 361, 367–80; Kido, 190.

14. Ike, 238. See also ibid., 3, 201–2; Kido, 250–51; Morley 1983, 281; Morley 1981, 92–93, 117–19, 255, 293–94; Elsbree, 16–22; Cohen 1949, 111; Millett, III, 294. Tojo believed "the honor of the Empire [will] be lost" also. Browne, 123.

15. Ike, 131. See also ibid., xxv, 4, 106, 130–31, 148, 202; Morley 1980, 118–19, 256, 258–63, 275–76; Cohen 1949, 48–51; Kido, 296–97, 300, 309, 320–21; Togo, chap. 1, 79, 141, 181; Millett, III, 13.

16. Some useful discussions of these issues are Wilensky, viii; Deitchman, 134; Shafer, 11–13; Betts 1977, 185–91.

17. Circulating fairly widely but ignored was the astonishingly prescient and detailed account of modern war that the Russian banker, Ivan Bloch, published in major languages at the turn of the century, describing how the next war would be one of unprecedented static defense and attrition lasting long enough to ruin its participants economically and socially. See Bloch, passim. For the preceding issues, see Vagts, 364–65, 383; Cooper, I, 147; Snyder, 85–87, 98–99, 104–5; Miller 1985, 109, 136–37; Porch, 231; Michon, 96–97; Liddell Hart 1938, 8; German Comm. of Inquiry, 67; Gooch 1938, 658; Gooch 1926, 24–25; Kautsky, 247; Farrar, 21; Chamberlin, 64–65; Strong, 61; Berghahn, 170–71; Fischer 1967, 50; Fischer 1975, 470; Ropp, 200–201.

18. These issues are assessed in Strong, 16–18, 73; Cohen 1990, 41, 119–20; Watts 1973, 120; Shrader, 123; Zhukov, 235, 267, 272–79; Cecil, 50–51, 129; Hinsley, 20–21; Garrett, 167–77; Taylor, 16–29; Palmer 1978, passim; Smith 1989, 182ff.; Stockwell, 43, 90; Deitchman, 400–401; Halberstam, 222–23, 248–49, 628; McChristian, 34–39; Colby, 184; Turner, 117.

### Chapter 3. Officers: The Eclipse of Warrior Castes

1. For Britain, see Beckett, 26, 40, 43, 65–67; Lloyd, 16–20; Spiers, 3–4, 15–17, 28–29; Bond 1972, 17; Baynes, 32–33; Keegan, "Regimental Ideology," 220–21; Travers, 4–7, 11, passim; Millett, I, 52–53.

2. For Germany, see Hughes, 12, 18–20, 70, 82, 92, 127, 147; Endres, 296; Kitchen, 22, 27; Rosinski, 97–99; Demeter, 318–19; Fischer 1975, 117–19; Millett, I, 83–85; Berghahn, 14–15, 112–13; Porch, 194, 227.

3. For Russia, Stone 1975, 20–23; Wildman, xvi, 7–24, 40; Shrader, 86–87.

4. Istvan Deak in Kiraly, 85–94; Serman, 8–10, 84; Ralston, 339; Bond 1972, 16–17; Porch, 1–8, 17; Barnett, 206; Miller 1985, 110–12; Nobecourt, 7ff.

5. These issues are ably discussed in Barnett, 194–99; and Kocka in Iggers, 122. See also Geyer, passim; and Eley, passim.

6. For Britain, Keegan, 272–73; Travers, 23–70; Higham in Kiraly, 49; Beckett, 70, 89. For Germany and France, Vagts, 411; Nobecourt, 47, 52–53; Rosinski, 147; Geyer, 196; Grunberger, 137. For Russia,

Chamberlin, 65, 224; Stone 1975, 166–67; Wildman, 100–101; Florinsky, 214.

7. For useful insights on these themes, see Howard, 18, 20, 44, 85; Kocka, 134–35; King, 34–35, chaps. 5 and 6; Florinsky, 214; Katkov, 35–36; Chamberlin, 224; Wildman, 106–7; Stone 1975, 167–68; Cruttwell, 48; Kiraly, 92; Beckett, 65, 84–85; Travers, 23ff.

8. Bessel, 21–22, 28; Müller, 23–24; Mühlberger, 18, 286ff.; Chabod, 25–31.

9. Beckett, 91; Barnett, 206–7; Keegan, 272; Howard, 124–25; Nobecourt, 227–30.

10. For Germany, see Creveld 1983, 22–23; Müller, 25, 35–41; Rosinski, 202–7; Hoffmann, 25–27, 40; and esp. Wheeler-Bennett, 21–34, 159–79, 210ff., passim.

11. White 1974, 4–5, 47; Kolko 1969, 43–47; Krepinevich, passim; U.S. Senate, Comm. on Armed Services, 85, 316, 359–70; Halberstam, 223–30, 248–49, 344, 441ff.

## Chapter 4. War Organization: The Dilemma of Managing Modern War

1. For prewar planning, see Kitchen, xxix, 36–37; Berghahn, 6–7; Millett, I, 84–85; Creveld 1977, 110–13, 124–25; Vagts, 282–23; Müller, 9, 46–47; Frumkin, 163–64; Lloyd George, 124ff.; Adams 1978, 2–4, 13–14; King, 34–35.

2. For Germany, Kocka, 30, 132–35, 151–61; Feldman, 8, 30–33; Wall, 38–40; for the U.S., Cuff, 2ff., 272ff.; Koistinen 1967, passim; for France, Kuisel, 34–50; Joffre, II, 331–32; Wall, 36–37; Godfrey, 214–25, 257–58, 296–97; for Britain, Adams 1978, 54–55, 171–73; Hurwitz, 150–64; Vagts, 256–57; for Russia, Florinsky, 51–53; Stone 1975, 208–9.

3. Kocka, 31–33, 138–41, 152–53; Feldman, 469; Kuisel, 32, 35, 49; Godfrey, 214–15, 224, 257–58; Waites, 100–103.

4. For the U.S., see Koistinen 1970, passim; Koistinen 1973, 443–49; for Germany, Müller, 9ff.; for Japan, Cohen 1949, 28–32; Bisson, passim.

5. There is a rich literature on Germany, but most important for this discussion is Speer, 202–3, 216, 223ff., 255–56, 382; Milward 1965, 8–11; Milward 1977, 128–30, 157–59; Carroll, 170, 198, 246–48; Orlow, 20–21, 159; Klein, 170–71, 200–201, passim; Goebbels 1948, 364–65; Millett, III, 185–86; Gillingham 1985, 1–3, 83–84, 112–13, 139–47, 158–70; Gillingham 1977, 44–48, 57, 76–78, 112–13; Hayes, 191–92, 216–17, 347, 365–81; Hancock 1991, passim. Some interesting questions also arise in Caplan, 137, 262–65, 328–29.

6. For Japan, see Bisson, 159–61, 199–201; Cohen 1949, 1–3, 101–3; for the U.S., see Adams 1955, 84–85, 117, 120; U.S. Senate, Special Comm., 6, 29, 37–39, 46–49.

7. Adams 1955, 106; Kolko 1969, 20–25, 33, 44–46; U.S. Congress,

Joint Economic Comm., 3–7, 16; U.S. House, Comm. on Government Operations, 41–48; U.S. Senate, Comm. on Judiciary, 2–3.

### Chapter 5. World War One: The Impact on European Society

1. Basic sources of European historical economic and demographic data for these and other chapters are Ambrosius, and Mitchell 1975. For England, see Winter in Wall, 36, 49–53; Dewey in Wall, 202–11; Marwick 1965, 191; Williams 1972, 190ff.; Routh, 134; for France, Gallie, 229–31; Augé-Laribé; 33, 39, 55, 171, 190, 194, 249–308; Winter in Wall, 10; Fridenson in Wall, 239; Scholliers in Wall, 139–48; Becker, 206; Bowley, 71, 120; Oualid 1928, 360; Cobb, 26–29.

2. For Italy, Bowley, 71, 117; Seton-Watson, 468, 486–87; Clough, 187, 196; Neufeld, 540; for Germany, Winter in Wall, 31; Triebel in Wall, 160, 163; Deist, 42–43; Hancock 1949, 19–20; Grebler, 27, 61, 80–81; Bowley, 71; Bry, 74; Kocka, 23–25; Feldman, 472.

3. Pastor, 113. See also ibid., 145; Reinhard J. Sieder in Wall, 110–12, 117; Auerbach, 19–20, 475.

4. Stone 1975, 288–99; Clarkson, 236–43; esp. Florinsky, 49–50, 117–22, 150–51; Chamberlin, 154; Thompson, 11; Ferro 1972, 22; Keep, 46.

5. Oualid 1923, 149, 155–56; Gallie, 232; Armeson, 59–62, 103; Adams 1987, 90–243; McInnes, 15; Kocka, 18; Grebler, 27–28; Moore, 280; Augé-Laribé, 39–40, 115.

6. International Labor Office, 3, 14; Robert in Wall, 254, 262; Thom in Wall, 306; Daniel in Wall, 269, 274–78; Routh, 120; Grebler, 29–30; Kocka, 18, 23; Becker, 17–21; Augé-Laribé, 39–40.

7. For France, Augé-Laribé, 115–19; Ducasse, 263; Oualid 1923, 173–75; Becker, chaps. 6 and 7, esp. 229–32; Marwick 1988, 3; for Italy, Seton-Watson, 468; Clough, 189; for Austro-Hungary, Schreiner, 87–89; Pastor, 113; Auerbach, 475; for Germany, Feldman, 463–64; Lutz 1932, 188–95; for Russia, Stone 1975, 292–96; Trotsky, I, 46; Keep, 33, 185; Florinsky, 49–50.

8. The preceding economic trends are assessed in Grebler, 64–66; Feldman, 469; Chabod, 23–24; Bowley, 120, 139; Ambrosius, 74; Waites, 87–89; Pastor, 113; Becker, 121; Perreux, 293ff.; Ducasse, 260–62, 296–97; Smith 1969, 311; Kocka, 39; Marwick 1965, 128.

9. Dewey in Wall, 197ff.; Waites, 114–15, 279; Ambrosius, 71; Ferro 1972, 22; Florinsky, 120–22; Becker, 325; Chabod, 23–25, 31; Perreux, 138–39; Triebel in Wall, 159–89; Feldman, 465–69; Kocka, 39, 48, 115; Mendelssohn, 11–12; Mommsen in Marwick 1988, 26–43.

10. Military losses are taken from Cruttwell, 630–31; Dumas, 137, 145; Golovine, 94; Aldcroft, 13; Becker, 6, 331; Bowley, 41; Gallie, 229.

11. Civilian losses from Waller, 93, 481; Kulischer, 70–71; Aldcroft, 16;

Winter in Wall, 30–31; Becker, 6. Crosby, 27, 206–7, 215, claims that world flu deaths may have been as much as twice the 21 million usually given.

12. For economic data, see Renouvin, 604; Bowley, 122; Cobb, 10–41; Cruttwell, 400–401; Gide, 170–73; Sauvy, 106; Augé-Laribé, 55; Cépède, 418; for demographic changes, see Florinsky, 118; Oualid 1923, 164–65, 176–77; Gide, 195, 198; Fridenson in Wall, 237; Kulischer, 54–55, 62–64, 70–71.

### Chapter 6. World War One: Transforming Europe's People

1. Mendelssohn, 217. For the labor market, see Adams 1987, 1, 97–98; Hurwitz, 104–9; Gallie, 232–33; Armeson, 8, 59–62, 103; Wildman, 99; Becker, 206–7, 233, 247; Lutz 1934, 98–99; Kocka, 41; Marwick 1965, 203–7; Oualid 1923, 179.

2. These trends and events are documented in Haimson, 627, 634–36; Gallie, 232; Fridenson in Wall, 227, 243; Pastor, 145; Ferro 1969, 306–7; Neufeld, 547; Oualid 1928, 330, 360, 370–71; Armeson, 100–101, 110–11; Kocka, 48–49, 58, 65; Becker, 210–11; Sieder in Wall, 125; Grebler, 33, 59; Feldman, 128–29, 459; United Kingdom, Ministry of Labour, Economic Notes, No. 40, 15 (hereafter, *German Economic Notes*).

3. For Germany, see Schorske, 76–77, 85, 116–17, 124–27, 144–45, 265–66, 292–94; Feldman, 19, 129–30, 450–53, 522–23; Armeson, 110–11; Kocka, 41–44, 58–61, 66; Lutz 1934, 97–98; Scheidemann, I, 341, passim; Mendelssohn, 216; Levy, 21, passim; Deist, 46; *German Economic Notes*, No. 31, 13.

4. For France, Becker, 3, 7, 248, 290–94; for Britain, Hurwitz, 263; Reid in Wall, 228–29; Waites, 16–17, 114–15; Marwick 1965, 202–3; Adams 1987, 202–3, 227–28.

5. For the German middle class, see Kocka, 77–90, esp. 87, 91–113; Gordon in Emsley, 95–96; Feldman, 464–68; Mendelssohn, 217; for the social composition of the Nazis, see Kater 1983, chaps. 1–3; Childers, passim; Hamilton, passim; for Italy and France, Lyttelton, 50, 60–61; Becker, 227, 230, 248, 325.

6. For Russia, Golovine, 202–3; for Italy, Lyttelton, 24–25; Smith 1969, 310–13, 327; Neufeld, 253, 256–62; Seton-Watson, 470–71; Thayer, 330.

7. Liebknecht, 121. See also Thayer, 330; Scheidemann, I, 205–7, 218–19.

8. Kissin, 191. See also Kissin, 184–93, 246–48; Lutz 1934, 97–105; Feldman, 449.

9. Becker, 177. See also ibid., chaps. 4–6, 194–95, 220–21; Ferro 1969, 6–33; Bordeaux, IV, 6ff.

10. Becker, 248, 303. See also ibid., 225, 239, 247; Musée, 65–67.

### Chapter 7. Soldiers and the Crisis of World War One

1. Adams 1987, 174; Bidwell, 22, 41–42; Baynes, 34–35; Spiers, 45–46; Berryman, 34–37; Grebler, 77; Vagts, 233, 411; Speier, 256; Cépède, 14; Augé-Laribé, 115; Clough, 186–87; Spriano 1975, 10

2. Knox, xxxiv. See also ibid., xxxi; Chamberlin, 65–66; Stone 1975, 130–31, 144–45, 212–13, 285; Golovine, 22–23, 69; Wildman, 27–29, 36, 95, 99, 102; Katkov, 45; Florinsky, 207.

3. Stone 1966, 99; Beckett, 24; Lloyd, 78–79; Chamberlin, 106; Knox, 350; Stone 1975, 168–71; Katkov, 273–74, 281; Florinsky, 154, 166; Becker, chaps. 6 and 7; Deist, 56–57; Whalen, 75–77; *German Economic Notes*, No. 25, 30.

4. Falkenhayn, 40. See also ibid., 41; Rosinski, 138.

5. Binding, 27, 39. For the problems of British morale, Leed, 98–103, 166–67; Lloyd, 31ff.; Holmes, 204–5; Keegan, 228–36, 244–45, 255–56; Baynes, 70ff., 88–93; Ellis, 156, 176; Cruttwell, 263; Beckett, 23–24; Playne, 58–59; one-seventh of all British disability discharges were for nervous illness, and 70,000 pensions went to such cases, Englander, 599; Cooper, I, 331–33; for France, Pedroncini, 61, 67n, 83, 87; Ducasse, 97; Duhamel, 26–30; for Russia, Browder, 7–9; Golovine, 126–27; Chamberlin, 65; Wildman, 77–79.

6. Quoted in Cruttwell, 277. See also Binding, 66; Rosinski, 146–50; Falkenhayn, 226; Keegan, 230–34.

7. Cooper, I, 368–69; II, 174–75, 362–63; Cruttwell, 276, 400–401, 522; Renouvin, 550–51; Whalen, 122–28; Lutz 1934, 81–83.

8. Lloyd, 79–81; Playne, 69, 79; Cruttwell, 108–9; Ducasse, 92–94; Bordeaux, IV, 320.

9. For Italy, see Millett, I, 183; Seton-Watson, 474–79; Bond 1983, 124–25; for Britain, see Englander, 595–97; Allison, 12, 58–61, 91, 107; Beckett, 25; Leed, 201–3.

10. Cooper, II, 134. For France, see Pedroncini, 236–39, 280, passim; Becker, 217; Musée, 70; Keegan, 71; for Germany, Binding, 66.


### Chapter 8. World War One and the Emergence of the Left

1. Pares, 419; Knox, 349–50; Golovine, 98, 171–73; Millett, I, 279; Stone 1975, 288; Wildman, 115, 235; Katkov, 282; Chamberlin, 223: Florinsky, 239–40.

2. Chamberlin, 73, 235–36; Ferro 1972, 188–89, 209–10, 231–32; Katkov, 236, 271–74, 282; Rabinowitch, xxvi–vii, 52; Browder, 21–23; Wildman, xvii, 170ff.

3. Ferro 1972, 155–56, 184–87; Chamberlin, 228–29, 235, 266; Browder, 23, 71–74; Keep, ix–x; Katkov, 363–65; Liebman, 156–57; Pares, 418–19; Wildman, xix.

4. Haimson, 635–40; Browder, 26–27; Chamberlin, 266; Ferro 1972, 98–99, 114–17.

5. Lutz 1932, 233. See also ibid., 101; Ryder, 98–99, 117–18; Feldman, 449–51.

6. Sturmthal, 43–44; Lutz 1934, 97, 122–23; Kissin, 246–48; Liebknecht, 121ff.; Schorske, 318–23.

7. Whalen, 108–25; Lutz 1932, 85; Lutz 1934, 84–85, 122; Fischer 1948, 15, 55ff.; Ryder, 10–12, 101–2, 140; Leed, 198; Carsten, 32–33, 323; Renouvin, 550–51; Cruttwell, 587–89; Wheeler-Bennett, 28; Scheidemann, II, 251–55, 280–81.

8. Ryder, 150–53, 160–63; Scheidemann, II, 240–44, 254; Fischer 1948, 62; Waite, 2–6; Cruttwell, 598; Carsten, 39; Moore, 290–94; Wheeler-Bennett, 20–27; Carsten, 33, 55–70, 133; Bessell, 21–22.

9. Waite, 2, 9, 11–14, 35–41, 47–49, 53–78, 183–89; Carsten, 73, 128–39, 327, chap. 6; Ryder, 162–64; Wheeler-Bennett, 33–37; Fischer 1948, 70–74; Moore, 303–4; Scheidemann, II, 254–55; Sturmthal, 44.

10. Waite, 79–90; Mitchell 1965, chap. 10, passim; Gruber, 170–90; Fischer 1948, 102–3; Carsten, chap. 7; Sturmthal, 49–51.

11. Ryder, 231, 270–72; Sturmthal, 47–48; Gruber, 174; Scheidemann, II, 247; Carsten, 247.

12. Sieder in Wall, 110–31; Sturmthal, 53–56, 189–91; Gruber, 191–96; Carsten, 22–32, 123, 324.

13. Pastor, 119, 145, 157, 161–62; Mayer, 529n; Károlyi, 434–35, 444ff.; Carsten, 238–39; Gruber, 135–41, 150–63.

14. Mayer, 527, 532, 541–44, 555, 852, chaps. 21 and 24; Gruber, 150–63; Károlyi, 299; Carsten, 239–47; Pastor, 157–63; Hoover, 136ff.; Tokes, 214–15.

15. Neufeld, 256, 263, 540, 547; Kulischer, 208–9, 216; Spriano 1975, 10–11, 42–44; Seton-Watson, 503, 520–23; Lyttelton, 37, 523; Smith 1969, 326.

16. Neufeld, 256–58, 264–65; Smith 1969, 327–28; Seton-Watson, 524, 564–65; Lyttelton, 28–30; Chabod, 36–40; Spriano 1975, 32–33, 60–61.

17. Neufeld, 263–69; Sturmthal, 184–87; Mühlberger, 10–13, 18, 33; Lyttelton, 37–40, 44–57; Seton-Watson, 567; Kulischer, 208.

18. Katkov, 32.

19. Chamberlin, 73.

20. Pares, 422–23. See also ibid., 418–19; Chamberlin, 101, 154–55, 235–36; Ferro 1972, 84ff., 98–99, 158, 279–83; Golovine, 195; Florinsky, 239–40.

21. Trotsky, I, 324, 435. See also Haimson, 639; Katkov, 28–31.

22. Trotsky, I, 285. See also Kissin, 233–37; and Sprenger, passim, on Leninism.

23. Rabinowitch, xxix–xxxii, 63–70; Trotsky, I, 285, 316, 325; Stone 1975, 283; Thompson, 123; Chamberlin, 114–16.

24. Rabinowitch, 37. See also ibid., xxiii–xxiv, xxx–xxxiii, 16–21, 34–35, 70–71; Kissin, 240–43; Chamberlin, 117, 144–46, 152, 166, 172–73, 184–87; Stone 1975, 301; Thompson, 79–85.

25. Rabinowitch, 60–63, 90ff., 125–71, 180–81, 191–94, 210–18, 225–72, 311–14; Stone 1975, 301; Mohrenschildt, 96–97; Thompson, 123–24.

### Chapter 9. World War Two and European Life and Society

1. Deist, 282–95, 304–5; Millett, III, 182–84, 191; Rich, 82, 146–47; Watt 1973, 116; Watt 1989, 385; Weinberg, 18–19, 36–37, 557, 582; Cecil, 137; Klein, 26–27, 77, 186–87; Homze, 14–15; Mason 1971, 226–28, 236; Walrimont, 3–93.

2. Rich, 208–09; Cecil, 76, 110–11, 124–29, 146–47; Walrimont, 140–41, 208; Klein, 184, 207–9; Speer, 184–91; Millett, III, 194–95, 200–203; Homze, 67–68; Harvey, passim.

3. Montgomery, 49. See also Frankland, 48; Milward 1977, 40; Milward 1965, 2–3; Klein, 99–101.

4. Loewenheim, 235.

5. White 1974, 2. See also ibid., 4, 47.

6. Parkinson 1974, 293. See also ibid., 279–93; Matloff, 522–23; Kolko 1990, passim; Frankland, 57–62, 103; Sherry, 261; Boog, passim; Garrett, chaps. 1–3.

7. Speer, 214. See also ibid., 214–19; Millet, III, 184; Walrimont, 203–9, 278.

8. See esp. Hans Umbreit in Dejonghe 1987, I, 5–40; Speer, 219; Milward 1970, 27, 41; Millett, III, 183–84; Gillingham 1977, 87; Rings, 32–33.

9. Gillingham 1977, 40. For Belgium and Denmark, see also ibid., 7, 39–41, 87, 94; Semelin, 167–68; Littlejohn, 70–79; Brandt, 616; Willequet, 63–83; Baudhuin, 288–90; Dejonghe 1987, I, 318.

10. For France, see Hirschfeld 1989, 6, 11, 18–19; Milward 1970, 35ff., 80–82, 111, 271–73, 283; Sauvy, 98, 105, 208–09; for Poland, Wolowski, 81ff., 158–62; Gross, 91; for German imports, see Brandt, 7, 610; for foreign labor, see Homze, 200, 232–33; Arnoult, 59; Hirschfeld 1988, 220–21; Struye, 38; Milward 1970, 114, 122, 274; Gillingham 1977, 84, 90; Kulischer, 262.

11. Goebbels 1948, 64. See also ibid., 75, 196, 225; Millett, III, 189–90. For German living standards, see Brandt, 235; Deist, 47–51; Marwick 1988, 62; Speer, 220–22, 256–57; Studnitz, 166–67; Hancock 1949, 500; Klein, 88–89, 154; Morsomme, 246; Grunberger, 214; Mitchell 1975, 254; League 1944, 10–11; League 1946, 25–26, 36; for real income and hours, see Hachtmann, 51, 159. Older data by Bry, 48, 264, 279, on real income is essentially similar but not as complete for hours worked. For labor conditions, see also Hancock 1949, 152; Homze, 8–9, 232; Marwick 1988, 61;

Klein, 136–37; McInnis, 16; Emsley, 305; Mason 1993, 338–60; Salter, 96–108.

12. Baudhuin, 201–3, 209–22, 235, 382–84; League 1946, 21, 25–26, 36; Mitchell 1975, 250, 330; Dejonghe 1988, II, 592–95; Struye, 157–59; Brandt, 479; Cobb, 51–52; Gillingham 1977, 102–21, 137–38, 190–93; Jacquemyns, 164ff.

13. Cépède, 65, 70, 235, 324, 332, 350, 418–19; Brandt, 561, 566–67, 613; Dejonghe 1979, 49–50; Mitchell 1975, 253, 330, 356; Sauvy, 192–93, tables III–X; Arnoult, 69; League 1946, 21, 25–26; Milward 1970, 288–89; Amouroux 1961, 166–68, 175–83; Ehrmann, 265–70; Debû-Bridel, 45–49.

14. Coles, 772. For the black market, see Crémieux-Brilhac, I, 427–31; Gross, 152–53; Debû-Bridel, 56–59, 116; Walter, 96–97, 126–29; Amouroux, 168–69, 182; Sauvy, table VIII.

15. League 1946, 26, 36–37; Mitchell 1975, 259, 331, 357; Brandt, 419, claims 25,000 plus deaths, Hirschfeld, 53, 20,000 plus including deficiency symptoms, van der Zee, 305–7, claims 18,000.

16. Coles, 318. See also ibid., 307, 310–11; League 1946, 21, 36–37; Brandt, 584–85; U.S. Office of Strategic Services (hereafter "OSS"), Oct. 27, 1943, 1; OSS, Jan. 1, 1944, 2.

17. OSS, Oct. 27, 1943, 1, 22–23; OSS, Jan. 1, 1944, 2–3; Coles, 310–12, 318; Neufeld, 540; OSS, July 31, 1944, passim.

18. The Greek events, including varying estimates of the famine's toll, may be found in Brandt, 235–48, 614; Iatrides 1981, 66–75; Kitsikis, 23ff.; Henry, 747; Chiclet, 28, 286; Woodhouse, 161–62; Hondros, 70–78; Mazower 1993, 37–41, 48–72.

19. Bédarida, 156–59, 170–72, 192–93; Brandt, 9, 31–32, 611–14; Gross, 104–6, 109–13, 145–55; League 1946, 18–21, 25–26, 36; Deist, 51; Wolowski, 68–71, 144–47, 158–63, 260.

20. For migration, see Kulischer, 264–66, 302–3; Henry, passim; Milward 1977, 213–14; Gross, 72; Brandt, 36, 43; Kedward 1978, 7; Amouroux, chaps. 1 and 2; Bordeaux, XII, 22ff.; Vidalenc, passim; for forced labor, Kulischer, 263; Bartov 1986, 153; Gross, 78–79; Homze, 24–25; for postwar refugees, Kulischer, 272–73, 302; Milward 1977, 214–15.

21. For the air war, see Milward 1977, 334; Mierzejewski, 55; Rumpf, 167; Groehler in Boog, 291–92; Messerschmidt in Boog, 304–7; Terraine in Boog, 489; Garrett, 18–21; Millett, III, 61; Sherry, 259–62; Frankland, 103; Parkinson 1974, 450–51; Ehrman, VI, 239–40. For war costs, Baudhuin, 288–90; Milward 1970, 111, 279; Marwick 1988, 82; Sauvy, 99–100, 105, table I; Arnoult, 63–64.

22. For the USSR, see Kulischer, 276; Bartov 1986, 153; Milward 1977, 211; for Jews and Poland, see Kulischer, 279–80; Henry, 744, 747; Milward 1977, 211; for Germany, Sauermann, 103; Henry, 747; Bartov 1986, 153; Kulischer, 279n; Milward 1977, 211; League 1946, 110–11; for France,

Bourgeois, passim; Arnoult, 65; Sauvy, 194–95; League 1946, 110–11; Henry, 746–47; Kulischer, 276, 280; see also Milward 1977, 210.

23. Stouffer, Combat, 150. See also ibid., 71, 81, 108–9, 149–53, 201–4, 561, 571, 576; Stouffer, Adjustment, 226–27, 440–41; Crémieux-Brilhac, I, 456–72, II, 363–68, 439–69; Paxton, 240n; Ellis, 10–11, 316, 335, passim; Fussell, 17–19, 100ff., 283, chap. 10; Bidwell 1973, 210–13; Marshall, 16–18, 53–55; Creveld 1983, 167–68.

24. Speer, 184.

25. Goebbels 1948, 37. See also Millett, III, 202–3; Creveld 1983, 4; Bartov 1991, 17, 73–74; Cecil, 147.

26. Studnetz, 68. See also Creveld 1983, 5, 65–66, 173; Henry, 746; Milward 1965, 113.

27. Goebbels 1948, 37. See also Bartov 1986, 60–61, passim; Bartov 1991, 28–31, passim; Creveld 1983, 22–23, 75, 86–87, 131–32, 155–65; Kater 1992, passim; Mazower 1992, 132ff.

28. Goebbels 1948, 514. See also Mazower 1992, 150–51, passim.

29. Pogue, 448. See also Bartov 1991, 95–100; Milward 1965, 113; Goebbels 1977, 72, 89, 134.

30. Klein, 137; Homze, 100–101, 232; Mason 1976, I, 87, II, 21–22; International Labor Office, 3, 14; Cohen 1949, 1, 290; Emsley, 305; Routh, 5, 179; Milward 1965, 112; Marwick 1988, 71; McInnes, 16.

31. Reck-Malleczewen, 106. For Germany, see ibid., 105–6; Steinert, 9, 339–40; for Poland, see Gross, 173, 291; Wolowski, 260–63; for Greece, Iatrides 1981, 66–67, 73–74, 302–5, 316–17; for France and Belgium, Amouroux, 165, 181–82, 471–72; Crémieux-Brilhac, I, 427–31; Debû-Bridel, 58–59; Walter, 102–3; Baudhuin, 267–68; Dejonghe 1979, 50.

32. Titmuss, 84–87; Morsomme, 167–79; Emsley, 255–75; Kolko 1962, passim.

### Chapter 10. European Responses to World War Two

1. Bédarida, 156–59, 170–72, 192–93; Semelin, 32; Umbreit in Dejonghe 1987, I, 30.

2. Dejonghe 1987, I, 7, 24–25, 66–71; Hirschfeld 1989, 6–11; Baudhuin, 25–29, 372n; Hoffmann, 517, 530; Hirschfeld 1988, chap. 1, 14–15, 27–36, 55–57, 132–38, esp. 154; Gillingham 1977, chap. 1.

3. This number excludes Ukranians recruited into military auxiliaries that were also assigned to killing Poles, Jews, and Soviet citizens. See Gross, 132–35, 186–94, 302–3.

4. See Haestrup, 136–41; Michel 1972, 204–5; Semelin, 60–64 for insights.

5. Amouroux, chap. 17; Baudot, 1–2; Marjolin, 55, 104; Emsley, 240; Paxton, passim; Hirschfeld 1989, 3.

6. Noguères 1967, 25, 52–53, 74; Paxton, 18, 334–36; Kedward 1978,

21; Cobb, 64–65, 103, 119; Baudot, 42–43; Dejonghe 1987, I, 105–16, 397, 417; Dejonghe 1988, II, 755, 833–56; Hirschfeld 1989, 3, 8–10, 19; Rings, 76–77, 83.

7. Cobb, 58–61, 83–84, 96–98, 147–49; Hirschfeld 1989, 17; Paxton, 17–19, 237; Sauvy, 182–85; Walter, 60–61; Amouroux, 469.

8. Baudhuin, 114, 129–30, 201–10, 267–72, 293, 298; Dejonghe 1987, I, 66–99, 371; Struye, 91, 148, 157–59; Willequet, 67–68, 96–101, 151–53, 238–39, 262; Gillingham 1977, 24–30, 72–77, 129, 152–53, 175–76, 189–90; Gillingham 1985, chap. 7.

9. Hirschfeld 1988, 5–6, 34–36, 42, 56, 133–39, 170–208, 266, 293–95, 321–25; Rings, 74–75, 96.

10. Wolowski, 68–72, 185–86, 260–62; Gross, 114–15, 132–35, 144–48, 160–67, 179–94, 302–3; Rings, 83.

11. Trunk, xxxii, 34, 51, 327, 432–33, 455ff., 490–526.

12. Grunberger, 201. See also Peukert, 106–25, 139–40; Engelmann, 51–54, 312; Allen, 286–87, chap. 12; Kershaw 1983, 75–92; Seydewitz, 38–39, 156; Emsley, 305; Hoffmann, 529; Kater 1983, fig. 1.

13. Kershaw 1987, 140. See also ibid., 219, passim; Peukert, 68–71; Kershaw 1983, 268–69, 304; Steinert, 7, 146, 334–35; Seydewitz, 50; Deist, 294; Engelmann, 249; Reck-Malleczewen, 105; Salter, 90–94.

14. Steinert, 81–83, 123, 188, 202ff., 217, 240–41, 259, 339–40; Kershaw 1983, 108–10, 222–23, 290–95, chap. 8; Peukert, 63, 246–47; Goebbels 1948, 325, 389, 401; Engelmann, 40, 127–29; Studnetz, 25; U.S. Dept. of State, May 27, 1946. For the ephemeral, ambiguous nature of the resistance, see the essays by Broszat, Peukert, and Mommsen in Large.

15. For Holland, Hirschfeld 1988, 6, 57; 179–80; Warmbrunn, 104–11; Rings, 80–81; for Belgium, Struye, 16–38, 91, 116, 148, 165, 182–83; Dejonghe 1987, I, 325–29.

16. Crémieux-Brilhac, I, 20, 9. See also ibid., 403–4.

17. Ibid., 59, 419–20, 618–19; Amouroux, chap. 17; Paxton, 235–41, 294–95; Sweets, 149, 152, 160, 229; Michel 1962, 11; Rousso, 287; Baudot, 1–6, 24–34, 70–71, 90–91; Noguères 1967, 442; Cobb, 45–54; Madjarian, 58–59; Semelin, 135–37; Dejonghe 1988, II, 994; Laborie, 258–70, 310–19.

18. Semelin, 46–47; Rings, 1–12; Michel 1972, 71–72 are especially thoughtful.

19. Battaglia, 77. See also Urban, 162, 166; Gallerano, 66–67; Wilhelm, passim.

20. Debyser, 114–15. See also Delzell, 290–96; Judt, 89–91, 95; Battaglia, 88, 166–67; International Conference, 88–89; Legnani, 52–53; Gallerano, 67; Harris, 276; Kogan, 111; Urban, 168; Coles, 528; Kesselring, 225–28; Chabod, 108; Michel 1972, 286; OSS, March 31, 1945, 4.

21. Judt, 90; Delzell, 208–9, 304–5; Chabod, 109; Battaglia, 88–89; and esp. Collotti, 32–33.

22. Gross, 283. See also ibid., 166, 171, 212ff., 259–68, 281–84; Kolko 1990, 117; Wolowski, 170–82, 197–98; Haestrup, 224.

23. Kedward 1978, 274–77; Noguères 1967, 438–42; Hawes, 102–5; Amouroux, 241, 551, 554; Tillon, 320–21, 327, 339; Bourdrel, 103; Guingouin 1982, 43–45, 194–96; Baudot, 112–14, 140–44; Semelin, 161; Kolko 1990, 78; Dejonghe 1988, II, 842–56, 874–76; Gillingham 1985, 156; Haestrup, 123; Sainclivier, 46–55.

24. Amouroux, 307; Haestrup, 12, 359; Semelin, 133–37; Hirschfeld 1989, 13; Paxton, 294; Rings, 210–11; Noguères, III, 295, 302–6, IV, 54; Marcot, 91–96; Michel 1962, 308; Michel 1972, 275; Ehrman, V, 324–26; Guingouin 1982, 180, 194; Kedward 1993, 2, 19–48, 82, 129, 158, 204, 219.

25. Kolko 1990, chap. 4; Michel 1962, 59; Amouroux 1988, 123ff., passim; Ehrman, V, 326–28; Noguères, III, 558–59, IV, 92ff., 160–62, 199; Kriegel-Valrimont, 70–71, 107, 167, 176, 216–17; Baudot, 144, 170ff.; Madjarian, 62.

26. Noguères, IV, 55; Paxton, 294; Rioux, 476, note 33; Sweets, 227; Guingouin 1974, 227; Guingouin 1982, 54; Kolko 1990, 88; Kriegel-Valrimont, 71; Rings, 211; Tillon, 359; Ehrman, V, 326; Coles, 770, Baudot, 210–11.

27. Hirschfeld 1988, 154. For Holland, see ibid., 220–21; Warmbrunn, 58–61, 73, 100–102, 118–20, 132, 185ff., 264–71; Michel 1972, 353; for Belgium, see Gotovich in Dejonghe 1988, II, 809–32; Haestrup, 224; Willequet, 10, 217; Gillingham 1977, 177–79; Baudhuin, 371–72; Struye, 132–34, 140, 165, 178–79; Dejonghe 1987, I, 325–29.

### Chapter 11. European Communism and the Political Consequences of World War Two

1. Chiclet, 31, 47, 50, 99–100; Lazitch, 212; Eudes, 19, 28; Woodward 1971, 387; Sarafis, lxi–lxiii, 47, 67, 100n, 320–21; Bærentzen 1987, 121–22; Kédros, 90–93, 122–23, 362; Iatrides 1981, 38; Woodhouse, 8–9, 24–27; Papastratis, 121–22; Kolko 1990, 175; Kofos, 120–31; Hondros, 98–121, 133; Mazower 1993, 305–9; Vlavianos, 19–21.

2. Iatrides 1981, 41; Woodhouse, 44–45, 97; Wheeler, 77–78; Chiclet, 29–35, 50; Eudes, 19, 28, 169, 205–6; Sarafis, lxi, 48–49, 100–101, 154, 272, 320–21, 425–26; Kédros, 49; Vukmanovic, 23; Hondros, 77–78, 111–21, 139–44; Mazower 1993, 305–21. Chiclet, 34n, claims there were 1,070 *capetans* in September 1944.

3. Kolko 1990, 173–74; Iatrides 1972, 22; Iatrides 1981, 10–11, 27; Chiclet, 30–31; Woodhouse, 135.

4. Spriano 1985, 198. See also ibid., 178–203; Judt, 42–43; Kolko 1990, chap. 8.

5. Churchill 1962, VI, 65. See also Kolko 1990, 37–42, 50–53, 129–31, 141; Woodward 1971, 117ff.

6. Churchill 1962, VI, 181. See also Kolko 1990, 142ff.; Woodward 1971, 119–24.

7. Churchill 1962, VI, 196ff.; Kolko 1990, 144–46; Woodward 1971, 147–53, 350.

8. Stavrakis, 33. See also ibid., 28; Wittner, 5–7; Seraphis, 223–25; Kolko 1990, 180–81.

9. Churchill 1962, VI, 610. See also Eudes, 203–5; Stavrakis, 28–33; Wittner, 8–9; Kolko 1990, 181–82.

10. Wittner, 27. See also Stavrakis, 38.

11. Iatrides 1981, 13; Dedijer, 293.

12. Churchill 1962, VI, 247. See also Chiclet, 47, 69, 94–95, 121; Kédros, 290, 472–73; Eudes, 168–69, 235–37; Vukmanovic, 12–13; Woodward 1971, 410–11; Wittner, 8–9; Woodhouse, 98; Iatrides 1981, 200; Kolko 1990, 185; Ehrman, V, 86–87; Hondros, 234–39; Bærentzen, "The German Withdrawal. . . ." 256–58.

13. Churchill 1962, VI, 249. See also Woodhouse, 97, 127, 130–31; Kolko 1990, 182–88; Iatrides 1972, 161–64; Chiclet, 106–7; Eudes, 218–19; Hondros, 239–47; Bærentzen 1978, passim.

14. Kolko 1972, 224. See also Kolko 1990, 189–92; Woodhouse, 135; Wittner, 34–35.

15. Kolko 1972, 221–25; Eudes, 316–17, 324ff., 336, 343–44; Kolko 1990, 192–93, 429–31; Wittner, 28–29; United Kingdom 1946, 10ff.; Bærentzen 1987, 46; Iatrides 1981, 178; Woodhouse, 141; Sarafis, lxiii; Vukmanovic, 87–89, 140–41; Hondros, 248–50.

16. Woodward 1971, 438; Kolko 1990, 429; Vlavianos, chap. 3.

17. Coles, 770. See also Lazitch, 193; Michel 1972, 358–59; Madjarian, 122ff., 146–49, 167; Buton, 405–12.

18. On deaths, see Paxton, 329; Amouroux 1988, 558; Sauvy, 197–98; Bourdrel, 325–27 and rear cover; Lottman, 272–75; Buton, 422; see also Coles, 770–71; Bourdrel, 103, 107; Guingouin 1974, 227, 231–32; Sainclivier, 54; Baudot, 140–44; Tillon, 362, 370, 493n; Kedward 1978, 275; Kedward 1993, 418–19; Guingouin 1982, 43–45, 54, 182, 218–21; Taubmann, 65–98, 120–24; Jacques Duclos, report, Sept. 2, 1944, Marty Papers, reel 7.

19. Bourdrel, 91–92, 103–5; Madjarian, 99–100, 109–11, 122, 167, 180–81; Buton, 415–19; Taubmann 104–14 Duclos, report Sept. 2, 1944, 3–4, Marty Papers, reel 7.

20. Kolko 1990, 94. See also Tillon, 409; Spriano 1985, 178–80; Giraud, 145–49, 158–63, 185–86; Rieber, 15, 26; Urban, 193.

21. U.S. Dept. of State, Foreign Relations 1944, 723. See also ibid., 634–35; Aguhon, 72; Tillon, 409, 416.

22. U.S. Dept. of State, Foreign Relations 1944, 733. See also ibid., 742–43; Tillon, 405.

23. Agulhon, 71ff.; Madjarian, 99–100; Rieber, 131–36; Giraud, 185–86, 199; Michel 1962, 319; Kriegel-Valrimont, 134ff., passim; Noguères, V, 238–48, 493–94.

24. Duclos report, Sept. 5, 1944, 6, Marty Papers, reel 7. See also Duclos report, Sept. 2, 1944, 3–4, Marty Papers, reel 7; Tillon, 419–21; Willard, 102–3; Spriano 1985, 229–30; Madjarian, 130–31, 147–48, 195ff.; Rioux, 39–56; Buton, 418–19; Thorez, 181–89, 194–95, 201.

25. Duclos report, Dec. 30, 1943, Marty Papers, reel 6; Duclos report, Sept. 5, 1944, Marty Papers, reel 7; Tillon, 406, 413, 417; Reale, 81–82, 160ff.; Kolko 1990, 93–96, 439ff.; Kolko 1972, 154–55; Dedijer, 295–96; Willard, 96ff.; Agulhon, 84–85.

26. Coles, 620; Collotti, 32–33; Chabod, 129.

27. Sefarty, 28. See also ibid., 87; Judt, 90–91; Michel 1972, 248–49; Collotti, 29–31; Domenico, 57–58, 118, 192, 209; Miller 1986, 155–56; Coles, 566; Federazione Genovese del PCI, "I Comunisti per il Popolo Italiano," n.d., in PCI leaflets.

28. Communist success was to be greatest, both in terms of Party membership and electoral support, in the vast, contiguous region directly north of Rome: Tuscany, Umbria, the Marches, and Emilia. Here the Communists became, and largely remained, the party in power. In the Piedmont, Lombardy, and the Veneto in the far north the Socialists were considerably stronger. But in the aggregate the Communists were successful in turning their membership into a durable force in local governments, which over decades gave them the patronage as well as the prestige essential to sustain their organization. See PCI leaflets, passim; Urban, 175, 180, 190, 212–15; Lazitch, 225; Chabod, 126–29; Sefarty, 28; Gallerano, 67n; Sefarty, 21–28, 87.

29. Coles, 114. See also ibid., 115, 118, 160.

30. Ibid., 387. See also ibid., 373–75, 384–88, 560; Harris. 3, 79, 147–48, 284–87; Domenico, 55, 74–75, 89, 201, 208–10; Miller 1986, 133–35, 140.

31. Churchill 1962, V, 86. See also Kolko 1990, 45–57.

32. OSS, March 31, 1945, 13–14; Miller 1986, 144–45; Coles, 526–27.

33. Toscano, esp. 275, 266–89, 293; Badoglio, 121, 128–29; Harris, 141–42.

34. Macmillan, 489. See also Urban, 191–94; Kolko 1990, 52; Kogan, 64–65.

35. Woodward 1971, 129.

36. Kolko 1990, 438. See also Toscano, 267–77, 301–3; Urban, 156–60, 186–87; Dedijer, 296.

37. Badoglio, 147. See also Urban, 153, 158–59, 174–77, 200–203; Sefarty, 23–24; Kolko 1990, 54.

38. Urban, 169–71, 185, 195, 204; Judt, 21; Sefarty, 24; Kolko 1990, 54.

39. Coles, 542. See also ibid., 538ff.; Delzell, 304–5, 515–20.

40. Churchill 1962, VI, 267.

41. Coles, 544. See also ibid., 539–42; Miller 1986, 139ff.; Delzell, 451–53, 464–65, 474–76; Colletti, 32; Urban, 199; Kolko 1990, 62–63.

42. Kolko 1990, 376.

43. Ibid., 385.

44. Coles, 564. See also Coles, 548; Kolko 1990, 437.

45. Coles, 560. See also ibid., 373–74, 384, 560, 565–66; Miller 1986, 140; Delzell, 551–53; Harris, 305, 310, 359; Kolko 1990, 437; Domenico, 141, 148–49, 153.

46. Coles, 566.

47. Ibid., 622. See also ibid., 616, 623.

48. Ibid., 614, 625. See also Woodward 1971, 484–85.

49. Willard, passim.

50. Kogan, 122.

## Chapter 12. China: War, Society, and Revolution

1. Dower, chaps. 8, 10; Morley 1984, passim; Millett, III, 15; Crowley, 288ff., 370–73; Morley 1983, 280–81, 290–91; Morley 1980, 254–79, 292–95; Kido, 190, 320–21; Elsbree, 22; White 1946, 62–63, 70; Ike, 76–77, 148.

2. Ike, 283. See also ibid., 152–53; Elsbree, 26–27, 44, 50–51, 68–69; Browne, 105, 121–23; Morley 1980, 117–19; Crowley, 371–72; Thorne, 149–56, 259; Silverstein, 28–29.

3. Togo, 263. See also Iriye, 176, 182; for economic trends, Cohen, 275, 354, 375, 386, 415, 521.

4. Kolko 1990, 550.

5. Fairbanks 1986, 547n. See also ibid., 29.

6. Ch'i, 221; Fairbanks 1983, 50; Chang 1967, 66; White 1946, 60; Young, 139, 152, 300–301, 358; Chou, 91–93, 260–61.

7. Young, 11–27, 53–54, 266, 317–26; Chang 1958, 60–64; Chou, 15, 244; Ch'i, 155, 165–67, 176; White 1946, 69; Fairbanks 1986, 35–37.

8. For prewar China, see Fairbanks 1986, 17–19, 30–34, 239, 255–60; Ch'i, 139, 146–51; Peck 1967, 19–21; Esherick, 10; Selden, 5–7; Fairbanks 1983, 81–83; Chen, 134–37; for wartime, see Chou, 243; Fairbanks 1986, 267–68; Chang 1958, 60–63; Eastman, 5–6, 46, 58–59.

9. Romanus, 369, 242. See also ibid., 10, 66–67; Ch'i, 54, 59, 161–64, 170; Esherick, 6; Peck 1967, 216–17.

10. Romanus, 245. See also ibid., 242–47; Fairbanks 1986, 574–75; Ch'i, 162; White 1946, 132–38; Chang 1958, 63; Young, 318–20; Eastman, 152.

11. Eastman, 68–69, 152; Fairbanks 1986, 32–34, 257, 268–69, 565; Esherick, 11–15, 36–37; White 1946, 60–66, 143, 174–76; Selden, 5–6; Ch'i, 159–60; Peck 1967, 21–22.

12. Eastman, 137.

13. Ibid., 142–43, 162; Ch'i, 97, 104, 171; Romanus, 12, 66–67; White 1946, 72, 139–42; Young, 318–19; Peck 1967, 20.

14. Eastman, 4–5.

15 Romanus, 10. See also Kataoka, 289; White 1946, 69–71; Eastman, 10, 131–33, 141–43, 162; Peck 1967, 3, 19–21; Selden, 189; Ch'i, 238–39; Stilwell, passim.

16. For prewar discontent, see Fairbanks 1986, 278–81, 301–6, 326; Selden, 65–66; for wartime events, see Eastman, 68–69, 85; Esherick, 14, 20–21; Ch'i, 97, 160; Peck 1967, 23.

17. Johnson, passim; Dirlik, passim; Kataoka, passim; Fairbanks 1986, 322–23; Chen, xix; Shum, 2–15, 232–33; Lewis, 264; Kolko 1990, 236ff.; Selden, 65–95ff., 190.

18. Kolko 1990, 240. See also Kataoka, 28–31, 47, 117ff.

19. Chen, 122, 129, 155–61, 182, 188–89, 220–22; Schurmann, 432–33; Kolko 1972, 266, 550–51.

20. Shum, 5ff.; Schurmann, 129; Selden, 212ff.; Johnson, 14; Lewis, 264–66.

21. Eastman, 160. See also Chassin, 19, 22; Kataoka, 308; Chen, 78; Kolko 1972, 248–55, 552.

22. Schurmann, 129; Kolko 1972, 248, 266, 274, 534, 539, 548, 553.

## Chapter 13. War, Revolution, and Reaction in Southeast Asia

1. Lockhart, 108–9; Martin, xvii; Tonnesson, 37.

2. Gaudel, 208–31; Decoux, 267, 448–49; Khanh, 292–93; Buttinger, 240, 581; Woodside, 139–41, 158–59; Kolko 1985, 15; Lockhart, 110; Long, 131–32, 222–27; Martin, 100.

3. Lockhart, 111–12; Hammer, 145; Long, 130–33, 228–29; Khanh, 300–301; Isoart, 154; Decoux, 267; Giap, 39; Buttinger, 240.

4. Mordant, 112; Commission 1972, 14–15, 36–37, 55–56, 64, 95–96; Kolko 1985, 31; Trullinger, 29, 33–34; Khanh, 182–83, 270–75, 283–88; Lockhart, 75, 84–93; Tonnesson, 344–45; Woodside, 234–36.

5. Commission 1972, 76. See also ibid., 72ff.; Khanh, 304, 308–14.

6. Commission 1980, 70–71. See also Khanh, 313; Commission 1972, 89–95.

7. Commission 1972, 85, 94–95. See also Khanh, 311–12; Lockhart, 117–21.

8. Giap, 15. See also Lockhart, 104–5; Khanh, 312; Commission 1972, 83–96.

9. Commission 1972, 95–96, 134–35, 172–75; Devillers, 135–37; Isoart, 162–70; Khanh, 320–28; Lockhart, 137–43; Tonnessen, 375–76, 379ff.; Patti, 164–67.

10. Giap, 73.

11. Commission 1980, 72, 95–96; Khanh, 332; Kolko 1985, 40, 46; Hammer, 145–46; Buttinger, 350; Trullinger, 45–46.

12. Constantino 1975, 321ff.; Wolters, chaps. 1–3.

13. Twenty years later General Douglas MacArthur, the American commander, stated that he gave no instructions whatsoever, but even if true this left the local authorities free to collaborate. No one told them to resist. See Steinberg, 32–33; Hartendorp, I, 226n; Recto, 76.

14. Japanese, 2. See also Steinberg, 37–61; Cannon, 13–14.

15. OSS, Nov. 25, 1944, 4.

16. Japanese, 1–2. See also Recto, 74–77; OSS, Nov. 25, 1944, "Recto"; Kerkvliet, 65; Steinberg, 90–91; Willoughby, 286–87, 342–45; Hartendorp, I, 190–91; Constantino 1978, 84–93; Agoncillo, 458–63; Dower, 46; Cannon, 17.

17. Steinberg, 106–9, 114, 122; Apostol, 10, 18; Hartendorp, II, 557n, 604; Willoughby, 343–44; Taruc, 142–43; Kerkvliet, 76–77; Agoncillo, 459–65; Constantino 1978, 101ff.

18. Taruc, 58. See also ibid., 56; Hartendorp, I, 431.

19. U.S. Army, 12. See also Hartendorp, I, 431, II, 609, 642; Constantino 1978, 87; Friend, 207, 227.

20. Willoughby, 264.

21. Cannon, 14. See also Willoughby, 442.

22. Willoughby, 446.

23. Willoughby, 266–67, 464, 452. See also Cannon, 17.

24. Kerkvliet, 18–25, 40–59; Larkin, 215, 292–305; Paige, 45, 58–60.

25. Taruc, 129. See also ibid., 56–58, 130, 143; Kerkvliet, 79, 98.

26. Taruc, 52–53. See also ibid., 60–61, 70–72, 142–58, 177; Hartendorp, II, 642; U.S. Army, 12–15; Kerkvliet, 97.

27. Taruc, 110. See also Kerkvliet, 100–101.

28. Laurel, 17. See also Kerkvliet, 102–4; Taruc, 126, 143.

29. Taruc, 190. See also ibid., 185–98; Kerkvliet, 111–13, 124; Edgerton, 40–53.

30. Kolko 1988, 27. See also Edgerton, 26–28, 150–62; Steinberg, 115–16, 130–31.

## Chapter 14. Repression, Rebellion, and the Limits of Military Power, 1945–1953

1. Woodhouse, 163. See also ibid., 172; Bærentzen 1987, 46, 52–53.

2. United Kingdom 1947, 4.

3. Woodhouse, 142, 162, 184, 208, 266; Kousoulas, 240; United Kingdom 1947, 12–16; Wittner, 49–51, 69, 167–73, 183–84; U.S. House, Select Comm., 193–99; Sweet-Escott, 132–33.

4. Woodhouse, 183–87, 194, 215; Bærentzen 1987, 160, 166–67, 171, 184–87; Iatrides 1993, 209–11; Eudes, 340, 351, 354, 356, 360; Stavrakis, 90–91; Vukmanovic, 103, 128–29; Vlavianos, 99, 105.

5. Heinz Richter in Bærentzen 1987, 187. See also ibid., 162–65, 184–87; Vukmanovic, 93–99, 104; Kolko 1972, 223, 226; Woodhouse, 164–77, 183–84; Eudes, 354; Iatrides 1981, 178–79, 206–7; Wittner, 45; Vlavianos, chap. 5.

6. U.S. House, Select Comm., 193. See also Wittner, 108, 113–15, 162–65, 225.

7. U.S. Dept. of State, Foreign Relations 1948, 118–19. See also Woodhouse, 209, 215; Wittner, 137–38, 144, 155, 163; Smith 1949, 237.

8. Wittner, 140–41, 162, 165, 245, 283, 401; Bærentzen 1987, 62–73, 95, 98; Eudes, 466; Kofos, 186; Kousoulos, 284.

9. Woodhouse, 186, 222, 262; Eudes, 360, 386; O'Ballance, 127, 142, 158–59; Iatrides 1993, 227–28; Laiou in Bærentzen 1987, 55, 60; Kofos, 176; Wittner, 107, 231; Smith in Bærentzen 1987, 174–76.

10. Elisabeth Barker in Bærentzen 1987, 272–73. See also ibid., 263ff., 303; Sweet-Escott, 53–54; Wittner, 56–58; Iatrides in Bærentzen 1987, 246–47; Vukmanovic, 93–98; Iatrides 1993, 213, 222–23, 228; Kofos, 163–64; Vlavianos, 69–71.

11. U.S. Dept. of State, Foreign Relations 1948, 1084–85. See also ibid., 100–106, 129–30; Wittner, 108, 113–18, 162–65, 171–84, 189–90, 223–53, 263–65; Iatrides 1993, 212–13, 226–29; Barker in Bærentzen 1987, 272–74, 305; O'Ballance, 176–77; Woodhouse, 238–43; Vlavianos, 239, 244.

12. Barker in Bærentzen 1987, 295. See also ibid., 276–77, 286, 290–93, 304–5; Eudes, 465–66, 472–73; Wittner, 263, 267, 272–79; U.S. Dept. of State, Foreign Relations 1948, 115–17, 248–49; Bærentzen 1987, 312–13; Shulman, 71–73.

13. Landé, passim; Edgerton, 226–27, 244, 290ff.; Kerkvliet, 120–21, 135; Constantino 1978, 207.

14. Officials in Manila, trying to convince the U.S to supply military aid, claimed that the Huk army in late 1946 numbered between 9,500 and 10,000, but although this figure was far too large, it was nonetheless still only one-third of its wartime peak strength; Kerkvliet, 192. See also ibid., 124, 143–48, 153, 159, 168–74, 186, 196–98; Taruc, 227–32, 236–37, 242, 249; Wolters, 149, 186–95; Constantino 1978, 208–11.

15. Kerkvliet, 140–41, 150–51, 170, 178–87, 205; Taruc, 208–14; Constantino 1978, 208–15; Kolko 1988, 28–29; Edgerton, 340.

16. Kerkvliet, 179–90, 200–211; Taruc, 230, 248–49, 259–64; Constantino 1978, 214–22, 236–37; Cullather, passim.

17. Kerkvliet, 177–78, 203–7, 216–17, 227–33, 238–48; Kolko 1988, 64–66, passim; Constantino 1978, 231–36.

18. U.S. NSC-68, 28, 31, 36, 21, 56. See also ibid., 57–65.

19. Kolko 1972, 477–84, 502–8, 558–77; Goulden, xvii; Simmons, 118, 129; Suh, 319–29; Scalapino, 246–47, 257, 289, 327, 376–83, 409–10; Cumings, II, 293; Weathersby, 5, 19–32.

20. Kolko 1972, 568. See also ibid., 567–68, 573–77; Schnabel, 29, 38; Simmons, 108–9.

21. Kolko 1972, 570, 575ff.; Schnabel, 64; Simmons, 118–25; Shulman, 140ff.; Weathersby, 22–32.

22. Futtrell, 195. See also ibid., 102.

23. Pearson, 150. See also Mrozek, 1, 24; Momyer, 62; Kaufman, 84–85; Collins, 144–45; Goulden, 234–37; Rees, 100.

24. Kaufman, 86–88; Schnabel, 177–82, 222; Appleman, 607–8; Kolko 1972, 594–605.

25. Hermes, 283–84, 337, 340, 477–78, 501, 508; Futtrell, 689–92; White 1974, 5; Rees, 440–41; Kolko 1972, 615.

26. Futtrell, 628. See ibid., 316, 337–40, 411, 424–25; Hermes, 205, 283, 332, 367, 510–11.

27. Futtrell, 485–89, 501, 504, 629; Rees, 166–68, 194; Goulden, xvi.

28. Collins, 250. See also ibid., 251; Rees, 404–6, 418; Goulden, xxv; Futtrell, 529; Hermes, 499.

29. Hermes, 461. See also ibid., 63–64, 214, 436–46; Goulden, xvii, 636–37; Rees, 422; Futtrell, 667.

30. Futtrell, 669. See also ibid., 666–70.

31. Peck 1962, 100; Mueller, 45–47; Collins, 388–89.

### Chapter 15. Warfare at an Impasse: The United States Confronts the World, 1954–1991

1. Kolko 1988, 50. See also Kolko 1972, 671, 705–7.

2. Kolko 1972, 671–72; Bitzinger, passim; Gaddis, 139–45.

3. Kolko 1972, 706–7; Kolko 1988, 48–52, 293; Gaddis, 130–31, 144–45, 151; Shafer, chap. 5.

4. Blechman, 30–52; Shafer, chap. 2, 279; Betts 1977, 202–3, chap. 10; Betts 1978, 62ff.; Kolko 1988, 49–54; Booth, 26; Janvry, 416; Bairoch 1979, 671ff.

5. Kolko 1985, 15, 39–41, 60–67, 93–94, 99, 130; Trullinger, 91ff.; Bergerud, 55ff., 76, 335.

6. Kolko 1985, 143–44, 180–81, 194–95; Mrozek, chap. 2; Momyer, 80–95; U.S. Senate, Comm. on Armed Services, 316; Smith 1989, 182ff.; McChristian, passim; Halberstam, passim; Deitchman, 113, 134; Betts 1977, 185–91; Wilensky, passim.

7. Krepinevich, xi. See also ibid., 126–27; Mrozek, 164–65, 178–79, esp. 184.

8. Kolko 1985, 189–92, 357; Palmer 1984, 58, 62; Krepinevich, 127.

9. Taylor, 17–18.

10. Kolko 1985, 197. See also ibid., 284ff.; Halberstam, 733–40, 782–83; Taylor, 25; Palmer 1978, passim; Heiser, 22–23, 48, 60–61.

11. Heiser, 23. See also Palmer 1984, 70–71, 168–69.

12. Mueller, 54–57, 124–25, 130, 138–39; Kolko 1985, 172; U.S. Senate, Comm. on Armed Services, 580–92.

13. Kolko 1985, 359–64.

14. Halberstam, 667. See also Kolko 1985, 200–201.

15. Palmer 1984, 167. See also ibid., 168.

16. Kolko 1985, 144–45, 200–202; Mrozek, 132–45.

17. Kolko 1985, 202–7.

18. Trullinger, 143–44, 182–203; Deitchman, 386–403; Bergerud, 295–96; Mrozek, 178–79, 184.

19. Kolko 1985, 234–36, 253–60, 523ff.

20. Philippines, 22, 26, 29; Booth, 138–42; Janvry, 396ff.; Bairoch 1979, 677; Williams 1986, 198, passim; Brockett, 55.

21. Inter-American 1989, 121; Roberts, 7, 94, 174; Binnendijk,118–19; *Financial Times* [London], Sept. 9, 1991, Oct. 1, 1992, Nov. 24, 1992; *Far Eastern Economic Review*, July 26, 1990, 48.

22. *Finance & Development* [IMF], Dec. 1990, 18, Sept. 1992, 3, 9–12; *IMF Survey*, Sept. 10, 1990, 258–59; Inter-American 1989, 3, 127, 129; Inter-American 1991, 103.

23. Cardoso, 22–26; Inter-American 1991, 99; Jain, passim.

24. Turner, chap. 10; Shafer, chap. 2; Betts 1978, 63ff.; Hyland, 130.

25. Stockwell, 90. See also Binnendijk, 10, 36–39.

26. Stockwell, 43. See also Binnendijk, 307; Blechman, 33, 52; Kolko 1988, 209, 294.

27. Builder, 3–5; U.S. Senate, Comm. on Armed Services, 3–8, 15, 313–497; Hosmer 1990, 30–31; Hosmer 1987, 124, 155; Kolko 1991, 17.

28. Levine, viii. See also ibid., v–ix; Hosmer 1990, 30–31; Hosmer 1987, 127, 154; for South Africa, see Woodward 1987, 269; Stockwell, 187.

29. U.S. Commission, 13. See also ibid., 16.

30. John S. Fulton, *Military Review*, Feb. 1986, 61. See also Krepinevich, 269–72; Shafer, 283ff.; Simon, 1–3; Kolko October 1988, passim.

31. Schwarz, 49. See also ibid., vi–xiv, 20–23, 29; Bacevich 8, 21, 34–35, 56, 70; and esp. Taw, passim, for the army's doctrinal impasse.

32. *Los Angeles Times*, Feb. 26, 1992. See also Hiro, 71–84, 90–91, 119ff., 186–211; *New York Times*, Jan. 26, 1992; *Los Angeles Times*, Feb. 23, 1992; Akin letter in *Washington Post* [weekly ed.], Nov. 9–15, 1992.

33. *Washington Post* [weekly ed.], July 8–14, 1991, April 20–26, 1992, May 4–10, 1992; *Los Angeles Times*, April 11, 1992; *International Herald Tribune*, June 11, 1991, Feb. 24, 1992, April 11–12, 1992.

34. Hyland, 242. See also Blechman, 36.

35. *Department of State Dispatch*, Oct. 7, 1991, 739. See also Hosmer 1990, vff.; Simon, 1ff.; U.S. Commission, 13.

36. Richard Haass [special assistant to the president], text of speech,

U.S. Information Service, London, "Official Text," Sept. 24, 1991. See also David Binder, *New York Times*, Feb. 7, 1993.

37. Michael Mandelbaum in *New York Times*, Dec. 22, 1990. See also Kolko 1991, 23.

38. Remarks by Boren, National Press Club, April 3, 1990, 3–4 [ms].

39. *Department of State Dispatch*, Oct. 7, 1991, 739. Most informative regarding U.S. fears of the negative consequences of the dissolution of the USSR, is Beschloss, 106–7, 123, 170–77, 192, passim.

40. U.S. Joint Chiefs, 1–2.

# REFERENCES

Adams, R. J. Q. *Arms and the Wizard: Lloyd George and the Ministry of Munitions, 1915–1916.* College Station, Tex., 1978.

——, and Philip P. Poirier. *The Conscription Controversy in Great Britain, 1900–1918.* London, 1987.

Adams, Walter, and Horace M. Gray. *Monopoly in America: The Government as Promoter.* New York, 1955.

Agoncillo, Teodoro A., and Milagros C. Guerrero. *History of the Filipino People.* Quezon City, 1970.

Agulhon, Maurice. "Les Communistes et la Libération de la France." In *La Libération de la France.* Comité d'histoire de la Deuxième Guerre Mondiale, ed. Paris, 1976.

Aldcroft, Derek H. *From Versailles to Wall Street, 1919–1929.* London, 1977.

Allen, William Sheridan. *The Nazi Seizure of Power: The Experience of a Single German Town, 1922–1945.* New York, 1989.

Allison, William, and John Fairley. *The Monocled Mutineer.* London, 1978.

Ambrosius, Gerald, and William H. Hubbard. *A Social and Economic History of Twentieth-Century Europe.* Cambridge, Mass., 1989.

Amouroux, Henri. *La Vie des Français sous l'occupation.* Paris, 1961.

——. *Joies et douleurs de peuple libéré: 6 juin–1 septembre 1944.* Paris, 1988.

Apostol, José P. "Some Effects of the War on the Philippines." Philippine Council, Institute for Pacific Relations, 1947.

Appleman, Roy E. *South to the Naktong, North to the Yalu: June–November 1950 [U. S. Army in the Korean War].* Washington, 1961.

Armeson, Robert B. *Total War and Compulsory Labor: A Study of the Military-Industrial Complex in Germany During World War.* The Hague, 1964.

Arnoult, P., et al. *La France sous l'Occupation.* Paris, 1959.

Auerbach, Bertrand. *L'Autriche et la Hogrie pendant la Guerre*. Paris, 1925.

Augé-Laribé, Michel, and Pierre Pinot. *Agriculture and Food Supply in France During the War*. New Haven, 1927.

Bacevich, A. J., et al. "American Military Policy in Small Wars." Kennedy School of Government, Harvard University, March 1988.

Badoglio, Pietro. *Italy in the Second World War: Memories and Documents*. London, 1948.

Bærentzen, Lars. "The Demonstration in Syntagma Square on Sunday the 3rd of December, 1944." *Scandanavian Studies in Modern Greek* 2 (1978), 3–52.

——. "The German Withdrawal from Greece in 1944 and British Naval 'Inactivity'." *Journal of Modern Greek Studies* 5 (October 1987), 237–65.

——, et al., eds. *Studies in the History of the Greek Civil War, 1945–1949*. Copenhagen, 1987.

Bairoch, Paul. *Diagnostic de l'évolution économique du Tiers-monde, 1900–1966*. Paris, 1967.

——. "Le Volume des productions et du produit national dans le Tiers monde." *Revue Tiers Monde* 20 (October–December 1979), 669–91.

Barnett, Correlli. "The Education of Military Elites." In *Governing Elites: Studies in Training and Selection*. Rupert Wilkinson, ed. New York, 1969.

Bartov, Omer. *The Eastern Front 1941–45: German Troops and the Barbarisation of Warfare*. New York, 1986.

——. *Hitler's Army: Soldiers, Nazis, and War in the Third Reich*. New York, 1991.

Battaglia, Roberto. *The Story of the Italian Resistance*. London, 1957.

Baudhuin, Fernand. *L'Économie belge sous l'occupation, 1940–1944*. Brussels, 1945.

Baudot, Marcel. *L'Opinion publique sous l'occupation: l'exemple d'un département français (1939–1945)*. Paris, 1960.

Baynes, John. *Morale: A Study of Men and Courage—The Second Scottish Rifles at the Battle of Neuve Chapelle, 1915*. London, 1967.

Becker, Jean-Jacques. *The Great War and the French People*. New York, 1986.

Beckett, Ian F. W., and Keith Simpson, eds. *A Nation in Arms: A Social Study of the British Army in the First World War*. Manchester, 1985.

Bédarida, François, ed. *La Politique Nazi d'extermination*. Paris, 1989.

Bergerud, Eric M. *The Dynamics of Defeat: The Vietnam War in Hau Nghia Province*. Boulder, 1991.

Berghahn, V. R. *Germany and the Approach of War in 1914*. London, 1973.

Berryman, Sue E. *Who Serves? The Persistent Myth of the Underclass Army*. Boulder, 1988.

Beschloss, Michael R., and Strobe Talbott. *At the Highest Levels: The Inside Story of the End of the Cold War*. Boston, 1993.

Bessel, Richard. "The Great War in German Memory: The Soldiers of the First World War, Demobilization, and Weimar Political Culture." *German History* 6 (April 1988), 20–34.

Betts, Richard K. *Soldiers, Statesmen, and Cold War Crises*. Cambridge, Mass., 1977.

———. "Analysis, War, and Decision: Why Intelligence Failures Are Inevitable." *World Politics* 31 (October 1978), 61–89.

Bidwell, Shelford. *Modern Warfare: A Study of Men, Weapons and Theories*. London, 1973.

———, and Dominick Graham. *Fire-power: British Army Weapons and Theories of War, 1904–1945*. London, 1982.

Binding, Rudolf. *A Fatalist at War*. London, 1929.

Binnendijk, Hans, ed. *Authoritarian Regimes in Transition*. Washington, 1987.

Bisson, T. A. *Japan's War Economy*. New York, 1945.

Bitzinger, Richard A. *Assessing the Conventional Balance in Europe, 1945–1975* [Rand Corp. N-2859]. Santa Monica, 1989.

Blechman, Barry M., and Stephen S. Kaplan. *Force Without War: U.S. Armed Forces as a Political Instrument*. Washington, 1978.

Bloch, Jean de. *La Guerre: La Guerre future aux points de vue technique, économique et politique*. 6 vols. Paris, 1898–1900.

Bond, Brian. *The Victorian Army and the Staff College, 1854–1914*. London, 1972.

———. *War and Society in Europe, 1870–1970*. London, 1983.

Boog, Horst, ed. *The Conduct of the Air War in the Second World War: An International Comparison*. New York, 1992.

Booth, Anne, and R. M. Sundrum. *Labour Absorption in Agriculture: Theoretical Analysis and Empirical Investigations*. Delhi, 1984.

Bordeaux, Henry. *Histoire d'une vie*. Vols. 4, 12. Paris, 1957, 1970.

Bourdrel, Philippe. *L'Épuration sauvage, 1944–1945*. Paris, 1988.

Bourgeois, Jean. "La situation démographique." *Population* 1 (January–March 1946), 117–42.

Bowley, Arthur L. *Some Economic Consequences of the Great War*. London, 1930.

Brandt, Karl. *Management of Agriculture and Food in the German-Occupied and Other Areas of Fortress Europe: A Study in Military Government*. Stanford, 1953.

Brockett, Charles D. *Land, Power, and Poverty: Agrarian Transformation and Political Conflict in Central America*. Boston, 1988.

Browder, Robert Paul, and Alexander F. Kerensky, eds. *The Russian Provisional Government 1917*. Stanford, 1961.

Browne, Courtney. *Tojo: The Last Banzai*. New York, 1967.

Bry, Gerhard. *Wages in Germany, 1871–1945*. Princeton, 1960.

Builder, Carl H. *The Masks of War: American Military Styles in Strategy and Analysis*. Baltimore, 1989.

Burk, Kathleen, ed. *War and the State: The Transformation of British Government, 1914–1919*. London, 1982.

Buton, Philippe. "L'État restauré." *La France des années noires: De l'Occupation à la Libération*. Jean-Pierre Azéma and François Bédarida, eds., 405–28. Paris, 1993.

Buttinger, Joseph. *Vietnam: A Dragon Embattled*. Vol. 1. New York, 1967.

Cairns, John C. "International Politics and the Military Mind: The Case of the French Republic, 1911–1914." *Journal of Modern History* 25 (September 1953), 273–85.

Cannon, M. Hamlin. *Leyte: The Return to the Philippines* [U.S. Army in World War II]. Washington, 1954.

Caplan, Jane. *Government Without Administration: State and Civil Service in Weimar and Nazi Germany*. Oxford, 1988.

Cardoso, Eliana, and Ann Helwig. "Below the Line: Poverty in Latin America." *World Development* 20 (January 1992), 19–37.

Carroll, Berenice A. *Design for Total War: Arms and Economics in the Third Reich*. The Hague, 1968.

Carsten, F. L. *Revolution in Central Europe, 1918–1919*. Berkeley, 1972.

Cecil, Robert. *Hitler's Decision to Invade Russia, 1941*. London, 1975.

Cépède, Michel. *Agriculture et alimentation en France durant la Deuxième Guerre mondiale*. Paris, 1961.

Chabod, Federico. *A History of Italian Fascism*. London, 1963.

Chamberlin, William Henry. *The Russian Revolution, 1917–1921*. Vol. 1. New York, 1935.

Chang, John K. "Industrial Development of Mainland China, 1912–1949." *Journal of Economic History* 27 (March 1967), 56–81.

Chang, Kia-Ngau. *The Inflationary Spiral: The Experience in China, 1939–1950*. Cambridge, Mass., 1958.

Charteris, John. *Field-Marshal Earl Haig*. New York, 1929.

Chassin, Lionel Max. *The Communist Conquest of China: A History of the Civil War, 1945–1949*. Cambridge, Mass., 1965.

Chen, Yung-fa. *Making Revolution: The Communist Movement in Eastern and Central China, 1937–1945*. Berkeley, 1986.

Ch'i, Hsi-sheng. *Nationalist China at War: Military Defeats and Political Collapse, 1937–1945*. Ann Arbor, 1982.

Chiclet, Christophe. *Les communistes grecs dans la guerre: histoire du parti communiste de Grèce de 1941 à 1949*. Paris, 1987.

Childers, Thomas. *The Nazi Voter: The Social Foundations of Fascism in Germany, 1919–1933*. Chapel Hill, 1983.

Chou, Shun-hsin. *The Chinese Inflation, 1939–1949*. New York, 1963.

Churchill, Winston S. *The World Crisis 1911–1914*. New York, 1923.

———. *Closing the Ring* [*The Second World War*, vol. 5]. Bantam ed. New York, 1962.

———. *Triumph and Tragedy* [*The Second World War*, vol. 6]. Bantam ed. New York, 1962.

Clarkson, Jesse D., and Thomas C. Cochran, eds. *War as a Social Institution: The Historian's Perspective*. New York, 1941.

Clough, Shepard B. *The Economic History of Modern Italy*. New York, 1964.

Cobb, Richard. *French and Germans, Germans and French: A Personal Interpretation of France Under Two Occupations, 1914–1918/1940–1944*. Hanover, N.H., 1983.

Cohen, Eliot A., and John Gooch. *Military Misfortunes: The Anatomy of Failure in War*. New York, 1990.

Cohen, Jerome B. *Japan's Economy in War and Reconstruction*. Minneapolis, 1949.

Colby, William. *Lost Victory: A Firsthand Account of America's Sixteen-Year Involvement in Vietnam*. Chicago, 1989.

Coles, Harry L., and Albert K. Weinberg. *Civil Affairs: Soldiers Become Governors* [*U.S. Army in World War II*]. Washington, 1964.

Collins, J. Lawton. *War in Peacetime: The History and Lesson of Korea*. Boston, 1969.

Collotti, Enzo. "L'Occupation allemande, la résistance, les alliés: essai d'historiographie." *Revue d'histoire de la Deuxième Guerre mondiale* 23 (October 1973), 21–33.

Commission for the Study of the History of the Party. *History of the August Revolution*. Hanoi, 1972.

———. *50 Years of Activities of the Communist Party of Vietnam*. Hanoi, 1980.

Constantino, Renato, and Letizia R. *The Philippines: A Past Revisited*. Quezon City, 1975.

———. *The Philippines: The Continuing Past*. Quezon City, 1978.

Cooper, Duff. *Haig*. 2 vols. Toronto, 1935.

Crémieux-Brilhac, Jean-Louis. *Les Français de l'an 40*. 2 vols. Paris, 1990.

Creveld, Martin van. *Supplying War: Logistics from Wallenstein to Patton*. Cambridge, 1977.

———. *Fighting Power: German and U. S. Army Performance, 1939–1945*. London, 1983.

Crosby, Alfred W., Jr. *Epidemic and Peace, 1918*. Westport, Conn., 1976.

Crowley, James B. *Japan's Quest for Autonomy: National Security and Foreign Policy, 1930–1938*. Princeton, 1966.

Cruttwell, C. R. M. F. *A History of the Great War, 1914–1918*. Oxford, 1936.

Cuff, Robert D. *The War Industries Board: Business-Government Relations During World War I*. Baltimore, 1973.

Cullather, Nick. "America's Boy? Ramon Magsaysay and the Illusion of Influence." *Pacific Historical Review* 62 (August 1993), 305–38.

Cumings, Bruce. *The Origins of the Korean War*. 2 vols. Princeton, 1981, 1990.

Debû-Bridel, Jacques. *Histoire du marché noir (1939–1947)*. Paris, 1947.

Debyser, F. "Une publication et des chiffres officiels sur la guerre des partisans." *Revue d'histoire de la Deuxième Guerre mondiale* 5 (January 1955), 112–15.

Decoux, Amiral. *A la barre de l'Indochine: Histoire de mon gouvernement Général (1940–1945)*. Paris, 1949.

Dedijer, Vladimir. *Tito*. New York, 1953.

Deist, Wilhelm, ed. *The German Military in the Age of Total War*. Leamington Spa, 1985.

Deitchman, Seymour J. *The Best-laid Schemes: A Tale of Social Research and Bureaucracy*. Cambridge, Mass., 1976.

Dejonghe, Étienne. "Le Nord isolé: occupation et opinion (mai 1940–mars 1942)." *Revue d'histoire moderne et contemporaine* 26 (January–March 1979), 48–97.

——, ed. *L'Occupation en France et en Belgique, 1940–1944*. 2 vols. Lille, 1987, 1988.

Delzell, Charles F. *Mussolini's Enemies: The Italian Anti-Fascist Resistance*. Princeton, 1961.

Demeter, Karl. *Das deutsche Offizierkorps in Gessellschaft und Staat, 1650–1945*. Frankfurt, 1964.

Devillers, Philippe. *Histoire du Vîet-Nam de 1940 à 1952*. Paris, 1952.

Dirlik, Arif. *The Origins of Chinese Communism*. New York, 1989.

Domenico, Roy Palmer. *Italian Fascists on Trial, 1943–1948*. Chapel Hill, 1991.

Dower, John W. *War Without Mercy: Race and Power in the Pacific War*. New York, 1986.

Ducasse, André, et al., eds. *Vie et mort des français, 1914–1918: Simple histoire de la grande guerre*. Paris, 1959.

Duhamel, Georges. *Civilisation, 1914–1917*. Paris, 1918.

Dumas, Samuel, and K. O. Vedel-Petersen. *Losses of Life Caused by War*. Oxford, 1923.

Eastman, Lloyd E. *Seeds of Destruction: Nationalist China in War and Revolution, 1937–1949*. Stanford, 1984.

Edgerton, Ronald K. "The Politics of Reconstruction in the Philippines: 1945–1948." Ph.D. dissertation, University of Michigan, 1975.

Ehrman, John. *Grand Strategy: August 1943–September 1944*. Vol. 5. London, 1956.

——. *Grand Strategy: October 1944–August 1945*. Vol. 6. London, 1956.

Ehrmann, Henry W. *French Labor: From Popular Front to Liberation*. New York, 1947.

Eley, Geoff. *From Unification to Nazism: Reinterpreting the German Past*. Boston, 1986.

Ellis, John. *The Sharp End of War: The Fighting Man in World War II*. Newton Abbot, 1980.

Elsbree, Willard H. *Japan's Role in Southeast Asia's Nationalist Movements, 1940 to 1945*. Cambridge, Mass., 1953.

Emsley, Clive, et al., eds. *War, Peace and Social Change in Twentieth-Century Europe*. London, 1989.

Endres, Franz Carl. "Soziologische Struktur und ihr entsprechende Ideologien des deutschen Offizierskorps vor dem Weltkriege." *Archiv für Sozialwissenschaft und Sozialpolitik* 58 (1927), 282–319.

Engelmann, Bernt. *In Hitler's Germany: Daily life in the Third Reich*. New York, 1986.

Englander, David, and James Osborne. "Jack, Tommy, and Henry Dubb: The Armed Forces and the Working Class." *Historical Journal* 21 (1978), 593–621.

Esherick, Joseph W., ed. *Lost Chance in China: The World War II Despatches of John S. Service*. New York, 1974.

Eudes, Dominique. *Les Kapetanios: la guerre civile grecque de 1943 à 1949*. Paris, 1970.

Fairbanks, John K., ed. *The Cambridge History of China: Republican China, 1912–1949*. Pt.1 [Vol. 12]. Cambridge, 1983.

———, and Albert Feuerwerker, eds. *The Cambridge History of China: Republican China, 1912–1949*. Pt. 2 [Vol. 13]. Cambridge, 1986.

Falkenhayn, Erich von. *General Headquarters, 1914–1916, and Its Critical Decisions*. London, n. d.

Farrar, L. L., Jr. *The Short-War Illusion: German Policy, Strategy and Domestic Affairs, August–December 1914*. Santa Barbara, 1973.

Feldman, Gerald D. *Army, Industry, and Labor in Germany, 1914–1918*. Princeton, 1966.

Ferro, Marc. *La Grande Guerre, 1914–1918*. Paris, 1969.

———. *The Russian Revolution of February 1917*. Englewood Cliffs, N.J., 1972.

Fischer, Fritz. *Germany's Aims in the First World War*. London, 1967.

———. *War of Illusions: German Policies from 1911 to 1914*. New York, 1975.

Fischer, Ruth. *Stalin and German Communism: A Study in the Origins of the State Party*. Cambridge, Mass., 1948.

Florinsky, Michael T. *The End of the Russian Empire*. New York, 1931.

Frankland, Noble. *The Bombing Offensive Against Germany: Outlines and Perspectives*. London, 1965.

Friend, Theodore. *Between Two Empires: The Ordeal of the Philippines, 1929–1946.* New Haven, 1965.

Fromkin, David. *A Peace to End All Peace: The Fall of the Ottoman Empire and the Creation of the Modern Middle East.* New York, 1989.

Fussell, Paul. *Wartime: Understanding and Behavior in the Second World War.* New York, 1989.

Futtrell, Robert Frank, et al. *The United States Air Force in Korea, 1950–1953.* New York, 1961.

Gaddis, John Lewis. *Strategies of Containment: A Critical Appraisal of Postwar American National Security Policy.* New York, 1982.

Gallerano, Nicola. "Le front intérieur (1942–1943)." *Revue d'histoire de la Deuxième Guerre mondiale* 23 (October 1973), 55–68.

Gallie, Duncan. *Social Inequality and Class Radicalism in France and Britain.* Cambridge, 1983.

Garrett, Stephan A. *Ethics and Airpower in World War II: The British Bombing of German Cities.* London, 1993.

Gaudel, André. *L'Indochine française en face du Japon.* Paris, 1947.

German National Constituent Assembly, Committee of Inquiry. *Official German Documents Relating to the World War.* 2 vols. New York, 1923.

Geyer, Michael. "The Past as Future: The German Officer Corps as a Profession." In *German Professions, 1800–1950.* Geoffrey Cocks and Konrad H. Jarausch, eds. New York, 1990.

Giap, Vo Nguyen. *Unforgettable Days.* Hanoi, 1975.

Gide, Charles, and William Oualid. *Le bilan de la guerre pour la France.* Paris, 1931.

Gillingham, John. *Belgian Business in the Nazi New Order.* Ghent, 1977.

———. *Industry and Politics in the Third Reich: Ruhr Coal, Hitler and Europe.* London, 1985.

Giraud, Henri-Christian. *De Gaulle et les communistes: l'alliance, juin 1941–mai 1943.* Paris, 1988.

Godfrey, John F. *Capitalism at War: Industrial Policy and Bureaucracy in France, 1914–1918.* Leamington Spa, 1987.

Goebbels, Joseph. *The Goebbels Diaries, 1942–1943.* Garden City, N.Y., 1948.

———. *The Goebbels Diaries: The Last Days.* London, 1977.

Golovine, Nicholas N. *The Russian Army in the World War.* New Haven, 1931.

Gooch, G. P., and Howard Temperley, eds. *British Documents on the Origins of the War, 1898–1914: The Outbreak of the War.* Vol. 11. London, 1926.

———. *British Documents on the Origins of the War, 1898–1914: The Last Years of Peace.* Vol. 10, pt. 2. London, 1938.

Gordon, Michael R. "Domestic Conflict and the Origins of the First World

War: The British and German Cases." *Journal of Modern History* 46 (June 1974), 191–226.

Goulden, Joseph C. *Korea: The Untold Story of the War*. New York, 1982.

Grebler, Leo, and Wilhelm Winkler. *The Cost of the World War to Germany and Austria-Hungary*. New Haven, 1940.

Gross, Jan Tomasz. *Polish Society Under German Occupation: The General gouvernement, 1939–1944*. Princeton, 1979.

Gruber, Helmut, ed. *International Communism in the Era of Lenin*. New York, 1967.

Grunberger, Richard. *The 12-Year Reich: A Social History of Nazi Germany*. New York, 1971.

Guingouin, Georges. *Quatre ans de lutte sur le sol limousin*. Paris, 1974.

——, and Gérard Monédiare. *Georges Guingouin: premier maquisard de France*. Limoges, 1982.

Hachtmann, Rüdiger. *Industriearbeit im "Dritten Reich": Untersuchungen zu den Lohn-und Arbeitsbedingungen in Deutschland, 1933–1945*. Göttingen, 1989.

Haestrup, Jorgen. *European Resistance Movements, 1939–1945: A Complete History*. Westport, Conn., 1981.

Haimson, Leopold. "The Problem of Social Stability in Urban Russia, 1905–1917." *Slavic Review* 23 (December 1964), 619–41; 24 (March 1965), 1–21.

Halberstam, David. *The Best and the Brightest*. New York, 1972.

Hamilton, Richard F. *Who Voted for Hitler?* Princeton, 1982.

Hammer, Ellen J. *The Struggle for Indochina, 1940–1955*. Stanford, 1966.

Hancock, Eleanor. *National Socialist Leadership and Total War, 1941–45*. New York, 1991.

Hancock, W. K. *British War Economy*. London, 1949.

Harris, C. R. S. *Allied Military Administration of Italy, 1943–1945*. London, 1957.

Hartendorp, A. V. H. *The Japanese Occupation of the Philippines*. 2 vols. Manila, 1967.

Harvey, S. "Mobilisation économiques et succès militaires pendant la seconde guerre mondiale." *Revue d'histoire de la Deuxième Guerre mondiale* 36 (April 1986), 19–35.

Hawes, Stephen, and Ralph White, eds. *Resistance in Europe, 1939–1945*. London, 1975.

Hayes, Peter. *Industry and Ideology: I. G. Farben in the Nazi Era*. Cambridge, Mass., 1987.

Hayne, M. B. *The French Foreign Office and the Origins of the First World War, 1898–1914*. Oxford, 1993.

Heiser, Joseph M., Jr. *Logistic Support* [U.S. Department of the Army. *Vietnam Studies*]. Washington, 1974.

Henry, Louis. "Évolution démographique de l'Europe 1938–1947." *Population* 4 (1949), 743–47.

Hermes, Walter G. *Truce Tent and Fighting Front* [*U. S. Army in the Korean War*]. Washington, 1966.

Hinsley, F. H., et al. *British Intelligence in the Second World War: Its Influence on Strategy and Operations.* Vol. 3, pt. 2. London, 1988.

Hiro, Dilip. *The Longest War: The Iran-Iraq Military Conflict.* New York, 1991.

Hirschfeld, Gerhard. *Nazi Rule and Dutch Collaboration: The Netherlands Under German Occupation, 1940–1945.* Oxford, 1988.

——, and Patrick Marsh, eds. *Collaboration in France: Politics and Culture during the Nazi Occupation, 1940–1944.* Oxford, 1989.

Hoffmann, Peter. *The History of the German Resistance, 1933–1945.* Cambridge, Mass., 1977.

Holmes, Richard. *Acts of War: The Behavior of Men in Battle.* New York, 1986.

Homze, Edward L. *Foreign Labor in Nazi Germany.* Princeton, 1967.

Hondros, John Louis. *Occupation and Resistance: The Greek Agony, 1941–44.* New York, 1983.

Hoover, Herbert. *The Ordeal of Woodrow Wilson.* New York, 1958.

Hosmer, Stephen T. *Constraints on U.S. Strategy in Third World Conflicts.* New York, 1987.

——. *The Army's Role in Counterinsurgency and Insurgency* [Rand Corp. R-3947]. Santa Monica, 1990.

Howard, Michael, ed. *Soldiers and Governments: Nine Studies in Civil-Military Relations.* London, 1957.

Hughes, Daniel J. *The King's Finest: A Social and Bureaucratic Profile of Prussia's General Officers, 1871–1914.* New York, 1987.

Hurwitz, Samuel J. *State Intervention in Great Britain: A Study of Economic Control and Social Response, 1914–1919.* New York, 1949.

Hyland, William G. *Mortal Rivals: Superpower Relations from Nixon to Reagan.* New York, 1987.

Iatrides, John O. *Revolt in Athens: The Greek Communist "Second Round," 1944–1945.* Princeton, 1972.

——. "The Doomed Revolution: Communist Insurgency in Postwar Greece." In *Stopping the Killing:How Civil Wars End.* Roy Licklider, ed., 204–32. New York, 1993.

——, ed. *Greece in the 1940s: A Nation in Crisis.* Hanover, N.H., 1981.

Iggers, Georg, ed. *The Social History of Politics: Critical Perspectives in West German Historical Writing Since 1945.* Leamington Spa, 1985.

Ike, Nobutake, ed. *Japan's Decision for War: Records of the 1941 Policy Conferences.* Stanford, 1967.

Inter-American Development Bank. *Annual Report 1989.* Washington, 1990.

———. *Annual Report 1991*. Washington, 1992.

[1st] International Conference on the History of the Resistance Movements. *European Resistance Movements, 1939–1945*. New York, 1960.

International Labor Office. *The War and Women's Employment: The Experience of the United Kingdom and the United States*. Montreal, 1946.

Iriye, Akira. *Power and Culture: The Japanese-American War, 1941–1945*. Cambridge, Mass., 1981.

Isoart, Paul, ed. *L'Indochine française, 1940–1945*. Paris, 1982.

Jacquemyns, G. *La Société Belge sous l'Occupation Allemande, 1940–1944: Alimentation*. Brussels, 1950.

Jain, Shail. *Size Distribution of Income: A Compilation of Data*. Washington, 1975.

Janvry, Alain de, et al. "Land and Labour in Latin American Agriculture from the 1950s to the 1980s." *Journal of Peasant Studies* 16 (April 1989), 390–423.

Japanese Military Administration [Philippines], Department of General Affairs. *The Official Journal of the Japanese Military Administration*. 2nd ed. Vol. 1, no. 1. Manila, 1942. [Copy in the Hoover Institution Library, Stanford, Calif.]

Joffre, J. J. C. *The Personal Memoirs of Joffre: Field Marshal of the French Army*. 2 vols. New York, 1932.

Johnson, Chalmers. *Peasant Nationalism and Communist Power: The Emergence of Revolutionary China, 1937–1945*. Stanford, 1962.

Judt, Tony, ed. *Resistance and Revolution in Mediterranean Europe, 1939–1948*. London, 1989.

Károlyi, Michael. *Fighting the World: The Struggle for Peace*. New York, 1925.

Kataoka, Tetsuya. *Resistance and Revolution in China: The Communists and the Second United Front*. Berkeley, 1974.

Kater, Michael H. *The Nazi Party: A Social Profile of Members and Leaders, 1919–1945*. Cambridge, Mass., 1983.

———. *Different Drummers: Jazz in the Culture of Nazi Germany*. New York, 1992.

Katkov, George. *Russia 1917: The February Revolution*. London, 1967.

Kaufman, Burton I. *The Korean War: Challenges in Crisis, Credibility, and Command*. New York, 1986.

Kautsky, Karl. *Outbreak of the World War* [*German Documents Collected by Karl Kautsky*, 1-vol. ed.]. New York, 1924.

Kédros, André. *La Résistance grecque (1940–1944)*. Paris, 1966.

Kedward, H. R. *Resistance in Vichy France: A Study of Ideas and Motivation in the Southern Zone, 1940–1942*. New York, 1978.

———. *In Search of the Maquis: Rural Resistance in Southern France, 1942–1944*. Oxford, 1993.

Keegan, John. *The Face of Battle*. London, 1976.

———. "Regimental Ideology." In *War, Economy and the Military Mind*. Geoffrey Best and Andrew Wheatcroft, eds. London, 1976.

Keep, John L. H. *The Russian Revolution: A Study in Mass Mobilization*. New York, 1976.

Keiger, John F. V. *France and the Origins of the First World War*. London, 1983.

Kennedy, Paul M. *The Rise and Fall of the Great Powers: Economic Change and Military Conflict from 1500 to 2000*. New York, 1987.

———, ed. *The War Plans of the Great Powers, 1880–1914*. Boston, 1985.

Kerkvliet, Benedict J. *The Huk Rebellion: A Study of Peasant Revolt in the Philippines*. Berkeley, 1977.

Kershaw, Ian. *Popular Opinion and Political Dissent in the Third Reich: Bavaria 1933–1945*. Oxford, 1983.

———. *The "Hitler Myth": Image and Reality in the Third Reich*. Oxford, 1987.

Kesselring, Field-Marshal [Albert]. *Memoirs*. London, 1953.

Khanh, Huynh Kim. *Vietnamese Communism, 1925–1945*. Ithaca, 1982.

Kido, Marquis. *The Diary of Marquis Kido, 1931–1945*. Frederick, Md., 1984.

King, Jere Clemens. *Generals and Politicians: Conflict Between France's High Command, Parliament and Government, 1914–1918*. Berkeley, 1951.

Kiraly, Béla K., and Walter S. Dillard, eds. *The East European Officer Corps, 1740–1920: Social Origins, Selection, Education, and Training*. Boulder, 1988.

Kissin, S. F. *War and the Marxists: Socialist Theory and Practice in Capitalist War, 1848–1918*. London, 1988.

Kitchen, Martin. *The German Officer Corps, 1890–1914*. Oxford, 1968.

Kitsikis, Dimitri. "La famine en Grèce (1941–1942): les Conséquences politiques." *Revue d'histoire de la Deuxième Guerre mondiale* 19 (April 1969), 17–41.

Klein, Burton H. *Germany's Economic Preparations for War*. Cambridge, Mass., 1959.

Knox, Alfred W. F. *With the Russian Army, 1914–1917*. London, 1921.

Kocka, Jürgen. *Facing Total War: German Society, 1914–1918*. London, 1984.

Kofos, Evangelos. *Nationalism and Communism in Macedonia*. Thessaloniki, 1964.

Kogan, Norman. *Italy and the Allies*. Cambridge, Mass., 1956.

Koistinen, Paul A. C. "The 'Industrial-Military' Complex in Historical Perspective: World War I." *Business History Review* 41 (Winter 1967), 378–403.

——. "The 'Industrial-Military' Complex in Historical Perspective: The Inter-War Years." *Journal of American History* 56 (March 1970), 819–39.

——. "Mobilizing the World War II Economy: Labor and the Industrial-Military Alliance." *Pacific Historical Review* 42 (November 1973), 443–78.

Kolko, Gabriel. *Wealth and Power in America: An Analyis of Social Class and Income Distribution.* New York, 1962.

——. *The Roots of American Foreign Policy: An Analysis of Power and Purpose.* Boston, 1969.

——, and Joyce Kolko. *The Limits of Power: The World and United States Foreign Policy, 1945–1954.* New York, 1972.

——. *Anatomy of a War: Vietnam, the United States, and the Modern Historical Experience.* New York, 1985.

——. *Confronting the Third World: United States Foreign Policy, 1945–1980.* New York, 1988.

——. *Le Monde Diplomatique.* Paris, October 1988.

——. *The Politics of War: The World and United States Foreign Policy, 1943–1945.* Rev. ed. New York, 1990.

——. "The Gulf and Afterwards: The Future of American Foreign Policy." *Studies in Political Economy* 34 (Spring 1991), 7–28.

Kousoulas, D. George. *Revolution and Defeat: The Story of the Greek Communist Party.* London, 1965.

Krepinevich, Andrew F., Jr. *The Army and Vietnam.* Baltimore, 1986.

Kriegel, Annie. *Aux origines du communisme français, 1914–1920.* Vol. 1. Paris, 1964.

Kriegel-Valrimont, Maurice. *La Libération: les archives du COMAC (mai–août 1944).* Paris, 1964.

Kuisel, Richard F. *Capitalism and the State in Modern France.* New York, 1981.

Kulischer, Eugene M. *Europe on the Move: War and Population Changes, 1917–1947.* New York, 1948.

Laborie, Pierre. *L'Opinion française sous Vichy.* Paris, 1990.

Landé, Carl H. *Leaders, Factions, and Parties: The Structure of Philippine Politics* [Yale University Southeast Asia Studies No. 6]. New Haven, 1964.

Large, David Clay, ed. *Contending with Hitler: Varieties of German Resistance in the Third Reich.* New York, 1991.

Larkin, John A. *The Pampangans: Colonial Society in a Philippine Province.* Berkeley, 1972.

Laurel, R. Kwan. "The Life of Commander Hizon." *Midweek* (Manila), November 6–13, 1991, 16–17.

Lazitch, Branko. *Les partis communistes d'Europe, 1919–1955.* Paris, 1956.

League of Nations, Economic, Financial and Transit Department. *Food Rationing and Supply, 1943/44*. Geneva, 1944.

———. *Food, Famine and Relief, 1940–1946*. Geneva, 1946.

Leed, Eric J. *No Man's Land: Combat and Identity in World War I*. New York, 1979.

Legnani, Massimo. "La société italienne et la Résistance." *Revue d'histoire de la Deuxième Guerre mondiale* 23 (October 1973), 37–54.

Levine, Robert A. *The Arms Debate and the Third World* [Rand Corp. N-3523]. Santa Monica, 1987.

Levy, Carl, ed. *Socialism and the Intelligentsia, 1880–1914*. London, 1987.

Lewis, John Wilson, ed. *Peasant Rebellion and Communist Revolution in Asia*. Stanford, 1974.

Liddell Hart, B. H. *Through the Fog of War*. New York, 1938.

———. *The Tanks: History of the Royal Tanks Regiment and Its Predecessors*. Vol. 1. London, 1959.

Liebknecht, Karl, Rosa Luxemburg, and Franz Mehring. *The Crisis in German Social Democracy (The "Junius" Pamphlet)*. New York, 1918.

Liebman, Marcel. *The Russian Revolution: The Origins, Phases and Meaning of the Bolshevik Victory*. London, 1970.

Littlejohn, David. *The Patriotic Traitors: A History of Collaboration in German-Occupied Europe, 1940–1945*. London, 1972.

Lloyd, Alan. *The War in the Trenches*. London, 1976.

Lloyd George, David. *War Memoirs*. Vol. 1. London, 1933.

Lockhart, Greg. *Nation in Arms: The Origins of the People's Army of Vietnam*. Sydney, 1989.

Loewenheim, Francis L., et al., eds. *Roosevelt and Churchill: Their Secret Wartime Correspondence*. New York, 1975.

Long, Ngo Vinh. *Before the Revolution: The Vietnamese Peasants under the French*. New York, 1992.

Lottman, Herbert R. *The Purge*. New York, 1986.

Lutz, Ralph H., ed. *Fall of the German Empire, 1914–1918*. 2 vols. Stanford, 1932.

———. *The Causes of the German Collapse in 1918*. Stanford, 1934.

Lyttelton, Adrian. *The Seizure of Power: Fascism in Italy, 1919–1929*. New York, 1973.

Macmillan, Harold. *The Blast of War, 1939–1945*. London, 1967.

Madjarian, Grégoire. *Conflits, pouvoirs et société à la libération*. Paris, 1980.

Magnus, Philip. *Kitchener: Portrait of an Imperialist*. London, 1958.

Marcot, M. "Pour une Enquête sur les Maquis: Quelques Problemes." *Revue d'histoire de la Deuxième Guerre mondiale* 33 (October 1983), 89–100.

Marjolin, Robert. *Architect of European Unity: Memoirs, 1911–1986*. London, 1989.

Marshall, S. L. A. *Men Against Fire: The Problem of Battle Command in Future War*. New York, 1947.

Martin, François. *Heures tragiques au Tonkin*. Paris, 1949.

Marty Papers. Manuscripts of André Marty in the Hoover Institution Library.

Marwick, Arthur. *The Deluge: British Society and the First World War*. New York, 1965.

——. *War and Social Change in the Twentieth Century: A Comparative Study of Britain, France, Germany, Russia and the United States*. London, 1974.

——, ed. *Total War and Social Change*. London, 1988.

Mason, Timothy W. *Social Policy in the Third Reich: The Working Class and the "National Community."* Providence, 1993.

——. "The Legacy of 1918 for National Socialism." In *German Social Democracy and the Triumph of Hitler*. Anthony Nicholls and Erich Matthias, eds., 215–39. London, 1971.

——. "Women in Germany, 1925–1940: Family, Welfare and Work." *History Workshop* 1 (Spring 1976), 74–113; 2 (Autumn 1976), 5–32.

Matloff, Maurice. *Strategic Planning for Coalition Warfare, 1943–1944* [*U.S. Army in World War II*] Washington, 1959.

Maurice, Frederick. *Lessons of Allied Co-operation: Naval, Military and Air, 1914–1918*. London, 1942.

Mayer, Arno J. *Politics and Diplomacy of Peacemaking: Containment and Counterrevolution at Versailles, 1918–1919*. New York, 1967.

Mazower, Mark. *Inside Hitler's Greece: The Experience of Occupation, 1941–44*. New Haven, 1993.

——. "Military Violence and National Socialist Values: The Wehrmacht in Greece, 1941–1944." *Past and Present* 134 (February 1992), 130–58.

McChristian, Joseph A. *The Role of Military Intelligence, 1965–1967* [U.S. Department of the Army. *Vietnam Studies*]. Washington, 1974.

McInnes, Colin, and G. D. Sheffield, eds. *Warfare in the Twentieth Century: Theory and Practice*. London, 1988.

Mendelssohn-Bartholdy, Albrecht. *The War and German Society: The Testament of a Liberal*. New Haven, 1937.

Michel, Henri. *Les courants de pensée de la résistance*. Paris, 1962.

——. *The Shadow War: Resistance in Europe, 1939–1945*. London, 1972.

Michon, Georges. *La préparation à la Guerre: La loi de trois ans (1910–1914)*. Paris, 1935.

Mierzejewski, Alfred C. *The Collapse of the German War Economy, 1944–1945: Allied Air Power and the German National Railway*. Chapel Hill, 1988.

Miller, James E. *The United States and Italy, 1940–1950: The Politics and Diplomacy of Stabilization*. Chapel Hill, 1986.

Miller, Steven E., ed. *Military Strategy and the Origins of the First World War*. Princeton, 1985.

Millett, Allan R., and Williamson Murray, eds. *Military Effectiveness*. Vols. 1, 3. Boston, 1988.

Milward, Alan S. *The German Economy at War*. London, 1965.

———. *The New Order and the French Economy*. Oxford, 1970.

———. *War, Economy and Society, 1939–1945*. Harmondsworth, 1977.

Mitchell, Allan. *Revolution in Bavaria, 1918–1919: The Eisner Regime and the Soviet Republic*. Princeton, 1965.

Mitchell, B. R. *European Historical Statistics, 1750–1970*. London, 1975.

Mohrenschildt, Dimitri von, ed. *The Russian Revolution of 1917: Contemporary Accounts*. New York, 1971.

Momyer, William W. *Airpower in Three Wars*. Washington, D.C., 1978.

Montgomery, Viscount [Bernard Law]. *Memoirs*. London, 1958.

Moore, Barrington, Jr. *Injustice: The Social Bases of Obedience and Revolt*. White Plains, 1978.

Mordant, Eugène. *Au service de la France en Indochine, 1941–1945*. Saigon, 1950.

Morley, James William, ed. *The Fateful Choice: Japan's Advance into Southeast Asia, 1939–1941*. New York, 1980.

———. *The China Quagmire: Japan's Expansion on the Asian Continent, 1933–1941*. New York, 1983.

———. *Japan Erupts: The London Naval Conference and the Manchurian Incident, 1928–1932*. New York, 1984.

Morsomme, Albert. *Anatomie de la guerre totale: ses aspects économiques et financiers*. Brussels, 1971.

Mrozek, Donald J. *Air Power and the Ground War in Vietnam: Ideas and Actions*. Maxwell Air Force Base, Ala., 1988.

Mueller, John E. *War, Presidents and Public Opinion*. New York, 1973.

Mühlberger, Detlef, ed. *The Social Basis of European Fascist Movements*. London, 1987.

Müller, Klaus-Jürgen. *The Army, Politics and Society in Germany, 1933–1945: Studies in the Army's Relation to Nazism*. Manchester, 1987.

Musée d'Histoire Contemporaine. *Images de 1917*. Paris, 1987.

Nef, John U. *War and Human Progress: An Essay on the Rise of Industrial Civilization*. Cambridge, Mass., 1950.

Neufeld, Maurice F. *Italy: School for Awakening Countries; The Italian Labor Movement in Its Political, Social, and Economic Setting from 1800 to 1960*. Ithaca, 1961.

Nobecourt, Jacques. *Une Histoire politique de l'armée: De Pétain à Pétain, 1919–1942*. Paris, 1967.

Noguères, Henri. *Histoire de la Résistance en France: Juin 1940–Juin 1941*. Paris, 1967.

————, and Marcel Degliame-Fouché. *Histoire de la Résistance en France de 1940 à 1945.* Vols. 3, 4, 5. Paris, 1972, 1976, 1981.

O'Ballance, Edgar. *The Greek Civil War, 1944–1949.* New York, 1966.

Orlow, Dietrich. *The Nazis in the Balkans: A Case Study of Totalitarian Politics.* Pittsburgh, 1968.

Oualid, William. "The Effect of the War Upon Labour in France." In *Effects of the War upon French Economic Life.* Charles Gide, ed. Oxford, 1923.

————, and Charles Picquenard. *Salaires et tarifs, conventions collectives et grèves.* Paris, 1928.

Paige, Jeffery M. *Agrarian Revolution: Social Movements and Export Agriculture in the Underdeveloped World.* New York, 1975.

Palmer, Bruce, Jr. *The 25-Year War: America's Military Role in Vietnam.* Lexington, Ky., 1984.

Palmer, Gregory. *The McNamara Strategy and the Vietnam War: Program Budgeting in the Pentagon, 1960–1968.* Westport, Conn., 1978.

Papastratis, Procopis. *British Policy Towards Greece During the Second World War, 1941–1944.* Cambridge, 1984.

Pares, Bernard. *My Russian Memoirs.* London, 1931.

Parkinson, Roger. *Blood, Toil, Tears and Sweat: The War History from Dunkirk to Alamein, Based on the War Cabinet Papers of 1940 to 1942.* London, 1973.

————. *A Day's March Nearer Home: The War History from Alamein to VE Day Based on the War Cabinet Papers of 1942 to 1945.* London, 1974.

Pastor, Peter, ed. *Revolutions and Interventions in Hungary and Its Neighbors, 1918–1919.* Boulder, 1988.

Patti, Archimedes L. A. *Why Vietnam: Prelude to America's Albatross.* Berkeley, 1980.

Paxton, Robert O. *Vichy France: Old Guard and New Order, 1940–1944.* New York, 1972.

"PCI Leaflets." Italian Communist party collection in the International Institute of Social History, Amsterdam.

Pearson, Lester B. *Mike: Memoirs of the Right Honorable Lester B. Pearson.* Vol. 2. Toronto, 1972.

Peck, Graham. *Two Kinds of Time.* 2nd ed. Boston, 1967.

Peck, Merton J., and Frederic M. Scherer. *The Weapons Acquisition Process.* Boston, 1962.

Pedroncini, Guy. *1917: les mutineries de l'armée française.* Paris, 1968.

Perreux, Gabriel. *La Vie quotidienne des civils en France pendant la grand guerre.* Paris, 1966.

Peukert, Detlev J. K. *Inside Nazi Germany: Conformity, Opposition and Racism in Everyday Life.* London, 1987.

Philippines Department of Agriculture, Bureau of Agricultural Statistics.

*Agricultural Development Trends in the 80's: Philippines vs. Other Selected Countries.* Manila, n.d. [1990].

Phillips, Gregory D. *The Diehards: Aristocratic Society and Politics in Edwardian England.* Cambridge, Mass., 1979.

Playne, Caroline E. *Society at War, 1914–1916.* London, 1931.

Pogue, Forrest C. *The Supreme Command: The European Theater of Operations* [U. S. Army in World War II]. Washington, 1954.

Porch, Douglas. *The March to the Marne: The French Army, 1871–1914.* Cambridge, 1981.

Rabinowitch, Alexander. *The Bolsheviks Come to Power: The Revolution of 1917 in Petrograd.* New York, 1976.

Ralston, David B. *The Army of the Republic: The Place of the Military in the Political Evolution of France, 1871–1914.* Cambridge, Mass., 1967.

Reale, Eugenio. *Avec Jacques Duclos.* Paris, 1958.

Reck-Malleczewen, Friedrich P. *Diary of a Man in Despair.* New York, 1970.

Recto, Claro M. *Three Years of Enemy Collaboration.* Manila, 1946.

Rees, David. *Korea: The Limited War.* New York, 1964.

Renouvin, Pierre. *La crise européenne et la grande guerre (1904–1918).* Paris, 1934.

Rich, Norman. *Hitler's War Aims: Ideology, the Nazi State, and the Course of Expansion.* Vol. 1. New York, 1973.

Rieber, Alfred J. *Stalin and the French Communist Party, 1941–1947.* New York, 1962.

Rings, Werner. *Life with the Enemy: Collaboration and Resistance in Hitler's Europe, 1939–1945.* Garden City, N.Y., 1982.

Rioux, Jean-Pierre. *The Fourth Republic, 1944–1958.* Cambridge, 1987.

Ritter, Gerhard. *The Schlieffen Plan: Critique of a Myth.* New York, 1958.

Roberts, Bryan. *Cities of Peasants: The Political Economy of Urbanization in the Third World.* Beverly Hills, 1978.

Romanus, Charles F., and Riley Sunderland. *Time Runs Out in CBI: China-Burma-India Theater* [U.S. Army in World War II]. Washington, 1959.

Ropp, Theodore. *War in the Modern World.* Durham, N.C., 1959.

Rosinski, Herbert. *The German Army.* New York, 1966.

Rousso, Henry. *The Vichy Syndrome: History and Memory in France since 1944.* Cambridge, Mass., 1991.

Routh, Guy. *Occupation and Pay in Great Britain 1906–79.* London, 1980.

Rumpf, Hans. *The Bombing of Germany.* London, 1963.

Ryder, A. J. *The German Revolution of 1918: A Study of German Socialism in War and Revolt.* Cambridge, 1967.

Sainclivier, Jacqueline. "Sociologie de la Résistance: quelques aspects méthodologiques et leur application en Ille-et-Vilaine." *Revue d'histoire de la Deuxième Guerre mondiale* 30 (January 1980), 33–74.

Salter, Stephen. "Structures of Censensus and Coercion: Workers' Morale and the Maintenace of Work Discipline, 1939–1945." In *Nazi Propaganda: The Power and the Limitations*. David Welch, ed., 88–116. London, 1983.

Sarafis, Stefanos. *ELAS: Greek Resistance Army*. London, 1980.

Sauermann, Heinz. "Demographic Changes in Postwar Germany." *Annals of the American Academy of Political and Social Sciences* 260 (November 1948), 99–107.

Sauvy, Alfred. *La vie économique des Français de 1939 à 1945*. Paris, 1978.

Scalapino, Robert A., and Chong-Sik Lee. *Communism in Korea*. Vol. 1. Berkeley, 1972.

Scheidemann, Philipp. *The Making of New Germany: Memoirs*. 2 vols. New York, 1929.

Schnabel, James F. *Policy and Direction: The First Year* [*U. S. Army in the Korean War*]. Washington, 1972.

Schorske, Carl E. *German Social Democracy, 1905-1917: The Development of the Great Schism*. Cambridge, Mass., 1955.

Schreiner, George A. *The Iron Ration: Three Years in Warring Central Europe*. New York, 1918.

Schurmann, Franz. *Ideology and Organization in Communist China*. Berkeley, 1966.

Schwarz, Benjamin C. *American Counterinsurgency Doctrine and El Salvador: The Frustrations of Reform and the Illusions of Nation Building* [Rand Corp. R-4042]. Santa Monica, 1991.

Selden, Mark. *The Yenan Way in Revolutionary China*. Cambridge, Mass., 1971.

Semelin, Jacques. *Sans armes face à Hitler: La résistance civile en Europe, 1939–1943*. Paris, 1989.

Serfaty, Simon, and Lawrence Gray, eds. *The Italian Communist Party: Yesterday, Today, and Tomorrow*. Westport, Conn., 1980.

Serman, William. *Les officiers français dans la nation, 1848–1914*. Paris, 1982.

Seton-Watson, Christopher. *Italy from Liberation to Fascism, 1870–1925*. London, 1967.

Seydewitz, Max. *Civil Life in Wartime Germany: The Story of the Home Front*. New York, 1945.

Shafer, D. Michael. *Deadly Paradigms: The Failure of U.S. Counterinsurgency Policy*. Princeton, 1988.

Sherry, Michael S. *The Rise of American Airpower: The Creation of Armageddon*. New Haven, 1987.

Shrader, Charles A., ed. "The Impact of Unsuccessful Military Campaigns on Military Institutions, 1860–1980" [U.S. Army Center of Military History]. Washington, 1984.

Shulman, Marshall D. *Stalin's Foreign Policy Reappraised*. Cambridge, Mass., 1963.

Shum, Kui-kwong. *The Chinese Communists' Road to Power: The Anti-Japanese National United Front, 1935–1945*. Hong Kong, 1988.

Silverstein, Josef, ed. *Southeast Asia in World War II: Four Essays* [Yale University Southeast Asia Studies No. 7]. New Haven, 1966.

Simmons, Robert R. *The Strained Alliance: Peking, Pyongyang, Moscow and the Politics of the Korean Civil War*. New York, 1975.

Simon, John. *Revolutions Without Guerrillas* [Rand Corp. R-3683]. Santa Monica, 1989.

Smith, Denis M. *Italy: A Modern History*. Ann Arbor, 1969.

Smith, Howard K. *The State of Europe*. New York, 1949.

Smith, Russell Jack. *The Unknown CIA: My Three Decades in the Agency*. Washington, 1989.

Snyder, Jack. *The Ideology of the Offensive: Military Decision Making and the Disasters of 1914*. Ithaca, 1984.

Speer, Albert. *Inside the Third Reich: Memoirs*. New York, 1970.

Speier, Hans. *Social Order and the Risks of War: Papers in Political Sociology*. Cambridge, Mass., 1952.

Spiers, Edward M. *The Army and Society, 1815–1914*. London, 1980.

Sprenger, Rudolf. *Bolshevism: Its Roots, Role, Class View and Methods*. New York, n.d. [1937?].

Spriano, Paolo. *The Occupation of the Factories: Italy 1920*. London, 1975.

———. *Stalin and the European Communists*. London, 1985.

Stavrakis, Peter J. *Moscow and Greek Communism, 1944–1949*. Ithaca, 1989.

Steinberg, David J. *Philippine Collaboration in World War II*. Ann Arbor, 1967.

Steiner, Zara S. *Britain and the Origins of the First World War*. London, 1977.

Steinert, Marlis G. *Hitler's War and the Germans: Public Mood and Attitude During the Second World War*. Athens, Ohio, 1977.

Stilwell, Joseph W. *The Stilwell Papers*. New York, 1948.

Stockwell, John. *In Search of Enemies: A CIA Story*. New York, 1978.

Stone, Norman. *The Eastern Front, 1914–1917*. London, 1975.

———. "Army and Society in the Habsburg Monarchy, 1900–1914." *Past and Present* 33 (April 1966), 95–111.

Stouffer, Samuel A., et al. *The American Soldier: Combat and Its Aftermath*. Princeton, 1949.

———. *The American Soldier: Adjustment During Army Life*. Princeton, 1949.

Strong, Kenneth. *Intelligence at the Top: The Recollections of an Intelligence Officer*. London, 1968.

Struye, P. *L'Évolution du sentiment publique en Belgique sous l'occupation allemande*. Brussels, 1947.

Studnitz, Hans-Georg von. *While Berlin Burns, 1943–1945*. London, 1964.

Sturmthal, Adolf A. *The Tragedy of European Labor, 1918–1939*. New York, 1943.

Suh, Dae-Sook. *The Korean Communist Movement, 1918–1948*. Princeton, 1967.

Sweet-Escott, Bickham. *Greece: A Political and Economic Survey, 1939–1953*. London, 1954.

Sweets, John F. *Choices in Vichy France: The French under Nazi Occupation*. New York, 1986.

Taruc, Luis. *Born of the People*. New York, 1953.

Taubmann, Michel. *L'Affaire Guingouin*. Limoges, 1994.

Taw, Jennifer Morrison, and Robert C. Leicht. *The New World Order and Army Doctrine* [Rand Corp. R-4201]. Santa Monica, 1992.

Taylor, Leonard B. *Financial Management of the Vietnam Conflict, 1962–1972* [U.S. Department of the Army. *Vietnam Studies*]. Washington, 1974.

Thayer, John A. *Italy and the Great War: Politics and Culture, 1870–1915*. Madison, Wis., 1964.

Thompson, John M. *Revolutionary Russia 1917*. New York, 1981.

Thorez, Maurice. *Œuvres*. Vol. 20. Paris, 1960.

Thorne, Christopher. *The Far Eastern War: States and Societies, 1941–45*. London, 1987.

Tillon, Charles. *On chantait rouge*. Paris, 1977.

Titmuss, Richard M. *Essays on "the Welfare State."* London, 1958.

Togo, Shigenori. *The Cause of Japan*. New York, 1956.

Tokes, Rudolf L. *Béla Kun and the Hungarian Soviet Republic: The Origins and Role of the Communist Party of Hungary in the Revolutions of 1918–1919*. New York, 1967.

Tonnesson, Stein. *The Vietnamese Revolution of 1945: Roosevelt, Ho Chi Minh and de Gaulle in a World at War*. London, 1991.

Toscano, Mario. *Designs in Diplomacy: Pages from European Diplomatic History in the Twentieth Century*. Baltimore, 1970.

Travers, Tim. *The Killing Ground: The British Army, the Western Front and the Emergence of Modern Warfare, 1900–1918*. London, 1987.

Trotsky, Leon. *The History of the Russian Revolution*. 3 vols. Ann Arbor, 1957.

Trullinger, James Walker, Jr. *Village at War: An Account of Revolution in Vietnam*. New York, 1980.

Trunk, Isaiah. *Judenrat: The Jewish Councils in Eastern Europe Under Nazi Occupation*. New York, 1972.

Turner, Stansfield. *Secrecy and Democracy: The CIA in Transition*. Boston, 1985.

United Kingdom. Foreign Office. *Report of the British Parliamentary Delegation to Greece.* August 1946. London, 1947.

————. Ministry of Labour. *Economic Notes from German and Austrian Newspapers* (October 26, 1914–December 1919). [Copy in the Hoover Institution Library.]

————. Parliament. *Report of the British Legal Mission to Greece, 17th January 1946.* Cmd. 6838. London, 1946.

U.S. Army. Pacific Forces, Military Intelligence Section. "The Guerrilla Resistance Movement in the Philippines." Vol. 1. April 15, 1946.

U.S. Commission on Integrated Long-Term Strategy. *Report: Discriminate Deterrence.* Washington, January 1988.

U.S. Congress. Joint Economic Committee. *Report: The Economics of Military Procurement.* 91:1. Washington, 1969.

U.S. Department of State. *Foreign Relations of the United States.* 1944, vol. 3; 1948, vol. 4. Washington, 1965, 1974.

————. Office of Research and Intelligence. "Status and Prospects of German Trade-Unions and Works Councils." No. 3381. May 27, 1946.

U.S. House of Representatives, Select Committee on Foreign Aid. *Final Report on Foreign Aid.* 80:2. May 1, 1948. Washington, 1948.

————. Committee on Government Operations. *Report: Organization and Management of Missile Programs.* 86:1. Washington, 1959.

U.S. Joint Chiefs of Staff. *1991 Joint Military Net Assessment.* Washington, March 1991.

U.S. National Security Council. "United States Objectives and Problems for National Security." No. 68. April 14, 1950 [numbering as in original ms.].

U.S. Office of Strategic Services. Research and Analysis Branch. "Food Distribution in Italy." R. & A. No. 1371. October 27, 1943.

————. "Food Resources of North Italy." R. & A. No. 1400.4. January 1, 1944.

————. "Food Rations and Prices in Italy Before and After Allied Invasion." R. & A. No. 2324. July 31, 1944.

————. "Biographical Reports" (Philippines). November 25, 1944.

————. "Contributions of the Italian Partisans to the Allied War Effort." R. & A. 2993. March 31, 1945.

U.S. Senate. Committee on Armed Services. *Report: Defense Organization: The Need for Change.* 99:1. Washington, 1985.

————. Committee on the Judiciary. *Report: Concentration Ratios in Manufacturing Industry, 1963.* 89:2. Pt. 1. Washington, 1966.

————. Special Committee to Study Problems of American Small Business. *Report: Economic Concentration and World War II.* 79:2. Washington, 1946.

Urban, Joan Barth. *Moscow and the Italian Communist Party: From Togliatti to Berlinguer.* Ithaca, 1986.

Vagts, Alfred. A *History of Militarism: Romance and Realities of a Profession*. New York, 1937.

Vidalenc, Jean. *L'exode de mai–juin 1940*. Paris, 1957.

Vlavianos, Haris. *Greece, 1941–49: From Resistance to Civil War: The Strategy of the Greek Communist Party*. London, 1992.

Vukmanovic, Svetozar. *How and Why the People's Liberation Struggle of Greece Met with Defeat*. London, 1985.

Waite, Robert G. L. *Vanguard of Nazism: The Free Corps Movement in Postwar Germany, 1918–1923*. Cambridge, Mass., 1952.

Waites, Bernard. *A Class Society at War: England, 1914–1918*. Leamington Spa, 1987.

Wall, Richard, and Jay Winter, eds. *The Upheaval of War: Family, Work and Welfare in Europe, 1914–1918*. Cambridge, 1988.

Waller, Willard, ed. *War in the Twentieth Century*. New York, 1974.

Walter, Gerard. *Paris Under the Occupation*. New York, 1960.

Warlimont, Walter. *Inside Hitler's Headquarters, 1939–45*. London, 1964.

Warmbrunn, Werner. *The Dutch Under German Occupation, 1940–1945*. Stanford, 1963.

Watt, Donald Cameron. *Too Serious a Business: European Armed Forces and the Approach to the Second World War*. London, 1973.

———. *How War Came: The Immediate Origins of the Second World War, 1938–1939*. New York, 1989.

Weathersby, Kathryn. "Soviet Aims in Korea and the Origins of the Korean War, 1945–1950: New Evidence from Russian Archives." Cold War International History Project, Woodrow Wilson Center, November 1993.

Wehler, Hans-Ulrich. *The German Empire, 1871–1918*. Leamington Spa, 1985.

Weinberg, Gerhard L. *The Foreign Policy of Hitler's Germany: Starting World War II, 1937–1939*. Chicago, 1980.

Whalen, Robert W. *Bitter Wounds: German Victims of the Great War, 1914–1939*. Ithaca, 1984.

Wheeler, Mark C. *Britain and the War for Yugoslavia, 1940–1943*. Boulder, 1980.

Wheeler-Bennett, John W. *The Nemesis of Power: The German Army in Politics, 1918–1945*. London, 1967.

White, Theodore H., and Annalee Jacoby. *Thunder out of China*. New York, 1946.

White, William D. *U.S. Tactical Air Power: Missions, Forces, and Costs*. Washington, 1974.

Wildman, Allan K. *The End of the Russian Imperial Army: The Old Army and the Soldiers' Revolt (March–April 1917)*. Princeton, 1980.

Wilensky, Harold D. *Organizational Intelligence: Knowledge and Policy in Government and Industry*. New York, 1967.

Wilhelm, Maria de Blasio. *The Other Italy: Italian Resistance in World War II.* New York, 1988.

Willard, Germaine, et al. *De la guerre à la libération: la France de 1939 à 1945.* Paris, 1972.

Willequet, Jacques. *La Belgique sous la Botte: Résistances et Collaborations, 1940–1945.* Paris, 1986.

Williams, John. *The Home Fronts: Britain, France and Germany, 1914–1918.* London, 1972.

Williams, Robert G. *Export Agriculture and the Crisis in Central America.* Chapel Hill, 1986.

Williamson, Samuel R., Jr. *The Politics of Grand Strategy: Britain and France Prepare for War, 1904–1914.* Cambridge, Mass., 1969.

Willoughby, Charles A., ed. *The Guerrilla Resistance Movement in the Philippines: 1941–1945.* New York, 1972.

Winter, J. M., ed. *War and Economic Development: Essays in Memory of David Joslin.* Cambridge, 1975.

Wittner, Lawrence S. *American Intervention in Greece, 1943–1949.* New York, 1982.

Wolowski, Alexandre. *La vie quotidienne à Varsovie sous l'occupation Nazi, 1939–1945.* Paris, 1977.

Wolters, Willem. *Politics, Patronage and Class Conflict in Central Luzon.* Quezon City, 1984.

Woodhouse, C. M. *The Struggle for Greece, 1941–1949.* London, 1976.

Woodside, Alexander B. *Community and Revolution in Modern Vietnam.* Boston, 1976.

Woodward, Bob. *Veil: The Secret Wars of the CIA 1981–1987.* New York, 1987.

Woodward, Llewellyn. *Great Britain and the War of 1914–1918.* London, 1967.

———. *British Foreign Policy in the Second World War.* Vol. 3. London, 1971.

Young, Arthur N. *China's Wartime Finance and Inflation, 1937–1945.* Cambridge, Mass., 1965.

Zee, Henri A. van der. *The Hunger Winter: Occupied Holland, 1944–45.* London, 1982.

Zhukov, G. K. *Reminiscences and Reflections.* 2 vols. Moscow, 1985.

# INDEX